Competitive Government: Public Private Partnerships

Series Editors

Simon Hakim, Center for Competitive Government, Temple University, Philadelphia, PA, USA

Adrian Moore ⓘ, Policy, Reason Foundation, LOS ANGELES, CA, USA

Robert M. Clark, University of Cincinnati, Cincinnati, OH, USA

A shift from monopolistic government to a competitive setting is expected to improve efficient production and stimulate innovation. That shift has typically been in the form of Public-Private Partnerships (PPP), where each partner contributes its share of comparatively advantaged resources towards the production and delivery of the services. The shift to PPP, the types of services, and the methods used in the shift are increasing and becoming ever more sophisticated. This book series intends to capture a state of the art of such PPPs and present a guide for the implementation of such ventures.

The book series will present, evaluate, and suggest policy implications based upon PPP experiences in fields like: police, prisons, courts, water and wastewater, telecommunications, air and water ports, rail, highways, schools, garbage collection, postal services, cyber security, foster care and child adoption, and homeland security management. The audience of this book series are advanced undergraduate/graduate students students in courses on privatization and public finance, consultants and researchers in both government and the private sector, and members of think tanks that promote the ideas of more-focused government, competitive government, and privatization.

The series welcomes proposals for monographs, edited volumes, and handbooks. Please contact the responsible editor for more information. All proposals submitted undergo single-blind evaluation by the series editors and/or external peer reviewers prior to acceptance and publication.

Erwin A. Blackstone • Simon Hakim
Brian Meehan
Editors

Handbook on Public and Private Security

 Springer

Editors
Erwin A. Blackstone
Department of Economics and Center
for Competitive Government
Temple University
Philadelphia, PA, USA

Simon Hakim
Department of Economics and Center
for Competitive Government
Temple University
Philadelphia, PA, USA

Brian Meehan
Department of Accounting,
Economics, and Finance
Berry College
Mount Berry, GA, USA

ISSN 2524-4183 ISSN 2524-4191 (electronic)
Competitive Government: Public Private Partnerships
ISBN 978-3-031-42405-2 ISBN 978-3-031-42406-9 (eBook)
https://doi.org/10.1007/978-3-031-42406-9

This Springer imprint is published by the registered company Springer Nature Switzerland AG
The registered company address is: Gewerbestrasse 11, 6330 Cham, Switzerland

Paper in this product is recyclable.

This volume is dedicated to our wives, Marijane Blackstone, Galia Hakim, and Katrina Meehan, and to our children and grandchildren.

Acknowledgments

Funding for this project was provided by the John Templeton Foundation and the Institute for Humane Studies (IHS) at George Mason University. Without their support this volume would not have been possible. Special thanks are extended to Maria Rogacheva and Hailey Lesué at IHS for organizing and administering a workshop for the authors.

Contents

List of Editors and Contributors

Editors

Erwin A. Blackstone Department of Economics and Center for Competitive Government, Temple University, Philadelphia, PA, USA

Simon Hakim Department of Economics and Center for Competitive Government, Temple University, Philadelphia, PA, USA

Brian Meehan Department of Accounting, Economics, and Finance, Campbell School of Business, Berry College, Mount Berry, GA, USA

Contributors

Colleen Arnold GardaWorld, Customer Services Excellency, Quebec, Canada

Barak Ariel Institute of Criminology, University of Cambridge, Cambridge, UK
Institute of Criminology, The Hebrew University of Jerusalem, Jerusalem, Israel

Bruce L. Benson Florida State University, Tallahassee, FL, USA

Erwin A. Blackstone Department of Economics and Center for Competitive Government, Temple University, Philadelphia, PA, USA

Benjamin Blemings Dyson School of Applied Economics and Management, Cornell University, Ithaca, NY, USA

Mark Button School of Criminology and Criminal Justice, University of Portsmouth, Portsmouth, UK

Gregory DeAngelo Claremont Graduate University, Claremont, CA, USA

Simon Hakim Department of Economics and Center for Competitive Government, Temple University, Philadelphia, PA, USA

David R. Hines Hanover County, Virginia, Sheriff's Office, Hanover, VA, USA

Steve Jones Allied Universal, Conshohocken, PA, USA

Jonathan Klick University of Pennsylvania, Philadelphia, PA, USA

Pieter Leloup Ghent University, Ghent, Belgium

Vrije Universiteit Brussel, Brussels, Belgium

Wei Long Department of Economics, Tulane University, New Orleans, LA, USA

John MacDonald University of Pennsylvania, Philadelphia, PA, USA

Brian Meehan Department of Accounting, Economics, and Finance, Campbell School of Business, Berry College, Mount Berry, GA, USA

Tim Prenzler School of Law and Society, University of the Sunshine Coast, Sippy Downs, QLD, Australia

Logan Puck Department of Political Science, The George Washington University, Washington, DC, USA

Ryan Quandt Claremont Graduate University, Claremont, CA, USA

Louis B. Salz Trinity University, San Antonio, TX, USA

Rick Sarre Division of Justice and Society, University of South Australia, Adelaide, SA, Australia

Garett Seivold International Security Ligue, Zollikofen, Switzerland

Taylor Smith DWS Group, Chicago, IL, USA

Alexander Specht Claremont Graduate School, Claremont, CA, USA

Steve Somers GardaWorld, Operation-Security Services U.S., New York, NY, USA

Edward Peter Stringham Shelby Cullon Davis Professor of American Business and Economic Enterprise, Trinity College, Hartford, CT, USA

Terry L. Sullivan Hanover County, Virginia Sheriff's Office, Hanover, VA, USA

William Wyatt Claremont Graduate University, Claremont, CA, USA

Frank Vram Zerunyan USC Sol Price School of Public Policy, Director of Executive Education, The Bedrosian Center on Governance, USC ROTC and Nautical Science Programs, Los Angeles, CA, USA

An Overview of Private Security and Policing in the United States

Erwin A. Blackstone, Simon Hakim, and Brian Meehan

Abstract This paper is a presentation on recent trends and a survey of recent research on private security, and its relationship with policing in the United States. Recent research suggests a larger role for private security in crime deterrence efforts than was previously assumed. This research suggests that increases in some forms of private security generate reductions in some types of crime, and that private security can act as complements or substitutes for police in different environments. We also review the industry structures for private security and detectives, and do the same for public police and detectives. In addition, we examine how private security is regulated in the U.S. and the limitations of these regulations.

1 Introduction

A substantial body of economic literature exists on the role of crime deterrence investments and criminal behavior. Starting with Becker (1968), this literature examines the role of apprehension and punishment in affecting criminal behavior. Becker advanced this rational choice model of crime asserting that individuals weigh the expected benefit of a particular criminal activity vs. the expected cost. As perceptions of these costs change, criminal activity changes. These expected costs include the probability of getting caught while engaging in the activity, and the expected punishment that accompanies the crime if caught, as well as the opportunity cost of outside options (e.g. labor market options) available to individuals. As expected costs of a criminal activity increase, either through an increase in the

E. A. Blackstone · S. Hakim
Department of Economics and Center for Competitive Government, Temple University, Philadelphia, PA, USA

B. Meehan (✉)
Department of Accounting, Economics, and Finance, Campbell School of Business, Berry College, Mount Berry, GA, USA
e-mail: bmeehan@berry.edu

© The Author(s), under exclusive license to Springer Nature Switzerland AG 2023
E. A. Blackstone et al. (eds.), *Handbook on Public and Private Security*,
Competitive Government: Public Private Partnerships,
https://doi.org/10.1007/978-3-031-42406-9_1

1

probability of getting caught, or increased expected punishment, the amount of the activity engaged in should fall. It appears that the probability of apprehension has a larger impact on criminal activity than changing punishment (see Lee & McCrary, 2009; Grogger, 1991). Efforts aimed at increasing the probability of apprehension include both private and public security measures aimed at identifying and catching perpetrators, and stopping the activity before it happens. For example, a public police officer stationed on the side of a busy road both increases the probability of catching a speeding car on that road, and also deters the activity itself as potential speeders notice the police car before engaging in speeding. Private deterrence efforts can achieve similar goals, cameras and burglar alarms allow for quicker response to burglaries and increased chances of identification of the perpetrator. Security guards stationed outside a jewelry store could dissuade a burglary before it is even attempted. Much of the deterrence research has focused on the impact of public police on crime, but recently a surge in studies on privately purchased security has examined the role of private deterrence investments. Private security in the U.S. and around the world has risen in recent decades (Blackstone & Hakim, 2010). Some estimates suggest that private security are more than three times as prevalent as public police within the U.S. (Joh, 2004). Security investments to deter crime come in many forms such as; burglar alarms, monitoring devices, private investigators, and private security guards. This paper will focus on recent U.S. trends and research findings regarding private security and public police services, how they interact, and how they could interact more efficiently moving forward. In Sect. 2 we examine U.S. trends for public and private security professions over time, Sect. 3 takes a deeper dive into investigative services, while Sect. 4 does the same for guard and patrol services, Sects. 5 and 6 deal with the impact of private security and police on crime, Sect. 7 adds some discussion and Sect. 8 concludes.

2   Recent Trends

US national data were collected for the years 1997 through 2021; these data include: GDP, reported crime, public and private security employment and wages, Internet related crime figures, and employment and wage figures on information technology security analysts. We present diagrams to examine relationships among these variables. The objective is to show overarching trends in these industries relative to aggregate economic and crime conditions in the U.S., and to speculate on possible supply and demand determinants for both police and private security employment.

Staring with public police, Fig. 1 shows annual changes in police employment are somewhat unrelated to both GDP and crime, but more closely related to GPD growth. Figure 2 indicates that police employment and expenditures are a relatively constant percentage of state and local employment. Indeed, the ratio of spending on police and total state and local spending (which includes spending on education by the state and local governments) ranges narrowly between 3.67 and 3.81 percent. Further, police employment as a percentage of total state and local

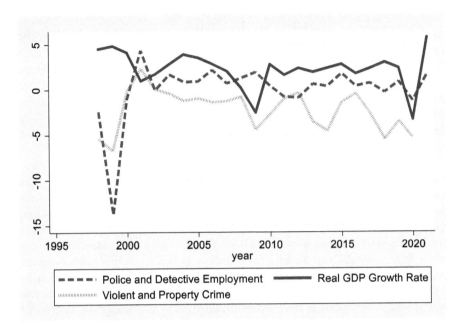

Fig. 1 Annual changes in GDP, crime, and police

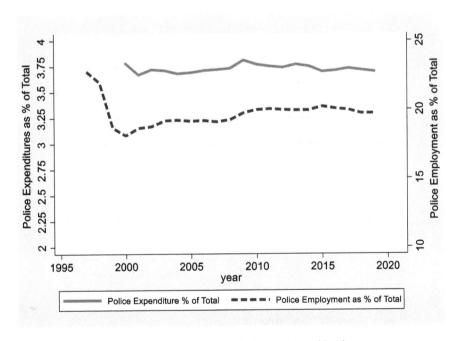

Fig. 2 Police expenditures and employment as a % of total state and local

employment remains steady around 22 percent over the data period. Figure 2 shows how closely parallel both expenditures and employment move. Control of crime is a major responsibility of police. Specifically, property crimes declined from 1978 through 2021, and violent crimes declined through 2016 but then increased through 2021. However, both the decline and the rise in crimes were not met with respective changes in police manpower or budgets. The implication is that the supply of available funding appears to be a significant determinant of police employment, while the demand variable stemming from changing crime levels for police protection seems not to be driving changes in policing expenditures and employment.

Figure 3 shows complaints to the Federal Trade Commission for identity theft, fraud and other cybercrime and reflects the rapid growth of these "new crimes". The employment of IT security professionals rises similar to the increase of these crimes but unfortunately, data categorizing pure cybercrime do not exist. Most local communities and even states do not have the professional manpower or the interest in handling cybercrimes like identity theft, and these crimes can emanate from anywhere in the world. Even the FBI has difficulty in handling crimes that originate outside the U.S. Addressing these crimes, which are growing at a faster rate than the eight traditional FBI Uniform crimes (violent and property crimes), has not been an easy job for governments at any level to handle. Perhaps that is why we observe the growth in private sector IT security employment that mirrors these complaints (Fig. 3).

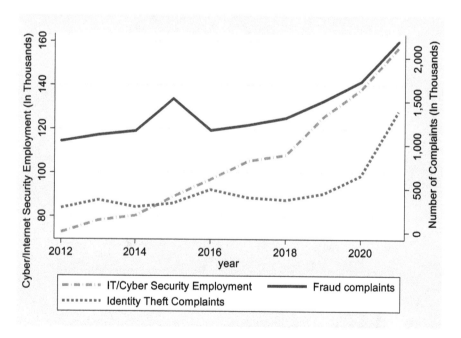

Fig. 3 FTC cyber crime complaints and IT/cyber security employment

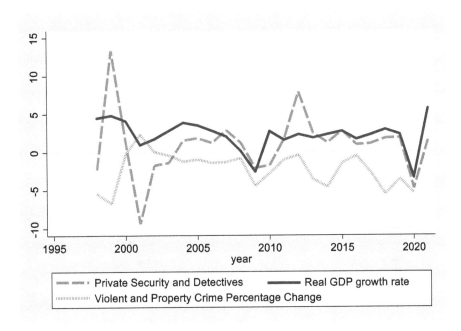

Fig. 4 GDP, crime, and private security annual employment changes

Private security employment appears to be positively related to GDP fluctuations and behaves like a "normal good,"[1] hence the employment in private security changes in the same direction as GDP (Fig. 4). For example, between 2019 and 2020, during the COVID-19 pandemic, real GDP declined by 3.4 percent while private security employment declined by 1.8 percent. There does not appear to be a robust relationship between private police employment and crime. But, as with any measure of security (both public and private) the relationship between crime and security is endogenous, in particular at such an aggregated level. Increasing crime may increase demand for police or private security services, but an increase in these security services may reduce crime. Thus, there is an ambiguous relationship between aggregate measures of crime and security.

Figure 5 provides trends on average hourly wages for security professions over time. Private detective wages were 71 percent higher in 2021 than private guards, while police detective wages were just 33 percent higher than patrol officers. Further, police investigators and patrol officers' wages in 2021 were 68 percent and 116.5 percent, respectively, higher than private investigators and guards. Guards include a wide gamut from stationary guards to private sworn officers, where the majority are probably in the lower end category. For example, only about 10 percent of private guards are armed, presumably usually sworn officers, and they earn higher wages than unarmed guards (Perry, 2020). The rapid growth in the "new crimes" is

---

[1] Demand increases as income levels increase for a normal good, if income falls, demand also falls.

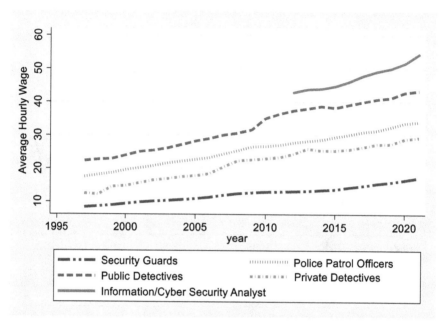

Fig. 5 Average wages for security professions

expected to be handled by IT security professionals who have the highest average wages of all security professions listed. Between 2012 and 2021 IT security employment experienced the largest growth in earnings of 29 percent compared with 11 percent for police detectives. It seems unlikely that significant new demand for private detective services will arise over time. There is a greater chance that patrol and guard could experience a significant growth via colleges and healthcare institutions including hospitals. Perhaps the most significant buyer could be government where some security services might well be shifted from police. These issues will be further developed in the following sections.

3   The US Investigative Services Industry

In this section we analyze how competitive the private detective and investigative industries are, how the concentration of these industries has changed over time, how they are expected to function in the future, and whether private security is expected to grow by providing some existing police services.

The investigative service industry (NAICS 561611) has been and remains unconcentrated. Table 1 shows that the industry is highly competitive where the 4 firm concentration ratio is well below 40 percent, which is the beginning range of oligopoly, according to Industrial Organization teachings (Oxford, n.d.). Moreover,

Table 1 US Investigative Services Industry (NAICS 561611)

	1997	2002	2007	2012	2017
Sales ($ 000)	1,819,015	2,585,756	3,887,203	4,903,574	5,893,086
Payroll ($ 000)		1,044,361	1,379,590	1,557,236	2,052,939
Total Establishments	5077	4975	5015	4637	4186
Total Firms				4340	3920
Share of Top 4 (%)	7.2	18.4	27.0	36.2	20.8
Share of Top 8 (%)	10.1	22.2	33.6	42.8	33.5
Share of Top 20 (%)	15.7	29.2	44.0	52.3	47.4
Share of Top 50 (%)	24.1	37.7	53.7	62.1	60.9
HHI					176.3
Payroll/Sales (%)		40.4	35.5	31.8	34.8
Establishments/Firms				1.068	1.068
Sales/Establishment ($)	358.286	519,750	775,115	1,057,408	1,407,808

Source: Bureau of the Census, Department of Commerce. Concentration in American Industry

the HHI (Herfindahl-Hirschman Index, see Hirschman, 1964) of 176.3 indicates that this industry is equivalent to one with at most 56 equal size firms. Even if the industry is composed of local or regional markets, the large number of firms competing suggests low concentration. For example, Pennsylvania with 2180 private defectives in 2021 and an average size of firm in the industry of 3 employees, means that Pennsylvania could have 726 companies. Further confirmation is the statement by IBISWorld (2020) that no major national players exist in the industry. The data provided on investigators by the BLS is only for these small independent firms. However, the number of in-house investigators in law firms and insurance companies are not included in these statistics. The BLS (2022, A) reports that only 36 percent of private investigators are employed by such firms. This means that the data for this market is substantially undercounted. Perry (2020) estimated that the overall security market is $15–20 billion larger than the data indicate. Law firms and management companies compete for some of the services offered by private investigative firms, suggesting even more competition than indicated by the concentration figures alone.

The average sales per private investigative firm in 2017 was $1.4 million, compared with $1.18 Million for just one lawyer, which is indicative of the small size of these firms. Further, there is no obvious trend towards larger establishments (C. Barnes, 2021) suggesting the absence of economies of scale or scope. Most investigative firms have just one establishment with an average of three employees, and a market share of less than one percent. For example, All State Investigations Inc. has a market share of 0.7 percent, North American Investigations has a market share of 0.2 percent, and Pinkerton, which is now a division of the Swedish based Securitas has merely 0.1 percent (IBISWorld, 2020). The number of establishments has decreased by 20 percent since 1997 and the number of firms has diminished by 10 percent in the 5 years ending in 2017. These declines reflect limited entry into the industry, which is highly competitive, suggesting low profitability. Also, there seem to be limited economies of scale and scope since the industry remains comprised of small firms. Between 1997 and 2017, the industry grew in current dollars by 220 percent while GDP grew by 228 percent. In real terms the industry grew in this period by 1.24 times while GDP grew 1.9 times. Thus, the investigative industry grew slightly below GDP, which explains why entry to the industry is not especially attractive.

Entry barriers are relatively low, when compared to other U.S. Industries. Investigative firms appear to incur low start-up and overhead costs. Most start-ups can begin at home with initial capital required below $3000 (Caramela, 2022). Regulation varies among states. Most states require detectives seeking licensure to have work experience in a related field, licensees to undergo a background check, and some require a test. Additional requirements are imposed for those who wish to be armed (IBISWorld, 2020). Thus, when demand rises (falls), new small firms enter (exit) with a short delay.

A survey of private investigators revealed that the most common specialties and services offered were background checks (34%), civil investigations (33%), and surveillance (26%). Other less common services included insurance investigations (19%), fraud (17%), corporate investigations (13%), accident reconstruction (17%), domestic investigations (13%), infidelity (13%), and other (19%) (Faber, 2013). The low industry concentration and its high degree of competition along with low entry barriers yields firms offering a multitude of services with limited specialization.

The high competitiveness of the private investigators industry suggests normal competitive profits with limited resources to invest into major technological innovations. As, in theory, within a perfectly competitive market, normal profits leave no or limited resources for research and development and no or limited technological progress. Since there are no public corporations that reveal profits in this industry, we report margins for the firms. The margins reflect the operating profits before interest, taxes, depreciation, and amortization. The margins before interest and taxes were estimated at only 5.2 percent in 2020. Comparing this industry to the S & P-500-listed companies shows that the S&P margins are 11–14 percent, substantially above the private investigative industry and reflecting again its highly competitive nature. Further, 10 percent or higher is generally considered to reflect good profitability (Wiblin, 2021). Recognizing that 2020 may be a low profit year and the industry's low capital intensity, nevertheless the substantial difference in profitability compared to benchmarks suggest a low or normal profitability industry.

Finally, private detectives do not appear to take profits in the form of high wages. Private detectives average wage in 2021 was $28,860 while an average police investigator's wage was $107,890 in 2021. The median salary of private detectives was $45,500 whereas the top 10 percent made more than $85,000.

4   The US Guard Services Industry

The guard services are the largest part of the private security industry. In 2017, total sales were five times, and total wages 9.3 times, larger than the investigative segment of the industry. Between 1997 and 2017, the 4 firm concentration ratio grew to 40.7 percent, which, according to a general rule of thumb for Industrial Organization economics (See Oxford Reference, four-firm concentration ratio), approaches the bottom of an oligopoly classification. The second four firms each had an average market share of 1.45 percent, indicating the small size of most of the industry's firms. The HHI in 2017 indicates that the industry had the equivalent of about 19 equal size firms. The government standard is that an industry of at least seven equal size firms is unconcentrated (U.S. department of Justice, Horizontal Merger Guideline, 2010). Another indication of the concentration is the statement by Perry (2020: 53) that the combined market shares of G4S, Securitas, and Garda in 2019 was 30 percent. Along with Allied Universal, it is reasonable that the concentration in 2019 remains about the same as in 2017 and is considerably higher than the private investigation industry. Like the private investigators industry, the data provided here refer to 61 percent of guards employed in such firms and as casino surveillance officers (BLS, B, 2022). Finally, the industry is more nationally oriented than the detective industry.

Mergers in the guard industry have contributed to the increase in concentration. Most of the acquisitions have been of larger firms acquiring small firms. For example, since its founding in 1972, Securitas has been making a large number of acquisitions worldwide but not in the US. The acquisitions include companies which specialized in guards, cash collection using armored vehicles, electronic security, security consulting, security technology, video security, cloud based and automation services (Securitas AB, 2021). Two advantages for such acquisitions are penetrating additional geographical markets and achieving economies of scope where one service yields reduced costs of other services. All Securitas acquisitions have not directly increased concentration of the guards or any other security services in the US.

Mergers have played a major role in the growth of leading US guard firms. For example, a small Philadelphia guard service for sporting events named SpectaGuard was bought by two partners in the 1990s and then proceeded, in 2000, to buy Allied Security, followed by acquisition of additional large companies including Barton Protective, at the time with $350 million in revenues, and Initial Security with $225 million in revenues. The newly named AlliedBarton made 10 additional acquisitions. Then, in 2016, AlliedBarton with revenues of $2.5 billion merged with Universal Protection with revenues of $2.3 billion. Finally, in 2021 G4S, with $9 billion in revenue, originally a Danish company that went through a series of similar worldwide mergers, was bought for $5.3 billion by Allied Universal (Perry, 2020). Allied Universal paid a 68 percent premium for G4S shares after a bidding rivalry with Garda and gained the unique technology of G4S and its customer base (Perry, 2021). Neither the US antitrust authorities nor the EU competitive commission challenged the merger. Suggesting that the authorities did not view this merger as anti-competitive.

Observing the profits in the form of EBITDA (earnings before interest, taxes, depreciation, and amortization) reveals that small guard companies earned 8 percent profits in 2009 while showing losses between 2018 and 2021. Regional guard companies showed steady 7 percent profits for the same period while the large national/international firms exhibited a slight rise throughout the period from 6 percent in 2009 to 8.5 percent in 2021 (Perry, 2021: 65). As of 2021, these profit margins reflect modest profitability even for the large companies. It is important to note that the data were gathered from hundreds of companies where the small companies usually provided guard services while the large companies had a major guard component but, also provided mixture of other security services requested by their customers. However, there were some companies that provided services like those that used armored cars for cash transfer that are not part of this industry. Given these qualifications, the data indicate that the profitability of guard companies rises with size, reflecting a likely decline in the future share of the small companies. It also suggests that guard companies' long-term existence depends on the demand side, on the provision of related services. It may also suggest, on the supply side, economies of scale and scope and buying power on costs of insurance, uniforms, and automobiles. The existing trend of the last twenty plus years suggests that the share of the small companies could continue shrinking, with the larger firms becoming more technologically oriented, providing a wide mix of security services. Thus, it is likely that the improved services of the large companies could mean their market shares might well continue to increase, and their increased mix of security services will enhance contracting out security by government and business. On the other hand, some consumers may prefer dealing with a smaller firm, offering more personal services.

It appears that much of the growth in the industry occurred mostly in the five largest firms that gained market share at the expense of the other smaller companies. Overall, the growth of the guard's industry between 1997 and 2017 in real dollars was 124 percent while GDP grew 189 percent. Thus, this industry has grown less than the entire economy while at a similar rate as the investigative services industry. Entry barriers could also contribute to increasing concentration and are discussed below, and while entry barriers to this industry would appear modest in some states, competing with the large firms anywhere would require more capital and technological knowhow. Entry by foreign firms is also possible. For example, Prosegur, a Spanish firm is a recent entrant. Finally, a low-level concentrated oligopoly may be an optimal market structure, large enough to be innovative but still competitive enough to have near competitive profits (Table 2).

As mentioned above, another factor that contributes to increased concentration for private security firms is regulation. Private security in the U.S. is primarily regulated at the state level. Some states require occupational licenses to enter into the industry and others do not. But, the requirements for these licenses vary across states and over time. Meehan (2015) documents how more stringent licensing requirements impact the size of firms and average wages of security guards at these

Table 2 US Guard Services Concentration (NAICS 561612)

	1997	2002	2007	2012	2017
Sales ($ 000)	9,132,633	14,763,333	18,799,306	23,940,418	29,616,794
Payroll ($ 000)		10,115,867	12,628,781	15,520,045	19,146,998
Total Establishments	6644	7365	5015	10,171	9457
Total Firms					6711
Share of Top 4 (%)	28.3	32.7	30.6	35.1	40.7
Share of Top 8 (%)	35.7	39.8	38.7	43.1	46.5
Share of Top 20 (%)	45.9	49.6	48.1	53.4	55.7
Share of Top 50 (%)	54.6	58.2	58.0	63.4	64.3
HHI					538.2
Payroll/Sales (%)		68.5	67.2	64.8	64.6
Establishments/Firms					1.41
Sales/Establishment ($)	1,374,568	2,004,526	3,748,615	2,393,792	3,131,792

Source: Bureau of the Census, Department of Commerce. Concentration in American Industry

firms. Bonding and insurance requirements, law enforcement experience require-ments, and training requirements were shown to increase the average wage of secu-rity guards in at least one of the paper's empirical specifications. Most of these requirements also had disproportionately negative impacts on firms with less 100 employees, and disproportionately positive impacts on firms that had more than 100 employees. As they tend to increase, these entry requirements increase the propor-tion of firms that have more than 100 employees while decreasing the proportion of firms that have less than 100 employees. It appears that these regulations tend to increase the proportion of private security firms that are relatively large.

Examining the regulatory supply side of this issue can help explain some of the occupational licensing patterns across the U.S. In some states, private security licenses are just simple business licenses, but in other states an entire separate regu-latory bureaucracy is set up to evaluate and propose new requirements for entry. In states where specific licensing boards are set up that include licensed security guards or security guard firm owners, requirements tend to be much more stringent. In particular, this type of regulatory infrastructures is associated with much higher training and experience requirements after controlling for state and time level fixed effects. The analysis also indicates that examination requirements are around 60% more likely when private security guards control the licensing boards than when no specific authority is given control of the licensure requirements. From a public choice perspective, it is argued that these self-interested security guard board mem-bers want to increase these requirements to reduce entry and thus stifle competition for their services. Sometimes these licensing requirements are left to the public police. When public police are involved with overseeing these licensing require-ments, the law enforcement experience requirements tend to be higher than when no specific regulatory authority existed. Bonding and insurance requirements also tended to be higher as well as the likelihood of an exam requirement. With the exception of the law enforcement experience requirement, the results suggest that the most stringent requirements occurred when licensed private security guards were in control of these regulatory institutions (Meehan & Benson, 2015). Thus, it may not be desirable to have a possible substitute for private security in control of licensing when licensing requirements act as substantial barriers to entry.

5 Private Security Guards and Crime

Becker argued that private security was probably a specific crime deterrent but did not generate a large impact on general deterrence; instead, potential criminals would simply substitute unprotected targets for targets that were protected by private security (Becker, 1968, 201). In a process now often called displacement, as this thinking goes, areas that increase private security measures displace crime to other areas, actually producing a negative externality on these other areas in terms of increased crime. Much of the recent empirical research on private security and crime does not support this hypothesis, and some actually finds the direct opposite externality exists, that private security generates positive spillovers, as crime in entire cities and states declines as private security increases. Thus, this research suggests that private security plays a role as a general crime deterrent.

As mentioned above, investments in private security come in many forms. This section will draw primarily from the literature on private security guards and patrol officers. But, studies on other forms of privately purchased security are informative in showing how private investments can generate spillovers. An illustration of a private investment that generated general crime deterrence was highlighted by Ayres and Levitt (1998). They laid out the interesting case of Lojack, a hidden radio transmitter that can be installed on automobiles. Because there is no visible indication that a vehicle is equipped with Lojack, a potential car thief cannot identify if Lojack is installed on a targeted vehicle. Lojack greatly reduced the expected loss for car owners who use them, as 95 percent of the cars equipped with these devices are recovered compared to 60 percent for non-Lojack equipped cars. They also found that it acted as a general deterrent, it had a significant crime reducing effect, as a one percentage point increase in installations of the device in a market was associated with a 20 percent decline in auto thefts within large cities, and a five percent reduction in the rest of the state. Since other crime rates are not correlated with the drop in auto theft and installation of Lojack, the obvious implication is that many potential auto thieves are aware of the increased probability that they will be arrested, and are deterred as a consequence. These results are also consistent with a more recent investigation of the introduction of Lojack in Mexican states (Gonzalez-Navarro, 2013).

A relatively early cross-sectional study by Zedlewski (1992) found that greater levels of employment in private security firms was associated with lower crime rates. This analysis included 124 SMSA's in the U.S., and results suggested that private security generated positive spillovers. And thus, the presence of private security resulted in general crime deterrence. This study's findings should be interpreted with caution, as it did not control for the endogenous relationship between crime and security. This endogenous relationship between security measurers is highlighted by Ehrlich (1973). Security investments might have a negative impact on crime, but demand for these security investments also rise as crime increases, as people demand more protection. So more recent empirical studies have focused on how to separate the security-determines-crime relationship from the crime-determines security relationship (Meehan & Benson, 2017).

Improving on the cross-sectional analysis and addressing the endogeneity concerns, Benson and Mast (2001) used a panel of U.S. county level data from 1977–1992. This study used the number of firms and employees in 23 different industries that were expected to have relatively high demand for private security as instrumental variables in estimating private security presence in a county. Benson and Mast also included NRA membership, and lagged percentages of the state level republican vote within their estimation. The results suggested that increases in private security guard employees were associated with lower burglary and rape rates. This study used U.S. Census County Business Patterns data to account for the private security guard employee measures.

One issue with the Benson and Mast paper, as well as many other local level crime studies, is that they employed the FBI's county level crime counts published in the annual Uniform Crime Reports (UCR). These statistics are fraught with error. The count data are self-reported by local police departments, and departments that actually report data vary wildly from year to year. Much of the variation in these statistics is from these underreporting errors and not from changes in the underlying crime conditions themselves. After a thorough review of this county level data, Maltz and Targonski comment (2002, 298): "we conclude that county-level crime data [UCR-data], as they are currently constituted, should not be used, especially in policy studies." The annual state-level UCR data are considered to be better. The state level data used are estimated crime rates that attempt to correct for underreporting by police departments. When police agencies fail to report crime statistics for a given year, their data are replaced with equivalent data formed from what the FBI considers "similar" agencies. The county level data do not correct for these underreporting problems and simply report the error filled crime counts. Another advantage of state level studies is that they are less likely to have results impacted by displacement. The larger geographic areas make it less likely that potential criminals are just substituting unprotected targets by engaging in criminal activity in a completely different state.

Both Zimmerman (2014) and Meehan and Benson (2017) use the state level measures in panel studies to examine the impact of private security on crime. Zimmerman uses the Arellano and Bond (1991) estimation technique to account for the endogeneity of crime and private security. This technique uses lagged values of private security employees to instrument for current period numbers. The paper results suggest some deterrence impact for private security for murder and larceny, although these results are sensitive to estimation specification choice.

Meehan and Benson (2017) use occupational licensing requirements as instrumental variables to address endogeneity concerns. Findings suggest that increases in private security generate reductions in robbery and burglary rates (significant at the 5% level) and for larceny and motor vehicle theft (significant at the 10% level). The occupational licensing requirements used were: law enforcement experience, bond and insurance, training, and examination requirements. These licensing requirements tended to be firm level license requirements. The goal was to find the regulations that served as entry conditions for an independent contractor or firm and not as an employee of an existing firm. Overall the results suggested that private security had a large role in deterring property crime, as a 30% increase in the instrumented private security firms was associated in an 11.8% decrease in property crimes. The occupational licensing regulations examined looked at unarmed guards, and were intended to be a lower bound for entry into this industry. Many states have additional requirements for armed guards. Most security guards are not armed in the U.S. and around the world. Estimates of the proportion of security guards that are armed ranges from 20% to 30% (Graduate Institute of International Development Studies, 2011) to less than 10% (Cunningham & Taylor, 1985) in the U.S.

As an alternative to the county and state level panel data approaches, MacDonald et al. (2016) focused their analysis on a small section of the city of Philadelphia. This analysis attempts to measure the impact of sustained geographic variations in police officers, and the sustained impact on crime. The study explores geographic variations in police, examining police levels and subsequent crime levels on either side of a private police patrol boundary around the University of Pennsylvania by pooling city block level around this boundary from 2006 and 2010. The authors argue that this boundary is a historical artifact and blocks on either side of this boundary are believed to be very similar in their sociodemographic characteristics. The number of actively patrolling private police within the University of Pennsylvania's Police patrol zone was more than double number of publicly funded police in the neighborhood blocks just outside the boundary. The natural variation was the larger (private) police force patrolling one side of this area. The number of private police was more than twice the number of public police on the other side of the boundary. This larger private police force was associated with a 45–60% reduction in all reported crimes in the neighborhoods on the Penn Police patrol side of the boundary. The study estimated elasticities for these private police of −0.7 for violent crimes and −0.2 for property crimes. They also address displacement concerns with the following statement:

> We also estimated our models by using yearly block level data and obtained substantively similar findings. Because crime rates dropped overall in the University City district between 2005 and 2010 this provides evidence that the addition of Penn Police did not simply displace crime to other parts of the University City district. (pg. 834)

6   The Relationship Between Police and Private Security

If private security can act as a general crime deterrent, what is the mechanism by which it works? Does it produce these results as a stand-alone service or does it act as a complement to public police efforts? Private security and public police could substitute for one another as crime deterrents in some roles. The presence of security guards tends to increase the costs of attacking a specific target much like the presence of public police officers would. Private security guards often operate in similar ways to police through patrol and increase the probability of potential criminals becoming apprehended. But in some areas, private security guards have provided substitutes for many of the duties typically assigned to public police.

Governments often shed services or contract out depending on the nature of the service. Theoretically, when government provides a service that aids an individual entity and imposes no positive or negative externalities on others, it is providing a private good which could be shed for market provision. For example, some local governments provide animal control services, like capturing a bird caught in a chimney, where the service seems not to have any effects beyond the individual site and thus should be shed by police. If police offer such service, it will usually not be provided by private firms. On the other hand, when the service is a public good, shifting its provision from monopolistic police to competitive market provision could yield more efficient production, which may also reflect lower costs of inputs. For example, police response to a domestic dispute may generate positive externalities for the community, but the use of a professional psychologist or social worker may be more effective than a response of sworn officer or other typical first responders (see Cacciatore et al. 2011 for an example program involving social workers teamed with fire department first responders). In both cases of contracting-out and shedding, police could be allowed to compete with the private firms for the provision of the service. Such police involvement requires that it is conducted "under level playing field rules." Contracting out public good services requires that the output can be clearly quantified in the contract, and that the demand for such a service is greater than the minimum threshold for normal profits. In the case of shedding, government no longer assumes responsibility for the service. Indeed, shedding is the greatest degree of privatization. In both shedding and contracting out the objective is to increase efficiency, where competition replaces monopolistic police.

Obviously, private security can also provide similar or enhanced versions of the services provided by public police. For example, police patrol provides deterrence and faster response to crimes than police dispatch. However, merchants of a particular shopping area may wish to enhance security beyond the "standard" police level to attract customers and, therefore, they hire a private security company to complement police presence. This is a privately provided public good, which is effectively a Public Private Partnership.

An example of shedding is the case of burglar alarm response in Salt Lake City, Utah. When police respond to burglar alarm activations, 94 to 99 percent of the time they are false alarms. Blackstone et al. (2020) argue that such responses to false activations are a private good where only the alarm owner benefits, and such service must be shed. Police could choose to compete with private response companies if they do so on a leveled playfield. Indeed, Salt Lake City (SLC) changed its alarm ordinance to require verification of an actual or attempted burglary before police will respond. The initial response to the alarm in this scenario is by a contracted security guard service. The results of this Verified Response policy in SLC were a decrease in the number of police responses to false alarms by 87 percent. Also, police responses to high priority calls improved, as it declined from an average of 12:04 minutes to 4:05 after the policy was implemented. While response to lower priority calls also improved, as on average it fell from 11:52 minutes to 8:37 minutes between 2000 and 2003. Burglaries also declined in the relevant period by 26 percent relative to burglaries in a control group of cities. Since response to high priority calls, including valid burglar alarms, significantly declined, burglary deterrence increased. In addition to faster police responses, the community benefited by having alarm owners pay for the costs they initially imposed on police and the subsequent savings in police expenditures generated crime reduction benefits, while specialization occurred in the competitive market for private alarm response that developed.

Contracting out specific police services is illustrated by two following examples. In 2019, Milwaukee announced a plan that instead of hiring additional officers, to add cameras and to employ a private security company to assist the police to fight crime. Also, in 2019 Virginia signed a contract for a private security firm to transport mental health patients instead of using sworn officers. In both these examples, private security companies substituted for police in performing a public good service (Perry, 2020: 51). Competition is here introduced through the open and widely advertised bidding for the service. Contracting out is the intermediate degree of privatization. The ultimate solution where possible, is to allow consumers sovereignty as discussed in the Salt Lake City example. However, where the services are public goods, government is more likely to be responsible for their provision and should do so for a given quality at the lowest costs. Thus, contracting out using open bidding is a potential solution for this public goods provision where feasible.

Hybrid models are the most common and growing form of Public Private Partnership (PPP) where both police and private security participate in the delivery of a public good. In this category, the supply level of police services is insufficient for the consumers who demand more and supplement police with private security. Two major employers for such cooperation and complementarity are hospitals and educational institutions, which according to BLS (2022, B) are the largest employers (at 6 percent each) of private security guards other than security firms.

With the rise of attacks on the medical staff in hospitals,[2] police response tends to be relatively slow and demand for supplementary private security has became

---

[2] For anecdotal evidence of this problem, see Robert Javlon and Stephan Dafazio, "Police ID Suspect in Attack on Doctoe, Nyrses in LA Hospital", Associated Press June 4, 2022. https://www.usnews.com/news/us/articles/2022-06-04/man-held-in-attack-on-doctor-nurses-at-california-hospital

acute. One indication of the security problem in hospitals is the recent Occupational Health and Safety Administration (OHSA) report, which states: "almost 75 percent of workplace violent victims are employed in healthcare settings" (Shah et al., 2022). Healthcare workers suffer more than 5 times the risk of workplace violence than workers in general. Hospitals are especially vulnerable for both patients and medical staff (Shah et al., 2022). Emergency rooms and psychiatric wards are especially vulnerable. A survey of 340 US hospitals revealed that 72 percent employed non-sworn officers, 18 percent employed sworn officers, 21 percent of hospitals had public police officers, 3 percent used contract security guards of whom 28 percent were non-sworn. Almost half of private security officers had the power of arrest (Schoenson & Pompeii, 2016).

Colleges and universities compete for students and therefore need to address the major considerations of parents and the prospective students. In a survey of parents, a safe environment was found to be a top concern with 74.5 percent saying it was the most important consideration (Youngblood, 2015). Universities and colleges are also inviting targets for those who want to commit property or violent crimes. The Clery Act of 1990 requires colleges and universities to collect and publish statistics on crime in and around their campuses. Since its passage, rising numbers of colleges and universities have employed security services of their own. In the academic year 2011/12 75 percent of campuses had their own sworn and armed officers growing from 68 percent 7 years earlier. Overall, 94 percent of sworn officers were armed. The campus private officers usually have full police powers, and often patrol areas surrounding the campus. Seventy percent of the campus police have a cooperative agreement with the outside law enforcement agencies in their communities (Reaves, 2015). Campus police may request the City's police help investigating crime, and the Campus officers patrol the neighborhood and sometimes respond to 911 calls. When a city officer stops a driver or a suspect, campus police may assist the officer. Another form of private supplementing, used in addition to both city and campus police, is when parents hire a private force to patrol the vicinity of the students' residences (Armstrong, 2022).

In Washington DC, New Orleans,[3] San Francisco, Los Angeles, and Portland Oregon neighborhoods and business districts have hired private security companies to enhance public police protection. On occasion, sworn officers work as private security to supplement their police earnings. Residents of some wealthy neighborhoods, retail business districts or chain stores, and critical infrastructure augment standard police protection with private police. On private property, private security has the same powers as the owner, which is substantial, while on public property private security can exercise citizens' arrest power and then turn the perpetrator over to police. In New York City, for example, off duty police officers guard local retail chains where the payments by the merchants are funneled through the city and paid as overtime to the officers (Akinnibi & Holder, 2022).

---

[3] See Chapter "How to Fight Crime by Improving Police Services: Evidence from the French Quarter Task Force" by Long in this volume.

The San Francisco Patrol Special Police was founded in 1847 and includes non-sworn officers that are under the regulatory control of the San Francisco police commission. The patrol provides a variety of private security services and are paid by the clients on an hourly basis. They attend civic and merchant meetings to stay aware of the needs of the community. A 2009 survey conducted by Stringham showed that the Special Police force made the neighborhoods where they operate safer than other neighborhoods (Wikipedia, 2022). This private group relieves the police of dealing with low priority private matters that prevent police in other communities from concentrating on their main mission. The services provided by the Special Police are mostly private goods and usually do not involve externalities. The exceptions include the response to valid 911 calls, apprehending law breakers, or aiding public police in emergencies.

Since most services provided by the Special police are private or client oriented, free entry should be allowed to create a more competitive market. In the case above of Salt Lake City, its Verified Response (VR) policy allowed free entry of burglar alarm response companies so that alarm owners could choose among them. This free entry policy increased social welfare, which is reduced in the San Francisco practice since the Special Police seem to have monopolistic power for low priority responses. However, even with this deficiency the San Francisco practice is still superior to most other communities where response for private services in funded and conducted by public police.

7 Discussion

The private investigation industry is small and is composed of small firms, limited use of technology, 2.1 percent growth, which is roughly similar to or slightly below US GDP average growth. The industry has modest profitability and likely lacks economies of scale and scope. The average wage of private detectives over time has been around 45–47 percent of police detectives. There has been no significant contracting out of detective tasks from government over time. Police detectives have been trained and employed as patrol officers before being promoted to detectives. The state regulations for private detectives have been generally modest compared with the training of public detectives. Thus, there is no apparent reason for police to contract out services to private detectives. There is another group of investigators employed by large law or accounting firms for which no data exist and therefore is not addressed here.

One growth area for private investigators is closely related to counterfeit goods and fraud, where brand named companies hire private detectives and then provide the evidence to the district attorney to pursue criminal charges. Identity thefts, which most often extend beyond local jurisdictions are not addressed by police or the district attorney's office, and often require professional private help. The rapid growth of such crimes may provide opportunities for highly professional private detectives. It is evident, however, that the existing industry is not yet equipped to address this expected growing demand. In fact, police have in many cases shed enforcement of these laws, forcing victims to seek private help.

In 2022, public detectives are usually hired after successfully serving as a line police officer with considerable professional experience. Also, to be promoted to detective, police officers must pass a test. Private detectives usually must meet more modest requirements. Further, the small size of such firms and their limited capital and technology make less likely contracting out from police, district attorneys, and federal agencies. However, retired police detectives are the prime candidates for entering the private detective industry to improve its performance. Further, to address crimes like identity thefts, fraud, and other cyber related crimes an investigative firm needs in-house accountants, lawyers, IT professionals, and good investigators. Demand by victims and contracting out by public agencies must grow significantly to enable this industry to hire such high-income professionals. The current fragmented and highly competitive industry shows few signs of meeting the challenge.

The growth of both the investigative and the guard industries has been similar and modest over this period and even below GDP growth. The guard segment of the industry has been adopting technology, witnessed mergers that may well result in, and lead to, more technological and managerial innovations but that also may have been the result of regulatory incentives. The ability of the guard industry to adopt new technology and procedures as well as its flexibility to change may have contributed to government at all levels to contract out services to them. On the other hand, investigative services seem to remain structurally as small firms and show limited signs for technological and managerial innovations. Technological gains in security services can be witnessed on many fronts, security companies introducing new cameras, alarms, and equipment. It appears that investigative services haven't been as active in these endeavors, perhaps that is why there is a reluctance by individuals and government to contract out these services.

Forecasting the near future is risky, but it is reasonable to assume that the guard services, which appear to innovate and have moved to the low end of regulatory or technologically induced oligopoly, and as such exhibit a greater chance of economic profits and further growth. Thus, this trend seems to provide incentives for government and police to contract out services to the large private guard companies and even establish Public Private Partnerships (P3) relationships. On the other hand, government seems not to gain from either contracting out or establishing P3 relationships with the private investigative industry, which suggest that this industry is not expected to experience significant growth. One possible exception may arise from the rapidly growing new types of internet crimes where state and local authorities refrain from addressing, and thus shift victims to the private investigation industry. However, since dealing with such IT crimes requires professional efforts that are missing in the "traditional" small investigation companies, it is reasonable to conclude that addressing such crimes will be in IT companies or large law or accounting companies and will not yield any significant demand to the existing investigative industry.

The guard industry provides direct preventive and deterrence services to clients, where they address the specific client requirements. The number of private guards is estimated to be 20 percent higher than all officers at local, state, and federal law enforcement agencies (BLS, A & B).

The guard industry is modestly concentrated where the share of the largest firms is likely to grow somewhat. The firms have adopted technology to be able to provide integrated security services that clients demand. Their purchasing flexibility unlike the rigid and bureaucratic public police, their large size which allows them to potentially utilize economies of scale, and their lower wages than public police together enables them to provide services at lower costs than public police. Further, the competition among the large firms encourages adoption of new technology and efficiency in the delivery of services. Thus, we expect more contracting out of specific security services by government including even the police. For example, it is possible to reduce or complement patrolling with cameras spread throughout the community, as was planned for in most of London (Satariano, 2020). The system could even be integrated with drones. In case of a serious event, a task force or nearby patrol officer could be dispatched to the site. Such a service would likely deter burglars and other law breakers because of the high visibility and quicker response. It may be conducted by local police or, because of significant technological efficiencies, be contracted out to private security. A national security company that installs and operates such systems in many places may resolve problems that local police may be unable to do. One cautionary note is that the industry concentration now is modest but it would be undesirable for regulation to make entry difficult so that competition is threatened. Allowing police or existing security companies to exercise control over entry of a potential competitors is also problematic (Meehan & Benson, 2015).

Police officers are often extensively trained for some the tasks they perform, but not well trained for others. Specialization in the areas that they are better trained, or areas where they have a comparative advantage (dealing with violent crime deterrence and investigation perhaps) may increase efficiency. Police often perform tasks for which they overqualified and overpaid relative to alternative service providers. For example, sworn officers work as clerks, write parking tickets, guarding municipal facilities, directing traffic, or helping children cross the street. Such tasks can be contracted out under competitive bidding to lower paid guards of private companies. On the hand, officers are often underqualified to manage technology or investigate financial frauds that require highly paid professionals whose salaries are beyond government levels (see Fig. 5 for IT/cyber security service wages). This again creates an opportunity for contracting out, or complete shedding, of such services and increased specialization by existing police forces.

The wages of all police officers vary in a small range depending on rank and seniority. There is only limited room for merit pay for performance. Thus, it is not unusual that officers are over or under paid for their task and their individual productivity. On the other hand, workers in private companies are usually compensated by their task and productivity. Unlike monopolistic police, private security companies are motivated by increasing profits and thus improve productivity and seek to obtain additional clients while competing with other similar companies. Finally, monopolistic police do not have to respond to consumer preferences as much as private companies in a competitive environment.

Introducing the mere possibility of competition will encourage police to improve their performance to preserve their jobs. To conclude, introducing competition to a government monopoly that is normally slow to innovate and respond to consumer preferences is especially likely to improve overall performance.

8 Conclusion

This chapter presented and analyzed the trends in US public and private security, their hypothesized causes from both the demand and supply factors, the private security markets for both guards and detectives, and suggested future trends and policy implications. Spending and employment of public police seem to closely relate to state and local budgets and employment while being unrelated to traditional crime rates and the new internet related crimes. On the other hand, private security employment has a closer relationship to real GDP changes, or the resources available for their clients, while somewhat unrelated to crime fluctuations.

We also analyzed private security and detective market structures including concentration and entry barriers between 1997 and 2017. We find that the guard segment has experienced increased concentration, and borders on oligopoly. The investigative services industry remains relatively unconcentrated, comprised of small firms. Mergers in the guard segment have led to larger firms with more advanced technology which allows them to offer integrated security services. The flexibility of operations, adoption of technology, pecuniary economies of scale and possible economies of scope along with a market structure conducive to modest profitability and strong innovation bodes well for the future of the industry. On the other hand, the unconcentrated private detective industry with an average firm size of three employees, earning at best normal profits and using limited technology is not likely to exhibit significant growth in the coming years. The sources of growth for the security industry overall are likely to come from colleges and universities, healthcare including hospitals and in particular government at all three levels. Contracting out security by these three sectors and businesses in general depends on lower costs and improved quality of service. Government has contracted out guard services but not investigative services and is likely to continue to do so. Large businesses, in general, contract out non-core activities in order that their management can concentrate on the core activities.

The evidence presented above also suggests that private security acts as a general crime deterrent and may possibly act as a complement to public police efforts. If private security generates positive spillovers (as general deterrence would suggest) this would indicate that there is probably an underinvestment in private security relative to what would be the efficient level. Meehan and Benson (2017) demonstrated the negative impacts of occupational licensing regulations on the number of private security firms, which was subsequently correlated with increasing property crime. Thus, the impacts of private security regulation and regulatory formation are of interest to policy makers.

U.S. State law makers should be careful when allocating power to occupational licensing boards dominated by already licensed practitioners or controlled by potential substitute providers. In particular, in areas where underinvestment already exists. These licensed industry members may erect barriers to entry, via licensing requirements, to reduce competition for their services. In the case of private security guards, this comes with another cost to the U.S. criminal justice system, as positive spillovers in the prevention of crime and efficient allocation of public police resources may be sacrificed.

Police training includes coverage of most issues police confront. Sworn officers who are paid significantly more than private guards are often assign to activities that could be fulfilled by lower paid individuals. Examples include officers doing clerical work, officers directing or controlling traffic, guarding municipal facilities, helping children cross the street or escorting funerals. Private guards could be contracted for all such activities. On the other hand, police officers often lack the knowledge to handle Internet related fraud or identity theft that their constituents face, and subsequently a small industry of high paid IT/cyber security experts has emerged to address these issues.

Indeed, government, colleges and universities, among others, already contract private security companies, primarily guard companies that specialize in their specific requirements. These demands are expected to grow, leading to improved managerial and technological innovations of such companies, while the competition among them could provide competitive priciness for their services. The current generally lower professional level of private investigators in comparison to public law enforcement makes difficult significant joint efforts of the two sectors. Unlike the private guard service, the private investigation industry is not expected to grow soon.

References

Akinnibi, F., & Holder, S. (2022, Feb 23). NYC businesses hire off-duty police to blunt uptick in violent crime. *Bloomberg US Edition*. https://www.bloomberg.com/news/features/2022-02-23/new-york-city-businesses-hire-off-duty-police-officers-to-blunt-crime-increase. Last visited 5-27-2022.

Arellano, M., & Bond, S. (1991). Some tests of specification for panel data: Monte Carlo evidence and an application to employment equations. *The Review of Economic Studies, 58*(2), 277–297.

Armstrong, J. (2022, March 3). Temple mom was right to hire off-Temple security. *The Philadelphia Inquirer*: A13.

Ayres, I., & Levitt, S. D. (1998). Measuring positive externalities from unobservable victim precaution: An empirical analysis of Lojack. *The Quarterly Journal of Economics, 113*(1), 43–77.

Becker, G. S. (1968). Crime and punishment: An economic approach. *Journal of Political Economy, 76*(2), 169–217.

Benson, B. L., & Mast, B. D. (2001). Privately produced general deterrence. *Journal of Law and Economics, 44*(2), 725–746.

Blackstone, E. A., & Hakim, S. (2010). Private policing: Experiences, evaluation, and future direction. In B. L. Benson & P. R. Zimmerman (Eds.), *Handbook on the economics of crime*. Edward Elgar.

Blackstone, E. A., Hakim, S., & Meehan, B. (2020). Burglary reduction and improved police performance through private alarm response. *International Review of Law and Economics, 63*, 1–13.

Bureau of Labor Statistics (BLS, A). (2022, April 18). *Occupational outlook handbook*. Private Investigators. https://www.bls.gov/ooh/protective-service/private-detectives-and-investigators.htm#tab-3. Last visited 5–25–2022.

Bureau of Labor Statistics (BLS, B). (2022, April 18). *Occupational outlook handbook*. Private Guards and Gambling Surveillance Officers. https://www.bls.gov/ooh/protective-service/security-guards.htm#tab-3. Last visited 5–25–2022.

Cacciatore, J., Carlson, B., Michaelis, E., Klimek, B., & Steffan, S. (2011). Crisis intervention by social workers in fire departments: An innovative role for social workers. *Social Work, 56*(1), 81–88.

Caramela, S. (2022, April 14). Startup costs: How much cash will you need?. *Business News Daily*. https://www.businessnewsdaily.com/5-small-business-start-up-costs-options.html

C. Barnes & Co. (2021). *U.S. Industry and market report: NAICS 561611: Investigation Services Industry*.

Cunningham, W. C., & Taylor, T. H. (1985). *Crime and protection in America: A study of private security and law enforcement resources and relationships*. U.S. Department of Justice, National Institute of Justice.

Faber, K. (2013, Nov 5). *The 10 most common specialties of private investigators*. PInow.com. https://www.pinow.com/articles/1737/the-10-most-common-specialties-of-private-investigators. Last visited 5-19-2022.

Ehrlich, I. (1973). Participation in illegitimate activities: A theoretical and empirical investigation. *Journal of Political Economy, 81*, 521–565.

Gonzalez-Navarro, M. (2013). Deterrence and geographical externalities in auto theft. *American Economic Journal: Applied Economics, 5*(4), 92–110.

Graduate Institute of International Development Studies. (2011). *Small arms survey: States of security*. Graduate Institute of International Development Studies.

Grogger, J. (1991). Certainty vs. severity of punishment. *Economic Inquiry.*, Western Economic Association International, *29*(2), 297–309.

Hirschman, A. O. (1964). The paternity of an index. *The American Economic Review*. American Economic Association, *54*(5), 761–762.

IBISWorld. (2020, Nov). *Private detective services, Industry Report OD4407*.

Joh, E. E. (2004). The paradox of private policing. *Journal of Criminal Law and Criminology.*, *95*(1), 49–132.

Lee, D., & McCrary, J. (2009). *The Deterrence effect of prison: Dynamic theory and evidence*. No. 1168. Princeton University, Department of Economics, Center for Economic Policy Studies.

MacDonald, J. M., Klick, J., & Grunwald, B. (2016). The effect of private police on crime: Evidence from a geographic regression discontinuity design. *Journal of the Royal Statistical Society A, 179*(3), 831–846.

Maltz, M. D., & Targonski, J. (2002). A note on the use of county-level UCR data. *Journal of Quantitative Criminology, 18*(3), 297–318.

Meehan, B. (2015). The impact of licensing requirements on industrial organization and labor: Evidence from the US private security market. *International Review of Law and Economics, 42*(C), 113–121.

Meehan, B., & Benson, B. L. (2015). The occupations of regulators influence occupational regulation: Evidence from the US private security industry. *Public Choice, 162*(1–2), 97–117.

Meehan, B., & Benson, B. L. (2017). Does private security affect crime?: A test using state regulations as instruments. *Applied Economics, 49*(48), 4911–4924.

Oxford Reference. (n.d.). *Four-Firm Concentration Ratio*, https://www.oxfordreference.com/view/10.1093/oi/authority.20110803095831707#:~:text=The%20four-firm%20ratio%20is,held%20to%20indicate%20an%20oligopoly

Perry, R. H. (2020, Aug). *U.S. Contract Security Industry*. Robert H. Perry & Associates, Inc. https://www.nasco.org/wp-content/uploads/2020/09/2020_White_Paper_FINAL.pdf. Last visited 5-23-2022.

Perry, R. H. (2021, April 12). *Analysis of Allied Universal Merger of G4S*. Security Information. com https://www.securityinfowatch.com/security-executives/protective-operations-guard-services/article/21218234/analyst-allied-universals-acquisition-of-g4s-a-deal-of-historic-proportions. Last visited 5-23-2022.

Reaves, B. A. (2015). *Campus Law Enforcement, 2011–12*. Special Report, U.S. Department of Justice, Office of Justice Programs, Bureau of Justice Statistics, January.

Satariano, A. (2020, Jan 24). London police are taking surveillance to a whole new level. *New York Times*, https://www.nytimes.com/2020/01/24/business/london-police-facial-recognition.html. Accessed 5 June 2022.

Schoenson, A. L., & Pompeii, L. A. (2016). Security personnel practices and policies in U.S. hospitals. *Workplace Health & Safety, 64*(11), 531–542.

Securitas AB. (2021, July 30). *Securitas AB: Company Profile*. http://www.marketing.comcessed/. May 19, 2022.

Shah, Y., et al. (2022, May 22). *Gun violence in a hospital*. Philadelphia Inquirer, G2.

U. S. Department of Justice. 2010 Horizontal Merger Guideline. (2010). https://www.justice.gov/atr/horizontal-merger-guidelines-08192010. Last visited June 4, 2022.

Wiblin, B. (2021, Nov 8). What is EBITDA and how to calculate it. *Life & Money*, https://www.firstrepublic.com/articles-insights/life-money/build-your-business/what-is-ebitda-and-how-to-calculate-it. Last visited 5-20-2022.

Wikipedia. (2022). *San Francisco Patrol Special Police*. https://en.wikipedia.org/wiki/San_Francisco_Patrol_Special_Police. Last visited 5-28-2022.

Youngblood, J. (2015). *Report: What do parents want from colleges?*. https://www.noodle.com/articles/report-what-do-parents-want-from-colleges. Last visited 5-26-2022.

Zedlewski, E. W. (1992). Private security and controlling crime. In G. W. Bowman, S. Hakim, & P. Seidenstat (Eds.), *Privatizing the United States Justice System: Police adjudication, and corrections services from the private sector*. McFarland & Company.

Zimmerman, P. R. (2014). The deterrence of crime through private security efforts: Theory and evidence. *International Review of Law and Economics, 37*, 66–75.

Part I
General Security Issues

Allocating Police and Security: Comparing Public and Private Processes and Consequences

Bruce L. Benson

Abstract Most resource, including police and private security labor and capital, are scarce so they must be allocated (rationed) among alternative uses. There are many ways to allocate scare resources. A lottery might be used, for instance, a coercive authority (government including a legislature, court, executive or executive bureaucracy; the Mafia or other organizations) might impose an allocation, first-come-first serve means allocating by queuing (waiting) and/or search, so the allocation reflects the willingness to spend time waiting or searching. Those not willing to pay the time price often simply opt out, choosing not to pursue the good or service. With prices, if people are willing to pay the market price for some type of good or service, they can obtain it. This process tends toward efficient allocation if regulations do not prevent it. Each of these rationing processes affect incentives of people involved.

Private security is allocation through market prices. This market need not result in efficiency, however, because there are numerous regulations in some security markets limiting the types of security that can be provided, limit entry into some markets, and so on. Public policing involves numerous allocation mechanisms. One is the political process, so groups and perhaps individuals who have the most political influence tend to get more and better public policing services. Another police rationing mechanism is first-come-first-serve. The victims of many crimes wait forever because their cases are not ever considered by police investigators. This means that many people who are crime victims do not enter the queue (report crimes). It also implies another rationing mechanism. When there is excess demand, the suppliers (police officials, prosecutors, legislatures) have considerable discretion to decide which crimes will be considered and which will not. That decision will reflect a supplier's personal objectives and the political pressures they face. The allocation may reflect the police officer's prejudices, or monetary incentives (corruption and bribery, asset seizures in some situations). Many victims get no attention

B. L. Benson (✉)
Florida State University, Tallahassee, FL, USA
e-mail: bbenson@fsu.edu

© The Author(s), under exclusive license to Springer Nature Switzerland AG 2023
E. A. Blackstone et al. (eds.), *Handbook on Public and Private Security*,
Competitive Government: Public Private Partnerships,
https://doi.org/10.1007/978-3-031-42406-9_2

27

because of their race, gender, or sexual orientation. Many get attention because they are a different race, gender, sexual preferences, or they have income (e.g., to bribe), political influence, or they are attractive, friendly, etc. This chapter explores the economic and equity implications of these allocations procedures.

1   Introduction[1]

Public policing is often alleged to be a public good. Samuelson (1954, 1955) developed the "public good" concept, and subsequent theoretical clarifications (see McNutt, 2000) resulted in economists' general understanding of the terminology (McNutt, 2000, 927–928): a public good is non-rivalrous in consumption, and non-excludable, which combine to produce free riding incentives, and therefore, voluntary private provision will not occur because a supplier cannot expect full payment; therefore, coercive power is necessary to collect payments (e.g., taxes). One implication of a public good is that a rationing process not required. Scarcity implies tradeoffs, so scarce resources/goods generally must be allocated (rationed) among competing uses, but this is not relevant for a public good, because it is non-rivalrous in consumption.[2] Indeed, since a public good also is non-excludable, rationing is not possible.

If the characterization of policing as a public good is accurate, private security apparently is very different from policing, since it is privately provided and rationed through market prices. The following presentation demonstrates that there are, in fact, tradeoffs in the allocation of public policing resources, and that public policing is rationed. In this sense, private security and public police actually have much in common. However, the rationing mechanism for public police and private security are quite different, creating different incentives, and leading to differences in police and security personnel behavior.

A "private good" generally refers to private ownership.[3] Non-owners can be excluded because of enforceable property rights,[4] even if the good is physically non-rivalrous in consumption. Since exclusion can occur through legal actions, a non-owner desiring legal access has to negotiate with the owner.[5] The owner can allow

---

[1] Parts of this paper draws from Benson (1988, 2010, 2014), and Benson and Meehan (2018).

[2] If the resources used to produce a true public good are scarce, then there are tradeoffs at the pre-production stage, and some method is required to allocate the scarce resources between production of the public good and alternatives.

[3] Within the public-goods literature, private goods often are assumed to be completely rivalrous in consumption. Physical consumption certainly is one method of exclusion, but there are others.

[4] Demsetz (1970) shows that when exclusion is possible, non-rivalrous consumption will not prevent private provision. Following his article, "many economists conclude that non-excludability is generally the only serious problem in the provision of public goods" (Cowen, 1988, 9).

[5] Goldin (1977) explains that there are actually no inherently public goods because there are always institutional choices available that can be used to exclude.

simultaneous access by others, but the good is only non-rivalrous to those granted access. In fact, the owner can choose to exclusively use the physically non-rivalrous good repeatedly. On the other hand, when property rights are not defined, so a substantial number of people have free or "common" access to a good/resource, a common pool arises. The provider may be nature (a natural resource) or a supplier who chooses to give it away without receiving a money price (often a government). Excess demand and shortages arise with any price below the market clearing level, including a zero money price (free access) because there are people willing to pay a positive price but who cannot get it. Excess demand and shortages demonstrate that consumption is rivalrous. This creates incentives for potential users to rush in to the commons in order to capture benefits without spending too much time waiting in a queue (before others enter and diminish net benefits for everyone due to crowding/congestion). Indeed, free access to a good does not mean it is free, since time must be spent, and as the time price for obtaining the good rises, demand falls. Rationing is by first-come-first-serve.[6]

When a price is paid with time rather than money, and each entrant diminishes the benefits (creates a negative externality) for all users.[7] A shortage and rising time costs (congestion/crowding) implies deterioration in net value and availability means if the shortage is great enough, some people who want the good may end up not being able to get it (they are crowded out) or what they do get is not worth the time it takes to obtain it.[8] Others who recognize what is going on decide to opt out, choosing not to pursue the good/resource. The "tragedy of the commons" (Hardin, 1968) of crowding (congestion), overuse, and rapid depletion (relative to what would be efficient) is a negative externality problem because no user is fully liable for the cost of use.[9]

Deterioration in quality and availability of common pools might be at least partially offset with appropriate investments in maintenance or improvements, but individuals do not have incentives to make such investments because they cannot prevent others with free access from consuming the resulting benefits. This underproduction of maintenance is a positive externality problem. While it might be contended that "public goods" and "common pools" are simply two terms for the same

---

[6] Allocation through violence is actually likely unless everyone has similar capacity for violence or effective policing maintains order by limiting violence..

[7] The pool may be large enough to accommodate a number of users before external costs begin to materialize, so the common pool may initially appear to be abundant (not scarce), and therefore, perhaps a public good. However, with a zero money price, entry by consumers continues and inevitably rivalrous consumption occurs, causing congestion. In this context, Benson (1994) contends that in reality there are few if any true public goods because entry virtually always continues beyond the point where rivalrous consumption and crowding arise. Thus, most so-called public goods become common pools.

[8] Those willing to wait, hoping to get the good, place a very high value on the good, or people who have a low value of time.

[9] People have incentives to develop limits on access to a commons, so a common pool should persist only if the cost of limiting access is higher than the benefits, perhaps because a coercive power forces free access (Johnson & Libecap, 1982).

concept because the same nonpayment incentives arise, this inference is inappropriate. Free riding is a decision to consume without paying for personal benefits, while common pool underinvestment is an unwillingness to pay for benefits others will capture. These are very different motivations.

When an good or service is underpriced (e.g., apartments under rent controls, a free access publicly provided service), the resulting excess demand means that suppliers (e.g., landlords, public bureaucrats) often have considerable discretion to decide which demanders will get some portion of the good or resource. In other words, setting up a rationing process based on waiting time, often leads to rationing according to supplier discretion. Suppliers facing persistent excess demand while not being allowed to or choosing not to raise prices, naturally develop discriminatory rules and processes to decide how to allocate the underpriced good. An apartment owner in a rent-controlled city or a bureaucrat may require a bribe, or choose not to ration apartments or services to students, racial minorities, people with pets, and so on. If she feels the rule will be seen as meritorious, she may provide information about her rationing criteria. Merit rationing in general reflects the supplier's subjective choice of an allocation based on something she can justify as meritorious (e.g., civil service jobs are rationed, at least in part, by performance on exams; in many states, private security licenses also require performance on an exam along with other indicators of merit – see below).

There are many ways to allocate scare resource and rationing mechanism determines the nature of the competition to guide resource use. Private security resources are primarily allocated through market processes (price rationing). Scarce public police resources are generally not rationed by willingness to pay a money price (unless corruption is present), so they must be rationed in some other way (Shoup, 1964), such as, but not necessarily exclusively, by first-come-first-serve and supplier discretion or preferred merit criterion. After rejecting characterization of policing as a public good in Sect. 2, the relevant rationing methods for and behavioral consequences for public police and private security are examined in Sects. 3 and 4.[10] Section 5 concludes.

2   Is Policing a Private Good, Public Good, or Something Else?

Police and private security are expected to prevent (deter) crimes. Obviously, not all crimes are prevented, so police are also expected to investigate committed crimes, and to pursue offenders. Private security's role in investigation and pursuit appears to be relatively small, in part at least, because government regulations limit the

---

[10] The evidence employed in this presentation is virtually all drawn from observations of policing and security in the United States, so some of the conclusions may not generalize to other countries where institutions and constraints affecting police and/or security rationing differ from those that dominate in the U.S.

potential for successful production and sale of such private services. Nonetheless, there are specialized markets for private investigation and pursuit, as illustrated below.

Crimes reported to police provide a very imperfect indicator of crimes not prevented by police or security. In the U.S., the Federal Bureau of Investigation's (FBI) annual *Uniform Crime Report* (UCR) provides data on reported murder and manslaughter, rape, aggravated assault, robbery, burglary, larceny, motor vehicle theft and arson, the so called "Index I" crimes. 2019 estimates of nationally reported crimes are provided in Table 1, as well as calculated "crime rates" per 100,000 population, implying reported crimes are reasonable measures of crime levels. Unfortunately, reported crimes do not come close to total crimes. According to the 2019 U. S. *Victimization Survey*, only 40.9 percent of total violent crimes and 32.5 percent of property crimes were reported by victims (reporting percentages for specific crimes are in Table 1) (Morgan & Thompson, 2021).[11] Police success in arresting criminals responsible for reported crimes is crudely measured by total arrests, or by clearance rates, both also listed in Table 1.[12]

Table 1 2019 U.S. Reported Index I crimes, crime rates, arrests, clearance rates and victim reporting rates

Crime	Reported crimes	Crime rate	Total arrests	Clearance rate	% Reported by victims
Murder & non-negligent manslaughter	16,425	5.0	11,060	61.4%	a
Rape	139,815	42.6	24,986	32.9%	33.9%
Robbery	267,988	81.6	74,547	30.5%	46.6%
Aggravated assault	821,182	250.2	385,278	52.3%	40.9%
Burglary	1,117,696	340.5	171,590	14.1%	51.4%
Larceny–theft	5,086,096	1549.5	813,075	18.4%	26.8%
Motor vehicle theft	721,885	219.9	80,636	13.8%	79.5%
Arson	32,981	10.9	9068	23.4%	a

Source: US Department of Justice, Federal Bureau of Investigation, Criminal Justice Information Services division, *Crime in the United States, 2019*, Table 25 https://ucr.fbi.gov/crime-in-the-u.s/2019/crime-in-the-u.s.-2019/topic-pages/tables/table-25; Table 1, https://ucr.fbi.gov/crime-in-the-u.s/2019/crime-in-the-u.s.-2019/topic-pages/tables/table-1; and Table 29
aMurder victims cannot report crimes, and essentially all arsons are reported to fire departments

---

[11] Non-reporting by police agencies also reduces the reliability of reported crime statistics. Many police departments, the source of data in Table 1, do not provide their data to the FBI. Missing data must be estimated. In 2019, The FBI received data from 15,334 of 18,674 law enforcement agencies in the country, but they only used data from 9991 jurisdictions to produce their crime estimates. https://crime-data-explorer.app.cloud.gov/pages/explorer/crime/crime-trend

[12] The clearance rate does not equal reported crimes divided by arrests, in part because some arrests clear multiple crimes, and some arrests made in one time period clear crimes reported in earlier time periods, etc.,

2.1   What Else Do Police Do?

Tables 1 illustrates that police resources are scarce, and that at least for crime victims, policing is rivalrous in consumption. Some portion of criminals involved in each type of crime are arrested, meeting at least part of the demands of some victims, but most are not. Part of the reason is illustrated in Table 2 which provides arrest data for categories of Non-Index I arrests, and for comparison, total Index I arrests derived by summing numbers from Table 1. Importantly, only about 15.5 percent of total arrests are for Index I crimes. However, even the expanded arrest statistics in Tables 2 reveal only part of the competing demands for scarce police resources.

Table 2   Estimated numbers of arrests in the US, 2019

Index I (Reported Violent and Property Crimes) Arrests (from Table 1)	
Total Reported Violent Crimes	**485,871**
Total Reported Property Crimes	**1,074,367**
Total Index I	**1,560,238**
Index II (Other Crimes) Arrests	
Other assaults	1025,711
Forgery and counterfeiting	45,183
Fraud	112,707
Embezzlement	13,497
Stolen property; buying, receiving, possessing	88,272
Vandalism	180,501
Weapons; carrying, possessing etc.	153,161
Prostitution and commercialized vice	26.713
Sex offenses (except rape and prostitution)	40,796
Drug abuse violations	1,558,862
Gambling	2458
Offenses against the family and children	85,687
Driving under the influence	1,024,508
Liquor laws	175,548
Drunkenness	316,032
Disorderly conduct	310,331
Vagrancy	21,896
All other offenses	3,318,453
Suspicion	579
Curfew and loitering law violations	14,653
Total Index II Arrests	**8,515,548**
Total Index I plus Index II Arrests	**10,075,786**

Source: US Department of Justice, Federal Bureau of Investigation, Criminal Justice Information Services division, *Crime in the United States 2019*, National Arrest Data, Table 29, https://ucr.fbi.gov/crime-in-the-u.s/2019/crime-in-the-u.s.-2019/topic-pages/tables/table-29

Police are also allocated to perform many activities that do not deter any crimes or directly produce any arrests. Reaves (1992, 4) surveyed police departments and found that: 96 percent were responsible for accident investigation, over half performed telephone and radio emergency communications and dispatch services for fire, ambulance, search and rescue and other emergency response services, 43 percent had animal control duties, 33 percent did search and rescue, 18 percent had responsibility for emergency medical services, 18 percent provided court security, 14 percent did civil defense, 10 percent provided civil process serving, and so on. With so many crimes and other expected services, scarce public policing resources are simply unable to effectively deal with many of the crimes.

2.2   What About Policing (and Security) Services That Actually Are Non-rivalrous and Non-excludable?

Some police services may appear to be both non-rivalrous and non-excludable. Police patrols presumably deter crime. Everyone in the area benefit from deterrence, so it apparently is non-rivalrous. Non-excludability appears to apply since everyone in the area should benefit whether they pay or not, creating free rider incentives. Another source of deterrence arises when police successfully arrest criminals who are then successfully prosecuted and punished. Potential criminals recognize the risk of committing crimes, so some choose not to commit such crimes, and the probabilities of victimization declines for everyone in the community. While these seem like examples of "public-goods", they do not stand up to close scrutiny.

First, benefits from public police like deterrence are largely localized. People outside a neighborhood or community that increases patrols or arrests do not gain substantial benefits. Second, policing in a local area may generate external costs for people outside the area due to the "displacement effect": increased policing in one area encourages criminals to relocate to less-intensively policed areas (Rasmussen et al., 1993; Bronars & Lott, 1998). Third, private security presumably is not a public good, but it also can generate general deterrence.

Private security often focuses on specific locations which tend to be small geographically (relative to most towns, cities, counties, or states with public police), but some types of security (e.g., outside security cameras, improved lighting, security patrols) also often deter crime against nearby locations. A relatively large-scale example is documented by MacDonald et al. (2012), who estimate that the University of Pennsylvania's 200 percent increase in private university police patrolling generated a 45–60 percent reduction in reported violent and property crime, both on campus and in surrounding neighborhoods.[13] As with public policing, however, when

---

[13] Several studies offer empirical support for the hypothesis that private security deters specific crimes within political jurisdictions, including Benson and Mast (2001), Zimmerman (2014), and Meehan and Benson (2017) although which crimes appear to be deterred varies across studies. Deterrence may arise because increases in private security raise the costs of finding soft targets.

private security hardens specific targets, some criminals have incentives to move to (substitute) softer targets, perhaps nearby, but perhaps in another area (e.g., criminals deterred by Penn's increased security might move to areas around other Philadelphia universities). Public police and private security both can generate positive and negative externalities.

Profit-seeking firms want to get paid for benefits produced so they have incentives to develop technological or institutional innovations to internalize positive externalities. Similarly, those who are harmed by external costs have incentives to force internalization (make the private party producing external costs liable for them). The cost of internalization may exceed the benefits (Demsetz, 1967), so internalization does not always occur, but incentives to do so remain, encouraging search for effective internalization innovations. Not surprisingly, improvements and innovations in private security technology have resulted in increasing investments in new security options, leading to expanding markets for a growing array of security equipment and services.[14]

Even though most shared benefits of policing are localized, they still must be paid for. People may well want to free ride, although social pressures in small groups, and institutional changes including privatization can induce payment. Through innovation, private security has eliminated or reduced free riding in the production of a great deal of deterrence, and there is little doubt that the market would willingly provide more (see discussion below), if not for government-imposed barriers to entry (see below).

2.3   Rivalrous Use of Policing

The rapid increase in illicit drug enforcement in the US between late 1984 and 1989 led Benson and Rasmussen (1991) to hypothesize that reallocation of resources to increase drug enforcement will result in a reduction in enforcement efforts directed at other crimes, and those crimes will increase. Since then, a substantial number of empirical studies have supported this hypothesis.[15] These empirical studies use different data sets, different data periods, and different empirical techniques, but sup-

Note that Meehan and Benson (2017) find support for deterrence effects for robbery and all property crimes. Most private security is employed to protect property and owners of property.

[14] For discussion of the rapid growth and wide array of private security services in the U.S., see Benson (1998, 2014), and Blackstone and Hakim (2010). Joh (2004) suggests that there were approximately three times as many private security personnel in the US as public police, up from an estimated ratio of one-to-one in the early 1970s (public police employment has been relatively constant).

[15] Benson et al. (1992) find that increased drug control draws resources away from control of property crime, leading to increases in such crime. Rasmussen et al. (1993) also find a significant tradeoff relationship between drug enforcement and violent crime. These findings have been corroborate by a number of studies including Sollars et al. (1994), Brumm and Cloninger (1995), Benson et al. (1998), Miron (1999), Resignato (2000), Mendes (2000), and Shepard and Blackley

port for the hypothesis is robust.[16] The results of these studies also clearly reject the assumption that policing resources are non-rivalrous. Allocation decisions clearly determine who gets services and who does not (see more discussion below).

2.4 Excludability and Police Services

The non-excludability assumption also does not hold, at least for many policing actions. Consider the "scathing examination" of this New Orleans Police Department by the city's Office of Inspector General, which

> found that of 1,290 sex crime "calls for service" assigned to five New Orleans police detectives from 2011 to 2013, 840 were designated as "miscellaneous," and nothing at all was done. Of the 450 calls that led to the creation of an initial investigative report, no further documentation was found for 271 of them.
> .... The report described how victims' charges of sexual assault were ignored, referrals from medical personnel were dismissed, and evidence was not processed; in some cases, the detective would mark down in a report that evidence had been sent to the state laboratory, though no records could be found that the laboratory received anything (Robertson, 2014).

(2005, 2010). Reviews of the literature appear in Shepard and Blackley (2010), and Werb et al. (2011).

[16] A related hypothesis is that recreational-marijuana legalization should free up policing resources to enforce other crimes, and empirical analysis of this proposition has begun to appear. The resulting evidence is mixed, Makin et al. (2019) find a positive impact of legalization on clearance rates in Colorado and Washington while Jorgensen and Harper (2020) find no meaningful changes in Colorado or Washington clearance rates. Wua et al.'s (2022) examination of Oregon data also suggests a positive impact of legalization on violet-crime clearance rates. However, Wua et al. (2022) also considered the relationship between legalization and crime rates, finding that "recreational marijuana legalization was associated with a marginally significant increase in overall violent crime... and aggravated assault... in the OR counties relative to counties in the non-legalized states." They also suggest that the consequences of marijuana legalization could differ across states. After all, legislation varies across states. For instance, some states have imposed very high taxes on recreational marijuana production, sales, and consumption. High taxes push activities into underground markets, just as prohibition does. The same holds for imposition of onerous regulations including significant barriers to entry. This suggests that states with low taxes and modest regulation should see stronger positive impacts of legalization, while states with substantial regulation and/or taxation may see no significant impact, or ever negative impacts, depending on how substantial the incentives are to remain in or move to underground markets. Dills et al. (2021) examine changes in violent crime over time in 11 states, both before and after legalization. Most of the 11 state's trends track the U.S. trend before legalization. After legalization, a number of states continued to track the national trend, although violent crime in Maine and Nevada decreased by 90 and 178 crimes per 100,000 respectively, compared with the national trend. On the other hand, violent crime rates in Alaska and Massachusetts increased post-legalization by 152 and 57 percent more than the national trend. They conclude that "Overall, violent crime has neither soared nor plummeted in the wake of marijuana legalization." Without statistically controlling for other factors like changes in taxes and imposition of regulations, it is not surprising that a common relationship across all states is not evident.

The report focuses on five detectives, perhaps suggesting that this is an unusual case, but as Robertson notes, problems with police discretion have a long history in the city. In fact, the New Orleans police force was placed under federal court supervision after US Department of Justice investigators examined its performance in 2010 and 2011. The DOJ found "a pattern of inefficient, abusive and corrupt police work" and reported that "the police routinely discouraged sexual assault victims from pursuing prosecution and that reclassifying rapes as miscellaneous charges was so common that it had the effect of "shutting down investigation for a significant proportion of possible sex crimes" (Robertson, 2014).[17]

3   Rationing Public Police

The brief discussion of police treatment of sexual assault suggests key resource allocation mechanisms for public police: rationing by waiting, and discretionary allocations by police officials and officers, both of which are discussed further below. There is a third – political influence and legislation - which is considered first.

3.1   Politics, Legislation and Police Rationing

Policing is a free access service because of political decisions, not because of some physical characteristic. Furthermore, political decisions driven by the demands of special interest groups partially guide the use of policing resources. Berk et al.'s (1977, 11, 200–205) detailed and careful study, concludes that one of the two lobby groups shaping California crime legislation, year after year, is the law-enforcement lobby, led by the California Peace Officers Association. This lobby group induces significant changes leading to increasing criminalization, and more resources for police.[18] In fact, however, criminalization also reflect the pursuit of more resources (budgets) and power for police. After all, as Breton and Wintrobe (1982, 146–154)

---

[17] This issue is not unique to New Orleans. For instance, San Francisco's "Police Department … has come under increasing scrutiny for how it handles and investigates sexual assault cases" (Mark, 2019). Of the 864 sexual assaults reported in 2017, for instance, only 88 went to prosecutors for review and only 35 were prosecuted (the DA's office did not provide data on how many of those prosecuted were convicted). A spokesman for the DA's office emphasized that their prosecution rate [35/88 = 39.8 percent] is above the national average of 19 percent (Mark, 2019), but the relevant number for victims is 35/864 = 0.04 percent.

[18] The other major lobby group pursuing criminal justice legislation is the Civil Liberties Lobby led by the America Civil Liberties Union, which stresses limits on police powers (and more judicial discretion). Neither group gets everything it demands: "the horse trading endemic to the legislative process often produced criminal law that diluted and often distorted original intent…. [W]hat might have begun as incipient law soon became a hybrid whose content reflected what was politically acceptable" (Berk et al., 1977, 276). In fact, as Berk, et al. (1977, 85–86) explain, the creation

explain, one bureaucratic strategy in competing for budgets is to "generate" demand for the bureau's own services. More crimes to control requires additional funding and increased police power. Implications are discussed below.

3.2   Interest Group Strategies by Police

Police spokesmen often engage in misleading political rhetoric (just as other interest groups including other bureaucrats do – so do politicians, of course) (Rolles, 2011 59). Furthermore, "individuals are drawn to information that is vivid, negative, or signals a potential threat. The greater the reliance on these types of cues, the more likely are people to draw incorrect inferences about the world around them" (Jerit & Barabas, 2006, 281). Rhetoric justifying many police objectives exploits these cues (Jerit & Barabas, 2006). In addition, bureaucratic strategies also include "(i) alterations in the flows of information or commands . . .; (ii) variations in the quality or quantity of information leaked to the media, to other bureaus . . . to special interest groups, and/or to opposition parties and rival suppliers; and (iii) changes in the speed of implementation of policies" (Breton & Wintrobe, 1982, 37–38). These strategies and other selective behavior are possible because of the way complex hierarchies work, including the fact that monitoring is very costly. Indeed, such strategies generally increase monitoring costs.

Legislatures deal with several issues affecting the allocation of policing resources, but as suggested above, an important focus by police is criminalization to justify larger budgets and more power. In this context, Stuntz (2001, 512) distinguishes between two types of crimes. "Core crimes" are the offenses "used to compile the FBI's crime index [see above] – murder and manslaughter, rape, robbery, arson, assault, kidnapping, burglary, larceny, and auto theft." Stuntz' second type of crime "consists of everything else. Criminal law courses, criminal law literature, and popular conversation about crime focus heavily on the first. The second dominates criminal codes: "Legislators create new crimes regularly."[19]

Criminalization has been occurring for a very long time, as illustrated in Fig. 1. As a result, in the US "There are so many criminalized actions that no one has been able to determine a definitive count, including the Justice Department, the principal federal law enforcement agency" (Larkin Jr., 2013, 726). What appears to be the

---

of criminal legislation is an agreed bill process. Lobbyists from affected interests and a few members or staff from relevant legislative committees negotiate directly in making important decisions.

[19] Law enforcement is not the only source of demand for criminalization. Politically defined crimes may involve efforts to prohibit behavior that offends moral, religious, or ideological beliefs or the self-interest of interest groups. While police are likely to cooperate in seeking criminalization of many such activities if they expect to be involved in enforcement, other groups may take the lead in pursuing them. Politically defined crimes also include actions that violate/circumvent politically created requirements or restrictions, such as taxes, and a long list of regulations. Some of these crimes are enforced by regulators or specialized agencies but some also are enforced by police.

most recent published estimate of federal criminalization suggests that about 4450 federal crimes existed in 2008, along with around 300,000 regulatory violations with criminal penalties (Baker, 2008, 5).[20] By increasing demand for policing services, criminalization also provided a justification for budget growth.

While increasing criminalization has a long history, the areas attracting criminalization legislation have changed over time. By the first third of the twentieth century, however vice was the primary focus.[21] This included criminalization of drug market activities, as well as alcohol prohibition. Regulatory crime also became a focus in the second third of the century, along with racketeering, while the last third saw focused on "white-color" regulatory crime along with drug production, possession and use (Stuntz, 2001, 515).

The role of law enforcement in criminalization of drugs is easy to illustrate. One example suggests that once a bureaucracy is created, incentives arise to ensure its continued existence by expanding bureau size and scope, is from federal drug legislation. The early twentieth century saw federal prohibition enforcement for both alcohol and narcotics captured by the Treasury Department. The 1914 Harrison Act was essentially a narcotics tax act which was then interpreted by the Treasury Department's newly created enforcement bureaucracy to prohibit use of narcotics

Fig. 1 Federal Criminalization

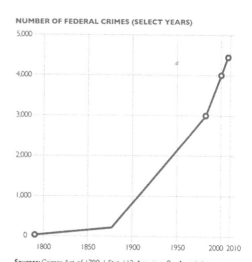

NUMBER OF FEDERAL CRIMES (SELECT YEARS)

Sources: Crimes Act of 1790, 1 Stat. 112; American Bar Association, "The Federalization of Criminal Law," 1998; John S. Baker, Jr., "Revisiting the Explosive Growth of Federal Crimes," Heritage Foundation Legal Memorandum, No. 26, June 16, 2008.

🐘 heritage.org

---

[20] I recently spoke to the author of this study. He is engaged in a new count, and expects that there are now more than 5000 federal crimes,

[21] Early nineteenth century state-level criminal codes included "statutes that were immensely more intrusive into private and family life, and non-commercial public behavior ... than exist now" (Brown, 2011, 662). As criminalization of these acts declined, criminal regulation of commercial and economic activities increased, as did regulation of property uses and labor (see Brown (2011)).

like methadone to treat addicts. Not surprisingly, from the 1920s to the early 1960s the nation's program for handling the "drug problem" is one "which, to all intents and purposes, was established by the decisions of administrative officials of the Treasury Department" (Lindesmith, 1965, 3) and the Department's Bureau of Prohibition. For instance, with repeal of alcohol prohibition by the twenty-first amendment in 1933, the Bureau was in need of a new *raison d'etre* (in fact, the bureau's budgets began falling in 1931). One result of the Bureau's lobbying is the Marijuana Tax Act (1935). The campaign leading to this Act (1935) "included remarkable distortions of the evidence of harm caused by marijuana, ignoring the findings of empirical inquiries" (Richards, 1982, 164; also see Lindesmith, 1965, 25–34, and many more).[22] Rolles (2011, 59) explains that the role of misleading and even false rhetoric coming from law enforcement continues to support expansion of the drug war:[23]

> The... "war on drugs" ... has been predicated on the concept of drugs as an existential 'threat' ... Prohibitionist rhetoric frames drugs as menacing not only to health but also national security (our borders), and not infrequently, to the moral fabric of society itself, using the 'drug threat' to children as the specific rhetorical vehicle ... and the sinister drug dealers who prey on the young and vulnerable (lurking at the school gates, etc.). While there are of course, very real risks for children and young people associated with both drug use and illegal drug markets, perception of these risks has been dramatically distorted by the populist fearmongering ..., aided and abetted by a sensation-hungry mainstream media.

The budgeting decision affects police allocation decisions directly because justification for budget size and increases often requires politically acceptable "evidence" of both the need for police and the fact that police are producing output that appears to be associated with pursuing such output. The number of crimes actually prevented

---

[22] See Benson and Meehan (2018) for discussion and references.

[23] Reallocation of police can also be induced by legislation that changes police incentives. For example, this occurred after passage of the 1984 federal Crime Act. One section of the Act, lobbied for by law enforcement, mandated that proceeds from assets seized in a joint investigation involving state or local policing agencies cooperating with a federal agency must be shared among the agencies involved. Soon after passage it became clear that the "Equitable Sharing" process was being used by police to circumvent state laws. A number of states directed forfeiture proceeds to non-law-enforcement activities, including general funds as well specific programs (e.g., county school funds in North Carolina). State and local police were making seizures under the federal law so the revenues would go to police instead. The Department of Justice (DOJ) began treating state or local seizures "as if" they involved federal agency participation, by "adopting" seizures and then passing them back to the state or local agency, minus 20 percent. Some states subsequently modified their forfeiture laws to allow state and local police to retain revenues without going through the federal adoption process. "With local, state and federal law enforcement agencies suddenly able to keep all the proceeds from forfeiture standards, the value of assets confiscated [in the U.S.] surged from just over $100 million in 1983 to $460 million in 1990" (Drug Policy Alliance, 2015, 9). The ability to keep seized assets also had a dramatic impact on drug enforcement. Total U.S. drug arrests in 1983 were estimated to be 661,400. Five years after the law was in place, estimated 1989 drug arrests were 1,361,700. It might be argued that this enforcement increase was not a response to the opportunity to keep seizures, but empirical studies find that police do in fact respond to incentives created by the ability to retain proceeds from assets seizure (e.g., Mast et al., 2000; Baicker & Jacobson, 2007).

cannot be quantified, so police need other measurable outputs as indicators of police "productivity" (Sherman, 1983, 156). The number of arrests is one of the primary "statistics" police focus on in the budget negotiation process. As a result, the budget process rewards those who successfully dispose of cases after crimes are committed more than those who prevent crimes. In this context, another measurable dimension of police activity is response times following emergency calls. Thus, there are strong incentives to wait until crimes are committed in order to quickly respond in hopes of making arrests. Police engage in a great deal of "waiting to respond" rather than "watching to prevent."

The importance of arrests in the budget negotiation process also makes criminalization of vice and drug crimes particularly attractive for police, as Blumberg (1970, 184–185) emphasizes: there is a "bureaucratic fetish . . . to ferret out . . . cases which can be most easily processed . . . As a result, we have spent much of our limited resources . . . [to arrest] addicts, alcoholics, prostitutes, homosexuals, gamblers, and other petty offenders, simply because they are readily available and produce the desired statistical data."

The "easy" narcotics and vice arrestees often are minor players in the relevant illegal markets such as street prostitutes, street-level drug dealers and drug users, of course, not organized crime bosses, human traffickers, drug wholesalers, major drug smugglers and money launderers. While the Blumberg quote is dated, and there also are incentive to make high profile arrests that attract a lot of attention, the attraction of "soft target law enforcement" remains (Barrett, 2011, 6).

As an illustration of the focus on making large numbers of easy arrests, which also demonstrates Rolles' (2011) point about framing the prohibition paradigm for vice "as a moral crusade against an evil". Consider the Los Angeles County Sheriff's Department's (LASD) "Operation Reclaim and Rebuild", allegedly to combat "human trafficking." This operation, employed the previous six years as well, involved "more than 80 participating federal, state, and local law enforcement agencies, and task forces from across California," including the FBI and Homeland Security, and the National Center on Sexual Exploitation (Brown, 2022). The LASD reported, on February 15, that over a one-week period (which included the date of the Super Bowl, February 13, held in the Los Angeles area), the operation produced arrests of 214 people for allegedly selling sex, 201 people for allegedly trying to pay for sex, and 53 for alleged pimping, pandering, or supervising prostitution. It does not appear, however, that "any of these individuals were engaged in anything that we might think of as abusive or non-consensual behavior - aka sex trafficking" (Brown, 2022). Nonetheless, the Los Angeles Times headline declared, "Nearly 500 arrested in statewide human trafficking operation."[24] Many similar large-scale oper-

[24] An alternative breakdown of arrests provided by the LASD implies, but does not explicitly say that trafficking, actually was involved as a minor component of the operation: 445 arrests were for misdemeanors, eleven of which had nothing to do with sex, and 49 arrests involved felony allegations, eight of which were not related to either human trafficking or sex, while seven arrests were for unspecified sexual offenses related to a minor, and 34 involved "either human trafficking, pimping, or pandering." A breakdown of arrests for "trafficking, pimping or pandering" was not

ations focus on drug crimes too.[25] Note that the easy drug and vice arrests are not for core (Index I) crimes, so while these arrests are measures of output, they are not likely to have a major deterrent effect on violent and property criminals. Indeed, violent and property crime rates tend to rise as police shift resources to focus on drug crimes: core crime rates rise and police are producing a lot of arrests, as suggested above.

The preceding discussion emphasizes that the political process, and its consequences significantly influence the rationing of police resources and police behavior. The huge number of activities that have been criminalized makes anything close to effectively policing all crimes impossible. Instead, police officials and often, individual officers, are given tremendous discretion to decide how to allocate policing across all of these crimes. Preferences and prejudices of individual police officers determine many of the rationing choices made, and since police officers' preferences are subjective and varied (like everyone else), the result is uneven and selective enforcement. Another rationing process used to allocate police also enhances their discretion.

3.3 Rationing by Time or Merit: Excess Demand and Police Discretion

Several years ago, I was involved in a minor traffic accident. Both vehicles were damaged, the police were called, and we were told that we would have to wait at least 45 minutes for an officer to arrive, because the Tallahassee police department

---

provided, "despite the differing implications in each charge" (Brown, 2022). Furthermore, arrested prostitutes have incentives to claim that they are victims of human trafficking in order to avoid arrest for selling sex, so even if some arrests were reported as such, it is not clear that any trafficking was discovered.

[25] Denwalt (2022) describes an episode earlier this year, led by the Oklahoma Bureau of Narcotics (OBN) and involving a multi-agency raid of three residences and nine marijuana growing locations. Over 200 state, federal and local law enforcement officers were involve in executing the relevant search and arrest warrants. The result was the "largest marijuana-related bust in Oklahoma history," although eight of nine growers raided were licensed. Production, sales and consumption are legal in the state for medical purposes. There are over 900 licensed Oklahoma growers (it is much less costly to legally engage in marijuana production in Oklahoma than virtually any other state). Oklahoma growers supply black markets in other states where marijuana is illegal, like Texas, and where marijuana is legalized but high taxes and/or costly regulations undermine legal production and sales, such as California. It is not clear how Oklahomans are being harmed by this, however, so the investment of police resources to carry out the operation is difficult to defend, but not to explain: The OBN had plans to "file asset forfeiture cases against multiple vehicles, bank accounts, cash, equipment and at least eight of the properties involved" (Denwalt, 2022)

only had two officers allocated to traffic issues. This may appear to be trivial, but rationing by first-come-first-serve is widely used for publicly supplied goods and services, including police resources.

Police resources have to be allocated across a huge number of crimes and non-criminal activities. Many requests for service get no police attention because too many others are ahead of them. There can be efforts to sort many of these demands according to the perceived importance so some move up in the waiting line, but that also means that some move down, and never get any attention. For instance, about the time of my accident mentioned above, the *Tallahassee Democrat* newspaper explained that, of 15,900 crimes reported to the city's police during the previous year that required investigation if they were to be solved, roughly 11,000 were not assigned to an investigator. About 7000 reported crimes allegedly had no obvious leads for investigators to follow, so no investigator was assigned to deal with them. One might expect that one purpose of an investigator is to find leads, but these reports apparently were simply filed away and ignored. This is not surprising. Many who report crimes are never adequately served. Backlogs of thousands of supposedly open police cases actually receive little or no attention. In fact, another 4000 cases that actually had leads were not assigned to Tallahassee police investigators, perhaps because they were not considered to be important enough to merit attention (or perhaps because the person reporting was belligerent, or black, or unattractive, etc.). Only 4900, less than a third of these reported cases, were assigned to investigative personnel. Police probably would characterize this as rationing by merit.

Merit rationing is common in many situations (e.g., hiring and promotions are often rationed in this way[26]). One criteria in Tallahassee apparently was that only cases with existing evidence merited investigation. Someone or some group has to decide what the merit criterion is, a decision that can reflect the subjective preferences and prejudices of those making the decision. Should drug crimes or burglaries get the most attention from investigators? Does the availability of assets to seize matter, or characteristics of the victim or alleged offender (race, social status, neighborhood of residence, etc.)? There are also incentives for interested groups (including police) to influence that decision, often bringing the political process into play. The merit process can formalize discretionary decisions (e.g., to emphasize drug and vice control) if credible arguments can be made, or they can be informal but widely recognized among relevant police. The 4900 cases assigned to investigators were the only cases with any chance of being investigated, but some other criteria must also apply to separate the 4000 and 4900 cases. Furthermore, individual police investigators often do not have sufficient time to effectively deal with their assigned caseloads, so each investigator has to ration her time among cases assigned to her. This rationing often depends on individual police officers' assessments, preferences, and prejudices. For instance, recall the discussion of the New Orleans Police Department's failure to investigate hundreds of sex crimes. One of the New Orleans

---

[26] Presumably, the most meritorious allocation results, so competition takes the form of trying to meet the merit requirements (Krueger, 1974).

guilty detective allegedly told many people that simple rape should not be a crime (Robertson, 2014).

Another implication of on-going excess demand is that the supplier can reduce the quality of the good or service, reducing costs, because there are demanders who will still want it, even if it is of low quality. A landlord may reduce maintenance, reduce the quality of appliances and furnishings, slow repairs, and so on. Similarly, those who report a crime by phone or in person may have to wait for an officer's attention, and then the interviewer may be indifferent, doubtful, biased, impatient, or verbally abusive. And when/if an officer is dispatched the quality of the service may also be determined by the police officer. The U.S. annual Victimization Surveys routinely indicate that over 60 percent of the crimes against persons and property are never reported to the police (see discussion above). Reporting also varies across types of crime. This does not mean that those who opt out no longer want resolution of the crimes they suffered; they simply see the expected costs of reporting the crime to exceed the expected benefits.[27]

3.4 Will Increase Budgets Solve the Problems of Excess Demand and Police Discretion?

If policing is a public good, adding more police presumably generates benefits for everyone. If policing is a common pool however, adding more police will only benefit a few people but never solves the various problems of the system. Adding more police may lead to more crimes being investigated and temporarily reduce the time spent for some victims queuing up to report crimes. However, other victims, seeing that time costs and police discretion has been reduced and perhaps that services are improving, opt back into the queue (e.g., report crimes). More individuals are served, which is certainly a benefit, but excess demand increases and police discretion and resulting behavior does not change. Observable excess demand (queues,

---

[27] Several reasons have been proposed to explain victims' non-reporting. For the most part, however, the failure of the public-sector-dominated criminal justice system to capture and arrests most criminals (including abusive police) after crimes have been committed, to prosecute many alleged criminals who have been arrested, and to effectively punish many criminals who are successfully arrested, underlies these reasons for non-reporting. All of these failures reflect the common pool nature of the criminal justice system (Benson, 1998, 55–7). Court time, prison space, probation officers are all scarce. Just as police decide which reported crimes to investigate, ignoring many victims, prosecutors decide which arrested criminals to charge, ignoring many victims. They also decide which crimes go to court. 90–95 percent of convictions are plea bargained by dropping several charges or reducing the seriousness of charges, thereby reducing the severity of punishment. Thus, prosecutors and judges have free access to prison and probation commons. They crowd the prisons with too many inmates, forcing the use of alternative sentences such as probation, or early release (e.g., parole, good-time credit). The probation (and parole) system is crowded too, so probation (parole) officers cannot effectively supervise their caseloads. With such crowding at every stage of the criminal justice process, victims are often dissatisfied, and realizing this, many simply choose not to enter the commons.

inactive files) ends up being roughly the same as it was before and unseen excess demand, those who opt out, continues. It generally would take a massive, probably inconceivable, infusion of government spending to respond to all victim demands, particularly when police are expected to deal with additional crimes that have been created by legislatures, as well as the non-crime-related duties that are expected to perform.[28]

3.5   Police Discretion and Discrimination[29]

Given excess demand and significant discretion, along with similar preferences and prejudices among police, widespread discrimination may be observable. Large numbers of media outlets and research reports suggest that police systematically mistreat specific racial groups. Oppel Jr et al. (2016), for instance, report that the Justice Department found that the Baltimore Police Department has, for years "hounded Black residents who make up most of the city's population, systematically stopping, and searching their cars, often with little provocation or rationale. In a blistering report, coming more than a year after Baltimore erupted into riots over the police-involved death of a 25-year-old black man, Freddie Gray, the Justice Department was sharply critical of policies that encouraged police officers to charge black residents with minor crimes". Similarly, young African-American and Latino men make up 4.7 percent of New York City's population, but African-American and Latino males between the ages of 14 and 24 accounted for 41.6 percent of stops in the City's "Stop-and-Frisk" program in 2011 (New York Civil Liberties Union, 2011, 2, 15I). In addition, a number of recent studies find that police are significantly more likely to kill Black and Hispanic civilians, relative to Whites (e.g., DeAngelis, 2021; Fagan & Campbell, 2020).[30]

Fryer Jr (2019) statistically examines four data sets in an effort to explain apparent discriminatory police behavior: (1) New York City's Stop, Question, and Frisk program, (2) the Police-Public Contact Survey, a triennial national survey with a representative sample of civilians. (3) a random sample of police-civilian interaction from police files including all incidents in which an officer discharges his weapon at civilians from Austin, Dallas, Houston, Los Angeles County and six large

---

[28] Furthermore, an increase in police resources and arrests adds to crowding problems for other parts of the system (courts, jails and prisons, probation and parole programs, all of which are also crowded (Benson, 1998)).As suggested above, the criminal justice system is a complex vertically and horizontally linked system of common pools. Changes at one level or function change demands on other levels and for other functions.

[29] See the discussion of discretionary non-responses to large numbers of rape victims in New Orleans and San Francisco.

[30] There are huge literatures on police discretion, police discrimination and police abuse. No attempt is made here to even provide a summary or overview of these literatures. The purpose simply is to explore the relationships between rationing processes and police behavior.

Florida counties, and 4) a 300 variables-incident, random sample of police-civilian interactions with the Houston Police department from arrests codes in which lethal force is more likely to be justified. Together, these data allowed Fryer to consider numerous characteristics of police contact with citizens, including voluntary, involuntary, non-violent, non-lethal violent, and lethal situations. Fryer (2019, 39) concludes that:

> On non-lethal uses of force, there are racial differences – sometimes quite large– in police use of force, even after accounting for a large set of controls designed to account for important contextual and behavioral factors at the time of the police-civilian interaction. Interestingly, as use of force increases from putting hands on a civilian to striking them with a baton, the overall probability of such an incident occurring decreases dramatically but the racial difference remains roughly constant. Even when officers report civilians have been compliant and no arrest was made, blacks are 21.2 percent more likely to endure some form of force in an interaction. Yet, on the most extreme use of force – officer-involved shootings – we are unable to detect any racial differences in either the raw data or when accounting for controls.
>
> We argue that these facts are most consistent with a model of taste-based discrimination in which police officers face discretely higher costs for officer-involved shootings relative to non-lethal uses of force.[31]

Fryer's conclusion that there are reasons to expect that discrimination is taste-based implies that discrimination is not driven by the design (or evolving characteristics) of the system, but instead it reflects the preferences (tastes) of individual officers. This implication, while tentative, is consistent with predictions stressed above, which focus on the implications of excess demand and individual police-officer discretion, implying that individual preferences (tastes) determine targets for discriminatory treatment. The system plays a role because it has been set up to ration by time and other methods that do not legally involve money prices, thereby creating excess demand. Nonetheless, the individual police officers respond to these incentives in light of their own prejudices.

---

[31] Fryer Jr (2019) explains that there are a number of potential concerns with his efforts, one of which is important in the context of arguments made here:

> First, all but one dataset was provided by a select group of police departments.... There may be important selection in who was willing to share their data. The Police-Public contact survey partially sidesteps this issue by including a nationally representative sample of civilians, but it does not contain data on officer-involved shootings.

> Relatedly, even police departments willing to supply data may contain police officers who present contextual factors at that time of an incident in a biased manner – making it difficult to interpret regression coefficients in the standard way. It is exceedingly difficult to know how prevalent this type of misreporting bias is.... accounting for contextual variables recorded by police officers who may have an incentive to distort the truth is problematic. Yet, whether or not we include controls does not alter the basic qualitative conclusions. And, to the extent that there are racial differences in underreporting of non-lethal use of force (and police are more likely to not report force used on blacks), our estimates may be a lower bound.

3.6   Discretion and Police Abuse

Discrimination is only one example of discretionary abuse of power. Police frequently "have lied, stolen, dealt drugs, driven drunk", used excessive force (frequently, discriminatorily) including lethal force, and engaged in other illegal activities (Kelly & Nichols, 2019). In most police departments, less than ten percent of officers are investigated for misconduct (Kelly & Nichols, 2019), but it is not clear how much misconduct does not attract investigations. If it is anything close to the portion property and violent crimes that go unreported, or the portion of reported crimes that are never investigated or cleared, misconduct is likely to be very widespread. Even if that is not the case, ten percent is not a trivial portion. Furthermore, a great deal of officer misconduct that has come to the attention of police departments is not reported outside the department. For instance, *USA TODAY* and its affiliated newsrooms joined with the Invisible Institute, a Chicago nonprofit, and spent more than a year creating a huge volume of more than 200,000 incidents of alleged police misconduct from thousands of state agencies, prosecutors, police departments and sheriffs (including 110,000 internal affairs investigations). This collection contains around 85,000 individuals. While many of the records involve "routine" infractions, whatever that means, there are "tens of thousands of cases of serious misconduct and abuse", including 22,924 investigations of officers using excessive force, as well as 3145 allegations of rape, child molestation and other sexual misconduct" by officers (Kelly & Nichols, 2019); in addition, "Dishonesty is a frequent problem. The records document at least 2227 instances of perjury, tampering with evidence or witnesses or falsifying reports." Nonetheless, the collection is incomplete because several states did not supply records. Unions representing law enforcement officers have been especially outspoken opponents of such data releases. California is one of the non-reporting states, for instance, and the union representing Los Angeles County sheriff's deputies went to court to stop the department from disclosing 300 deputies with misconduct histories.

Some officers are repeatedly under investigation. Almost 2500 of the 85,000 have been investigated for ten or more charges. Some have faced 100 or more allegations but have been able to keep their badges for many years. Many officers with repeated abuse are allowed to, after minor punishments, return to the same department. Other misbehaving officers, including a number small-town police chiefs, have been fired and/or decertified in one jurisdiction, but then hired in another because of insufficient background checks.[32] As a result, "Thousands of people have faced criminal charges or gone to prison based in part on testimony from law

---

[32] Pilcher et al. (2019) report that "The USA TODAY Network identified 32 people who became police chiefs or sheriffs despite a finding of serious misconduct, usually at another department. At least eight of them were found guilty of a crime. Others amassed records of domestic violence, improperly withholding evidence, falsifying records or other conduct that could impact the public they swore to serve."

enforcement officers deemed to have credibility problems by their bosses or by prosecutors" (Reilly & Nichols, 2019).[33]

3.7 Barriers to Disciplining Police for Abuse: Unions, Qualified Immunity, and Indemnification

How do so many police repeatedly abuse the system, victims, or suspects? A major reason is that police unions have gained many barriers to investigating abuse and punishing police, as implied above. For instance, Rushin (2017) compiled police-union collective-bargaining contracts from 178 cities with populations over 100,000 and found at least one provision in 156 of the contracts that make it more difficult to discipline officers. Such Protections appear to have substantial impacts on police behavior. Dharmapala et al. (2017) examined results from a Florida Supreme Court decision that extended collective bargaining rights (already obtained by municipal police) to sheriffs' deputies. These rights led to a 27 percent increase in misconduct complaints.

Another way that unions protect police officers from discipline is by pursuing state legislation such as a Law Enforcement Officer's Bill of Rights (LEOBOR). At least thirteen states have statutory LEOBORs (Rushin, 2017). LEOBORs provide due-process privileges for officers who are being investigated for conduct that could be disciplines by their departments, as well as for criminal misconduct. These due-process requirements, which are substantially more protective than those provided to civilians, include things like restrictions on how soon after an incident an officer may be interrogated, who and how many people may perform the interrogation, the manner in which the investigation takes place, the incentives that interrogators may offer, and a requirement that all other witnesses be questioned first. Some LEOBORs prohibit certain interrogation tactics police use on civilians, limit the kind of language used in an interrogation, require that interrogation periods be limited, allow rest periods, and so on. 87 of 178 largest cities in the U.S. and 3 states with LEOBORs have provisions that erase records of complaints, even involving

---

[33] For instance, fifteen years of discipline files for Little Rock police officers were compared to court records, revealing that officers determined by the department to have lied or committed crimes were witnesses in at least 4000 cases (Kelly & Nichols, 2019). One officer filed a false report claiming that he did not injure anyone even though video evidence contradicted him. He was suspended for 30 days. Since then he has testified in at least 687 criminal cases. Another officer was suspended for 30 days for lying to internal affairs investigators about his seizure of a cellphone during an arrest that was never turned as evidence. He also did not report the arrest, but his sworn statements have been used in 256 criminal cases.

In this context, the National Registry of Exonerations indicates that in 2021 161 people were exonerated for crimes they had been convicted for (Shackford, 2022). The average prison sentence served by those exonerated is about 11.5 years. Official misconduct played a role in 102 of the convictions of those exonerated, including over 75 percent of the 2021 murder convictions. The Registry reports that there have been at least 3061 exonerations since 1989.

substantiated misconduct, after a specified period (Rushin, 2017). Such protections combined with relatively low probability of investigation and punishment, and the limits on potential punishment, tend to make some (many?) police more inclined to be abusive, whether because of prejudices, preferences (e.g., for exerting power over others), or other factors (e.g., having a bad day, interaction with a non-cooperative or unlikable individuals).

Criminal justice is not the only way to discipline abuse police. Civil lawsuits seeking damage awards can be filed in state courts under common law torts, or in federal court under Title 42, Section 1983 (the Civil Rights Act) of the US Code for violation of constitutional protections. Unfortunately, it can be difficult to get a judgement against police officers themselves, however. One of the barriers (created as a court precedent in 1982) as police have been granted an entitlement to "qualified immunity" if the plaintiff does not demonstrate that his rights were clearly established. In practice that means that the plaintiff must point to a factually similar previous case, or to a broader principle that applies. Police have been protected by a steady stream of qualified immunity ruling in recent years.[34] This liability rule also reduces police officers' incentives to avoid abuse. Furthermore, police officers are almost always indemnified by their department or relevant government (city, county, etc.) against payment of tort damage awards.

A survey of 72 large law enforcement agencies in the US (44 responded), along with 70 randomly selected small to mid-sized agencies (37 responded), regarding the total number of civil cases filed against sworn officers from 2006–2011, found that police officers only paid .02 percent of total awards for misconduct in the 44 large cities (Thomson-DeVeaux et al., 2021). The 37 smaller agencies reported that officers paid none of their police-misconduct damages. As a result, many millions of dollars in damage awards are paid by cities as Table 3 illustrates (these data do not include legal fees and other litigation costs). Column 3 lists the total payments by the cities in column 1, accumulated over the number of years for which data are available, provided in Colum 2. Since the number of years of data varies across cities, column 4 lists the average annual payments for each city. These payments comes from taxpayers. There probably is no way to determine how accurate many of the payment numbers in Table 3 are, however. As Thomson-DeVeaux et al. (2021) note:

---

[34] For instance, several Denver police officers searched a man's tablet even though they did not have a warrant, because they wanted to delete a video that the tablet owner took of them beating a suspect (Binion, 2021). The officers' actions violated the Denver Police Department's own rules and training, which stresses that people have a First Amendment right to record them. The officers were granted qualified immunity because there was no "clearly established" prior court ruling against such behavior. A driver in Shreveport, Louisiana, was pulled over in 2016 because he had a broken brake light and license plate light. Before he was arrested he found himself on the ground as officers punched and kicked him (King, 2022). A federal court ruled, in 2021, that the officers had qualified immunity. Fresno police officers allegedly stole $225,000 when they were executing a search warrant, but they were given qualified immunity because there was no court precedent that expressly established that stealing, under those exact circumstances, is unconstitutional (Binion, 2021).

Table 3 City payments for police abuse

City	Number of Years	Total Amount	Yearly Average	Number of Officers, 2017	Payments per officer[a]
New York City	10	$1,704,120,487	$170,412,049	36.378	$4684
Chicago	10	$467,586,464	$46,758,646	12,383	$3776
Los Angeles	10	$329,925,620	$32,992,562	9988	$3303
Washington, D.C.	9	$114,841,449	$12,760,161	3836	$3326
Philadelphia	11	$116,881,088	$10,625,553	6558	$1620
Detroit	9	$57,702,989	$6,411,443	2499	$2566
Milwaukee	10	$40,017,822	$4,001,782	1.824	$3515
Baltimore	5	$18,432,748	$3,686,550	2516	$1465
San Francisco	10	$27,873,298	$2,787,330	2332	$1195
Springfield, MA	15	$32,846,089	$2,189,739	448	$4488
Indianapolis	10	$13,149,775	$1,314,977	1625	$809
Memphis	7	$8,772,884	$1,253,269	1972	$635
Boston	10	$11,905,482	$1,190,548	2205	$540
Atlanta	5	$4,761,182	$952,236	1621	$587
Paterson, NJ	10	$7,742,498	$774,250	400	$1936
Miami	11	$7,284,684	$662,244	204	$3246
St. Louis	5	$3,117,847	$623,569	1188	$2624
Orlando	9	$3,611,879	$401,320	714	$562
New Orleans	10	$3,510,642	$351,064	1101	$318
North Charleston, SC	10	$3,333,750	$333,375	339	$983
Baton Rouge	10	$2,879,795	$287,979	641	$449
Fort Lauderdale, FL	9	$2,471,384	$274,598	503	$546
Waterbury, CT	9	$2227,250	$247,472	277	$893
Cincinnati	11	$2,472,787	$224,799	1025	$219
Charleston, SC	10	$1,520,250	$152,025	439	$346
Columbia	10	$1,352,435	$135,244	301	$449
Little Rock	10	$943,950	$94,395	509	$185
Richmond, VA	10	$748,500	$74,850	695	$108
Roanoke, VA	10	$132,500	$13,250	254	$52
Cambridge, MA	10	$114,000	$11,400	278	$41

Sources: Thomson-DeVeaux et al. (2021) for columns 1, and 3, and US Department of Justice, Federal Bureau of Investigation, Criminal Justice Information Services Division, Crime in the United States (2017) Table 78: "Full-time Law Enforcement Employees, by State by City, 2017" for column 4. https://ucr.fbi.gov/crime-in-the-u.s/2017/crime-in-the-u.s.-2017/tables/table-78/table-78.xls/view

[a]Column 5 is a rough estimate of payments per officer: the average annual payments divided by police officer in 2017. It is intended to provide an indication of the variation in per-officer city costs of corruption for cities reported on in Thomson-DeVeaux et al. (2021)

In many cases, the cities told us they weren't keeping records in a form that would allow them — or anyone else — to easily analyze how much money was going out the door for police misconduct. A handful of places responded to our … request with a sheaf of court documents and told us to figure out the totals on our own. Others sent easier-to-analyze data with the caveat that some relevant incidents might still be excluded — and then refused to elaborate on how, or why, the data was incomplete.

Table 3 also includes column 5 showing the total number of police officers employed in each city for 2017 (the year is chosen somewhat randomly because it is one of the early years in of payment data for the shortest number of years in column 2 (5)). Column 6 provides somewhat crude estimates of payments per officer for illustrative purposes, calculated by dividing the average annual payments in column 4 by the number of officers from column 5. Clearly, some cities pay for much more police abuse than others. In fact, New York's annual average payment per officer is roughly 114 times higher than Cambridge, Massachusetts. This variation probably depends on each city's institutional arrangements for hiring, monitoring, and punishing officers, as well as police wages and benefits, union power, crime levels, city characteristics (it appears that large cities tend to have larger abuse payments, for instance, but that may reflect institutional differences across departments of various size), and so on.

One of the most important types of police abuse in corruption. Corruption means that someone with public power (authority) takes actions to capture personal gain. This includes police officers accepting bribes for unique services (e.g., extra patrols in a particular area, directing an investigation towards or away from particular individuals or organizations), as well as for not arresting (or ticketing, detaining, etc.) someone for a crime. Corruption also includes direct personal involvement by an officer in criminal activities such as thefts from crime victims or offenders, illegal sales (e.g., of drugs seized from dealers or producers) extortion or shakedowns, and accepting kickbacks or payoffs for ignoring criminal activity, or directly providing protection for criminals, perhaps by preventing competitive entry by individuals or organizations wanting to compete with existing criminals.[35] Essentially, corruption reallocates policing resources, and the combination of power and discretion create many opportunities for police to take actions that results in material and subjective benefit for themselves (Benson, 1988, 1998; McChesney, 2010).

The typical rhetoric coming from police is that corruption (and other forms of abuse) involves a "few bad apples" and that the huge majority of police do not engage in any corruption at all. There is no way to know if this is correct or not. After all, the only countable statistics about corruptions arise when corrupt officers get reported or caught (e.g., complaints, investigations, arrests, charges and convictions). Recall the discussion of reported crimes above, however. If corruption is like

---

[35] Corruption of authority also includes small payoffs like free coffee or meals from restaurants, or gifts. By accepting such gifts, the officer is implicitly agreeing that whoever gave it to her will receive something in return (extra vigilance, quicker responses, letting trucks parked illegally to unload, etc.). Some of this behavior might seem like simple friendly reciprocity, but if so, the question becomes, where to draw is the line between corruption and acceptable behavior?

other crimes in that most victims do not report it, and most of what is reported does not lead to arrest or conviction, then the few bad apples that are observed are just the top layer of a barrel with lots of less visible rotten apples. In fact, serious investigations following major corruption scandals often reveal much more pervasive corruption than police claim exists (e.g., Knapp, 1972). There are reasons to believe that corruption is like other crimes in this regard. In fact, corruption may actually be less likely to be reported than many crimes (Benson, 1988, 1998). Many who might be in a position to observe and report corruption also may fear retaliation, and fellow officers recognize that a public perception of police corruption may negatively impact police budgets (they may also be involved in corruption or want to keep the corruption option open). Reports of corruption by fellow officers also can lead to ostracism and worse for the "snitch".

The key to understanding police corruption is that the public rationing processes at work create excess demand, shortages, and therefore, police discretion (Benson, 1988). That discretion allows them to ration by "selling" services to some people and/or withholding them from others. Corruption often is simply a market using price rationing for illegal services and privileges. While this appears to be similar to legally rationing through market prices, legal price rationing creates very different incentives than corrupt public police face.

4   Allocation of Private Security and Resulting Behavior

In markets coordinated by the price mechanism, the plans of producers tend to mesh with the plans of consumers. Market price rationing means that if people are willing to pay the market-determined price for some type of scarce resource (or product produced with scarce resources) and people who control (own) the resource are willing to sell at that price, a voluntary exchange can occur (this is true for both legal and illegal markets). Purchasers are willing to pay a particular price only if their expected value generated by their preferred use of the scarce resource exceeds the value that could be obtained from alternative uses of their funds. Similarly, those who initially control the resource (or good) are willing to sell if the price exceeds the value that an alternative allocation of the resource will generate. Under certain legal conditions (e.g., respected property rights, enforceable contracts, free entry and exit, no relative-price-altering taxes or regulations), resources are allocated to their highest valued uses.[36]

In order for "demanders" to guide resources to their preferred uses with price rationing, individuals compete to obtain money by selling scarce resources they own (e.g., labor time, minerals, timber, etc.), or goods and services they produce

---

[36] These ideal conditions are rarely met in the real world, of course, and they are not necessarily met in the private security market for reasons discussed below. Thus, when comparing government and private provision of a particular good or service, such as policing, we are comparing two imperfect alternatives.

with scarce resources they own (there are other ways to obtain money, of course: e.g., theft, corruption, extortion, protection' money, taxation and transfers) which can change the allocation from what would be a resource's highest valued uses. On the supply side, the profit motive creates incentives to sell at a price that maximizes net revenues (profit) but in a free market that price is constrained by competition among sellers and entry of new sellers. Seller whose prices are higher than other sellers' prices for similar products will not be able to find buyers. Competition with free entry also drives the price of a resource (or good) down to the level that just covers minimized production costs (including normal but not excess profits for entrepreneurs). Furthermore, when a seller is planning on being in business in the future, the value of her reputation influences profit by attracting new buyers and keeping existing customers. In order for sellers to build and maintain reputations, they have incentives to provide relatively high-quality goods at relatively low prices compared to competitors, to live up to promises in exchange (behave honestly), and so on. Constraints on competition, whether they are imposed illegally (e.g., through extortion or corruption) or legally (e.g., through government regulations), mean that prices are higher than they would with free competition, and inefficient (i.e., high cost) suppliers can survive.

Profit seeking in competitive markets also creates strong incentives to develop new products that consumers will find to be attractive, and to find more cost-effective ways to produce goods and services being provided. In other words, innovation is common in free markets. As suggested above, there is a wide variety of private security options, and new and improved options are regularly being brought to the market. Many privately provided security options are specialized to focus on specific security threats. Private security firms patrol specific areas,[37] guard locations, provide highly trained experts in defense to protect potential targets for corporate espionage or terrorism, including many government facilities, install alarms and/or security cameras for individual homes or provide the equipment for the customer to install, provide alarm response services, operate armored cars for banks and other high-cash flow businesses, provide bodyguards for people threatened by kidnappers or other criminals, develop complex high tech security systems including monitoring (closed circuit TV, video cameras, computer based monitoring, security lighting) and alarms (sensors and detectors), background investigations, access control (including electronic and biometric technology) and badges/IDs (including photo, fingerprint, facial recognition, etc.), electric or electromagnetic locks and

---

[37] An interesting example of private patrols is the San Francisco "Patrol Special Police" which started in 1851 and continue to operate (Fixler Jr. & Poole, 1992; Stringham, 2015). These 65 police-academy graduated patrol specials are "peace officers" who own their beats and can carry firearms and make arrests. They are paid by individual businesses, homeowners, and landlords located within the area of their patrols, with the services required by each customer determining their prices. Critical Intervention Services (CIS) provides a revealing example. CIS offers services specializing in deterring crime for landlords who have apartment complexes with low-income tenets (Boyce, 1996). They started in 1991 in Tampa, and by 1996 they were providing security for over 50 apartment complexes in Miami, Jacksonville, and Orlando, in addition to Tampa. Crime in these complexes fell by an average of 50 percent between 1991 and 1996.

entry systems, vehicle or fleet tracking, guard stations and communication technology, safes and vaults, computer and network security systems and other information-security for corporate headquarters or production facilities, and so on.

Markets, including security markets, are generally quite flexible in quickly responding to new demands. For instance, after 9/11, the demand for security at the country's 104 nuclear reactors and around 15,000 major chemical plants increased considerably, and the private security market responded. Chemical plants increased their security measures well beyond government requirements, and nuclear facilities are protected by very reputable security firms' highly-trained guards equipped with powerful weapons (Blackstone & Hakim, 2010). Another example developed after a Temple University Student told his mother about an armed robbery outside his house. The mother started a Facebook group by asking if other parents would like to contribute to hiring a private security firm. Dozens of parents did so and the patrol has expanded to cover "15th to 19th streets and Diamond to Master streets" (6abc Digital Stafff and Perez, 2022). Another recent development involves private security for domestic violence victims (Harkin, 2020). This includes working in partnership with domestic violence services, security-technology companies offering services to domestic violence victims, and governments contracting with private companies to provide victim security.[38] Private security companies tend to offer practical support along with a variety of security strategies, individually tailored and more focused on the question: "what can be done to make you feel safe?" In contrast, police officers tend to challenge the credibility of the victim, often trivializing and minimizing the complaint (Harkin, 2021). Police focus on investigating what happened, determining the merits of the complaint, and assigning guilt, while private security provides advice and security based on the victim's wishes and needs.

4.1 Private Investigation and Pursuit

There is a substantial "private investigator" market, but much of the work focuses on non-criminal investigations (e.g., search for evidence in divorces and other civil litigation) because that is what clients pay for, not because that is all private investigators could do. Private investigation of crime does occur, however. Insurance companies investigate many crimes, for instance, and organizations like the American

---

[38] This is not surprising. Government influences the allocation of private security as a major consumer it the security market. Wackenhut is a leading supplier of security services to governments, for instance, providing the entire police force for 1600 acres nuclear test site in Nevada and the Kennedy Space Center, and a wide range of other public facilities (Poole, 1978, 41–42; Reynolds, 1994). Numerous other examples exist. In fact, many local city governments contract for activities traditionally done by police employees, like crime labs, maintenance, parking meter patrols, communications and dispatch, fingerprinting, background checks, transporting prisoners, guarding prisoners in hospitals, guarding public buildings like court houses and convention facilities, patrolling public housing projects, guarding mass transit facilities such as metro rail systems and so on (Fixler Jr. & Poole, 1992; American Society of Industrial Security Foundation, 2005).

Banking Association and the American Hotel-Motel Association have contracted with detective agencies. Many Universities also have their own private police forces which investigate crimes on campuses. Railroad police trace back to the mid-1800s, but they were officially established at the end of World War I as complete and autonomous private police forces in the U.S. and Canada. By the end of WWII there were about 9000 railroad police officers in North America, but reductions in passenger services, the shift of freight to trucks and other changes, resulted in this police force shrinking to about 2300 (Miller & West, 2008). While railroad police often are involved in routine patrol of rail yards, depots, and railroad property, they also are responsible for "conducting complex investigations involving cargo theft, vandalism, theft of equipment, arson, train/vehicle collisions, and they even investigate assault and murders that may spill over onto railroad property" (Miller & West, 2008). In 1992, U.S. railroad police cleared about 30.9 percent of the crimes reported to them, while public police cleared about 21.4 percent of reported crimes (Reynolds, 1994, 11–12). However, an estimated 75 percent of crimes against railroads were reported to railroad police compared to 39 percent of crimes reported to public police. Therefore, adjusted for reporting, the clearance rate for railroad police (23.2) was 286 percent higher than that for public police (8.1).

Another example of private investigation and pursuit is in the bail-bonding market. Many alleged criminals must be released prior to trial due to court delay, limited jail space, and constitutional guarantees of bail. Helland and Tabarrok (2004, 93) report that at the time of their study about a quarter of all pre-trial releases (about 200,000) failed to appear at trial and after a year about 30 percent of those still had failed to appear. Over half of accused felons are released on some sort of public bond such as small deposit bonds, unsecured bonds (no initial deposit is made), or simply on their own recognizance (ROR), promising to appear at their trial. Many promises to appear under these condition apparently are not be credible. Others accused of crimes make a stronger commitment to appear. Some post property or full cash bonds themselves, but many do not have sufficient funds or property to do this (less than five percent of pretrial releases are under property or cash bonds). Public police are responsible for pursuing fugitives released under public bonds (deposit bonds, unsecured bonds, and ROR) as well as full property and monetary bonds.

Prisoners who are not ROR cannot pay full cash or property bonds, but they can contract with commercial bail bondsmen, who post surety bonds in exchange for fees. About 33 percent of prisoner releases before trial between 1990 and 2004 had surety bonds (Cohen & Reaves, 2007, 7). There were about 14,000 bondsmen in the U.S., and about 2,000,000 defendants with surety bonds at the time (Cohen & Reaves, 2007, 4). Bondsmen lose the full bonds if defendants fail to appear, however, and they report that at least 95 percent of their clients must appear in order to break even (Helland & Tabarrok, 2004, 97). Bondsmen generally are given from 90 to 180 days to deliver clients after a failure to appear, before the full bonds are forfeited. Therefore, if someone with a security bond flees, a national network of private 'bounty hunters' is notified. These bounty hunters search for (investigate and pursue) fugitives with surety bonds.

Cohen and Reaves (2007, 9) examine data on pretrial releases from state courts in the 75 largest counties in the U.S., and report that over the 1990–2004 period, about 30 percent of defendants released with unsecured bonds fail to appear when their trial date arrives, as do 26 percent of those who are ROR. By comparison, only 18 percent of those with surety bonds do not appear.[39] Fugitive rates after a year are even more revealing, as just three percent of those under surety bonds remain at large, compared to four percent for property bonds, seven percent for both cash and deposit bonds, and eight and ten percent respectively under ROR and unsecured bonds (Cohen & Reaves, 2007, 9). Helland and Tabarrok (2004) reach similar conclusions, reporting, for instance, that fugitives released under surety bonds are 28 percent less likely to fail to appear than those who are ROR. Furthermore, for those who fail to appear, surety-bond fugitives are 53 percent less likely than ROR fugitives to remain at large for long periods. Clearly, private bondsmen and the system of private bounty hunters are more effective in getting defendants to court than public alternatives.

4.2 Abuse by Suppliers of Private Crime Control

There are abusive private security guards and investigators.[40] Determining how many is impossible, however, since there is no publicly available depository for information about such abuse that I am aware of. I did a google search for "abuse by private security" and many pages of links came up. However, the first actual detailed example of abuse was on the sixth page (a few were alluded to earlier but without details). Instead, multiple links on the first pages were actually not about abuse by private security, as they explored the growing use of private security protecting domestic abuse victims, as indicated above. There were also links to information about abuse of private security personnel such as assault of security guards. Many of the links also discussed abuse by private mercenary firms employed by governments and engaged in various military actions around the world. These mercenary firms often call themselves security firms (indeed, some also provide private security in the US to deter crime), but the abusive situation occurs during military actions. Some links also led to discussions without evidence, about why the writers expect that there should be abuse (typical incorrect claims about markets, such as profit seeking leads to cost cutting and low-quality services, as well as issues insufficient government oversight, lack of training, etc.).

---

[39] This is a better appearance rate than the 20 percent for full cash bonds and the 22 percent with deposit bonds. Only about 14 percent of those with property bonds failed to appear, but use of this option by the courts is relatively rare since most individuals waiting for criminal trials do not have sufficient property for such bonds.

[40] Some abusive actions by "private security" involve police officers moonlighting as a security guards (e.g., Pilcher et al., 2019; Costello & Glowicki, 2022).

Many individuals, whether publicly or privately employed, might abuse their positions by cutting costs, doing poor quality work, bullying and so on, if they can. The institutional arrangements within which *people* perform their tasks determine whether or not such abuses can be carried out, however, and profit seeking firms in competitive markets with clearly defined property rights, including liability for harms, are one of the best institutional arrangements for discouraging abusive behavior. Private firms facing competition must satisfy customers to stay in business. Furthermore, they can be held liable for harms that their employees inflict. Thus, security firms generally are bonded and/or buy liability insurance to cover this contingency, but if abuse is a serious and frequent problem for a particular firm, such insurance can be extremely costly if available at all. Therefore, a security officer who is abusive will not be a security officer for long. Security firms also have strong incentives to screen employees if they can. Firms in private competitive markets, and their employees, are not nearly as likely to abuse their powers as is frequently claimed.

Recall from Sect. 3.7 that an individual who is not liable for the negative consequences of his actions is likely to be relatively unconcerned about those consequences. In this contest, an important difference between private security and public police is the allocation of liability. If a private security officer abuses a customer, an alleged criminal, or anyone else, whether intentionally or accidently, the security officer and/or firm owner is likely to be liable for the harms. They do not get qualified immunity. Firms in turn purchase insurance or are bonded to protect themselves from large payouts. In most legitimate tort claims filed, the employee, firm, insurance company, and injured party (or the lawyers representing them) negotiate an acceptable compensation payment. A firm with large numbers of tort claims filed against it will face high insurance, legal and/or liability costs. Abusive employees also are likely to sued, fired, and depending on the nature of the abuse, charged with a crime, such as assault. Failure to change employee incentives suggests that more abuse will occur. As information about the abusiveness of a firm's employees spreads, demand for the firm's services declines, leading to bankruptcy. Naturally, firm owners want to avoid liability by trying to avoid hiring potentially abusive employees. Not surprisingly, security firms take precautions that are intended to limit the likelihood of abuse. For instance, unlike public police, most private security personnel are not armed. The Graduate Institute of International Development Studies (2011, 111–116) examined much of the existing data and reports ranges of estimates of firearms per private security company personnel for several countries. For instance, the ratio for Australia is between 0.02 and 0.15, while the US ratio is between 0.2 and 0.3. Security service customers often request armed guards, but many of these requests are discouraged by security providers, both because they feel that weapons are generally not needed and because they face higher insurance costs when their employees are armed (Cunningham & Taylor, 1985: 20). Some potential targets protected by private security may require armed guards, of course, but in these cases, the guards come from a different labor pool, made up of individuals with experience and/or training in the safe use of firearms. They are instructed to take precautions to avoid dangerous uses of firearms, while many public police appear to be trained to immediately react by drawing a firearm at the slightest hint of aggravation, hostility or reluctance to follow police orders. Perhaps more significantly, Cunningham and Taylor's (1985, 67) extensive survey "tends to confirm other research indicating that most private security personnel are drawn from different labor pools than law enforcement officers, and their personal characteristics differ." Thus, while security companies actively "discourage employees from detention, searches, and the use of force" (Cunningham & Taylor, 1985: 34), they also try to employ people who are not inclined to be abusive. For example, Donovan and Walsh (1986: 47–49) report that 96.30 percent of Starrett City private security officers had a "service orientation," compared to 59.57 percent of NYPD officers. Indeed, 94.44 percent of the security officers reported that they always comply with Starrett City residents' requests while only 30.60 percent of NYPD officers said that they always comply with citizens' requests. In light of these findings, it is not surprising that 81.46 percent of Starrett City officers felt that citizens respected them compared to 49.64 of the NYPD officers, and that 80.77 percent of the Starrett City security force believed that they got adequate support from citizens while only 40.60 percent of the police officers considered this to be the case.[41]

4.3 Political Interference in Markets for Private Security

Coercion may be required to enforce the rules of the market (e.g., those establishing property rights and backing contractual obligations), but coercion also can be employed to undermine competition. Government mandated price ceilings or price floors dramatically distort market allocations, for instance, as do other politically imposed limits on competition. Raising barriers to entry (e.g., occupational licensing, exclusive franchises, quotas, import taxes, etc.) allow existing sellers to charge non-competitively high prices and/or reduce quality.

Statutes in many states mandate that private security personnel cannot engage in various policing actions.[42] This can mean that private security cannot gather evidence for trial, cite suspects in court, and/or take people into custody. Some states grant limited numbers of private security personnel partial and even full police powers, but typically only within confined areas, such as manufacturing plants, retail stores or malls, and campuses.[43] A somewhat dated survey of medium-to-large

---

[41] Indeed, the "concern shown by security personnel for care of property and prevention of disorder as well as the safety of residents and visitors" explains the high level of reporting in Starrett City (Donovan & Walsh, 1986: 36).

[42] For the most part, security firms and employees have no more authority than an average citizen. The political justification for this is that security officers act on behalf of the person, business, corporation, or other entity that hires them, so that entity's basic right to protect persons and property is transferred to the security officer, but additional police powers are not.

[43] In New York, for example, retail security personnel can apprehend suspects, cite them in court, and preserve evidence if they have completed an approved training course. Washington, DC secu-

police departments indicates that about 25 percent grant special police powers to some private security personnel by "deputizing" them, although most of the deputized officers are employed in-house by large firms or developments rather than by security firms (Cunningham & Taylor, 1985, 40). Therefore, most security firms and personal are not allowed to perform many police services.

Occupational licensing limits competition by restricting entry and creates artificially protected profits (e.g., Kliener & Krueger, 2013). These barriers result in higher prices and reduced provision levels. Licenses for private security firms and their employees are issued at the state level, and the requirements vary considerably across the U.S. In some states, no regulations or regulatory bodies exist, while in other states, licenses are issued by bureaus that deal with business licensing in general (Departments of Commerce, State, Professional Regulation, or Consumer Affairs). Finally, some states have boards established specifically to oversee the private security licensing process. The composition of these boards varies, however, with some but not all including private security personnel, public police officers, or both. Meehan and Benson (2015) explore the relationship between these different regulatory institutional structures and the characteristics of the subsequent licensing requirements. Empirical results suggest that requirements for entry into the security market tend to be relatively strict when active private security personnel are in control of licensing, and that different patterns of regulation generally apply when police or non-specialized agencies control licensing. Recall research discussed above which implies that allocating more resources to private security reduces crime, and that relatively stringent licensing requirements limit entry, thereby increasing crime (Meehan & Benson, 2017). This suggests that the patterns of regulation that arise when active private security personnel control licensing are limiting competitive entry.

Public police officers frequently "moonlight" as security guards, thereby competing directly with the employees of private security firms. If police representatives on regulatory commissions want to protect this moonlighting market they may support regulations that raise barriers to entry by non-police. Many retired public police officers also enter the private security market, so regulators may want to avoid setting regulations that raise their own costs of entry (e.g., insurance/bonding requirements, testing, or additional training), while supporting constraints on the entry of firms established by individuals who are not former police officers. This expectation

---

rity personnel can make arrests if they are licensed as "special police officers" after meeting specified qualifications, while Maryland's governor can appoint "special policemen" with full police powers, given that they work on the premises of certain businesses. North Carolina has a similar law, and Las Vegas security guards can be appointed as "special deputy sheriffs" (Fixler Jr. & Poole, 1992, 35–36). Oregon's governor can appoint "special policemen" who work for the railroad and steamboat industries, and the Texas Department of Public Safety can commission security personnel who work for private employers as "special rangers" with full police powers. A number of states grant varying degrees of police power to campus security personnel, both for public and private universities. The railroad police discussed above were originally given police powers by the federal government because of the interstate nature of the industry, but since then a number of states have also granted them police powers.

is born out in Meehan and Benson (2015). For instance, licensing requirements generally make police training a substitute for the guard training and public police experience a substitute for private security guard experience, so police of security regulatory boards set high training and experience requirements. Police officers who moonlight as private security guards or who want to enter the market after they retire are likely to have more than enough training and experience to meet these high requirements while other potential entrants are less likely to qualify. Regulatory boards with police also tend to oppose testing requirements. Potential entrants who are former police officers (and/or moonlighting officers) do not want to take exams regarding private security procedures and rules they are not familiar with. Evidence in Meehan and Benson (2015) indicates that public police presence on a private security licensing board is associated with higher law enforcement experience requirements in order to qualify for a license, while the probability that passing an exam is required is much lower if police are on the state's licensing board.

The evidence presented in Meehan and Benson (2015) also supports the contention that occupational licensing limits competition by restricting entry, and creating artificially protected profit, when existing security firms dominate regulations. Meehan (2015) finds that three particular licensing requirements – the training, experience, and testing requirements – reduce the number of private security firms per 100,000 people in a state, and tend to reduce the prevalence of relatively small firms. Due to limits on entry, firms that were established before licensing was instituted or who already successfully obtained a license, expand to meet market demand at prices above the competitive level. Established firms, including those represented on licensing boards, have additional advantages in states that have explicit "Grandfather" clauses that exclude existing license holders from meeting new stricter licensing requirements. Established firms also benefit by making licensing renewal requirements less strict than entry requirements. In fact, when licensing requirements are made more stringent renewal requirements often are not changed.

5 Conclusions

A non-politicized market-driven defund-the-police process has been going on for decades. Sherman pointed out, back in 1983, that "Few developments are more indicative of public concern about crime – and declining faith in the ability of public institutions to cope with it – than the burgeoning growth of private policing.... Rather than approving funds for more police, the voters have turned to volunteer and paid watchers" (1983, 145–149). Indeed, governments are increasingly contracting with private security firms for various functions that police departments historically have performed, such as guarding courthouses, transporting prisoners, parking control, and even patrolling (Benson, 1998, 2014).[44]This has continued. Employment of private security personnel has been increasing dramatically since at least the early 1960s while employment of public police personnel has been relatively constant.

Substantially more privatization is clearly possible, particularly if the market is deregulated in order to increase entry and increase the types of prevention, investigative and pursuit activities that private security can offer. For instance, after his extensive examination of the evidence on police and security performance, Sherman concludes that voluntary and paid security patrols are both more effective providers of crime prevention than police. Therefore, for cost effectiveness reasons, public police should not be primary providers of crime prevention. Sherman (1983, 58) proposes that the organization and use of both voluntary watch groups and paid private security should be encouraged and public police should focus on other tasks. This could happen naturally if the competitive playing field for public and private policing is leveled. Then if public police can effectively compete they should be able to continue to attract funding. Part of this leveling must include changes in liability rules. Public police should be held accountable for their abusive behavior. If a police officer's action, whether intentional or accidental, harms someone, that person should be able to sue the officer and her employer under tort law. Such personal liability rules would create incentives for police and their employers to take more precautions against abuse. In addition, private security and public police generally should have the same powers under similar conditions. This is likely to involve giving some additional power to private security (e.g., to make arrests, to gather and present evidence) to deal with some, but not all, criminal activities, and removing some power from public police (e.g., no-knock entry, ease of and immediacy of firearm use by all police officers in all circumstances – police should not carry firearms under many circumstances, as illustrated in England[45]). Concerns about private police becoming just as abusive as public police are not warranted, given the appropriate institutional environment, including competitive markets and appropriate liability rules. Abuse by public police should also decline if they face completion and personal liability.

Another policy action that would also reduce police abuse is to reduce discretion, at least to a degree, through large-scale decriminalization. Decriminalization does not necessarily mean legalization. In fact, even the core violent and property offences designated as crimes in modern societies were not always crimes. They were illegal but treated as offences against individuals (torts) rather than against 'society' or the state. Successful prosecution resulted in compensation to victims

---

[44] If police see this as a threat to their jobs, it provides another reason for police to seek limits on security-market entry.

[45] These issues have not been discussed here, but they all are sources of abuse by public police. Perhaps most importantly, the actions of police officers should be shifted from the current aggressive approach for virtually every issue to one of selective aggression under limited circumstances. Such changes should naturally develop by removal of firearms in dealing with many issues, demilitarization, adding liability for all abuses and so on.

(restitution) rather than fines and confiscations going to the state, physical punishment, and/or imprisonment.[46] Potential restitution creates strong incentives for victims to pursue prosecution, often by contracting with private individuals or firms specialized in investigative and pursuit services. This suggests a spontaneous expansion of private policing (assuming government regulations do not stifle such a development), and over time, reliance on public police could naturally decline.[47]

---

[46] It is often claimed that these offences were ultimately designated as crimes for 'public interest' reasons (e.g., state pursuit, prosecution and punishment allegedly is more efficient and/or more equitable). This is not correct. These changes reflect private interests of individuals and groups with coercive power and/or political influence, including kings and aristocracy in medieval societies, in order to shift payments from restitution for victims, to fines and confiscations for the king or lord. See Benson (1994, 1998, 203–26, 315–18).

[47] For instance, the limited use of private pursuit clearly results, at least in part, because government regulations limit the rights and incentives to invest in such private policing, including the fact that crime victims virtually never receive restitution. If they did that would create incentives to invest in pursuit (Benson, 1994, 1998, 2014). Historically, when victims had rights to restitution, voluntary investment in private policing is prevalent (Benson, 1994, 1998). Judges in many states are now allowed to order restitution as a punishment, but it often is not included in judgements, and even if it is, it is often not collected by police. For instance, a Nebraska study reported that in 2013, just 5 percent of felony prison sentences, 4 percent of felony jail sentences, and 20 percent of felony probation sentences included restitution orders (CSG Justice Center, 2015). Thirty percent of those sentenced to probations did not pay any of the restitution they owed while 70 percent made at least some partial payments. Similarly, Iowa's Division of Criminal Justice Planning examined data from 2010 through 2017 and found that only 34 percent of the criminals on probation with court ordered restitution paid at least half the restitution and just 6 percent of incarcerated prisoners paid half or more of the restitution owed (Beisoner, 2018). After eight years, approximately 17% of restitution obligations had been paid. In 2013, the Minnesota Legislature ordered the Department of Public Safety (DPS) to form a working group to study how restitution is requested, ordered, and collected in the state. The resulting report (Minnesota Restitution Working Group, 2015) followed all adult convictions in 2010 for a minimum of three years and four months and a maximum of four years and four months. Just seven percent of the total 2010 criminal cases that were disposed of had restitution orders. The report breaks this total into cases involving property crime, crimes against persons, DWI, drug crimes, and other crimes and the portion of each category's dispositions including restitution, are 36 percent, 8 percent, 2 percent, 4 percent and 2 percent respectively. Restitution orders were given in 22 percent of convictions for felonies, 7 percent of gross misdemeanors, and 0.3 percent of petty misdemeanors. Minnesota judges ordered $24,988,398 in restitution but $12,744,083 (about 51 percent) was still outstanding at the end of the study period. Restitution orders also can be reduced or adjusted after a verdict, and $5,097,338 (about 21 percent) of the restitution assessments were eliminated through these procedures. Another $499,768 was credited but not paid, so only $6,247,100 (about 25 percent) was actually paid.

References

6abc Digital Staff and Walter Perez. (2022, March 15). Concerned parents band together, hire private security near Temple University Campus, *6abc.com*, https://6abc.com/temple-university-philadelphia-police-gun-violence-north-philly-crime/11651332/

American Society of Industrial Security Foundation. (2005). *The ASIS Foundation security report: Scope and emerging trends*. ASIS Foundation. http://www.asisonline.org/foundation/trendsin-securitytudy.pdf

Baicker, K., & Jacobson, M. (2007). Finders keepers: Forfeiture laws, policing incentives, and local budgets. *Journal of Public Economics, 91*, 2113–2134.

Baker, J. S. (2008, June 16). Revisiting the explosive growth of federal crimes. *Heritage Foundation Legal Memo No. 26*.

Barrett, D. (2011). Introduction: Counting the costs of the children's drug war. In D. Barrett (Ed.), *Children of the war on drugs: Perspectives on the impact of drug policy on young people*. International Debate Education Association.

Beisoner, K. (2018). *Iowa restitution paid*. Iowa Division of Criminal and Juvenile Justice Planning.

Benson, B. L. (1988). Corruption in law enforcement: One consequence of the 'Tragedy of the Commons' arising with public allocation processes. *International Review of Law and Economics, 8*, 73–84.

Benson, B. L. (1994). Are public goods really common pools: Considerations of the evolution of policing and highways in England. *Economic Inquiry, 32*(2), 249–271.

Benson, B. L. (1998). *To serve and protect: Privatization and community in criminal justice*. New York University Press.

Benson, B. L. (2010). The allocation of police. In B. L. Benson & P. R. Zimmerman (Eds.), *Handbook on the economics of crime*. Edward Elgar.

Benson, B. L. (2014). Let's focus on victim justice, not criminal justice! *The Independent Review, 19*, 209–238.

Benson, B. L., & Mast, B. D. (2001). Privately produced general deterrence. *Journal of Law and Economics, 44*, 725–746.

Benson, B. L., & Meehan, B. (2018). Predatory public finance and the evolution of the war on drugs. In A. Hoffer & T. Nesbit (Eds.), *For your own good: Taxes, paternalism, and fiscal discrimination in the twenty-first century*. Mercatus Center.

Benson, B. L., & Rasmussen, D. W. (1991). The relationship between Illicit drug enforcement policy and property crimes. *Contemporary Policy Issues, 9*, 106–115.

Benson, B. L., Kim, I., Rasmussen, D. W., & Zuehlke, T. W. (1992). Is property crime caused by drug use or drug enforcement policy? *Applied Economics, 24*, 679–692.

Benson, B. L., Kim, I., & Rasmussen, D. W. (1998). Deterrence and public policy: tradeoffs in the allocation of police resources. *International Review of Law and Economics, 18*, 77–100.

Berk, R., Brackman, H., & Lesser, S. (1977). *A measure of justice: An empirical study of changes in the California Penal Code, 1955–1971*. Academic.

Binion, B. (2021, May 19). Cops who beat a man after pulling him over for broken lights receive qualified Immunity, *Reason.com*, https://reason.com/2021/05/19/qualified-immunity-cops-shreveport-louisiana-assaulted-gregory-tucker-5th-circuit-court-of-appeals/

Blackstone, E. A., & Hakim, S. (2010). Private policing: Experiences, evaluation, and future direction. In B. L. Benson & P. R. Zimmerman (Eds.), *Handbook on the economics of crime*. Edward Elgar.

Blumberg, A. (1970). *Criminal justice*. Quadrangle Books.

Boyce, J. N. (1996, Sept 18). Landlords turn to Commando Patrol. *Wall Street Journal*, B1–B2.

Breton, A., & Wintrobe, R. (1982). *The logic of Bureaucratic Control*. Cambridge University Press.

Bronars, S. G., & Lott, J. R. (1998). Criminal deterrence, geographic spillovers, and the right to carry concealed handguns. *American Economic Review, 88*, 475–479.

Brown, D. K. (2011). Criminal law's unfortunate triumph over administrative law. *Journal of Law, Economics and Policy, 7*, 657–683.

Brown, E. N. (2022, Feb 16). 214 Sex workers arrested in Super Bowl 'Human Trafficking' Mission, *Reason.com*, https://reason.com/2022/02/16/214-sex-workers-arrested-in-super-bowl-human-trafficking-mission/?utm_medium=email

Brumm, H. J., & Cloninger, D. O. (1995). The drug war and the Homicide rate: a direct correlation. *Cato Journal, 14*, 509–517.

Cohen, T. H., & Reaves, B. A. (2007). *Pretrial release of Felony Defendants in State Courts, Bureau of Justice Statistics special report*. U.S. Department of Justice, Office of Justice Programs.

Costello, D., & Glowicki, M. (2022, Jan 31). 6 LMPD officers accused of working private security jobs during patrol shifts. *Louisville Courier Journal*. https://www.yahoo.com/news/6-lmpd-officers-accused-working-222504967.html

Cowen, T. (1988). Introduction. Public goods and externalities: Old and new perspectives. In T. Cowen (Ed.), *The theory of market failure*. George Mason University.

CSG Justice Center Staff. (2015). *Victim advocates improve justice reinvestment in Nebraska*. Council of State Governments.

Cunningham, W. C., & Taylor, T. H. (1985). *Crime and protection in America: A study of private security and law enforcement resources and relationships*. U.S. Department of Justice, National Institute of Justice.

DeAngelis, R. T. (2021). Systemic racism in police killings: New evidence from the mapping police violence database, 2013–2021. *Race and Justice*, 1–10.

Demsetz, H. (1967). Toward a theory of property rights. *American Economic Review, 57*, 347–359.

Demsetz, H. (1970). The private production of public goods. *Journal of Law and Economics, 13*, 293–306.

Denwalt, D. (2022, Feb 22). Law enforcement officers conduct massive raid of Black Market Marijuana, issue arrest warrants, *Oklahoman*, https://www.yahoo.com/news/law-enforcement-officers-conduct-massive-183907087.html

Dharmapala, D., McAdams, R. H., & Rappaport, J. (2017). *The effect of collective bargaining rights on law enforcement: Evidence from Florida*. Social Science Research Network. https://papers.ssrn.com/abstract=3095217

Dills, A., Goffard, S., Miron, J., & Partin, E. (2021). *The effects of State Marijuana Legalizations: 2021 update*. Cato Institute Policy Analysis Number 908.

Donovan, E. J., & Walsh, W. F. (1986). *An evaluation of Starrett City security services*. Pennsylvania State University.

Drug Policy Alliance. (2015). *Above the law: An investigation of civil asset forfeiture in California* (Drug Policy Alliance ed.).

Fagan, J. A., & Campbell, A. D. (2020). Race and reasonableness in police killings. *Boston University Law Review, 100*, 951–1016.

Fixler, P., Jr., & Poole, R. (1992). Can police be privatized? In G. Bowman, S. Hakim, & P. Seidenstat (Eds.), *Privatizing the United States Justice System: Police, adjudication, and corrections services from the private sector*. McFarland & Co.

Fryer, R. G., Jr. (2019). An empirical analysis of racial differences in police use of force. *Journal of Political Economy, 127*, 1210–1261.

Goldin, K. (1977). Equal access vs. selective access: A critique of public goods theory. *Public Choice, 29*, 53–71.

Graduate Institute of International Development Studies. (2011). *Small arms survey: States of Security*. GIIDS.

Hardin, G. (1968). The tragedy of the commons. *Science, 162*, 1243–1248.

Harkin, D. (2020). *Private security and domestic violence: The risks and benefits of private security companies working with victims of domestic violence*. Routledge.

Harkin, D. (2021). The uncertain commodity of 'Security': Are private security companies 'Value for Money' for domestic violence services? *Journal of Criminology, 54*, 532–538.

Helland, E., & Tabarrok, A. (2004). The Fugitive: Evidence on public versus private law enforcement from bail jumping. *Journal of Law and Economics, 47*, 93–122.

Jerit, J., & Barabas, J. (2006). Bankrupt Rhetoric: How misleading information affects knowledge about social security. *Public Opinion Quarterly, 70*, 278–303.

Joh, E. E. (2004). The paradox of private policing. *Journal of Criminal Law and Criminology, 95*, 49–132.

Johnson, R. N., & Libecap, G. D. (1982). Contracting problems and regulation: The case of the fishery. *American Economic Review, 72*, 332–347.

Jorgensen, C., & Harper, A. J. (2020). Examining the effects of legalizing Marijuana in Colorado and Washington on clearance rates: A quasi-experimental design. *Journal of Experimental Criminology*. Advance online publication. https://doi.org/10.1007/s11292-020-09446-7

Kelly, J., & Nichols, M. (2019, May 23). We found 85,000 cops who've been investigated for misconduct, *USA TODAY*, https://www.usatoday.com/in-depth/news/investigations/2019/04/24/usa-today-revealing-misconduct-records-police-cops/3223984002/

King, J. (2022, Feb 14). I was beaten by the police for no reason. Now the Supreme Court should give me Justice, *Reason.com*, https://reason.com/2021/05/19/qualified-immunity-cops-shreveport-louisiana-assaulted-gregory-tucker-5th-circuit-court-of-appeals/

Kliener, M., & Krueger, A. (2013). Analyzing the extent and influence of occupational licensing on the labor market. *Journal of Labor Economics, 31*, S173–S202.

Knapp, W. (Chairman). (1972). *The Knapp Commission report on police corruption*. George Braziller.

Krueger, A. (1974). The political economy of the Rent-Seeking Society. *American Economic Review., 64*, 291–303.

Larkin, P. J., Jr. (2013). Public choice theory and overcriminalization. *Harvard Journal of Law & Public Policy, 36*, 715–791.

Lindesmith, A. (1965). *The addict and the law*. Vintage Press.

MacDonald, J. M., Klick, J., & Gunwald, B. (2012). The effect of privately provided police services on crime. *Faculty Scholarship at Penn Law, 430*. https://scholarship.law.upenn.edu/faculty_scholarship/430

Makin, D. A., Willits, D. W., Wu, G., DuBois, K. O., Lu, R., & Stohr, M. K. (2019). Marijuana legalization and crime clearance rates: Testing proponent assertions in Colorado and Washington State. *Police Quarterly, 22*, 31–55.

Mark, J. (2019, May 22). Rape survivors feel re-victimized by the SFPD, despite department's pledge to improve, *Mission Local*, https://missionlocal.org/2019/05/rape-victims-say-they-feel-re-victimized-by-the-sfpd-despite-departments-pledge-to-improve/

Mast, B., Benson, B., & Rasmussen, D. (2000). Entrepreneurial police and drug enforcement policy. *Public Choice, 104*, 285–308.

McChesney, F. S. (2010). The economic analysis of corruption. In B. L. Benson & P. R. Zimmerman (Eds.), *Handbook on the economics of crime*. Edward Elgar.

McNutt, P. (2000). Public goods and club goods. In B. Bouckaert & G. De Geestm (Eds.), *Encyclopedia of law and economics*. Edward Elgar.

Meehan, B. J. (2015). The impact of licensing requirements on industrial organization and labor: Evidence from the U.S. Private Security Market. *International Review of Law and Economics, 42*, 113–121.

Meehan, B. J., & Benson, B. L. (2015). The occupation of regulators influences occupational regulation: Evidence from the U.S. Private Security Industry. *Public Choice, 162*, 97–117.

Meehan, B. J., & Benson, B. L. (2017). Does private security affect crime? a test using state regulations as instruments. *Applied Economics, 49*, 4911–4924.

Mendes, S. M. (2000). Property crime and drug enforcement in Portugal. *Criminal Justice Policy Review, 11*, 195–216.

Miller, P., & West, M. (2008). *The railroad police*, http://www.therailroadpolice.com/history.htm

Minnesota Restitution Study Group. (2015). *Report to the legislature*. Office of Justice Programs, Minnesota Department of Public Safety.

Miron, J. A. (1999). Violence and the U.S. Prohibition of drugs and alcohol. *American Law and Economics Review, 1*, 78–114.

Morgan, R. E., & Thompson, A. (2021). *Criminal victimization, 2020.* U.S. Department of Justice, Office of Justice Programs, Bureau of Justice Statistics. https://bjs.ojp.gov/sites/g/files/xyckuh236/files/media/document/cv20.pdf

New York Civil Liberties Union. (2011). *Stop-and-frisk 2011: NYCLU Briefing.* NYCLU. http://www.nyclu.org/files/pub...

Oppel, Jr., Richard, S. G. S., & Spuzzoaug, M. (2016, Aug 10). *Justice Department to release blistering report of racial bias by Baltimore police,* https://www.nytimes.com/2016/08/10/us/justice-department-to-release-blistering-report-of-racial-bias-by-baltimore-police.html?action=click&contentCollection=U.S.&module=RelatedCoverage&region= Marginalia&pgtype=article

Pilcher, J., Hegarty, A., Litke, E., & Nichols, M. (2019, Oct 14). Fired for a Felony, again for Perjury. Meet the New Police Chief, *USA TODAY Network,* https://www.yahoo.com/news/fired-felony-again-perjury-meet-011524150.html

Poole, R. W. (1978). *Cutting back City Hall.* Free Press.

Rasmussen, D. W., Benson, B. L., & Sollars, D. L. (1993). Spatial competition in illicit drug markets: The consequences of increased drug enforcement. *Review of Regional Studies, 23,* 219–236.

Reaves, B. A. (1992). State and local police departments. *Bureau of Justice Statistics Bulletin, 4,* 1–14.

Reilly, S., & Nichols, M. (2019). Hundreds of police officers have been labeled liars, some still help send people to prison. *USA TODAY.* https://www.yahoo.com/news/hundredspolice-officers-labeled-liars-002015295.html

Resignato, A. J. (2000). Violent crime: a Function of drug use or drug enforcement? *Applied Economics, 32,* 681–688.

Reynolds, M. O. (1994). *Using the private sector to deter crime.* National Center for Policy Analysis.

Richards, D. A. J. (1982). *Sex, drugs, death, and the law: An essay on human rights and over criminalization.* Rowman and Littlefield.

Robertson, C. (2014, Nov 13). New Orleans Police routinely ignore sex crimes, report finds, *New York Times,* http://www.nytimes.com/2014/11/13/us/new-orleans-police-special-crimes-unit-inquiry.html

Rolles, S. (2011). After the war on drugs: How legal regulation of production and trade would better serve children. In D. Barrett (Ed.), *Children of the Drug War.* International Debate Education Association.

Rushin, S. (2017). Police union contracts. *Duke Law Journal, 66,* 1191.

Samuelson, P. A. (1954). The Pure Theory of public expenditure. *Review of Economics and Statistics, 36,* 387–389.

Samuelson, P. A. (1955). Diagrammatic exposition of a theory of public expenditure. *Review of Economics and Statistics, 37,* 350–356.

Shackford, S. (2022, April 13). Imagine having a decade of your life erased. It happened to 161 people exonerated from prison in 2021, *Reason.com,* https://reason.com/2022/04/13/imagine-having-a-decade-of-your-life-erased-it-happened-to-161-people-exonerated-from-prison-in-2021/

Shepard, E. M., & Blackley, P. R. (2005). Drug enforcement and crime: Recent evidence fom New York State. *Social Science Quarterly, 86,* 323–342.

Shepard, E. M., & Blackley, P. R. (2010). Economics of crime and drugs: Prohibition and public policies for illicit drug control. In B. L. Benson & P. R. Zimmerman (Eds.), *Handbook on the economics of crime.* Edward Elgar Publishing.

Sherman, L. W. (1983). Patrol strategies for police. In J. Q. Wilson (Ed.), *Crime and public policy.* Institute for Contemporary Studies Press.

Shoup, C. (1964). Standards for distributing a free government service: Crime prevention. *Public Finance, 19,* 383–392.

Sollars, D. L., Benson, B. L., & Rasmussen, W. (1994). Drug enforcement and deterrence of property crime among local jurisdictions. *Public Finance Quarterly, 22,* 22–45.

Stringham, E. (2015). *Private governance: Creating order in economic and social life*. Oxford University Press.

Stuntz, W. J. (2001). The pathological politics of criminal law. *Michigan Law Review, 100*, 505–600.

Thomson-DeVeaux, A., Bronner, L., & Sharma, D. (2021, Feb 22). Cities spend millions on police misconduct every year. Here's why it's so difficult to hold departments accountable. *FiveThirtyEight*. https://fivethirtyeight.com/features/police-misconduct-costs-cities-millions-every-year-but-thats-where-the-accountability-ends/

Werb, D., Rowell, G., Guyatt, G., Kerr, T., Montaner, J., & Wood, E. (2011). Effect of drug law enforcement on drug market violence: A systematic review. *International Journal of Drug Policy, 22*, 87–94.

Wua, G., Yongtao, L., & Xiaodong, L. (2022). Effects of recreational Marijuana legalization on clearance rates for violent crimes: Evidence from Oregon. *International Journal of Drug Police, 100*, 1–6.

Zimmerman, P. R. (2014). The deterrence of crime through private security Efforts. *International Review of Law and Economics, 37*, 66–75.

Public Space Crime Prevention Partnerships: Reviewing the Evidence

Tim Prenzler and Rick Sarre

Abstract This chapter reviews studies on public-private crime prevention partnerships in public spaces. The focus of the chapter is on successful case studies, while also addressing ethical issues and practical obstacles. The first section provides brief accounts of the development of policies regarding partnerships in security, including a variety of examples in practice, outlining how the work of the security industry fits within a successful situational and problem-oriented crime prevention framework. The chapter then considers the potential role of private security in foot patrols supporting police and in Business Improvement District programs. The focus then shifts to six evaluated case studies, addressing development processes, interventions, and impact measures. The final section reviews the likely ingredients for success, with the provision of a set of guidelines for ensuring accountability and optimal outcomes in police-security collaboration, including through optimal regulation of the security industry.

1 Background: Public-Private Partnerships & Crime Theories

Public-private partnerships have a long history but appear to have become a policy virtue in the wash up from the controversial privatisation agenda of the 1980s. Privatisation involved selling government services – often considered natural monopolies entailing major public goods – to private for-profit companies in the interests of improved efficiency. Partnerships, on the other hand, provide a less

T. Prenzler (✉)
School of Law and Society, University of the Sunshine Coast, Sippy Downs, QLD, Australia
e-mail: tprenzler@usc.edu.au

R. Sarre
Justice and Society, University of South Australia, Adelaide, SA, Australia
e-mail: rick.sarre@unisa.edu.au

radical and less controversial way for governments to reduce financial outlays, improve outputs, spread risk, create employment, and mobilise expertise, while remaining substantially in control of programs and assets (van Buuren & den Boer, 2009). Public-private partnerships can take a variety of forms from simple short-term commercial arrangements between a government department and a private provider to long-term complex contractual or voluntary agreements involving numerous stakeholders. Participants can include different levels of government and different government departments, not-for-profit organisations, citizen groups, residents, businesses, professional associations, and labour unions.

Policing has seen very little in the way of any large-scale replacement of police personnel by private operators, and it appears there are few documented cases of privatisation or outsourcing of policing tasks showing clear public benefits. In one case, Connors et al. (1999) described a program in which the city council of Kentwood, Michigan, engaged a private company to investigate complaints about bad checks. The program reportedly cleared a large backlog of cases, assisted businesses to recover losses, and freed up police time for other tasks (p. 11). In another example, the city of Phoenix contracted out security and crowd control work at its city centre and other council buildings. Apart from the lower cost, the private providers were reportedly more effective than police in focusing on crime prevention rather than simply responding to incidents as they occurred (pp. 19–20).

Another example of police outsourcing occurred in the United Kingdom in the early 2010s. In response to a public debt crisis, the government announced a 20 percent cut to police budgets and required police to outsource 'non-core' tasks with a view to 'freeing up the police to fight crime more effectively and efficiently' (Home Office, 2011: 5). Most prominently, in 2011, Lincolnshire Police entered a £200 million ten-year 'strategic partnership' with security firm G4S. The arrangement included a relocation of 575 non-police staff in areas such as offender custody, enquiries management and control room operations. One report on the scheme claimed numerous achievements, including savings of £5 million, an increase in call centre customer satisfaction (to 94 percent), an increase in calls answered within ten seconds (from 89 percent to 93 percent) and a reduction in crime (by 14 percent compared to eight percent nationally) (Boyd, 2013; Lincolnshire Police/G4S, 2013). A flagship program was the G4S prisoner escort service – 'Street to Suite' – which allowed police to stay on patrol or at a crime scene following an arrest, saving 1876 hours of police time over 11 months. Elsewhere in the UK, the police privatisation agenda received less enthusiastic support. A 2012 report, *Increasing Efficiency in the Police Service: The Role of Collaboration*, found that cooperation across the 43 police forces in England and Wales was largely between public sector agencies. Most partnerships involving the private sector were limited to the fields of information technology and processes relating to finance (HMIC, 2012).

1.1 Types of Police/Private Security Collaboration

Despite the general lack of appetite for outsourcing police tasks, the concept of extending police resources through various forms of partnerships with private providers has considerable currency. The idea of natural synergies between police and the security industry was given increased support during the period of increasing crime rates from the 1970s to the 1990s. However, a variety of obstacles to formal cooperation were also identified, including conflicting principles – e.g., impartial public service versus private profit – and the lower levels of training and regulation of private security staff (Kakalik & Wildhorn, 1971). At the same time, a degree of privatisation of policing occurred internationally by default through growth in demand for commercial providers, with private security outstripping public policing services in personnel numbers and in interactions with the public (UNODC, 2011). Security providers were increasingly seen supplying frontline crime prevention services, including being a visible presence in 'public-private' spaces such as shopping malls, transport hubs, residential complexes, sporting arenas, entertainment venues and festivals. During the recent COVID19 pandemic, private providers played crucial security roles at testing clinics and vaccination hubs, and in enforcing restrictions on entry to premises (ASIAL, 2021).

Two overlapping areas of potential co-operation have been intelligence-sharing and communications. A Spanish study by Gimenez-Salinas (2004) found that police and private security providers could work well together on a routine basis through a communications coordination room in areas such as licence checks on suspect vehicles, information about suspect persons, recovery of stolen vehicles, back-up assistance to security officers, and shared intelligence about organised crime. Another example is the 'Eyes on the Street' program in Perth, Australia (Crime Stoppers, 2022). The program involves a partnership between the Western Australia Police, local government, businesses, and the security industry, focusing on members reporting suspicious persons and events to police. Security personnel are considered key players and report to an Eyes on the Street Team or directly to police. An evaluation found strong support from participants, with over 100 agencies involved covering approximately 4000 employees (Crime Research Centre, 2008). More than 200 arrests were attributed to Eyes on the Street intelligence between 2004 and 2007.

The post 9/11 2001 counter-terrorism agenda added to the case for information-sharing. The 9/11 Commission noted that '85 percent of our nation's critical infrastructure is controlled not by government but by the private sector' and recommended much greater engagement of the sector in anti-terrorism planning (National Commission on Terrorist Attacks upon the United States, 2004: 317). In 2005, the U.S. Department of Justice issued a report, *Engaging the Private Sector to Promote Homeland Security: Law Enforcement-Private Security Relationships*. Among other things, the report recommended that police prioritise formal relationships with private security (National Institute of Justice, 2005: 6). The report included a case study of a communications system run by the Law Enforcement and Private Security Council of Northeast Florida, which managed radio frequencies for direct contact between private security and police. Another example was the Las Vegas Police Department's Tourist Safety Unit, targeting fraudsters and pickpockets through information sharing between police and hotel security.

Access to private surveillance data has been another mechanism of private-public cooperation, although the flow of data appears to largely favour police, and research on the field is highly limited (Ashby, 2017). One study in the United Kingdom found that British Transport Police claimed that footage – obtained from the transport companies via a central CCTV Hub – was useful in solving cases in 65 percent of the 45 percent of cases in which footage was available (Ashby, 2017). Also in the UK, in a major investigation, police considered CCTV a 'crucial weapon' in identifying and prosecuting upwards of 3000 individuals involved in the 2011 London Riots (Evison, 2015: 524).

The largest area of cooperation would appear to be in extending the deterrent and rapid intervention functions of police through links with private guarding services. In that regard, the main attraction of private security has been its lower costs compared to police – as much as half the cost of labour as reported in one study (Sarre & Prenzler, 2011). Venue security and mass-transit security are the most obvious personnel-based partnerships experienced by most people. Both formats now cover many decades of successful experience, with established contractual arrangements and protocols for collaboration. For example, Sarre and Prenzler (2011) analysed arrangements between police and private security at sports stadiums in Australia. Much of the violence of the past had been reduced through the deployment of security officers amongst the crowds, as well as at entry checkpoints and perimeter security, and in CCTV monitoring stations. A smaller police contingent served in a back-up role when arrests or higher levels of force were required (see also van Steden, 2021).

Another example of collaboration in this area is Project Griffin – now known as ACT (Action Counter Terrorism) Awareness – established by the London Metropolitan Police in 2004 and adopted in the UK and internationally, including Singapore, Australia, Canada and the United States (Project Griffin, 2018). The scheme involves specialist 'Griffin-trained' private security officers available to assist police with major incidents, such as a terrorist attack, in areas such as perimeter access control and crowd management (CoESS, 2011). Training modules include threat assessments, responding to suspicious conduct and dealing with bomb threats (Project Griffin, 2018).

Shopping centre security also provides examples of close cooperation between police, private security, and other parties. For example, Crawford et al. (2005) described innovations in the enormous retail and leisure complex MetroCentre in Northumbria in the United Kingdom. In 2002, centre management formed a partnership with the local police in which it funded the employment of eight police officers as 'community beat managers' to staff a small police station, provide patrols and work with centre management and retailers on crime prevention (p. 102). The partnership included employing a security firm, with 64 officers complementing the police. The security program also included a smaller in-house security team (See also van Steden, 2007, Chapter 10).

1.2 Crime Prevention Theory and the Security Industry

The limits on police capacity to prevent crime and the effectiveness of private security are consistent with opportunity theories of crime and prevention. Public spaces, such as town centres and entertainment hubs, attract people involved in shopping, working, relaxing, exercising and travelling. The combination of large numbers of diverse goods and services, and different types of distracted persons, creates numerous opportunities for predation, and typically generates concentrations or 'hot spots' of crime. The disinhibiting effects of alcohol often escalate these risks. The potential for crime in areas where people congregate is best understood within Routine Activity Theory, entailing 'the convergence in space and time of … 1. motivated offenders, 2. suitable targets, and 3. the absence of capable guardians' (Cohen & Felson, 1979: 589). The 'crime triangle' – Fig. 1 – is a model that usefully captures the core elements of victim-offender encounters, with countervailing elements to reduce opportunities. The inner triangle summarises the three primary ingredients for crime: an offender, a target, and a place. The outer triangle shows human agents who can facilitate or inhibit crime by their actions, with a potentially important role for private security personnel, especially as place managers and guardians.

Traditionally, police have tended to be seen as the primary guardians of society. However, the growth in crime from the 1970s to the 1990s and the spread of the security industry have challenged this position. Research has shown that a typical police force is entirely incapable of providing the type of on-site 24-7 guardianship necessary to effectively deter offenders or intervene to stop crimes in progress (Felson, 1998: p. 9). In contrast, the owners and managers of premises have a vested interest in self-protection and an area of manageable responsibility where they can match protections to threats. Furthermore, managers of premises have legal powers

Fig. 1 The Crime Prevention Triangle. (Source: Clarke & Eck, 2003: 9. Used with permission)

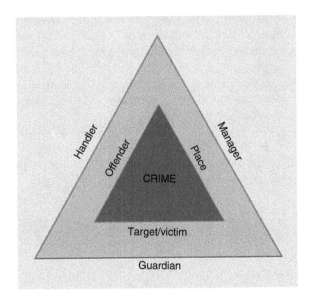

to control access, remove offenders, install security devices, and use reasonable force to protect people and property within their sphere of influence (Sarre, 2014).

The uptake of private security provided a major contribution to the international decline in crime from the 1990s through the adoption of policies of 'self-protection' and 'responsive securitization' (van Dijk, 2012: 10–11; Farrell, 2013). The security industry has been at the forefront of the application of the best attested means of reducing crime through situational prevention measures by making crime 'more difficult and riskier, or less rewarding and excusable' (Clarke, 1997: 4). This includes adopting many of the 25 techniques of situational prevention as a routine business tool, including 'target hardening' with security devices; 'assisting compliance' through communication, advice and directions; and 'extending guardianship' and 'strengthening formal surveillance' through audio-visual technologies and the deployment of security officers (Cornish & Clarke, 2003: 90).

Several additional theoretical frameworks support the idea of police capitalising on these techniques through partnership arrangements. The more significant models are as follows.

- Problem Oriented Policing emphasised the importance of police analysing crime problems to find effective preventive interventions (Goldstein, 1990). In many cases, this would involve projects that include the input of third parties.
- Community Policing put forward the idea that police are unable to reduce crime on their own. They need to work closely with their local communities, including commercial entities, in a genuine power-sharing arrangement (Trojanowicz & Bucqueroux, 1990).
- Reassurance Policing focused on the problem of public insecurity and argued that police should do more to make people feel safe. It proposed that police target 'signal crimes' which trigger anxiety, and operationalise 'control signals' which show that legitimate and capable guardians are present (Innes & Fielding, 2002).
- Quality-of-Life Policing, based on Broken Windows Theory, argued that signs of disorder signal the absence of guardians, deter law-abiding persons and attract offenders (Bratton, 2015). Authorities should work together to reduce signs of neglect and target what are often considered minor crimes, such as public nuisance offences. Preventing minor crimes should make people feel safer and go out more; and dealing effectively with minor crimes should help stop offenders escalating to major crimes.
- Crime Prevention Through Environmental Design (CPTED) is a form of situational prevention focused on designing open malls, parks, streets, buildings, and other locations in ways that facilitate 'defensible space' and 'territoriality' (Crowe, 1991).

2 Police and Security Foot Patrols

The deployment of security officers in stationary and mobile guarding roles has been a mainstay of the security industry. Applied to public places, the practice entails an application of the Reassurance Policing agenda, and the operationalisation of the situational prevention concepts of 'extend guardianship' and 'strengthen formal surveillance' – representing a type of democratic response to public expectations about visible authority and protection. Wakefield's (2006) review of 13 police foot patrol programs found they could positively influence citizens' feelings of safety. Their primary functions in deterring crime and providing assistance are preferred over aggressive 'stop and search' and arrest-focused strategies, and the absence of foot patrols appears as a source of public dissatisfaction with police (Metcalf & Pickett, 2018; Wakefield, 2006). In that regard, a recent report on policing in the United Kingdom by the Police Foundation (2020), emphasised a growing mismatch in crime policy between police priorities and public priorities, as evidenced in focus group studies. This was manifested most noticeably in the decline of a visible police presence, and a strong sense of disorder and danger in public spaces (p. 54):

> the desire for a greater police presence was expressed most often in the context of a general sense of 'deterioration' in the quality and atmosphere of familiar local public spaces (such as town centres, parks, and shopping precincts). In many locations respondents identified empty shops, civic disrepair, street homelessness and visible drug and alcohol misuse as signs of a local 'turn for the worse' and saw these changes as indicators of increased threat. The instinctive response to this increased sense of nearby malignancy was often to call for a greater deterrent police presence.

Responsibilities assigned to police for reducing fear of crime, and studies showing some successes by foot patrols in crime reduction, suggest that a problem-solving framework is the most likely way to achieve success. This can be done by matching the type of service to local conditions and involving local communities (Braga et al., 2019; Wakefield, 2006). In addition, foot patrols can be conducted by security officers or both security officers and police in partnership. The security officers can be government employees, commercial in-house staff, or the employees of contract security firms. Public opinion surveys suggest that most people find the presence of security officers to be reassuring (van Steden & Nalla, 2010). However, the nature of interactions mediates these views, leading to the conclusion that 'the industry needs to incorporate elements that heighten the security guards' image, as well as their utility to be an effective and trusted presence in quasi-public spaces where a large amount of public life takes part' (van Steden & Nalla, 2010: 219; also Nalla et al., 2017).

3   Business Improvement Districts

Business Improvement Districts (BIDs) seek to improve commerce and the enjoyment of public spaces by enhancing the amenity, civility and safety of a business precinct, utilising Community Policing and Reassurance Policing principles. Funds from government and/or business groups are used to upgrade open areas, remove graffiti, repair vandalised property, improve lighting, and expand police and security patrols with a view to attracting legitimate users and deterring offenders.

Evaluations of BIDs have shown variable results but several successes in reducing crime without displacement effects (Brooks, 2008; Clutter et al., 2019; Han et al., 2017; MacDonald et al., 2009, 2010). One review stated that, 'based on available statistics, most neighbourhoods with established BID security programs have experienced double-digit reductions in crime rates (sometimes up to 60 percent) in the years following their creation' (Vindevogel, 2005: 237). Police support is considered essential to the success of security operations in BIDs, along with the deployment of security guards. An economic assessment of the impact of BIDs found that they could provide significant public value, apart from reducing victimisation. For example, by reducing crime they also reduced the costs of criminal justice processing of arrested offenders (Cook & MacDonald, 2011; also Welsh et al., 2015).

BIDs also help to make police more accountable by focusing business owners' expectations of a police response, and by channelling calls for assistance through one phone link. At the same time, the evidence appears to support the idea that BIDs will ultimately reduce calls to police and demands on police time. The process, along with associated benefits, is described by Vindevogel (2005: 250):

> Even if police officers in the field do have to respond to the solicitations of the BIDs and react to such problems as disorderly youths or street peddling, there is no doubt that BID security officers take appropriate measures more often. They not only take on a whole array of responsibilities that police officers have to assume in the absence of other easily identifiable 'guardians' (they give directions, help find lost property, assist lost children, etc.) but they also take charge of all these quality-of-life violations that police officers traditionally dislike handling because, as they argue, it diverts them from 'real police work'. More importantly, thanks to their deterrent visibility and communication skills these security officers also anticipate problems and prevent tensions from escalating: they stop disputes before they degenerate into fights, create safety corridors between high schools and subway stations, etc. Finally, BIDs centralize requests: when local retailers or corporate security directors have safety-related concerns, they frequently solicit BID instead of calling 911 or their precinct.

Los Angeles has seen the creation of numerous BIDs. These are generally 'chartered and regulated' by local government, and 'managed and operated by private non-profit organisations' (Cook & MacDonald, 2011: 448). In the Los Angeles case, the city government provided financial assistance for planning BID programs. BIDs in the city tend to be focused on sanitation and crime: '"Clean" and "safe" are common terms used by BIDs in LA (p. 448). Cook and MacDonald reported that, 'eleven of the 30 BIDs operating in LA in 2005 spent more than $200,000 a year on private security operations, with nearly equal amounts being spent on sanitation services' (2011: 448). The researchers also provided some detail on the Figueroa Corridor BID in downtown Los Angeles (p. 499):

> The Figueroa Corridor BID was formed in 1998 by business property owners in direct response to economic decline and a concern with area crime. From the outset its efforts were focused on improving community safety by employing uniformed private security workers (Safety Ambassadors) who patrol the district on foot, bike and evening vehicle patrols and assist in keeping order. It spends close to $500,000 a year, or almost half of its operational budget, on these officers.

BIDs can include a variety of other features. The BID-Malmö program in Sweden incorporates community gardens, while security assessments and upgrades of premises result in reduced insurance premiums (Kronkvist & Ivert, 2020). A BID in Newark, New Jersey, included a police 'substation', which served as a base for intensified foot and vehicle patrols (Piza et al., 2020).

4 Evaluated Intervention Case Studies

This section provides accounts of six successful crime prevention partnerships involving police and in-house and contract security providers in diverse settings. Where possible, information is provided about the nature of the relationships between parties, the mechanisms of success and measures of impacts. However, some reports simply describe the tandem deployment of police and security officers and lack detail about the nature of the relationship. The studies are mostly 'within group' – that is, lacking matched control groups – although the context of the interventions suggest that it is reasonable to infer a crime reduction effect from the interventions (cf., Pawson & Tilley, 2004).

1. *Upgraded security in the Mitchellhill public housing estate*

This was a place-based program designed to address high crime rates and resident alienation in the large Glasgow City Council Mitchellhill housing estate – consisting of five 19-story tower blocks (Davidson & Farr, 1994). Police had reportedly been reluctant to attend calls and often refused to leave their vehicles unattended. The program, introduced in 1989, involved the following measures (based on consultation with, and a commitment from, police):

1. an on-site manager and assistant,
2. 12 building concierges who provided 24-hour security-oriented services to residents,
3. security hardware such as solid doors with barrel locks rekeyed for new tenants,
4. improved lighting,
5. CCTV,
6. controlled entry to foyers,
7. removal of internal landing doors that provided hiding places,

8. increased police patrols,
9. a 'multi-watch' system for residents to report issues to the concierges or police,
10. improvements to the attractiveness of the estate with renovations and provision of furnished flats, and
11. tenant representation on the tenant selection committee.

An initial evaluation of the program found that the total number of police-recorded crimes fell by 62 percent from 141 to 53 in 15 months following the introduction of the concierge scheme (Davidson & Farr, 1994: 26). In the same time periods, burglaries were reduced by 71 percent, and theft of vehicles and theft from vehicles reduced by 72 percent. Large reductions in maintenance costs, mainly associated with vandalism, were also recorded, along with increased demand for flats, increased occupancy, and increased rental income. Demands on police time were reduced. Crime rates remained stable over the same period in a nearby comparable area. A brief follow-up evaluation, using 1991 and 1992 data, showed a partial regression, with the overall crime rate back up to approximately 50 percent of the pre-intervention rate. However, the large reductions for burglary and vehicle-related crime held firm (p. 33).

2. Shared security at the Enschede-Haven industrial estate

In the late-1980s, the Area Entrepreneur Association of the Dutch Enschede-Haven industrial site requested police provide increased patrols to counter criminal activity (van den Berg, 1995). The police produced a crime profile for the area and suggested a partnership arrangement in which they supported private security patrols. The Association established a cooperative; with membership from the majority of the 410 companies on the site; and police set up a Project Agency to coordinate the work of the cooperative, the police and the local government. Start-up funds were obtained from the national government. Further assistance was provided by a government employment agency which subsidised the appointment of unemployed people as security guards, with training provided by police. The key element of the project was the stationing of a security guard on the estate outside business hours, who checked alarm activations before contacting police. The local council also improved lighting and the amenity of the area, while signage about the project was designed to deter offenders. An evaluation of the project found that security incidents were reduced by 72 per cent, from 90 per month in the 18 months before the project to 25 per month in the 18 months after it was established. The partnership continued as a self-funded project once the initial subsidy expired. A similar project on the Vianen industrial site generated similar results.

3. CCTV in King's Lynne

CCTV cameras were introduced into different parts of the town centre of King's Lynn (UK) in 1992 (Brown, 1995). The monitoring station, located in council premises, was operated 24 hours a day by private security staff who relayed observations to a police communications centre. Images could also be transferred to a monitor at the police centre. The centre staff assessed the calls and made decisions on police dispatches to incidents or to arrest wanted persons. The system also operated on a two-way basis in that police would send requests for information to the monitoring centre. Recordings could also be checked for evidence in investigations. The main concentration of 19 cameras was around ground-level carparks, with a focus on reducing theft of and from motor vehicles and damage to vehicles. These cameras also captured adjacent venues and thoroughfares. The cameras were also used to monitor litter and parking, and flooding of the local river. The system was funded by a small surcharge on parking tickets and funds from local businesses.

The evaluation by Brown (1995) examined rolling averages per quarter for five crime categories across four quarters before the introduction of the carpark area cameras and seven quarters following, comparing these data to those for the remainder of the Police Division and the remainder of the Police Force area. Overall, the evaluation identified large reductions in crime post-intervention. Although theft from vehicles was declining pre-intervention, reaching an average of 13 cases per quarter, the number declined to approximately five at the end of the final quarter (−62 percent). Similarly, theft of vehicles had been in decline pre-intervention, but the camera system most likely contributed to further reductions, almost eliminating the problem. In the final quarter pre-intervention, the quarterly average was seven thefts of vehicles, with a figure of one at the end the evaluation period (−86 percent). Large reductions post-intervention were also identified in burglary, and wounding and assault, with a moderate fall in criminal damage. The trends for the comparative areas involved moderate increases and moderate falls. The evaluation also found that the cameras were associated with 80 arrests for property offences and just under 100 arrests for public order crimes. In addition, the screening system greatly reduced the number of unnecessary urgent responses by police.

4. *The Surfers Paradise Safety Action Project*

The Surfers Paradise Safety Action Project was established in 1993 as a multi-partner initiative designed to reduce violence within and around licensed venues in the major tourist area of Surfers Paradise, Australia. Periodic police crackdowns had proven unsuccessful, with mounting community and business concerns. The initiative for the project came from a criminologist who obtained cooperation from key stakeholders and a federal grant to support the work as a demonstration project (Homel et al., 1997). The project was managed through a steering committee involving the Gold Coast City Council, state health department, state liquor regulator, police, the local chamber of commerce, a tourism promotion body, and a university research team. A project officer coordinated the day-to-day operations and stakeholder liaison. An initial assessment of the nature and causes of the problem led to the introduction of interventions focused on reducing intoxication and improving guardianship, including responsible service of alcohol; improved venue amenity, food and entertainment; and greater responsibility taken by venue security.

The project included a Security and Policing Task Group that brought together a range of security-oriented stakeholders including police and venue security providers, with a focus on the areas outside licensed venues. Better training of security staff in de-escalation was a major outcome of the Group's work, along with joint street patrols and the introduction of a shuttle bus to assist with transport out of the entertainment area – reducing frustration, violence and drink driving. Security officers were also deployed at taxi ranks, and venue managers employed more security officers, taking pressure off police.

The evaluation involved multiple sources including field observations of 18 nightclubs over two summers in 1993 and 1994 (pre- and post-intervention). The observation data revealed significant reductions in incidents of verbal abuse (−82 percent) and arguments (−68 percent) (Homel et al., 1997: 70). Observations also found security officers to be more engaging and more effective in enforcing age requirements for entry. Police records showed reductions in incidents of 'drunk and disorderly' conduct across comparable five-month periods pre- and post-implementation – from 258 to 146 (−43 percent) – and assaults – from 50 to 33 (−34 percent).

5. *Strike Force Piccadilly in Sydney*

Strike Force Piccadilly was set up in 2005 by the New South Wales (Australia) Police Property Crime Squad to counter a dramatic upsurge in Automatic Teller Machine (ATM) ram raids in the greater Sydney area – most occurring in public spaces. In mid-2006, the Piccadilly team convened a stakeholder forum, which led to the establishment of an ongoing partnership between police and security managers from the ATM Industry Association, the Australian Bankers' Association, cash-in-transit firms, and the Shopping Centre Council of Australia (Prenzler, 2017). Research and information sharing identified key situational vulnerabilities around machines, including easy vehicle access and frequent false alarm activations that delayed police responses. The analysis led to a commitment to implement the following primary opportunity reduction measures: (1) a police priority response number (based on multiple alarm activations vetted by a private sector monitoring company), and (2) the installation of situational prevention measures, including ATM relocations, specialist bollards and anti-ramming devices,

These changes were effective in producing large reductions in 'successful' raids (where cash was obtained) and 'unsuccessful' raids (involving considerable property damage). The rapid response system closed the raiders' timeframe, the relocations and bollards reduced access, and the anti-ramming devices made removal of ATMs more difficult. The reduced time frames assisted investigations, which led to the arrest and incapacitation of 97 persons between August 2005 and June 2007. Over the longer-term, there was a 100% reduction in successful raids, with no cases after August 2009. Unsuccessful raids declined by 84% from the initial peak period. In 2008, a shift in offender tacts to explosive gas attacks – or 'bam raids' – was successfully countered by adjustments to the priority alarm system, introduction of gas disabling equipment, and arrests of offenders with assistance from the commercial partners with CCTV footage and crime scene preservation (Prenzler, 2017).

6. *The Adachi Ward Partnership*

Hino and Chronopoulos (2021) evaluated a crime prevention partnership involving the Adachi Ward government and the Tokyo Metropolitan Police, introduced in

2008. In the early-2000s, the ward 'experienced the highest crime rates in central Tokyo and was perceived as a crime-ridden area' (p. 342). The program includes a policing focus on minor crimes, beautification and improvement of public spaces, a bicycle security program, citizen patrols, private security patrols, resident access to a crime map, and security cameras. The security contract is awarded on a competitive basis, involving 24-7 patrols in 3–4 marked vehicles. Patrol routes are determined between the security company, ward office and police, with police briefings to patrol officers. Private security officers report incidents to police, they do not engage in arrests. (Information supplied by Kimihiro Hino 7 March 2022). According to Hino and Chronopoulos (2021), Adachi Ward experienced a 62.6% decline in crime from 2007 to 2019, the largest reduction amongst 23 wards in Tokyo. By 2013, a majority of residents surveyed described security as 'good'.

5 Best Practice Principles

The analysis above suggests an optimistic scenario for reducing crime in common and open spaces through partnerships between public police, private security, and other government and non-government entities. Formal public-private partnerships meet many of the criteria for best practice approaches to crime prevention, including Situational Prevention, Problem-Oriented Policing, Community Policing, Reassurance Policing, Quality-of-Life Policing and CPTED. Key areas with significant potential include lower cost private security officers engaged in frontline foot and vehicle patrols, working in a coordinated fashion with police to deter crime and provide a rapid response to incidents. The installation and monitoring of CCTV in public places also allows police to harness cutting edge technology developed in the commercial sector to extend formal surveillance, deterrence and response capabilities. Additionally, private security assessments of alarm activations have shown potential to focus police responses and reduce the wastage of police time responding to false alarms. Formal agreements – such as accords or memoranda-of-understanding – also provide assurance to commercial security that police will provide the responses and back up they need to optimise their site-specific deterrence, de-escalation and target-hardening functions. A commitment by private providers to improve security officer training and professionalism is another potentially highly productive outcome. Intelligence sharing by both sides, based on mutual respect and trust, means that strategic decisions are made on the best possible data. Police partnerships adds legitimacy to private sector security services which have a specific public interest dimension.

On the basis of these arguments and experiences, the idea that police and private security should work together has become a commonplace policy position adopted by many police and other government departments worldwide (UNODC, 2011). However, examples in practice are not well documented – especially in relation to public space projects – as this chapter has shown. In some cases, partnerships have been initiated by police, but police leaders are often reluctant to take the first step.

In that regard, there are numerous opportunities for third parties to take the initiative, including in the key task of brokering funds. Local governments are particularly well placed to take the lead, given their close proximity to their constituents and concern for public order and safety in town centres and at local events. Transport departments can also initiate partnerships, as can other government departments with specific portfolios, such as counter-terrorism or sports. One specific means is by councils and government departments appointing crime prevention officers with a brief that includes fostering partnerships (Crawford et al., 2005).

In terms of policies and actions that facilitate partnerships, the United Nations has published several useful guides (e.g., United Nations, 2010). UN support is based in part on the idea of increasing equality in security. The report *Civilian Private Security Services: Their Role, Oversight and Contribution to Crime Prevention and Community Safety* (UNODC, 2011) recommends creating specialist bodies to implement programs along with investments in research and training. The UN guidelines also emphasise the importance of effective licensing systems to ensure adequate competency and integrity in the security industry. Government facilitated demonstration projects can be an important way of showcasing success and encouraging similar projects. One previous review of factors involved in a wider set of crime prevention partnerships identified the following ingredients likely to lead to successful outcomes (Prenzler & Sarre, 2016: 163):

- a common interest in reducing a specific crime or crime set,
- effective leadership, with personnel with authority from each partner organisation driving participation,
- mutual respect,
- information sharing based on high levels of trust in confidentiality,
- formal means of consultation and communication; such as committees, forums and e-mail networks,
- willingness to experiment and consider all ideas,
- formal contractual relationships are not always essential,
- additional legal powers are not always necessary on the security side,
- data-rich projects appear more likely to generate effective interventions and demonstrate success.

Maintenance of partnerships involves a major challenge, as does ongoing accountability through reporting on performance. Only one of the case studies included here – Strike Force Piccadilly – involved long-term evaluation and public reporting (Prenzler, 2017). One of the partnerships covered in some depth – the Surfers Paradise Safety Action Project – fell apart when the project coordinator position ended. Venue management put profits over safety in promoting liquor consumption and the government regulator failed to enforce standards (Homel et al., 1997). A permanent project manager position, with a liaison role between all parties, might therefore also be a key ingredient for success.

Security industry regulators and government departments also need to manage ethical risks associated with partnerships. Conflicts of interest need to be avoided altogether or carefully managed if this is not possible. As one example, police departments can ban officers from working in the security industry or holding a financial interest in the sector or they can require specific approval and monitoring for working in the industry outside rostered hours. A specialist government unit that facilitates partnerships can also have a role in guarding against conflicts of interest, vetting parties and ensuring there is no bias or special interest benefits in contracts and agreements. A robust anti-corruption agency should ideally have responsibility for oversighting all partnerships.

Partnerships can also involve strategies that lead to oppressive actions against disadvantaged groups, including excluding them from public spaces. Wherever possible, these groups, or their representatives, should be involved in the development and management phases of a security partnership. Arrests and banning orders should be considered as last resort strategies, with crime reduction methods focused as much as possible on facilitating compliance and providing support. A public interest test needs to be part of the development and monitoring processes. Several crime prevention guides include standards around community consultation, social inclusiveness, observance of human rights, and democratic accountability (see Mazerolle & Prenzler, 2004).

6   Conclusion

The private sector is a key player in the fight against crime, including at critical infrastructure sites and through the reach of the private security industry into almost every aspect of people's lives. Despite different operating principles, it is possible to develop public-private partnerships that address crime problems in ways that benefit a variety of stakeholders, including the public and taxpayers. Considerable caution, however, should be exercised in moving to private involvement in policing, especially in protecting the universal mission of the police. Nonetheless, available evidence indicates that a variety of productive public-private relationships can operate effectively in safeguarding public spaces.

References

Ashby, M. (2017). The value of CCTV surveillance cameras as an investigative tool: An empirical analysis. *European Journal on Criminal Policy and Research, 23*(3), 441–459.

ASIAL. (2021). *Security 2025: A roadmap for the future.* Australian Security Industry Association Limited.

Boyd, D. (2013). *Developing public private partnerships that work.* ASIAL Security Conference, Sydney, June 24.

Braga, A., Welsh, B., & Schnell, C. (2019). *Disorder policing to reduce crime: A systematic review.* Campbell Collaboration.

Bratton, W. (2015). *Broken windows and quality-of-life policing in New York City.* http://www.nyc.gov/html/nypd/downloads/pdf/analysis_and_planning/qol.pdf

Brooks, L. (2008). Volunteering to be taxed: Business improvement districts and the extra-governmental provision of public safety. *Journal of Public Economics, 92*(1–2), 388–406.

Brown, B. (1995). *CCTV in town centres: Three case studies.* Home Office.

Clarke, R. (Ed.). (1997). *Situational crime prevention: Successful case studies.* Harrow and Heston.

Clarke, R., & Eck, J. (2003). *Become a problem-solving crime analyst in 55 small steps.* Jill Dando Institute of Crime Science, University College London.

Clutter, J., Henderson, S., & Haberman, C. (2019). The impact of business improvement district proximity on street block robbery counts. *Crime and Delinquency, 65*(8), 1050–1075.

CoEss. (2011). *Private security services in Europe, Coess facts and figures 2011.* Confederation of European Security Services.

Cohen, L., & Felson, M. (1979). Social change and crime rate trends: A routine activities approach. *American Sociological Review, 44*, 588–608.

Connors, E., Cunningham, W., & Ohlhausen, P. (1999). *Operation cooperation: A literature review of cooperation and partnerships between law enforcement and private security organizations.* US Bureau of Justice Assistance.

Cook, P., & MacDonald, J. (2011). Public safety through private action: An economic assessment of BIDS. *The Economic Journal, 121*, 445–462.

Cornish, D., & Clarke, R. (2003). Opportunities, precipitators and criminal decisions. *Crime Prevention Studies, 16*, 41–96.

Crawford, A., Lister, S., Blackburn, S., & Burnett, J. (2005). *Plural policing: The mixed economy of visible patrols in England and Wales.* Policy Press.

Crime Research Centre. (2008). *Evaluation of the eyes on the street program.* University of Western Australia.

Crime Stoppers. (2022). *Supporting eyes on the street.* https://www.crimestopperswa.com.au/supporting-eyes-on-the-street/

Crowe, T. (1991). *Crime prevention through environmental design.* Butterworth-Heinemann.

Davidson, J., & Farr, J. (1994). Mitchellhill estate: Estate-based management (concierge) initiative. In S. Osborn (Ed.), *Housing safe communities: An evaluation of recent initiatives* (pp. 22–33). Safe Neighbourhoods Unit, Greater London Council.

Evison, M. P. (2015). The third forensics—Images and allusions. *Policing and Society, 25*(5), 521–539.

Farrell, G. (2013). Five tests for a theory of the crime drop. *Crime Science, 2*(5), 1–8.

Felson, M. (1998). *Crime and everyday life.* Pine Forge Press.

Gimenez-Salinas, A. (2004). New approaches regarding private/public security. *Policing and Society, 14*(2), 158–174.

Goldstein, H. (1990). *Problem-oriented policing.* McGraw-Hill.

Han, S., Morçöl, G., Hummer, D., & Peterson, S. (2017). The effects of business improvement districts in reducing nuisance crimes: Evidence from Philadelphia. *Journal of Urban Affairs, 39*(5), 658–674.

Hino, K., & Chronopoulos, T. (2021). A review of crime prevention activities in a Japanese local government area since 2008: Beautiful windows movement in Adachi Ward. *Crime Prevention and Community Safety, 23*(1), 341–357.

HMIC. (2012). *Increasing efficiency in the police service.* Her Majesty's Inspectorate of Policing.

Home Office. (2011). *Annual report and accounts 2010–11.* Home Office.

Homel, R., Hauritz, M., Wortley, R., McIlwain, G., & Carvolth, R. (1997). Preventing alcohol-related crime through community action: The surfers paradise safety action project. *Crime Prevention Studies, 17*, 35–90.

Innes, M., & Fielding, N. (2002). From community to communicative policing: 'Signal crimes' and the problem of public reassurance. *Sociological Research Online, 7*(2), 1–22.

Kakalik, S. J., & Wildhorn, S. (1971). *The private police industry: Its nature and extent.* RAND.

Kronkvist, K., & Ivert, A. (2020). A winning BID? The effects of a BID-inspired property owner collaboration on neighbourhood crime rates in Malmö, Sweden. *Crime Prevention and Community Safety, 22*, 134–152.

Lincolnshire Police/G4S. (2013). *The G4S Lincolnshire Police strategic partnership – One year on*. The Police and Crime Commissioner for Lincolnshire.

MacDonald, J., Bluthenthal, R., Golinelli, D., Kofner, A., Stokes, R., Sehgal, A., Fain, T., & Beletsky, L. (2009). *Neighborhood effects on crime and youth violence: The role of business improvement districts in Los Angeles*. RAND.

MacDonald, J., Golinelli, D., Stokes, R., & Bluthenthal, R. (2010). The effect of business improvement districts on the incidence of violent crimes. *Injury Prevention, 16*(5), 327–332.

Mazerolle, L., & Prenzler, T. (2004). Third party policing: Considering the ethical challenges. In M. Hickman, A. Piquero, & J. Greene (Eds.), *Police integrity and ethics* (pp. 163–187). Wadsworth.

Metcalf, C., & Pickett, J. (2018). The extent and correlates of public support for deterrence reforms and hot spots policing. *Law and Society Review, 52*(2), 471–502.

Nalla, M., Maxwell, S., & Mamayek, C. (2017). Legitimacy of private police in developed, emerging, and transitional economies. *Journal of Crime, Criminal Law and Criminal Justice, 25*(1), 76–100.

National Commission on Terrorist Attacks upon the United States. (2004). *The 9/11 Commission Report including executive summary: Final report of the National Commission on terrorist attacks upon the United States*. National Commission on Terrorist Attacks upon the United States.

National Institute of Justice. (2005). *Engaging the private sector to promote homeland security: Law enforcement-private security partnership*. US Department of Justice.

Pawson, R., & Tilley, N. (2004). Realistic evaluation. In S. Matthieson (Ed.), *Encyclopaedia of evaluation* (pp. 362–367). SAGE.

Piza, E., Wheeler, A., Connealy, N., & Feng, S. (2020). Crime control effects of a police substation within a business improvement district: A quasi-experimental synthetic control evaluation. *Criminology and Public Policy, 19*(2), 653–684.

Prenzler, T. (2017). Reducing property crime and fraud: Twelve case studies. In T. Prenzler (Ed.), *Understanding crime prevention: The case study approach* (pp. 107–120). Australian Academic Press.

Prenzler, T., & Sarre, R. (2016). Public-private crime prevention partnerships. In T. Prenzler (Ed.), *Policing and security in practice: Challenges and achievements* (pp. 149–167). Palgrave Macmillan.

Project Griffin. (2018). *Project Griffin*. https://www.gov.uk/government/publications/project-griffin/project-griffin

Sarre, R. (2014). Legal powers, obligations and immunities. In T. Prenzler (Ed.), *Professional practice in crime prevention and security management* (pp. 149–162). Australian Academic Press.

Sarre, R., & Prenzler, T. (2011). *Private security and public interest: Exploring private security trends and directions for reform in the new era of plural policing*. University of South Australia, Australian Research Council Linkage Report.

The Police Foundation. (2020). *Public safety and security in the 21st century*. https://www.policingreview.org.uk/wp-content/uploads/phase_1_report_final-1.pdf?mc_cid=d7d15e595c&mc_eid=5a36b24a10

Trojanowicz, R., & Bucqueroux, B. (1990). *Community policing: A contemporary perspective*. Anderson.

United Nations. (2010). *Handbook on the United Nations crime prevention guidelines*. United Nations Office on Drugs and Crime.

UNODC. (2011). *Civilian private security services: Their role, oversight and contribution to crime prevention and community safety*. United Nations Office on Drugs and Crime.

van Buuren, J., & den Boer, M. (2009). *A report on the ethical issues raised by the increasing role of private security professionals in security analysis and provision*. International Peace Research Institute and European Commission.

van den Berg, E. (1995). Crime prevention on industrial sites: Security through public-private partnerships. *Security Journal, 6*(1), 27–35.

van Dijk, J. (2012, June). *Closing the doors: Stockholm Prizewinners lecture 2012.* Paper presented at the Stockholm Criminology Symposium, Stockholm.

van Steden, R. (2007). *Privatizing policing: Describing and explaining the growth of private security.* BJU Legal Publishers.

van Steden, R. (2021). Theorising and illustrating the collaborative practices of plural policing: An analysis of three cases in The Netherlands and Belgium. *International Journal of Comparative and Applied Criminal Justice.* published online, *47,* 1–17.

van Steden, R., & Nalla, M. (2010). Citizen satisfaction with private security guards in The Netherlands. *European Journal of Criminology, 7*(3), 214–234.

Vindevogel, F. (2005). Private security and urban crime migration: A Bid for BIDs. *Criminal Justice, 5*(3), 233–255.

Wakefield, A. (2006). *The value of foot patrol: A review of research.* The Police Foundation.

Welsh, B., Farrington, D., & Gowar, B. (2015). Benefit-cost analysis of crime prevention programs. *Crime and Justice, 44*(1), 447–516.

Australian Public and Private Crime Prevention Partnerships in Cyberspace

Rick Sarre and Tim Prenzler

Abstract This chapter explores the growing trends in cybercrime and the role that public and private partnerships can and do play in addressing the scourge of criminal activity in cyberspace. The amount of digital information stored and available to the world expands exponentially. Global technological innovations are ubiquitous and growing. The nature and quality of data are changing. Each of these trends, however, threatens to leave policing in its wake as digital information becomes vulnerable to improper usage and theft. That being the case, the private sector has been and will continue to be co-opted in the public policing spheres. In significant ways its assistance has been desirable and useful. There is a developing trust between public and private agencies, for example, in relation to the collection, use and storage of metadata and the monitoring of visual digital data. However, given the potential of some corporate entities, particularly in the processing, use and storage of private digital data records, to push legal and ethical boundaries, governments cannot adopt a 'hands-off' approach. In the quest to defeat cybercrime, governments must continue to develop partnerships with a clear over-arching framework to require the compliance of private owners of surveillance tools and data managers in the same way as controls are in place to protect the private nature of government-collected data. These partnerships are not just with private entities committed to the business of policing. Partnerships must be developed with those who are vulnerable to cybercrime, and that is everyone's business. In this way, governments must enhance the capacity of potential victims to be self-policing. This chapter explores these relationships, the legislative initiatives that are now in place in Australia, and the imperatives that flow therefrom.

R. Sarre (✉)
University of South Australia, Adelaide, SA, Australia
e-mail: Rick.Sarre@unisa.edu.au

T. Prenzler
University of the Sunshine Coast, Sippy Downs, QLD, Australia
e-mail: tprenzler@usc.edu.au

E. A. Blackstone et al. (eds.), *Handbook on Public and Private Security*,
Competitive Government: Public Private Partnerships,
https://doi.org/10.1007/978-3-031-42406-9_4

1 Introduction

Global technological innovations are ubiquitous and growing. The nature and quality of data are changing too. The amount of digital information stored and available to us expands exponentially, and the consequences for each one of us are significant. Societies today are completely dependent upon the developments of the digital age. The massive changes in societal expectations of connectivity and the shifts in technology that have accommodated that demand, are mind-boggling. For example, The Economist reported that

> [collections of data are] no longer mainly stocks of digital information – databases of names and other well-defined personal data, such as age, sex and income. The new economy is more about analysing rapid real-time flows of unstructured data: the streams of photos and videos generated by users of social networks, the reams of information produced by commuters on their way to work, the flood of data from hundreds of sensors in a jet engine. ... The world will bristle with connected sensors so that people will leave a digital trail wherever they go ... (Economist, 2017, p. 24)

So it is that the digital world, and the data it produces, expands exponentially year by year (Kirkpatrick, 2018). In 2016, Amazon, Alphabet (Google) and Microsoft together spent nearly US $32 billion in capital expenditure and capital leases, up 22 percent over the previous year. According to market research firm IDC, the digital universe (the total of the bits of data created and copied each year) will reach 180 zettabytes (180 followed by 21 zeros) in 2025 (Economist, 2017). This estimate appears to be on track. According to Australian government sources, the global 'data sphere' will, in the 5 years from 2019 to 2024, increase from 45 zettabytes to 143 zettabytes (Australian Government, 2021a, p 11).

However, there is a significant downside of this data-driven, digital revolution: the willingness and aptitude of those who share our cyberspace to engage in criminality (Sarre et al., 2014; Australian Crime Commission, 2015). The expansion of cyberspace threatens to leave us vulnerable to the serious worldwide problem of cybercrime (Broadhurst, 2017; Broadhurst & Chang, 2013) and cyberterrorism (Australian Government, 2021a). Cybercrime costs the global economy countless billions of dollars annually. Actual estimates are impossible, as the field changes so rapidly, but hints at the speed and spread of losses can be gleaned from a recent report from the Australian Cyber Security Centre (2022). The Centre reports that in the financial year 2020–2021 in Australia, a cybercrime was reported every 8 min, an increase of 13 percent on the previous year. Economic losses in the year were reported as amounting to AU$33 billion (Toh et al., 2022). Globally, 623 million ransomware attacks were recorded in 2021, that is, 20 attacks every second, and more than triple the number recorded in 2019 (SonicWall, 2022).

The pain of cybercrime continues unabated. In October 2022 Medibank Private, a company that covers one-sixth of Australians with health insurance, admitted that an unidentified person had stolen personal information of customer as part of a theft of 200 gigabytes of data (Reuters, 2022). The Data Breaches Report from the Australian Government (2021b) shows the Office of the Australian Information

Commissioner (OAIC) received 464 data breach notifications from July to December 2021, an increase of 6% compared with the previous period. Malicious or criminal attacks remain the leading source of breaches, accounting for 256 notifications (55% of the total). The health sector remains the highest reporting industry sector notifying 18% of all breaches, followed by finance (12%).

Cyberterrorism, either state-sanctioned or prompted by international blackmailers, presents a future scenario that is appalling to contemplate.

> Open-source reporting has observed foreign powers actively seeking to gain access to data that is valuable, such as intellectual property, to gain strategic and commercial advantages .... Data is also a key vehicle to enable countries to progress geo-political agendas. This includes non-likeminded countries who wish to do us harm or access Australian data as a means to conduct espionage or foreign interference. Prioritising security in the application and use of data is vital to ensure the protection of our most valuable data from foreign adversaries. (Australian Government, 2021a, p. 7)

The significant consequences for policing give rise to several questions. How best can this new crime landscape be monitored and policed? How can we protect private businesses from falling victim to cybercrime through their own foolishness? Do public and private policing partnerships work? Before we deal with these questions, it is important to examine more closely the nature of the phenomenon itself.

2 The Modern Phenomenon of Cybercrime

Cybercrime has been variously referred to as 'computer crime', 'computer-related crime', 'hi-tech crime', 'technology-enabled crime', 'e-crime', or 'cyberspace crime' (Chang, 2012). Grabosky (2007, Chapter 3) helpfully classified three general forms, including crimes where the computer is used as the 'instrument' of crime, crimes where the computer is 'incidental' to the offence, and crimes where the computer is the 'target' of crime. McGuire and Dowling (2013) developed a similar idea, classifying cybercrime into 'cyber-enabled' crime and 'cyber-dependent' crime. Cyber-enabled crimes are traditional crimes facilitated using computers, for example, extortion, stalking and the dissemination of child exploitation materials. Cyber-dependent crimes are those crimes that would not exist without the technology, such as website defacement, denial of service attacks, ATM fraud and dissemination of malicious codes. Another useful classification is the one devised by Gordon and Ford (2006) who divided activities into Type I and Type II offences (Sarre, 2022). Type I cybercrimes are crimes which are more technical in nature (for example, hacking). Type II cybercrime is crime that relies on human contact rather than technology (for example, illegal online gambling).

Regardless of how cybercrime is classified, there is little doubt that its range is broad—it includes fraudulent financial transactions, identity theft, romance scams, theft of electronic information for commercial gain, drug-trafficking, money-laundering, aberrant voyeuristic activities, image-based sexual abuse, harassment, stalking and other threatening behaviours (Sarre et al., 2018). While these activities have always been classified as criminal, they are now so much easier to pursue with a computer and a modem, and they can be conducted from anywhere in the world, targeting victims in another corner of the globe. In large part, the increasing number of data breaches is being driven by the growth of a global illicit industry that trades in online data. Hackers known as "initial access brokers" specialize in illegally gaining access to victim networks and then selling this access to other cyber criminals (Martin & Whelan, 2022). These activities make personal fraud a daily occurrence. The Australian Bureau of Statistics (ABS) reveals 11% of Australians experienced personal fraud in 2020–21, up from 8.5% in 2014–15. The increase was driven by a rise in credit card fraud (from 5.9% to 6.9%) and scams (from 2.4% to 3.6%). Credit card fraud was the most common fraud type experienced in 2020–21 (6.9%). In the 5 years prior to the 2021 survey, an estimated 2.8% of Australians aged 15 and above (570,900) experienced identity theft. The majority (93% or 529,600) reported their most recent incident to an authority, most commonly a bank or financial institution (71%) (ABS, 2021).

In 2018–19, the estimated direct and indirect cost of identity crime in Australia was $3.1b. In 2019 the total losses reported by Australian Institute of Criminology (AIC) online survey respondents alone was $3.6 m, an increase of 80% over the previous year (Franks & Smith, 2020).

Cybercrime includes terrorist recruitment, terrorist communications, and terrorist financing. It includes implementing malware attacks designed to disrupt a business by destroying its database. It includes the activities of the 'hacktivist,' someone who protests an organization's actions or policies by orchestrating a denial of service (Sarre et al., 2018). The cybercriminals of today can carry out their criminal activity without the need for high-level technical skills. In fact, the internet will sometimes assist the perpetration of these crimes, for example, by providing hands-on 'do-it-yourself' malware kits that are available in online forums. The borderless nature of the internet makes law enforcement not only challenging, but, in some instances, almost impossible (Sarre, 2008).

A threat report in 2017 by the Australian Cyber Security Centre (ACSC), for example, noted that 'malicious cyber activity against Australia's national and economic interests is increasing in frequency, scale, sophistication and severity' (Australian Cyber Security Centre, 2017, p. 16). The ACSC 2020–21 Annual Cyber Threat Report noted a 15 per cent increase in ransomware-related cybercrime compared to the previous financial year. Indeed in 2020–21, the ACSC responded to nearly 160 cyber security incidents related to ransomware (Australian Cyber Security Centre, 2022). The MinterEllison summary of the Annual Cyber Threat Report 2020–21 identified several trends in the threat environment. It repeated the information that:

> one-quarter of ACSC recorded cyber incidents in 2020–21 affected Australia's critical infrastructure, including essential services such as education, health, communications, electricity, water, and transport. In 2021, a ransomware attack affected one of Melbourne's larger metropolitan public health services. An effective and coordinated incident response

minimized disruption. In December 2021, the ACSC alerted Australians to the significant Apache Log4j vulnerability… If unaddressed, the vulnerability could allow cybercriminals to break into an organization's systems, steal login credentials, extract sensitive data and infect networks with malicious software. (MinterEllison, 2022, p. 11)

There is no doubt that cybercrime remains an escalating problem for national and international police and security agencies.

3   Policing Cybercrime

The police role in tackling cybercrime is an important yet difficult one. There are several factors that militate against effective prevention in this domain. The first is the difficulty associated with jurisdictional boundaries. It is exceedingly problematic for police in one nation to assume control over an investigation in another nation, especially if the other nation denies that the crime emanated from within their country. No other field of criminality finds international borders more permeable than they are in cyber criminality (Holt, 2018, p. 141).

The second is the lack of expertise of law enforcement when pitted against some of the best information-technology minds in the (ill-gotten gains) business (Holt, 2018, p. 144). Moreover, just when the police-resourced teams catch up, capacity-wise, the cybercrime operatives shift into opaque and lawless territory again.

The third factor is the rising cost, in dollar terms, of enforcement. Resourcing high-tech crime abatement (particularly where there may be only one or two – albeit badly financially bruised – victims) is an expensive task, especially when there are other more highly visible calls upon the law enforcement budget (Holt, 2018). Indeed, there is no guarantee that the funding will ever be adequate to meet the growing demand for prophylactic measures, especially given the highly versatile and transitory nature of cyber criminality. Consider also that local police lack incentives to act on behalf of potential victims elsewhere where the likelihood of achieving any satisfactory outcome is very small. Police may well believe (with good reason) that allocating resources to cybercrime is not a good use of their scarce resources.

When one considers the above factors, it should come as no surprise that, in a time of fiscal restraint, there is a general reluctance of governments to do all of the heavy lifting. Other non-governmental resourcing is needed. Luckily, the demand is being met enthusiastically by a resource that is highly amenable to the task at hand: the private sector (Sarre & Prenzler, 2021), both in terms of the specialist skills that it has to offer, and the readiness to shore up vulnerabilities and weaknesses such that it does not, too, fall prey to online criminality.

4 The Specialist Private Sector in Cybercrime Prevention

A great deal of the responsibility of policing the world of cybercrime has been shifted to the private sector, not only in terms of the discrete roles it can play in industry regulation, but in challenging the sector not to fall victim to the hustlers of cyberspace. In other words, the private component in cybercrime prevention not only involves private security firms doing policing and patrolling activities, but encouraging all private entities to remain vigilant and engage in self-policing.

Moreover, the private gains of providing highly visible and successful security for customers provides strong incentives for private firms to offer high quality service. Marketing a solid reputation invariably results in greater business turnover. In house reputation scores internalize the benefits of good security and is an effective regulator of online activity.

That is not to say that there is no role for legislative incentives too. In the wake of 2022 data breaches, the Australian Government introduced legislation that exponentially increases the financial penalties entities face for allowing cybercriminals to expose these entities to repeated or serious privacy breaches. In October 2022 Attorney General Mark Dreyfus introduced the Privacy Legislation Amendment (Enforcement and Other Measures) Bill 2022 which significantly increases the existing maximum penalty to whichever is the greater of an AU\$50 million fine; three times the value of any benefit obtained through the misuse of information; or 30% of a company's adjusted turnover in the relevant period (ACSM, 2022).

There are two examples of fields of endeavour where public and private sector cooperative efforts have a vital role to play in meeting the task of preventing or forestalling cybercrime: digital imaging and metadata retention. Let us examine each in turn here.

4.1 Digital Imaging and Other Surveillance Tools

Visual imaging has played an important role in reducing criminal offending. The most pervasive of electronic surveillance is the digital camera, linked to a closed-circuit television (CCTV) system. These cameras are now widespread throughout the world. CCTV can accommodate overt and covert cameras, traffic flow cameras, speed infringement cameras and red-light intersection cameras. Casinos, department stores, convenience and fuel shops, streets and car parks, reserves and nature parks, railway and bus stations, universities and sports arenas are all likely candidates for CCTV surveillance. CCTV can be, and has been, deployed by national, regional, and local governments in public areas, and by the private sector on and around private property. The vast majority are operated and monitored by private security personnel to whom such responsibilities have been outsourced by contractual arrangements.

The main application of CCTV is the monitoring and reviewing of recorded scenes, principally as a crime prevention tool. In retail shops and market precincts, CCTV has become indispensable, with widespread business support for their potential value as a means of crime reduction (Prenzler & Sarre, 2016). Such cameras, loaded with 'search' software, allow police, building owners, sportsground managers and retail proprietors (to name a few) to watch and count people moving past a certain point. Such systems can track children, or people wearing certain distinctive clothing, which can be helpful in search and rescue situations, or in following up matters pertaining to the commission of a crime. Having accurate time and date stamps on digital recordings can contribute significantly to supporting a police investigation.

In the not-too-distant past, the market for CCTV was limited by the size of the investment required to install and use the technology. The high cost of cameras, their security housings, along with switching and control equipment, recorders, and cabling required to support their operation was frequently too great for a user to justify choosing CCTV above other available security options. However, advances in camera technology (especially with aerial 'drone' capability) have been phenomenal; supply has increased to meet demand, and prices have plummeted accordingly (Sarre, 2015). There is now a massive capacity to store data in even the simplest and cheapest of CCTV models. CCTV systems no longer need to be purchased from specialty security contractors. Sophisticated systems can now be purchased from retail outlets, such as hardware stores. The prices are now affordable for the average householder. The consequence is that the main players in the digital surveillance space are private operators, not governments (Sarre et al., 2014).

There has been some academic interest in the potential for abuse of CCTV, principally by virtue of the public intrusiveness exercised by those who operate and monitor the cameras (Prenzler & Sarre, 2017) and the potential misuse of the images collected and stored by CCTV hardware. However, these technical limitations no longer apply. YouTube, Vimeo, Instagram, Twitter, Facebook, TikTok, X, and other social media platforms now provide instructions for ease of use, and mechanisms for the almost immediate world-wide distribution of recorded moving and static images.

These advances bring opportunities to use images in innovative ways to manage and respond effectively to crises and crime risks, but they also raise privacy concerns. The Australian 'Reef' casino in 2011, for example, was exposed as an employer that allowed its security staff to collect and copy CCTV footage of patrons and other staff for their own prurient interests and in clear defiance of privacy courtesies (if not rights) and company policy (Sarre, 2014, p. 760). The vision included footage of a couple having sex on a bench outside the casino and a group of female dancers getting changed (Channel Nine, 2011).

4.2 Metadata Retention

A key vehicle through which governments have sought to target cybercrime, is by the accessing, monitoring and storage of digital data through what is referred to as 'metadata retention' which relies heavily upon the cooperation of the private telecommunications sector (Australian Parliament, 2017) and which is well assisted by taxpayer dollars (Sarre, 2017a). Branch (2014) defines 'metadata' as data 'that puts other data into context'. Metadata provides the record of a phone call. But even if one does not have the contents of the call the metadata provides a unique indicator that provides answers to all of these questions. Metadata information relating to phone usage does not contain content. It is simply information about the telephone numbers or message links involved in the communication, the location of the caller and receiver, the date and time of the calls, and the length of the conversation.

Hence the collection and retention of metadata provides an electronic 'building block' that can be used in investigations into any form of cybercrime such as terrorism, organized crime, and crimes that are carried out online. Metadata records can now be accessed by national, state, and local government departments under recent Australian legislation (Sarre, 2017a).

It includes data pertaining to Short Message Service (SMS) text messages sent and received. However, Uniform Resource Locators (URLs) and world-wide-web (www) browsing histories are said to be specifically excluded from the Australian metadata retention law, although the Internet Protocol (IP) addresses of users' devices are accessible. What this means is that the locations of the devices that are sending messages can be tracked. Getting a warrant to access telecommunications (conversation) data is much more difficult than accessing metadata, hence the great interest shown by law enforcement agencies in the gathering, storing, and analyzing of the latter.

To frustrate and block those who would orchestrate organised crime, or who would perpetrate violence in the name of some particular ideology, governments (including the Australian government) have the capacity to keep track of metadata by enlisting the compliance of private sector telecommunications companies (Kowalick et al., 2018). Indeed, in 2015, new laws came into force in Australia requiring telecommunications service providers to retain and store their metadata so that it remains available for analysis by anti-terrorism strategists and organized crime fighters (Gal, 2017; Sarre, 2017b). The new laws were not universally welcomed, however. Senator Scott Ludlum was scathing.

> [I]n the few years I've been working up close to government, I've learned one important lesson: Governments cannot be trusted. This government, the one before it, the one that will come after it. (Ludlam, 2015)

The vehicle for the change in Australian policy was the *Telecommunications (Interception and Access) Amendment (Data Retention) Act 2015*. This Act came into effect in October 2015. Under the Act, all telecommunications providers were given 18 months (to 13 April 2017) to put in place a capacity to retain their customers' metadata for 2 years, making it available to government agencies (principally police agencies) without complaint and upon request. Until this legislation was in place, metadata was kept for various periods by communications providers on an *ad hoc* basis simply for the purpose of billing their customers, and available on an *ad hoc* basis for law enforcement agencies if they made demands. The new legislation regularized this process, circumventing any objection by the public that, contractually, their metadata was private between them and their telecommunications provider (Grattan, 2015; Sarre, 2018). The literature on its effectiveness is silent. There are two reasons for this. The first is that governments are loath to reveal what they determine to be state secrets, although a sceptic might consider silence as hiding revelations of failure. The second is that a policy of deterrence is very hard to test. How does one determine how much terrorism and state crime has been prevented, and if there has been a reduction in crime, how does one determine, in the absence of assistance from the agency itself whether that specific intervention of policy has been the reason for the change?

5   Concerns about Public/Private Partnerships

The above examples illustrate that there is now in Australia, if not elsewhere in the world, a strong record of cooperation between governments and private security and other commercial companies, sometimes for mutual benefit (prompted by the private sector), and sometimes with one-way, top down, government dictates (albeit with a governmental payment to defray the private costs associated with the task). This trend continues to go hand in hand with private sector policing and security cooperation that has operated under the aegis of government agencies for years, and across most nations of the world (Prenzler & Sarre, 2016). However, in the fight against cybercrime, there is good reason for apprehension in the public/private cooperative space. Concerns about dubious ethical practices and the regularity of instances of 'over-reach' by private companies were heightened by the March 2018 revelations that the information company Cambridge Analytica had manipulated and exploited the data of Facebook user profiles.

The data were collected through an app entitled "This Is Your Digital Life". A series of questions were asked which allowed psychological profiles on users to be built. Thereupon the personal data of the respondents' Facebook friends were linked. 87 million Facebook profiles were built. Cambridge Analytica admitted using the data to provide analytical assistance to the 2016 presidential campaigns of Republican candidates Ted Cruz and Donald Trump (Manokha, 2018). Just 46 days later, Cambridge Analytica announced it would close its doors. So, too, did its parent company, SCL Elections. Facebook admitted that it was (unwillingly and unwittingly) complicit in this clear breach of privacy. Other commentators called out the potential conflicts of interest.

> It might seem inherently incompatible with democracy for that knowledge to be vested in a private body. Yet the retention of such data is the essence of Facebook's ability to make money and run a viable business … Maybe the internet should be rewired from the grassroots, rather than be led by digital oligarchs' business needs. (Joseph, 2018)

Mark Zuckerberg, Facebook CEO, later admitted to the United States Congress that Facebook routinely gathers data on non-members, and the only way for a person to remove or correct that data is to join Facebook. Commentators are now suggesting that there is a new era of 'surveillance capitalism' brewing.

> The outcry against Cambridge Analytica has not attempted to sanction, nor even to question, the existence of digital platforms and other actors which depend on the ever more extensive acquisition and monetisation of personal data. If anything, the Cambridge Analytica story has unintentionally contributed to the further normalisation of surveillance and the lack of privacy that comes with being an internet user nowadays. Even the web pages of the sites that broke the story (The Observer and New York Times) allow dozens of third-party sites to obtain data from the browser of the user accessing the articles. It was 75 and 61 sites, respectively, last time I checked …. (Manokha, 2018)

The case of Cambridge Analytica provides a sobering reminder of why the relationship between government policing agencies and the private sector needs to be kept under constant scrutiny (Holt, 2018, p. 153). We have struggled to determine how best any society finds an acceptable balance between the rights of its citizens to enjoy freedom from the prying eyes of government, and the legitimate interests that the state might have in monitoring them. In July 2015, the then Australian Communications Minister (and later Prime Minister) Malcolm Turnbull expressed the challenge in this way.

> [W]e need to recognize that getting the balance right is not easy (not least because the balance may shift over time) and we are more likely to do so if there is a thoughtful and well-informed public debate – weighing up the reality of the national security threat, the effectiveness of particular proposed measures and then asking whether those measures do infringe on our traditional freedoms and if so whether the infringement is justifiable. (Turnbull, 2015)

However, there is now an added complication. When those prying eyes are not subjected to the scrutiny of parliamentary inquiries and governmental oversight, but are found in 'outsourced' private corporations, how is that balance to be determined and maintained, consistent with democratic principles? It is to that question that we now turn.

6   The Right Balance

An appropriate equilibrium must be struck between forestalling crime and terrorism using all available electronic means (public and private), while not unduly curtailing the legitimate rights to privacy that citizens in modern democracies currently expect to enjoy. What controls should society employ over the private sector to monitor its engagement in cyber surveillance? What degree of intrusion is acceptable? There are no easy answers to these questions, especially given that modern society appears uncertain about what levels of privacy its citizens demand and expect, and the extent to which its citizens trust private operators to manage their private data.

On the one hand, there is the view that we should safeguard strictly the privacy of the personal data held by private companies, given that digital data can spread worldwide in a matter of seconds, or can be hacked, or can be used to target potential voting preferences. On this view, we should be very cautious of any covert surveillance that allows an emboldening of private agencies to spy upon the legitimate activities of those whom they (or any other authorities) deem 'undesirable.' Indeed, the case of *Schrems v The Data Protection Commissioner and Digital Rights Ireland Ltd* (Case C-362/2014) illustrates that we have good reason to be cautious. In this case, the European Court of Justice was asked to determine a challenge to what is referred to as the 'Safe Harbor' agreement. This agreement, between the European Union and the United States, was formed in 2000, and was designed to protect private data collected by internet companies. Specifically, it protects data collected in Europe when that data is then shared with US providers. The court found that US legislators fell short of providing the sort of privacy guarantees that their European subsidiaries were bound by, hence the agreement was unsustainable. In other words, the 'Safe Harbor' agreement could not proceed because it did not comply with European human rights law. The *Schrems* case provides us with a reminder that data security cannot be trifled with. We should not always trust those who tell us that their databases are secure. Government statements get no special privileges.

On the other hand, there is a strong sense that citizens' lives can be enhanced by having a ready supply of data available to anyone who wishes to access it. The new generations of digital users appear to be ambivalent about how much privacy they are willing to sacrifice in the rush to maintain contemporaneous contact with the world (Sarre, 2014). Access to internet sites and messaging services such as Instagram, Facebook, Facetime, WhatsApp, Viber, and Tango, for example, has enhanced the communication channels across the globe. They provide instantaneous and useful information. Each can act as a safety and protection tool, too, when, say, a user is lost, or fearful, or has become a victim of crime.

It is becoming more and more clear that police need to co-opt private sector communication networks to assist in the fight against cybercrime. Experience has shown that private companies, however, cannot be trusted unequivocally to deal with our data in a manner that befits our privacy, and meets our expectations (Gal, 2017). What, then, is to be done? Let us now examine the co-option process more closely.

7 Co-opting Private Sector Prevention

In addition to enlisting the specialist private sector, governments are now recognising the importance of putting in place resources for private companies such that they are exhorted to join the fight just by their own vigilance. Below we cite recent Australian legislation that has sought to mandate this vigilance, and then outline a case study of successful public/private cooperation.

7.1   Legislation

The *Security Legislation Amendment (Critical Infrastructure) Act 2021* (First Amending Act) came into force in Australia in December 2021. The Federal Minister, Karen Andrews, offered the following regarding its importance to national security:

> The Australian Government is seeking [business] help to improve data security measures and close the gaps that exist in our data settings. We want to ensure that governments, businesses, and communities are informed and resourced to protect their data. This is why I am committed to delivering Australia's first National Data Security Action Plan .... (Australian Government, 2021a, p. 3)

The First Amending Act amends the scope of the *Security of Critical Infrastructure Act 2018* (SOCI Act), which underpins a framework for managing risks relating to critical infrastructure. This Act extends the obligations under the SOCI Act to a broad range of sectors, now 11 in total: namely, communications data and storage or processing, financial services and markets, water and sewerage, energy, healthcare and medical, higher education and research, food and grocery, transport, space technology, and the defence industry. On 31 March 2022, the Australian Government passed the *Security Legislation Amendment (Critical Infrastructure Protection) Act 2022* (Second Amending Act). This Act demands that private entities that are responsible for critical infrastructure assets adopt and maintain a critical infrastructure Risk Management Program. The Act sets out the process by which the Minister can declare a critical infrastructure asset to be a System of National Significance (SoNS) and prescribes enhanced cyber security obligations for SoNS. The Act introduces information-sharing provisions for regulated entities. This legislation indicates the commitment of the Australian government to significant prophylactic measures and the key role of private instrumentalities in carrying out these measures.

The effectiveness of these new provisions can best be determined by the Annual Reports distributed by the Department of Home Affairs. The 2020–2021 Report provides a sanguine overview. There appears to be a productive level of engagement with private providers:

> In the 2020–21 financial year, the Department has continued to engage with state and territory and industry, through stakeholder meetings, telephone, email and formal website enquiries. The Department has participated in numerous teleconferences and face-to-face meetings, and answered frequent enquiries from industry and state and territory government stakeholders. (Australian Government, 2022, p. 6)

The Report noted that there had been no contraventions of civil penalty provisions of the Act during that period (Australian Government, 2022, p. 6).

7.2   Case Study: Project Sunbird

Project Sunbird ran from 2013 to early-2017 in Western Australia, a joint venture of the Police Major Fraud Squad and the Department of Commerce Consumer Protection Division (Emerson, 2017; Prenzler & Sarre, 2021). Project Sunbird was focused on preventing repeat online fraud, particularly from scams originating in West Africa. Bank account holders with suspicious payments – flagged by a 'financial intelligence' system – received warning letters and offers of assistance. Official accounts claim that approximately 50 new victims were identified each month from data provided by private financial institutions, and approximately three-quarters of victims stopped sending money, saving tens of millions of dollars over the life of the Project (Cross, 2016; Department of Commerce, 2017, p. 29; Mischin, 2017). Despite this success, however, the Project was shut down. The Western Australia Police cited 'resource priorities' for putting a halt to their analysis of the data.

Regrettably, the ACCC shut down a similar 'National Scams Disruption Project' in 2017 (see Cross, 2016; ACCC, 2019) although their online 'Scamwatch' website (ACCC, 2022a) provides a regular snapshot of fraudulent online activities that continue to prey upon vulnerable Australians (for example, Cross et al., 2022). However, simply putting in place information on likely 'scam' activities does not overcome the misconceptions that exist in the minds of victims regarding the relationship between the Australian Federal Police and state/territory police and *who* can investigate *what* (Cross, 2020). Nor did it provide any assistance for victims other than referring to the victims' financial institutions in the event that recovery of moneys paid to cybercriminals could be recovered. Creating the Australian Cybercrime Online Reporting Network in 2014 as the 'one-stop-shop' for reporting was a welcome step, but it has not fixed the issue. Improvements are needed regarding awareness of victims and police alike in order to reduce unnecessary trauma to victims of fraudulent online activities (Cross, 2020). Sadly, despite the best endeavours of financial institutions to warn clients of the risks of cybercriminality, the message does not appear to be getting through to Australians. In 2021 Australians lost a record amount of more than AU$2 billion to scams, despite government, law enforcement, and the private sector disrupting more scam activity than ever before. Investment scams were the highest loss category (AU$701 million) in 2021, followed by payment redirection scams (AU$227 million), and romance scams (AU $142 million (ACCC, 2022b).

8   What Is to Be Done?

There is a way through this dilemma, we affirm, if nations pursue the adoption of the following imperatives. We list them here by way of five Strategic Foci' (or 'dictates'):

Strategic Focus 1: Determine what we want and expect from cyberspace technology through public debate.

This requirement of policymakers insists that citizens need to decide what they can and cannot abide with the innovations that arise from technology, and how much they are prepared to sacrifice in the privacy versus connectedness dichotomy.

> [This] means more innovative forms of public debate. And it means that the most influential institutions in this space – …governments, technology firms and national champions – need to listen and experiment with the goal of social, as well as economic and technological, progress in mind. (Davis & Subic, 2018)

Strategic Focus 2: Put appropriate rules in place and finance them accordingly.

The rules to be put in place by policymakers need to ensure that citizens can enjoy the benefits of the digital age without bringing them closer to a 'surveillance society' in which our every move is monitored, tracked, recorded, and scrutinized by the governments and private interests (Rodrick, 2009). Nations must build in more safeguards as the technology becomes more widespread and spend the required money to keep them going. In March 2022, the Australian Government allocated AU\$9.9 billion over 10 years to the Australian Signals Directorate to deliver a Resilience, Effects, Defence, Space, Intelligence, Cyber and Enablers package. This is the largest ever investment in Australia's intelligence and cyber capabilities (MinterEllison, 2022, p. iii). One can only hope that an empirical evaluation of regarding the effectiveness of these rules will be a high priority for those responsible for implementation of the package.

Strategic Focus 3: Encourage and adopt governmental guidelines.

Policymakers have made the Australian experience on this front worth emulating. On May 8, 2017, the Australian Government tabled the Productivity Commission's *Data Availability and Use Inquiry* (Australian Government, 2018). The Inquiry made 41 recommendations designed to shift from policies based on risk avoidance towards policies based on value, choice, transparency, and confidence. A year later, on May 1, 2018, the Australian Government committed to establishing an office of the National Data Commissioner, introducing legislation to improve the sharing, use and reuse of public sector data while maintaining the strong security and privacy protections the community expects, and introducing a Consumer Data Right to allow consumers of data to share their usage with private service competitors and comparison services. The government has enshrined in legislation that data sharing and release is only for authorized for specified purposes (such as informing and assessing government policy and research and development with public benefits), and provided that data safeguards are met (Flannery, 2019).

Strategic Focus 4: Engage the private sector but be suitably wary of its power and motives.

Policymakers must be on guard to ensure that the private sector is thoroughly accountable for its cybercrime-prevention efforts. Private corporations are being trusted with vast amounts of sensitive personal data that will be generated as they 'police' the internet. But there are some commentators who are not confident that this trust is well-placed.

> There are ... serious unintended consequences that may result from the various extralegal measures employed by industry and corporate entities. Specifically, they have no legal or constitutional remit to enforce national laws or the interests of any one country. Industrial involvement in transnational investigations ... may lead some to question whether they have overstepped their role as service providers into order maintenance based on their economic interests only. (Holt, 2018, p. 152)

Strategic Focus 5: Engage the private sector to be vigilant and engage in self-policing.

Policymakers must ensure that the right incentives are in place to enjoin those entities that are vulnerable to cybercrime to act in their own self-interest and put in place their own shields from potential threats (Prenzler & Sarre, 2022).

9   Conclusion

Police cannot go alone in the fight against cybercrime. The other significant way in which private cooperation has been encouraged (and in some respects mandated) is illustrated by how governments have enjoined and continue to enjoin (mainly by legislative mandate) private entities to reduce their vulnerability. That being the case, the private sector has been and will continue to be co-opted. In significant ways its assistance has been fruitful. There is considerable trust between public and private agencies in relation to the fight against cyber criminality. However, given the excesses of some corporate entities, and their propensity to allow hackers access to their data, particularly in the processing and storage of digital data records, government agencies cannot adopt a 'hands-off' approach and allow the private sector free rein in their quest. Instead, they must develop a clear over-arching framework to require compliance of private owners of surveillance tools and data managers in the same way as controls are in place to protect the private nature of government-collected data. Critical infrastructure and private companies cannot remain vulnerable to cyber incursion. Cyber security is everyone's business.

  The future security of every nation depends upon the decisions we make regarding the prophylactic strategies we adopt today. The important take-away message from the above evidence is that governments cannot act alone. The internationalization of cybercrime requires an international focus, stretching and reaching beyond governments, a focus that is well within the ambit of a properly regulated private sector, a sector that is more than keen to be involved.

References

ABS. (2021). *Finance fraud financial year 2020–2021*. Australian Bureau of Statistics.

ACCC. (2019). *Targeting scams: Report of the ACCC on scams activity 2018*. Australian Competition and Consumer Commission.

ACCC. (2022a). *Scamwatch website*. Retrieved May 18, 2022, from https://www.scamwatch.gov.au/. Australian Competition and Consumer Commission.

ACCC. (2022b). *Targeting scams*. Retrieved May 18, 2022, from https://www.accc.gov.au/publications/targeting-scams-report-on-scam-activity/targeting-scams-report-of-the-accc-on-scams-activity-2021. Australian Competition and Consumer Commission.

ACSM. (2022). Australian government to increase data breach penalties. *Australian Cyber Security Magazine, 24*, 2000. https://australiancybersecuritymagazine.com.au/australian-government-to-increase-data-breach-penalties/

Australian Crime Commission. (2015). *Organized crime in Australia report*. Commonwealth of Australia.

Australian Cyber Security Centre. (2017). *Australian cyber threat report 2016–2017*. Retrieved May 18, 2022, from: https://www.cyber.gov.au/acsc/view-all-content/reports-and-statistics/acsc-threat-report-2017

Australian Cyber Security Centre. (2022). *Annual cyber threat report 2020–2021*. Retrieved May 21, 2022, from https://www.cyber.gov.au/sites/default/files/2021-09/ACSC%20Annual%20Cyber%20Threat%20Report%20-%202020-2021.pdf

Australian Government. (2018). *New Australian Government Data Sharing and Release Legislation,* Issues Paper for Consultation. Department of Prime Minister and Cabinet.

Australian Government. (2021a). *National data security action plan, discussion paper,* Retrieved May 22, 2022, from https://www.homeaffairs.gov.au/reports-and-publications/submissions-and-discussion-papers/data-security

Australian Government. (2021b) *Notifiable data breaches report*. Office of the Australian Information Commissioner.

Australian Government. (2022). *Security of critical infrastructure act 2018 annual report 2020–2021*. Department of Home Affairs.

Australian Parliament. (2017). *Review of the implementation period of the telecommunications (interception and access) amendment (data retention) act 2014*. Joint Parliamentary Committee on Intelligence and Security.

Branch, P. (2014). Surveillance by metadata. *Issues, 109*(December), 10–13.

Broadhurst, R. (2017). Cybercrime. In A. Deckert & R. Sarre (Eds.), *The Palgrave handbook of Australian and New Zealand criminology, crime and justice* (pp. 221–236). Palgrave Macmillan.

Broadhurst, R., & Chang, L. Y. C. (2013). Cybercrime in Asia: Trends and challenges. In J. Liu, B. Hebenton, & S. Jou (Eds.), *Handbook of Asian criminology* (pp. 49–63). Springer.

Chang, L. Y. C. (2012). *Cybercrime in the greater China region: Regulatory responses, and crime prevention across the Taiwan Strait*. Edward Elgar Publishing.

Channel Nine. (2011, August 31). *A current affair, Reef Casino Cairns Queensland*. http://www.youtube.com/watch?v=WRL6fM42UXE

Cross, C. (2016). Using financial intelligence to target online fraud victimisation: Applying a tertiary prevention perspective. *Criminal Justice Studies, 29*(2), 125–142.

Cross, C. (2020). 'Oh we can't actually do anything about that': The problematic nature of jurisdiction for online fraud victims. *Criminology and Criminal Justice, 20*(3), 358–375.

Cross, C; Holt, K & O'Malley, R.L. (2022). 'If u don't pay they will share the pics': Exploring sextortion in the context of romance fraud. *Victims & Offenders: An International Journal of Evidence-based Research, Policy, and Practice*. https://doi.org/10.1080/15564886.2022.2075064.

Davis, N. & Subic, A. (2018, 18 May). Hope and fear surround emerging technologies, but all of us must contribute to stronger governance. *The Conversation*. Retrieved May 18, 2022, from https://theconversation.com/hope-and-fear-surround-emerging-technologies-but-all-of-us-must-contribute-to-stronger-governance-96122

Department of Commerce. (2017). *Final report 2016–2017*. Government of Western Australia.

Economist. (2017). Data is the new oil. *Weekend Australian, 6–7*, 24.

Emerson, D. (2017). Love scam plea: Romance scam squad disbanded. *The West Australian, 16*, 4.

Flannery, A. (2019). *Public sector data: The proposed data sharing and release act and implications for governments*. Retrieved May 18, 2022, from http://www.mondaq.com/article.asp?article_id=772966&signup=true

Franks, C. & Smith, R. (2020). *Identity crime and misuse in Australia: Results of the 2019 online survey*. Statistical Report no. 27. Australian Institute of Criminology.

Gal, U. (2017, June16). The new data retention law seriously invades our privacy – And it's time we took action. *The Conversation*. Retrieved May 18, 2022, from https://theconversation.com/the-new-data-retention-law-seriously-invades-our-privacy-and-its-time-we-took-action-78991?sa=pg2&sq=metadata&sr=1

Gordon, S., & Ford, R. (2006). On the definition and classification of cybercrime. *Journal of Computer Virology, 2*, 13–20.

Grabosky, P. (2007). *Electronic crime*. Prentice Hall.

Grattan, M. (2015, May 12). $131 million for companies' metadata retention in budget boost to counter terrorism. *The Conversation*. Retrieved May 18, 2022, from https://theconversation.com/131-million-for-companies-metadata-retention-in-budget-boost-to-counter-terrorism-41637

Holt, T. J. (2018). Regulating cybercrime through law enforcement and industry mechanisms. *The Annals of the American Academy of Political and Social Science, 679*(1), 140–157.

Joseph, S. (2018, April 3). Why the business model of social media giants like Facebook is incompatible with human rights. *The Conversation*. Retrieved May 18, 2022, from https://theconversation.com/why-the-business-model-of-social-media-giants-like-facebook-is-incompatible-with-human-rights-94016

Kirkpatrick, D. (2018). Technology. *Time Magazine, 23*, 38–41.

Kowalick, P., Connery, D., & Sarre, R. (2018). Intelligence-sharing in the context of policing transnational serious and organized crime: A note on policy and practice in an Australian setting. *Police Practice and Research: An International Journal, 19*(6), 596–608.

Ludlam, S. (2015, February 27). *Data retention: We need this opposition to oppose*. ABC *The Drum*. Retrieved May 18, 2022, from http://www.abc.net.au/news/2015-02-27/ludlam-we-need-this-opposition-to-oppose/6269504

Manokha, I. (2018, 3 May). *Cambridge analytica's closure is a pyrrhic victory for data privacy*. The Conversation, Retrieved May 18, 2022, from https://theconversation.com/cambridge-analyticas-closure-is-a-pyrrhic-victory-for-data-privacy-96034

Martin, J. & Whelan, C. (2022, 27 October). Why are there so many data breaches? A growing industry of criminals is brokering in stolen data. *The Conversation*. Retrieved October 27, 2022, from https://www.aic.gov.au/publications/tandi/tandi344

McGuire, M. & Dowling, S. (2013, October). *Cybercrime: A review of the evidence: Summary of key findings and implications*. Home Office Research Report 75. Home Office.

MinterEllison. (2022). *Perspectives on cyber risk*. https://www.minterellison.com/articles/perspectives-on-cyber-risk-new-threats-and-challenges-in-2022

Mischin, M. (2017, January 18). *WA victims lose $10 million to scams in 2016*. Retrieved from https://www.mediastatements.wa.gov.au/Pages/Barnett/2017/01/WA-victims-lose-10-million-to-scams-in-2016.aspx

Prenzler, T., & Sarre, R. (2016). Public-private crime prevention partnerships. In T. Prenzler (Ed.), *Policing and security in practice: Challenges and achievements* (2nd ed., pp. 149–167). Palgrave Macmillan.

Prenzler, T., & Sarre, R. (2017). The security industry and crime prevention. In T. Prenzler (Ed.), *Understanding crime prevention: The case study approach* (pp. 165–181). Australian Academic Press.

Prenzler, T. & Sarre, R. (2021). Community safety, crime prevention and 21st century policing. In P. Birch, M. Kennedy & E. Kruger (Eds.) *Australian policing: Critical issues in 21st century police practice* (pp. 283–298). Routledge.

Prenzler, T., & Sarre, R. (2022). Facilitating best practice in security: The role of regulation. In M. Gill (Ed.), *Handbook of security* (pp. 777–799). Palgrave Macmillan.

Reuters. (2022). *Australia's No. 1 health insurer says hacker stole patient details.* Retrieved October 20, 2022, from https://www.reuters.com/technology/after-telco-hack-australia-faces-wave-data-breaches-2022-10-20/

Rodrick, S. (2009). Accessing telecommunications data for national security and law enforcement purposes. *Federal Law Review, 37*(3), 375–415.

Sarre, R. (2008). Privacy and cyber forensics: An australian perspective. In A. Marcella & D. Menendez (Eds.), *Cyber forensics: A field manual for collecting, examining, and preserving evidence of computer crimes* (2nd ed., pp. 231–240). Taylor & Francis.

Sarre, R. (2014). The use of surveillance technologies in the fight against crime: What are the trends, opportunities and threats? In E. Pływaczewski (Ed.), *Current problems of the penal law and criminology* (Vol. 6, pp. 755–767). Temida Publishing House.

Sarre, R. (2015). Eyes in the sky. *Drone Magazine, 1*, 48–51.

Sarre, R. (2017a). Metadata retention as a means of combatting terrorism and organized crime: A perspective from Australia. *Asian Journal of Criminology, 12*, 167–179.

Sarre, R. (2017b). The surveillance society: A criminological perspective. In E. Viano (Ed.), *Cybercrime, organized crime, and societal responses: International approaches* (pp. 291–300). Springer.

Sarre, R. (2018, June 8). Revisiting metadata retention in light of the government's push for new powers. *The Conversation.* Retrieved May 18, 2022, from https://theconversation.com/revisiting-metadata-retention-in-light-of-the-governments-push-for-new-powers-97931

Sarre, R. (2022). Policing cybercrime: Is there a role for the private sector? In J. Eterno, B. Stickle, D. Peterson, & D. Das (Eds.), *Police behavior, hiring and crime fighting* (pp. 217–227). Routledge.

Sarre, R., & Prenzler, T. (2021). Policing and security: Critiquing the privatisation story in Australia. In P. Birch, P. M. Kennedy, & E. Kruger (Eds.), *Australian policing: Critical issues in 21st century police practice* (pp. 221–233). Routledge.

Sarre, R., Brooks, D., Smith, C., & Draper, R. (2014). Current and emerging technologies employed to abate crime and to promote security. In B. Arrigo & H. Bersot (Eds.), *The Routledge handbook of international crime and justice studies* (pp. 327–349). Routledge.

Sarre, R., Lau, L., & Chang, L. (2018). Responding to cybercrime: Current trends. *Police Practice and Research: An International Journal, 19*(6), 515–518.

SonicWall. 2022. *2022 SonicWall cyber threat report. https://www.sonicwall.com/medialibrary/en/white-paper/2022-sonicwall-cyber-threat-report.pdf*

Toh, W.-L., Simmonds, R., & Neary, M. (2022, September). *Cyber risk and the role of insurance,* green paper. Actuaries Institute.

Turnbull, M. (2015). *Magna Carta and the rule of law in the digital age.* Speech to the Sydney Institute, Sydney, 7 July. Retrieved May 18, 2022, from https://www.malcolmturnbull.com.au/media/speech-to-the-sydney-institute-magna-carta-and-the-rule-of-law-in-the-digit

Private Security Confounds Estimates of Public Police and Crime

Benjamin Blemings, Gregory DeAngelo, Ryan Quandt, and William Wyatt

Abstract The effectiveness of public policing has become an important issue given recent discussions of defunding law enforcement. This has also led to a discussion about the role of private security in potentially filling the void of creating public safety in the absence of public security. Thus, it is implicitly assumed that private security and public police are substitutes for one another. Alternatively, these two forms of security could complement each other. Causally determining whether private security and public police are complements or substitutes for one another is complicated by numerous layers of endogeneity. Nevertheless, excluding the presence of private security from a causal analysis of the effect of public police on crime could result in omitted variable bias. In this work we utilize survey data on private security and public police, as well as crime data, by county over the period 2006–2019 to explore the extent that omitting private security confounds an analysis of public security and crime. Our results indicate that it is a non-trivial omission to exclude private security from such analyses.

1 Introduction

Ensuring the safety of communities is often attributed to publicly funded law enforcement agencies. Indeed, our societies are so ingrained in tax funded public safety that many community members expect police to handle nearly all social

B. Blemings (✉)
Dyson School of Applied Economics and Management, Cornell University, Ithaca, NY, USA
e-mail: btb77@cornell.edu

G. DeAngelo · R. Quandt · W. Wyatt
Department of Economic Sciences, Claremont Graduate University, Claremont, CA, USA
e-mail: gregory.deangelo@cgu.edu; ryan.quandt@cgu.edu; william.wyatt@cgu.edu

© The Author(s), under exclusive license to Springer Nature Switzerland AG 2023   103
E. A. Blackstone et al. (eds.), *Handbook on Public and Private Security*,
Competitive Government: Public Private Partnerships,
https://doi.org/10.1007/978-3-031-42406-9_5

issues, including mental health, substance abuse, homelessness, and so on.[1] But, tax-funded police resources are not the only form of security.

Publicly funded law enforcement is not omnipresent and is often merely reacting to criminal behavior that is already in progress. Public law enforcement often calls on the community to assist in deterring and clearing crimes (Nicholson-Crotty & O'Toole, 2004; Renauer et al., 2003; Tolman & Weisz, 1995; Weitzer et al., 2008; Zhao et al., 2002). Because there is a desire to prevent criminal behavior from occurring, citizens often engage in practices to deter crime. While locks on homes, cars, bikes, etc. have been common for quite some time, more recent reductions in the cost of simplified home video surveillance installation have resulted in more evidence of criminal conduct. But, surveillance is often not enough to deter criminal behavior, resulting in the utilization of private security, including armored cars, corporate security, bodyguards, parking security, casino security, investigative services, private security in a homeowner's association, and even guard dogs (Gill, 2015; Maskaly et al., 2011; Nemeth, 2017; Noaks, 2000).

Private security is assumed to arise in circumstances where the presence of publicly funded law enforcement falls short of the level desired by a private entity. This can occur for a variety of reasons, including the remoteness of a location, the movement of a desired asset (e.g., money) that is hard for police to track and protect, or a personal preference for a higher level of security than can be provided by tax-funded law enforcement. Other instances of an absence of either law or law enforcement have been well-documented in the literature (Ellickson, 1991). These scenarios often give rise to private solutions to resolve issues between disagreeing parties, as seen in the diamond industry (Bernstein, 1992), trading partners before real-time monitoring existed (Greif, 1993), cattle ranching (Ellickson, 1985), whaling (Ellickson, 1989), prison order (Skarbek, 2011), hockey (DeAngelo et al., 2017), and maritime pirates (DeAngelo & Smith, 2020).

Security can also arise in a form other than private security. For example, community watch groups have been established to identify suspicious behavior. And with the onset of smart phones, many community watch groups have been replaced by applications such as the "Next Door" app, which quickly disseminates information that is pertinent to public safety (Kurwa, 2019; Patton et al., 2019; van Steden & Mehlbaum, 2021). Additionally, laws have empowered community members to protect their wellbeing and property under the principle known as the "Castle Doctrine." However, Cheng and Hoekstra (2013) and McClellan and Tekin (2012) note, these laws have largely led to increases in murders and manslaughters without reducing burglary or theft.

Whether private and public security are complements or substitutes for one another remains an open question. Certain contexts (e.g., Prenzler and Sarre (2012) and MacDonald et al. (2016)) have found that the combination of private and public security has led to increased deterrence of proscribed behavior. Other contexts (e.g., Williams (2004) and DeAngelo et al. (2017)) have found no statistically significant

---

[1] See Wood et al. (2017), Fry, O'Riordan, and Geanellos (2002), and Krameddine and Silverstone (2016) for a non-exhaustive representation of this literature.

relationship between public and private security. And still other research (Helsley & Strange, 2005; Lee & Pinto, 2009) has found that public and private security could work in opposition to one another.

The difficulty in empirically examining the relationship between public and private security is the non-random presence of both forms of security. As noted in the economics of crime literature, an endogenous relationship exists between police and crime such that reverse causality makes estimating the causal effect of police on crime complicated. Nevertheless, quasi-experimental methods have unearthed a negative relationship between police and crime.[2] The relationship between private security and crime is less well understood in the literature. To start, it is not clear that private security is more likely to be deployed in high crime areas, as these regions tend to be poorer with fewer resources to employ private security. Alternatively, wealthier areas have the resources to deploy private security, but face lower levels of criminal behavior because of publicly funded law enforcement efforts to deter criminal acts in these regions.

The endogenous relationship between crime and security is further complicated when one considers the impact of private and public security, independently and in conjunction with one another, on proscribed behavior. High levels of public and private security in a region should presumably reduce crime unless the levels of security have been deployed because the region experiences high levels of crime. If the region has low levels of public and private security, presumably this is because the region has low levels of crime and needs fewer security resources. But it could also be the case that the region is poor and, due to political pressure, receives fewer government resources and has higher levels of crime. Or, regions with high levels of private security and low levels of public security could arise as a response to the absence of tax-funded police resources.

Incentives facing law enforcement agencies also complicate the relationship between crime rates and police. Law enforcement agencies that face incentives to raise funds that support their efforts, typically in the form of citations and asset forfeitures, could be impacting the empirical relationship between crime rates and police presence.[3] If so, crime rates may be a function of incentives rather than crimes committed. Similarly, crime rates may be higher in areas with greater police presence due to greater probability of apprehension and detection, quicker response times, or proactive policing. On the other hand, these elements may deter would be criminals.

Unpacking the causal relationship between private security, public security and criminal behavior is beyond the scope of the current research. Nevertheless, we believe that a preliminary analysis of the effect of different forms of security, independently and in conjunction with one another, on crime is merit-worthy for a few reasons. First, it is not clear that quasi-experimental methods can identify as-if

---

[2] See Levitt (1997), Di Tella and Schargrodsky (2004), Draca et al. (2010), DeAngelo and Hansen (2014) and DeAngelo et al. (2018) for examples of this work.

[3] See Baicker and Jacobson (2007), Figlio and O'Sullivan (2001), Kantor et al. (2021), and Makowsky et al. (2019) for work in this space.

random assignment of both public and private security. While it is likely possible to isolate as-if random assignment of public security, the choice of when and where to deploy private security is likely in response to the level of public security and corresponding criminal behavior. Second, understanding the endogenous interaction effects of private and public security on criminal behavior can still shed light on the net effect of investment in these resources on public safety. Indeed, even a well-identified estimation strategy would likely violate the stable unit treatment value assumption, as private deterrence efforts likely result in spillover effects. Finally, this research can provide a platform upon which future work can benchmark the empirical relationship between public funding for security and private investment in reducing proscribed behavior.

In the next section we discuss the various data sources utilized in our research and present basic descriptive statistics. In Sect. 3 we discuss the empirical model that we use to estimate the effect of security on criminal behavior. Our main empirical results are presented in Sect. 4, which examines both aggregate, and separately, violent and property crimes. Finally, Sect. 5 concludes with a discussion of our results and areas of future research.

2   Data

Our research question pertains to the relative contributions and interactive effects of public police and private security on crime deterrence. This requires, at a minimum, observing both types of security and criminal activity at sufficient levels of disaggregation. While data on crime and public police employment at disaggregated levels are regularly collected and employed, less has been done with private security. A reason there is less national research on private security is because private entities are not required to report their activities and their scope. To overcome the difficulties in measuring private security from public sources, we obtain data from the American Community Survey (ACS) that is disaggregated by county and year across the entire United States. This enables a nationwide characterization of private and public security and their contributions to deterrence.

The ACS is a weighted average sample, where the smallest region spans 100,000 citizens across cities and, in some instances, counties. As a result, counties with less than 100,000 residents are excluded from our sample. ACS observes weighted individuals such that each observation represents 100 persons in a county. To aggregate, we subset the data to include only individuals whose primary occupation is either private security or policing, weights are applied, and then the data are aggregated at the county and year level.[4]

---

[4]Private security comprises a wide range of roles, from bank security and mall cop to a privately hired armed guard. Since the data only contains primary occupation, this count excludes those who have a second or part-time security job.

Although ACS also includes information about police employment, we sourc public police from UCR since it is more likely to be accurate due to it being a within-department census rather than a general survey.[5] For our purposes, an individual is counted as a police officer only if they carry a firearm and badge, have full arresting power, and are paid by government funds allocated to sworn law enforcement. We drop other staff, such as office workers since they likely do not have any direct deterrence effects.

The UCR crime data are constructed to contain yearly counts of crime levels for a unique police agency. The resulting dataset was then merged with UCR's police employment data. Of the 241,658 observations from the UCR crime and police employment data for the years 2006–2019, 79% of the data matched according to agency and year. The other 21% lacked either crime records or police employment and were dropped. Using a crosswalk to match agencies to their respective counties, we collapse the data to make each observation an aggregate of crime and police employment across agencies within a county for a given year. We use U.S. Census Bureau estimates to determine each county's population and then use these estimates to normalize police employment, private security, and our crime variables to generate per capita measures of police, private security, and crime.

Finally, we merge UCR and ACS data for our main dataset and drop observations with either missing values for police or private security, or observations that have a value of zero for police,[6] resulting in 5593 county-year observations. The resulting data are still an unbalanced panel with some counties missing years. To ensure our results are not skewed by variation in unobserved years, we drop all observations that lack more than 1 year of observations. The resulting sample includes 324 counties from 2006–2019, with a total of 4529 observations. 317 counties have data in each year of our sample and 7 counties are missing 1 year.

Table 1 presents the number of police and private security employment per 1000 people. On average, we observe approximately 2000 private security guards within a county, or 3.7 private security guards per 1000 people. UCR and ACS data for police employment are similar. On average, we observe 1000–1200 police within a county, or 1.9–2.6 police per 1000 people.

To control for poverty, we use the Small Area Income and Poverty Estimates (SAIPE) dataset from the U.S. Census Bureau. The SAIPE dataset defines a threshold of poverty at the county-year level. Combining the dataset, SAIPE completely matched with the merged IPUMS and FBI UCR datasets. The result is a poverty threshold for every county and year. We take the median income for the county and

---

[5] Numbers between sources of police employment are comparable. As stated in the note to Table 1, the sources have similar counts of police per capita. The ACS numbers are higher for both police and private security. This may mean the ACS overestimates the count or UCR underestimates. Or the difference may be due to the agencies that do not report in the UCR data, and so the counties in our subset match both sources. Police employment is voluntarily submitted to the FBI with 83% of the nation's 15,875 agencies reporting their number of sworn officers and employees in 2017.

[6] Since the counties we observe have over 100,000 residents, it is unlikely that counties have no police.

Table 1 County Level Summary Statistics of Police and Private Security (2006–2019)

	Mean	Std. Dev.	Observations
Security (IPUMS)	3.71	2.242	4529
Police (UCR)	1.909	1.831	4529
Police (IPUMS)	2.636	1.993	4529
Violent Crime	3.453	3.021	4529
Property Crime	24.96	13.44	4529
Property plus Violent Crime	28.41	15.88	4529
Percent Counties in Poverty	.3464	.4759	4529

Note: This table displays summary statistics on private security, police, as well as crime and poverty. All variables, except poverty, are measured per 1000 persons in the relevant county. Our poverty variable measures the percentage of counties that have 50% of the population in poverty measured defined by the SAIPE threshold. For comparison, police employment through the ACS is as follows: mean of 2.636, standard deviation of 0.993, and 4529 observations. Counties in our sample have more than 100,000 residents per census, policing and crime data from the UCR through the period of our panel, and private security data from ACS. A list of counties is included in the appendix

use that to determine if the county is below the SAIPE poverty threshold. This gives us a dummy variable that indicates if the 50*th* percentile for income is below the SAIPE poverty threshold.

3 Models

The primary goal of this analysis is to examine the separate and interactive effects of police and private security on criminal behavior. As a first step, we run a series of two-way fixed effects regressions with the model below. Due to the endogeneity issues mentioned earlier, this model will not isolate causal effects, but will describe the correlation between public and private security with respect to crime rates. The results indicate whether the presence of private security may bias estimations of policing on crime rates if a strong correlation is present. Our primary specification is:

$$Crime_{ct} = \beta_1 PubPol_{ct} + \beta_2 PrvSec_{ct} + \beta_3 \left(PubPol_{ct} \times PrvSec_{ct} \right) \\ + \beta_4 Poverty_{ct} + \lambda_c + \kappa_t + \epsilon_{ct} \tag{1}$$

where *PrvSec* represents private security and *PubPol* represents public police. We include county (λ_c) and year (κ_t) fixed effects, *c* represents the county and *t* represents the year. We also control for the poverty level by including an indicator variable if the median income in the county is below the poverty line. The outcome variable, *Crime*, includes violent crime, property crime and combined (property and violent) crime. All the values are per capita so the coefficients should be interpreted as marginal changes to the density of public police and private security. We use robust standard errors clustered at the county level.

To further explore the interaction between private security and police, we employ a slight modification to the model presented above. Specifically, we examine the interaction effects across different quantiles of police per capita. We first partition police per capita into intervals, $I_i = [0, 2.5), [2.5, 5), [5, 7.5), [7.5, \infty)$. We then interacted these police per capita indicator variables with the level of private security per capita to construct our interaction variables. Police per capita are broken into eight intervals with corresponding dummy variables I_i. The regression is identical to Eq. 1 except that we replace $PublicPolice_{ct}$ and the interaction term, $(PublicPolice \times PrivateSecurity)_{ct}$, with the following:

$$\sum_{4}^{i=1} \left[\gamma_i I_i PubPol_{ct} + \delta_i I_i \left(PubPol_{ct} \times PrivSec_{ct} \right) \right], \tag{2}$$

where I_t is one when the value of $PubPol_{ct}$ is within the specified interval, zero otherwise. With these changes, our more complex model becomes:

$$Crime_{ct} = \sum_{4}^{i=1} \gamma_i I_i PubPol_{ct} + \beta_2 PrivSec_{ct} +$$
$$\sum_{4}^{i=1} \delta_i I_i \left(PubPol_{ct} \times PrivSec_{ct} \right) + \beta_4 Poverty_{ct} + \lambda_c + \kappa_t + \epsilon_{ct} \tag{3}$$

As illustrated in Fig. A.1, we are unable to disentangle the endogeneity between crime levels, public police, and private security. This is because the number of police will influence crime and the amount of crime will influence the quantity of police. An area with low crime may be inherently safe or it may be that the quantity of police or security guards make the area safer. To isolate the direct effects of police or security guards on crime requires a quasi-exogenous shock to both police and private security. As stated in our introduction, the stable unit treatment value assumption likely threatens even well-identified estimation strategies. So, endogeneity may persist even with a quasi-exogenous shock. Other relevant variables are also unobserved, such as, for example, the location and time of day of these crimes, and the jurisdiction of private security, which could be impacting our analysis.

4 Results

We now turn to empirically examining the effects of private security and police on criminal behavior. As noted in Fig. A.1, dependencies between private and public security impact the level of crime in a particular region. For example, individuals, housing associations, retail businesses and banks may hire patrol officers to prevent and respond to break-ins. The decision to hire private security likely follows from the level of criminal behavior in a region, which is a function of the level and effectiveness of police resources. This endogeneity impacts any estimate that is obtained in our analysis. Still, these results provide a starting point upon which future

Table 2 The effect of police and private security on property and violent crime

	(1)	(2)	(3)	(4)
Police (UCR)	1.694	1.355	1.019	1.019
	(1.577)	(2.253)	(1.889)	(1.886)
Security (IPUMS)	0.304	−0.798*	−0.908**	−0.905**
	(0.440)	(0.458)	(0.372)	(0.371)
Police (UCR) × Security (IPUMS)	0.434**	0.537**	0.467**	0.466**
	(0.218)	(0.260)	(0.209)	(0.209)
Mean Crime Rate	28.41	28.41	28.41	28.41
Observations	4529	4529	4529	4529
Region FE	No	Yes	Yes	Yes
Time FE	No	No	Yes	Yes

Note: Table 2 shows our estimate of the effect of public and private security on combined crime using various empirical specifications. Column (1) includes no controls or fixed effects, while column (2) adds county fixed effects. Column (3) adds time fixed effects and column (4) includes time and county fixed effects as well as poverty controls
Robust standard errors in parentheses. Clustered at county level
$^*p < 0.10$, $^{**}p < 0.05$, $^{***}p < 0.01$

estimates can be compared. Importantly, the results below suggest that the presence of private policing at certain levels of police employment may influence crime rates. So, while we cannot overcome endogeneity in this analysis, the results of our analysis cast doubt on prior research that has examined the deterrence effect of police on crime that omit private security.

4.1 Descriptive

The results of our first series of regression estimates of Eq. 1 are reported in Table 2. We start by analyzing total crime and then turn to examining property and violent crime separately. Column 1 includes no fixed effects, while column 2 includes county fixed effects. Column 3 includes both county and year fixed effects and column 4 adds the poverty control. We cannot precisely estimate the effect of police per capita on overall crime rates, although prior causal estimates (e.g., Levitt (1997), DeAngelo et al. (2017), Mello (2019)) have established a negative relationship. Our variable of interest is the interaction coefficient.

The more saturated model specifications (columns 3 and 4) identify a negative relationship between private security per capita and combined crime rates. A one unit increase in security guards per capita (approximately 27.0% increase) yields a 0.9 reduction (about 3.2% decrease) in crime rates, indicating that private security does.

not have a meaningful impact on overall crime rates. The interaction effect between public police and private security is relatively stable across all specifications in Table 2. The positive coefficient on the interaction term indicates that, holding police levels constant, crime rates are higher in areas where private security is more prevalent. Again, holding police levels constant at their average level (approximately 2 per 1000 persons), the results in Table 2 indicate that a one unit increase in private security leads to 0.46 (1.4%) more crimes per capita.

The positive correlation of the interaction coefficient suggest that private security may influence crime, yet does not determine whether private security substitutes for police or complements them due to the endogeneity of the model. That is, our model cannot isolate whether increased private security presence enables police to redistribute due to private security coverage of certain areas (banks, schools, malls, colleges), and so substitutes for policing, or private security assists police in certain vulnerable locations. This is an important distinction insofar as the public and government bodies consider replacing police with private security, or reallocating certain functions to private entities. If private security cannot substitute for police but merely complement their functions, replacing police with private security cannot be expected to ensure the same level of public safety. But, again, the positive coefficient of the interaction variable cannot isolate substitution. Also, to be clear, the data utilized in this analysis do not include public-private partnerships between law enforcement agencies aimed at providing public safety.

On the other hand, the sign of the coefficient suggests a negligible influence of private security on crime rates. Prior estimates of police deterrence are likely unaffected by the presence of private security generally. However, this result is insufficient since private security may have a stronger correlation in counties with less police, but a weaker correlation in counties with more police. On the average, these differences would wash out. For example, if police reallocate resources in response to private security presence, crime rates may hold as police arrest in other areas or for other crimes. Greater specificity is required to determine if private security is biasing estimates of police deterrence. One way to see if there is any difference across counties relative to police density is binning counties via the interval measures presented above for police employment. We report our results of such an exercise next.

With our values for public police and their respective interaction term partitioned we can evaluate the interaction coefficient for each of the seven intervals we have for public police density. In Fig. 1 we plot the interaction coefficients δ_i on the y-axis and the public police indicator, I_i, on the x-axis. We find that between 0 and 5 police per 1000 people, the interaction coefficient is approximately 0.5 crimes per capita and statistically significant. The interaction effect drops to zero when there are more than 5 police per 1000 people. Therefore, the positive interaction effect that we observed in Table 2 is driven by regions with low public police presence. As public police levels rise, the interaction effect of public police and private security leads to reductions in overall crime rates. Police density does influence the correlation between private security and crime rates, though, again, results across bins cannot isolate whether private security substitute for, or complement, policing.

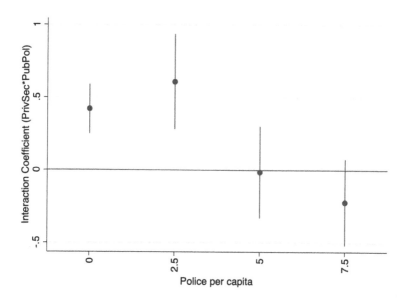

Fig. 1 Combined crime interaction effects

Note: In this figure the x-axis is the intervals of police per 1000 people. For example at 0 we have the counties with between [0, 2.5) police per 1000 people. The y-axis is the interaction coefficient, δ_i from Eq. 2 on the term $PublicPolice_{ct} \times PrivateSecurity_{ct}$. The errors are clustered on county. In this figure the left hand side of our regression is the summed amount of property and violent crimes per capita

4.1.1 Property Crime

The presence of private security and public police could have different effects on criminal behavior, depending on the type of crime. Since private security is typically hired with specific aims (e.g., protect merchandise within a store from theft, provide personal security, etc.), they arguably have different objectives than public police. Private security are not intended to deter or respond to any crime, but those crimes a private entity deems threatening to themselves or their property. Thus, it seems reasonable to expect private security to have more influence on specific types of crimes that fall within its purview. Comparing property crime to violent crime after considering their sum is a first step toward isolating trends for specific types of crime.

In Table A.1 we examine the effect public police and private security on property crimes. The first column omits county and year fixed effects, which are added in the middle two columns. Column 4 includes our control for poverty. The results are similar to those in Table 2, which may be unsurprising since property crimes are roughly eight times more common than violent crimes. The more saturated models report a negative and statistically significant relationship between private security and crime, while the interaction coefficient is positive and statistically significant across models. Note that, although the coefficient values are nearly the same as before, the mean of property crime rates is lower such that these values present greater effect sizes. Namely, an increase in 1 private security guard per capita correlates with 0.8 fewer property crimes per capita, which translates to a 3.2% reduction. The positive coefficient on our interaction term also suggests that private security influences crime rates relative to public policing (without isolating substitution or complementarity, again) and that the net effect of private security in an area is approximately zero (at the mean level of public policing).

Similar to Fig. 1, we present the results of our modification of column 4 according to different quantiles of police per capita in Fig. A.2a. The results support the expectation that private security has more influence on property crime, at least when there are 2.5 police per capita (approximately the average level of policing), a finding that is consistent with Meehan and Benson (2017). Surprisingly, there is a steep decline as police density increases and the interaction coefficients fall to zero when there are more than 5 police per capita. Thus, it appears that there is a threshold at which private security may have less influence on crime rates relative to policing, but for reasons mentioned above, there may be multiple explanations for this decline.

4.1.2   Violent Crime

Since property crimes are more prevalent than violent crime, it is unsurprising that the results in Table 2 and Table A.1 are quite similar. Still, it is worthwhile to compare the earlier results with violent crime rates and the results for such an analysis are reported in Table A.2. As seen before, we do not observe a statistically significant effect of public police on violent crime, likely due to endogeneity. However, we do observe a negative and statistically significant effect of private security on violent crime rates: a one unit increase in private security per 1000 persons in the population produces a -0.1 reduction in violent crime rates, which translates to a 3% reduction. Thus, we do not find statistically different results for the effect of private security on property versus violent crime rates.

Once again, we explore the interaction effect of private security and public police on violent crime rates and find that the interaction effects are strikingly similar to what we observed in the property crime results. Namely, holding public police constant at the mean of 2 police per 1000 citizens, the net effect of private security is nearly zero. When we explore the interaction effect by estimating separate coefficients in Fig. A.2b, we continue to see that higher levels of private security are associated with higher violent crime rates in locations with 0–5 police per 1000 citizens. However, as the number of public police increases, we observe a steep decline in the interaction coefficient.

Parallel results between property and violent crime suggest that private security has a negligible effect on police deterrence since, if there was an effect, we would expect different results. Most private security agencies aim to prevent property crime rather than violent crime. These results are inconclusive, however, given the high level of aggregation of crime types within a county. Private security is employer-bound unlike policing, and so may deter crimes relative to their employer or location. It may be that counties with higher levels of police and more crime reallocate resources to respond to high crime levels, and so depend upon the deterrence of private security in select locations.

4.2   An Attempt at Causal Estimates

So far the results do not incorporate any sources of quasi-random variation, limiting the interpretation of our estimates to correlations. To fit our results into the existing causal results (Mello, 2019), we examine how the measurement of private security at the county level is consequential for the effect of public security on crime. We examine how controlling for private security affects the relationship between quasi-randomly assigned police, via COPS grants as seen in Mello (2019), and crime.

4.2.1   Method and Data

We utilize two stage least squares regression estimates in which COPS grants serve as an instrumental variable for public police to examine the interactive effects between public police and private security. Under certain assumptions, notably a strong association between funding and police hiring (first stage) and that public police hiring is the only channel through which COPS grants affect crime (exclusion), COPS grants could be a valid instrument. The empirical validity of these assumptions are not the main focus of this paper, because they have already been addressed in the prior literature. Nevertheless, we present diagnostics for the first stage strength and discuss the role of our fixed effects in weakening the exclusion restriction. The main research interest is whether omitting private security biases the effect of police on crime.

Our first stage regression is:

$$Police_{cy} = \phi_1 COPS\ Dollars_{cy} + \mu_c + \rho_y + u_{cy}. \tag{4}$$

The new variable is COPS spending, which we describe in Appendix B.[7] All other subscripts and variable definition are as described in Sect. 2. We then estimate our second stage equation, which is specified:

$$Crime_{cy} = \beta_1 \widehat{Police}_{cy} + \mu_c + \rho_y + e_{cy}, \tag{5}$$

in which $Police$ are the predicted values for police from Eq. 4. This is the replication we perform in our dataset.

---

[7] COPS spending is at the agency-level which we aggregate up to the county level.

4.2.2 Not Holding Private Security Constant

Table 3 shows the first stage association between COPS grants and police staffing levels. A one million dollar increase in COPS grants is associated with between 0.003 and 0.086 additional police. Table 4 shows the association between COPS grants award amounts and total crime. We find statistically significant, positive associations between COPS grants and crime for most specifications. These effect sizes vary; an increase of $1 million dollars of COPS grants is associated with an additional 0.184–2.21 total crimes per 1000 people in a given county. This is consistent with the notion that additional police are able to identify more crime in an area, and potentially increasing deterrence of future criminal conduct (Table 5).

Table 3 First stage results

	Crime	Crime	Crime	Crime	Crime
Police	28.805***	25.875***	96.996	15.540	25.840***
	(6.905)	(5.295)	(145.674)	(15.244)	(3.981)
Observations	972	972	972	972	972
RKF-stat	3.411	3.629	0.321	1.177	6.790
Year-FE	–	X	–	X	X
County-FE	–	–	X	X	–
State-FE	–	–	–	–	X

Note: This table compares the independent variable of the amount of COPS Funding in millions of dollars to the dependent variable of the number of police per 1000 people within 324 counties across 3 years, 2009–2011. In columns 2–4 we add clustered standard errors on the county. In columns 2 we add year fixed effects and column 3 we add county fixed effects. Our final columns is the fully saturated model. These is a total of 972 observations in each model with an average of 2 police per 1000 people in a county

Cluster-robust standard errors in parentheses

$^*p < .1, ^{**}p < .05, ^{***}p < .01$

Table 4 Reduced form results

	Crime	Crime	Crime	Crime	Crime
Award millions	1.594***	1.609***	0.303**	0.184	2.211***
	(0.432)	(0.455)	(0.144)	(0.144)	(0.771)
Observations	972	972	972	972	972
Year-FE	–	X	–	X	X
County-FE	–	–	X	X	–
State-FE	–	–	–	–	X

Note: This table compares the independent variable of the amount of COPS Funding in millions of dollars to the dependent variable of the total crime count per 1000 people. There is a total of 324 counties across 3 years, 2009–2011. In columns 2–4 we add clustered standard errors on the county. In columns 2 we add year fixed effects and column 3 we add county fixed effects. Our final columns is the fully saturated model. These is a total of 972 observations in each model with an average total crime of 63 per 1000 people for each county

Cluster-robust standard errors in parentheses

$^*p < .1, ^{**}p < .05, ^{***}p < .01$

Table 5 Association between COPS funding and private security

	Priv. Sec.	Priv. Sec.	Priv. Sec.	Priv. Sec.	Priv. Sec.
Award millions	0.161***	0.169***	0.046***	0.048***	0.170***
	(0.022)	(0.024)	(0.016)	(0.017)	(0.038)
Observations	972	972	972	972	972
Year-FE	–	X	–	X	X
County-FE	–	–	X	X	–
State-FE	–	–	–	–	X

Note: This table compares the independent variable of the amount of COPS Funding in millions of dollars to the dependent variable of the number of private security per 1000 people. There is a total of 324 counties across 3 years, 2009–2011. In columns 2–4 we add clustered standard errors on the county. In columns 2 we add year fixed effects and column 3 we add county fixed effects. Our final columns is the fully saturated model. These is a total of 972 observations in each model with an average number of 4 private security per 1000 in a county
Cluster-robust standard errors in parentheses
$^*p < .1, ^{**}p < .05, ^{***}p < .01$

Table 6 IV officers and private results

	Crime	Crime	Crime	Crime
Police	15.540	14.682	25.840***	22.955***
	(15.019)	(14.930)	(3.981)	(4.761)
Priv. Sec.		0.210		1.448*
		(0.227)		(0.762)
RKF-stat	1.258	1.179	6.790	5.608
AR	E	E	[17.5,37.0]	[13.3,37.5]
State-FE	–	–	X	X
County-FE	X	X	–	–

Note: We compare 324 counties over 3 years for 972 observations in each column. Our first stage estimates the number of police by the amount of money from COPS funding in millions of dollars. Our second stage then correlates that to the total crime. Columns 1–2 use county fixed effects whereas columns 3–4 use state fixed effects. In columns 2,4 we add in private security as a control. The last column has positive statistically significance coefficient for private security under a 95% confidence interval. Across all columns we have a mean total crime of 63 per 1000 people in a county. RKF-Stat stands for the Kleibergen-Paap F-Statistic. The AR row represent the Anderson-Rubin Confidence set where E is short for the entire grid
Cluster-robust standard errors in parentheses
$^*p < .1, ^{**}p < .05, ^{***}p < .01$

Our two stage results, that do not account for private security, are presented in columns 1 and 3 of Table 6. We present the results without county fixed effects in column 1. As evidenced by the low first stage F-statistic of 1.258, the COPS grant instrument is weak when county fixed effects are added. This causes the relationship between police and crime to be statistically insignificant, though the coefficient is not intuitively small. The lack of significance with county fixed effects is likely due to there being only 3 observations per county and limited variation within county in either crime or COPS spending.

Removing county fixed effects and adding state fixed effects, as shown in column 3, police do have a statistically significant, positive association (at 99% confidence) with crime. Increasing police by 1 is associated with an increase of 25.8 crimes per 1000 people in a county. This coefficient may be partially biased, due to the mild strength of the relationship between COPS spending and police staffing that is demonstrated by a first stage F-statistic of 6.7. The increase in the first stage F-statistic, when state fixed effects are substituted for county fixed effects, suggests that at least some of the insignificance from column 1 is due to it being too difficult to find a within-county relationship between COPS spending and policing levels in this data. To address the possibility that the instrument strength leads to biased estimates, we present the Anderson-Rubin (AR) confidence set which is efficient for potentially weak instruments and is recommended for just-identified regressions (Anderson et al., 1949; Andrews et al., 2019). Using this weakinstrument robust procedure, we find strong evidence that a coefficient of 0 can be ruled out as the confidence set spans 17.5–37. While it would be ideal for there to be greater precision in these estimates, they provide an adequate benchmark for investigating how they change when private security is added to the model.

4.2.3   Association Between COPS Grants and Private Security

The literature and our replication exercises above ignore the potential that COPS grants are associated with private security. In fact, the association between COPS grants and private security is impossible to sign a priori. It could be that COPS grants and private security are positively associated if an area has high crime that private actors seek to address. Alternatively, public security investment could obviate the need for private security, making them negatively associated. This makes it impossible to sign the potential bias that results from omitting private security from regressions of crime on police, theoretically. If either of these situations were true, then regressions that estimate the effect of public security provided by COPS grants would be biased.

We estimate the empirical relationship between private security and COPS grants award amounts with the following regression:

$$Private_{cy} = \beta COPS\ Dollars + \mu_c + \rho_y + u_{cy}. \tag{6}$$

Table 5 shows the results. Regardless of which fixed effects are included, there is always a statistically significant (at 99% confidence), positive association between COPS funding and private security. Increasing COPS grants by one million dollars is associated with between 0.046 and 0.17 additional private security. This suggests there could be an issue since the association between COPS grants and private security is larger than the association between COPS grants and public police (which ranges from 0.003–0.086). This finding suggests that two stage regressions of crime on COPS-funded public security are, at best, biased without controlling for private security and, at worst, unidentified.

4.2.4   Public Security and Crime, Holding Private Security Constant

Next, we examine how holding private security constant affects the relationship between COPS-funded police and crime. Our final regression is specified:

$$Crime_{cy} = \beta_1 \widehat{Police}_{cy} + \beta_2 Private_{cy} + \mu_c + \rho_y + e_{cy}, \tag{7}$$

in which police are quasi-randomly assigned from COPS Grants and private security is held constant in both regressions. This is important because we still only have estimated one part of the omitted variable bias formula. While we have shown that $corr(private, COPS) > 0$, which implies that $corr(private, public) > 0$, we still do not know of a causal result that estimates $corr(private, crime)$. It is possible that this correlation could be either positive or negative, so it is necessary to see how β_1 changes when private security is added.

In the best case, identification can be restored by also controlling for private security. Next, we present the two stage results which implement this solution. Column 2 shows how controlling for private security affects the estimates of police on crime. The estimate on police drops to 14.6 (a reduction of 0.9) and remains statistically insignificant.

In column 4, we use state fixed effects which still account for many differences in enforcement and crime across states in large counties. While this comes at the potential cost of not controlling for county level characteristics, it does increase the precision of our estimates by a substantial amount. As shown in column 4, the estimate on public security is larger, but the standard errors are also smaller, such that the estimate would be significant even if it did not get larger. Additional police are associated with an additional 22.9 crimes and the AR confidence set, which is efficient for potentially weak instruments, finds a range of 13.3–37.5. The minimum of 13.3 is smaller than 17.5, which is the bottom of the confidence set when private security is not included. This implies that omitting private security may lead to upward bias on estimates of the association between police and total crime. While it is unlikely to be appropriate to attach a causal interpretation to the private security coefficient, we find that private security is also positively associated (at 90% confidence) with total crime. As shown in Table 7, these conclusions are broadly similar for both violent and property crimes.

5   Conclusion

This chapter is the first study to form a nation-wide dataset of public police and private security to examine whether private security can substitute for policing. It employs three models of analysis. First, an Ordinary Least Squares model that interacts police per capita with private security per capacity. We find a slightly negative coefficient on our interaction term, which suggests that an increase in private

Table 7 IV officers and private results

	Violent	Violent	Violent	Violent	Property	Property	Property	Property
Police	2.190	2.156	2.696***	2.404***	5.487	5.095	10.177***	9.029***
	(1.654)	(1.678)	(0.441)	(0.526)	(6.127)	(6.089)	(1.606)	(1.915)
Priv. Sec.		0.008		0.147*		0.096		0.576*
		(0.020)		(0.082)		(0.104)		(0.309)
RKF-stat	1.258	1.179	6.790	5.608	1.258	1.179	6.790	5.608
AR	D	D	[1.77,3.93]	[1.42,4.05]	E	E	[6.81,14.6]	[5.16,14.7]
State-FE	–	–	X	X	–	–	X	X
County-FE	X	X	–	–	X	X	–	–

Note: We compare 324 counties over 3 years for 972 observations in each column. Our first stage estimates the number of police by the amount of money from COPS funding in millions of dollars. Our second stage then correlates that to the violent crime in columns 1–4 and property crime in columns 5–8. Columns 1–2 and 3–6 use county fixed effects whereas columns 3–4 and 7–8 use state fixed effects. In columns 2,4 we add in private security as a control. RKF-Stat stands for the Kleibergen-Paap F-Statistic. The AR row represent the Anderson-Rubin Confidence set where E is short for the entire grid and D means the confidence set is disjoint over zero
Cluster-robust standard errors in parentheses
$^*p < .1, ^{**}p < .05, ^{***}p < .01$

security, holding police employment constant, correlates with a decrease in crime. However, when we distinguish between property crime and violent crime, the coefficient has a negligible difference. Since we expect private security to influence property crime, given the aims of most private security contracts, but such security to influence violent crimes less, our results suggest private security may have an overall negligible influence. Next, we bin (group) counties by their police density and run a similar analysis. Lower levels of police density result in a stronger positive correlation between a one unit increase in private security and crime, while the coefficient sharply declines to zero for counties with higher police density. Due to endogeneity, however, we cannot isolate the possible deterrence effect of private security for counties with sparser police density.

This research provides a comprehensive analysis of the effect of public police and private security, independently and in conjunction with one another, on community safety. Leveraging data on public police from UCR, private police from IPUMS, and crime information from UCR, we find that public police and private security are complements to one another. We also find that private security is significantly more negatively correlated with property crime than violent crime.

This work builds on previous theoretical work (e.g., Helsley and Strange (2005) and Lee and Pinto (2009)) that discerns the effect of private and public security on public safety, noting that increases in private policing reduce aggregate expenditure on traditional policing. While we do not test this hypothesis directly, the implications are the essence of the main analysis presented in this work.

Although the current research is not able to unearth causal relationships between private security, public police, and crime, we highlight an important omitted variable that likely confounds any analysis that aims to estimate the casual effect of public police on crime. Specifically, we note that the omission of private security in the estimation of public police on crime likely leads to an upward bias on estimates of public police on crime. Thus, our research notes that previous estimates of the effect of police on crime that do not account for the presence of private security should be viewed with skepticism.

Our research contains a couple important policy implications. First, knowledge about the presence of private security could lead to significant improvements in public safety if publicly funded law enforcement agencies could leverage the whereabouts of private security. While private security is unlikely to have a large impact on violent crime directly, allowing public security to reallocate scarce resources toward situations that are more prone to violent crime could generate an effect. Second, as conversations about the appropriate levels of publicly funded policing continue to occur, it is important that discussions of private security are incorporated into these discussions. While the omission of private security in empirical estimates of public police on crime are likely overstating the impact, it is important that the channel through which private security is impacting the police-crime relationship is better understood. Private security does not offset the role of public police, but might deter some property crime, which enables law enforcement to devote their time to more serious offenses.

While our work finds that private security likely confounds the estimated relationship between public police and crime, we must reiterate that our results should be viewed as suggestive, but not causal. Thus, future work would significantly benefit from leveraging quasi-experimental environments where as-if random shocks to both private and public security occur to determine the independent and interdependent effects of security on public safety. We caution, however, that studies which examine the effects of private security in small geographic regions (e.g., MacDonald et al. (2016) and Cheng and Long (2018)) might not produce externally valid findings.

Appendix

A. Additional Tables and Figures (Tables A.1 and A.2)

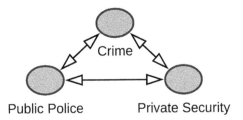

Fig. A.1 Relationship between crime, public police, and private security
Note: This figure shows the endogenous relationships between public police, private security and crime that make it difficult to disentangle the causal impact public security of private police on crime rates

Table A.1 Effect of public and private security on property crime

	(1)	(2)	(3)	(4)
Police (UCR)	1.615	1.213	0.902	0.903
	(1.294)	(2.017)	(1.686)	(1.684)
Security (IPUMS)	0.409	−0.696*	−0.805**	−0.803**
	(0.366)	(0.412)	(0.333)	(0.333)
Police (UCR) × Security (IPUMS)	0.255	0.478**	0.415**	0.414**
	(0.180)	(0.234)	(0.187)	(0.187)
Mean Crime Rate	24.96	24.96	24.96	24.96
Observations	4529	4529	4529	4529
Region FE	No	Yes	Yes	Yes
Time FE	No	No	Yes	Yes

Note: OLS estimates with property crime on the left hand side. Through each column we include our various fixed effects to show that our estimates change for private security
Robust standard errors in parentheses. Clustered at county level
$*p < 0.10, **p < 0.05, ***p < 0.01$

Table A.2 Effect of public and private security on violent crime

	(1)	(2)	(3)	(4)
Police (UCR)	0.0792	0.142	0.116	0.117
	(0.295)	(0.236)	(0.203)	(0.202)
Security (IPUMS)	−0.105	−0.102**	−0.103**	−0.102**
	(0.090)	(0.048)	(0.041)	(0.041)
Police (UCR) × Security (IPUMS)	0.179***	0.0587**	0.0528**	0.0524**
	(0.043)	(0.028)	(0.024)	(0.024)
Mean Crime Rate	3.453	3.453	3.453	3.453
Observations	4529	4529	4529	4529
Region FE	No	Yes	Yes	Yes
Time FE	No	No	Yes	Yes

Note: In this table we regress with the left hand side being violent crime. The result is surprising because we would not really expect statistical significance in security guards stopping violent crime
Robust standard errors in parentheses. Clustered at county level
$*p < 0.10, **p < 0.05, ***p < 0.01$

(a) Property Crime: Police per 1,000 with Interaction Coefficient

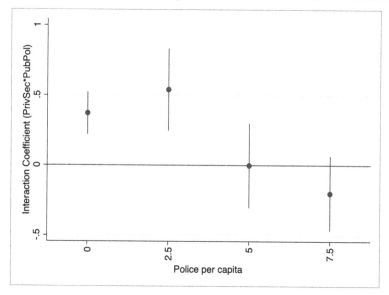

(b) Violent Crime: Police per 1,000 with Interaction Coefficient

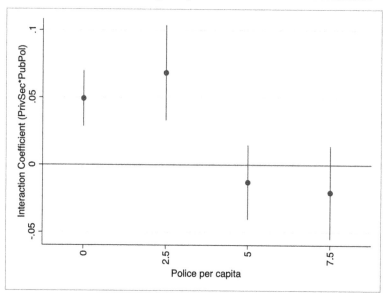

Fig. A.2 Interaction coefficients compared to property and violent crime. (**a**) Property Crime: Police per 1000 with Interaction Coefficient. (**b**) Violent Crime: Police per 1000 with Interaction Coefficient

Note: In both of there figures the x-axis are intervals of police per 1000 people. For example at 0 we have the counties with between [0, 2.5) police per 1000 people. The y-axis is the interaction coefficient, δ_i from Eq. 2 on the term $PublicPolice_{ct} \times PrivateSecurity_{ct}$. The errors are clustered on county. In the Fig. A.2a the left hand side is the amount of property crime per capita. In contrast, Fig. A.2b has violent crime per capita on the left hand side

B. COPS Replication Data

Our primary source of data for this study is from Steve Ross, who was kind enough to provide the original FOIA requested data. The dataset is simple dataset containing the agency's ORI, agency name and the amount of award from COPS funding received, along with their COPS score. The COPS dataset is identified by ORI for each agency. The issue with this dataset is that there are 2169 observations that had a broken ORI that did not match with the FBI UCR ORI. This is because the agency either does not have an ORI or the ORI was not well defined. As a result, we needed a method for mapping the agencies into a FIPS without an ORI and given the name, so we turned to geocoders.

Recovering Data

Given the 2169 observations across all years that did not have a FIPS, there was only 1441 of agencies without a FIPS code (this is collapsing on year). We still did have that agency's name and state. We formulated a query string using the name and state and processed it through Google's geocoder to find a latitude and longitude for each of the agencies. Then we used a open-source reverse-geocoder called Pelias to map the latitude and longitude into a county and find the corresponding FIP code. After this process, we were able to find FIPS to 2040 out of the 2168. We dropped the last 129 observations that we were unable to match to a FIPS.

COPS Summary Statistics

Now that we have our COPS dataset finalized we can review some of the basic summary statistics. First, we want to know how much money was actually distributed. In total, we calculate $2.68 billion dollars sent through the COPS program where $2.10 billion dollars were just within 2009–2011. Most of this money seems to be awarded through the first few years, between the years of 2009–2011. There is a total of 9111 agencies that received funding from 2009–2016 and 8803 of these were between the years of 2009–2011 (Fig. B.1).

Next we want to ask, if the same agencies are being funded over the years. To do this we look at the distribution of funding over the years so see if agencies have [received funding? Finish the sentence.]

As you can see in Fig. B.2 that most agencies received funding between the years of 2009–2011 that is because that is the main year that the 2009 President Obama signed the American Recovery and Reinvestment Act which provided the allocated $1 Billion dollars directed towards hiring police officers through the COPS program between the years of 2009–2011. The COPS program continued to exist but these are the years that the funding was directed towards.

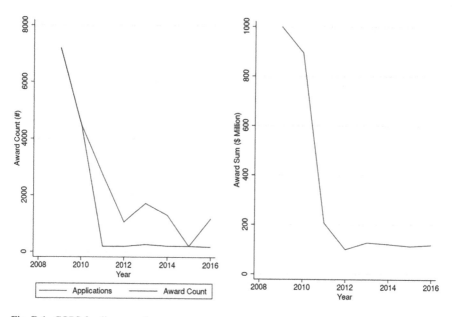

Fig. B.1 COPS funding over the years

Note: On the left we show the number of awards and applicants for the COPS program and on the right we show the total value in millions of dollar awarded throughout the years

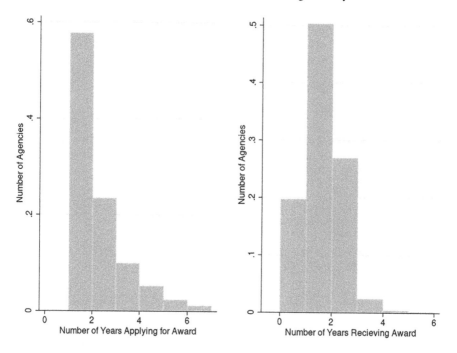

Fig. B.2 COPS funding over the years

Note: Both of these plots have the x-axis showing the number of year the agency has been on record. On the left we show the number of times they applied to cops and their percentage on the y-axis; on the right we show how many years the agency would receive funding. On the left you can see that most of the agencies applied for the COPS funding for 1 year the it drops off proportionate to some power-law distribution. On the right you can see that most commonly, these agencies would receive funding for 2–3 years

Matching to UCR and IPUMS

Lastly, we want to compare estimates of COPS data to our values from IPUMS and UCR. To do this we aggregate our COPS data onto the FIPS level. We do this by summing the award of each ORI for a given FIP. We isolate our research to the years of 2009–2011 when the shock actually occurred. We are left with the 531 awards and a total of 913 FIPS that we have data on. In our further results we use state fixed effects because by comparing FIPS we are comparing counties. Some FIPS are non-county entities but all of the ones in our dataset are have an isomorphic county to FIPS mapping. Next, we want to show some of our results to compare it to the original results found in other papers.

References

Anderson, T. W., Rubin, H., et al. (1949). Estimation of the parameters of a single equation in a complete system of stochastic equations. *Annals of Mathematical Statistics, 20*(1), 46–63.

Andrews, I., Stock, J. H., & Sun, L. (2019). Weak instruments in instrumental variables regression: Theory and practice. *Annual Review of Economics, 11*, 727–753.

Baicker, K., & Jacobson, M. (2007). Finders keepers: Forfeiture laws, policing incentives, and local budgets. *Journal of Public Economics, 91*(11), 2113–2136. Retrieved from https://www.sciencedirect.com/science/article/pii/S0047272707000539. https://doi.org/10.1016/j.jpubeco.2007.03.009

Bernstein, L. (1992). Opting out of the legal system: Extralegal contractual relations in the diamond industry. *The Journal of Legal Studies, 21*(1), 115–157.

Cheng, C., & Hoekstra, M. (2013). Does strengthening self-defense law deter crime or escalate violence? Evidence from expansions to castle doctrine. *The Journal of Human Resources, 48*(3), 821–853. Retrieved 2022-04-07, from http://www.jstor.org/stable/23799103

Cheng, C., & Long, W. (2018). Improving police services: Evidence from the French quarter task force. *Journal of Public Economics, 164*, 1–18.

DeAngelo, G., & Hansen, B. (2014, May). Life and death in the fast lane: Police enforcement and traffic fatalities. *American Economic Journal: Economic Policy, 6*(2), 231–257. Retrieved from http://www.aeaweb.org/articles?id=10.1257/pol.6.2.231. https://doi.org/10.1257/pol.6.2.231

DeAngelo, G., & Smith, T. (2020). Private security, maritime piracy and the provision of international public safety. *Journal of Risk & Uncertainty, 60*, 77–97.

DeAngelo, G., Humphreys, B. R., & Reimers, I. (2017). Are public and private enforcement complements or substitutes? Evidence from high frequency data. *Journal of Economic Behavior & Organization, 141*, 151–163.

DeAngelo, G., Gittings, R. K., & Ross, A. (2018). Police incentives, policy spillovers, and the enforcement of drug crimes. *Review of Law & Economics, 14*(1), 20160033.

Di Tella, R., & Schargrodsky, E. (2004). Do police reduce crime? Estimates using the allocation of police forces after a terrorist attack. *American Economic Review, 94*(1), 115–133.

Draca, M., Machin, S., & Witt, R. (2010). Crime displacement and police interventions: Evidence from London's "Operation Theseus". In *The economics of crime: Lessons for and from Latin America* (pp. 359–374). National Bureau of Economic Research. Retrieved from https://ideas.repec.org/h/nbr/nberch/11849.html

Ellickson, R. C. (1985). Of Coase and cattle: Dispute resolution among neighbors in Shasta county. *Stanford Law Review, 38*, 623.

Ellickson, R. C. (1989). A hypothesis of wealth-maximizing norms: Evidence from the whaling industry. *The Journal of Law, Economics, & Organization, 5*, 83.

Ellickson, R. C. (1991). *Order without law*. Harvard University Press.

Figlio, D. N., & O'Sullivan, A. (2001). The local response to tax limitation measures: Do local governments manipulate voters to increase revenues? *The Journal of Law and Economics, 44*(1), 233–257.

Fry, A. J., O'Riordan, D. P., & Geanellos, R. (2002). Social control agents or front-line carers for people with mental health problems: Police and mental health services in Sydney, Australia. *Health & Social Care in the Community, 10*(4), 277–286. Retrieved from https://onlinelibrary.wiley.com/doi/abs/10.1046/j.1365-2524.2002.00371.x.   https://doi.org/10.1046/j.1365-2524.2002.00371.x

Gill, M. (2015). Senior police officers' perspectives on private security: Sceptics, pragmatists and embracers. *Policing and Society, 25*(3), 276–293.

Greif, A. (1993). Contract enforceability and economic institutions in early trade: The Maghribi traders' coalition. *The American Economic Review, 83*, 525–548.

Helsley, R. W., & Strange, W. C. (2005). Mixed markets and crime. *Journal of Public Economics, 89*(7), 1251–1275.

Kantor, S., Kitchens, C. T., & Pawlowski, S. (2021). Civil asset forfeiture, crime, and police incentives: Evidence from the comprehensive crime control act of 1984. *Economic Inquiry, 59*(1), 217–242. Retrieved from https://onlinelibrary.wiley.com/doi/abs/10.1111/ecin.12952. https://doi.org/10.1111/ecin.12952

Krameddine, Y. I., & Silverstone, P. H. (2016). Police use of handcuffs in the homeless population leads to long-term negative attitudes within this group. *International Journal of Law and Psychiatry, 44*, 81–90. Retrieved from https://www.sciencedirect.com/science/article/pii/S0160252715001442. https://doi.org/10.1016/j.ijlp.2015.08.034

Kurwa, R. (2019). Building the digitally gated community: The case of Nextdoor. *Surveillance & Society, 17*(1/2), 111–117.

Lee, K., & Pinto, S. M. (2009). Crime in a multi-jurisdictional model with private and public prevention. *Journal of Regional Science, 49*(5), 977–996.

Levitt, S. D. (1997). Using electoral cycles in police hiring to estimate the effect of police on crime. *The American Economic Review, 87*(3), 270–290. Retrieved from http://www.jstor.org/stable/2951346

MacDonald, J. M., Klick, J., & Grunwald, B. (2016). The effect of private police on crime: Evidence from a geographic regression discontinuity design. *Journal of the Royal Statistical Society: Series A (Statistics in Society), 179*(3), 831–846.

Makowsky, M. D., Stratmann, T., & Tabarrok, A. (2019). To serve and collect: The fiscal and racial determinants of law enforcement. *The Journal of Legal Studies, 48*(1), 189–216.

Maskaly, J., Donner, C. M., Lanterman, J., & Jennings, W. G. (2011). On the association between SROs, private security guards, use-of-force capabilities, and violent crime in schools. *Journal of Police Crisis Negotiations, 11*(2), 159–176.

McClellan, C. B., & Tekin, E. (2012, June). *Stand your ground laws, homicides, and injuries* (NBER Working Papers No. 18187). National Bureau of Economic Research, Inc. Retrieved from https://ideas.repec.org/p/nbr/nberwo/18187.html

Meehan, B., & Benson, B. (2017). Does private security affect crime? A test using state regulations as instruments. *Applied Economics, 49*(48), 4911–4924.

Mello, S. (2019). More COPS, less crime. *Journal of Public Economics, 172*, 174–200.

Nemeth, C. P. (2017). *Private security and the law*. CRC Press.

Nicholson-Crotty, S., & O'Toole, J., Laurence J. (2004, 01). Public management and organizational performance: The case of law enforcement agencies. *Journal of Public Administration Research and Theory, 14*(1), 1–18. Retrieved from https://doi.org/10.1093/jopart/muh001

Noaks, L. (2000). Private cops on the block: A review of the role of private security in residential communities. *Policing and Society: An International Journal, 10*(2), 143–161.

Patton, E. A., et al. (2019). *Knowing your neighbors: An analysis of the social media app "Nextdoor" and human interaction* (Unpublished doctoral dissertation).

Prenzler, T., & Sarre, R. (2012). Public-private crime prevention partnerships. In *Policing and security in practice* (pp. 149–167). Springer.

Renauer, B. C., Duffee, D. E., & Scott, J. D. (2003). Measuring police-community co-production: Trade-offs in two observational approaches. *Policing: An International Journal of Police Strategies & Management, 26*(1), 9–28.

Skarbek, D. (2011). Governance and prison gangs. *American Political Science Review, 105*(4), 702–716.

Tolman, R. M., & Weisz, A. (1995). Coordinated community intervention for domestic violence: The effects of arrest and prosecution on recidivism of woman abuse perpetrators. *Crime & Delinquency, 41*(4), 481–495.

van Steden, R., & Mehlbaum, S. (2021). Do-it-yourself surveillance: The practices and effects of WhatsApp neighbourhood crime prevention groups. *Crime, Media, Culture, 18*(4), 543–560.

Weitzer, R., Tuch, S. A., & Skogan, W. G. (2008). Police–community relations in a majority-black city. *Journal of Research in Crime and Delinquency, 45*(4), 398–428.

Williams, J. W. (2004, 09). Reflections on the private versus public policing of economic crime. *The British Journal of Criminology, 45*(3), 316–339. Retrieved from https://doi.org/10.1093/bjc/azh083

Wood, J. D., Watson, A. C., & Fulambarker, A. J. (2017). The "gray zone" of police work during mental health encounters: Findings from an observational study in Chicago. *Police Quarterly, 20*(1), 81–105. Retrieved from https://doi.org/10.1177/1098611116658875 (PMID: 28286406)

Zhao, J., Scheider, M. C., & Thurman, Q. (2002). Funding community policing to reduce crime: Have COPS grants made a difference? *Criminology & Public Policy, 2*(1), 7–32.

Public-Private Security Partnerships. Can They Meet the Growing Challenges of Law Enforcement?

Frank Vram Zerunyan

Abstract Police powers, like other powers of the federal government, are limited under the United States Constitution. Through the Tenth Amendment of that constitution, states, on the other hand, enjoy extensive police powers. Each state constitution delegates this authority to municipalities, which include counties and cities. While public and private collaborations exist and are indispensable, critical functions of law enforcement, like detentions, arrests, and incarceration, still reside in the public sector and specifically with sworn peace officers. In this chapter, we explore the role of each sector and the possible expansion of functions with existing examples, which make these partnerships very valuable.

Abbreviations

ALPR	Automatic License Plate Reader
BSIS	Bureau of Security and Investigative Services
CA	California
COAST	Cash Overtime Allotment for Scheduling and Timekeeping
HOA	Home Owners Association
LAPD	Los Angeles Police Department
MHART	Mental Health and Response Team
MOU	Memorandum of Understanding
MPTFWP	Motion Picture Television Filming Work Permit
POST	Peace Officer Standards and Training
PSO	Public Safety Officer
RHE	Rolling Hills Estates

F. V. Zerunyan (✉)
USC Sol Price School of Public Policy, Director of Executive Education, The Bedrosian Center on Governance, USC ROTC and Nautical Science Programs, Los Angeles, CA, USA
e-mail: frank.zerunyan@usc.edu

© The Author(s), under exclusive license to Springer Nature Switzerland AG 2023   129
E. A. Blackstone et al. (eds.), *Handbook on Public and Private Security*,
Competitive Government: Public Private Partnerships,
https://doi.org/10.1007/978-3-031-42406-9_6

SCOTUS   Supreme Court of the United States
UT   University of Texas

1 Introduction

Police powers are generally the critical ability of governments to preserve peace through laws for the public good. The police power of the United States federal government is limited to its enumerated powers under the Constitution.[1] On the other hand, the broad police powers are delineated in the Tenth Amendment, which states, "[t]he powers not delegated to the United States by the Constitution, nor prohibited by it to the states, are reserved to the states respectively, or to the people."[2] This delegation of power is the central tenet of our federalism. Decentralized governance, also known as federalism, finds its roots in the Articles of Confederation. They declare, "each state retains its sovereignty, freedom and independence, and every power, jurisdiction and right, which is not by this confederation expressly delegated to the United States, in Congress assembled."[3] The Tenth Amendment is the natural progression the Federalists had advocated during the adoption of the Constitution.[4]

Therefore, the state's regulatory power under its constitution is extensive. The United States Supreme Court (SCOTUS) in Berman v. Parker (1954)[5] described the traditional application of these police powers to include "[p]ublic safety, public health, morality, peace and quiet, law and order." Today these applications are even broader. In 2019, the California Supreme Court expanded "[t]he inherent local police power" to include "broad authority to determine, for purposes of the public health, safety, and welfare, the appropriate uses of land," and even "the authority to establish aesthetic conditions for land use."[6] The Massachusetts supreme court found the state's police power to be so fundamental that "the legislature cannot surrender its broad authority to regulate matters within its core police power," including regulating gambling even if legally permissible.[7]

These broad powers represent a significant challenge to state and municipal governments, which find it difficult to overcome the challenge independently. Therefore, the intergovernmental collaborations facilitated by the "Lakewood Plan" have become the staple of law enforcement activities in the State of California and a few other states. On the other hand, while private security collaborations have their own

---

[1] U.S. CONSTITUTION Article I Section 8.
[2] U.S. CONSTITUTION amend. X.
[3] ARTICLES OF CONFEDERATION of 1781, art II.
[4] See THE FEDERALIST No. 45 (James Madison).
[5] U.S. Supreme Court. Berman v. Parker, 348 U.S. 26 (1954).
[6] T-Mobile West LLC v. City and County of San Francisco (2016) 3 Cal.App.5th 334.
[7] Abdow v. Attorney General (2014) 468 Mass. 478.

constitutional and democratic difficulties, partnerships are also inevitable and necessary. These partnerships, especially considering the current context to re-imagine police powers and law enforcement.

This chapter discusses policing in general at the state level—the distinction between independent and contract cities in California, and the various public and private partnership regulations to further implement public safety with first responders. Finally, the chapter concludes with a few twenty-first-century re-imagination of law enforcement using public and private first responders deployed currently at universities which may become the model for the future of law enforcement.

2   Sources of California City Powers and the Lakewood Plan

California cities derive their powers directly from the California Constitution. That document in Article XI describes cities and counties and their ability to make and enforce all local, police, sanitary, and other ordinances and regulations not in conflict with general laws within their city limits.[8] Part of this Article is known as the "police power" and is the source of counties' and cities' regulatory authority to protect public health, safety, and welfare.[9] While other city and county powers are also described in the California Constitution, the focus of this chapter is the "police power" and the collaborations designed or permitted by statute in California to protect the public.

3   The "Lakewood Plan" and California Law on "Contracting"

The governance model of the Lakewood Plan, or Contracting Model, encourages inter-organizational networks of public and private sectors to solve policy and public administration problems jointly. The "Lakewood Plan," named after its birthplace, the city of Lakewood, California, was devised to facilitate the incorporation of newer cities that sought to control their neighborhoods. The so-called Contracting Model was created by the Lakewood Plan to allow public agencies and private organizations to collaborate in the delivery of municipal services. The model relies on the sharing of resources by various actors but also counts on each actor's strengths in the collaboration to bring efficiencies in the delivery of public services.[10]

---

[8] For a comprehensive review of California's Local Governance see Frank Vram Zerunyan, *The Evolution of the Municipal Corporation and the Innovations of Local Governance in California to Preserve Home Rule and Local Control*, 44 Fordham Urb. L.J. 217 (2017).

[9] Cal. CONSTITUTION Article XI Section 7.

[10] Zerunyan, F. V., & Pirnejad, P. (2014, April 2). From contract cities to mass collaborative governance. *American City & County*.

The motive behind the incorporation of Lakewood was to retain local control over the intensity and nature of services provided locally. The purpose of what became known as the "Lakewood Plan" was merely to eliminate duplication and rely on the efficiencies of various government service providers to deliver public administration cost-effectively.

Several California statutes facilitate the implementation of the Contracting Model. First, Government Code Section 54981 provides,

> The legislative body of any local agency may contract with any other local agency for the performance by the latter of municipal services or functions within the territory of the former.[11]

Rather than having a traditional city police department, more than 30% of California's 482 cities[12] contract with their county sheriff's department for law enforcement services. For example, The Los Angeles County Sheriff's Department is one of the largest providers of contract law enforcement services in the world. The earliest forms of intergovernmental contracts in California are traced back to 1891. The California Legislature allowed cities to contract with counties "for the performance of property assessment and tax collection." La Verne, California, was the first city to use this statute in 1907.[13]

Intergovernmental contract services in Los Angeles County expanded exponentially in 1954. The City of Lakewood and The Los Angeles County Sheriff's Department entered into the very first agreement for one government entity to provide services to another independent government entity in law enforcement. While most cities contract with the Los Angeles County Sheriff Department, contracting inter-jurisdictions is also possible. For example, the City of Santa Fe Springs in 1995 became the first municipality in Los Angeles County to contract with an adjoining city (City of Whittier) for police services. In 2003, Cudahy ended its contract with the Los Angeles County Sheriff Department and contracted with the neighboring Maywood Police Department for police services. However, that contract ended when Maywood's department disbanded, forcing Cudahy back to the Sheriff's Department.[14]

Since 1954, all but one of the cities incorporated in Los Angeles County have adopted the Lakewood Plan. Intergovernmental law enforcement contracting in Los Angeles County has expanded to include transit authorities, school districts, court security, and custody services. While other services are also provided by typically a larger municipal organization like the county, they are outside the purview of this chapter. Still, they include fire suppression, public works, animal control, plan check for building or remodeling, etc.

---

[11] California Code, Government Code, Section 54981.

[12] https://sgf.senate.ca.gov/sites/sgf.senate.ca.gov/files/city_facts_2016.pdf

[13] Misner, G. E. (1961). The police service contract in California. An instrument of functional integration. *The Journal of Criminal Law, Criminology, and Police Science, 52*(4), 445–452.

[14] https://www.laalmanac.com/crime/cr69.php

The intergovernmental contract system offers a wide range of services at a reduced cost, allowing each Contract City, governmental authority, or special district to choose a level of service that best meets the needs of its constituency. Duplicate costs are avoided because contract cities, authorities, and special districts draw upon the full potential of their sheriff's department, sharing support resources and paying only their proportionate "user costs." As a result of this "cost-sharing" concept, contract cities, authorities, or special districts can obtain an optimum level of police service for a lesser cost than would be required to maintain their own police department.

In addition to intergovernmental contracts, California law under the Contracting Model also allows private organizations to participate in the delivery of municipal services, including law enforcement.

In the context of California's Contracting Model today, the relevant statutes facilitating collaboration are in the California Government Code, which provides:

> The legislative body may contract with any specially trained and experienced person, firm or corporation for special services and advice in financial, economic, accounting, engineering, legal or administrative matters,[15]

and

> The legislative body of any public or municipal corporation or district may contract with and employ any persons for the furnishing to the corporation or district special services and advice in financial, economic, accounting, engineering, legal, or administrative matters if such persons are specially trained and experienced and competent to perform the special services required.[16]

Typically, these private sector organizations contracting with municipalities include trash haulers, street sweepers, engineers, accountants, and auditors. Law enforcement contracts are with private code enforcement officers, prosecuting attorneys, and some private security services, especially during major events. Most act under the color of law and authority of the municipalities they serve with qualified immunity within the scope of their employment. However, one exceptional and critical distinction is that they are not sworn peace officers with the power to search, detain, and arrest. This power is reserved for the sworn peace officer protecting the public.

4   Who Is a Peace Officer?

Peace officers, most generically, are law enforcement officials with the duty to enforce laws and preserve the peace for all people. California's Criminal Code defines this person as "who otherwise meets all standards imposed by law on a peace officer ... no person other than those designated in this chapter is a peace officer."[17]

---

[15] California Code, Government Code, Section 37103.
[16] California Code, Government Code Section 53060.
[17] California Penal Code Section 830.

The California Commission on Peace Officer Standards and Training ("POST")[18] requires individuals applying to be peace officers to achieve minimum standards prescribed by law. These standards include fingerprints and background checks, citizenship and residency, good moral character, psychological evaluation, reading and writing abilities, and minimum high school graduation or equivalency, which is being challenged today, perhaps requiring a college education. While these may be the state's minimum standards, the law in California allows local hiring authorities to set higher standards. This local hiring may vary from department to department. For example, some agencies will only hire individuals after graduating from a basic law enforcement academy. In contrast, others will employ individuals and send them through an academy as trainees or cadets. Some agencies require that an individual attend the agency's academy regardless of the previous completion of another academy.[19]

The Penal Code in California generally defines a peace officer as "[A] sheriff, undersheriff, or deputy sheriff, employed in that capacity, of a county, a chief of police of a city or chief, director, or chief executive officer of a consolidated municipal public safety agency that performs police functions, a police officer, employed in that capacity and appointed by the chief of police or chief, director, or chief executive of a public safety agency, of a city, a chief of police, or police officer of a district." These districts include airports and port districts.[20]

The authority of these peace officers extends to the entire state as described by the Penal Code. This authority is for a peace officer to search lawfully, detain or arrest anyone for a crime committed or where probable cause for the commission of a crime exists.[21] This authority is critical in the differentiation between sworn peace officers and private security engaged in law enforcement.

The definition of a peace officer is further extended to the State Attorney General and his agents at the Department of Justice, the Highway Patrol, the University of California and California State University police, Department of Correction, Department of Fish and Game, Parks and Recreation, Forestry, Department of Alcoholic Beverages, State Fair, Cannabis Control, all departments of Consumer Affairs, etc.[22]

California law also empowers few other non-traditional "peace officers" to exercise the powers of arrest.[23] These include cemetery and health facilities personnel designated under the Health and Safety Code,[24] security officers for independent institutions of higher education, individuals employed by transit authorities, and code enforcement officers to enforce laws related to illegal waste dumping or littering. The arrest must occur during employment, and each officer must successfully

---

[18] https://post.ca.gov/how-do-I-become-a-peace-officer
[19] Ibid.
[20] California Penal Code Section 830.1.
[21] California Penal Code Section 830.1 (1).
[22] California Penal Code Sections 830.2 and 830.3.
[23] California Penal Code Section 830.7.
[24] California Health and Safety Code Sections 8325 and 1250.

complete a course.[25] In addition, all these employers must sign a memorandum of understanding (MOU) with their respective local law enforcement jurisdictions to retain the rights of a "peace officer."[26] For example, the University of Southern California (USC), located in Los Angeles, maintains an MOU with the Los Angeles Police Department. The "Public Safety Officer" (PSO) of USC's Department of Public Safety (DPS) wears a distinctive uniform, is armed, and is trained at a POST-accredited training academy.[27]

5   Who Is a Private Security Guard or Officer?

A private security guard/proprietary private security officer is assigned to protect specific people and property. Their function is generally to observe and report. They enjoy no greater authority than an ordinary citizen vis a vis another. This limitation on power may include detecting some of the same offenses that would cause a peace officer to act, such as a fight or burglary. Still, they have no constitutional authority to detain or arrest. However, most states have statutes facilitating the process commonly referred to as a "citizen's arrest." This same right is theoretically available to private security guards or officers, but most private organizations avoid this process for civil liability reasons.

Citizen arrests are lawful in certain limited situations, such as when a private citizen personally witnesses a violent crime and then detains the perpetrator. This scenario means that any person can physically detain another to arrest them. Detention could be as simple as preventing the perpetrator from leaving or physically holding the perpetrator. Any physical resistance to such a lawful citizen's arrest may add criminal assault to the list of crimes committed by the perpetrator.[28]

In California, "[A] private person may arrest another:

1. For a public offense committed or attempted in his presence.
2. When the person arrested has committed a felony, although not in his presence.
3. When a felony has been in fact committed, and he has reasonable cause for believing the person arrested to have committed it."

But for this law, any detention of another creates civil tort liability in an assault, battery, and false imprisonment. This serious potential risk of harm and damage makes private security guards, officers, and their employers pause. For this reason, every security guard company rigorously trains its employees on the "power to arrest," leaving the responsibility to a peace officer.

---

[25] California Penal Code Section 832.

[26] California Penal Code Section 830.7.

[27] https://dps.usc.edu/about-dps/types-of-officers/

[28] See People v. Garcia (1969) 274 Cal.App.2d 100.

A security guard/proprietary private security officer may also be responsible for maintaining specific company rules established by their employer. Typically empowered by the property owner, the guard or private security officer may prevent trespassers from entering private property. They may require employees to show badges and the content of purses or containers. They may monitor safety standards, report hazards, block exits, perform fire safety measures, or otherwise manage the proper use of the property. No matter the function, the roles are never the same. A peace officer is charged with the enforcement of laws and the protection of all people. A security guard or proprietary private security officer is responsible for protecting only specific people or property they are hired to protect.

In California, the business and Professions Code defines a security guard or private security officer as "an employee of a private patrol operator, or an employee of a lawful business or public agency who is not exempted pursuant to Section 7582.2, who performs the functions as described in subdivision (a) on or about the premises owned or controlled by the customer of the private patrol operator or by the guard's employer or in the company of persons being protected."[29]

To be eligible to apply for a security guard registration, the applicant must be of 18 years of age, undergo a background check, and complete the "Power of Arrest" training.[30] The applicant must complete this training before issuing any registration by the California Bureau of Security and Investigative Services.[31] In addition, a security guard registrant must complete "not less than 32 hours of training in security officer skills within 6 months from the date an initial registration is issued." A security guard registrant must complete 16 of the 32 hours within 30 days from the date the registration is issued. The remaining 16 hours must be completed within 6 months from the registrant's employment date. Finally, the guard must complete eight training hours annually.[32]

A private patrol security firm is an organization, which for any consideration, "[A]grees to furnish, or furnishes, a watchman, guard, patrolperson, or other person to protect persons or property or to prevent the theft, unlawful taking, loss, embezzlement, misappropriation, or concealment of any goods, wares, merchandise, money, bonds, stocks, notes, documents, papers, or property of any kind; or performs the service of a watchman, guard, patrolperson, or other person, for any of these purposes."[33]

A proprietary private security employer is an organization or person with "one or more employees who provide security services for the employer and only for the employer."[34] And a proprietary security officer is an "unarmed individual who is employed exclusively by any one employer whose primary duty is to provide secu-

---

[29] California Business and Professions Code Section 7582.1(e).

[30] California Business and Professions Code Sections 7582.8, 7581, and 7583.9.

[31] California Business and Professions Code Sections 7583.6, and 7583.8.

[32] California Business and Professions Code Section 7583.6 and California Code of Regulations Section 643.

[33] California Business and Professions Code Section 7582.1(a).

[34] California Business and Professions Code Section 7574.01(e).

rity services for his or her employer."[35] Under this statute, the officer who interacts with the public while performing his duties must wear a distinctive uniform visibly identifying the individual as a security officer.

6   Los Angeles Police Department (LAPD) Examples of "On-Duty" "Off-Duty" "In Uniform" "Out of Uniform"

Visible identification can blur authority in some instances. LAPD policy[36] allows active and retired police officers to work in and out of uniform under certain circumstances. The Board of Police Commissioners has deemed the security of various Los Angeles venues to serve the city's best interest and public safety. Therefore, active-duty police officers may be assigned to these venues off regular duty hours. Supervisors approve and fill these assignments through the Cash Overtime Allotment for Scheduling and Timekeeping (COAST) Overtime Detail Guidelines. The venues include iconic venues such as Dodger Stadium, Los Angeles Memorial Coliseum, Hollywood Bowl, Nokia Theater and Los Angeles Live, Los Angeles Convention Center, etc. While the LAPD officers at these venues may be technically off their regular duty, for their police powers, they are considered "on-duty" when working COAST overtime. Therefore, they retain their total obligations to protect the public and remain responsible for following all LAPD Department rules, policies and procedures.

LAPD Department policy allows active and retired police officers to work in uniform at motion picture filming locations provided they applied and obtained a Motion Picture/Television Filming Work Permit (MPTFWP). Off-duty Los Angeles police officers often perform security duties at movie production locations in uniform. The MPTFWP permit is limited to performance of traffic and crowd control at those times and places authorized in the permit issued under the Los Angeles Administrative Code.[37]

Recently enacted Los Angeles Municipal Code sections give the Chief of Police the authority and responsibility to regulate the conduct and dress of both active and retired police officers at filming locations within the City of Los Angeles.[38] Field supervisors are tasked to take immediate corrective action in the event of misconduct, or violation of any departmental policy.

Law enforcement agencies are not liable for the actions of peace officers that are engaged in off-duty private employment as security guards while wearing plain-clothes or the uniform of the private employer. In California, a peace officer who

---

[35] California Business and Professions Code Section 7574.01(f).

[36] Interview with Captain Alejandro Vargas, LAPD (the Author thanks Captain Vargas for his collaboration).

[37] Los Angeles Administrative Code Section 22.350.

[38] Los Angeles Municipal Code (LAMC) sections 52.28, 80.03 and 80.03.1.

works as a security guard for pay by a private employer does not act as a peace officer during that private employment.[39]

However, part time off-duty peace officers working as private security guards may exercise the powers of a peace officer concurrently with the private employment. They must, however, be in uniform, their part-time employment is authorized by the law enforcement agency they work for, and they follow the rules and regulations of their law enforcement agency.[40]

LAPD warns its employees to weigh the risks of private employment. The City of Los Angeles will not defend or indemnify off-duty officers when they act on behalf of private security organizations unless the off-duty officer fully complies with the requirements of Penal Code Section 70.

7 The Private Security Field Is Highly Regulated

The Bureau of Security and Investigative Services ("BSIS") licenses and regulates private security services and other related industries. As a consumer protection agency, the mission of BSIS is to protect and serve the public and consumers of California through "effective regulatory oversight of the professions" within BSIS's jurisdiction.

The regulation of private security firms began in 1915 when California enacted licensing requirements for private investigators. The industry's history dates to 1850, when Allan Pinkerton founded the Chicago-based Pinkerton National Detective Agency (Pinkerton), quickly becoming the industry standard in private protection. In the mid to late 1800s, Pinkerton performed many duties today associated with federal and state law enforcement. Pinkerton guarded railroads and stagecoach shipments and protected banks and other businesses often targeted by outlaws. President Lincoln hired Pinkerton as his personal security and to spy against the confederacy. At its peak, Pinkerton was the largest law enforcement agency in the nation. In the twentieth century, Pinkerton re-branded itself as a risk management firm.[41]

In 1943 California added a new category for private patrol operators to the Private Investigator Act in the Business and Professions Code. Later the law evolved to address the importance of regulation in private security and proprietary security services under two specific acts bearing those titles. They are generally in Chapters 11.4 and 11.5 of the Act in the Business and Professions Code, including Sections 7574–7576 and 7580–7588.8.[42] As a regulatory agency BSIS also promulgates

---

[39] Melendez v. City of Los Angeles, 63 Cal.App.4th 1.

[40] California Penal Code Sections 70 (d) and (c).

[41] https://pinkerton.com/our-story

[42] California Business and Professions Code Sections 7574–7588.8.

regulations to address the industry's and consumers' ongoing needs.[43] Legislation in 1993 consolidated and formally renamed BSIS in 1994 as the Bureau of Security and Investigative Services.[44] BSIS, as one of the largest agencies of its kind, issues licenses, registrations, certificates, and permits to more than 380,000 licensees.[45] Among the permits issued are firearms, tear gas, and baton. These permits require additional scrutiny in background checks, appropriate training, and qualifying written and range examinations.[46]

8   The Critical Requirement of Training

Given the risk of civil and even criminal liability for possessing an unpermitted weapon, for example, BSIS and every major private security organization emphasize the "Power of Arrest," skills training, and the appropriate accreditation for additional licenses to carry weapons.

Every lesson plan emphasizes the difference between a peace officer with the power to arrest versus a security guard or a private security officer without such power or at least with the statutory right of any other private citizen. The emphasis on the private security officer is the protection of persons or property they are hired to protect.[47] The goal is prevention. The primary tools are observation and reporting. A security guard's or a private security officer's registration card in California does not allow them to carry a weapon.[48] A security guard must train and certify to carry a firearm, tear gas, or a baton. Even with that certification, both the guard and employer are required under law to "deliver to the director [of BSIS] a written report describing fully the circumstances surrounding any incident involving the discharge of any firearm in which he or she was involved while acting within the course and scope of his or her employment, within 7 days after the incident."[49] A private property security officer (as opposed to a security guard with proper training and certification) cannot be issued a firearm or baton permit. A violation of these rules carries significant civil and potentially criminal liabilities for the individual guard, security officer, and employer.[50]

---

[43] https://www.bsis.ca.gov/about_us/laws/bsis_regulations.pdf
[44] California Assembly Bill 936, Chapter 1263, Statutes of 1993.
[45] https://www.bsis.ca.gov/about_us/strategic_plan.pdf
[46] https://www.bsis.ca.gov/forms_pubs/fire_fact.shtml
[47] California Business and Professions Code Section 7582.1.
[48] California Business and Professions Code Section 7583.3(c) and (e).
[49] California Business and Professions Code Section 7583.4.
[50] California Code of Regulations, Title 16 Sections 601.6 et Seq.

9 The Collaboration Necessary Between Peace Officers and Private Actors

Law enforcement clearly needs peace officers to conduct their duty to protect the public. "Life, liberty, and the pursuit of happiness" guaranteed by the Declaration of Independence are not possible without lawful and appropriate enforcement of the laws. While this phrase may not be legally binding, it is seen as the inspiration for governments to protect the people. Peace officers as public actors fulfill this vital duty that security guards or security officers as private actors cannot or are not designed to deliver. However, the collaboration today of the public sector with the private sector is more important than ever.

American society in the twenty-first century continues to evolve. Changing demographics, cultural norms, values, and technologies raise the importance of these collaborations to address the root causes of criminal conduct. American law enforcement agencies and private security are increasingly faced with challenges regarding loss of community confidence, growing rates of violence and gun crime in urban centers, and cybercrimes. As a result, governments are turning to security, safety, technology, and health care providers to help navigate the threats and disruptions they now face.

The private sector is critical to cybercrime investigations. Experts admit that law enforcement cannot address cybercrime without collaborating with the private sector. Cybercrime is now one of our biggest threats in society. In 2021, cybercrime costs were $6 trillion in damages globally. The growth over previous years is partly attributed to increased "organized crime gang hacking activities." Recent schemes demonstrate today's cybercriminals are working in large groups across the globe to perpetuate their crimes. Thus, law enforcement is joining forces with the private sector to augment and extend its investigative power.

The private technology community is also instrumental in public safety enhancement programs. The Automatic License Plate Reader (ALPR) camera system is designed and installed by the private sector to support law enforcement in California cities. The Palos Verdes Peninsula and neighboring cities[51] signed a memorandum of understanding (MOU) to install and operate a comprehensive public safety platform of ALPR (Fig. 1) to add additional support toward enhancing the safety of their communities. ALPR are high-speed camera systems that photograph license plates, convert the numbers and letters into machine-readable text, tag them with the time and location, and upload that data into a database for retrieval. Law enforcement agencies that use ALPR compare plates to a "hot list" of plates suspected of being connected to crimes or stolen vehicles. The program's success is remarkable over only 3 years of operation, with more than 100 arrests and recovery of stolen vehicles, several residential burglary arrests, several missing persons located, and several criminal warrant arrests.

---

[51] Rolling Hills Estates, Palos Verdes Estates, Rolling Hills, Rancho Palos Verdes, Lomita, and Torrance (See Appendix A for a sample MOU).

Fig. 1 Illustration of ALPR camera placements

Based on the success of these public safety enhancement programs, the City of Rolling Hills Estates, California, has also created a matching fund grant program to facilitate the installation of neighborhood entryway high-resolution cameras in partnership with Homeowners Associations and Neighborhood Watch programs. A simple application[52] allows the city to address this neighborhood's needs efficiently. These enhancements are typically combined with private security patrol organizations to further secure communities.

The re-imagination of law enforcement further supports the collaboration of the public with the private sector. While we may need new laws to accommodate some of these changes, examples of cooperation at high school diversion programs and university departments of public safety may be the new model for public law enforcement to emulate.

The inspiration for these programs and some grant funding are available through the Crime Control and Law Enforcement Act.[53] This federal act allows states, local governments, and tribal organizations to apply for grants to fund collaborative programs, which "promote public safety by ensuring access to adequate mental health and other treatment services for mentally ill adults or juveniles that are overseen cooperatively."[54] While the program promotes diversion as an alternative to prosecution and sentencing, the underlying purpose is to recognize "mental illness" and "Mental health disorder" as diagnosable mental, behavioral, or emotional disorders warranting intervention more suited for the private sector rather than public law enforcement.

---

[52] See Appendix B.
[53] 34 USC 10651.
[54] Ibid.

10   The Los Angeles County Teen Court Program

Teen Court is a juvenile diversion and prevention program.[55] It links high school students, schools, teachers, parents, teen offenders, probation officers, and the Los Angeles Superior Court to reduce recidivism and encourage first-time juvenile offenders to accept responsibility for their actions and to stay out of the juvenile court system. Young offenders in the program receive their sentence (appropriate consequences for their action) through a jury of their peers-other teenagers.

Teen Court offers the juvenile who is found guilty the opportunity, upon successful completion of their sentence within 6 months, to have no record of a criminal conviction. A local law school accommodates the hearings, supervised by a sitting Los Angeles Superior Court judge. The Court currently operates 38 Teen Courts in high schools throughout Los Angeles County. Over 70 judges preside over Teen Courts and typically hear trials one to two afternoons each month.[56] The program hopes to correct criminal behavior and detect any potential disorder that could be addressed outside the criminal justice system. The program also hopes to instill in students legal responsibility and the importance of the law. This California State Bar-sponsored award-winning program also trains and supports teenagers interested in the judicial system and a career in the law.[57]

11   Mental Health and Response Team (MHART) Programs Are Launched at Universities

Armed peace officers responding to calls for mental health crises have had some disastrous consequences. While 911 or law enforcement is called during a public safety concern or potential criminality, peace officers are trained to search, detain, and arrest. They are also trained and authorized by law to respond to physical threats if in the "totality of circumstances" they are "defending against the imminent threat of death or serious bodily injury."[58] Sadly to err is human, and the line between imminent threat and no threat is blurred in emotionally charged encounters, especially when peace officers are not trained to recognize mental, behavioral, or emotional disorders.

In response to this lose/lose framework in peace officer encounters and those suffering a mental health crisis, the University of Texas (UT) and the University of

---

[55] Butts, J. A., Buck, J., & Coggeshall, M. B. (2002). *The impact of teen court on young offenders.* Urban Institute Justice Policy Center and Stickle, W. P., Connell, N. M., Wilson, D. M., et al. (2008). An experimental evaluation of teen courts. *Journal of Experimental Criminology, 4,* 137–163.

[56] https://www.lacourt.org/generalinfo/communityoutreach/GI_CO010.aspx

[57] https://www.legalprofessionalsinc.org/los-angeles-lascs-teen-court-program/

[58] California Penal Code Section 835a (c) (1).

Southern California (USC) launched two successful programs in 2021 and 2022 to create collaborative response teams to address public safety in a more holistic approach. Dr. Siegel, the department chair for Psychiatry and Behavioral Sciences at the USC Keck School of Medicine, summed it up by saying, "The impetus for the program is that we want students in crisis—or potentially in crisis—that are having mental health issues to interact primarily with mental health clinicians as an alternative to law enforcement [peace officers]."[59]

This concept developed and implemented by both universities puts mental health providers front and center in any response team to interact with the person and help through the crisis, while peace officers are there to support them. Aside from providing immediate intervention, MHART connects persons with mental health crises to university and community resources. More importantly, MHART diverts the mentally ill from the criminal justice system.

Each university's respective programs promote support for the university community, de-escalation practices, and care for those in crisis. In both universities, MHART is a grand collaboration between administrators, faculty, students, health care providers, and law enforcement. Each university designed and implemented policies and procedures to field calls and dispatch professionals.[60]

MHART does not stop there. MHART will seek the student's consent for further assessment. In the alternative, MHART will determine if the student needs hospitalization or care because they represent a danger to themselves or others. MHART is proactive. If there is a known concern about a member of the university community, MHART will assess wellness under an umbrella of confidentiality and recommend appropriate actions. Many other organizations and networks stand ready to help students academically and socially.

12   Conclusion

The broad police powers of states and municipalities remain inadequate to preserve their constituents' safety, security, and well-being. The twenty-first-century challenges are difficult to overcome independently. Therefore, intergovernmental, and sectoral collaborations are inevitable. These partnerships, especially considering the current context to re-imagine police powers and law enforcement, are critical for advancing policy in the public and private sectors.

Historically a private organization like Pinkerton had expansive law enforcement powers to protect banks and even the president of the United States. Over time as public law enforcement agencies improved, governments scaled back these powers—most states, like California, highly regulated private functions of law

---

[59] https://studenthealth.usc.edu/mhart-pilot-program-launches-to-help-students-experiencing-mental-health-crises/

[60] https://president.utexas.edu/messages-speeches-2021/supporting-mental-health-on-campus-introducing-mhart

enforcement. Given the challenges of our century, especially with cybercrime, the policy may need to be revisited on empowering and immunizing the private sector in these highly specialized digital spaces. Various models using MOUs with University DPS (USC) and local jurisdictions (LAPD) and specialized partnerships like the MHART programs already exist. They may need to be expanded to contemplate the critical importance of inter-sectoral collaborations. Socio-economic and political change is difficult to implement. However, human ingenuity and innovative programs like the Teen Court or MHART are staples of good change to address the needs of a changing society. Finally, promoting sectoral collaborations is critical to solving some of the most vexing problems of our times.

Appendix A: Memorandum of Understanding Between the City of Torrance and the City of Rolling Hills Estates (ALPR Cameras)

This Memorandum of Understanding ("MOU"), effective as of July, 2019 ("Effective Date"), sets forth the terms of the agreement between the City of Torrance (**"Torrance"**) and the City of Rolling Hills Estates (**"RHE"**) for the installation and operation of automated license plate reader cameras (**"ALPR Cameras"**) at certain locations near the boundary of Torrance and RHE.

1. **RECITALS**

    A. RHE has approved a program to purchase and place ALPR Cameras at various locations to monitor ingress traffic into RHE. These locations include sites located on certain property owned by Torrance (**"Torrance Property"**).
    B. Torrance wishes to cooperate with RHE in using and placing ALPR Cameras in the interest of providing mutual security for both Torrance and RHE.
    C. To further these mutual interests, RHE will fund the installation and certain annual costs for three ALPR Cameras at the Torrance Property: one at the intersections of Rolling Hills Road at Crenshaw Boulevard, as specifically described in Exhibit A, and two at the intersection of Rolling Hills Road at Hawthorne Boulevard, as specifically described in Exhibit B. The parties anticipate that the cost for the three cameras will consist of the cost of camera hardware, installation, annual service, warranty, maintenance, and related services from the camera provider, and data services from a separate telecommunication services provider.

2. **TERM.** The MOU will be effective for an initial term 3 years from the Effective Date, and will automatically renew upon the third anniversary of the Effective Date for additional 1-year periods, until June 30, 2030, unless either party elects to terminate this MOU with no less than 30 days' notice before any annual renewal.

3. **FUNDING.** RHE will provide funding for the purchase, installation, and operation of the ALPR cameras in exchange for the use of the Torrance Property and mutual access to the ALPR Cameras, as set forth below.

   A. Purchase and Installation. RHE will provide payment to camera vendor for the purchase and installation of three ALPR Cameras that will be installed at the Torrance Property. Torrance will coordinate with camera vendor and Rolling Hills Estates for the installation of such ALPR Cameras, which includes maintenance services, and ensure that the ALPR Cameras will be set up in a manner that allows RHE and the Los Angeles County Sheriff's Department access to such ALPR Cameras and their data.

   B. Power or Electrical Utility Service. Torrance will be responsible for all charges incurred for public utility services used to provide electricity to the ALPR Cameras.

   C. Telecommunication Services. RHE will pay wireless company directly for telecommunications service for the ALPR Cameras, which consists of monthly data costs for internet connections to, and sim cards for, the ALPR Cameras.

   D. Removal. Torrance, at its sole cost, will be responsible for the removal of the ALPR Cameras upon termination of this MOU.

4. **CIVIL CODE ALPR COMPLIANCE.** Each party acknowledges and agrees that Title 1.81.23 commencing with Section 1798.90.5 of the California Civil Code (**"ALPR Title"**) establishes certain security procedures and practices to protect automated license plate recognition (ALPR) information from unauthorized access, destruction, use, modification, or disclosure. Each party agrees to comply with all applicable provisions of the ALPR Title applicable to an "ALPR operator" as defined in the ALPR Title.

5. **INDEMNIFICATION.** Each party will indemnify, defend, and hold harmless the other party, including its elected and appointed officers, employees, agents, attorneys, and designated volunteers, from and against any and all liability, including, but not limited to demands, claims, actions, fees, costs, and expenses (including reasonable attorney's and expert witness fees), arising from or connected with the respective acts of each party arising from or related to this MOU; provided, however, that no party is obligated to indemnify the other party for that party's own negligence or willful misconduct.

6. **NOTICE.** Any notices, bills, invoices, or reports relating to this MOU, and any request, demand, statement, or other communication required or permitted here must be in writing and delivered to the representatives of the parties at the addresses set forth in this MOU. Parties must promptly notify each other of any change of contact information, including personnel changes. Notice will be deemed to have been received on (i) the date of delivery, if delivered by hand during regular business hours; or (ii) on the third business day following mailing by registered or certified mail (return receipt requested) to:

RHE: _____ Administrative Analyst
              City of Rolling Hills Estates
              4045 Palos Verdes Drive North, Rolling Hills Estates, CA 90274

Torrance: _____, Captain
              City of Torrance Police Department
              3300 Civic Center Drive, Torrance, CA 90503

7. **COOPERATION.** Each party will fully cooperate with the other party to attain the purposes of this MOU.

8. **ADMINISTRATION.** For the purposes of this MOU, the city manager of each party, or their designee, will administer the terms and conditions of this MOU on behalf of their respective party.

9. **AMENDMENT.** The terms and provisions of this MOU may not be amended, modified, or waived, except by an instrument in writing signed by all parties.

10. **COUNTERPARTS.** This MOU may be executed in counterparts, which together will constitute the same and entire MOU.

THE UNDERSIGNED AUTHORIZED REPRESENTATIVES OF the parties hereby execute this MOU as follows:

CITY OF TORRANCE   CITY OF ROLLING HILLS
ESTATES

                               ATTEST:

APPROVED AS TO FORM: APPROVED AS TO FORM:

Exhibit A to Appendix A

Phase 1 Location 3 – Rolling Hills Road at Crenshaw Blvd. (one camera)

Exhibit B to Appendix A

Phase 2 Location 2 – Rolling Hills Road at Hawthorne Blvd. (two cameras)

Appendix B

 Homeowner Association Neighborhood Entryway Camera
Grant Program Application

Homeowner Association(s): _____

Designated Homeowner Association Representative(s): _____
*Please attach proof of HOA, letter of interest, HOA minutes or resolution

Phone Number: _____ E-mail: _____

Proof of purchase from approved vendor: Yes ☐   No ☐

Proposed Security Camera Location Information

Cross Streets: _____

Private Property: Yes ☐   No ☐   Public Right of Way: Yes ☐   No ☐
*If yes for public right-of-way, completes eparate application, and agreement

Location where power will be placed (specify exact location): _____

Installation Equipment Options Pole: Yes ☐   No ☐

Preliminary Site Visit Conducted by City Staff: Yes ☐   No ☐

Date of Site Visit: _____

I,_____(designated HOA Board Member) on behalf of the
_____(HOA Name), agree to abide to the City of Rolling Hills Estates'
Homeowner Association Neighborhood Entryway Camera Grant Program license agreement,
terms, and the conditions of all City-issued permits for this project. The HOA acknowledges and
agrees to the following grant program conditions: the HOA is the owner of the security camera
system purchased or leased from Obsidian Integration, Flock Safety, or Vigilant Solutions; is
responsible for all equipment and installation costs, ongoing operating costs, warranty fee and
maintenance service fee(s); and for the removal of all camera installation improvements from
the public right-of-way should the camera no longer be needed. Compliance with the grant terms
requires that the Los Angeles County Sheriff's Department be provided the ability to locate,
review and download video from the security camera system for law enforcement purposes. The
HOA further agrees to submit the required documentation to the City of Rolling Hills Estates to
receive a one-time City grant in the amount of $ _____ for each installed security camera
system unit per HOA entrance.

_____
Signature of HOA Board representative

Permits:
Permit/Plan Check Application Required: Yes ☐   No ☐
If yes, approved by RHE staff on: _____ Zone Clearance No.: _____
If yes, approved by RHE Building and Safety Department on: _____
Date of Final Site Visit: _____
Staff Initials: _____

OFFICE USE ONLY

Proof of purchase or contract: Yes ☐   No ☐
Security camera location eligible per City requirements: Yes ☐   No ☐
Camera Right-of-Way Application Required: Yes ☐   No ☐
*If yes, complete separate application and agreement Fee: $ _____
Approved- Rolling Hills Estates Staff Member: Yes ☐   No ☐

_____
Staff Name, Title, and Signature   Date

Part II
National Case Studies

The COVID-19 Pandemic and Its Impact on Public-Private Partnership in Policing: Experiences from Within the Belgian and Dutch Security Industry

Pieter Leloup

Abstract After the initial outbreak of a novel coronavirus was reported in March 2020, the European private security sector emphasized its essential role in dealing with the crisis, and in enforcing health and safety measures alongside the public police sector. The crisis, as was stated by the Confederation of European Security Services (Better recognition of private security for safe and secure economic recovery in the COVID-19 situation. Position paper, 2020b), *proved the important character of private security*". However, most research has hitherto been carried out on the involvement of the public law enforcement agencies, with particular reference to policing the Coronavirus outbreak. Notwithstanding the private security sector actively highlighted its relevance, little is known about the actual role of the private security sector throughout the several stages of the COVID-19 pandemic and lockdown. This contribution describes how the security industry emphasized its support in monitoring measures of public health, safety and social and economic recovery, by focusing on developments in two European countries: Belgium and the Netherlands. In particular, the chapter will explore private sector involvement in the protection of vaccination centres in the two countries. Research data are drawn from three main sources: (1) semi-structured interviews with representatives from the private security industry, public officials, policy makers and police officers; (2) (policy) documents and reports on COVID-19 from both public and private agencies; (3) legislation (e.g., on private security and civil safety). The findings of this chapter will make an important contribution to the fields of public and private security, public-private cooperation and crisis management.

P. Leloup (✉)
Ghent University, Ghent, Belgium

Vrije Universiteit Brussel, Brussels, Belgium
e-mail: Pieter.Leloup@Ugent.be

© The Author(s), under exclusive license to Springer Nature Switzerland AG 2023
E. A. Blackstone et al. (eds.), *Handbook on Public and Private Security*,
Competitive Government: Public Private Partnerships,
https://doi.org/10.1007/978-3-031-42406-9_7

Abbreviations

APROSER	Asociación Profesional de Compañias Privadas de Servicios de Seguridad
BVBO	Beroepsvereniging van Bewakingsondernemingen
BDSW	Bundesverband der Sicherheitswirtschaft e.V.
BSIA	British Security Industry Association
CoESS	Confederation of European Security Services
NHO	Service og Handel
NV	De Nederlandse Veiligheidsbranche
PPP	Public-private partnership

1 Introduction

Throughout several stages of the COVID-19 pandemic and lockdown, the Confederation of European Security Services (CoESS) emphasized the function and advantages of private security to ensure compliance with measures of public health and safety and support the recovery of the social and economic life. From the early stages of the COVID-19 pandemic, the organization urged European governments on different occasions to reach out to the private sector for enhanced partnership support in policing the crisis:

> Cooperation and exchange of information are crucial, and CoESS' national associations stand ready for an enhanced public-private partnership in these challenging times and to discuss a common way forward with competent authorities in the Member States (CoESS, 2020a)

The private sector's aim to enhance coordination between state and non-state agencies was certainly not new. In the years preceding the COVID-19 crisis, the European and national security industries had regularly emphasized the benefits of a close public-private cooperation for the security and protection of, amongst others, critical infrastructures (CoESS, 2016; BVBO, 2011). However, (security) crises have been mostly regarded by the industry – and governments – as key moments when private security could be called upon. In such moments, the state, local governments, the police and the security industry have been increasingly looking at the creation of public-private partnerships (PPPs) to tackle issues of crime, disorder, and insecurity.

In particular, in the post-2001 security environment, the role of the security industry and the extent of public-private cooperation in this area, became a more pervasive aspect of, for example, Homeland Security (U.S. Department of Justice, 2005). Additionally, in the aftermath of the 2005 London bombings, the British government stated that the development and deliverance of their counter-terrorism strategy depended upon the successful establishment of public-private partnerships (HM Government, 2006). After the terrorist attacks on public spaces in Europe in

2015 and 2016, the role of the private sector as a resource for security provision significantly grew, while public-private partnerships increased (Leloup & White, 2022). Likewise, during the 2015 European migration crisis the private security sector became more involved in managing refugee and migrant flow, and other migration control tasks (Davitti, 2020; Pacciardi & Berndtsson, 2022).

Deeper forms of collaboration between public and private police forces, however, have, been enabled in realms beyond security crises. In 2008, the global financial crisis and subsequent politics of austerity prompted UK police forces to explore, what White (2014, 1002), describes as, *"radical new budget-reducing policies, including outsourcing key service areas to the private sector on an unprecedented scale"*. Similarly, the recent global public health crisis which emerged in early 2020, was seized upon by European and national security industries as a crucial moment for accelerated cooperation and dialogue between the police and the private security industry (e.g., BSIA, 2020; CoESS, 2020a, d; Nederlandse Veiligheidsbranche, 2020).

Notwithstanding the industry's efforts to promote its crucial role during the COVID-19 pandemic in general and the need for enhanced PPPs in particular, little research has been conducted on the actual impact of the crisis on the public-private cooperation of security actors in policing the crisis. This is especially pertinent given that some research had suggested that the public health crisis had the potential to create new opportunities to increase the role of commercial actors in the provision of security (e.g., Chen, 2020; Deckert et al., 2021; Leloup & Cools, 2022; White, 2022). That said, there has been no detailed investigation into the degree of outsourcing police tasks to the private sector, or the extent of actual (local) PPPs in policing as a result of the COVID-19 pandemic, and the security business' experiences with these state collaborations.

This study explores and, accounts for, the experiences of public-private cooperation in policing the pandemic in Belgium and the Netherlands. It considers the extent to which the recent crisis affected and shaped relations between the public sector and the market in policing, and the methods and risks that can arise when PPPs are entered into during a crisis event. Due to the localize, 'loose' and largely ad hoc nature of the policing partnerships that emerged during the pandemic, the concept of 'PPP' in this chapter is interpreted in its broad sense. It refers to the wide range of informal and formal partnerships where public and private actors work(ed) alongside, and not strictly, for one another under the terms of a contract. As a case study, the protection of infrastructures such as vaccination centers in cooperation with or besides the police, will be explored in Belgium and the Netherlands.

1.1 Methodology

Drawing upon, and developing, research carried out as part of a study on the long-term changes and their causes in policy and regulation in Continental-European countries, mostly in Belgium and the Netherlands. It does not simply describe the broad area of all PPPs in the domain of policing and security provision that existed during COVID-19, rather, it explores the views from inside the private security sector on the building and maintenance of such a PPP. By doing this, the study adds to the knowledge of a group often written about in academic research, yet whose inside views and perspectives are seldom articulated (Leloup et al., 2022) and who are most likely to be on the side that must adapt, rather than steer, in the public-private field. Moreover, by analyzing the relationship between the private security industry, public authorities and police forces, insights into the actual collaborations that are being established will be identified.

To achieve this, a considerable number of interviews were conducted with international experts and representatives, including the Director-General of CoESS, and the chairmen of 4 national private security associations[1] from the private security sector over a 2 year period. In the case of Belgium and the Netherlands, approximately 20 additional interviews with experts and representatives were conducted during the course of 2021–2022, mostly managers from the Dutch and Belgian branches of the private security companies Securitas and G4S. The study used qualitative semi structured interviews, offering an in-depth understanding of the experiences of private security managers and representatives of policing the crisis. The questions asked about the pre-COVID-19 role of private security in each country; its place besides public police forces; regulation and control of the sector; the impact of COVID-19 on the industry, its function and its activities; and forms and degrees of cooperation between the public and private police, and related challenges.

The information collected from the interviews has been supplemented by a wide range of published and unpublished sources, largely from the security industry, including (policy) documents and private security research. Overall, research data are drawn from three main sources: (1) semi-structured interviews with representatives from the private security industry, public officials, policy makers and police officers; (2) (policy) documents and reports on COVID-19 from both public and private agencies; (3) legislation (e.g., on private security and civil safety).

1.2 Structure

In this chapter, the following section provides a brief overview of private security in Belgium and the Netherlands, with a specific focus on the size and regulation of the industry, followed by a description of pre-COVID-19 forms of PPP to provide a contextual outline of the field of policing in both countries. A third section gives a detailed account of one particular case study: the involvement of the private security sector in the protection of vaccination centers in Belgium and the Netherlands during the coronavirus pandemic. Based on the evidence of this case, the fourth section develops an overview of possible challenges stakeholders and policymakers need to

---

[1] i.e. BVBO – Beroepsvereniging van Bewakingsondernemingen (Belgium), APROSER – Asociación Profesional de Compañias Privadas de Servicios de Seguridad (Spain), BDSW - Bundesverband der Sicherheitswirtschaft e.V. (Germany), NHO Service og Handel (Norway)

take into account, and what lessons can be learned from for public-private cooperation in the field of security and private sector involvement in policing the COVID-19 crisis respectively.

2 Private Security in Belgium and the Netherlands

Belgium and the Netherlands are geographically situated within Western continental Europe between France, Germany and the UK, and share similar political and economic systems. Although important similarities do exist (Leloup & White, 2022), state-market interactions across security provision in Western continual European countries, differs from Anglo-Saxon countries such as North America, and England and Wales (Terpstra, 2017). In the former, private security tends to be less present than public security, while their security industries are more highly regulated (Button & Stiernstedt, 2016).

Although providing exact figures on the size of the private security sector in Europe poses important methodological issues – i.e., dissimilar definitions of private security are used across different countries – CoESS has published the most complete overview. In 2008, about 1,453,636 private security employees were active in the larger Europe,[2] with an average of 1 private security guard per every 624 citizens, in contrast to an average ratio of 1 police officer per 244 citizens (CoESS, 2009). In 2013 – one of the last years in which figures for the European private security sector have been available, a total of 2,299,922 private security guards were active in 34[3] European countries (CoESS, 2015). This rise has been mainly attributed to the increasing security needs of a growing number of private and public clients, like critical infrastructure facilities, transport hubs (e.g., airports, train stations), and governmental agencies and institutions (e.g., embassies, universities) (CoESS & UNI-Europe, 2014).

When compared to other European countries, the ratio between private security officers and police officers in Belgium and the Netherlands is low (Fig. 1). Based on figures by CoESS for the year 2013 (2015), the ratio for both countries registers at around 0,44, although one other study projected a more even ratio for the Netherlands (0,88) (Devroe & Terwel, 2015).

In the case of Belgium, with a current population of 11,590,000 inhabitants, exact figures on, and the evolutions in the size, of the security industry are very difficult to obtain, and given numbers often vary – even within the same year. However, broader trends can be identified. Where the number of (officially licensed) private security guards varied around 11,000 in 1990 (Leloup, 2021), the industry in 2018 consisted of almost 200 private security companies that employed 18,885 private

---

[2] The then 25 EU-countries and six additional European countries (Bosnia-Herzegovina, Croatia, Macedonia, Norway, Serbia, Switzerland and Turkey).
[3] i.e. the then 28 EU Member States and six additional European countries (Bosnia & Herzegovina, Macedonia, Norway, Serbia, Switzerland and Turkey).

security officers, of which 1468 were allowed to carry a weapon. Armed security activities in Belgium mostly relate to the protection of cash-in-transit, bodyguarding, and providing security at NATO buildings and embassies. While this demonstrates a slow increase over the past decades, private security has increasingly become relied upon as a professional security partner. In recent years, the private security sector has steadily expanded its activities and powers, including the new law of October 2, 2017 that regulates private security. Any person wishing to work as a private security officer is required to undergo training at an institution approved by the Minister of the Interior; only after the successful completion of a basic training course consisting of 139 teaching hours can the trainee receive his or her license.

Figures on the private security sector in the Netherlands tend to be more accurate. In total, approximately 3000 licensed private security companies, investigation agencies, alarm centers, cash-in-transit companies, in-house security services and other security organizations are involved in private security activities (Fig. 1). Based on figures from the *Nederlandse Veiligheidsbranche* (Nederlandse Veiligheidsbranche (2022), a yearly average of approximately 28,000 private security personnel has been operating since 2002 (cf. Fig. 2). Where police employed 63,131 police officers in 2021, the number of private security personnel for the same year was 24,896 (Nederlandse Veiligheidsbranche, 2022). Although this indicates a visible decline in the number of personnel over the past decade, the annual turnover of the Dutch market in private security and criminal investigation in 2021 was still calculated at 1348 billion euros (Nederlandse Veiligheidsbranche, 2020, 2022).

In the Netherlands, the number of private security companies grew from 151 to 317 between 1992 and 1998, with an increase in the number of private security guards from 10,000 to 21,000 for roughly the same period (De Waard, 1999; van

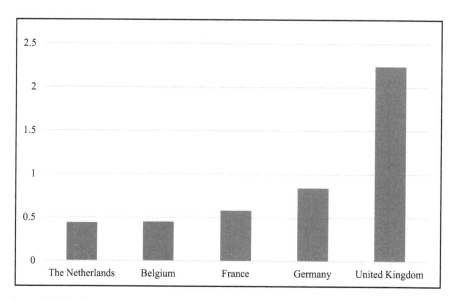

Fig. 1 Ratio private security guards to police officers (2013)

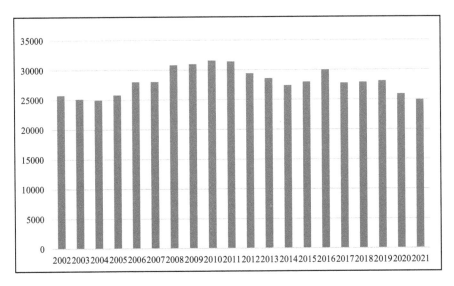

Fig. 2 Private security personnel (the Netherlands)

Steden, 2007). It is not entirely illogical, then, that most researchers situate the creation of a sector-specific public policy at that juncture, where both the economic utility and the security function of the private sector were increasingly recognized publicly and politically (Cools & Verbeiren, 2004; Leloup & White, 2022). In the Netherlands, public-private partnerships were steadily increasing within the security domain (van Steden, 2007). This was grasped by the Dutch Legislature when drafting the Private Security Organisations and Private Investigation Agencies Act in 1997, which recognized the useful function that private security companies could perform. To protect the interests and rights of citizens, the then legislature necessitated a licensing and monitoring system to ensure the competence and reliability of such companies. While the Minister of Justice and Security is responsible for granting licenses, the police are charged with monitoring compliance with the law. With the exception of protecting merchant ships against piracy, Dutch private security personnel are not allowed to carry any firearms.

3 Public-Private Partnerships in the Field of Policing

3.1 Definition

Quite often, PPPs are defined in ways consistent with the characterization of the Organisation for Economic Co-operation and Development (OECD), which refers to *"long term contractual arrangements between the government and a private partner whereby the latter delivers and funds public services using a capital asset, sharing the associated risks*" (2012). PPPs can be put in place to achieve a wide range of objectives – e.g., investments, risk sharing, maintenance duties – in a range of public services, such as transport, telecommunication, social housing, healthcare, education and research. Influenced by budgetary motivations and ideas surrounding New Public Management, interest in the concept and practice of PPPs increased from the 1980s and 1990s onwards, where they were originally used in connection to infrastructure projects, finances and economic renewal (Hodge & Greve, 2007), they have become a tool for providing a much wider range of public services "*with less public financial input and more private participation*" (Arthur et al., 2022, 16).

In the extant literature, several potential benefits are put forward for implementing such public-private collaborations. They can offer substantial public benefits by offering important additional funding and saving costs, by improving efficiency, maintenance and service levels, by sharing risks with the private sector, and by combining public and private expertise (Bloomfield, 2006, 400; Cheng, 2019). At the same time, authors have warned of contradictory results regarding the actual evaluation of these potential benefits. In practice, it is claimed, PPPs do not always provide adequate value-for-money, are subject to delays, downgrade employment conditions and service levels, etc. (Clark & Hakim, 2019; Lam, 2019).

3.2   Public-Private Partnerships in Policing

Since the late twentieth century, PPPs have emerged as part of a broader trends towards plural policing within the security landscape. Indeed, in large parts of the Western world security provision – and the actors involved – changed considerably and became more complex. Far-reaching shifts in late modern policing and security provision have attracted much academic attention, with authors referring to these phenomena in terms of 'privatization' and 'hybridization' (Dupont, Grabosky, & Shearing, 2003; Johnston, 1992, 1993), 'multilateralization' (Bayley & Shearing, 2001) and 'pluralisation' (Jones & Newburn, 2006; Loader, 2000). Intrinsic to this was the establishment of mostly local PPPs or 'security networks', which steered the sole responsibility of crime control away from the state (Jones et al. 2009; Terpstra, 2008; Cools & Pashley, 2018), especially since the 1980s, when they, "*developed under the tutelage of the Home Office in Britain, and largely by private enterprise and local government in the USA*" (Garland, 2001, 17–18). Such partnership arrangements were designed to pursue more effective crime prevention strategies and to enhance community safety (Garland, 2001; Gilling, 1997).

Even in Continental-European countries, such as the Netherlands, Germany and Belgium where security provision has regularly been characterized by more state-oriented approaches (Cools & Verbeiren, 2004; Cools & De Raedt, 2015; Devroe & Terwel, 2015; Devroe & Terpstra, 2015), whilst similar collaborations, as part of community policing strategies, were discussed and created from the early 1990s onwards.

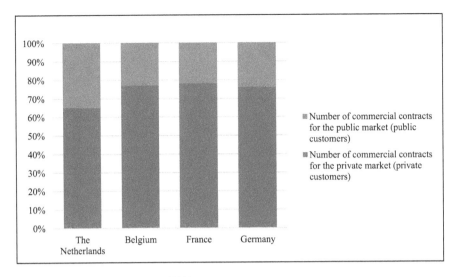

Fig. 3 Private security contracts (2011)

A survey by CoESS (2012) (cf. Fig. 3) showed that for the Netherlands, 35% of the private security sector's clients were public in nature. In Belgium, the public sector was the client in only 23% of the contracts with private security companies; a number close to this of France (22) and Germany (24).

In Germany, for instance, mobile private security staff reports about suspected persons and vehicles in the area of critical infrastructures sites to their operations centers, where the information is then shared with local police forces who use the security industry as a second pair of eyes and ears (CoESS, 2016).

In the Netherlands, research demonstrated that 14% of the municipalities hire a private security company to conduct surveillance in the public domain (Terpstra et al., 2013). In these specific cases, however, operational control remains with the police. These private security agents cannot wear any visible features that can be traced back to their company, while they have to be recognizable as municipal officials. They can carry handcuffs, but they do not have any access to police and/or investigation systems.

In Belgium, for instance, PPPs and outsourcing became increasingly common for, amongst other things, the design, construction and finance of new prison infrastructures, security and the care services of forensic psychiatric centers for ill offenders, as well as so-called transition houses, electronic monitoring, and probation services (Gudders & Daems, 2018; Herzog-Evans, 2018; Vanhouche & Nederlandt, 2019).

More recently, partnerships have gradually increased between (local) police forces and private security companies as well, both in contractual and non-contractual forms. In 2018, the Antwerp Police launched a European tender process for the permanent surveillance and security of its headquarters. Since then, the buildings of the Antwerp local police have been surveilled by Securitas. It was the first police station in Belgium to outsource the security of its reception services to an external partner (De Standaard, 2018) including the provision of security officers, technological tools such as X-ray scanners and metal detection gates. The partnership between the Antwerp police and Securitas mainly covers two tasks: security and customer-care. On the one hand, security officers control access by identifying visitors and customers, and the presence of dangerous objects, whilst on the other, Securitas reception staff are responsible for greeting of visitors and customers and guiding them to the appropriate police departments. When required, the Antwerp police have the ability to use other 'on-demand' private security services from Securitas, such as dog patrols, mobile surveillance, drone cameras, telecommunication solutions, event surveillance assistance, or other technical aids. Similar, less formal collaborations have developed between Belgian police forces and private security companies in, for example, Ghent, where the local police force cooperate with security officers in their effect to tackle domestic burglary, and reports of suspicious vehicles (Vermeersch, 2015).

4   Policing the COVID-19 Pandemic: Results

4.1   The COVID-19 Pandemic: Background

The initial outbreak of a novel coronavirus was reported in China near the end of 2019. The first European cases of a novel coronavirus were reported in France and Germany on 24th and 28th January, and by the 22nd February, Italy had reported several clusters of cases in Lombardy, Piedmont and Veneto (WHO, 2 March 2020). In the following weeks, the number of cases of COVID-19 outside China increased 13-fold and cases were reported in several other European countries. On 11th March 2020, the Director-General of the World Health Organization (WHO) stated that COVID-19 could be characterized as a pandemic; the COVID-19 outbreaks that followed, posed significant implications for public health, while causing huge economic and societal disruptions.

4.2   Impact of COVID-19 on the Private Security Sector

Evidence suggests that the international trends that saw national governments increasingly turn toward the private security sector to deliver essential services, was a notable feature of the COVID-19 crisis. In regions such as Europe (CoESS, 2020d), North America (NASCO, 2020), Latin America (DCAF, 2020), Asia (Chen, 2020) and India (Financial Express, 2020), the security industry has been increasingly relied upon to respond to, and then manage, the crisis. In the first weeks of the coronavirus outbreak in Europe, the exact impact of the crisis on the industry, and its particular role in policing the public health crisis and lockdown measures, was unclear. Nonetheless, representatives of the security sector projected a set of possible challenges and tendencies, such as staff shortages and significant shifts in the demand for security personnel from their clients (Leloup & Cools, 2022). On European and national levels, the private security sector highlighted its particular function in access control, guarding locations, perimeter control, and to secure "*the transport of critical goods, such as protection gear or other medical goods*" (CoESS, 2020a). In the meantime, the European Commission, and some European countries, such as Belgium, the Netherlands, Spain and the UK, recognized private security as "essential services". This granted the industry with special 'rights', such as the free movement of workers and access to childcare services.

Altogether, the public health crisis had a considerable direct and indirect impact on the security industry and the services it offered; few of which can be considered as positive. Early in the crisis, there was an increase in demand for some of their services. In particular, specific health-security demands related to controlling the pandemic and the associated lockdown led to the emergence of new market segments, and the expansion of some existing ones (Leloup & Cools, 2022). In addition, the industry identified a growing public recognition for its engagement in countries such as Belgium, Germany and France (CoESS, 2020b). According to several of the industry's representatives, the crisis had proven that private security can make a major contribution to the safety of society, and that its legitimacy in the eyes of society had increased: "The security industry was able to show what its worth during the coronavirus pandemic [...] and these efforts were certainly noticed within society. A lot of people have been to the COVID-19 vaccination centers and have spotted the security guard and his duties" (Interview Managing Director G4S, 14 February 2022).

Notwithstanding these perceived successes, the industry did encounter new and demanding challenges. For example, in some European countries the private security sector witnessed a decline of 25–30% of its overall business activity compared to 2019, while 75% of CoESS members reported a lack of liquidity (CoESS, 2020c; CoESS & UNI, 2020). In particular, the aviation and event security businesses were badly hit by the coronavirus pandemic. Similarly, increased public fear, and consequent restrictions in the use of cash payments, led to severe financial losses for the Cash-in-Transit business. Therefore, the security industry urged governments and central banks to boost trust in – and promote the use of – cash (CoESS & UNI, 2020, 3). Furthermore, the security industries in many countries experienced significant shortages of necessary personnel. Taken together, the private sector's high expectations of increased public recognition, turned out to be lower than they had hoped for (White, 2022). The overall impact of the pandemic on the activities of the private security sector can be seen in the table below (Table 1).

Although the above effects would likely be replicated for any European countries where the private sector plays an important role in security provision, differences in economic emphasis and activities between countries can play a role. Thus, the economy in countries with a strong service-based industry built around tourism, cultural events and transportation, such as Spain, was more susceptible to the pandemic,

Table 1 (economic) impact on private security industry

Economic impact	Negative	Positive
Direct	Staffing shortages due to illness and/or exhaustion among security personnel	New security areas (health security cf. control at entrance; vaccination centers)
Indirect	Lower turnover due to reduction of clients' economic activities (tourist sector; events industry; transport sector, cash-in-transit, …) Lower turnover due to loss activities in favor of volunteers, … (other non-state security providers)	Higher turnover due to increase clients' economic activities (health care institutions; supermarkets and shops; critical infrastructures…) Private security as an 'essential service' Growing public recognition and legitimacy

indirectly leading to the security industry bearing more negative consequences in instances of lockdown.

In the end, however, and notwithstanding early expectations that the public health crisis would lead to greater structural public-private cooperation, a few representatives of the security industry stated that the actual establishment of PPPs failed to materialize in many countries. One of them mentioned that *"although private security today has been increasingly seen as a partner by the police, it has not resulted in any real partnerships"* (Interview manager SERIS Belgium, 9 June 2020). Indeed, the crisis did lead to some forms of ad hoc partnerships, but without being fully institutionalized (Interview Director-General CoESS, 12 January 2022). In the following section, one particular case of cooperation is discussed in more detail: the protection of vaccination centers.

4.3   Case Study: Private Sector Involvement in the Protection of Vaccination Centers

Over the last few decades, variant crises have had the potential to increase private sector involvement and partnerships in security provision (Hlouchova, 2020; Phelps, 2021; Morriss, 2006). This begs the question of how far partnership approaches were used to police the COVID-19 pandemic in Europe, in the domain of health security in general, and certainly the protection of vaccination centers in particular.

At the European level, CoESS indicated that "private security will help enforce many of the health and safety measures, which citizens will have to live with for the foreseeable future, in collaboration with or on behalf of public forces" (2020a). Likewise, national private security associations of several European countries, informed their governments that security firms were prepared to take a more prominent role in policing the lockdown and protecting the public health of their citizens (Leloup & Cools, 2022). In Germany, for example, security personnel took over the control of people flows in pedestrian zones due to a lack of police officers (Interview

Managing Director BDSW, 20 January 2022). In Norway, similar fears that COVID-19 would lead to staff shortages within the police, initiated monthly informative meetings between the National Police Directorate and the NHO, the Norwegian private security association. On these occasions, the industry informed the police of its available security guards, cars and other resources, that could support the police at times of emergency (Interview Managing Director NHO, 26 January 2022).

During the pandemic, the private security industry delivered a wide set of (health) protection services and products to prevent, detect and respond to COVID-19 threats. Besides installing fever detection systems, (automated) customer counting technology and applications, private security officers were trained to control compliance with physical distancing rules (Leloup & Cools, 2022).

In Belgium, industry representatives expressed their hope that the public health crisis could create additional opportunities to create new, or strengthen existing, public-private collaborations, while increasing the role of commercial actors in the provision of security (Interview Manager SERIS Belgium, 9 June 2020). Early in the pandemic, new formal and informal consultation structures between public and private security actors, were initiated to optimize inter-sectoral consultation in light of the crisis. For the first time in Belgian history, the private security industry were in direct communication with the national crisis management center (Interview representative BVBO, 30 March 2020). The sudden increased demand for hospital security in Belgium, and the consequent staff shortages, were covered by reductions to other private security activities and sectors (interview representative BVBO, 30 March 2020). According to the communication manager of one Belgian private security company, security guards helped with monitoring the implementation of and compliance with health measures (L'Avenir, 2020), whilst in the Netherlands, representatives of the Dutch security industry indicated that the crisis led to more consultation between police services and the private sector (Interview Managing Director G4S Netherlands, 14 February 2022).

While the corona-protests in Belgium remained peaceful, fiercer collective protests arose in the Netherlands, against the requirement to wear a mask, the prohibition of activities, gatherings and free movement, and the compliance with social distancing rules (Terpstra et al., 2021). Simultaneously, COVID-19 conspiracy beliefs acted as a barrier to the development of public support for health policies to address the pandemic (Earnshaw et al., 2020). Ultimately, when the vaccination program was launched in the second half of 2020, Dutch protesters also began to target vaccination centers. For instance, the testing facilities of the municipalities Urmond (Limburg province) and Urk (Flevoland province) were set on fire as one of the first in the Netherlands (e.g., AD, 2020; Het Parool, 2021; Leeuwarder Courant, 2021), and in addition, Dutch citizens suspected of involvement in planned terrorist activities against other vaccination centers, were arrested and put on trial (NH Nieuws, 2021). In an environment where vaccination centers, and the distribution and transportation of vaccines, became targets, public police forces lacked the capacity to impose nationwide protective measures. While there was a need to secure the transportation of vaccines to the medical provider and to the vaccination

centers, "*the Dutch government was not able to provide these services, [police]
capacity was not available*" (Interview Director Government G4S Netherlands, 19
January 2022). As a result, and largely from 2021 onwards, governments increasingly began to appeal to the private security sector to secure public health facilities
such as COVID-19 testing and vaccination centers in particular. In general, security
guards were employed for the control of access, securing the perimeter of buildings,
but also as escorts for the transport of critical and medical goods (CoESS, 2020a).

In the Netherlands, the government turned towards G4S, a company which – during the crisis – promoted its experience in setting up temporary infrastructures and
monitoring critical infrastructures, while managing and controlling crowd flows
(G4S, 2021). Given the unpredictable, and swift escalation of the crisis, the Dutch
partnership was established on a very ad hoc basis. Under normal conditions, a wide
range of very specific regulations and requirements steer the often lengthy process
of setting up public-private security contracts. During this crisis, however, the
agreement was sealed in a matter of days, leading to one of the largest outsourcing
contracts in the history of G4S Netherlands. The private security sector thus emphasized the advantage and ability they could bring to situations where gaps in security
services needed to be quickly filled. When the government was facing security
issues, one G4S representative stated that the added value of the private sector was
noticeable in its fast switching operations and moving quickly into action: "*on such
occasions, one way or another, it is clear the private sector is able to act more
quickly and in a more focused way*" (Interview Managing Director G4S Netherlands,
14 February 2022).

While the Dutch authorities mobilized the private security sector to protect their
vaccination facilities, the situation in Belgium developed differently. To some
degree, the authorities did rely on private security for the protection of testing and
vaccination centers in the capital of Belgium, Brussels, and the southern part of
Belgium, Wallonia, where private security companies engaged in functions related
to securing vaccination centers. The security firm Protection Unit was present in 6
of the 49 facilities situated in Brussels and Wallonia. From February 2021 onwards,
the company was responsible for one of the largest Belgian vaccination centers –
with a daily number of 5000 visitors. Security officers provided access controls,
managed queues and crowd flows within the center, and set-up a 24-hour surveillance of the vaccine storage area (Protection Unit, 2021). In Flanders, the northern
part of Belgium, security personnel mostly undertook night patrols in some of the
94 existing facilities. In Bruges, Securitas provided surveillance through the use of
a temporary Mobilecam, the which images from which were monitored in the control room. In addition, a security guard, who also provided support for guiding visitors, monitored the site 24/7 (Securitas, 2021). In general, however, private security
was less engaged in keeping vaccination centers and vaccination transports safe,
than was the case in the Netherlands. This can be explained by two principal reasons.

On the one hand, although surveys showed increases in (physical) aggression
towards medical staff at such facilities throughout 2021 (Domus Medica, 2021),
violent protest and acts of arson against coronavirus testing centers remained relatively low. On the other hand, securing critical infrastructures– as stated by some

representatives of the security industry – was seen as less of a priority for the Belgian authorities, even when acts of arson grew in neighboring countries like the Netherlands, Germany and France. In Belgium, local authorities largely appealed to the event industry to support the rapid construction and organization of vaccination locations and facilities. Although this industry had the necessary expertise to build accommodations which could handle high numbers of visitors, security needs were less catered for. According to a representative from the private security sector: *"When the planning of the 'ideal type' vaccination center was drawn out by the event industry, security itself was not taken into consideration"* (Interview representative BVBO, 27 May 2022).

At the same time, the decentralization of pandemic management toward regional levels, in particular the practical organization of vaccinations and building of related facilities, was seen as less favorable from a strict security perspective. This was unlike previous national crises which had mostly been met by the Department of Internal Affairs and the national crisis center, which collects and analyzes relevant information – such as instances of arson against foreign critical infrastructures. Throughout this public health crisis, however, responsibilities were shifted to the regions, which were – as stated by security industry actors, *"less involved with and informed about possible safety and security issues"* (Interview representative BVBO, 27 May 2022). In addition to this, both the public and private sector increasingly relied on other commercial security actors to enforce social distancing restrictions in testing and vaccination facilities, control access and inform visitors. Similar to strategies adopted in supermarket and shops (Leloup & Cools, 2022), those responsible began to rely on unpaid volunteers rather than security officers for such tasks.

5   Challenges and Requirements: Some Policy Recommendations

While often presented as a solution to a wide range of security challenges, scholars have identified a set of potential restraints to police forces successful implementing PPPs. Often, these relate to media scaremongering and public fears of privatization trends, cultural resistance from within the police, inexperience of the often-complex contracting-out processes, and staffing issues (Rogers, 2017, 52–54; White, 2014). Given that the benefits and necessities to form PPPs can be different in any situation, our research, and interviews with industry representatives, allows the identification of a range of challenges and requirements public-private cooperation in the field of security needs to overcome. These findings run parallel with earlier research on interprofessional cooperation in similar environments (e.g., Cools & Pashley, 2018; Loyens et al., 2021), and in other settings (e.g., Goldman & Xyrichis, 2020), which can help policy makers to create the appropriate framework. Most notably, these relate to the pursuit of a common goal, (working) experience with each other, trust between the parties involved and willingness to share information – within the appropriate legal framework – and the necessity of respectable personal relations. Undeniably, overlap and mutual influence have some bearing between these factors.

Overall, stable societal and economic conditions need to be in place before the benefits of PPPs are likely to be recognized by the public sector. As earlier research has demonstrated, periods of economic crisis, (local) governments and police forces facing budgetary restrictions, and a pro-market government, are all pressures which can force the public sector to engage more rapidly with the private sector (Leloup & White, 2022). In that sense, and in more practical terms, the pursuit of a common goal between the sectors is also of vital importance. For instance, the private security sector often takes the initiative in promoting its existing services and products to its clients. While this supply-driven business strategy could work for non-state clients, it might be less efficient for state clientele. Adapting to the particular security needs of public authorities, and aiming at providing solutions for their needs, might be more beneficial. During the 1980s and 1990s in Belgium, false alarms placed a considerable strain on police capacity. At that time, privately run alarm centers from the security industry offered a solution by filtering (false) alarm signals, which ultimately left only 3% of alarms reaching the police. (Interview representative BVBO, 27 May 2022). Through this positive collaboration which saw the successful offering of a private solution to a public problem, the alarm system industry gained much more legitimacy.

Secondly, both parties should have had at least some experience of setting up and maintaining a public-private cooperation. In this regard, small-scale, informal and loose forms of cooperation between the police and the private security sector can act as valuable stepping-stones for future official and contractual partnerships. During COVID-19, private sector involvement in the Netherlands was partly attributed to the degree of prior consultation and cooperation, the professionalization of the sector and the awareness among police authorities that the private sector could support in policing the crisis (Interview Managing Director G4S Netherlands, 14 February 2022). Since 2015, Oslo has successfully used private security personnel alongside regular police in public places such as train stations and public parks, which has expanded to other police districts in Norway in recent years. In other words, positive experiences from partnerships that were established and successful during the pre-COVID-19 era, led to faster and more efficient cooperation during the pandemic (Interview Managing Director NHO, 26 January 2022).

Thirdly, trust between the actors involved is essential, both in setting up a partnership and throughout its implementation. Trust can be gained in several ways, for example through successful experiences, and satisfaction with, earlier, small-scale PPPs as noted above. Mutual knowledge about each other's organization, roles, powers, strengths and weaknesses, can also lead to greater levels of trust and recognition between those involved, hence the importance for a preparatory phase ahead of the actual formation of the collaboration (Cools & Pashley, 2018). This allows time to establish a strong, structural framework – accepted by all of the involved (security) partners – which elaborates and delineates their respective missions, roles, responsibilities and – of major importance – their legal and operational limits.

Expectations towards each other also have to be discussed and decided on in preparation for the partnership. Jointly sharing information about each of the security partners, their duties, tasks and the like, has often been identified as a crucial step. The professionalization of the security industry in general, and its training of security officers in particular, has also increased trust within the public sector to cooperate with private agents during the COVID-19 pandemic. While representatives of the industry acknowledged the importance of these trends in light of PPPs, earlier research came to similar results (Nalla & Hummer, 1999).

In the policing landscape, however, where debates regarding the balance between the state and the market has mainly centered around a broad range of opposing ideological positions, the establishment of PPPs is still largely steered by personal motives and relationships between several of the stakeholders (Interview Secretary-General APROSER, 9 January 2022). Personal and ideological differences between the public and private sector, as well as opposing objectives and perspectives towards security provision, have acted as barriers for the foundation of PPPs on various occasions (Interview representative BVBO, 30 March 2020). Often arising from public sector fears about the outsourcing and privatization of former police tasks, police departments are sometimes unwilling to leave the door open for cooperation. Among police officers, questions regarding the objectives and ethics of the security industry, the security training, and the degree of control to name just a few, are still raised (Waelput et al., 2021).

Finally, laws and regulations must provide the necessary framework in which PPPs could develop. Within the context of public-private cooperation, it is essential to facilitate the exchange of necessary data and information between the sectors, yet information exchange between the public and private sectors has been a longstanding issue over several decades (De Corte & Van Laethem, 1997), which became even more apparent since GDPR. Prohibitions regarding the disclosure of governmental information towards the private sector, challenge – according to some respondents – the effective operations of PPPs. Notwithstanding this, practical realities can sometimes stall ad hoc cooperation structures or limit the effectiveness of the foreseen public-private policing, certainly in the public domain. For instance, in controlling public conduct to the coronavirus measures, the lack of police powers hindered the daily operations of security personnel, who had no jurisdiction to instruct people to wear their masks or maintain social distance (Interview Managing Director BDSW, 20 January 2022).

As important as the availability of the legislation can be, the implementation of it is a significant matter. This is illustrated by the following example. When new private security regulations were introduced in Belgium in 2017,[4] the legislation provided authorities with the opportunity to rely on private security in the public domain, in case of an emergency. In such moments, security officers would be able to guard certain perimeters in order to prevent unauthorized entry into a particular

---

[4]Law of 2 October 2017 regulating private and particular security.

area, and to protect the work of the emergency and police services.[5] However, Belgian authorities have been reluctant to use private security resources during such events. On 14–16 July 2021, eastern Belgium was hit by extreme rainfall leading to severe flooding along the river Meuse, resulting in 38 fatalities and damage to at least 38,000 buildings. In the immediate aftermath of the event, and regardless of police presence, looting took place in abandoned houses and shops. One interviewee noted that neither any public administration, neither any crisis center, called upon the private security sector to contribute to the security of the damaged areas: "*All the while the police lacked manpower to do so. In other words, the legal arsenal to initiate support from the private security sector is at their disposal, but it is not operationalized. It is not being utilized*" (Interview representative BVBO, 27 May 2022).

6 Conclusion

Despite continuous efforts, the extent to which the coronavirus pandemic has led to (contractual) PPPs in policing has been rather limited, although private security did provide health-related security services, such as for the protection of vaccination centers. That said, representatives from the European and national private security sector have indicated that, although the pandemic has undeniably confirmed the public role of the private sector, their increased visibility and function has not always led to a more fundamental recognition of the sector in practice, and the establishment of a significant number of structural partnerships between the private sector and police forces and (local) governments.

Several practices were highlighted, however, that could support the establishment and elaboration of such linkages in the future. For example, to succeed, the discussion and initiation of such partnerships need to take place within a clearly defined framework, in which the missions, objectives, roles, expectations and limits of all partners must be discussed and defined. Developing meaningful knowledge about each other, especially in sectors that sometimes indicate that they fundamentally do not know each other, is crucial. In countries where systematic meetings take place between the stakeholders, rather than through mere ad hoc consultations, the chances of success of PPPs increase significantly.

Knowledge exchange between the different stakeholders is also often highlighted as important, but albeit difficult to achieve due to the legislative constraints. In the private sector, therefore, interviewees often commented about one-way communication, with information flowing to the public sector but with little, if anything, coming back. When sharing publicly accessible information, speed is of the essence so that the private security industry can also move quickly in the event of a crisis. Moreover, the practical, organizational and legal frameworks within which

---

[5] Art. 118, Law of 2 October 2017 regulating private and particular security.

partnerships are established, must be future-oriented if they are to be capable of responding appropriately to new crises.

References

AD. (2020, December 16). *Poging brandstichting bij coronatestlocatie in Limburgs dorp Urmond.* https://www.ad.nl/limburg/poging-brandstichting-bij-coronatestlocatie-in-limburgs-dorp-urmond~aef7a93a/

Arthur, I. K., Agyemang, E., & Nikoi, E. G. A. (2022). Evaluating the viability of the Ghan Airport Cargo Centre as a public-private partnership project. In S. Hakim, R. M. Clark, & E. A. Blackstone (Eds.), *Handbook on public private partnerships in transportation, Vol I. Competitive government: Public private partnerships.* Springer. https://doi.org/10.1007/978-3-030-83484-5_2

Bayley, D., & Shearing, C. (2001). *The new structure of policing: description, conceptualization, and research agenda.* Washington: U.S. Department of Justice. National Institute of Justice.

Bloomfield, P. (2006). The challenging business of long-term public-private partnerships: Reflections on local experience. *Public Administration Review, 66*(3), 400–411. http://www.jstor.org/stable/3843920

BSIA. (2020). *The British Security Industry Association and COVID-19: Fighting the pandemic.* Fire Safety Matters. Available from: https://www.fsmatters.com/BSIA-responds-to-Coronavirus-pandemic

Button, M. & Stiernstedt, P. (2016). Comparing private security regulation in the European Union. *Policing and Society, 28*(4), 398–414. https://doi.org/10.1080/10439463.2016.1161624

BVBO. (2011). Activiteitenverslag 2010–2011. Beroepsvereniging van Bewakingsondernemingen.

Chen, Q. (2020, May 11). *How's China's private sector helped the government fight coronavirus.* The Conversation. Available from: https://theconversation.com/how-chinas-private-sector-helped-the-government-fight-coronavirus-136100

Chen, Q. (2020). How's China's private sector helped the government fight coronavirus. *The Conversation,* May 11.

Cheng, E. W. L. (2019). Public–private partnerships for critical infrastructure development: The Hong Kong experience. In R. M. Clark & S. Hakim (Eds.), *Public-private partnerships. Competitive government: Public-private partnerships.* Springer. https://doi.org/10.1007/978-3-030-24600-6_11

Clark, R. M., & Hakim, S. (2019). Public–private partnerships and their use in protecting critical infrastructure. In R. M. Clark & S. Hakim (Eds.), *Public-private partnerships. Competitive government: Public-private partnerships.* Springer. https://doi.org/10.1007/978-3-030-24600-6_1

CoESS. (2009). *Private and public security in the Nordic Countries. 2nd white paper.* CoESS & ALMEGA Private Security.

CoESS. (2015). *The new security company. 5th white paper.* CoESS & BDSW.

CoESS. (2016). *Critical infrastructure security and protection. The public-private opportunity.* CoESS.

CoESS. (2020a, March 26). *Observations and recommendations on the COVID-19 situation.* Position paper.

CoESS. (2020b, April 29). *Better recognition of private security for safe and secure economic recovery in the COVID-19 situation.* Position paper.

CoESS. (2020c, May 4). *European business services call for sector-specific EU aid and coordination in the COVID-19 situation.* EU Affairs. Available from: https://www.coess.org/newsroom.php?news=European-Business-Services-call-forsector-specific-EU-aid-and-coordination-in-the-COVID-19-situation

CoESS. (2020d). *The new normal 2.0: Private security and COVID-19 in Europe. A strategic review and foresight.* White Paper. Wemmel: Confederation of European Security Services.

Coess & UNI Europa. (2014). *Buying quality private security services.* CoESS and UNI Europe.

CoESS and UNI Europe. (2020, May 8). *Ensuring business continuity and protection of workers in the COVID-19 pandemic.* Joint Declaration. Available from: https://www.uni-europa.org/2020/05/private-secruity-joint-declarationensuring-business-continuity-and-protection-of-workers-in-the-covid-19-pandemic/.

Cools, M., & De Raedt, E. (2015). Het outsourcen van politietaken naar de private veiligheid in een stroomversnelling? In P. Ponsaers, E. De Raedt, L. Wondergem, & L. G. Moor (Eds.), *Outsourcing policing* (pp. 33–45). Maklu.

Cools, M., & Pashley, V. (2018). *Private veiligheid in een stedelijke en gemeentelijke context: onderzoek naar de rol en samenwerkingsmogelijkheden in Mechelen-Willebroek.* Gompel&Svacina.

Cools, M., & Verbeiren, K. (2004). *Politie en privébewaking: samen sterk. Het spanningsveld tussen uitbesteding en publiek-private samenwerking inzake de politietaken.* Politeia.

Davitti, D. (2020). Beyond the governance gap: Accountability in privatized migration control. *German Law Journal, 21*(3), 487–505. https://doi.org/10.1017/glj.2020.19

DCAF. (2020). How is the private security industry in Latin America responding to COVID19? Webinar. Available from: https://www.dcaf.ch/how-private-security-industrylatin-america-responding-covid19

De Corte, T., & Van Laethem, W. (1997). *Grijze politie. Verklaringen voor problematische publiek-private interacties in de Zaak Reyniers,* Brussel, Politeia, 227 p.

Deckert, A., et al. (2021). 'Safer communities…together'? Plural policing and COVID-19 public health interventions in Aotearoa New Zealand. *Policing and Society, 31*(5), 621–637. https://doi.org/10.1080/10439463.2021.1924169

Devroe, E., & Terpstra, J. (2015). Plural policing in Western Europe. A comparison. *European Journal of Policing Studies, 2*(3), 235–244.

Devroe, E., & Terwel, P. (2015). De politiefunctie geprivatiseerd? Private beveiliging in België en Nederland. In P. Ponsaers, E. De Raedt, L. Wondergem, & L. G. Moor (Eds.), *Outsourcing policing* (Vol. 3, pp. 11–31). Maklu.

Domus Medica. (2021, July 29). *Wij zijn geen reisbureau.* https://www.domusmedica.be/actueel/wij-zijn-geen-reisbureau

De Waard, J. (1999). The private security industry in international perspective. *European Journal on Criminal Policy and Research, 7,* 143–174.

Dupont, B., Grabosky, P., & Shearing, C. (2003). The Governance of Security in Weak and Failing States. *Criminal Justice, 3*(4), 331–349.

De Standaard. (2018). Securitas gaat hoofdkantoor Antwerpse politie bewaken. *De Standaard.* August 31. Available via: https://www.standaard.be/cnt/dmf20180831_03693595

Earnshaw, V. A., et al. (2020). COVID-19 conspiracy beliefs, health behaviors, and policy support. *Translational Behavioral Medicine, 10*(4), 850–856. https://doi.org/10.1093/tbm/ibaa090

Financial Express. (2020). How Covid lockdown has made us realise the significance of unarmed security guards. *Financial Express,* 29 June.

G4S. (2021, January 19). *Professionele bijstand voor vaccinatiecentra.* https://www.g4s.com/nl-be/media/newsroom/2021/01/19/vaccination-centre

Goldman, J., & Xyrichis, A. (2020). Interprofessional working during the COVID-19 pandemic: Sociological insights. *Journal of Interprofessional Care, 34*(5), 580–582. https://doi.org/10.1080/13561820.2020.1806220

Garland, D. (2001). *The Culture of Control: Crime and Social Order in Contemporary Society.* Oxford: Oxford University Press.

Gilling, D. (1997). *Crime prevention; Theory, policy and practice.* London: UCL Press.

Gudders, D. & Daems, T. (2018). Privatisation of punishment in Belgium. In T. Daems & T. Vander Beken (Eds.), *Privatising Punishment in Europe* (pp. 65–83). London: Routledge.

Het Parool. (2021, January 24). *Hugo de Jonge: brand in testlocatie Urk gaat alle perken te buiten.*

Hlouchova, I. (2020). Countering terrorism in the shadows: The role of private security and military companies. *Security and Defence Quarterly, 31*(4), 155–169. https://doi.org/10.35467/sdq/130817

HM Government. (2006). *Countering international terrorism: The United Kingdom's strategy.* The Stationary Office.

Hodge, G. A., & Greve, C. (2007). Public-private partnerships: An international performance review. *Public Administration Review, 67*(3), 545–558. http://www.jstor.org/stable/4624596

Herzog-Evans, M. (2018). French probation and prisoner resettlement: involuntary 'privatisation' and corporatism. In T. Daems & T. Vander Beken (Eds.), *Privatising Punishment in Europe* (pp. 104-123). London: Routledge.

Johnston, L. (1992). *The rebirth of private policing.* London: Routledge.

Johnston, L. (1993). Privatisation and Protection: Spatial and Sectoral Ideologies in British Policing and Crime Prevention. *The Modern Law Review, 56*(6), 771–792.

Jones, T., & Newburn, T. (2006). *Plural Policing: A Comparative Perspective.* London: Routledge.

Jones, T., Steden, R. van, & Boutellier, H. (2009). Pluralisation of policing in England & Wales and the Netherlands: exploring similarity and difference. *Policing and Society, 19*(3), 282–299.

L'Avenir. (2020). En première ligne pour gérer le Covid. *L'Avenir*, 15 October.

Lam, P. T. I. (2019). Public–private partnerships for fire, police, and ambulance services. In R. M. Clark & S. Hakim (Eds.), *Public-private partnerships. Competitive government: Public-private partnerships.* Springer. https://doi.org/10.1007/978-3-030-24600-6_8

Leeuwarder Courant. (2021, November 21). *Testlocatie Van Schaikweg in Emmen moet sluiten door brand(stichting).*

Leloup, P. (2021). *De ontwikkeling van de private bewakingssector in België (1907-1990). Een historisch-criminologisch perspectief op transities in de veiligheidszorg.* Den Haag: Boom Uitgevers

Leloup, P., & Cools, M. (2022). (Post-)crisis policing, public health and private security: The COVID-19 pandemic and the private security sector. *Policing and Society, 32*, 748–763. https://doi.org/10.1080/10439463.2021.1970159

Leloup, P., & White, A. (2022). Questioning Anglocentrism in plural policing studies: Private security regulation in Belgium and the United Kingdom. *European Journal of Criminology.* https://doi.org/10.1177/14773708211014853

Leloup, P., Lenjou, F., Seron, V., & Cools, M. (Eds.). (2022). *Private veiligheidsactoren in België. De sector aan het woord.* Gompel&Svacina, 188 p.

Loyens, K., de Boer, N., & Schott, C. (2021). *Inspectiewerk tijdens de Coronacrisis. Een verkenning van praktijken, ervaringen en mogelijke interventies in de Belgische federale sociale inspectiediensten ten gevolge van de uitbraak van Covid-19.* USBO-advies.

Loader, I. (2000). Plural policing and democratic governance. *Social & Legal Studies, 9*(3), 323–345.

Morriss, A. (2006). The public-private security partnership: Counterterrorism considerations for employers in a post-9/11 world, 2. *Hastings Business Law Journal, 2*(2), 427–452.

Nalla, M. K., & Hummer, D. (1999). Relations between police officers and security professionals: A study of perceptions. *Security Journal, 12*, 31–40.

Nederlandse Veiligheidsbranche. (2020). *Visie op particuliere beveiliging in 2030. Veiligheid van Nederland in goede handen.* Nederlandse Veiligheidsbranche.

NH Nieuws. (2021, October 1). *Veranderde Ralph (38) van vreedzame coronademonstrant in potentieel terrorist?.*

NASCO. (2020). Recognizing the Essential Public Safety Role of Private Security During the COVID-19 Pandemic. *National Association of Security Companies NASCO*, April, 15. Available from: https://www.nasco.org/wp-content/uploads/2020/04/Recognizing-the-Essential-Public-Safety-Role-of-Private-Security-During-the-COVID-19-PR-for-Website.pdf

Organisation for Economic Co-operation and Development. (2012). *Principles of public governance of public-private partnerships.* OECD.

Pacciardi, A., & Berndtsson, J. (2022). EU border externalisation and security outsourcing: Exploring the migration industry in Libya. *Journal of Ethnic and Migration Studies, 48*, 4010–4028. https://doi.org/10.1080/1369183X.2022.2061930

Phelps, M. (2021). The role of the private sector in counter-terrorism: A scoping review of the literature on emergency responses to terrorism. *Security Journal, 34*, 599–620. https://doi.org/10.1057/s41284-020-00250-6

Protection Unit. (2021, February, 19). *Protection Unit in het hart van de gezondheidscrisis.* https://www.protectionunit.com/nl/protection-unit-in-het-hart-van-de-gezondheidscrisis/

Rogers, C. (2017). Plural policing. Theory and practice. Bristol: Bristol University Press.

Securitas. (2021, January, 17). *Veiligheid als topprioriteit voor vaccinatiecentra.* https://www.securitasnewsroom.be/veiligheid-voor-vaccinatiecentra/

Terpstra, J. (2008). Police, local government, and citizens as participants in local security networks. *Police Practice and Research: An International Journal, 9*(3), 213–225. https://doi.org/10.1080/10439463.2016.1161624

Terpstra, J. (2017). 'Not just one node among many' – plural policing in a state-dominated context: the case of Austria. *Policing and Society, 27*(1), 68–81. https://doi.org/10.1080/1043946 3.2015.1012169

Terpstra, J., Stokkom, B. A. M. van, & Spreeuwers, R. (2013). *Who patrols the streets? An international comparative study of plural policing.* The Hague : Eleven International Publishing.

Terpstra, J., de Maillard, J., Salet, R., & Roché, S. (2021). Policing the corona crisis: A comparison between France and The Netherlands. *International Journal of Police Science & Management, 23*(2), 168–181. https://doi.org/10.1177/1461355720980772

U.S. Department of Justice. (2005). *Engaging the private sector to promote homeland security: Law enforcement-private security partnerships.* Bureau of Justice Assistance.

van Steden, R. (2007). *Privatizing Policing: Describing and Explaining the Growth of Private Security.* Den Haag: Eleven International Publishing

Vanhouche, A-S. & Nederlandt, O. (2019). Eindelijk een onafhankelijk en effectief toezicht op de Belgische gevangenissen? *Fatik, 162,* 25–37.

Vermeersch, C. (2015). *Private en publieke politie, vriend of vijand? Een zicht op publiek-private samenwerking in Vlaanderen.* Bachelor thesis, Ghent University.

Waelput, L., Leloup, P., & Cools, M. (2021). *Hoe zien leidinggevenden van de lokale politie het imago van bewakingsagenten.* BlueConnect. Vanden Broele.

White, A. (2014). Post-crisis policing and public–private partnerships: The case of Lincolnshire police and G4S. *The British Journal of Criminology, 54*(6), 1002–1022. https://doi.org/10.1093/bjc/azu063

White, A. (2022). Critical workers? Private security, public perceptions and the Covid-19 pandemic. *Security Journal, 36,* 317–332. https://doi.org/10.1057/s41284-022-00339-0

Incorporating Non-state Security Actors into Public Security: Mexico's Failed Experiment

Logan Puck

Abstract Centralizing the use of coercion by subduing violence wielding non-state actors is an essential component of state formation. Incorporating these actors into public security forces is one strategy states can utilize to both enhance the capacity of the state and eliminate the threat those actors may pose to the state's monopoly on the legitimate use of force. Focusing on Mexico City, this study shows how state efforts to incorporate private watchmen into public police forces ultimately failed to improve state capacity. The piecemeal process of incorporation in Mexico City and the integration of watchmen into a corrupt and abusive police force led to the creation of an underequipped, poorly trained, underpaid, corrupt, and exploited hybrid force that makes the city money, but fails to improve the state's capacity to enforce the rule of law and provide safety to its citizens. Ultimately, the Mexican case highlights both the appeal of incorporation as a state-making and capacity enhancing strategy and its negative consequences when conducted in corrupted settings.

1 Introduction

As Tilly (1985) lays out, state formation is a long process involving the extraction of resources and the centralization of the use of coercion in which non-state actors are gradually stripped of their ability to legitimately wield force. States can use multiple strategies to confront the violent non-state actors, most notably the use of force, prohibition and criminalization, management and regulation, and direct incorporation. I use the term incorporation to describe actions taken by the state to convert private actors and/or entities into state actors. These actions may consist of presidential decrees, the passing of laws, or more informal measures, such as recruitment, that convert non-state security actors into public ones. Incorporation

L. Puck (✉)
Department of Political Science, The George Washington University, Washington, DC, USA
e-mail: logan.puck@gwu.edu

serves as an example of how states may attempt to develop their state capacity from outside sources instead of building it from the ground up. Through incorporation, states can ostensibly improve their capacity by expanding the size of their public security forces with actors possessing security-related experience while simultaneously eliminating competition for citizens' loyalty and any threat these actors may have posed to the state's monopoly on force. Incorporation can also create a "measure of uniformity" in regard to the type and quality of security services offered to the public (Bryett, 1994, 64).

The development and centralization of the Mexican state was a long and arduous process that involved repeated efforts to subdue, eliminate, and/or co-opt non-state violent actors. Beginning with the creation in the mid-nineteenth century of the *Rurales*, a federal rural police force, the police have served as a key actor tasked with this responsibility (Vanderwood, 1992). Various Mexican governments have attempted to confront violence wielding non-state actors by incorporating them into the state's public security forces in order to both subdue threats and enhance state capacity. For example, in the mid- to late nineteenth century, Mexican governors and later the president incorporated bandits into the *Rurales* in an effort to both eliminate the bandits as a security threat and bolster the strength of the police (Vanderwood, 1992). In the 1930s and 1940s, Mexico City and some Mexican states incorporated private watchmen into their police forces by creating special units that offered services to public and private clients. Incorporating these non-state actors into city and state police forces was seen as a way to strengthen the size and quality of the police as well as eliminate competition for the police and a potential threat to the state's power and legitimacy. Finally, in 2014, the Mexican government incorporated militias, called "*autodefensas*", into municipal police forces or a newly formed "rural defense corps," similar to the nineteenth century *Rurales*, that would be controlled by the military. The militias emerged in 2011 to fight against drug trafficking organizations ravaging local communities. These groups disarmed municipal police forces who they viewed as corrupt and took control over towns and cities in the region. In an effort to regain control of the region, subordinate the militias, and regain legitimacy in the area, the government signed an agreement with militia leaders to register their weapons and join the state security forces (Althaus & Dudley, 2014). Nevertheless, as scholars (Sabet, 2012; Davis, 2010; Muller, 2012) have demonstrated, the highly politicized and negotiated nature of the development of the Mexican police has created a fragmented, corrupt, abusive, and largely ineffective public security apparatus that has severely stunted efforts at effectively incorporating outside threats.

This chapter investigates the Mexican state's incorporation of night watchmen into Mexico City's police force in the mid-1940s and the consequences this action had on the watchmen, state capacity, and public – private security relations. I argue that the piecemeal process of incorporation in Mexico City and the integration of watchmen into a corrupt and abusive police force led to the creation of an underequipped, poorly trained, underpaid, corrupt, and exploited hybrid force that failed to improve the state's capacity to enforce the rule of law and provide safety to its citizens. Through a slow incorporation process that took decades to complete, the

Policía Auxiliar were exposed to the abusive practices of the Mexico City police force while also being held unaccountable to the public and unsupervised by the government. By removing watchmen from the streets through their incorporation, the state temporarily reduced challenges from non-state security providers to the state's monopoly on the use of force. However, the weakness of the Mexico City police force and its inability to fill security gaps permitted the emergence of new private security providers to fill the place of the incorporated watchmen. Thus, in the longer term, incorporation also failed to diminish threats to the state's monopoly on force and legitimacy. Furthermore, prior to incorporation, the quality of the watchmen's forces was variable, however, they clearly degraded after being converted into the *Policía Auxiliar*. Over time, the *Policía Auxiliar* became, arguably, the most disreputable force in Mexico City's police department. It became known for corrupt activity and the hiring of uneducated recruits who were then poorly trained, ill-equipped, overworked, and abusive. The state has, therefore, had to invest significant time, energy, and resources to improve the quality of the *Policía Auxiliar*, which is still commonly viewed as the least respected force in the city. Ultimately, incorporating non-state security actors into the state failed to build state capacity and impose law and order and increase citizen security in Mexico City.

I begin the chapter by describing the emergence of night watchmen in early twentieth century Mexico City, their rivalry with the Mexico City police department, and their eventual incorporation into the state as the *Policía Auxiliar*. I then describe the development of the *Policía Auxiliar* and the federal and Mexico City government's largely failed efforts to improve the force. In the second half of the chapter, I examine the current security landscape in Mexico City and the rise of the contemporary private security industry in Mexico. I discuss how the creation of hybrid police forces had the unintended consequence of placing public and private security providers in competition with each other, thus damaging their relationship.

2   The Watchmen Emerge

The *Policía Auxiliar* originated from private groups of watchmen that began to appear in Mexico City in the 1920s. The watchmen bore similarities to contemporary private security guards except watchmen were hired individually or as part of a union or association as opposed to being employees of a company. Due to rising crime rates, citizens began hiring watchmen to guard against car and home thefts (Secretaría de Seguridad Pública del Distrito Federal, n.d.). Mexico City's citizens often turned to these watchmen because they did not trust the city's highly corrupt and often criminally involved police forces, labeled *maffias* (sic) by the press (Gráfico, 1938, 12).

The Mexican Revolution (1910–1920) fundamentally altered the structure of Mexican government and society. As the conflict was winding down, President Venustiano Carranza became concerned that anti-revolutionary elements had too much control over the police and the courts. In response, the 1917 Constitution separated the police into two forces, the preventative and the judicial police, serving under different authorities. The preventative police were designed to serve as beat cops – patrolling the streets, preventing crimes from occurring, and maintaining order. The judicial police were charged with investigating crimes, arresting suspects, and prosecuting them. Notably, only the judicial police were given the authority to arrest suspects. The judicial police were put under the command of the *Ministerio Público*, which was supervised by the president's office. This action closely linked the judicial police force to the executive branch. The presidency, therefore, began giving the judicial police more responsibilities and funding (Davis, 2006, 63–64).

Links between the police and local communities were loosened due to the police's newfound autonomy (Piccato, 2001, 186; Davis, 2006, 64). Due to this distancing, the judicial police were able to escape accountability from the public. As Piccato (2001) explains, "Rather than a sign of greater security, the enhanced role of the judicial police often meant that police actions escaped public scrutiny" (186). As a result, police corruption surged along with citizen distrust of the institution. For example, policemen often asked for money from victims to search for suspects (Piccato, 2001, 187). Moreover, in an effort to control, as opposed to eliminate illegal markets, the new political regime coming out of the revolution forged links between the Mexico City police force and the criminal underworld (Alvarado, 2012, 209). The police force also had a paltry budget, which encouraged police officers to collect bribes. As Davis (2010) explains, "By the 1920s, there existed a well-established pecking order of bribery and corruption, ensuring that beat cops on the ground could not acquire or keep their jobs without direct payment to superiors". For example, the *Unión General de Comerciantes en Pequeño del Distrito Federal* (Small Business Owners Union) posted a bulletin stating that small business owners were being subjected to shake downs by the police five times a day (Universal, 1937b). Finally, the city's police force was small relative to the growing Mexico City population. A local press report called Mexico City, "*una de las ciudades peor vigiladas en el mundo*" ("one of the worst guarded cities in the world") (*Universal*, 1931). Residents complained that certain areas of the city, such as Tacubaya, Lomas de Chapultepec, and Colonia del Valle, had almost no police presence whatsoever in their neighborhoods (Universal, 1936, 1937a).

Over the next two decades, the number of watchmen operating in Mexico City exploded as the rapid expansion and growth of the capital created greater security gaps that the police were increasingly unable to fill. The Mexican Revolution ravaged the country's economy, leaving few job opportunities for Mexico City residents during the 1920s and 1930s. Veterans and others, therefore, flocked to the profession due to the high demand and low training requirements needed to be a watchman (Davis, 2010, 146; *Secretaría de Seguridad Pública del Distrito Federal*, n.d.). In 1933, a number of these unions and associations were brought together to form a civil association called the *Cuerpo de Vigilantes Auxiliares de la Policía del*

Distrito Federal (The Vigilante Corp Auxiliary to the Federal District Police).[1] They aligned with Mexico's labor movement and demanded improved workers' rights and security from the government. Their alignment with organized labor and position as competitors for security provision created for a highly contentious relationship with the Mexico City police (Davis, 2010, 147).

The relationship between watchmen and the state changed when Lazaro Cárdenas became president in 1934. Cárdenas ruled as a populist who embraced and mobilized Mexico's labor movement. Cárdenas instituted a regime that "established a new basis for state-labor relations" in which the state established and collaborated closely with umbrella organizations representing various sectors of the labor market (Collier & Collier, 1991, 236). As Demmers (2001) explains, "By incorporating strategic groups into the state apparatus, the regime is able to demobilize, 'deradicalize' and control their demands" (152). The state strove to control and dominate all sectors of society during this period. This approach included a campaign by Cardenas to nationalize major industries in Mexico, such as railroads, petroleum, and electricity. Following suit with these policies, Cardenas sought to incorporate watchmen into the state. Moreover, Cardenas' close association with labor led to a contentious relationship with Mexico City's police forces who were traditionally used to repress labor and peasants. Many of the watchmen were veterans of the Mexican Revolution who formed unions and associations aligned with communism and the far left. The watchmen's proclivity towards communism made them natural allies to Cárdenas' leftist politics and thus by incorporating them into the police forces he hoped to counterbalance the highly corrupt and conservative leaning preventative police (Davis, 2010, 146–147; AGN, LCR, 417–9 PA). Moreover, incorporating watchmen into the state served as an effort to monopolize the state's control over the legitimate use of force. Incorporation could both neutralize the watchmen as a potential threat to the state's legitimacy as the appropriate provider of protection within the city and could bolster the size, strength, and quality of the city's security forces, thus improving the state's capacity. As Davis (2010) explains, "At a minimum, [Cardenas] would offer urban residents a reinvigorated police force whose members were considered to be responsive to local communities and relatively unconstrained by existent networks of corruption" (147). The motives for incorporation were therefore multiple, but the outcome of this effort was determined by the poor quality of Mexico's police forces.

Yet, Cardenas never made an official decree incorporating the watchmen into the state. Therefore, these independent security providers continued to have a

---

[1] These groups included *la Union de Veladores del Comercio y Particulares, Cuerpo de Vigilantes de Vehiculos, Cuerpo de Vigilantes del Comercio y Particulares, Cuerpo de Vigilantes de la Policía de Atzcapotzalco, Veladores Independientes Unidos del Comercio y Particulares, Cuerpo de Veladores de la Unión de Cesantes, Cuerpo de Vigilancia de la Policia Privada de la Colonia del Valle, Servicio de Vigilancia autorizada de Mixcoac, Cuerpo de Vigilantes Nocturnos Particulares, Cuerpo de Veladores del Delegación de Atzcapotzalco, Policia Preventiva Auxiliar de la Colonia Industrial, Cuerpo de Veladores del Comercio y Particulares, Servicio de Seguridad Nocturna de Tlalpan,* and the *Policía Privada de las Lomas de Chapultepec* (AGN, ALR, 840/241).

contentious relationship with the police, especially as their ranks swelled to over 1400 independent watchmen by 1937. Watchmen frequently protested that they were being harassed by police officers. Members of the private police and watch-men's unions delivered numerous complaints against the police to the president and the press. In these complaints they argued that the police, at the behest of Mexico City's Chief of Police, were unfairly pursuing, arresting, and persecuting watchmen as well as attempting to regulate their activities to a degree that would essentially nullify their existence (AGN, LCR, 417–21; Universal, 1937a). Various unions across Mexico rallied in support of the watchmen by sending letters to the nation's president demanding a stop to the abusive treatment perpetrated by Mexican police officers against night watchmen (AGN, ALR, 334/529).

On the other side, representatives of the Mexico City police department accused watchmen of participating in illegal activities. For example, Mexico City's Chief of Police, Francisco Mártinez Montoya, publicly declared that "numerous" members of the *Cuerpos Auxiliares de la Policía* engaged in unlawful actions, such as assault-ing pedestrians, robbing drunks, and invading homes (Nacional, 1937a, 8). As a solution, he called for a centralization of the Mexico City police force in order to restrict the activities of watchmen and the private police (Nacional, 1937b, 8). Through centralization, the police could oversee and control the activities of the watchmen, thus removing these non-state actors as a rival and threat to the legiti-macy of the state's public security institutions. Please explain how centralization would solve the problem. Did the promise of centralization come with promises of more defined roles and more public oversight? The public had mixed views about the watchmen's units. A 1937 editorial in Universal described the night watchmen's services as "excellent" and praised their efforts to protect areas of the city where there was little police presence (Universal, 1937a, 9). Another editorial, however, called the night watchmen's promises of security "illusory" (*Universal*, 1938). As the following section explains, the government attempted to resolve this contentious relationship was through official incorporation.

3   Official Incorporation: But Only Partially

In 1941, President Manuel Ávila Camacho officially united the watchmen within a newly created force labeled the *Policía Auxiliar* (PA). According to the president's decree, the PA would serve as an auxiliary force to the newly re-organized Preventative Police of Mexico City. The PA would continue to provide services to private clients, but now served under the authority of Mexico City's Chief of Police. The newly created force was tasked with "the night surveillance of the residences individuals and commercial, industrial and banking establishments located in the District Federal, in order to prevent crimes and misdemeanors" although they were not provided with a weapons license or arrest powers (Diario Oficial, 1941). PA agents were also required to wear specific uniforms with a badge and insignia rep-resenting the force and they were mandated to assist the Mexico City police whenever required. Basic eligibility requirements were also specified for members of the new force. These included Mexican nationality, a record of good conduct, no history of property-related crimes, and clearance from contagious diseases, and other debilitating afflictions (Diario Oficial, 1941). In the decree, Camacho also recognized the *Policía Bancaria*, a separate security force founded by Colonel Arturo Godinez Reyes, in collaboration with the Association of Mexican Bankers, specifically tasked with protecting Mexican banks. Although recognized by the government, the banking police would continue to be funded by their clients (Espinosa Rasgado, 2013).

In 1949, despite protestations, the *Policía Auxiliar* were placed under the orders of the Mexico City Protection and Transit Directorate where they would remain for the next 30 plus years (Policía Auxiliar, n.d. 22–23).[2] Despite their location within the government, the *Policía Auxiliar* were only partially incorporated into the state and thus still maintained a high level of autonomy. Although the force was assigned a director and grouped together under one title, they continued to operate as separate individual units. The former watchmen's groups were distributed into "battalions" headed by police or military commanders. Each unit commander was designated a zone of the city in which to operate and made responsible for recruiting, training, and outfitting their agents (Chávez, 1995, 39). Additionally, their budgets were controlled by the heads of each unit and self-generated through their earnings from contracts with private clients. Thus, there was little oversight or regulation of the force's activities (Gaspar Torres, 2014; Former Policía Auxiliar Administrator, 2014).

The partial incorporation of the *Policía Auxiliar* negatively affected the former watchmen. Commanders of the various *Policía Auxiliar* units were already enmeshed in the corrupt networks of the Mexico City police department and thus the force was immediately drawn into them. Commanders demanded quotas from the rank-and-file and sent them up the hierarchical chain. Members of the rank-and-file had to resort to demanding bribes and engaging in criminal activities to both subsist and provide for their superiors. Mexico City's large informal economy gave the police ample opportunities to extract bribes from black market dealers. Smuggling, gambling, prostitution, and car theft were common activities that the police provided protection for in exchange for payments (Piccato, 2003).[3] Additionally, the illegal production and trafficking of mostly marijuana and opium, along with other drugs, began to significantly increase in Mexico in the 1930s and 1940s, making it a highly lucrative market. As Kenny and Serrano (2011) note, "By 1943, US authorities

---

[2] The Chief of the *Policía Auxiliar*, Colonel Leandro Castillo Villegas, sent letters of protest to President Aleman, arguing that the transportation department was not an appropriate location for the PA because the protective services offered by the force clearly made it more suitably located under the leadership of the police. Despite these protestations, the force was still transferred (AGN, MAV, 545.22/498).

[3] While official crime rates at the time were relatively low, actual levels of crime from that time are hard to measure due to a lack of trust in the criminal justice system, which limited citizens' willingness to report crimes. Additionally, the police and the courts' lacked the resources to respond to many complaints of crime when they were reported (Piccato, 2003).

estimated that Mexico's opium production had tripled within a decade" (32). The police, along with certain members of the military and the political elite, became heavily involved in the drug trade by providing traffickers and producers with protection in exchange for bribes and/or directly participating in the trafficking themselves (Kenny & Serrano, 2011).

In 1947, just a few years after their incorporation, members of the PA were already being called thieves (AGN, MAV, 545.22/498). Over time, the PA became ever more involved in the Mexico City police department's corruption schemes. As Davis explains, "by the early 1960s, a highly formalized system of kickbacks was in full swing" (Davis 2010, 152). Internal documents show that payments of $125,000 pesos were made to the head of the PA each month during this period (2010, 152). Some original watchmen who were incorporated into the PA in 1941 were also purged from the force as evidenced by a complaint signed by dozens of former agents claiming they had been unfairly and illegally discharged of their duties (AGN, DGIPS, 1477/22). By the late 1960s, academics and government officials began to call for a centralization of the police force in an effort to rein in or even eliminate extraneous units who were deemed unnecessary (Ravelo, 1968). These units, including the *Policía Auxiliar*, strongly resisted these demands for centralization, as they "sought to protect their autonomy and independent access to protection rackets" (Davis, 2010, 155).

Additionally, during this time and to the dismay of Mexico City officials, private policing outfits began to emerge throughout the city. In 1967, Mexico City's Attorney General, Gilberto Suárez Torres and the Chief of the Mexico City Police Department, Luis Cueto Ramírez, declared the need to eliminate the "illegal" private policing groups proliferating throughout the nation's capital. Cueto Ramirez said he would pursue and arrest members of these groups in an "energetic and definite manner" (Excelsior, 1967). Clearly, the *Policía Auxilar* had failed to fill security gaps in the city and their general corrupt nature and incompetence likely contributed to the problem. Thus, the incorporation of watchmen into the state's security apparatus did little to eliminate potential threats to the state's monopoly on the legitimate use of force as new non-state security providers emerged to rival city police.

Throughout the 1970s, the *Policía Auxiliar* maintained its autonomy and remained deeply involved in corrupt networks while continuing to exploit its officers on the ground. By 1983, the corrupt nature of the *Policía Auxiliar* was so blatant that during his swearing in ceremony, the newly appointed chief of the force, Enrique Soberanes Gamboa, emphasized honesty as the key principle that would guide his time in power (Aguilar, 1983). A newspaper article from that period describes the *Policía Auxiliar* rank-and-file as "humble, defenseless and exploited by their superiors" (Anaya Sarmiento, 1984). Officers were provided with only two uniforms per year and then had to purchase new ones if their own became damaged or worn out (*Universal*, 1984b). They also had to pay unaccounted for quotas to their superiors. Furthermore, they were still restricted from carrying firearms and therefore defenseless against criminals. Nevertheless, officers were held responsible if the car or house he or she was guarding was damaged or robbed (Anaya Sarmiento,

1984). The Policía Auxiliar became so poorly run that it was dubbed "los patitos feos" (the ugly ducklings) of the Mexico City police department (*Universal*, 1984b).

4   Centralization

In 1984, President Miguel de la Madrid Hurtado passed a sweeping new law restructuring the Mexico City police forces. The re-structuring came in light of a major corruption scandal centered around Arturo Durazo, Mexico City's police chief from 1976 to 1982 (Muller, 2012, 100–101). A number of PA commanders were caught up in the scandal, admitting to providing Durazo with significant sums of money during his reign. Beyond Durazo's corrupt activities, numerous complaints emerged about the unruly nature of the Mexico City police department. Reporters, civil society groups and opposition party members criticized the department for its excessive number of police forces, including the PA, many of which these critics claimed were unnecessary and even unconstitutional (Ramiréz Mendez, 1981; *Universal*, 1984a; Fuentes, 1984; Universal, 1984c).

The 1984 law replaced President Camacho's decree in 1941 that originally recognized the *Policía Auxiliar* and the *Policía Bancaria e Industrial* (née *Policía Bancaria*). Within de la Madrid's new law, the *Policía Auxiliar* and *Policía Bancaria e Industrial* were officially integrated into the Mexico City police department in an effort to better regulate, professionalize, and modernize these two forces as well as improve their coordination with the city's other police forces. The PBI and PA were integrated as members of the newly created *Policía Complementaria* under the direction and leadership of the Mexico City Secretariat of Public Security (SSPDF).[4] These forces now had to abide by the laws and regulations similar to the preventative police. They were also authorized to carry firearms through a weapons license acquired by the Mexico City Secretariat of Public Security. All of their income acquired from their contracts with public and private clients was to be directed to the Mexico City Treasury. Stricter enrollment requirements were implemented that pertained to recruits' age, height, weight, educational attainment, and psychological profile. Moreover, as complementary police forces, the PBI and PA were mandated to not only continue their regular practice of providing protective services to public and private clients, but also to assist the preventative police in cases of disasters and massive events, such as protests and demonstrations (Diario Oficial de la Federación, 1984). Nevertheless, most of these forces' earnings, 98% in the case of the PA, were returned to their commanders to be doled out for salaries and equipment, thus the PA and PBI continued to possess high levels of autonomy. The PA continued to be plagued by endemic corruption involving networks of PA commanders stealing hundreds of millions of dollars that were supposed to go towards paying the salaries

---

[4]Although housed under the title *Policía Complementaria*, the two forces remained separate from each other.

and benefits of the force's employees (Chavez, 1995, 39–40; Monge, 1999, 32–33). During the 1980s and 1990s, rank-and-file members of the *Policía Auxiliar* had multiple letters-to-the-editor published in news publications in which they accused their superiors of corruption and demanded bonuses they had been promised (Proceso, 1989; Proceso, 1994, 80). These men and women were still being abused by their superiors, working 10-hour days or more, and earning salaries just above minimum wage. Additionally, applicants only needed a bare minimum of education to enlist, and new recruits received only 1 week of basic training before being sent on patrol. As a result of all of these issues, the PA suffered a 50% annual desertion rate as many PA officers abandoned the police force to join the burgeoning private security market where companies offered higher salaries and better benefits (Hernández A. and Gómez F. 1993).

In 1997, steps were again taken to improve the force when Cuauhtémoc Cárdenas of the recently founded Party of the Democratic Revolution (PRD) was elected mayor of Mexico City in the city's first ever democratic election.[5] Cárdenas made "several high-profile efforts to call attention to police corruption," including the implementation of a change in leadership in the *Policía Auxiliar* and a public investigation into the disappearance of hundreds of millions of pesos from the force's coffers every year (Davis, 2006, 67; Rodriguez Castañeda, 1999). With revelations of the force's corrupt practices coming to light, the *Policía Auxiliar*'s rank and file protested against their commanders for falsely representing their interests and paying them only 67% of their deserved wages (Guizar, 2013; Bolaños et al., 2000). From 1999 to 2000, members organized and participated in five separate demonstrations of protest throughout the city. Members of the *Policía Auxiliar* blocked major highways for multiple hours and marched through different points of the city. Close to 800 *Policía Auxiliar* agents participated in one of the marches that demanded the firing of 26 commanders (Bolaños et al., 2000).

After these protests and investigations, the force was finally fully incorporated into the state under the leadership of Cardenas and his successors. First, resources were put under strict control by the Mexico City legislature (Ex-Administrator, 2014). Subsequently, the PA and PBI would subsist on a fixed budget annually, created and voted upon by the Mexico City legislature (Espinosa Rasgado, 2013; Guizar, 2013). Additional steps were also taken to improve the quality of personnel and services offered by the PA through stricter enrollment requirements and improved training methods and offerings. In order to join the PA, one must now possess Mexican citizenship, be between the ages of 18 and 30, possess a junior high school degree, and not have been dishonorably discharged from the police or the military. Finally, Atenógenes Gaspar Torres, the PBI's Executive Director and the Director of Operations, switched over to the PA in 2010 in order to re-shape the PA so that it more closely resembled the PBI, which has a much better reputation than the PA (Gaspar Torres, 2014).

---

[5] Previously, the mayor had been appointed by the nation's president.

5   The Policía Auxiliar and Mexico City's Security Landscape Today

Today, the PA has over 28,000 employees. The PA offers bodyguard services to government officials and individual citizens and transport of goods protection and armed guard services to private companies and public institutions. Half of the PA's contracts are with public institutions while the other half are with private companies. PA units can also be contracted out to individual neighborhoods and delegations to assist with or perform the duties of Mexico City's preventative police (Guizar, 2013; Secretaría de Seguridad Ciudadana, n.d.). The PA still comprises one half of the Mexico City Complementary Police. The other half continues to be the *Policía Bancaria e Industrial* (PBI). The PBI is a smaller force of around 17,000 employees. It is housed in its own headquarters and possesses a separate command structure. The PBI offers similar services as the PA, but it primarily serves private clients. Approximately 90% of their contracts are with private clients while 10% are with public institutions (Espinosa Rasgado, 2013).

The PA and PBI have a number of competitors for contracts, however. Despite the creation of the PA and PBI to head off the need for non-state security providers, the private security industry has blossomed over the past 40 years throughout the capital city and the country as a whole. Profit driven private security companies began to appear in the 1960s and 1970s. Some of the earliest companies were formed by retired generals and other military higher ups in collaboration with the government to combat Cold War threats. These companies would work with the government to repress leftist insurgent groups (Security Company Owner, 2014). More companies began to emerge in the 1970s offering their protective services to private clients. This emergence aligned with a global trend as private security companies started to appear in many parts of the world during this era. The industry in Mexico was still quite small, however, with just 40 private security firms operating in the country in 1970 (Regallado Santillán, 2002, 188–189). It continued to grow into the 1980s as multinational private security firms began establishing footholds in Mexico and massive police corruption scandals reduced citizen trust in the institution. While some of these firms worked locally, others operated throughout the country providing services to both public institutions and private clients. The true boom in private security began with the signing of the North American Free Trade Agreement (NAFTA) in the 1990s and has continued to the present day (Puck, 2022a). In 1999, the growth in private security provision in Mexico peaked with a 40% increase compared to the year before (Muller, 2010, 135–136). By 2000, over 1400 private security companies were registered with federal government and many more operated under the table (187).

Today, an estimated 500,000–600,000 private security guards work in Mexico and approximately 6000–8500 companies operate in the country today (Badillo, 2021; Forbes, 2020; Frutos, 2014). Currently there are 540 registered private security companies and hundreds more that are not registered that operate in Mexico City. Approximately 50% of all private security firms in Mexico are unregulated and an estimated 20–25% operate in Mexico City (La Prensa, 2022). Across the country, the industry has grown so large that it currently represents 1.4–2% of percent of the nation's GDP and growth remains steady (Forbes, 2020; Badillo, 2021). For example, in 2019, the industry is reported to have grown by a whopping 20% (Sanchez, 2020). According to the *Consejo Nacional de Seguridad Privada*, a Mexican private security association, the country's formal private security industry is worth close to $1.5 billion – a figure that is "180% higher than in 2012 and growing every year, even without accounting for the private security firms operating in the informal sector" (Kinosian & Bosworth, 2018, 5).

Mexico's private security sector is quite heterogenous. It is predominantly composed of local companies, but large multinational companies, such as G4S and Securitas, also operate in the country. The sector ranges from professionalized outfits offering high quality services from well-trained employees to small, unregulated firms that hire ex-police officers and provide little to zero training and low- quality uniforms and equipment to their agents. Private security firms in Mexico tend to specialize in the protection of goods and property, however, many firms also offer the protection of persons, transfer of goods and valuables, alarms and electronic monitoring, information security, and prevention and responsibility systems (Robert Straus Center 10, 2018). Firms are able to compete with the PA and PBI for contracts to protect public institutions. For example, the Mexico City International Airport has contracts with five different private security firms to provide various security services in the airport (Aeropuerto Internacional Ciudad de México, n.d.). Nevertheless, the industry tends to have a poor reputation due to widespread informality in the industry. As noted earlier, an estimated 50% of firms are unregulated in Mexico City and estimates are even higher for the country at large.

Due to built-in advantages, the PA is often able to outcompete private security firms. First, the PA has a weapons license, which is quite difficult to acquire in Mexico. Firearms licenses are granted by the Secretariat of National Defense (SEDENA) and the only gun store in the entire country is located on a heavily guarded military base in Mexico City. The process for acquiring a license is time-consuming, complicated, and expensive (Security Company Owner, 2014). Private security companies are required to pay 34,094 pesos (~$1853 USD) for a firearms license (*Secretaría de la Defensa Nacional,* n.d.). This is more expensive than the cost of a license to operate a private security firm in Mexico City. Furthermore, a weapons license must be revalidated annually for the same cost as the initial registration fee. It is also commonly understood that one must have connections within Mexico's security apparatus and/or political system to receive approval for a license (Security Consultant, 2014; Gutierrez, 2013). Additionally, the PA has policing powers, such as the right to detain suspects, which private security firms do not possess, and the force tends to provide better training, albeit still quite minimal, to its recruits in comparison to many private security firms (Puck, 2022b). As a result, the force has been able to earn significant millions of dollars for the Mexico City government each year. For example, in Mexico City's 2020 budget, the government estimated that the PBI would earn 5 billion pesos (~ $230 million USD) (Secretaría de Administración y Finanzas, 2020).

The neighboring State of Mexico has its own auxiliary force called *Los Cuerpos de Seguridad Auxiliares del Estado de México* (Cusaem) Similar to the PA, the

Cusaem is linked to the state security apparatus and provides paid protection to public and private clients. Unlike the PA, however, the Cusaem was never fully incorporated into the state, and therefore operates in a legal gray zone between public and private status. This status allows the force to avoid oversight of its finances, operations, and labor, hiring, and training standards. As a result, the force can undercut the security market by offering cheaper services while maintaining some of the advantages of the PA, such as possession of a weapon's license and special policing powers. The Cusaem's presence in Mexico City increased after Enrique Peña Nieto, the former Governor of the State of Mexico, was elected president in 2012 (Villamil, 2011). Under his presidency, the Cusaem garnered contracts with close to 70 federal entities, many of which are headquartered in Mexico City (Leon et al., 2017). With the 2018 election of Andres Manuel Lopez Obrador, however, the Cusaem's presence in Mexico City is likely to wane as the new president has challenged the legal status of the organization (Ramírez, 2022).

The presence of these hybrid forces has created resentment from representatives of the private security industry who view these forces as an unfair incursion by the state into the private security market. Alejandro Desfassiaux, the founder of one of the largest private security companies in Mexico and the former president of the *Consejo Nacional de Seguridad Privada* is one of the leading voices denouncing the PA and other hybrid police forces in Mexico. Desfassaiux and Julio Cesar Garcia Marin, the president of the *Sociedad Mexicana de Guardaespaldas*, have both criticized the Mexico City government for using these forces like a business when the state is constitutionally obligated to provide protective services to its citizens free of charge (Ramirez, 1998; La Crónica, 2011). At a meeting I attended between representatives of the private security industry and Mexico City officials, private security providers openly complained about hybrid forces, particularly the Cusaem, for unfairly competing in the market for security.

Despite the PA's ability to bring in money for the city treasury, the force continues to have a poor reputation and is generally considered the worst police unit in Mexico City. The force still lacks public respect, engages in corrupt practices, and the rank-and-file continue to suffer abuses (Guizar, 2013; Villanueva, 2014). One example of this corruption is the suspicious disappearance of over 31,000 ammunition cartridges from the force's ammunition depot (Proceso, 2014). Furthermore, officers continue to complain that their wages are too low, they are still forced to work excessively long shifts, some that last over 24 hours, and they lack the proper equipment to successfully perform their jobs (Villanueva, 2014). Throughout the 2000s, numerous members of the *Policía Auxiliar* submitted written complaints to the President of Mexico regarding corruption, abuse, sexism, ageism, reduced vacation time, and unjust firings as well as demands for re-cooped wages, compensation for unjust firings, and improved pensions (AGN, PCGA). In one particularly colorful letter submitted in 2003, two former PA officers lamented how they were treated like "animals or beasts," forced to work in the rain and cold with no concern from their superiors (AGN, PCGA Caja 413, exp 109098,). Female police officers within the PA filed numerous sexual harassment complaints against their superiors (Proceso, 2003). According to a report in the investigative journal, *El Proceso*, four out of ten women on the force received threats or pressure to accede to the sexual demands of their superiors, in exchange for not being dismissed or placed at the disposal of their managers (2003). Some officers threatened hunger strikes and public demonstrations have continued. In 2011, approximately 200 members of the *Policía Auxiliar* protested in the streets, calling for the dismissal of Group 52 Commander Marcos Martinez Salazer for poorly treating his subordinates and demanding quotas from them (Rivera, 2011). In 2012, members of the force organized a demonstration in the streets of Mexico City to protest their lack of medical care (Cruz, 2012). Overall, problems continue to plague the *Policía Auxiliar* as members of the rank and file continue to suffer poor treatment from their superiors and corruption remains rife throughout the force.

6 Conclusion

Overall, incorporating non-state security actors into public security forces proved unable to improve the state's capacity nor eliminate threats to the state's monopoly over the use of force. In the Mexico City case, watchmen were incorporated into a corrupt and abusive police force through the creation of the *Policía Auxiliar*. Members of the newly created *Policía Auxiliar* were exploited, poorly trained, recruited with low standards and thus the force became weak and ineffective. As a result, the creation of the *Policía Auxiliar* did little to improve the Mexico City police department's quality of security provision services and the state's capacity was not bolstered. Moreover, the incorporation of watchmen did little in the long run to eliminate competing security providers with the potential to challenge the state's monopoly on legitimate force. Private policing outfits emerged again soon after the incorporation of the *Policía Auxiliar*.

These incorporation efforts exhibit a larger pattern in Mexican history of attempting to improve state capacity from outside sources instead of building it from within. Whether dealing with bandits, private watchmen, or militia members, Mexican governments have used incorporation as a tool to both strengthen their own security forces and neutralize potential threats to the state's monopoly on force and competitors for the state's legitimacy. Without possessing strong, clean, well-operating state security institutions during the process of incorporation, these efforts are bound to fail and further exacerbate problems within those institutions.

References

Aeropuerto Internacional Ciudad de Mexico. (n.d.). Contratacion de Seguridad y Vigilancia. https://www.aicm.com.mx/contratacion-seguridad-y-vigilancia/v-empresas-contratadas

Aguilar, A. (1983, July 5). *Honestidad*, subrayó al nombrar al nuevo jefe de la Policía Auxiliar. *El Día*. Biblioteca Miguel Lerdo de Tejada. L06226: Policía México 1983 Julio – Diciembre.

Althaus, D., & Dudley, S.. (2014, April 30). Mexico's security dilemma: The rise of Michoacan's Militias. *Insight Crime*. http://www.insightcrime.org/investigations/mexico-security-rise-militias-michoacan. Accessed 10 Oct 2015.

Alvarado, A. (2012). *El Tamaño del Infierno: Un estudio sobre la criminalidad en la Zona Metropolitana de la Ciudad de México*. El Colegio de Mexico.

Anaya Sarmiento, R. (1984, November 7). La Policía Auxiliar. *El Día*. Biblioteca Miguel Lerdo de Tejada. L06226: Policia Auxiliar 1984 Aug-Dec.

Badillo, D. (2021). Operan en México alrededor de 3,500 empresas de seguridad 'patito.' *El Economista*.   https://www.eleconomista.com.mx/politica/Operan-en-Mexico-alrededor-de-3500-empresas-de-seguridad-patito-20210815-0002.html

Bolaños, A., Olayo, R., Llanos, R., & Salgado, A. (2000, November 16). Policías Auxiliares Bloquean Vías; Rebasan Protestas a sus Dirigentes. *La Jornada*. http://www.jornada.unam. mx/2000/11/16/039n1cap.html. Accessed 5 Dec 2013.

Bryett, K. (1994). Privatisation of policing. In K. Bryett & C. Lewis (Eds.), *Un-peeling tradition: Contemporary policing* (pp. 58–70). Macmillan.

Collier, R. B., & Collier, D. (1991). *Shaping the political arena: Critical junctures, the labor movement, and regime dynamics in Latin America*. Princeton University Press.

Cruz, L.. (2012, February 27). Protestan policías auxiliares del DF por atención médica. *Reforma*. http://noticias.terra.com.mx/mexico/df/protestan-policias-auxiliares-del-DF-por-atencion-medica. Accessed 5 Dec 2013.

Chavez. E. (1995, May 1). La asociacion civil de la Policia Auxiliar, saqueada por las autoridades. *Proceso*.

Davis, D. (2006). Undermining the rule of law: Democratization and the dark side of police reform in Mexico. *Latin American Politics and Society, 48*(1), 55–86. (Spring).

Davis, D. (2010). Policing and populism in the Cardenas and Echeverria administrations. In A. M. Kiddle & M. L. O. Muñoz (Eds.), *Populism in twentieth century Mexico: The presidencies of Lazaro Cardenas and Luis Echeverria* (pp. 135–158). University of Arizona Press.

Demmers, J. (2001). Neoliberal reforms and populist politics: The PRI in Mexico. In J. Demmers, A. Fernandez Jilberto, & B. Hogenbook (Eds.) Miraculous Metamorphoses: The Neoliberalization of Latin American Populism (pp. 150–181). Zed Books.

Diario Oficial de la Federación. (1941, March 13). *Reglamento del Cuerpo de Veladores Auxiliares de la Policía Preventiva del D.F.*

Diario Oficial de la Federación. (1984). *Reglamento de la Ley de Federal de Seguridad Privada*.

Espinosa Rasgado, E. (2013, November 26). Director of institutional communication, *Policía Bancaria e Industrial*. Mexico City.

Ex-Administrator. (2014, October 7). *Policia Auxiliar*. Guadalajara, Jalisco.

Excelsior. (1967, September 20). *Serán Eliminadas las Policías Ilegales y las Guardias de Empresas Particulares*. Biblioteca Miguel Lerdo de Tejada. L06209 Policía México 1961–1969.

Forbes. (2020, November 12). *Seguridad privada: prioridad en el mundo empresarial*. https:// www.forbes.com.mx/brand-voice/ad-seguridad-privada-prioridad-en-mundo-empresarial-multisistemas/. Accessed 7 Oct 2022.

Former Policía Auxiliar Administrator. (2014, October 1). Guadalajara.

Fuentes, M. (1984). Policía anticonstitucional. *Uno Más Uno*, August 5. Biblioteca Lerdo de Tejada. L06226: Policía México 1984 Agosto – Diciembre.

Frutos. M. (2014, November 28). Seguridad privada es 60% patito. *Reporte Indigo*.

Gaspar Torres, A. (2014, April 29). Executive Director of Operations, *Policia Auxiliar*. Mexico City.

Gráfico. (1938). Las Maffias Policiacas: Parecidas a las Maffias de los Enemigos de la Sociedad. April 1: 12. Biblioteca Miguel Lerdo de Tejada. L06207: Policía México 1936–1946.

Guizar, F. (2013, November 30). Director of Communication, *Policía Auxiliar*. Mexico City.

Gutierrez, G. (2013, April 3). Trafican permisos de portar armas. El Universal.

Hernandez, A. & Gomez F. (1993, March 11). La Policia Auxiliar, con salarios infimos y baja preparacion, base de un 'gran plan de seguridad.' *Uno Mas Uno*. Biblioteca Lerdo de Tejada. L062000: Policia Salarios 1932–1993.

Kenny, P., & Serrano, M. (2011). The Mexican state and organized crime: An unending story. In P. Kenney, M. Serrano, & A. Sotomayor (Eds.), *Mexico's security failure: Collapse into criminal violence* (pp. 29–53). Routledge.

Kinosian, S., & Bosworth, J. (2018). Security for sale: Challenges and good practices in regulating private military and security companies in Latin America. *Inter-American Dialogue.*

La Crónica. (2011, July 31). *Descarta Mondragón y Kalb ganancias en SSPDF por renta de seguridad.* http://www.cronica.com.mx/notas/2011/595679.html

La Prensa. (2022). *50% de empresas de seguridad privada son "patito".*

Leon, L., Pazos, F., & Nacar, J. (2017, September 17). CUSAEM, un hoyo negro en el Estado de Mexico. *Eje Central.*

Monge, R. (1999, June 20). La Controlaria del DF formaliza la investigación sobre la Policía Auxiliar. *El Proceso,* pp. 32–33.

Muller, M.-M. (2012). *Public security in the negotiated state: Policing in Latin America and beyond.* Palgrave Macmillan.

Muller, M.M. (2010). Private Security and the State in Latin America: The Case of Mexico City. *Brazilian Political Science Review, 4*(1), 131–151.

Nacional. (1937a). Se han dedicado a actividades que pena la ley. September 15: 8. Biblioteca Miguel Lerdo de Tejada. L06207 Policía México 1936–1946.

Nacional. (1937b). Centralización de las labores de la policía. August 21: 8. Biblioteca Miguel Lerdo de Tejada. L06207 Policía México 1936–1946.

Nacional. (1937, September 15). Se han dedicado a actividades que pena la ley. Biblioteca Miguel Lerdo de Tejada. L06207: Policia Mexico 1936–1946.

Piccato, P. (2001). *City of suspects: Crime in Mexico City, 1900–1931.* Duke University Press.

Piccato, P. (2003). *A historical perspective on crime in twentieth-century Mexico City* (USMEX 2003–2004 working paper series). Project on Reforming the Administration of Justice in Mexico, Center for U.S.-Mexican Studies, UC San Diego.

Proceso. (1989, June 19). *Abusos en la Policía Auxiliar.*

Proceso. (1994, December 12). *Demandan bono sexenal*: 80.

Proceso. (2003, August 31). *Acoso sexual en la Policía Auxiliar.* http://www.proceso.com. mx/?p=255680. Accessed 2 Oct 2014.

Proceso. (2014, June 6). *Investigan la desaparición de más de 31 mil cartuchos de la policía auxiliar del DF.* http://www.proceso.com.mx/?p=373995. Accessed 14 Oct 2014.

Puck, L. (2022a). Police, private security, and 'Patitos': The market for security in Mexico City. In D. Watson, S. N. Amin, W. C. Wallace, O. (M.). Akinlabi, & J. C. Ruiz-Vásquez (Eds.), *Policing the global south* (pp. 106–120). Routledge.

Puck, L. (2022b). The state in private security: Examining Mexico City's complementary police. *Democracy and Security, 18*(1), 1–25.

Ramirez, B. T. (1998, February 4). Las policias de la capital, utilizadas como "negocios", acusa Desfasioux. *La Jornada.* http://www.jornada.unam.mx/1998/02/04/policias.html.

Ramírez, P. (2022, July 2). Los mil millones de Cusaem. *Reforma.*

Ravelo, C. (1968, October 30). Policía Preventiva y Represiva. *Excelsior.* Biblioteca Lerdo de Tejada. L06209 Policía México 1961–1969.

Regallado Santillán, E. (2002). Public security versus private security? In J. Bailey & J. Chabat (Eds.), *Transnational crime and public security: Challenges to Mexico and the United States* (pp. 181–194). Center for U.S. – Mexican Studies at the University of California, San Diego.

Robert Strauss Center. (2018, April). *Regulating Mexico's private security sector.* http://www. strausscenter.org/images/pdf/MSI/MSI-CNS_Report_06.pdf

Rodriguez Castañeda, R. (1999, June 13). Gertz entra al sórdido laberinto de la policía auxiliar, y pone a su director bajo licencia por no documentar egresos. *Proceso.* pp. 22–26.

Rivera, R. (2011, October 6). Realizan paro 200 policias auxiliares del DF. *La Reforma.*

Ramirez Mendez, J. (1981, June 21). Son anticonstitucionales todos los cuerpos policiacos: PMT y PAN. *El Sol de Mexico.* Biblioteca Lerdo de Tejada. L06215: Policia Mexico 1981.

Sabet, D. (2012). *Police reform in Mexico: Informal politics and the challenge of institutional change.* Stanford University Press.

Sanchez, A. (2020, January 20). Industria de la seguridad privada crece 20% en México durante 2019. *El Financiero*. https://www.elfinanciero.com.mx/nacional/industria-de-la-seguridad-privada-crece-20-en-mexico-durante-2019/

Secretaría de Administración y Finanzas. (2020). *Ley de ingresos: Presupuesto 2020*. Gobierno de la Ciudad de Mexico. Retrieved from https://cdmxassets.s3.amazonaws.com/media/files-pdf/presupuesto-2020/LEY_DE_INGRESOS_2020.pdf

Secretaría de Seguridad Ciudadana. (n.d.). *Funciones*. https://www.ssc.cdmx.gob.mx/organizacion-policial/policia-complementaria/policia-auxiliar.

Secretaría de Seguridad Pública del Distrito Federal. (n.d.). *Policía Auxiliar: Historia*. http://www.ssp.df.gob.mx/OrgPolicial/PA/Pages/Historia.aspx.

Security Company Owner. (2014, November 19). Author interview. Monterrey, Mexico.

Security Consultant. (2014, April 29). Mexico City.

Tilly, C. (1985). War making and state making as organized crime. In P. B. Evans, D. Rueschemeyer, & T. Skocpol (Eds.), *Bringing the state back in* (pp. 169–191). Cambridge University Press.

Universal. (1931, November 17). Por el ojo de la llave: Desorganizacion policiaca. Biblioteca Migeul Lerdo de Tejada. L06205: Policia Mexico 1894–1935.

Universal. (1936, February 15). Deficiencias de Servicios: 9. Biblioteca Miguel Lerdo de Tejada. L06207: Policía México 1936–1946.

Universal. (1937a, September 25). Los Buenos Servicios de la Policía Auxiliar: 9. Biblioteca Miguel Lerdo de Tejada. L06207: Policía México 1936–1946.

Universal. (1937b, May 4). Catorce Mil Pesos Diarios a Gendarmes. Biblioteca Miguel Lerdo de Tejada. L06207: Policía México 1936–1946.

Universal. (1938, July 10). El eterno problema de la policia. Biblioteca Miguel Lerdo de Tejada. L06207: Policia Mexico 1936–1946.

Universal. (1984a, August 4) Salvo la PJF, PJDF y la Preventiva, todas las demas policias son anticonstitucionales: Vasquez Carrillo. Biblioteca Lerdo de Tejada. L06226: Policia Mexico 1984 Agosto - Diciembre.

Universal. (1984b, April 19). Confía la Policía auxiliar en dejar de ser muy pronto 'los patitos feos.' Biblioteca Lerdo de Tejada. L06226: Policía México 1984 Enero – Junio.

Universal. (1984c, September 3). Haran una encuesta para saber cuantas organizaciones policiacas hey en el DF. Biblioteca Lerdo de Tejada. L06226: Policia Mexico 1984 Agosto - Diciembre.

Vanderwood, P. (1992). *Disorder and progress: Bandits, police, and Mexican development*. Scholarly Resources.

Villamil, G. (2011, November 23). El miniejército de Peña Nieto. *Proceso*. http://www.proceso.com.mx/289079/el-miniejercito-de-pena-nieto-2. Accessed 17 Nov 2013.

Villanueva, J. (2014, June 26). Policías sin balas ni justicia. *Reporte Indigo*. http://www.reporteindigo.com/reporte/df/policias-sin-balas-ni-justicia.

The Substitutability and Complementarity of Private Security with Public Police: The Case of Violence Against Women and Girls in the Rail Network of the United Kingdom

Barak Ariel

Abstract The stack of evidence on ways in which private and public police can work collaboratively is mounting. From what we know, when the two spheres take a co-operative approach, effective crime control practices ensue. The use of private security in lieu of 'classic' policing roles is not just a matter of desirable reduced public expenditure; security guards, place managers, and many other non-state actors are often as effective, if not more, in crime management and security services than the police. We take the case of violence against women and girls (VAWG), specifically in the public transportation environment, to illustrate the substitutability and complementarity of private security with public police. In this chapter, we observe three 'units of analysis': crime locations, offenders, and victims. Examination of all three units reinforces the view that private and public police should not work in silos. 'VAWG Hotspots' can be identified by police records and then patrolled by security guards, in order to prevent VAWG; known and potentially recidivist VAWG offenders can be managed by both police and private security, using a focused deterrence approach; and VAWG victims can be given additional care through a 'call back' policy, provided conjunctly by the two systems. I conclude with a series of policy recommendations for applying these evidence-based approaches to deal with VAWG, with the British Transport Police and the United Kingdom's train operating companies in mind, as they are best equipped to carry out these policies.

B. Ariel (✉)
Institute of Criminology, University of Cambridge, Cambridge, UK

Institute of Criminology, The Hebrew University of Jerusalem, Jerusalem, Israel
e-mail: barak.ariel@mail.huji.ac.il

© The Author(s), under exclusive license to Springer Nature Switzerland AG 2023
E. A. Blackstone et al. (eds.), *Handbook on Public and Private Security*,
Competitive Government: Public Private Partnerships,
https://doi.org/10.1007/978-3-031-42406-9_9

1 Introduction

Since the turn of the century, the occurrence of unwanted sexual behaviour and, more specifically, Violence Against Women and Girls (VAWG[1]) on the United Kingdom's rail network, has risen to the forefront of the political agenda, and has attracted the attention of legal and health professionals while triggering a burgeoning scholastic enterprise. The need to curb both the incidence and level of harm caused by VAWG on the mass transit system mirrors a wider global movement to reduce all forms of VAWG everywhere (United Nations, 2022). Parties engaged in this work continuously seek cross-discipline, evidence-based solutions, including, but not limited to, mass public information campaigns, educational programmes, focused technological developments and creative enforcement strategies in the mass transit environment. This chapter proposes a method to address the latter by way of an innovative case study of dealing with (a) the offenders, (b) the victims and (c) the places where VAWG takes place in the mass transit system.

Both the public police and the private security contracted out by the train operating companies must be involved in the effort to address VAWG. Whilst each partner has its own unique strengths and weaknesses,[2] a more cohesive and interagency

---

[1] According to the UK government (2022), VAWG "covers a range of unacceptable and deeply distressing crimes, including rape and other sexual offences, stalking, domestic abuse, 'honour'-based abuse (including female genital mutilation, forced marriage and 'honour' killings), 'revenge porn' and 'upskirting', as well as many others." https://www.gov.uk/government/publications/violence-against-women-and-girls-national-statement-of-expectations-and-commissioning-tool-kit/violence-against-women-and-girls-national-statement-of-expectations-accessible#:~:text=Violence%20against%20women%20and%20girls%20(VAWG)%20covers%20a%20range%20of,upskirting'%2C%20as%20well%20as%20many

[2] Variations also include different costs, as security guards are significantly cheaper than police officers; differences in the power to arrest, etc. (see Ariel et al., 2017). However, one could argue following Coase theorem, according to which there should be an economic efficiency of an economic allocation in the presence of externalities, that it is up to the rail company and the passengers to determine the level of security. The rail companies are usually large international conglomerates who contract out security services to prevent and manage crime in the train environments in which they operate under long term governmental contracts. As such, the rail company has a legal liability to protect the physical locations under the contact. They may insure against such attacks, and the insurance company will demand that the rail company take appropriate precautions. In turn, the rail company contracts out security services in order for their premiums not to rise. However, we note that the true cost of security in the rail environment is presently unknown, so the transaction costs necessary for preventing these outcomes from happening cannot be quantified. We do not know how much money is paid to private security, as many franchises operate simultaneously, and they do not disclose security costs in a systematic way. We do however know that the cost of security is not cheap, but nevertheless cheaper than contracting out police services. The British Transport Police's annual budget for 2021 was 320.1M (https://www.btp.police.uk/SysSiteAssets/foi-media/british-transport-police/reports/annual-reports-2020-21/btp_annual_report_2020_21.pdf), and franchised train operator expenditure in 2020–21 was a total of £10.B, a £0.4B (3.3%) annual decrease. The £10.3B includes staff costs (£3.6B), rolling stock leasing costs (£3.0B), diesel fuel costs (£0.2B), traction electricity costs (£0.4B), and "other operating costs" (£3.0B), whereas the total rail industry income in 2020–21 was £20.7B, which consisted of £16.9B from

collaborative approach is likely to increase efficiencies (Benson, 1998; Ceccato & Newton, 2015; De Waard, 1999). For example, whilst the police have arrest powers, they lack the resources to secure specific locations within a transit station for long periods of time, as they must attend to other duty-related obligations and respond to emergency calls for service. Security companies, on the other hand, are uniquely positioned to protect such locations, for example, by positioning a guard at the entrance to a shop or the train station, but they lack the police officers' arrest powers. Collectively, I call for a collaborative approach by police and private security forces when tackling VAWG, where one or the other assumes responsibility for some aspects of the work while the two forces work in unison in other circumstances. This chapter summarises an evidence-based approach used to determine the various components of this plan through rigorous methodologies. In line with the aforesaid vision to suppress VAWG, and with a focus on identifying 'what works' (Sherman, 2013), a design is required that integrates both private and public security at the mass transit environment. The UK example is particularly interesting, as neither the police nor the private security companies are armed with firearms. Sections 3, 4, and 5 present the architecture for simultaneously dealing with the three units of analysis: VAWG incident locations; offenders; and victims, respectively.

Given the importance of the criminology of place (Weisburd et al., 2012), the first unit of interest should be the locations where VAWG occurs. Crime does not distribute randomly or equally across places, whether these are different stations, within the stations or on trains (Ariel, 2011). Capitalising on the Pareto curve[3] resulting from the spatial (and temporal) distribution of VAWG crime events (Harinam et al., 2022), we can recommend the targeting of specific VAWG hotspots within the rail system, rather than 'spreading the available resources' thinly across all stations and trains. Through careful and precise detection based on police data, it is possible to identify places on both trains ('moving targets') and at train stations where VAWG incidents typically occur. Importantly, however, testing of place-based intervention is required before it can be recommended as policy (Ariel et al., 2022a), which is precisely where interagency collaboration is possible; the police

---

government funding, £2.5B from passengers (£1.8B of fares and £0.6B of other train operator income), and £1.3B from other sources (https://dataportal.orr.gov.uk/media/2036/rail-industry-finance-uk-statistical-release-2020-21.pdf). Security costs would be included under 'other operating costs', but without detailing how much of these expenditures go out to security costs.

[3] A Pareto principle, or the '80%–20% rule', refers to the mathematical and empirical fact that in many phenomena about 80% of the consequences are produced by 20% of the causes—for example that 80% of crime is produced by 20% of offenders. The ratio (80–20) is not consistent across phenomena, but the disproportionate representations of some units in the phenomena is a steady and reliable occurrence, certainly in criminology: a small number of addresses, train stations, bus stops, pubs, nightclubs, road intersections in any city experience an overwhelming majority of crime (Eck et al., 2017; SooHyun et al., 2017; Weisburd, 2015); fewer than 5% of victims experience more than 80% of crime harm (Lay et al., 2023), and so on. This principle carries not only theoretical implications but dramatic policy implications: the concentrations enable us to target crime control resources to a more limited subset of the population. Whether we can predict these '20' that produce the '80', however, is another matter (see Bland & Ariel, 2020).

can identify the locations of VAWG hotspots, based on crimes reported to the police and intelligence data, and private security personnel can then be deployed to secure these places. This scientific approach can determine efficiencies in terms of targeted patrols at precise intervals and duration.

It is important to address the risk of displacement onto other areas. Logically, applying social control mechanisms in certain places will drive the criminal activity elsewhere, because the core sociopsychological factors are not inherently addressed when we apply interventions at the level of the place. Subsequently, if the police or private security companies patrol the hotspot, we may experience crime "moving around the corner" (Weisburd et al., 2006). Indeed, highly motivated offenders are likely to seek other places or avenues to commit crime, especially career criminals whose livelihood depends on the commission of crime (Reppetto, 1976).

However, evidence largely debunks the displacement hypothesis and show instead spatial diffusion of the benefits of social control onto adjacent locations around the targeted hotspots (Clarke & Weisburd, 1994; Guerette & Bowers, 2009; Hesseling, 1994; Johnson et al., 2014) as well as large-scale geographic areas (Telep et al., 2014). In other words, we see a reduction rather than an increase of crime around hotspots assigned to crime control mechanisms.

There are different speculations as to why crime does not move around the corner. Some evidence suggests that crime will get displaced under certain conditions when offenders can anticipate the whereabouts of the police (Ariel & Partridge, 2017), where opportunities to gain from crime are similar outside the hot spot (Weisburd et al., 2006), or where crime control is perceived to be limited in the new area. But since there is a 'coupling' between crime and place—that is, some locations 'attract' crime more than others—then even if crime were to be displaced, *most* of it does not, because the propensity for crime somewhere else that does not carry the same criminogenic features is diminished: not all crime is committed by highly motivated offenders; for many 'expressive crimes' like violence the 'moment is gone' once people disperse; there may be limited opportunities to gain from 'instrumental crimes' like theft in the new place; or other offenders may control the new 'turf' and pose risk to the offender looking for a new place to commit crime. Thus, spatial displacement is less common than popularly believed—though admittedly we still do not fully understand why.

The second unit of interest is the VAWG offenders. Targeting prolific VAWG offenders through increased scrutiny and proactive policing tactics, on a scale and in a style never previously attempted, is warranted. While most police forces have violent and sex offender registrar (VISOR) teams, these specialised teams often select the offenders they closely monitor based on clinical and practical experience, rather than by following a systematic or statistical model. In other words, people are often placed on these registries based on professional judgement, whilst the evidence recommends against this practice because the use of clinical models has low predictive validity – as opposed to prediction models based on actuarial models (Kahneman et al., 2022). Moreover, being placed on a registry does not translate into reduced recidivism relative to not being placed on these registries. Agan (2011:207) concludes, based on multiple databases, that "sex offender registries are not effective tools for increasing public safety," so having a list of offenders, per se, is not an efficient strategy. As far as we know, no evaluations have been conducted to date on the use of VISOR policing tactics in the train environment.

On the other hand, there is evidence that 'focused deterrence' does seem to work (Ariel et al., 2019; Braga et al., 2018; RAND, 2022; Schnobrich-Davis et al., 2021). This approach, also referred to as "pulling levers," is a focused strategy that attempts to deter specific criminal behaviour through fear of specific sanctions (or "levers"), as well as anticipation of benefits for not engaging in crime. However, it is not presently known whether targeting VAWG offenders using VISOR teams through a pulling levers programme, with a focused deterrence approach that incorporates both a carrot and a stick approach, will reduce involvement in further VAWG. Within this approach, transit security teams would act as guardians against 'VISOR offenders' who pose a high degree of risk. Guards, ticket enforcement officers, and security personnel would be provided with a tasking sheet based on police data, with identifying details, photos, and other information identifying high-risk VAWG offenders which would enable them to provide an additional level of security.[4]

Finally, any comprehensive VAWG plan ought to place victims at centre stage (Lay et al., 2023). Just as VAWG offenders comprise a heterogenous population, VAWG victims are equally diverse and broad – except that they are females. According to The World Bank (2022), gender-based violence affects one in three women in their lifetime. Globally, a third of women have experienced either

---

[4] Admittedly, this approach carries a large investment and has privacy concerns, but similar programs demonstrate the potential upside of this intervention. First, should the intervention lead to a demonstrable reduction in VAWG, which include some of the most heinous crimes in the penal code, then the intervention can be deemed cost-effective *regardless* of the dollar value of the resources put into the project—assuming that no cheaper and efficient alternative course of action exists. Economists can assume that at some point the trade-off could lead toward rejecting the project if the resource allocation meant sacrificing an amount of money that is insurmountable. Resources are fungible and resources invested by the public or private security measures have opportunity costs, as resources are directed away from *other* life-saving activities. Nevertheless, in the context of VAWG we are unaware of alternative projects that may be cheaper than the proposed project. Nevertheless, it does not seem like the proposed programme is insurmountable: the tracking and targeting of offenders is part of routine police operations, and awareness to wanted suspects is part of security guards' routines as well, so the real cost of the operation is in terms of missed opportunity costs for police and security organisations, rather than new moneys required.

Second, indeed targeting offenders with a preventative engagement based on their criminal record rather than immediate evidence of wrongdoing may be *prima facie* a violation of human rights: why would the police or the private sector be allowed to interfere with one's right of movement or other civil liberties based on an algorithm? However, IRB applications considered similar applications to target offenders based on their prior criminal records and approved it (e.g., The Metropolitan Police Service Research Ethics Committee (MPSREC)). The study attempts to divert potential offenders from offending, as well as prevent further victimisation. There is no additional criminalisation in the sense of a criminal record, and the surveillance is put in place due to the risk they pose, and if one's movement is tracked and supervised because they are likely to rape, for example, cannot be seen as arbitrary. As long as checks and balances are placed in the selection of cases based on a reasonably high likelihood of reoffending, in the fair administration of the interventions, and the ethical handling of the data, the investment does weigh against these potential costs in terms of direct costs and indirect costs to offenders.

physical or sexual intimidation, partner violence or non-partner sexual violence; 7% of women are sexually assaulted by someone other than a partner; and 200,000,000 women have experienced female genital mutilation. Domestic violence and online or digital violence also constitute VAWG, however these forms of abuse do not form part of the proposed policy as the interventions applied in these situations are inherently different from those used to address public domain VAWG (see reviews in Lewis et al., 2017, and Rozmann & Ariel, 2018). The most common types of VAWG we are interested in are: sexual harassment; rape; sexual, physical and emotional abuse; and gender-based property crime, that take place in the mass transit environment.

However, a problem arises when victims of VAWG who have reported their abuse are left dissatisfied by the process or by the outcomes of their complaints to the authorities. Many people complain to either the train operating companies or the police about experiencing VAWG, but in many cases their report does not progress further through the criminal justice system, for example, when the offender(s) cannot be identified. This leaves the victim without a criminal justice system outcome. This 'no-further-action' designation is common in law enforcement, as *most* reported victimisation incidents, including VAWG, do not advance through the system (see Clark et al., 2022). Given the ways in which the criminal justice system operates, we should not expect substantial changes in the number of offenders brought to justice (for a review, see Buchnik et al., 2023) – but we can expect the processes to improve, given the importance people place on procedural justice. One crucial aspect is providing enough information to victims about how valuable the intelligence they share with the police for the prevention of future crimes, even if their case does not result in the criminal conviction of an offender. Based on their reports, it is possible to identify hotspots, attempt to predict emerging crime patterns, or identify the *modus operandi* of habitual or types of offenders. VAWG victims and witnesses involved in discontinued cases need to be assured that their contribution to VAWG prevention is genuine, and they need to be given a voice to express their perceptions, fears, observations, and any emotive statement they are otherwise unable to express during usual police-public contacts (McKee et al., 2023).

The unique environment of the mass transit system, in which public and private entities naturally collaborate given their shared space and similar accountability, provides the optimal setting for a public-private collaboration. An evidence-based approach can be applied to the problem of mass transit-related VAWG by focusing on the aforesaid three units of research – the location of incidents, offenders, and victims. A plan is laid out below.

2   Targeting VAWG Hotspots

Research shows that crime is heavily concentrated in discrete places called hotspots (Sherman et al., 1989; Weisburd, 2015). Importantly, these hotspots are small – street blocks, specific addresses, or train stations. For example, about half of all mass transit related crimes reported to the police are concentrated in approximately 5% of stations in England and Wales, across multiple years (Ariel, 2011). A similar ratio exists for the London Underground, where approximately half of all such crime is reported to have occurred in less than 5% of Tube stations (Ariel, 2018). This same 'power few' phenomenon also exists for unreported crime. Based on South-West Trains (UK) data, the same proportion of approximately half of all incidents reported to the train operating company, but not necessarily to the police, took place in fewer than 5% of locations (Ariel & Partridge, 2017). Collectively, then, the evidence makes it clear that at least spatially, crime is not a random event; it can be traced to specific places whose features and characteristics are conducive to criminal activity (Weisburd et al., 2012).

Some hotspots have been shown to be relatively stable over time. Weisburd et al. (2004) found that Seattle street-segments with the highest level of recorded criminal activity at the beginning of their longitudinal study were similarly ranked at the end of it. Such micro-places may remain stable because they provide continuous opportunities for criminal activity that other areas lack (Brantingham & Brantingham, 1995; see also Weinborn et al., 2017; Norton et al., 2018). In the mass transit system environment, crime opportunities arise in situations of large crowds found in the large 'hub' stations such as Kings Cross & St Pancras, London Bridge, and Stratford stations in London, in close proximity to the night-time economy facilities around a station (see Eck et al., 2007), and during football (soccer)-related events (Giulianotti & Armstrong, 2002). The same 'law of concentration of crime in place' (Weisburd, 2015) ought to be observed for VAWG as well, though at much higher levels of concentration than other street offences involving property, drugs, or public disorder. Recently, Harinam, Bavcevic and Ariel (2022) demonstrated that 50% of all reported crimes occurred in approximately 0.5% of all hexagonal tessellations no longer than 124 m long in Toronto. Duffy (2022) found that more than half of all reported VAWG incidents in an entire City of London police jurisdiction occurred in one polygon with half a dozen night-time economy establishments. Pearcy, Harinam and Ariel (n.d.) found, based on a review of 24 months of VAWG which occurred in public spaces in Dorset Police, UK, that 446 out of 3291 (13%) of 100 m hexagons accounted for 35% of the 13,225 reported VAWG incidents; in the entire police force jurisdiction of more than 25 million 100 m^2 hexagons.

Certain locations have attributes that are correlated with higher frequencies of VAWG incidents. For example, the lack of a capable guardian is very often associated with more crime (Cohen & Felson, 2010). Similarly, certain types of establishments are found to experience higher incidences of crime; namely, facilities such as clubs, fast-food restaurants, and liquor stores (Block & Block, 1995; Brantingham & Brantingham, 1995). Specifically for VAWG, certain spatial attributes are associated with greater VAWG risk: Loukaitou-Sideris (2014:246) report that "good lighting, good visibility, maintenance and cleanliness, surveillance through CCTV, and the presence of people" are associated with reduced risk, whilst "isolation, poor lighting or darkness, poor visibility, confined and enclosed spaces, and poor maintenance, indicated by the presence of litter, graffiti, and vandalism" increases the risk level. Similarly, Ceccato (2014) argues that "seclusion, potential for an easy escape of the perpetrator, presence of tunnels linking to the transit setting, and proximity of alcohol-selling establishments" are linked to VAWG, as well as "stations that had dark corners, proximity to bicycle storage, commercial uses and restaurants, physical disorder and social disorder (drunkenness)" (see also Ceccato & Paz, 2017). Finally, Ceccato and Loukaitou-Sideris (2020) demonstrated that sexual harassment of college students in Bogota, Los Angeles, Manila, and Stockholm is more likely to take place in transit stations with poor lighting, litter, drunkenness, and vagrancy. These studies demonstrate that there are identifiable attributes of locations where VAWG crimes occur. These locations can be identified at a spatial level and enforcement efforts undertaken to reduce or eliminate the likelihood of continuing VAWG offences are then hypothesised to be effective.

There is evidence that increasing the presence of capable guardians in crime hotspots reduces the number of crimes committed at these locations relative to control conditions (Sherman & Weisburd, 1995). Across multiple situations and around the globe, focusing the police on hotspots results in a modest yet reliable 16% reduction of recorded crime (Weisburd et al., 2017). For example, experiments in the United Kingdom on 'hotspots policing' found that multiple 15-minute visits to a hotspot by enforcement officials are sufficient to significantly reduce crime and disorder (Ariel, Sherman & Newton, 2020; Ariel et al., 2016; see also Bland et al., 2021; however, compare to Barnes, 2022). This trend mirrors the overall literature, as meta-analyses of the evidence show that police presence and proactive activities in hotspots reduce crime, relative to other hotspots which are not subjected to policing activities (Braga et al., 2019; see also Carriaga & Worrall, 2015; Dau et al., 2021).

Surprisingly, hotspots policing, as defined by scholars (e.g., Sherman & Weisburd, 1995), is not commonly practiced. Despite its efficacy identified in dozens of rigorous experiments, hotspots policing by officers has not been sustained as common practice, mainly due to implementation issues related to motivation, organisational resistance, and technological failures and data accuracy (Ariel, 2022a). Surveys taken in multiple sites (Lum et al., 2012; Telep & Lum, 2014; Rogers et al., 2022), including police forces that had recently completed their own hotspots policing experiments, demonstrate that many police officers have never heard the term 'hot spot policing', are unsupportive of the idea of following a prescribed patrol plan, do not like to be tracked, and do not think they can 'afford' it, given other policing constraints (Ariel, 2022b). Police forces do not routinely attend small hotspots in a proactive way, let alone for the often prescribed "fifteen minutes" of presence at the hotspots (Koper, 1995). Thus, whilst the science supports hotspots policing, and evidence demonstrates that hotspots policing leads to reductions in crime, there are detrimental implementation hurdles that make its practice uncommon for most police services.

2.1   A Tested Intervention: The Southwest Trains Experiment

Hotspots policing implementation obstacles can be overcome through public-private collaboration. The job of 'cooling down' hot spots identified by police records can be "outsourced" to the private sector, with private security personnel serving as alternative visible guardians. This assumption has been tested and has shown promising results (Ariel, Bland and Sutherland, 2017; Ariel et al., n.d.).

As Ariel et al. (2017) found in their SouthWest Trains Experiment, given the growing desire for secure spaces, there is an increasing number of communal spaces to which police patrols are normally not allocated, given more urgent police priorities. Hence, "paid-for, non-state policing agents have taken over both surveillance and even investigative roles traditionally allotted to state policing agents. Because of this, private security agents appear to be everywhere, including schools, shopping malls, airports, mass transit systems, college campuses, residential communities, and parking facilities" (ibid: 5).

Ariel et al. (2017) used a randomised controlled trial (RCT) to investigate the utility of security personnel in crime prevention by randomly assigning entire train stations in the Southwest of England, with an impressive footfall of 188 million passengers per year, to treatment and control conditions. Over 6 months, 30 private security guards were tasked with proactively patrolling target locations, which were selected based on official crime records provided by the British Transport Police. For the purposes of this report, several outcome measures at different geographic levels within the station complexes were reviewed. The results of Ariel et al.'s (2017) experiment are presented in the two figures below—first with a focus on the mean crime figures of victim-reported and police-generated crimes at differing types of locations in treatment and control stations (Fig. 1), and then the treatment effect within crime categories in treatment and control stations (Fig. 2).

The effect of the private security patrols determined by police records can be shown at several levels (Fig. 1). First, we separated the victim-generated from the police generated incidents; victim-generated crimes are incidents reported to the police by a member of the public who have been victimised (or witnessed victimisation), whilst police-generated incidents are crimes discovered by the police. In criminology this distinction is vital: whereas we expect a deterrence effect from police patrols to reduce victim-generated crimes like robbery, burglary, violence and theft from person, an increase in police-generated crimes is a desirable outcome: more crimes otherwise undetected are discovered through the security guards, like carrying weapons, drugs, or stolen goods.

These expectations were indeed detected in this experiment. As presented in Fig. 1, we have detected meaningful and significant reductions in victim-generated crimes. Overall, a significant 16% reduction in victim-reported crimes throughout all station complexes was detected—with an effect that intensifies as the area of study increases (i.e., as we move outside the epicentre of the patrolled hotspot). We have thus detected a strong diffusion of this social control apparatus in areas in the train stations outside the targeted hotspots – which collectively translated into an overall reduction in victim-generated crimes at the treatment stations, relative to control stations. This finding, as shown in Fig. 2, debunks the displacement hypothesis and, instead, indicated that whilst the effect of security patrols takes place in the area where staff are deployed, it 'radiates' into adjacent areas in the train station.

As importantly, we also have found a 49% increase in police-generated detections at the target locations. This is important because it indicates that private security is not only effective in prevention of crime – or a reduction in victimisation – but also assists law enforcement in supressing crime through proactive enforcement. Particularly in the immediate area of the hotspot area, members of staff were able to assist in the apprehension of offenders for crimes that can only be detected through active enforcement. Specifically in the target locations, we have found that detection of crimes that the police would otherwise miss has almost doubled in the target locations – from 1 crime on average per hotspots to 1.95 crimes per hotspot. Perhaps unexpectedly, we did not see the same increase in police-generated crimes outside the target areas, because the security teams were not tasked to be proactive in other areas of the station. We note however, that this is a meaningful finding especially as it shows the benefit of a targeted, proactive private security apparatus in crime fighting – especially when the statistical analyses suggested 30% increase in drug arrests and a 12% increase in ticket fraud offences detection (Fig. 2).

Thus, we can conclude, albeit based on a single study, that whilst the expansion of the private policing role may have been born out of economic necessity or a demand from the public for additional layers of surveillance and supervision, the 'bottom line' from this experiment remains the same: the presence of a privatised

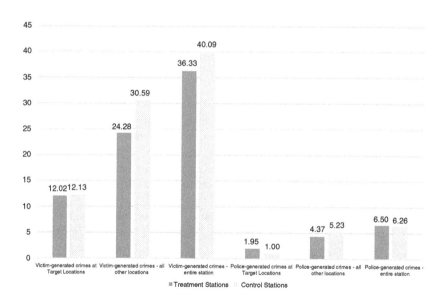

Fig. 1 Victim-generated and police-generated crimes (main effects): estimated marginal means. (*Source*: Ariel et al. (2017))

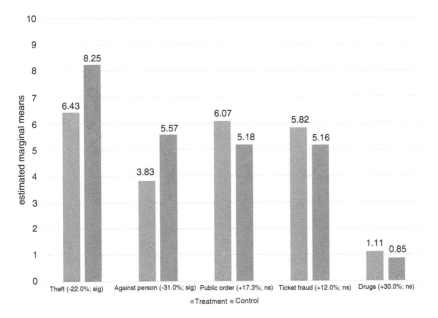

Fig. 2 Sub-group analyses: effect within crime categories (Entire station complex). (*Source*: Ariel et al. (2017))

police force can potentially lead to similar consequences as the presence of the state police force: less crime, disorder, and fear in communal spaces.

More recently, Ariel et al. (n.d.) presented a rigorous evaluation of state police and private security cooperation, which showed the degree to which collaboration increases efficiencies compared to working separately. In 2022-3, the British Transport Police shared intelligence with its partners at the large hub stations, including security guards, ticket enforcement personnel, ticket barrier enforcement, etc., and assigned specific tasks related to criminal 'elements' who were wanted for police questioning, vulnerable persons, and disorder risks. The results demonstrated that such a collaborative approach is cost-effective when compared with operating in silos (Reynald, 2010:358). The experiment indicated that police-led activities of security guards at large train hub stations across England and Wales increased reportage to the police in a beneficial way, reduced assaults against staff and reduced overall crime. Increase in solvability of crime relative to control conditions was particularly noteworthy, given the low overall solvability rates of non-injurious crimes (Coupe et al., 2019). The greater availability of capable guardians, operating in the right places, results in greater crime prevention, fewer state resources utilised, and an improved level of service to the public (see also Casciaro, Edmondson and Jang, 2019).

Thus, the evidence demonstrates that the concept of "capable guardians" in preventing crime at hotspots does not include only police constables (see also Felson, 1995; Hollis et al., 2013; Kamar et al., 2022; Leclerc & Reynald, 2017). Within the concept of effective guardianship lies the role of security guards, place managers, and non-police sentinels, who represent a major shift in the security terrain across the globe, who can both prevent crime and apprehend offenders at targeted locations. Private individuals, hired by for-profit companies whose primary responsibility is to their shareholders, can assist law enforcement to 'cool down' hotspots of crime. The increase in private guardianship is a crucial consideration because it brings to light a critical transition taking place in the way we understand social control theory: the monopoly on hot spot policing has decentralised, with a myriad of new actors playing the role of space-based policing.

3   Managing Habitual VAWG Offenders

VAWG related crimes are rare offences (Elkin, 2021), official recidivism rates are low (Hanson, 2002; Cortoni et al., 2010; Laajasalo et al., 2020), and the overwhelming majority of VAWG incidents are unreported to the police (Allen et al., 2022). However, these facts do not make the occurrence of these crimes unpredictable (Hanson & Bussiere, 1998; Quinsey et al., 1995). Research shows that with sufficient (and valid) data, rare events can be forecasted (Bland & Ariel, 2020). Ergo, we can identify VAWG offenders who are likely to commit VAWG crimes in the future (Persey, Harinam and Ariel, n.d.).

VAWG offenders comprise a heterogenous group, with many different types of deviant behaviours, ranging from verbal abuse and sexual harassment, through property damage and vehicle theft, to sexual arousal disorders (indecent exposure, voyeurism, etc.), rape and beyond (McKee et al. 2023). Some VAWG crimes are primarily alcohol-related, in the sense that they take place in certain social contexts, some are outright gendered, culturally motivated antiwomen attacks, whilst some are rooted in bio-psychological factors (Briken et al., 2005; Dawson et al., 2016; Hughes et al., 2016). What is important, however, is that a great deal of evidence exists on the habitual nature of VAWG and other offensive behaviour, with clear psychological components of sexually demeaning behaviour further strengthening the likelihood of recidivism (Williams, 2003 see more broadly Arango et al., 2014). For example, recently Pearcy, Harinam and Ariel (n.d.) have detected that amongst 43 high-harm VAWG offenders – that is, offenders who committed the most harmful crimes against women and girls – 46.5% have committed another VAWG offence *at the same* place where they have committed their prior VAWG crime. This concentration indicates that, for high harm VAWG offenders, there is a propensity for habitual offending—and these characteristics make VAWG predictable, and therefore susceptible to prevention (insofar as it is preventable; see Schmucker & Lösel, 2017; Wathen & MacMillan, 2003).

Thus, the best predictor of future behaviour is past behaviour. Even though police records lack external validity, namely, not all offences are reported or dealt with police, and whilst recidivism, as noted, is rare, available police records can be used to identify offenders who are most likely to reoffend by virtue of their prior criminal behaviour; that is, those who are at risk of causing additional harm to victims (i.e., secondary victimisation; see Hodgkinson et al., 2022). Therefore, existing police records, particularly those regarding individuals who have committed *two or more* VAWG offences[5] (the 'two strikes rule'), would provide a valuable list of VAWG offenders with whom engagement is likely to result in the prevention of future VAWG crimes and for whom interventions can be put in place.[6]

Beyond the two-strikes rule, agencies could capitalise on promising forecasting techniques based on machine learning like random forest modelling, to accurately forecast harm based on static data kept by the police. These techniques were explored in Philadelphia, USA (Berk, 2012). More recently, police forces, such as the one in Durham, have developed similar tools to forecast future harm (Oswald et al., 2018). Consequently, there is potential for using this strategy to forecast sexual offences based on arrest records. Random forest modelling can detect complex, non-linear patterns in datasets and set out a thorough framework for the comparison of different forecasting tools. In practical terms, the model comprises (1) a thorough establishment of which features are being compared, (2) comparisons based on data not used in the construction of the model, (3) appropriate comparison methods, (4) accurate characterisation, (5) comparable use of tuning parameters and (6) close attention to practical interpretation. Using this framework, random forest modelling is thus the strongest and most flexible option for creating a target list of habitual VAWG offenders who are the most likely to reoffend (see Bland & Ariel, 2020).

3.1   A Tested Intervention: Focused Deterrence

One way to deal with habitual offenders is to assign them an offender management programme: enhanced police supervision. This approach has been successfully applied to a variety of offenders at risk of recidivism, demonstrating its substantive impact in preventing future harm (Braga et al., 2018; Schnobrich-Davis et al., 2021). Within this 'focused deterrence' approach, a primary theoretical framework is deterrence: not through an ordinary punitive scheme of the judicial system but rather through the threat of apprehension for future transgressions. Rational

---

[5] Actual recidivism is hypothesised to be higher than reported in police records, given the psychopathologies involved, the sociology of gender, a lack of guardianship, or any combination thereof, so we ought to use multipliers to adjust for low official incidence rates (Leung et al., 2021)

[6] We note that non-clinical trials are unlikely to be available for state interventions, and lists of patients are unlikely to be shared with the police for preventative engagements (see Ariel et al., 2015; Boyle et al., 2013; Sutherland et al., 2021). There is a long tradition of not sharing data between police and the medical services and vice versa, even though there is a logical need to do so, including the prevention of additional harm to more victims – especially when it comes to VAWG. Additional datasets would enhance the external validity of the target list. At the same time, the view held by Bailey et al. (2020) regarding the utility of police records on violent offenders is relevant in the VAWG context as well: we ought to look no further for a substantive cohort of habitual VAWG offenders who are at an elevated risk of reoffending.

individuals prefer not to be caught, so a credible threat makes offending less probable when the risk of exposure as a repeat sex offender is perceived to be high (Ariel, 2012; Nagin, 2013; see also Hamilton, 2011; Ricciardelli & Moir, 2013). Therefore, if a potential offender believes that the risk of getting caught is elevated, he or she is less likely to commit a crime.

Deterrence theory suggests that there is often no need for additional punishment to deter prospective offenders from offending (Von Hirsch et al., 1999). Save in cases where incapacitation is required to prevent future harm, evidence suggests that the 'direct and specific warning' approach can be an effective prevention strategy (Erickson and Gibbs, 1975). This specific deterrence, where threats are made against individuals to prevent them from engaging in further criminal activity, can be efficient when the perceived cost of the crime outweighs the perceived benefits, or when the threat of punishment is perceived to be real, consequential, and probable, or carries 'meaningful' dosages of certainty of apprehension, severity of punishment, and celerity of execution (Nagin, 2013; Pratt & Turanovic, 2016).

As shown by Ariel et al. (2019) and Denley and Ariel (n.d.), within this mechanism, the state reacts to prior offending, namely, being arrested for sexual offending, but the threat of additional sanctions is then applied instead of punishment for the initial offence(s). The 'Sword of Damocles' message (Sherman et al., 2016) aims to dissuade the individual from continuing to offend, not through immediate punishment (i.e., arrest), but rather through the threat of future punishment (see Dunford, 1990). An emerging body of evidence supports this contention (see Bland & Ariel, 2020; Neyroud, 2018; Strang et al., 2017). We should note that in regard to increases in expected punishment, certainty of punishment tends to deter more than increases in the severity of punishment.[7] We can speculate that the harsh future sanctions, or the increased probability of being caught because of enhanced oversight is applied, or perhaps that the threat is perceived as a 'second chance' with the prospect of a turning point in an offender's trajectory. Evidence suggests that diversions in the spirit of the Sword of Damocles are beneficial (Blais et al., 2022; Bland et al., 2023; Hayhurst et al., 2015; Wilson et al., 2018; Wong et al., 2016), but again the precise mechanism is not clear—and more research is needed to disentangle these rather complex dimensions in decision making processes.

No studies have investigated the effects of specific deterrence on samples of VAWG offenders in the mass transit system. With "less conclusive evidence for the

---

[7] Some argue that this is a result of criminals having risk preferring or risk seeking preferences, as opposed to risk-neutral or risk-averse behaviour. Risk preferring behaviour is consistent with a person who will take the chance, or attempt the crime, in the lower probability of getting caught situation but not the higher probability of getting caught situation, even if the expected punishments are equal. For example, a 25% chance of being caught and facing a 4-year prison sentence and a 50% chance of getting caught accompanied by a 2-year prison sentence both result in an expected punishment of 1 year in prison, but a risk seeking individual is more likely to take the action or commit the crime in the 25% of a 4-year sentence as opposed to a 50% chance of a 2 year term. Such that increasing the certainty of punishment results in more deterrence relative to just increasing the severity of the punishment. While empirically this result seems to be true the behavioural motivations may not just be the result of risk preferences (see Mungan & Klick, 2015).

preventive effect of programmes for perpetrators" (Ellsberg et al., 2015:1555)), the VAWG policy should be based on evidence: a test is therefore required in order to dictate the work of the VISOR teams. VAWG offenders who have the propensity to reoffend (based on the two-strike designation plus actuarial forecasting offered by the random forest model) would be placed under increased surveillance. This is *not* akin to additional branding (the criminal tag has already been made by previous arrests for VAWG offences), excessive policing (the focused deterrence is not aimed at incarcerating the target, but rather to apply pressure on the individual in the form of additional police contact given the elevated risk they pose), or infringement of human rights (the need to protect women and girls outweighs the *habitual* offender's right to be left unsupervised). In short, the plan is to deter potential reoffenders by informing them that any future transgressions would be delt with swiftly and that additional supervision would be applied to increase the certainty of apprehension in the event of such new incidents.[8]

To clarify, the 'pressure' refers to police-led proactive contacts with the offender. A "pathways plan" would be designed, in which a police case manager would communicate a deterrence message to the offender that their behaviour is being monitored and a desistance plan could be drafted together with the offender. Similar to integrated offender management schemes (see Williams & Ariel, 2013), police action at certain "turning points" – points at one's life at which significant changes occur – can create the necessary conditions for crime desistance, even in the context of VAWG. Such police action would require identifying ways in which to halt persistent offending, including through reliance on social and counselling services. An essential aspect of this endeavour would be a threat of punishment issued by the police, by virtue of their being officers of the law (Ariel et al., 2019:839).

It is precisely at this point that the complementary role of private security could be applied: capable guardians could be made aware of the identities of the targeted habitual VAWG offenders who form part of the treatment group, so that they would be able to monitor habitual offenders' whereabouts and engage with them when necessary. The 'additional eyes' of the police's partner agencies compliments the message of deterrence, by elevating the perceived risk of apprehension for wrongdoing. For example, security guards in train stations could proactively engage with VAWG offenders as they enter the station, informing them that they are under close surveillance and therefore new VAWG offences would be detected and would not go unpunished. At least for VAWG offenders who already have legal orders banning them from British Transport Police's jurisdiction (e.g., restraining orders), security guards, ticket enforcement officers, and place managers would be in a position to further help enforce these orders, adding another layer of protection.

---

[8] To be sure, the plan ought to be executed according to the rules of procedural justice – meaning that engagements with the offender should be fair, polite, just, and for a valid reason. The importance of procedural justice cannot be overstated: without fairness in police-public engagement, there is a real risk of a backfiring effect, with increased rather than reduced involvement in VAWG or crime more broadly. On the merits of procedural justice, see Mazerolle et al., 2013).

4   Enhanced Service for Victims of VAWG

Studies from around the globe demonstrate the VAWG-risk associated with using public transportation. A 2020 review of gender-based violence determined that public transportation systems are the second most common place where sexual harassment occurs, after public streets (Williams et al., 2020). One characteristic of gender-based violence is that it knows no social or economic boundaries and affects women and girls of all socio-economic backgrounds who use the mass transit system. Based on interviews in Saltillo, Mexico, Infante-Vargas and Boyer (2022) report that women experience multiple effects resulting from the VAWG event, including limits on their mobility, and financial and emotional repercussions. The most frequently mentioned forms of harassment are "lascivious looks which 92.79 percent of participants reported experiencing, followed by whistling with 74.30 percent, and offensive or disrespectful words (including catcalling), with 72.83 percent. …[I]n 19.64 percent of violent episodes experienced within the last year the perpetrator(s) showed their genitals or masturbated in front of women. This number escalated to 29.3% when asked if this had ever happened since participants started using public transport" (p. 220–2). Similarly, interviews with 200 women and girls in Bangladesh reveals that "participants commonly used words such as 'unsafe', 'worried', 'helpless', 'vulnerable', 'afraid' and 'scared' when describing their journeys" (King et al., 2021:164) – with similar findings from Pakistan (Tabassum & Suhail, 2022), Ghana (Duvvury et al., 2021), Nepal (Neupane & Chesney-Lind, 2014), New York (see Ceccato, 2017), India (Anand & Nanda, 2022; Huq et al., 2021), and around the globe more broadly (see Ceccato & Loukaitou-Sideris, 2022; Loukaitou-Sideris & Ceccato, 2022).

There is a broad consensus that more should be done to help VAWG victims, particularly from the side of the criminal justice system (UN, 2022). There is a need to increase the reporting of VAWG, alongside the requirement to end its occurrence. However, once an incident has occurred, victims of VAWG are often left dissatisfied with the procedure of reporting their experiences (Vijayasiri, 2008). It has been found that, in various settings, victims who complain do not express positive feelings about the complaint experience (Wilkin, 2019). Yet one area where police can directly affect confidence – be it positively or negatively – is through personal contact (Bradford et al., 2009). For many members of the public, this contact takes the form of reporting a crime to the police as a victim. Their experience can provide an experiential foundation for perceptions of confidence in policing (Rosenbaum et al., 2015), which is why it is important to develop a more victim-centred approach that supports victims more efficiency and fairly.

Furthermore, victims have consistently reported that 'solving the case' may not be the most important factor in gauging satisfaction. The way police speak to and engage with victims often means more to them and helps to convey a sense of fairness (Bradford et al., 2008; Elliott et al., 2012) than solving the case. Victims want to be taken seriously, to have a voice (Strang & Braithwaite, 2017), whilst police effectiveness in terms of case solvability is less important (see Jonathan-Zamir &

Harpaz, 2018). This is a reasonable stand, because the rate of detection of crime – for most crimes including VAWG offences – is often low, usually less than one in five (see Coupe et al., 2019). As such, victims report that they rate their sense of satisfaction not just on the outcome of a case, but mainly on how they were treated. Consequently, the sense of fairness and procedural justice that reassurance and engagement with victims can provide is not only a key determinant of satisfaction but also affects wider confidence in, and legitimacy of police (Elliott et al., 2012; Hinds & Murphy, 2007). By ensuring that a sense of justice is felt by victims, the impact of negative influences on the wider society can be reduced (Hu et al., 2020).

4.1 A Tested Intervention: Reassurance Calls Backs to Victims

One method of operationalising fairness and increasing satisfaction – without a motivation of affecting case outcomes in terms of solvability – is through a policy of call backs. Following the reporting of an incident, the service provider – police, hospitals, restaurants, etc. – recontact the reporting party to ascertain the level of service received, to provide them with an additional forum to express their views, thoughts, or comments, and to convey a message of care.

Several studies, mainly in medicine and health care, show that call-backs reflect positively on patient care and wellbeing. A study of postoperative day surgery patients found that follow-up telephone contact improved patients' satisfaction and, consequently, health outcomes (Daniels et al., 2016). Similarly, nurse-led call-backs to sleep apnoea patients resulted in high levels of patient satisfaction (Walijee et al., 2020). Finally, there were also demonstrable benefits to be realised at low cost from conducting telephone follow-up calls to cancer patients (Mathew et al., 2017). We can learn from these examples as we attempt to increase the satisfaction of, create a sense of agency in, and enable closure for VAWG victims whose cases have been discontinued by the police.

In a study of fraud victims, it was found that those who received telephone support after reporting the crime reported greater wellbeing coupled with a reduced propensity to experience repeat victimisation (Cross, 2016). Recently, Clark et al. (2022) and McKee et al. (2023) conducted an experiment to assess the impact of telephone contact by police on victim satisfaction, specifically for victims who had reported crimes to the Metropolitan Police Service but whose criminal investigations had been closed without further action. Some lessons learned from this experiment may help our understanding of victims' dissatisfaction in VAWG situations, when the offending party is often not apprehended. After exclusion criteria were applied, victims were randomly assigned to treatment and control groups. Whilst all victims received the standard service given to victims of crime, those in the treatment group were telephoned by a local police officer, and offered reassurance. After this intervention, victims from both the treatment and control groups were surveyed and asked questions to assess their satisfaction with the police regarding their crime. The trial found that telephone follow-up contacts increased satisfaction. In most of the treatment group's responses to the survey questions, victims reported increases in satisfaction that were statistically significant.

The Metropolitan Police Service experiments discussed above (Clark et al., 2022; McKee et al., 2023) did not include VAWG offences, but it would be possible to increase satisfaction with, enhance the victim's perception of the performance of, and improve the overall ratings of train operating companies and the British Transport Police through a reassurance call, particularly for victims of offences that are unlikely to end up with the offender being charged, such as with the overwhelming majority of VAWG cases.

We should stress that the purpose of the reassurance call is not to solve the case. The premise of the intervention is to address the needs of the victims of the 'no-further-action', uncharged, and closed cases in instances where the outcome is not necessarily what the victim may have wished for. VAWG crimes, these comprise most cases. It is unlikely that police will be able to provide 'positive outcomes' for VAWG crime, so if satisfaction is to be influenced, it must be through improved procedures for victim engagement (which also should increase reporting rates in the future). It therefore follows that follow-up telephone contact can yield perceptual benefits, which are as important as material resolution of a crime that has already occurred.

5   Conclusions and Policy Implications

Based on the reviewed evidence, three policy recommendations can be drawn, focusing on VAWG places, offenders, and victims.

VAWG hotspots   The first step is to identify the VAWG hotspots using police records. There are multiple ways of identifying and mapping VAWG hotspots (see review in Eck et al., 2005; Wheeler & Reuter, 2021). The most straightforward way is to create heatmaps, polygons, or grids of land, and to select those units with the most crime relative to other units. In the case of the mass transit system, these units may be entire train stations or even specific areas within these stations. The number of units selected often depends on the availability of resources to patrol the designated areas; the choice is then a matter of pragmatism – how many VAWG hotspots can effectively be managed by the security guards, taking into account tasks within the hotspot, problem-solving initiatives, travel time between the hotspots, and the optimum length of time to spend in the hotspots.

It should be noted that there is no agreed optimal number of visits or length of time spent within the hotspots that would cause a significant effect. Some studies suggest visits of fifteen minutes (e.g., Koper, 1995), and some other studies implemented this threshold (e.g., Ariel et al., 2016; Telep, Mitchell, & Weisburd, 2014). However, there is no 'theory' behind this number of minutes, nor is there a discernible theory behind the necessary number of visitations to the hotspots, with suggestions ranging from just one visit per day (Bland et al., 2021), to 'sporadic' (Barnes et al., 2020); 'several' (Ariel, Sherman, and Newton, 2020), or more (Gibson et al., 2017). What is clear, however, is that increasing police visits to hotspots is sufficient to reduce crime relative to control conditions, as long as the 'dosage' is higher than the control conditions (see discussion in Ariel et al., 2022b). Once the number of visits to the hotspots is determined, the identification of which hotspots to visit becomes pragmatic; how many hotspots can be effectively targeted given existing resources.

Given some of the implementation issues raised above (see Ariel, 2023), including public expenditure austerity, I propose that the delivery of the intervention will be in the hands of security guards, not police constables. The purpose of this policy is to focus the security personnel on a prescribed task, which is a key part of the agenda. The security teams would be tasked to apply core prevention functionalities for the period of the test. The specific task of patrolling either the moving hotspots or the train stations would be the measure against which each team of security personnel would be assessed.

Finally, in addition to the allocation of the security personnel to specific VAWG areas, a bespoke tracking solution would be developed to follow through on the delivery of the operation. An encrypted and secure online portal in which security personnel can communicate the dosage they delivered, what precisely they did during their patrols in the hotspots, and any outcomes of these interventions, is required (on mobile devices, see Zahabi et al., 2020; Ariel, 2019; Wain & Ariel, 2014). Special attention would be given to ease of use, with as little additional bureaucracy and paperwork as possible. This tracking element is a critical component of the process's evaluation which, to our knowledge, has never been previously utilised in the context of VAWG.

VAWG offenders The first strategic objective is to present the police and their partners with a list of eligible offenders who, based on their habitual patterns and machine learning actuarial models, are likely to reoffend. The second broad strategic objective underpinning this policy recommendation includes implementing the VISOR strategy as an offender management approach. To maximise deterrence and desistance, police officers would manage individuals at risk of committing sexual offences on the rail network but would be supplemented by non-police capable guardians who would provide additional supervision support.

To identify a cohort of offenders to target, we propose using any contact with the police as the relevant data source. Arrests data are commonly used in criminology (e.g., Bland et al., 2022), and can be used in the case of VAWG offenders as well (e.g., Rothwell et al., 2022; however, *cf.* Fleury et al., 1998). Whilst arrests are not 'definitive' – that is, they are not criminal convictions in which guilt was proven beyond a reasonable doubt – they are more useful to our purposes given the low incidence of prosecutions in VAWG cases (see Loeber et al., 2008).

We note again the important eligibility criterion is having two or more VAWG-related arrests in one's criminal record. The habitualness of criminal behaviour against women and girls, which is signified by having at least two positive outcomes, gives the model an ethical grounding. Pearcy, Harinam and Ariel (n.d.) have found that out of 8692 VAWG offences in Dorset Police, UK over a three-year period, a named suspect was present in 3269 incidents. Within this category, 31.94% of prolific offenders have had an outcome against them (charged, received summons, penalty notices, etc.), compared to 22.17% of single offence VAWG offenders– a 44% difference, which gives an empirical justification to our inclusion criteria. Whilst this criterion limits the sample size quite dramatically, it is necessary to justify the intervention; a *pattern* of VAWG behaviour rather than a one-time arrest that resulted in no-further action indicates a form of recidivist behaviour that must be curtailed.

The intervention would consist of police contact at the offenders' abodes, with supplementary supervision by non-police capable guardians in the train station environment. The ingredients of the intervention would be both police and non-police enhanced supervision, with an unequivocal message to the habitual VAWG offenders: stop offending. This is meant to be delivered by, first, a 'knock on the door' of the offender where British Transport Police's VISOR constables proactively engage with the offender and inform him or her that, given their previous VAWG criminal history, he or she has been placed under enhanced surveillance. The intervention would have to be delivered in the most procedurally fair way possible (Langley et al., 2021), in order to forestall adversarial or otherwise negative feelings in the offender. The initial engagement would 'warn and inform' the target of the consequences of additional VAWG offending and provide the target with information related to available sources of assistance to address possible underlying issues.

The list of targets would then be communicated to the local mass transit police partners in the area where the offender resides or is employed so that they would be aware of the offender and his whereabouts. Security guards would be provided with a file on each treatment participant, including specific taskings the police wish them to undertake. These tasking sheets are akin to those used in previous experiments with police community support officers (Ariel et al., 2016), who were informed by neighbourhood police officers about local crime problems and certain individuals the police wished to inform that they are under community surveillance, given their criminal history and propensity to reoffend.

Finally, attention would be given to tracking the application of the interventions. One of the biggest challenges in applied criminal justice research is the ability to establish what resources are applied, when, where, and with what dosage. The issue of dosage, which is of significant concern in other evidence-based professions – health, engineering, and psychology – is largely missing from scholastic work on law enforcement (Wain & Ariel, 2014). When it comes to law enforcement, enhancing our knowledge base in this area requires meticulous and timely record-keeping. This goal would be achieved with the aid of technology by developing a bespoke instrument to measure the intervention(s). Unbiased measurement of the application of treatments would be required by both the police and security guards (e.g., egress. com). Meticulous record-keeping would be essential given the massive policy implications: At the very least, we ought to measure the following five families of variables: (a) the number of face-to-face meetings with each participant, including time, date, length of meeting, place, names of all attendees, and meeting outcomes using quantifiable measures; and (b) the number of interpersonal visits of any sort, including virtual and face-to-face. Participants' attendance at meetings, as well as dosage, like the number of meetings that were set up, would be of particular interest to any research project that seeks to examine the efficacy of the intervention programme; (c) any communications with participants through virtual means, including the number of contacts, number of times the participant accessed the website/account/Twitter, etc., and for how long; (d) any arrests, summons, or cautions, both formal and informal, that the participants accumulated, with dates, hours, and all other information that appears in these outputs, systematically recorded; and (e) any descriptive account of the police officers and security guards handling the case, such as gender, age, professional background, and experience. This is important in assessing the generalisability of the outcomes and deciphering the mechanisms of the causal link between treatment(s) and outcome(s).

Finally, outcomes of success should be measured, with the first and perhaps most important, family of outcome variables are criminal justice recidivism outcomes – arrests, convictions, cautions, prosecutions, charges, intelligence reports, etc. – for VAWG or crimes against persons more broadly. Arrests and other 'positive outcomes' (citations, notifications, etc.) are normally considered more reliable than other measures, as they are 'unfiltered' compared to outcomes that require legal or pseudo-legal decisions. It would be crucial to observe these official outcomes whilst separating arrests from new criminal events and violations of treatment conditions.

Increasing VAWG victims' satisfaction VAWG victims who have reported their incident to either the British Transport Police or the train operating company would be included under this proposed policy. However, in terms of eligible victims, certain categories of reports would be excluded: (a) VAWGs that were closed for any reason *other* than 'no further action', and/or VAWGs for which the offender was not charged; (b) Crimes where a secondary investigation has been initiated; (c) Crimes that are linked to another crime where a secondary investigation is taking place; (d) Crimes that have been 'flagged' as hate crimes or related to domestic abuse; and (e) VAWG reported by a third party where a victim cannot be identified. Two key datasets would be used: crime reporting system data for eligible VAWG, and the train operating company's internal records of eligible VAWG.

Based on our experiences working with data from train operating companies (Ariel et al., 2017), we can confirm that there are indeed many behaviours and events that take place in the mass transit system which are reported to members of train operating company staff but do not come up in crime records. These are the types of incidents that the call- or report-taker have deemed 'low level' or 'unharmful,' or that do not rise above a threshold that would require the incidents to be reported to the police. Once eligible cases are identified, they would receive a telephone call from an officer (police in the case of police-reported VAWG, or civil staff in the case of private security-reported VAWG). The caller would have a checklist of items to cover in the telephone call, including: (a) the fact that the caller has read the report of the VAWG crime; (b) an offer of reassurance that the report has been noted and will inform local enforcement deployments; (c) an offer of crime prevention advice to the victim; and; (d) asking the victim if they have any information about the VAWG that may help prevent a further occurrence of VAWG. Note that the caller would not offer to conduct a secondary investigation or re-open the case unless evidence that would justify such action comes to light during the conversation. If this occurs, then the case would be excluded from follow-up surveys, as an investigation would be ongoing and could therefore confound the results (Cook et al., 2002).

Satisfaction from the call-back would be measured via a telephone survey, using a series of graded questions to assess levels of satisfaction for each. Analysis of the responses would allow for improving the policy over time. The surveys would be conducted by persons independent of the treatment follow-up calls, and the interviewers would be blind to the nature of the survey to minimise interviewer bias (Murray et al., 2015).

Finally, a tracking process would be essential during both the intervention and the survey phases (MacQueen & Bradford, 2015; Neyroud, 2019), and we expect that reviews would be conducted every 10 days. This would provide a feedback loop and ensure that necessary changes would be quickly implemented (MacQueen & Bradford, 2015).

References

Agan, A. Y. (2011). Sex offender registries: Fear without function? *The Journal of Law and Economics, 54*(1), 207–239.

Allen, K., Barbin, A., Khan, A., & Ferreira, J. (2022). VAWG in public spaces: Barriers to reporting and impacts on women and girls. *British Society of Criminology Newsletter, 9.*

Anand, S., & Nanda, S. (2022). Violence in public spaces against women and girls: Narratives from India. *South Asian Journal of Law, Policy, and Social Research, 1*(2).

Arango, D. J., Morton, M., Gennari, F., Kiplesund, S., & Ellsberg, M. (2014). *Interventions to prevent or reduce violence against women and girls: A systematic review of reviews.*

Ariel, B. (2011, November 6). *Hot dots and hot lines: Analysis of crime in the London underground'.* Presented at the Annual American Society of Criminology, Washington, DC.

Ariel, B. (2012). Deterrence and moral persuasion effects on corporate tax compliance: Findings from a randomized controlled trial. *Criminology, 50*(1), 27–69.

Ariel, B. (2018). Not all evidence is created equal: on the importance of matching research questions with research methods in evidence based policing. *Evidence based policing: An introduction, 63.*

Ariel, B. (2019). Technology in policing. In D. Weisburd & A. A. Braga (Eds.), *Innovations in policing: Contrasting perspectives* (2nd ed., pp. 521–516). Cambridge University Press.

Ariel, B. (2022a). *Implementation issues with hot spots policing.* OSF.IO. Available at https://osf.io/t4xg9. Last accessed 7 Sept 2022.

Ariel, B. (2022b, July 12). *Integrated security and policing.* Presented at the 14th International Evidence-Based Policing Conference, Cambridge, 2022.

Ariel, B., & Partridge, H. (2017). Predictable policing: Measuring the crime control benefits of hotspots policing at bus stops. *Journal of Quantitative Criminology, 33*(4), 809–833.

Ariel, B., Weinborn, C., & Boyle, A. (2015). Can routinely collected ambulance data about assaults contribute to reduction in community violence? *Emergency Medicine Journal, 32*(4), 308–313.

Ariel, B., Weinborn, C., & Sherman, L. W. (2016). "Soft" policing at hot spots—Do police community support officers work? A randomized controlled trial. *Journal of Experimental Criminology, 12*(3), 277–317.

Ariel, B., Bland, M., & Sutherland, A. (2017). 'Lowering the threshold of effective deterrence'— Testing the effect of private security agents in public spaces on crime: A randomized controlled trial in a mass transit system. *PLoS One, 12*(12), e0187392.

Ariel, B., Englefield, A., & Denley, J. (2019). I heard it through the grapevine: A randomized controlled trial on the direct and vicarious effects of preventative specific deterrence initiatives in criminal networks. *Journal of Criminal Law and Criminology, 109,* 819.

Ariel, B., Sherman, L. W., & Newton, M. (2020). Testing hot-spots police patrols against no-treatment controls: Temporal and spatial deterrence effects in the London Underground experiment. *Criminology, 58*(1), 101–128.

Ariel, B., Bland, M., & Sutherland, A. (2022a). *Experimental designs.* Sage.

Ariel, B., Sutherland, A., Weisburd, D., Ilan, Y., & Bland, M. (2022b). Can the police cool down quality of life hotspots? A double-blind national randomized control trial of policing low-harm hotspots. *Policing: A Journal of Policy and Practice.*

Ariel, B., Gregory, A., Cronin, L., Ebbs, B., Wiffin, M., & Michel, N. (n.d.) *Routinising police-security collaborations: A prospective, mixed-methods experiment in British Train Stations.*

Bailey, L., Harinam, V., & Ariel, B. (2020). Victims, offenders and victim-offender overlaps of knife crime: A social network analysis approach using police records. *PLoS One, 15*(12), e0242621.

Barnes, G. (2022). New hot spots experiments from London and Australia. *Metropolitan Police Service.* Presented at the Center for Evidence-Based Crime Policy 2022 Symposium (George Mason University, 27/07/2022).

Barnes, G. C., Williams, S., Sherman, L. W., Parmar, J., House, P., & Brown, S. A. (2020). *Sweet spots of residual deterrence: A randomized crossover experiment in minimalist police patrol.*

Benson, B. L. (1998). *To serve and protect: Privatization and community in criminal justice* (Vol. 4). NYU Press.

Berk, R. (2012). *Criminal justice forecasts of risk: A machine learning approach.* Springer Science & Business Media.

Blais, E., Brisson, J., Gagnon, F., & Lemay, S. A. (2022). Diverting people who use drugs from the criminal justice system: A systematic review of police-based diversion measures. *International Journal of Drug Policy, 105,* 103697.

Bland, M. P., & Ariel, B. (2020). *Targeting domestic abuse with police data.* Springer.

Bland, M., Leggetter, M., Cestaro, D., & Sebire, J. (2021). Fifteen minutes per day keeps the violence away: A crossover randomised controlled trial on the impact of foot patrols on serious violence in large hot spot areas. *Cambridge Journal of Evidence-Based Policing, 5*(3), 93–118.

Bland, M., Ariel, B., & Ridgeon, N. (Eds.). (2022). *The crime analyst's companion.* Springer International Publishing.

Bland, M., Ariel, B. & Kumar, S. (2023). Criminal records versus rehabilitation and expungement: a randomised controlled trial. *Journal of Experimental Criminology.* https://doi.org/10.1007/s11292-023-09557-x

Block, R. L., & Block, C. R. (1995). Space, place and crime: Hot spot areas and hot places of liquor-related crime. *Crime and Place, 4*(2), 145–184.

Boyle, A., Ariel, B., & Weinborn, C. (2013). Can ambulance data be used to reduce community violence? Exploratory record linkage study. *Emergency Medicine Journal, 30*(10), 870–870.

Braga, A. A., Weisburd, D., & Turchan, B. (2018). Focused deterrence strategies and crime control: An updated systematic review and meta-analysis of the empirical evidence. *Criminology & Public Policy, 17*(1), 205–250.

Braga, A. A., Turchan, B. S., Papachristos, A. V., & Hureau, D. M. (2019). Hot spots policing and crime reduction: An update of an ongoing systematic review and meta-analysis. *Journal of Experimental Criminology, 15,* 289–311.

Briken, P., Habermann, N., Berner, W., & Hill, A. (2005). *The influence of brain abnormalities on psychosocial development, criminal history and paraphilias in sexual murderers*. ASTM International.

Bradford, B., Jackson, J., Hough, M. and Farrall, S. (2008). Trust and confidence in criminal justice: A review of the British research literature. In: Jokinen, A., Ruuskanen, E., Yordanova, M., Markov, D., Ilcheva, M. (Eds.), *Review of Need: Indicators of Public Confidence in Criminal Justice*.

Bradford, B., Jackson, J., & Stanko, E. A. (2009). Contact and confidence: Revisiting the impact of publicencounters with the police. *Policing & society, 19*(1), 20-46.

Brantingham, P., & Brantingham, P. (1995). Criminality of place: Crime generators and crime attractors. *European Journal on Criminal Policy and Research, 3*, 5–26.

Buchnik, E., Ariel, B., Domb, A., Treves, N., & Gafny, R. (2023). The role of DNA in criminal indictments in Israel. *Journal of Forensic Sciences*. https://doi.org/10.1111/1556-4029.15327

Carriaga, M. L., & Worrall, J. L. (2015). Police levels and crime: A systematic review and meta-analysis. *The Police Journal, 88*(4), 315–333.

Casciaro, T., Edmondson, A. C., & Jang, S. (2019). Cross-silo leadership. *Harvard Business Review, 97*(3), 130–139.

Ceccato, V. (2014). The nature of rape places. *Journal of Environmental Psychology, 40*, 97–107.

Ceccato, V. (2017). Women's victimisation and safety in transit environments. *Crime Prevention and Community Safety, 19*(3), 163–167.

Ceccato, V., & Paz, Y. (2017). Crime in São Paulo's metro system: Sexual crimes against women. *Crime Prevention and Community Safety, 19*, 211–226.

Ceccato, V., & Loukaitou-Sideris, A. (Eds.). (2020). *Transit crime and sexual violence in cities: International evidence and prevention*. Routledge.

Ceccato, V., & Loukaitou-Sideris, A. (2022). Fear of sexual harassment and its impact on safety perceptions in transit environments: A global perspective. *Violence Against Women, 28*(1), 26–48.

Ceccato, V., & Newton, A. (Eds.). (2015). *Safety and security in transit environments: An interdisciplinary approach*. Springer.

Clark, B., Ariel, B., & Harinam, V. (2022). "How should the police let victims down?" The impact of reassurance call-backs by local police officers to victims of vehicle and cycle crimes: A block randomized controlled trial. *Police Quarterly*. 10986111221128751

Clarke, R. V., & Weisburd, D. (1994). Diffusion of crime control benefits: Observations on the reverse of displacement. *Crime Prevention Studies, 2*(1), 165–184.

Cohen, L. E., & Felson, M. (2010). Social change and crime rate trends: A routine activity approach (1979). *In Classics in environmental criminology* (pp. 203–232). Routledge.

Cook, T. D., Campbell, D. T., & Shadish, W. (2002). *Experimental and quasi-experimental designs for generalized causal inference* (Vol. 1195). Boston, MA: Houghton Mifflin.

Cortoni, F., Hanson, R. K., & Coache, M. È. (2010). The recidivism rates of female sexual offenders are low: A meta-analysis. *Sexual Abuse, 22*(4), 387–401.

Coupe, R. T., Ariel, B., & Mueller-Johnson, K. (Eds.). (2019). *Crime solvability factors: Police resources and crime detection*. Springer Nature.

Cross, C. (2016). 'They're very lonely': understanding the fraud victimisation of seniors. *International Journal for Crime, Justice and Social Democracy, 5*(4), 60–75.

Dau, P. M., Vandeviver, C., Dewinter, M., Witlox, F., & Vander Beken, T. (2021). Policing directions: A systematic review on the effectiveness of police presence. *European Journal on Criminal Policy and Research*, 1–35.

Dawson, S. J., Bannerman, B. A., & Lalumière, M. L. (2016). Paraphilic interests: An examination of sex differences in a nonclinical sample. *Sexual Abuse, 28*(1), 20–45.

De Waard, J. (1999). The private security industry in international perspective. *European Journal on Criminal Policy and Research, 7*(2), 143–174.

Denley, J., & Ariel, B. (n.d.). *A 'Sticks and Carrots' approach to serious and organised crime: A cluster randomised controlled trial*.

Duffy, W. (2022). Reducing violence in City of London's Night Time Economy: A repeated cross-over trial. [University of Cambridge Thesis Dissertation]

Dunford, F. W. (1990). System-initiated warrants for suspects of misdemeanor domestic assault: A pilot study. *Justice Quarterly, 7*(4), 631–653.

Duvvury, N., Scriver, S., Gammage, S., & John, N. (2021). The impacts of violence against women on choice and agency: Evidence from Ghana and Pakistan. In *Women's studies international forum* (Vol. 89, p. 102536). Pergamon.

Eck, J., Chainey, S., Cameron, J., & Wilson, R. (2005). Crime hot spots: what they are, why we have them, and how to map them. In *Mapping Crime: Understanding Hotspots*, ch. 1. Washington DC: US National Institute of Justice.

Eck, J. E., Clarke, R. V., & Guerette, R. T. (2007). Risky facilities: Crime concentration in homogeneous sets of establishments and facilities. *Crime Prevention Studies, 21*, 225.

Eck, J. E., Lee, Y., & Martinez, N. (2017). Compared to what? Estimating the relative concentration of crime at places using systematic and other reviews. *Crime Science, 6*(1), 1–17.

Elliott, I., Thomas, S. D., & Ogloff, J. R. (2012). Procedural justice in contacts with the police: The perspective of victims of crime. *Police Practice and Research, 13*(5), 437–449.

Elkin, M. (2021). *Violence against women and girls: Helping to understand the scale and impact of the problem.* Office of National Statistics. https://content.govdelivery.com/accounts/UKONS/bulletins/2fdb7e6. Accessed 7 Sept 2022.

Ellsberg, M., Arango, D. J., Morton, M., Gennari, F., Kiplesund, S., Contreras, M., & Watts, C. (2015). Prevention of violence against women and girls: What does the evidence say? *The Lancet, 385*(9977), 1555–1566.

Erickson, M. L., & Gibbs, J. P. (1975). Specific versus general properties of legal punishments and deterrence. *Social Science Quarterly*, 390–397.

Felson, M. (1995). Those who discourage crime. *Crime and Place, 4*, 53–66.

Fleury, R. E., Sullivan, C. M., Bybee, D. I., & Davidson, W. S., II. (1998). What happened depends on whom you ask: A comparison of police records and victim reports regarding arrests for woman battering. *Journal of Criminal Justice, 26*(1), 53–59.

Gibson, C., Slothower, M., & Sherman, L. W. (2017). Sweet spots for hot spots? A cost-effectiveness comparison of two patrol strategies. *Cambridge Journal of Evidence-Based Policing, 1*(4), 225–243.

Giulianotti, R., & Armstrong, G. (2002). Avenues of contestation. Football hooligans running and ruling urban spaces. *Social Anthropology, 10*(2), 211–238.

Guerette, R. T., & Bowers, K. J. (2009). Assessing the extent of crime displacement and diffusion of benefits: A review of situational crime prevention evaluations. *Criminology, 47*(4), 1331–1368.

Hamilton, M. (2011). The child pornography crusade and its net-widening effect. *Cardozo L. Rev., 33*, 1679.

Hanson, R. K. (2002). Recidivism and age: Follow-up data from 4,673 sexual offenders. *Journal of Interpersonal Violence, 17*(10), 1046–1062.

Hanson, R. K., & Bussiere, M. T. (1998). Predicting relapse: A meta-analysis of sexual offender recidivism studies. *Journal of Consulting and Clinical Psychology, 66*(2), 348–362.

Harinam, V., Bavcevic, Z., & Ariel, B. (2022). *Spatial distribution and developmental trajectories of crime versus crime severity: Do not abandon the count-based model just yet* (Vol. 11). Crime Science.

Hayhurst, K. P., Leitner, M., Davies, L., Flentje, R., Millar, T., Jones, A., et al. (2015). The effectiveness and cost-effectiveness of diversion and aftercare programmes for offenders using class A drugs: A systematic review and economic evaluation. *Health Technology Assessment (Winchester, England), 19*(6), 1–168.

Hesseling, R. (1994). Displacement: A review of the empirical literature. *Crime Prevention Studies, 3*(1), 97–230.

Hinds, L., & Murphy, K. (2007). Public satisfaction with police: Using procedural justice to improve police legitimacy. *Australian & New Zealand Journal of Criminology, 40*(1), 27–42.

Hodgkinson, W., Ariel, B., & Harinam, V. (2022). Comparing panic alarm systems for high-risk domestic abuse victims: A randomised controlled trial on prevention and criminal justice system outcomes. *Journal of Experimental Criminology*, 1–19.

Hollis, M. E., Felson, M., & Welsh, B. C. (2013). The capable guardian in routine activities theory: A theoretical and conceptual reappraisal. *Crime Prevention and Community Safety, 15*(1), 65–79.

Hu, X., Dai, M., DeValve, M. J., & Lejeune, A. (2020). Understanding public attitudes towards the police: Covariates of satisfaction, trust, and confidence. *Canadian Journal of Criminology and Criminal Justice, 62*(1), 26–49.

Hughes, C., Marrs, C., & Sweetman, C. (2016). Introduction to gender, development and VAWG. *Gender and Development, 24*(2), 157–169.

Huq, M., Das, T., Devakumar, D., Daruwalla, N., & Osrin, D. (2021). Intersectional tension: A qualitative study of the effects of the COVID-19 response on survivors of violence against women in urban India. *BMJ Open, 11*(9), e050381.

Infante-Vargas, D., & Boyer, K. (2022). Gender-based violence against women users of public transport in Saltillo, Coahuila, México. *Journal of Gender Studies, 31*(2), 216–230.

Johnson, S. D., Guerette, R. T., & Bowers, K. (2014). Crime displacement: What we know, what we don't know, and what it means for crime reduction. *Journal of Experimental Criminology, 10*(4), 549–571.

Jonathan-Zamir, T., & Harpaz, A. (2018). Predicting support for procedurally just treatment: The case of the Israel National Police. *Criminal Justice and Behavior, 45*(6), 840–862.

Kahneman, D., Sibony, O., & Sunstein, C. R. (2022). *Noise* (pp. 38–46). HarperCollins UK.

Kamar, E., Maimon, D., Weisburd, D., & Shabat, D. (2022). Parental guardianship and online sexual grooming of teenagers: A honeypot experiment. *Computers in Human Behavior, 137*, 107386.

King, J., King, M., Edwards, N., Carroll, J. A., Watling, H., Anam, M., et al. (2021). Exploring women's experiences of gender-based violence and other threats to safety on public transport in Bangladesh. *International Journal for Crime, Justice and Social Democracy, 10*(4), 158–173.

Koper, C. S. (1995). Just enough police presence: Reducing crime and disorderly behavior by optimizing patrol time in crime hot spots. *Justice Quarterly, 12*(4), 649–672.

Laajasalo, T., Ellonen, N., Korkman, J., Pakkanen, T., & Aaltonen, O. P. (2020). Low recidivism rates of child sex offenders in a Finnish 7-year follow-up. *Nordic Journal of Criminology, 21*(1), 103–111.

Langley, B., Ariel, B., Tankebe, J., Sutherland, A., Beale, M., Factor, R., & Weinborn, C. (2021). A simple checklist, that is all it takes: a cluster randomized controlled field trial on improving the treatment of suspected terrorists by the police. *Journal of Experimental Criminology, 17*, 629–655.

Lay, W., Ariel, B., & Harinam, V. (2023). *Recalibrating the police to focus on victims using police records. Policing: A Journal of Policy and Practice, 17*, paac053. https://doi.org/10.1093/police/paac053

Leclerc, B., & Reynald, D. (2017). When scripts and guardianship unite: A script model to facilitate intervention of capable guardians in public settings. *Security Journal, 30*(3), 793–806.

Leung, P. C., Looman, J., & Abracen, J. (2021). To reoffend or not to reoffend? An investigation of recidivism among individuals with sexual offense histories and psychopathy. *Sexual Abuse, 33*(1), 88–113.

Lewis, R., Rowe, M., & Wiper, C. (2017). Online abuse of feminists as an emerging form of violence against women and girls. *British Journal of Criminology, 57*(6), 1462–1481.

Loeber, R., Farrington, D. P., & Jolliffe, D. (2008). Comparing arrests and convictions with reported offending. In *Violence and serious theft* (pp. 119–150). Routledge.

Loukaitou-Sideris, A. (2014). Fear and safety in transit environments from the women's perspective. *Security Journal, 27*(2), 242–256.

Loukaitou-Sideris, A., & Ceccato, V. (2022). Sexual harassment on transit: A global, comparative examination. *Security Journal, 35*(1), 175–204.

Lum, C., Telep, C. W., Koper, C. S., & Grieco, J. (2012). Receptivity to research in policing. *Justice Research and Policy, 14*(1), 61–95.

MacQueen, S., & Bradford, B. (2015). Enhancing public trust and police legitimacy during road traffic encounters: results from a randomised controlled trial in Scotland. *Journal of Experimental Criminology, 11*, 419–443.

Mathew, A. S., Agarwal, J. P., Munshi, A., Laskar, S. G., Pramesh, C. S., Karimundackal, G., ... & Deodhar, J.(2017). A prospective study of telephonic contact and subsequent physical follow-up of radically treated lung cancer patients. *Indian Journal of Cancer, 54*(1), 241–252.

Mazerolle, L., Bennett, S., Davis, J., Sargeant, E., & Manning, M. (2013). Procedural justice and police legitimacy: A systematic review of the research evidence. *Journal of Experimental Criminology, 9*(3), 245–274.

McKee, J., Ariel, B., & Harinam, V. (2023). "Mind the police dissatisfaction gap": The effect of callbacks to victims of unsolved crimes in London. *Justice Quarterly, 40*(5), 744–763.

Mungan, M. C., & Klick, J. (2015). Identifying criminals' risk preferences. *Indiana Law Journal, 91*, 791.

Murray, A., Mueller-Johnson, K., & Sherman, L. W. (2015). Evidence-based policing of UK Muslim communities: linking confidence in the police with area vulnerability to violent extremism. *International Criminal Justice Review, 25*(1), 64–79.

Nagin, D. S. (2013). Deterrence in the twenty-first century. *Crime and Justice, 42*(1), 199–263.

Neupane, G., & Chesney-Lind, M. (2014). Violence against women on public transport in Nepal: Sexual harassment and the spatial expression of male privilege. *International Journal of Comparative and Applied Criminal Justice, 38*(1), 23–38.

Neyroud, P. (2018). Out of court disposals managed by the police: a review of the evidence. *Commissioned by the National Police Chief's Council of England and Wales. University of Cambridge.*

Neyroud, P. (2019). Ethical Leadership in Policing: Towards a New Evidence-Based, Ethical Professionalism?. *Police Leadership: Changing Landscapes, 3–22.*

Norton, S., Ariel, B., Weinborn, C., & O'Dwyer, E. (2018). Spatiotemporal patterns and distributions of harm within street segments: The story of the "harmspot". *Policing: An International Journal, 41*(3), 352–371.

Oswald, M., Grace, J., Urwin, S., & Barnes, G. C. (2018). Algorithmic risk assessment policing models: Lessons from the Durham HART model and 'Experimental'proportionality. *Information & Communications Technology Law, 27*(2), 223–250.

Pearcy, J., Harinam, V., & Ariel, B. (n.d.). *Violence Against Women and Girls in Dorset, United Kingdom: Anepidemiological study of perpetrators and locations based on police records.*

Piza, E. L., Welsh, B. C., Farrington, D. P., & Thomas, A. L. (2019). CCTV surveillance for crime prevention: A 40-year systematic review with meta-analysis. *Criminology & Public Policy, 18*(1), 135–159.

Pratt, T. C., & Turanovic, J. J. (2016). Lifestyle and routine activity theories revisited: The importance of "risk" to the study of victimization. *Victims & Offenders, 11*(3), 335–354.

Quinsey, V. L., Lalumière, M. L., Rice, M. E., & Harris, G. T. (1995). Predicting sexual offenses. In *Assessing dangerousness: Violence by sexual offenders, batterers, and child abusers* (pp. 114–137).

RAND. (2022). *Focused deterrence in depth.* Available at https://www.rand.org/pubs/tools/TL261/better-policing-toolkit/all-strategies/focused-deterrence/in-depth.html

Reppetto, T. A. (1976). Crime prevention and the displacement phenomenon. *Crime & Delinquency, 22*(2), 166–177.

Reynald, D. M. (2010). Guardians on guardianship: Factors affecting the willingness to supervise, the ability to detect potential offenders, and the willingness to intervene. *Journal of Research in Crime and Delinquency, 47*(3), 358–390.

Ricciardelli, R., & Moir, M. (2013). Stigmatized among the stigmatized: Sex offenders in Canadian penitentiaries. *Canadian Journal of Criminology and Criminal Justice, 55*(3), 353–386.

Rogers, C., Pepper, I., & Skilling, L. (2022). Evidence-based policing for crime prevention in England and Wales: Perception and use by new police recruits. *Crime Prevention and Community Safety, 24*, 1–14.

Rosenbaum, D. P., Lawrence, D. S., Hartnett, S. M., McDevitt, J., & Posick, C. (2015). Measuring procedural justice and legitimacy at the local level: the police–community interaction survey. *Journal of Experimental Criminology, 11*, 335–366.

Rothwell, S., McFadzien, K., Strang, H., Hooper, G., & Pughsley, A. (2022). Rapid video responses (RVR) vs. face-to-face responses by police officers to domestic abuse victims: A randomised controlled trial. *Cambridge Journal of Evidence-Based Policing, 6*, 1–24.

Rozmann, N., & Ariel, B. (2018). The extent and gender directionality of intimate partner violence in different relationship types: A systematic review and meta-analysis. *Partner Abuse, 9*(4), 335–361.

Schmucker, M., & Lösel, F. (2017). Sexual offender treatment for reducing recidivism among convicted sex offenders: A systematic review and meta-analysis. *Campbell Systematic Reviews, 13*(1), 1–75.

Schnobrich-Davis, J., Swatt, M., & Wagner, D. (2021). Focused deterrence: Effective crime reduction strategy for chronic offenders? *Crime Prevention and Community Safety, 23*(3), 302–318.

Sherman, L. W. (2013). The rise of evidence-based policing: Targeting, testing, and tracking. *Crime and Justice, 42*(1), 377–451.

Sherman, L. W., & Weisburd, D. (1995). General deterrent effects of police patrol in crime "hot spots": Arandomized, controlled trial. *Justice Quarterly, 12*(4), 625–648.

Sherman, L. W., Gartin, P. R., & Buerger, M. E. (1989). Hot spots of predatory crime: Routine activities and the criminology of place. *Criminology, 27*(1), 27–56.

Sherman, L., Neyroud, P. W., & Neyroud, E. (2016). The Cambridge crime harm index: Measuring total harm from crime based on sentencing guidelines. *Policing: a Journal of Policy and Practice, 10*(3), 171–183.

SooHyun, O., Martinez, N. N., Lee, Y., & Eck, J. E. (2017). How concentrated is crime among victims? A systematic review from 1977 to 2014. *Crime Science, 6*(1), 1–16.

Strang, H., & Braithwaite, J. (2017). *Restorative justice: Philosophy to practice*. Routledge.

Strang, H., Sherman, L., Ariel, B., Chilton, S., Braddock, R., Rowlinson, T., et al. (2017). Reducing the harm of intimate partner violence: Randomized controlled trial of the Hampshire Constabulary CARA Experiment. *Cambridge Journal of Evidence-Based Policing, 1*(2), 160–173.

Sutherland, A., Strang, L., Stepanek, M., Giacomantonio, C., Boyle, A., & Strang, H. (2021). Tracking violent crime with ambulance data: How much crime goes uncounted? *Cambridge Journal of Evidence-Based Policing, 5*(1), 20–39.

Tabassum, S., & Suhail, K. (2022). Sexual harassment on public transport: A survey study of Rawalpindi, Pakistan. *Journal of Humanities, Social and Management Sciences (JHSMS), 3*(1), 258–266.

Telep, C. W., & Lum, C. (2014). The receptivity of officers to empirical research and evidence-based policing: An examination of survey data from three agencies. *Police Quarterly, 17*(4), 359–385.

Telep, C. W., Mitchell, R. J., & Weisburd, D. (2014). How much time should the police spend at crime hot spots? Answers from a police agency directed randomized field trial in Sacramento, California. *Justice Quarterly, 31*(5), 905–933.

Telep, C. W., Weisburd, D., Gill, C. E., Vitter, Z., & Teichman, D. (2014). Displacement of crime and diffusion of crime control benefits in large-scale geographic areas: A systematic review. *Journal of Experimental Criminology, 10*(4), 515–548.

The World Bank. (2022). *Gender-based violence (violence against women and girls)*. https://www. worldbank.org/en/topic/socialsustainability/brief/violence-against-women-and-girls. Last accessed 9 Sept 2022.

United Nations. (2022). *The spotline initiative*. https://www.un.org/sustainabledevelopment/ending-violence-against-women-and-girls/. Accessed 7 Sept 2022.

Vijayasiri, G. (2008). Reporting sexual harassment: The importance of organizational culture and trust. *Gender Issues, 25*, 43–61.

Von Hirsch, A., & Cambridge University. Institute of Criminology. Colloquium (1998: Bristol). (1999). *Criminal deterrence and sentence severity: An analysis of recent research* (p. 1). Oxford: Hart Publishing.

Wain, N., & Ariel, B. (2014). Tracking of police patrol. *Policing: A Journal of Policy and Practice, 8*(3), 274–283.

Walijee, H., Sood, S., Markey, A., Krishnan, M., Lee, A., & De, S. (2020). Is nurse-led telephone follow-up for postoperative obstructive sleep apnoea patients effective? A prospective observational study at a paediatric tertiary centre. *International Journal of Pediatric Otorhinolaryngology, 129*, 109766.

Wathen, C. N., & MacMillan, H. L. (2003). Interventions for violence against women: Scientific review. *JAMA, 289*(5), 589–600.

Weinborn, C., Ariel, B., Sherman, L. W., & O'Dwyer, E. (2017). Hotspots vs. harmspots: Shifting the focus from counts to harm in the criminology of place. *Applied Geography, 86*, 226–244.

Weisburd, D. (2015). The law of crime concentration and the criminology of place. *Criminology, 53*(2), 133–157.

Weisburd, D., Bushway, S., Lum, C., & Yang, S. M. (2004). Trajectories of crime at places: A longitudinal study of street segments in the city of Seattle. *Criminology, 42*(2), 283–322.

Weisburd, D., Wyckoff, L. A., Ready, J., Eck, J. E., Hinkle, J. C., & Gajewski, F. (2006). Does crime just move around the corner? A controlled study of spatial displacement and diffusion of crime control benefits. *Criminology, 44*(3), 549–592.

Weisburd, D., Groff, E. R., & Yang, S. M. (2012). *The criminology of place: Street segments and our understanding of the crime problem.* Oxford University Press.

Weisburd, D., Braga, A. A., Groff, E. R., & Wooditch, A. (2017). Can hot spots policing reduce crime in urban areas? An agent-based simulation. *Criminology, 55*(1), 137–173.

Welsh, B. C., Piza, E. L., Thomas, A. L., & Farrington, D. P. (2020). Private security and closed-circuit television (CCTV) surveillance: A systematic review of function and performance. *Journal of Contemporary Criminal Justice, 36*(1), 56–69.

Wheeler, A. P., & Reuter, S. (2021). Redrawing hot spots of crime in Dallas, Texas. *Police Quarterly, 24*(2), 159–184.

Wilkin, D. (2019). *Disability hate crime: Experiences of everyday hostility on public transport.* Springer Nature.

Williams, L. M. (2003). Understanding child abuse and violence against women: A life course perspective. *Journal of Interpersonal Violence, 18*(4), 441–451.

Williams, A. E., & Ariel, B. (2013). The Bristol Integrated Offender Management Scheme: A pseudo-experimental test of desistance theory. *Policing: A Journal of Policy and Practice, 7*(2), 123–134.

Williams, J. L., Malik, A. A., & McTarnaghan, S. (2020). Gender based violence on public transportation: A review of evidence and existing solutions. *USAID.* https://www.urban.org/research/publication/gender-based-violence-public-transportation. Last accessed 9 Sept 2022.

Wilson, D. B., Brennan, I., & Olaghere, A. (2018). Police-initiated diversion for youth to prevent future delinquent behavior: A systematic review. *Campbell Systematic Reviews, 14*(1), 1–88.

Wong, J. S., Bouchard, J., Gravel, J., Bouchard, M., & Morselli, C. (2016). Can at-risk youth be diverted from crime? A meta-analysis of restorative diversion programs. *Criminal Justice and Behavior, 43*(10), 1310–1329.

Zahabi, M., Pankok, C., Jr., & Park, J. (2020). Human factors in police mobile computer terminals: A systematic review and survey of recent literature, guideline formulation, and future research directions. *Applied Ergonomics, 84*, 103041.

Working with Private Policing to Enhance Public Policing: The Case of the United Kingdom

Mark Button

Abstract In the UK, public police are dwarfed by a substantial private policing sector that includes in-house provision, commercial for fee providers and Non-Governmental Organisations. The contribution of private policing ranges from the uncontroversial provision of uniformed security in private spaces such as shopping centres, office complexes and pleasure parks; the more controversial provision of prior state delivered services through contracts, such as police custody; to the more hidden functions of investigating fraud, corruption, and cybercrime. A patchwork of partnerships, official schemes and statutory interventions have emerged to frame these initiatives. This paper explores them through a typology. These will include *state facilitation* where the state has created standards and schemes to enable the public and private sectors to develop partnerships to better work together. This includes regulatory initiatives such as the regulation of private security, among others. Second there is *state delegation*, where the private sector has been brought in to deliver state functions but seeks to control the relationship. This includes the contracting out of prisoner transport and custody suites. Finally, there has been *state reinforcement* where from a position of weakness, the state has either acquiesced to, or even encouraged the growth of private contributions to fill the gap. This includes working with the private sector to enhance the policing of fraud and cybercrime. Such reinforcement has also varied in the degree to which the state controls and influences such capacity. This chapter will explore these in more depth offering detailed examples and critically evaluate these initiatives.

M. Button (✉)
School of Criminology and Criminal Justice, University of Portsmouth, Portsmouth, UK
e-mail: mark.button@port.ac.uk

© The Author(s), under exclusive license to Springer Nature Switzerland AG 2023
E. A. Blackstone et al. (eds.), *Handbook on Public and Private Security*,
Competitive Government: Public Private Partnerships,
https://doi.org/10.1007/978-3-031-42406-9_10

Acronyms

ACSO	Accredited Community Safety Officers
DCPCU	Dedicated Card and Payment Crime Unit
DPA	Deferred Prosecution Agreement
HMIC	Her Majesty's Inspectorate of Constabulary
IFED	Insurance Fraud Enforcement Department
PFI	Private Finance Initiative
PCSO	Police Community Safety Officer
RSPCA	Royal Society for the Protection of Animals
FACT	Federation Against Copyright Theft
SIA	Security Industry Authority
SFO	Serious Fraud Office
SAFO	Specified Anti-Fraud Organisation

1 Introduction

The traditional view of the public police as dominant in the provision of security has changed significantly in the last 30 years in the UK, with much greater appreciation of the significant role of the private sector. These changes can be explained by policy changes implemented by governments, which have directly encouraged the private sector; through societal changes, such as the changing nature of public and private spaces people use, and an inability of the state to cope with the policing demands of society, leading to the private sector filling the gap, such as in the patrol of public areas and investigation of certain crimes (which will be explored in more depth later). The growing interest of scholars in these areas of policing has also exposed private sector activity, that has been longstanding, but not appreciated, at least in academic circles. The picture of the provision of security in the UK today is much more a patchwork of public and private actors in the supply of policing and security with many different forms of private contribution (Button, 2019; Crawford & Lister, 2004; Jones & Newburn, 1998). Private security companies, consultancies, the in-house security, or proprietary, capabilities of organisations, alongside Non-Governmental Organisations and volunteer citizens in officially recognised schemes or more controversial vigilante actions, constitute that private contribution (see Table 1) (Button, 2019; Johnston, 1992). Complementing this are also initiatives where the state police have ventured into security markets, such as by charging for their services or in some cases soliciting funds for the provision of specialist units. Table 1 below illustrates this plurality of contributions beyond the state police in the UK (note most police officers in the UK are not armed).

The table above illustrates the substantial involvement of the private sector and juxtaposed against the 160,000 police officers employed in the UK. It reveals, at least in terms of size, the smaller size of the state police in comparison to the private

Table 1 Private provision in policing and security in the UK

Type	Examples	Size
Private security firms	Firms offering security and investigative services for fees to public and private sector clients (there are no armed private security officers in the UK)	In 2022 4000+ estimated firms, with 845 government approved contractors and 375,413 active licence holders (note: not all sectors of private security industry covered by Security Industry Authority (SIA) regulation). See page 4 for details
In-house (proprietary provision of organisations)	Many firms and public bodies employ their own security personnel such as uniformed guards and investigators	An SIA report in 2009 estimated 100,000 uniformed in-house guards
Non-governmental organisations	NGOs such as the Royal Society for the protection of animals, which polices crimes against animals and the Federation against copyright theft, which polices copyright theft against the movie and television industry	Difficult to determine complete size, but the RSPCA alone in 2022 had 273 inspectors and FACT circa 50 staff
Voluntary policing	Large numbers of citizens volunteer in capacities which support policing. Some of these are official such as the special constabulary or other police schemes; others could be considered more vigilante orientated such as paedophile hunters and scam baiters	In England and Wales there were 9147 special constables in 2021. Difficult to determine size of other voluntary contributions
Police commercial activities	The state police charge for a variety of services and there are some examples of specialist units been funded, such as the insurance fraud enforcement department (IFED) funded by insurers and the dedicated card and payment crime unit (DCPCU) funded by the banks	Relatively small numbers with IFED employing 34 in 2022

Sources: Button (2019); City of London Police (2022); House of Commons Library (2021); Royal Society for the Prevention of Cruelty to Animals (2022); Professional Security (2009); Security Industry Authority (SIA) (2022a, b)

contributions (House of Commons Library, 2021). The private security industry, which is regulated by the Security Industry Authority,[1] (SIA) a body established by the UK Government through legislation, has over 375,000 active licence holders and this is also only part of the picture. Some segments of the for fee private security

---

[1] The SIA licenses employees in designated sectors of the private security industry which currently includes security officers (contract), cash and valuables in transit (contract), door supervisors or 'bouncers' (contract and in-house), close protection or bodyguard (contract only) and CCTV operators (contract only). It also runs a voluntary scheme for firms/companies operating in these sectors called the Approved Contractors Scheme. Licensing of employees is based upon proof of identity, a character check and completion of approved training.

industry are not regulated, such as private investigators; some are regulated by other bodies, such as those offering custody and prison related services; and much of the in-house sector is exempt from regulation.

The huge range of activities of private policing means given the space constraints of this chapter the focus will be largely upon partnerships with the private security industry and in-house security counterparts. This chapter explores the three categories of working arrangement that have been identified: state facilitation, state delegation and state reinforcement. Then, these arrangements are evaluated.

2 Public Private Partnerships in Policing

There has been surprisingly little written about public-private partnerships based upon research in the UK. The following sections draw out some of the key studies. It will argue that the relationships can be characterised in three broad ways: *state facilitation*, where the state has simply through funding, legislation or just promotion encouraged private contributions; second, there is *state delegation*, where the state has given the role to the private sector through contracting or other statutory means; and finally there is *state reinforcement*, where the actions of the state, intentional or not, have led to the private sector filling the gap. In all these contexts a broad view of the state is taken to encompass acts of both government institutions and state policing agencies.

2.1 State Facilitation

State facilitation is where the state has enacted legislation or developed initiatives that encourage the growth of private contributions and/or inspire the public and private actors to work together. Central to this in many countries, and particularly the UK, has been the enactment of legislation to regulate private security. Indeed, in the White Paper setting out the case for regulation of the private security industry in England and Wales, it pointed to the importance of partnerships between the police and private security, the potential for the private security sector to assist the police in core functions such as patrol and highlighted:

> If the private security industry is to be given a greater role in our communities, then the police and local authorities will want to be sure that the industry is properly regulated and that the individuals who work within the industry are deserving of the trust placed in them (Home Office, 1999).

This culminated two years later in the Private Security Industry Act 2001, which established a regulatory system based upon individual licences for the those working in regulated sectors (principal sectors being: security guards - contract, security guards for cash and valuables in transit – contract, door supervisors (often known as 'bouncers') – in-house and contract, close protection officers – contract). Licensing is based upon a character or background check and completion of mandatory training. The Act also created a voluntary regulatory system for firms called the 'approved contractors' scheme whereby complying with the relevant standards they can be placed upon the Approved Contractors list, which provides commercial benefits. There were limitations with the legislation with some significant gaps such as in-house security guards (who are exempt) and the voluntary system for firms. There were also concerns over standards not being high enough (Button, 2007; White, 2015a). Nevertheless, there is evidence this legislation has provided the foundations to enable partnership, but also for private security to secure a bigger role in policing, which will be developed further in this paper. Indeed, one critical observer of the private security industry argued the legislation had in effect created a 'pimp' for the private security industry to boost the role of the private sector in security markets (Zedner, 2006). The private security industry itself has also been keen for such measures to give it greater legitimacy and an ability to undertake more of these tasks (Leloup & White, 2021; White, 2015b, 2022).

Regulatory initiatives directed at the wider private security industry, however, did not directly create a greater role for the private security industry. But, there have been other areas of intervention that specifically enhanced the role. For example, in 1991 the Criminal Justice Act was passed enabling contracting out of prisons to the private sector along with the transportation of prisoners. It also established special powers for certain court security officers, such as search and removal powers (to eject someone from court), to enable the contracting out of these functions (Jason-Lloyd, 2013). Additional legislation has facilitated this further, such that there is now a small but significant number of private prisons, along with several immigration detention centres. The administration of tagging (the electronic monitoring of offenders) orders for offenders is largely contracted out, and most serious offenders are transported by the private security companies. The legislation facilitated such private sector involvement by primarily enabling the state to allow private employees to conduct these functions, and setting regulation (Jason-Lloyd, 2013). The rationale for this contracting out was primarily cost reduction, but also an expectation the private sector would bring new innovative ways of working, which in turn would influence the remaining state delivered functions.

The privatisation of custody, although a boom for the private security industry, could be considered distinct from policing. However, in the UK, other legislation has moved the scope of potential private sector involvement into policing. Indeed, one year after the Private Security Industry Act, the Police Reform Act 2002 was passed, which at least on paper created much more significant scope for private sector involvement with the police. First, the legislation included provisions for chief police officers to designate civilian employees with powers, enabling contractors to perform some of these functions, particularly in custody and escorting of prisoners. The privatisations in custody pursued at a government level discussed earlier were in essence being placed as options chief police officers could pursue, with the expectation these would lead to lower costs and enable more police officers to be dedicated to frontline policing functions (rather than custody duties).[2] Some of this experience will be explored in more depth later in this chapter.

The other significant facilitating measure of Police Reform Act 2002 was to create accreditation schemes, which could be pursued at the discretion of chief police officers. The most relevant to private security was the 'community safety accreditation scheme'. This enables chief police officers to accredit private security, wardens etc. where they complete a special training course for which in return, they secure access to some special powers, such as to issue fixed penalty notices, require the name and address of a person, confiscate alcohol, and tobacco. The scheme also aimed to create a better relationship with the police in the micro context they operate and allowed accredited officers to wear a special badge on their lapels, indicating higher status (HM Government, 2012). This was the implementation of the former Metropolitan Police Commissioner's, Sir Ian Blair, ideas for police compliant security officers (Blair, 1998). The take up of these schemes has not been as popular as some hoped. In 2010, the Government published a survey of schemes in operation in 26 police force areas where the police chief chose to participate. It identified 2219 staff accredited in over 130 schemes covering largely warden schemes,[3] but also private security staff in shopping malls, hospitals and working for local authorities (HM Government, 2010). There has been surprisingly little research evaluating these schemes, bar one study which explored levels of public reassurance from different security actors, which noted the greater cost effectiveness of security officers (Rowland & Coupe, 2014).

It is not just by legislation the state has facilitated private sector involvement. The development of Project Griffin in 2004, which was rebranded as Action Counters Terrorism in 2016, was an attempt by the state to bring private security staff into the counter terrorism network by providing training on spotting signs of terrorist activity and what to do in the event of an incident (HM Government, 2016). The purpose of which was to expand the 'eyes and ears' of the private sector into the state counter terrorism structures. Reporting in 2013, the scheme boasted over 20,000 certificates of attendance issued, 1500 bridge calls (a conference telephone call connecting large numbers of people) with 500 alone in the City of London (City Security, 2013). There has been little formal evaluation of these schemes, which have expanded to other countries, but they clearly represent the state facilitating a larger role for the private sector in the prevention and response to terrorism.

There is a tendency for private policing scholars to focus upon uniformed private provision. But, in the field of investigation, particularly in relation to economic

---

[2] In the UK the average annual earnings in 2021 for a security guard was £23,307 (US$21,121) and for a police officer (sergeant and below) £41,552 (US$37,655) (ONS, 2021a). It is also important to note many security guards outside London are paid just above the minimum wage of £9.50 per hour (US$10.47) at £10.14 per hour (US$11.17), which compares to a police constables starting equivalent hourly rate of £12.55 per hour (US$13.83) which rises incrementally to £19.71 per hour (US$21.71) (Indeed, 2022; Northumbria Police Federation, 2020).

[3] Wardens are a form of local government security operative employed directly by the local authority who sometimes also possess powers to enforce local byelaws.

crimes surrounding money laundering, fraud, bribery and intellectual property, there is a substantial private policing component produced under state reinforcement, which is explored later in this chapter. In this context, the state has also sought to facilitate private sector involvement.

For example, the Serious Crime Act 2007 Section 68 contains a specific section on the prevention of fraud, with the focus on data-sharing. The essence of it is enabling public authorities to share information for fraud prevention with a "Specified Anti-Fraud Organisation" (SAFO). Among other provisions, it requires the Secretary of State to develop a Code of Practice related to this disclosure (Home Office, 2015). There are 11 SAFO organisations, which include bodies and companies such as Cifas (an NGO which holds largely financial services related fraud data), Call Credit, BAE Systems, Dun and Bradstreet, Equifax and Synectics Solutions. The legislation is essentially the state facilitating and helping to make more effective private sector involvement in the prevention, detection, and investigation of fraud. The success of the scheme is debatable, however. A National Fraud Authority (2010) report highlighted low uptake in the private sector, and a reticence of public authorities to share information, despite this legislation, for fear of breaching other privacy and data protections related regulations. A report by the Information Commissioners Office (2015) noted some gaps, such as some public bodies not sharing information and confusion among them of the status of SAFO.

2.2   State Delegation

In the *state delegation* category, the private sector has been given a role in the delivery of services through contracting out or through statutory direction. Prisons and prisoner escort were the pioneer areas in contracting out, which led to various policing and security functions being delivered privately. The areas of policing where the state mandates the private sector to engage in policing activity will also be briefly explored.

There are a wide range of functions within police organisations that have been contracted out to the private sector, many of which relate to back-room, administrative type functions, rather than front-line police. The rationale has been to secure cost-savings, free up more police officers for front-line policing and to stimulate innovation in service delivery. As noted earlier in the 1990s, the Criminal Justice Act 1991 and additional legislation paved the way for the contracting out of some prisons, prisoner escort, and magistrates court security. However, during this period there was relatively little interest in contracting out front-line police functions. The election of the Labour government in 1997, led to the substantial expansion of the private funding and provision of major capital projects. The capital was often supplied with services, such as cleaning, maintenance, facilities management, and security, to name some, locked in for often 25-year contracts. This Private Finance Initiative (PFI) was also embraced in small pockets in the UK police service. Writing in 2007, Button et al. noted 23 projects the majority of which were for the provision of buildings and associated facilities management functions. The only projects relating to front-line policing were:

- Cheshire Police for centralised custody suites (£185 million over lifetime) (US$204 million); and
- Sussex Police for centralised custody suites (£270 million over lifetime) (US$297 million).

In these projects purpose-built custody suites were constructed, and private security companies provided the staff to run the suites which were originally, Reliance in Sussex and a subsidiary of G4S, Global Solutions Ltd. in Cheshire.

The passage of PFI and the Police Reform Act 2002 were deemed to be pushing the police to greater private sector involvement. These combined seemed to suggest a move towards accelerated contracting out of police functions such as custody and escort and where this is not possible, the objective was workforce modernisation through greater civilianisation, with the additional areas of investigation and patrol (Loveday, 2007). It was, however, not until 2012 when a media storm emerged surrounding a proposal by West Midlands Police and Surrey Police for a £1.5 billion (US$ 1.65 billion) contract which was purported to cover politically sensitive services such as 'investigating crimes' and 'patrolling neighbourhoods' that the issue became significant (The Guardian, 2012). White (2015b) argues the plan was not as wide ranging as the media portrayed, but it nevertheless unleashed a storm of debate. Combined with the G4S failure to provide security to the expected level at the London Olympics and the move towards elected Police and Crime Commissioners, most of whom were opposed to police privatisation, this 'closed the window' for greater private sector involvement in these areas. Indeed, there is strong opposition to privatisation of the police from the Police Federation (the police trade union in the UK) and most of the political parties and even within the Conservative Party – which is the most inclined towards pursuing such policies.

However, under the radar of the controversy of West Midlands and Surrey, Lincolnshire Police had been pursuing an equally ambitious plan which between 2010 and 2012 had resulted in a £229 million (US$ 252 million) strategic partnership with G4S for 10 years with an option for a five-year extension (White, 2014). This partnership involves frontline services such as the force control room, custody, and front counters. (Please explain.) It also involves operational support functions such as the crime management bureau, firearms licensing, the identification unit, criminal justice unit, collisions unit and central ticket office, as well as a range of business support functions from fleet, human resources to facilities management.

White (2014 and 2015a, b) argues the 'window' of greater police privatisation closed for the time being and that Lincolnshire might be an atypical case. Indeed, a report by HMIC (2012) on money saving collaborations, found of 543 schemes only 34 involved the private sector and only custody (amongst software and IT) involved frontline police functions. It would seem contracting out of police frontline functions in the UK has not been significant, despite some evidence of cost savings in areas such as custody (Heath et al., 2009; Mawby et al., 2009).

There are some areas where the state has sought private sector action to deal with crime problems and has achieved this though legislation that effectively creates obligations on private entities to implement policing strategies. Airports, airlines, ports, ferry providers, railways, train operators and nuclear facilities, to name some, have been subjected to obligations to pursue specific security strategies and work with certain state agencies (Button & George, 2001). For example, the Railways Act 1993 Sections 119 to 121a gave powers to the Government to set minimum security standards on the railways.

One of the most significant areas of intervention, to direct private sector involvement in policing, relates to money laundering. Here the state has mandated specified actors (such as banks, casinos, estate agents etc) dealing with money to investigate potential clients and transactions and where they meet a threshold of suspicion, to report them to the authorities (Riccardi & Levi, 2018). This created an industry of compliance, some in-house some contracted, which has been described as a 'complex' (Verhage, 2009). Anti-bribery legislation in the UK has also created an offence of failing to prevent bribery for private entities, which requires them to have 'adequate procedures' as a defence against prosecution. This has effectively compelled high-risk organisations to develop capacity to secure their organisations (Wells, 2012). Prosecutions for this have been rare as the preferred option of the enforcement body, the Serious Fraud Office, has been to conclude a Deferred Prosecution Agreement (DPA) where the firm pays a fine and subjects itself to external scrutiny to avoid prosecution. The fines can be substantial, for example, in 2017 Rolls Royce paid £497.25 million (US$ 548 million) for various breaches, including failing to prevent bribery (Serious Fraud Office, 2017).

2.3   State Reinforcement

A strong current of thought in private policing scholarship has noted the fiscal constraint perspective, where the inability of the state police to satisfy public demands vis-à-vis policing and crime control have led to the private sector stepping up to fill the gap (Jones & Newburn, 1998; National Advisory Council on Criminal Justice Standards and Goals, 1976). The consequences of this fiscal constraint have been load shedding and avoidance of new loads by police. This has fuelled a substantial expansion of private sector involvement to fill this gap, in often what some might regard as controversial areas, which have received relatively little attention (Button, 2019; Johnston, 1992). Before some of this 'state reinforcement' is considered, it might be worth assessing the pressures the police have been under in the UK.

Since the financial crisis in 2008 there have been significant reductions in the resources available for public police. From 2010, police budgets that rely on the Home Office in England and Wales allocations, were cut 20 percent over four years, which had significant implications for most police forces (White, 2014). In 2010 there were 171,600 police officers (273.4 per 100,000) in the UK, by 2017 the number had fallen to 150,000, a 12.4 percent reduction (227.1 per 100,000). The 2002

Police Reform Act introduced the frontline uniformed supporting role of Police Community Support Officers (PCSO). In 2010 these had peaked at 16,918 officers in England and Wales and by 2017 had fallen substantially to 10,213, and by 2021 there were 9248 (House of Commons Library, 2017 and 2021). The election of the Conservative Johnson led government in 2019 has reversed this decline in police, and as was noted earlier, UK police strength has risen back to 160,000 (239.7 per 100,000).[4] But, this level of police recruitment must be set against rising demands, not least in crime. For example, traditional crime against individuals (theft, burglary, robbery etc) had declined from around 9.5 million incidents in 2010 to 4.8 million in 2021. In 2017 fraud and computer misuse related crimes were added to these statistics and in 2021 there were 11.6 million incidents. When fraud and computer misuse related crimes are the focus, state police have little interest and capability to deal with them (ONS, 2021b). These figures also exclude the large number of incidents against organisations.

The police have not withdrawn from patrolling public streets, but their decline in numbers – particularly PCSOs who have this as their main role, has meant that there is a thinner police presence on the streets, compared to what the public wants, which is a very high visible presence (BMG Research, 2019; Wakefield, 2006). The regular surveys by Her Majesty's Inspectorate of Constabulary including in the 2019 report based upon over 17,000 responses showed an increase in visibility of patrolling police officers on foot. But, in 2019 only 44% of those surveyed saw an officer at least once in 3 months, up from 29% in 2017, and 36% did not see one in 2018, down from 44% in 2017 (BMG Research, 2019). The gap between what the public wants and what is provided created an opportunity for the private sector to step in and fill the gap. Figure 1 illustrates the situation in the last decade (2010–2019), which included a substantial period of austerity in the UK after the 2008 financial crash. It shows a steady decline in police offers over this period of 6%, although police officers started to increase in 2019, while SIA active licence holders increased by over 23% during the same period. These don't represent the totality of private security personnel, but they represent a significant proportion, and this provides a useful gauge. Clearly as police numbers have been declining, the presence of private security has been increasing.

Another area of load shedding by the public police has been the response to intruder alarms. Traditionally the police would respond to any alarm activation. However, with the huge growth in the use of intruder alarms accompanied by a significant increase in false alarms and consequent drain on police resources, the police have sought to limit their response. Police will now only respond to intruder alarms/security systems fitted by approved installers (National Security Inspectorate or Security Systems Alarm Inspection Board approved installers), which are subject to annual maintenance and have paid the police for a Unique Reference Number (National Police Chiefs Council, 2015). The gap offered by the police withdrawal

---

[4] Rates per 100,000 derived by using UK population statistics from https://www.ons.gov.uk/peoplepopulationandcommunity/populationandmigration/populationestimates/timeseries/ukpop/pop

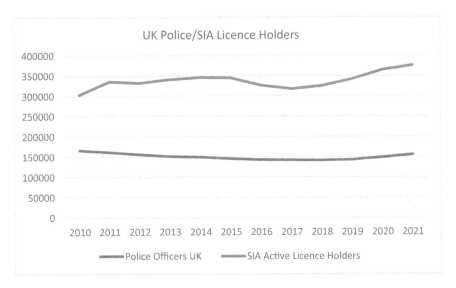

Fig. 1 Number of UK police officers v SIA active licence holders 2010–2021

has enabled the private security industry to step in and offer this response service for a fee. Unfortunately, there has been virtually no research assessing this change (see Cahalane, 2001).

A key area where gaps in police resources have led to opportunities for the private sector to fill the gap is in fraud investigation. In a government investigation into the policing, prevention, and punishment of fraud the following letter was published, detailing a response from a chief constable to a bank that had suffered a £100,000 (US$ 110,000) staff fraud:

> The investigation of fraud is extremely expensive in terms of hours spent obtaining statements and preparing a prosecution case. The Constabulary is required under the Crime and Disorder Act to produce a crime reduction strategy. Our strategy identifies priority areas and police resources are directed to those priority areas. Fraud is not one of them (Fraud Review Team, 2006, p 69).

Contrast this to a robbery of a bank, where a large police response would be very likely. There have been several other studies since which have shown the challenge of securing police interest to conduct a fraud investigation (Button et al., 2015). Indeed, the Police Foundation (2018, p4) noted:

> While 3.2 million frauds were estimated to have taken place in 2017–18, just 638,882 frauds were recorded by the police and industry bodies. For every crime reported just one in 13 was allocated for investigation and in that same period only 8313 cases resulted in a charge/summons, caution, or community resolution, representing just three per cent of the number reported to police.

The reality for most frauds against organisations of a certain size is that the police will require prima facie evidence before they become involved. If the investigation becomes public, it may cause negative publicity to the organization. Thus, organizations conduct internal investigation or contract private investigators to attempt to keep the case from becoming public. In some cases, the results of the private investigations are handed to the prosecutors to follow up with criminal charges (Button et al., 2015). The police have also been pleased not to investigate some fraud cases, which could be labour intensive, but pick up the benefits of a successful investigation by the private sector. Some areas of volume fraud, such as banking related frauds, have also traditionally been investigated by the bank's own fraud teams with only the most serious cases referred to the police, and even here the banking industry pays for its own police unit to deal with such cases: The Dedicated Card and Payment Crime Unit, which consists of sworn police officers paid for by the industry (Button, 2019).

It is not just fraud where the police are withdrawing from investigations. In 2015, Sara Thornton the new head of the National Police Chiefs Council caused controversy when she publicly stated the police may not attend to burglaries (BBC News, 2015). It was revealed in October 2017 that the Metropolitan Police Service in-order to save £400 million (US$ 441 million) would no longer conduct 'low level investigations' in a variety of areas which included: burglaries, thefts, and assaults. The Deputy Assistant Commissioner, Mark Simmons, was quoted as saying in the report:

> With the pressure on our resources, it is not practical for our officers to spend a considerable amount of time looking into something where, for example, the value of damage or the item stolen is under £50 (US$ 55), or the victim is not willing to support a prosecution. We need our officers to be focused on serious crime and cases where there is a realistic chance that we will be able to solve it. We also want them to be available to respond to emergencies and go to those members of the public that need our help the most. (The Guardian, 2017)

There are also some new roles that one would expect the police to undertake that they have avoided or sought to minimise involvement in. The most significant example of this has been the substantial increase in cyber related crime and fraud. As noted above, fraud is an area with limited state police response. For some cybercrimes it is even worse. For example, a person whose mobile device or laptop is infected and damaged with a malicious virus and seeks police interest is very unlikely to secure any serious support or investigation (Button et al., 2020). The reasons for lack of police interest in responding to cybercrimes includes both lack of expertise, lack of resources and pre-occupation with traditional crime (Button et al., 2022). Indeed, for organisational victims who can afford it, turning to the private sector, who can respond quickly and effectively for the right fees, is a much more efficient solution, particularly given the importance of information technology to the efficient running of most entities.

Historically, when there has been poor state preventive, deterrence, detection, and prosecution of criminals, voluntary and vigilante initiatives have emerged (Johnston, 1996). The huge increase in fraud has led to scambaiting (where people waste the time of fraudsters by playing along with the scam, but ultimately do not part with information or money to them) and other voluntary initiatives. Some simply support policing in providing valuable information, such as scam websites which should be closed, such as Petscams; others go further, effectively administering public humiliation as 'punishment' to the fraudsters, such as 419eater (Button

& Whittaker, 2021). For instance, on the 419eater website the of profiles of outed fraudsters, along with the often extensive (and sometimes humiliating) tasks the scambaiter has made them do, are publicly displayed. Similarly controversial have been paedophile hunter groups, who lure potential offenders by pretending to be victims and then arrange to meet, often promoting the confrontation online. Despite the controversy of these initiatives in 2018 it was revealed that many police forces in England and Wales have used the evidence gathered by such groups with 150 persons charged because of their evidence in the last year (BBC News, 2018). This illustrates the reinforcing nature of these initiatives.

The consequences of load shedding: direct and indirect are not as unambiguous as contracting out in most cases. Failure to investigate certain crimes might lead to some victims receiving no investigation or outcome, but for others with resources they may turn to other means, such as a private investigator or they may investigate themselves (Shepherd, 2021). Many victims observing the decline in police capacity may simply not even bother to report to the police and use an alternative means. The lack of visible police patrols might lead some persons to pay for a private security company to patrol their streets. Ultimately, however, these gaps have led to the private sector reinforcing the state.

3   Evaluating the Private Contribution to Policing

The three broad ways in which the private sector contributes to public policing illustrate a complexity of arrangements, which in many ways are hard to generalise. Contracting out police services, such as investigations, to commercial security companies is always going to be controversial, but private companies investigating crimes themselves solicit a much more sanguine response. There are several issues to consider.

It would not be possible for the state to supply all policing in a society, other than in a state dominated communist society. Therefore, the next question is where one draws the line in the boundaries between state and private provision? Such lines are inevitably influenced by political affiliations. But, if we consider a more practical approach driven by costs, there are many aspects of load shedding where given the demands in society upon the police and their costs it would not be economic or reasonable for the police to be conducting routine investigations for private companies, patrolling private shopping malls or responding to the alarm activations (where no other indicator exists of intrusion). In a liberal democracy with a mixed economy there is place for many of these activities, although there are important questions that arise about their quality, standards, and governance which we will return to shortly.

In some cases, private contributions may be more cost effective. In a study based upon shopping malls in the UK: police officers, PCSOs, Accredited Community Safety Officers (ACSO – security officers accredited under the community safety accreditation scheme) and security guards were compared (Rowland & Coupe,

2014). The study sought survey data from the people who visited these places and the costs of the different type of policing agents. This study noted several important findings. First, it found in comparison to the police and PCSOs a low recognition of security guards, as significantly more could recognise the police and PCSOs. Second, the police had three times greater perception of safety than the others. PCSOs had a slight advantage over security guards, with ACSOs worst of all. Although this was linked to the lack of recognition of status and symbols associated with the scheme. However, on the negative side, police officers led to greater fear of crime compared to the others. The authors then combined scores of reassurances with worry and their cost to produce an economic assessment. This produced a score where security guards were the most cost effective, 2.6 times more than police officers.

The delegation of roles to the private sector through activities such as contracting out has been more opaque in offering clear public savings. The Lincolnshire police contracting out was claimed to have saved the police £5 million (US$ 5.5 million) in the first year on a £200 million (US$ 220 million) contract over 10 years (BBC News, 2013). Independent verification of savings in the world of commercial confidentiality is harder to come by, but perhaps telling was the decision at the end of the contract not to renew it and Lincolnshire police to exploring options such as setting up their own company or taking the services in-house (Facilities Management Journal, 2020).

The HMIC report of 2012 also noted:

> Collaboration offers the potential to improve both efficiency and effectiveness. Forces are improving the service in some areas (such as protective services) and save money in others (£169m of savings planned by 2014/15). Savings, particularly those in non-front-line functions, assist forces in protecting their front-line service (p 56).

Note the phrase: "savings are not always a key driver of collaboration" and that innovation of transformation of services are often more important. Indeed, exposing public sector services to competition has been envisaged as a means to encourage police to innovate, without having to contract out. The Lincolnshire experiment may have achieved that enabling a return to a public model of delivery, but with more innovation.

It is also important to note that with *state facilitation, delegation,* and *reinforcement* there is evidence of reluctance and perhaps even resistance from the public police and related state agencies engaging with the private sector. The limited use of the police community accreditation scheme under the Police Reform Act 2002 was illustrated earlier, evidence of low uptake of the opportunities to contract out police functions, reluctance to share data and form constructive partnerships are all examples. Button et al. (2007) noted 'too many chiefs and not enough chief executives' in relation to Chief Constables and their attitude towards private sector involvement. Perhaps one of the barriers of working with the private sector for the police, at least when it means replacing public employees with private, is police culture, particularly that of the senior officers. This may in part be a response to some of the negative consequences of working with profit seeking enterprises.

Indeed, there are plenty of high-profile examples in this field which feed a reluctance to involve profit seeking companies and private initiative. G4S, one of the leading providers of contracted services in the UK, has been implicated in a number of high-profile scandals. For example, originally contracted to provide security for the London 2012 Olympics it over-promised and was unable to deliver the services it had been originally contracted for, resulting in several thousand guards short a month before the start, leading to the armed forces having to fill the gap (Reuters, 2012). Overcharging by G4S in a tagging contract (the electronic monitoring of offenders) for the Government also culminated in an investigation by the Serious Fraud Office (SFO) with the company admitting fraud and fined £44 million (US$48 million) (Guardian, 2020). Other commercial security firms have been implicated in poor standards that have resulted to deaths in custody, excessive force, racism, and sexism among others, although to what extent rates might be higher than the public sector is difficult to determine due to no easily available statistics providing comparison (see for example Metro, 2021; Mirror, 2021; Scotsman, 2011). The treatment of their own staff has also been criticised. In one case, a security firm was fined over £100,000 (US$110,000) after one of their own guards working at a remote windfarm froze to death while on duty (STV News, 2021). There have also been concerns over the quality of justice when private interests become involved. The scandal involving the Post Office, which has its own investigation and private prosecution capability, over 700 were wrongly prosecuted and convicted, in the UK's largest miscarriage of justice (BBC News, 2022). There are of course, many scandals to be found with the public police and other public bodies, perhaps even more than private forces, but what these scandals do is serve to create reference points which can be used to resist change in the public sector.

Ultimately, the private sector is needed in policing and the important question is where the line is drawn upon activities. The scandals and resistance frustrating greater private sector involvement reinforce the need for some of the measures that fell under *state facilitation*. If the private sector is to take on a much greater role in policing there is a need for regulation to ensure minimum standards and there is a requirement for legal frameworks to distinguish clear roles, enable powers and provide governance and accountability. And where the private sector does become involved and fails it is clearly held to account. There also needs to be more education about the respective sectors, perhaps facilitated by greater cross-over in senior managers taking time to work in both sectors.

4 Conclusion

This paper has explored how the state works with the private sector in policing in the UK. It did this by using a typology built upon three key areas. *State facilitation*, where the state has created standards and schemes to enable the public and private sectors to develop partnerships to better work together. *State delegation*, where the private sector has been brought in to deliver state functions, but the state seeks to control the relationship. Finally, there has been *state reinforcement* where from a position of weakness the private sector has filled the gap with varying levels of success and the state has either encouraged or acquiesced by not seeking to prohibit such activities. This chapter explored examples under each of these categories and then conducted a broad overview of this contribution. The paper has argued that ultimately private contributions are essential, the more significant questions are where to draw the line, maximising the effectiveness of private contributions and ensuring appropriate governance.

References

BBC News. (2013). *Private firm G4S 'saved Lincolnshire Police £5m'*. https://www.bbc.co.uk/news/uk-england-lincolnshire-23028812

BBC News. (2015). *Sara Thornton: Police may no longer attend burglaries*. Retrieved from http://www.bbc.co.uk/news/uk-33676308

BBC News. (2018). *'Paedophile hunter' evidence used to charge 150 suspects*. Retrieved from https://www.bbc.co.uk/news/uk-england-43634585

BBC News. (2022). *Post office scandal: What the Horizon saga is all about*. https://www.bbc.co.uk/news/business-56718036

Blair, I. (1998). *Where do the police fit into policing?* Speech delivered to ACPO Conference, 16th of July, 1998.

BMG Research. (2019). *Public perceptions of policing in England and Wales in 2017*. https://www.bmgresearch.co.uk//wp-content/uploads/2019/01/1578-HMICFRS-Public-Perceptions-of-Policing-2018_FINAL.pdf

Button, M. (2007). Assessing the regulation of private security across Europe. *European Journal of Criminology, 4*(1), 109–128.

Button, M. (2019). *Private policing* (2nd ed.). Routledge.

Button, M., & George, B. (2001). Government regulation in the United Kingdom private security industry: The myth of non-regulation. *Security Journal, 14*(1), 55–66.

Button, M., & Whittaker, J. (2021). Exploring the voluntary response to cyber-fraud: From vigilantism to responsibilisation. *International Journal of Law, Crime and Justice, 66*, 100482.

Button, M., Williamson, T., & Johnston, L. (2007). Too many chiefs and not enough chief executives' barriers to the development of PFI in the police service in England and Wales. *Criminology and Criminal Justice, 7*(3), 287–305.

Button, M., Wakefield, A., Brooks, G., Lewis, C., & Shepherd, D. (2015). Confronting the "fraud bottleneck": Private sanctions for fraud and their implications for justice. *Journal of Criminological Research, Policy and Practice, 1*(3), 159–174.

Button, M., Sugiura, L., Blackbourn, D., Shepherd, D. W. J., Wang, V., & Kapend, R. (2020). Victims of computer misuse: Main findings.

Button, M., Shepherd, D. W. J., Blackbourn, D., Sugiura, L., Kapend, R., & Wang, V. (2022). *Assessing the seriousness of cybercrime: The case of computer misuse crime in the United Kingdom and the victims' perspective* (p. 174889582211281). Criminology & Criminal Justice.

Cahalane, M. (2001). Reducing false alarms has a price—So does response: Is the real price worth paying? *Security Journal, 14*(1), 31–53.

City of London Police. (2022). IFED. https://www.cityoflondon.police.uk/police-forces/city-of-london-police/areas/city-of-london/about-us/about-us/ifed/

City Security. (2013). *Griffin by numbers*. https://citysecuritymagazine.com/police-partnerships/project-griffin-success-numbers/

Crawford, A., & Lister, S. (2004). The patchwork shape of reassurance policing in England and Wales: Integrated local security quilts or frayed, fragmented and fragile tangled webs? *Policing: An International Journal of Police Strategies & Management, 27*(3), 413–430.

Facilities Management Journal. (2020). *Lincolnshire police to end £200m deal with G4S in 2022.* https://www.fmj.co.uk/lincolnshire-police-to-end-200m-deal-with-g4s-in-2022/#:~:text=Lincolnshire%20Police%20Crime%20Commissioner%20(PCC,200%20million%20contract%20with%20G4S

Fraud Review Team. (2006). *Interim report.* http://www.lslo.gov.uk/pdf/Interim Fraud Report.

Guardian. (2017). *Low-level crimes to go un-investigated in Met police spending cuts.* Retrieved from https://www.theguardian.com/uk-news/2017/oct/16/low-level-crimes-to-go-uninvestigated-in-met-police-spending-cuts

Guardian. (2020). *G4S fined £44m by Serious Fraud Office over electronic tagging.* https://www.the-guardian.com/business/2020/jul/10/g4s-fined-44m-by-serious-office-over-electronic-tagging

Heath, G., Mawby, R. C., & Walley, L. (2009). Workforce modernization in police detention suites: The dilemmas of outsourcing in public services. *Policing: A Journal of Policy and Practice, 3*(1), 59–65.

HM Government. (2010). *A survey of employers involved in the community safety accreditation scheme completed October to December 2010.* Retrieved from https://assets.publishing.service.gov.uk/government/uploads/system/uploads/attachment_data/file/116966/survey-employers-csas-dec2010.pdf

HM Government. (2012). *Community safety accreditation scheme powers.* Retrieved from https://www.gov.uk/government/publications/community-safety-accreditation-scheme-powers

HM Government. (2016). *Project Griffin.* https://www.gov.uk/government/publications/project-griffin/project-griffin

HMIC. (2012). *Increasing efficiency in the police service.* HMIC.

Home Office. (1999). *The Government's Proposals for Regulation of the Private Security Industry in England and Wales.* https://assets.publishing.service.gov.uk/government/uploads/system/uploads/attachment_data/file/263537/4254.pdf

Home Office. (2015). *Data sharing for the prevention of Fraud Code of practice for public authorities disclosing information to a specified anti-fraud organisation under sections 68 to 72 of the Serious Crime Act 2007.* Retrieved from https://assets.publishing.service.gov.uk/government/uploads/system/uploads/attachment_data/file/415469/Data_Sharing_for_the_Prevention_of_Fraud_-_Code_of_Practice__web_.pdf

House of Commons Library. (2021). *Police service strength.* https://researchbriefings.files.parliament.uk/documents/SN00634/SN00634.pdf

Indeed. (2022). *Security guard salary in the United Kingdom.* https://uk.indeed.com/career/security-guard/salaries

Information Commissioners Office. (2015). *ICO review: Data sharing between the public and private sector to prevent fraud.* Retrieved from https://ico.org.uk/media/action-weve-taken/audits-and-advisory-visits/1043719/ico-review-data-sharing-to-prevent-fraud.pdf

Jason-Lloyd, L. (Ed.). (2013). *Quasi-policing.* Routledge.

Johnston, L. (1992). *The rebirth of private policing* (Vol. 63, pp. 341–349). Routledge.

Johnston, L. (1996). What is vigilantism? *British Journal of Criminology, 36*(2), 220–236.

Jones, T., & Newburn, T. (1998). *Private Security and public policing.* Clarendon Press.

Leloup, P., & White, A. (2021). Questioning Anglocentrism in plural policing studies: Private security regulation in Belgium and the United Kingdom. *European Journal of Criminology, 14773708211014853.*

Loveday, B. (2007). Re-engineering the police organisation: Implementing workforce modernisation in England and Wales. *The Police Journal, 80*(1), 3–27.

Mawby, R. C., Heath, G., & Walley, L. (2009). Workforce modernization, outsourcing and the "permanent revolution" in policing. *Crime Prevention and Community Safety, 11*(1), 34–47.

Metro. (2021). *Security guards sacked over sexual harassment of lone women at quarantine hotels.* https://metro.co.uk/2022/01/31/security-guards-sacked-over-sexual-harassment-at-quarantine-hotels-16018391/

Mirror. (2021). *Black rights campaigner grabbed by security and falsely accused of theft*. https://www.mirror.co.uk/news/uk-news/black-rights-campaigner-grabbed-shopping-24439066

National Advisory Committee on Criminal Standards and Goals. (1976). *Private security. Report of the task force on private security*. Government Printing Office.

National Fraud Authority. (2010). *Information sharing project report on data sharing for the prevention of fraud under Section 68 of the Serious Crime Act 2007*. Retrieved from https://assets.publishing.service.gov.uk/government/uploads/system/uploads/attachment_data/file/118464/info-sharing-serious-crime-act.pdf

National Police Chiefs Council. (2016). *National policing guidelines on charging for police services*. NPCC.

Northumbria Police Federation. (2020). *Pay scales*. https://www.norpolfed.org.uk/pay-scales-2020.pdf

ONS. (2015). *Public perceptions of the police*. Retrieved from https://www.ons.gov.uk/peoplepopulationandcommunity/crimeandjustice/compendium/crimestatisticsfocusonpublicperceptionsofcrimeandthepoliceandthepersonalwellbeingofvictims/2015-03-26/chapter1perceptionsofthepolice#section-2-visibility-of-the-police

ONS. (2021a). *UK earnings explorer*. https://www.ons.gov.uk/employmentandlabourmarket/peopleinwork/earningsandworkinghours/articles/ukearningsexplorer/2019-08-16

ONS. (2021b). *Crime in England and Wales: Year ending June 2021*. https://www.ons.gov.uk/peoplepopulationandcommunity/crimeandjustice/bulletins/crimeinenglandandwales/yearendingjune2021

Police Foundation. (2018). *More than just a number: improving the police response to victims of fraud*. Retrieved from http://www.police-foundation.org.uk/2017/wp-content/uploads/2010/10/more_than_just_a_number_exec_summary.pdf

Professional Security. (2009). *SIA In-house decision*. https://www.professionalsecurity.co.uk/news/news-archive/sia-in-house-decision/

Reuters. (2012). *Olympic failure leaves G4S in tatters, admits CEO*. https://www.reuters.com/article/uk-oly-4gs-hearing-idUKBRE86G0AU20120717

Riccardi, M., & Levi, M. (2018). Cash, crime and anti-money laundering. In *The Palgrave handbook of criminal and terrorism financing law* (pp. 135–163). Palgrave Macmillan.

Rowland, R., & Coupe, T. (2014). Patrol officers and public reassurance: A comparative evaluation of police officers, PCSOs, ACSOs and private security guards. *Policing and Society, 24*(3), 265–284.

Royal Society for the Prevention of Cruelty to Animals. (2022). *Facts*. https://www.rspca.org.uk/whatwedo/latest/facts

Scotsman. (2011). *Security gaffes led to death in custody*. https://www.scotsman.com/news/security-gaffes-led-death-custody-1678754

Security Industry Authority. (2022a). *SIA licence holder demographics: January 2022*. https://www.gov.uk/government/statistical-data-sets/sia-licence-holders

Security Industry Authority. (2022b). *SIA approved contractors: January 2022*. https://www.gov.uk/government/statistical-data-sets/sia-approved-contractors

Serious Fraud Office. (2017). *SFO completes £497.25m Deferred Prosecution Agreement with Rolls-Royce PLC*. https://www.sfo.gov.uk/2017/01/17/sfo-completes-497-25m-deferred-prosecution-agreement-rolls-royce-plc/

Shepherd, D. (2021). DIY fraud investigation and access to justice: A case study. *Policing: A Journal of Policy and Practice, 15*(4), 2165–2177.

STV News. (2021). *Companies fined nearly £900,000 after security guard froze to death*. https://news.stv.tv/west-central/companies-fined-nearly-900000-after-security-guard-froze-to-death

Verhage, A. (2009). Between the hammer and the anvil? The anti-money laundering-complex and its interactions with the compliance industry. *Crime, Law and Social Change, 52*(1), 9–32.

Wakefield, A. (2006). *The value of foot patrol: A review of Research*. Police Foundation.

Wells, C. K. (2012). Who's afraid of the Bribery Act 2010? *Journal of Business Law, 2012*(5), 420–430.

White, A. (2014). Post-crisis policing and public–private partnerships: The case of Lincolnshire police and G4S. *British Journal of Criminology, 54*(6), 1002–1022.

White, A. (2015a). The impact of the private security industry act 2001. *Security Journal, 28*(4), 425–442.

White, A. (2015b). The politics of police 'privatization': A multiple streams approach. *Criminology and Criminal Justice, 15*(3), 283–299.

White, A. (2022). Critical workers? Private security, public perceptions and the Covid-19 pandemic. *Security Journal*, 1–16.

Zedner, L. (2006). Liquid security: Managing the market for crime control. *Criminology & Criminal Justice, 6*(3), 267–288.

Part III
City and Maritime Security Experiences

Private Law Enforcement in New York City

Edward Peter Stringham and Louis B. Salz

Abstract New York City has a long and ongoing history with private police. State and city law allows for the existence of private peace officers with varying degrees of authority including the authority to carry firearms, use force, and make arrests. This chapter provides an overview of several types of deputized purely private law enforcement and hybrids of governmental and private law enforcement in New York City. One type of private law enforcement is in gated communities such as the Sea Gate Police Department. Another is in large housing developments or cooperatives such as the Co-op City Public Safety Department. Another type is the Hunts Point Department of Public Safety which polices America's largest wholesale food market and distribution hub. A somewhat governmental and somewhat private example is seen with the Battery Park City Authority, a public benefit corporation which contracts with the 800,000-employee security firm Allied Universal to hire a combination of private special police and unarmed security ambassadors. A major advantage of private law enforcement is that it is not a one-size-fits-all solution: different communities can hire more officers and different types of officers depending on their specific needs.

1 Introduction

Crime in New York City and many other American cities increased significantly after lockdowns starting in 2020. After city and state officials closed offices, restaurants, churches, schools, entertainment venues, and bars, the city took on

E. P. Stringham (✉) · L. B. Salz
Shelby Cullom Davis Endowment, Trinity College, Hartford, CT, USA
e-mail: Edward.stringham@trincoll.edu

© The Author(s), under exclusive license to Springer Nature Switzerland AG 2023
E. A. Blackstone et al. (eds.), *Handbook on Public and Private Security*,
Competitive Government: Public Private Partnerships,
https://doi.org/10.1007/978-3-031-42406-9_11

245

features of dystopian science fiction and has yet to fully recover. In 2020–2022 homicides on subways were 5.75 times more numerous than in the three years prior to lockdowns. Since ridership fell to 38% of the pre-lockdown figure, that means each rider became more than twenty times more likely to be murdered on the subway. Beside those intentionally working to foment civil unrest and the criminals themselves, nobody favors crime. But the most commonly invoked solution—government police—has lost popularity among Americans. Surveys show that confidence in government police fell from 64% of Americans in 2004 to 51% in 2021 (Gallup, 2021); among Black adults, just 27% have confidence in them.

Surveys typically present people with the question whether we should give more or less funding to government police, which may suggest the only choice is between funding government police and tolerating crime. A typically overlooked alternative, however, is private law enforcement. Paul Samuelson (1954) formalized the theory of public goods, and police are one of the most invoked examples of one. But in a subsequent article, "Should 'Public Goods' Be Public?," Samuelson (1967, p. 47) wrote, "The pure theory of public expenditure that I presented in the 1950s often uses the term 'public good' but cannot properly be interpreted to imply that private goods should be produced by private enterprise and public goods should be produced by government directly."

This chapter highlights how even a city not known for its recent commitment to private enterprise, New York, has a long and ongoing history of private law enforcement. Such law enforcement includes privately funded special patrolmen with peace officer status and arrest powers. This chapter provides an overview of several types of purely private law enforcement and hybrids of governmental and private law enforcement. The examples of private law enforcement we discuss are Sea Gate Police Department in Brooklyn, the Parkchester Department of Public Safety in the Bronx, the Co-op City Public Safety Department in the Bronx, and the Hunts Point Department of Public Safety in the Bronx. Officers are hired by their communities and have arrest powers in their communities. Similar examples that we do not cover include deputized private peace officers in LeFrak City, Big Six Towers, and Rochdale Village in Queens; Starret City in Brooklyn; and Stuyvesant Town and Peter Cooper Village in Manhattan. These officers have badges, uniforms, and patrol cars whose designs are very to those of government police, so it is likely that few people notice the difference. We also discuss the volunteer nondeputized security organization Boro Park Shomrim in Brooklyn, the hybrid Roosevelt Island Public Safety Department, the Brooklyn Rapid Transit Company's special police (operating a century ago), and the security patrol and fully deputized police run by Allied Universal in Battery Park City in Manhattan. Our study shows that varying degrees of private law enforcement already exist and that it can be looked upon as a model for communities concerned with reducing crime without relying more on government police.

2 Sea Gate Police Department

The Consolidated Laws of New York (2021, Chapter 11-A, Part 1) authorizes and distinguishes eighty-six types of peace officers.[2] Most types are government police, but some are private law enforcement. Types of private law enforcement include special patrolmen, special police, and specific categories such as "persons appointed as peace officers by the Sea Gate Association."[1] At the western tip of Coney Island in Brooklyn, Sea Gate is separated from the rest of the island by walls and gates, so it is almost completely isolated from the surrounding area—particularly at night,

---

[1] The terms *special police* and *special patrolmen* can refer to certain types of governmental law enforcement that are not regular police officers, but here we are focusing on law enforcement hired by private entities.

The specificity of the list ranges from very broad governmental police categories such as "1. Constables or police constables of a town or village" to very specific ones based on industry, geographic focus such as: "Special police officers for horse racing" or "Patrolmen appointed by the Lake George park commission."

Among the list of 86 types of peace officers, the terms special police officers, special patrolmen, and special officers often describes examples of private law enforcement. Private peace officers are likely to be found in the following categories:

"13. Persons designated as special police officers by the director of a hospital in the department of health pursuant to section four hundred fifty-five of the public health law."

"83. Members of the security force employed by Kaleida Health within and directly adjacent to the hospital buildings on the medical campus located between East North Street, Goodell Street, Main Street and Michigan Avenue."

"19. Harbor masters appointed by a county, city, town or village."

when entry is only granted to those with an ID and an invitation. It gained popularity in the late nineteenth century with the arrival of well-connected socialites such as the Vanderbilts and J. P. Morgan and the establishment (in 1898) of the Atlantic Yacht Club.

In 1899 Sea Gate was officially established and created the Sea Gate Association. The association constructed Sea Gate's external gates and walls and created Sea Gate Police Department. While the composition of Sea Gate's population has significantly changed—from wealthy socialites to primarily Jewish and Russian immigrants—the Sea Gate Police Department has not, making it one of the oldest continually operating privately funded police departments in the country and perhaps the oldest in New York City. While the surrounding area is mixed use (both commercial and residential), Sea Gate is exclusively residential, with the exception of its beach club. And because Sea Gate (population 4500) has a population density only about a third of Brooklyn's, it is more suburban than urban.

Sea Gate Police Department is privately funded but cooperates with the New York Police Department. It is primarily responsible for screening traffic and pedestrians entering Sea Gate and for enforcing standards of conduct within the community. At its inception, it exclusively comprised uniformed officers, but as it grew throughout the twentieth century, it expanded to include support staff, supervisors, and detectives. While Sea Gate police officers are not full-fledged New York City police officers, they are New York State peace officers under New York State Criminal Procedure Law Section 2.10, Subsection 46. This means they enforce the New York State Penal Law, New York State Vehicle and Traffic Law, New York State and New York City Environmental Protection Law (Engine Idling Law), and New York City Administrative Code within and around Sea Gate, giving them the power to make arrests and traffic stops on Sea Gate property and to carry firearms, handcuffs, tasers, and pepper spray. Sea Gate Police Department has twenty-five employees, many of which are retired New York Police Department officers working as New York State peace officers (Lexipol LLC, 2023).

While Sea Gate Police Department is responsible for policing within and at the perimeter of Sea Gate, its jurisdiction does not extend to the surrounding area of Coney Island. The New York Police Department also responds to major crimes

---

"27. New York city special patrolmen appointed by the police commissioner pursuant to subdivision c or e of section 434a-7.0 or subdivision c or e of section 14–106 of the administrative code of the city of New York."

"46. Persons appointed as peace officers by the Sea Gate Association."

"54. Special police officers appointed pursuant to section one hundred fifty-eight of the town law."

"55. Special patrolmen for sports facilities in the performance of sporting events, pursuant to the provisions of section one hundred six-b of the alcoholic beverage control law."

"77. (a) Syracuse University peace officers appointed by the chief law enforcement officer of the city of Syracuse."

"84. (a) Public safety officers employed by the University of Rochester who are designated as peace officers by the board of trustees of the University of Rochester pursuant to paragraphs (b), (c), and (d) of this subdivision."

committed on Sea Gate property. As peace officers, the department's members must hand in their weapons at the end of their shifts, a policy highly unpopular among them. While the division of power between Sea Gate Police Department and the New York Police Department allows the former to focus on issues specific to the Sea Gate community, the departments' relationship can be tense.

As New York State peace officers, under New York Criminal Procedure Law Section 140.25, Sea Gate Police Department officers have the same arrest authority within their jurisdiction as New York Police Department officers, as described under Section 140.15. However, their authority is restricted to Sea Gate and their hours on duty. As state-certified peace officers, they must undergo the same required training for legal certification as other such officers. According to state law, the peace officers must undergo a training course partly designed by the state government and partly designed by the Sea Gate Association. The state requires up to 180 h of state training in addition to the department's own training. As peace officers, Sea Gate Police Department officers may not carry a firearm unless they have completed a firearm training course (approved by the municipal-police training council) on deadly force and undergone annual firearms training.[2] In 2020 the Sea Gate Association spent $2,329,945 on salaries and wages, split across the roughly two dozen officers and the support staff and other employees (Nonprofit Metrics, 2023). The New York Police Department reports a starting salary of $42,500, and experienced officers may earn over $100,000 per year. Given the number of other Sea Gate employees, we estimate that Sea Gate officers earn less than New York Police Department officers.

Unlike the New York Police Department, which focuses on reported crimes, the Sea Gate Police Department focuses on preventing crimes by screening traffic and pedestrians. According to Sea Gate Police Department Officer Jeffrey Schnieder, "[Minor crimes] take the NYPD [New York Police Department] an hour to respond to unless it's a robbery-in-progress or something just as big," whereas the Sea Gate Police Department typically responds in a matter of minutes (Wallerson, 2015). Schnieder further states that policing in Sea Gate is "slower paced, but you're able to forge relationships because your main focus isn't combating crime, it's being there for residents." This emphasis on community policing fosters a closer relationship between the officers and residents, leading residents to offer passive support to the officers. While Sea Gate's police officers focus on fostering a safe neighborhood for the residents, they also buffer the community from the surrounding higher-crime neighborhood by checking visitors' IDs. According to Ryan Wallerspoon, a writer for Without a Badge, an organization that researches alternative policing arrangements, "Sea Gate officers are relics of a New York City long past, but with every resident interaction, they prove their value in maintaining the dynamic of Sea Gate as a secure and private community on the edge of one of New York City's most underserved areas" (Wallerson, 2015).

---

[2] Criminal Procedure Law, Section 2.30.

3 Parkchester Department of Public Safety

Parkchester is a planned community and one of the largest housing developments in the United States. Located in central Bronx, it is home to nearly sixty thousand residents in thirteen thousand residential units and features commercial spaces and parks. Like other parts of the Bronx, Parkchester has faced various challenges and median income there is half that of the rest of the city. Parkchester was developed in the early 1940s by MetLife, which also developed Stuyvesant Town–Peter Cooper Village in the early and middle 1940s. MetLife eventually sold to real estate investor Henry Helmsley, who failed to properly maintain it, causing it to slide into a state of high crime and disrepair throughout the 1970s and 1980s. However, in the 1990s the Parkchester Preservation Company was created, which purchased residential units from Helmsley and spent hundreds of millions of dollars on renovations, leading property values to significantly increase (Conde, 2020). Parkchester is known for its affordable property values and more ornate architecture than more modern developments. Unlike Sea Gate, it is not gated off from the surrounding area.

Parkchester Department of Public Safety traces its origins to two separate agencies founded in 1972 by the board members of Parkchester North and Parkchester South. After hiring former New York Police Department commanding officer Charles Ortiz, the departments merged to form Parkchester Department of Public Safety. Parkchester Department of Public Safety collaborates with the New York Police Department to protect and monitor the community's residents, guests, and businesses. Like Sea Gate Police Department officers, Parkchester Department of Public Safety officers are New York State peace officers granting them limited powers under the New York State Criminal Procedure Law and make warrantless arrests; and use physical force if necessary. Like Sea Gate, Parkchester requires all guards to meet the training requirements of all New York State peace officers and requires firearm-bearing officers to undertake additional training. Additionally, to apply for a job at Parkchester Department of Public Safety, candidates must have a valid

New York State security guard license with New York State eight- and sixteen-hour certifications.

Parkchester Department of Public Safety employs sixty-five patrolmen who patrol within the community and rely on the New York Police Department's Forty-Third Precinct for help with issues that go beyond day-to-day policing. Supervisors are issued a firearm after receiving a permit from the New York Police Department, and patrol officers are equipped with pepper spray, a baton, handcuffs, a flashlight, a two-way radio connected to the Parkchester Department of Public Safety dispatcher, and a body camera. Unlike many similar private security agencies, Parkchester Department of Public Safety also has a plainclothes anticrime unit and a special-operations unit responsible for investigating crimes alongside the New York Police Department and other agencies (City-Data, 2023).

4   Co-op City Public Safety Department

Co-op City is another large housing development in the Bronx that uses private law enforcement along with government police. Co-op City's first residents arrived in 1968, and the development finished construction in 1973. It was sponsored and built by the United Housing Foundation—an organization founded by the Amalgamated Clothing Workers of America—dedicated to providing affordable middle-income housing. With fifty thousand residents in 15,372 units across thirty-five high-rise buildings and seven townhouses, it is the largest cooperative housing development in the world The development is built on 320 acres of property, but only 20% of the property is developed, giving it significantly more open space and lower density than Parkchester. To purchase a unit in Co-op City, potential residents must fall under income thresholds, as the development is operated under New York State's Mitchell-Lama affordable-housing system. Applicants' household incomes must range between $26,778 and $167,225, depending on the size of the household. Additionally, a private investigative company is hired to conduct a household visit for all applicants to determine their suitability. In conjunction with the public-safety department, these rules are intended to create a safer and more controlled environment than the surrounding area (Co-op City, 2023c).

Like Sea Gate Police Department and Parkchester Department of Public Safety, Co-op City Public Safety Department is privately funded by the corporation that owns the property, and officers are certified New York City and New York State peace officers. Additionally, the department hires lobby attendants, who provide security for residents in high-rise buildings. As certified peace officers, the department's officers are authorized to carry firearms under New York Police Department permits and possess arrest authority. These peace officer powers are granted by the New York State Criminal Procedure Law and New York City Special Patrolman's Act, which is part of the New York City Administrative Code (Co-op City, 2023a). As state-certified peace officers, the roughly one hundred members of the force must complete a mandatory in-house training curriculum, approved by the New York State Division of Criminal Justice Services. Officers must also complete an annual firearms requalification to maintain their handgun permits. Emergency-service officers are another division of the force and are all certified emergency medical technicians. The department contains multiple units: a twenty-four-hour patrol-services department, a detective unit, an emergency-services unit, and a training unit. Additionally, bicycle-patrol, foot-patrol, community-affairs, and plainclothes units are deployed as needed. Online postings from anonymous employees report an average salary for officers of $104,000 per year, which is higher than a typical New York Police Department officer's salary (GlassDoor, 2023).

Co-op City Public Safety Department also provides services tailored to Co-op City residents that traditional police do not typically provide. Co-op City has more than six thousand senior residents, making it the largest naturally occurring retirement community in the nation (Co-op City, 2023b). Co-op City Public Safety Department, unlike traditional police forces, provides extra support for senior residents by offering emergency-medical-technician services and a unique service called *R U OK*, a free telephone-based reassurance program available to residents. Those enrolled in the program receive a daily checkup and receive emergency assistance when needed. The program provides a reliable and efficient way to check on residents who are homebound or have medical issues. In conjunction with the emergency-services unit, which provides twenty-four-hour medical coverage, R U OK provides an additional layer of security for elderly residents at risk of unchecked medical issues. Additionally, it provides medical assistance at a much lower cost than a traditional retirement community, granting medical access to underserved communities who otherwise might not access these services. Such benefits are recognized by those living in Co-op City, as the public-safety department seems more popular among online commentators than Parkchester's. While the prevalence of murder and assaults is roughly in line between the Bronx and Co-op City, residents of Co-op City suffer far fewer robberies and property crimes.

5 Hunts Point Department of Public Safety

The last modern example of private policing we discuss is somewhat different in that it is not in a residential area but in the world's largest food-distribution hub, the Hunts Point Food Distribution Center, consisting of three independent cooperative markets for produce, meat, and fish. Together the Hunts Point Cooperative Meat Market, the Hunts Point Terminal Produce Market, the New Fulton Fish Market, and some other tenants occupy 329 acres and employ eight thousand individuals (Hunter College New York City Food Policy Center, 2018; Kihss, 1974; New York City Economic Development Corporation, 2015). The markets operate as cooperatives owned by their member shareholders (Hunts Point Cooperative Market, 2023). The produce market moved from downtown in 1967, the meat market was set up in 1974, and the fish market joined them in 2005 when it had outgrown its space downtown (it now sees two million pounds of fresh seafood arrive daily) (Fulton Fish Market, 2023).

Although Hunts Point is served by the Forty-First Precinct of the New York Police Department, Hunts Point Food Distribution Center has its own Department of Public Safety to serve the needs of its members. The department was formed in 1985 and operates within the confines of the distribution center. It employs approximately forty peace officers, who are certified as special patrolmen under New York

State Criminal Procedure Law, Chapter §2.10 Sub 40, allowing them to make arrests and issue court summons while on Hunts Point property. Additionally, the department employs nondeputized security guards and emergency medical technicians. Officers undergo about seven weeks of training, like peace officers in other security departments. They are equipped with a baton, handcuffs, a flashlight, and a firearm after being approved and issued a handgun permit by the New York Police Department. Hunts Point is not the safest neighborhood in the city, with nearly twice the city average for serious crimes, so the focus of the Department of Public Safety is preventing crime within the distribution center. While crime statistics are unavailable for the distribution center, there is minimal evidence of crimes committed there.

6   Shomrim Volunteer Security

The Shomrim are a group of security agencies organized by Jewish communities in New York. In Hebrew, *Shomrim* means "watchers" or "guards." The three largest Shomrim organizations are the Brooklyn South Shomrim with 150 members, the Williamsburg Shomrim with 100 members, and the Flatbush Shomrim with 40 members. These three groups operate in the Brooklyn communities with the highest populations of Orthodox Jews. These organizations consist of unarmed civilian volunteers and are funded by a mixture of private donations from Orthodox communities and public grants. The Shomrim operate in the highly insular Orthodox Jewish communities in New York and are often preferred to the New York Police Department by these communities, as they solve issues within the community. Because of cultural barriers between the Orthodox communities and broader New York communities, the Shomrim "also act as intermediaries for the secular authorities, negotiating language barriers and complex social mores for a segment of the citizenry given to speaking Yiddish" (Levin, 2016). The Shomrim find themselves in a unique position, as they are neither police officers nor peace officers yet are often the first group to be called for emergency response in the Orthodox community.

Because of their widespread influence and nonpolice status, the Shomrim have an often-mutually-beneficial but sometimes-troubled relationship with the New York Police Department. While the Shomrim aid the New York Police Department by acting as an intermediary between the department and a culturally distinct community, the department has expressed frustration with how the Shomrim operate at times. Officers claim that the Shomrim have minimal accountability, as they do not have legal status as guards and thus do not undergo official training nor follow a standard rulebook. Additionally, the Shomrim are often reluctant to call for police backup, often waiting until an arrest needs to be made, which is beyond their power. Officers complain that at times the Shomrim hinder their work by withholding information and interfering with official investigations.

In 2011, a young boy named Leiby Kletzky went missing from an Orthodox community in Borough Park, Brooklyn and two days later he was found murdered. His mother reported his disappearance to the Boro Park Shomrim, which chose to investigate on its own rather than reporting the matter to the police. Police were only notified once his mother chose to dial 911 h later. According to a New York Police Department official with experience working with the Shomrim, they often "play cops" using their own files (on suspected individuals), which are not shared with the New York Police Department. The Boro Park Shomrim's response to Kletzky's disappearance and murder sparked criticism of the Shomrim and divided the community over their effectiveness and rationale for existence. While New York Police Department Commissioner Ray Kelly praised the Shomrim for mobilizing the Orthodox community in a search for Kletzky, others expressed strong dissatisfaction with the Shomrim's actions. Another New York Police Department official "told The Jewish Week it was 'unconscionable' for the Brooklyn South Shomrim (which covers Borough Park) to have not called the police immediately upon learning of young Leiby going missing" (Winston, 2011). This backlash has caused some within and outside the community to view the Shomrim's tactics as borderline vigilantism. Furthermore, unlike the organizations discussed above, the Shomrim are not a centralized group. Each Shomrim agency has its own protocol and purposes, and various Shomrim act as rivals.

Although the Shomrim are not certified by the city or state of New York as peace officers, they still receive funding from the city. Detractors have questioned why the city funds a department dedicated to protecting only one group (Orthodox Jews). A notorious example of public funding for the Shomrim came in 2012, when over $300,000 was secured to purchase a new mobile command center for the Boro Park Shomrim (Levin, 2016).

7 Roosevelt Island Public Safety Department

We now discuss a law enforcement agency that is mostly governmental but features certain attributes of private policing. The Roosevelt Island Public Safety Department is funded and operated by the Roosevelt Island Operating Corporation, a governmentally created public-benefit corporation. A public-benefit corporation in New York is similar to governmentally owned corporations such as the US Postal Service and Amtrak. Other well-known public-benefit corporations in New York include the United Nations Development Corporation, which assisted the United Nations in developing One, Two, and Three UN Plaza, and the Battery Park City Authority in downtown New York (Malesevic, 2015).

Located between Manhattan and Queens in the East River, Roosevelt Island is home to fourteen thousand residents. Your current authors know a famous economist who lives there and his family reports good things about safety there. Known as Varkens Eylandt (Hog Island) in the days of New Amsterdam and later as Blackwell's Island, it suffered tumult throughout he nineteenth and early twentieth centuries. Sold to the city in the early nineteenth century, it became home to Blackwell's Island Penitentiary, a workhouse and a mental asylum, leading to its rebranding as Welfare Island in 1921. Despite efforts to revamp, by the 1960s the island was largely uninhabited, with only two hospitals left with small intake populations (Berdy, 2015). The island was renamed Roosevelt Island in 1969 and the state then funded the development of two thousand middle-income housing units for five thousand residents, which were finished by 1975. The Roosevelt Island Operating Corporation was founded in 1984 and since this revitalization, the population has nearly tripled, leading to new developments including Cornell Tech's campus and Franklin Delano Roosevelt Four Freedoms Park (Berdy, 2015).

The Roosevelt Island Public Safety Department provides security services for residents and businesses on Roosevelt Island. Starting in 1976, the Roosevelt Island Development Corporation hired security guards from City Security Guards, Inc. However, in 1978 the contract was terminated, and a full police force of certified state officers, the Roosevelt Island Police Department, was formed in 1979. In 1981 the name was changed, and officers were transferred to the New York State Division of Housing and Community Renewal until 1985. Throughout this period, officers were armed and had arrest authority. However, once the Roosevelt Island Operating Corporation took over the development, it formed a security department with no special status. Soon after, residents demanded a more professional service, leading to the creation of the Roosevelt Island Public Safety Department, which operates to this day. While members of the force are certified peace officers, they do not carry firearms but do work closely with the New York Police Department's neighboring 114th Precinct in Queens. Members of the Roosevelt Island Public Safety Department are certified as special patrolmen under New York State Criminal Procedure Law, chapter §2.10 Sub 40, allowing them to make arrests and issue court summons while on Roosevelt Island property. Additionally, as certified peace officers, they must undergo equivalent training to that of other peace officers. The department is funded by the Roosevelt Island Corporation, which charges each landlord or building owner ground rent and a public-safety-reimbursement fee (Roosevelt Island Operating Corporation of the State of New York, 2023). The department spends $4 million per year and has forty-two employees (Stone, 2022).

8 Battery Park City

Another case is Battery Park City, which has experimented with different methods of security and policing over the last few years. Developed on landfill from the construction of the Twin Towers, the land under Battery Park City was developed by the public-benefit corporation Battery Park City Authority, which owns and charges rent on all the land. Its first residential buildings started construction in 1980, and it is now one-third greenspace and home to fourteen thousand residents, the World Financial Center (Brookfield Place), and the headquarters of American Express, Associated Press, Goldman Sachs, and the New York Mercantile Exchange. One of your present authors used to live there, as did Leonardo DiCaprio and Tyra Banks.

Until 2015, Battery Park City was patrolled by the New York City Parks Enforcement Patrol, which operated as a standard government-run security agency but hired the additional officers not with general taxpayer funds but with $2.5 million from rent charged by the Battery Park City Authority. The Parks Enforcement Patrol is a branch of the New York City Parks Department and consists of shielded and green-uniformed but unarmed officers. Members of the Parks Enforcement Patrol have jurisdiction to issue summonses and make arrests, as they are state-certified peace officers (New York City Department of Parks & Recreation, 2023).

Late in 2015, however, citing both budgetary and quality concerns, the Battery Park City Authority voted to replace the Parks Enforcement Patrol with private security provided by Allied Universal. With offices in forty-nine states and eight hundred thousand employees worldwide, Allied Universal has the third-most employees, just behind Amazon and Walmart, of all US-based companies. While some in the community originally opposed the change, it did alleviate issues with inconsistent patrolling and staffing by the Parks Enforcement Patrol. The initial contract with Allied Universal was $2.1 million per year (Glassman, 2015).

While Allied Universal presence has been praised for its heightened visibility and community presence, it initially lacked authority to enforce rules (Glassman, 2018). In 2018, the Battery Park City Authority decided to add Allied Universal officers with special patrol status. At the time the commanding officer of New York Police Department's District 1 stated, "I'll welcome anyone who wants to do enforcement here… Any additional people, agencies, peace officers that can help us with eyes and ears, they'll be more than welcome—so we're not the only ones doing the enforcement." (quoted in Glassman, 2018). Allied Universal operates in conjunction with the New York Police Department's First Precinct, which is responsible for responding to more serious issues. Along with the special patrolmen added in 2018, the ambassadors patrol to deter petty crime. Battery Park City harnesses contracted-out, unarmed private security and deputized private police provided by Allied Universal as complements to the New York Police Department, allowing for much stronger enforcement of minor crimes that are typically ignored by the New York Police Department. Battery Park City has one of the lowest crime rates in the city.

9 Brooklyn Rapid Transit Company Special Police

This last type of special police that we discuss no longer exists. Crime on the subways has become a major problem in the past three years, and with government police uninterested in or incapable of reining in the crime, peaceful riders must fend for themselves. This was not always the case. The subways were originally privately developed and run, mainly by the Brooklyn Rapid Transit Company (Brooklyn–Manhattan Transit Corporation) and the Interborough Rapid Transit Company.

Since crime was not good for business, in 1903 the Brooklyn Rapid Transit Authority deployed its own police. We quote one article from a 1906 issue of the *New York Daily Tribune* at length to portray what these private police officers did:

B. R. T. [Brooklyn Rapid Transit Company] Special Police:

"Seventy-Seven Detailed to Suppress Coney Island Ruffians

For a member of New York's Police force the average thug has a hearty respect. He knows that, properly wielded, the short "billy" is a very effective instrument. Of the special policeman employed by some private individual or company he is not so apt to stand in awe, until he has learned by experience that one is as dangerous to tackle as the other. For the special policeman, though he is not paid by the city, has the same legal authority in his own territory as the member of the city force, and is usually fully as well able to take care of himself. This is the lesson that is now being taught to a small portion of the crowds that already have begun to flock to Coney Island.

This is the third season that the Brooklyn Rapid Transit Company has had a police force of its own to guard passengers from rowdies and its property from thieves." (New York Daily Tribune, 1906, p. 6)

The *New York Daily Tribune* (1906, p. 6) went on to state that the private officers had increased in number from twelve to seventy and that they "differ from the regular policemen chiefly in the fact that they are paid by the company instead of by the city." The newspaper described how they were subject to the same laws and discipline as regular police and carried billy clubs. The article concluded, "In the last two years, indeed, the unruly have fairly well learned that a special officer is a formidable as a city policeman, and the fruit of this knowledge is apparent in the marked decrease in rowdyism on the cars."

A search through early twentieth-century newspapers for "Transit Special Police" brings up many colorful stories about fare beaters unceremoniously removed from subway cars. Unfortunately for these private subway companies, government-imposed price controls forced them into bankruptcy and the government took them over by 1940. A major advantage of putting the subways back in the hands of private owners would be the incentive of the owners to ensure safety in their cars.

10   Summary and Discussion

With the recent increase in crime in New York, many people are looking to increase spending on the New York Police Department and calling on the mayor and governor to take action. But the choice is not between more government police and more crime. Many private arrangements exist. New York State and New York City law allows for the existence of private peace officers with varying degrees of authority including the authority to carry firearms, use force, and make arrests. A major advantage of private law enforcement is that it is not a one-size-fits-all solution: different communities can hire more officers and different types of officers depending on their specific needs. Moreover, not all officers need to be armed to keep their communities safe. Table 1 summarizes some of the main features of the arrangements we discussed.

While deputized peace officers appear to provide a valuable service and have a good relationship with many residents, they are not immune from criticism. The most common criticisms we found were from outside residents who were subject to sanction or arrest. We should recognize that private officers who make arrests put people into jail and the criminal justice system, which of course are fraught with abuse. Our sense is that although they have arrest powers, many of the above departments do not use it frequently. Regarding the related legal question whether private officers have qualified immunity, we have found conflicting decisions by the courts. An appellate court in Maryland overturned an earlier decision that said qualified immunity does not apply to private actors. The court stated that private actors who are enforcing the law are acting as state agents when doing so and are thus entitled to qualified immunity.[3] Recently New York City passed a law placing limits on qualified immunity for police in general; the law explicitly states the new limits also apply to special patrolmen.[4] The second most common criticism we found came from employees who registered dissatisfaction with their employer.

---

[3] Callahan v. Bowers, 131 Md. App. 163, 748 A.2d 499 (2000).

[4] The law states its intent to "establish a local right of security against unreasonable search and seizure and against excessive force regardless of whether such force is used in connection with a search or seizure. If an NYPD employee, or a person appointed by the Police Commissioner as a special patrolman, allegedly deprives a person of this right, the person would be able to bring a civil action against the employee or appointee, as well as against the employee or appointee's employer, within three years after deprivation of the right. The employee or appointee (or their employer) would not be allowed qualified immunity, or any substantially equivalent immunity, as a defense."

Table 1 Characteristics of Law Enforcement Departments in New York

Department	Official certification (police officer/ peace officer)	Source of funding	Firearm permit	Jurisdiction	Arrest powers
NYPD	Police officer	Public	Yes	Entirety of New York City	Yes
Sea Gate Police Department	Peace officer	Dues paid by residents	With NYPD permit	Within Sea Gate	Yes
Parkchester Department of Public Safety	Peace officer	Dues paid by residents	With NYPD permit	Within Parkchester	Yes
Co-op City Public Safety Department	Peace officer	Dues paid by residents and public funding for the community	With NYPD permit	Within Co-op City	Yes
Boro Park Shomrim	Neither	Private donations and public funding	No, but privately obtained by some	No official jurisdiction. Unofficially 66th Precinct	No
Hunts Point Department of Public Safety	Peace officer	Dues paid by coop members	With NYPD permit	Within Hunts Point Food Distribution Center	Yes
Roosevelt Island Public Safety Department	Peace officer	Public-safety-reimbursement charges from Roosevelt Island Operating Corporation to buildings	No	Within Roosevelt Island	Yes
Brooklyn Rapid Transit Company Special Police	Neither	Paid by Brooklyn Rapid Transit Company	No	Trains and stations operated by BRTC	No
Battery Park City	Combination of peace officers and nonstatus patrolmen	Local ground rent paid by commercial landlords and 14,000 Battery Park City residents	No	Within Battery Park for special patrolmen; no official jurisdiction for ambassadors	Deputized peace officers have arrest powers; security ambassadors do not

In previous research about private policing elsewhere, we surveyed customers and found that the people hiring the police were satisfied with them (Stringham, 2015, p. 123). If one puts normative weight on the preferences of business owners whose property such private law enforcement is hired to protect, then one could conclude that private law enforcement is, for the most part, normatively good. As the examples in this chapter show, New Yorkers need not be faced with choosing between more government police and more crime. For something as crucial as the protection of safety and security, many non-monopolized private alternatives exist.

References

Berdy, J. (2015). The rocky history of Roosevelt Island. *Politico*. June 13, 2015.
City Data. (2023). *10462 zip code (New York, NY) detailed profile*. City-Data.
Conde, E. G. (2020). *Parkchester 80 years later: A brief history of a city within a city*. Welcome2TheBronx. May 13, 2020.
Consolidated Laws of New York. (2021). *Persons designated as peace officers*. Consolidated Laws of New York Criminal Procedure Chapter 11-A, Part 1, Title A, Article 2.
Co-op City. (2023a). *Co-op city public safety department*. Co-op City.
Co-op City. (2023b). *Co-op City shareholders and residents*. Co-op City.
Co-op City. (2023c). *Riverbay residential sales application*. Co-op City.
Fulton Fish Market. (2023). *About Fulton fish market*. Fulton Fish Market.
Gallup. (2021). *In U.S., black confidence in police recovers from 2020 low*. Gallup. July 14, 2021.
GlassDoor. (2023). *How much does co-op city department of public safety pay in 2023?* GlassDoor.
Glassman, C. (2015). Private security firm hired to replace most battery park city 'PEP' officers. *Tribeca Trib*. October 27, 2015.
Glassman, C. (2018). In pilot program, battery park city to add security with enforcement powers. *Tribeca Trib*. January 10, 2018.
Hunter College New York City Food Policy Center. (2018). *Spotlight on the produce market*. Hunter College New York City Food Policy Center.
Hunts Point Cooperative Market. (2023). *The World's Largest Food Distribution Center*. Hunts Point Cooperative Market.
Kihss, P. (1974). Work Starts at Hunts Point in October on Long-Planned Fulton Fish Market. *New York Times*, August 21.
Levin, J. (2016). Brooklyn's Private Jewish Patrols Wield Power. *T.O.T. Private Consulting*, June 17, 2016.
Lexipol, L. L. C. (2023). *Sea gate police department—Brooklyn, New York*. Police1.
Malesevic, D. S.. (2015). Battery Park City to Privatize Security. amNY Metro, November 5, 2015.
New York City Department of Parks & Recreation. (2023). *Parks enforcement patrol*. New York City Department of Parks & Recreation.
New York City Economic Development Corporation. (2015). *NYCEDC announces major expansion of Baldor specialty foods in Hunts Point Food Distribution Center*. New York City Economic Development Corporation.
New York Daily Tribune. (1906). B. R. T. Special Police. *New York Daily Tribune*, June 3, 1906, p. 6.
Nonprofit Metrics. (2023). *Sea gate association*. Cause IQ.
Roosevelt Island Operating Corporation of the State of New York. (2023). *Public safety department*. Roosevelt Island Operating Corporation of the State of New York.
Samuelson, P. A. (1967). Indeterminancy of Governmental Role in Public-Good Theory. *Papers on Non-Market Decision Making*, 3(1):47.

Stone, D. (2022). Right-sizing RIOC now: Cut bloated public safety staffing. *Roosevelt Island News*, October 6, 2022.

Stringham, E. P. (2015). *Private governance: Creating order in economic and social life*. Oxford University Press.

Wallerson, R. (2015). Sea gate PD: An integral element of New York's first gated community. *Without a Badge*, May 12, 2015.

Winston, H. (2011). Tragedy in Borough Park puts Shomrim under scrutiny. *Jewish Telegraphic Agency*, July 19, 2011.

Private Security and Deterrence

Jonathan Klick and John MacDonald

Abstract Quasi-experimental estimates indicate that police are a deterrent to crime. Benefit-cost analysis using those estimates indicate that hiring more police is more than justified, with one prominent study indicating that many U.S. cities are under-policed. Less is known about the deterrence potential of private security options. Considering budget pressures and political calls to de-emphasize or even defund the police, examining the relative efficacy of private security guards compared to police takes on added importance. We present results from college campuses suggesting that private police generate deterrence comparable to that of public police, but we do not find evidence that private security guards hired by colleges generate comparable deterrence.

1 Introduction

As "defund the police" became one of the rallying cries of the "Great Awokening",[1] progressive commentators started indicating that police do not deter crime. The ACLU's Paige Fernandez declared, "We have little evidence, if any, to show that more police surveillance results in fewer crimes and greater public safety."[2] In an article titled "Police don't stop crime, but you wouldn't know it from the news,"

---

[1] https://www.vox.com/2019/3/22/18259865/great-awokening-white-liberals-race-polling-trump-2020

[2] https://www.aclu.org/news/criminal-law-reform/defunding-the-police-will-actually-make-us-safer

---

J. Klick (✉) · J. MacDonald
University of Pennsylvania, Philadelphia, PA, USA
e-mail: jklick@law.upenn.edu; johnmn@sas.upenn.edu

PRISM, "an independent and nonprofit news outlet led by journalists of color,"[3] stated that "Police don't stop or prevent crime, but you wouldn't know that from how the mainstream media discusses them as the solution, parroting talking points directly from police departments. If larger police forces make us safe, then by that logic, the U.S. would already be the safest society in the world …".[4]

This theme was not just touted by progressive activists. Even mainstream news outlets cited the absence of correlation between police spending and reduced crime as evidence against the efficacy of police. For example, writing for the Washington Post, Philip Bump noted, "If we look at how spending has changed relative to crime in each year since 1960, comparing spending in 2018 dollars per person to crime rates, we see that there is no correlation between the two. More spending in a year hasn't significantly correlated to less crime or to more crime. For violent crime, in fact, the correlation between changes in crime rates and spending per person in 2018 dollars is almost zero."[5] Adding academic heft to the police skepticism, writing on the Brookings Institution blog, senior fellow Howard Henderson and coauthor Ben Yisrael called the evidence that police reduce or prevent crime "minimal."[6] Perhaps the most damning criticism came from Ben and Jerry's when they asked "Data Shows No Correlation Between Policing Spending and the Crime Rate—So Why Is Funding Going Up?"[7] When the police have lost the confidence of the nation's foremost number-crunching, policy-analyzing, monkey-chunking ice cream purveyors, it's all over.

These claims are misguided in principle and are wrong in their description of what research shows. Modern empirical designs demonstrate that police generate crime deterrence. Quasi-experimental methods consistently yield a statistically significant and practically important negative relationship between the number of police patrolling an area and crime. Research designs using data from across the U.S., as well as in many other countries, replicate this finding. In addition, a number of field experiments show that placing more police in high crime areas leads to significant reductions in crime with little evidence of displacement.[8] There is little doubt anymore that increasing police presence causally reduces crime.

That said, just because police reduce crime does not mean they do so in a cost-effective way. A finding that police causally reduce crime is likely a necessary condition for it to make sense to hire more officers (or even maintain current levels of police coverage), but it is not sufficient. Many rigorous benefit-cost analyses do

---

[3] https://prismreports.org/about/our-team/

[4] https://prismreports.org/2022/02/23/police-dont-stop-crime-but-you-wouldnt-know-it-from-the-news/

[5] https://www.washingtonpost.com/politics/2020/06/07/over-past-60-years-more-spending-police-hasnt-necessarily-meant-less-crime/

[6] https://www.brookings.edu/blog/how-we-rise/2021/05/19/7-myths-about-defunding-the-police-debunked/

[7] https://www.benjerry.com/whats-new/2022/03/crime-and-police-spending

[8] https://www.nationalacademies.org/our-work/proactive-policing-effects-on-crime-communities-and-civil-liberties-in-the-united-states

suggest police are a good investment in basic public finance terms with their monetized deterrence benefits exceeding at least their budgetary costs. However, there are at least two limitations with these benefit-cost tests. First, they generally compare the net benefit of hiring additional officers to not hiring officers, as opposed to making alternative social investments. Second, the benefit-cost analyses focus entirely on budgetary costs without considering other economic costs of hiring police.

In the recent push to defund the police, progressive rhetoric reveals concerns with both limitations. Activists often indicate that police funding ought to be moved to education, mental health treatment, and a range of other social programs the activists assert would do more to improve crime rates. Also, while claiming police engage in corrupt, violent, and biased behavior, many commentators indicate these costs are made worse by constraints on reforming or disciplining police such as qualified immunity in civil trials and employment protections that limit firing police for bad behavior.

Private police and security guards of various types may hold promise on both dimensions. Given that private alternatives such as security guards are often much cheaper than public police, even if they are not quite as effective in generating deterrence, they might be more efficient on the margin. Also, because private security personnel do not receive liability protections like qualified immunity, nor civil servant employment protections, they may prove easier to incentivize or discipline than the public policing alternatives.

This chapter presents some preliminary evidence that publicly certified private police can be just as effective in deterrence terms as the estimates provided in the literature on public policing. However, our evidence indicates that the much lower cost security guards, who operate without arrest powers, do not appear to generate any deterrence at all. Although private police are not generally cheaper than public police in budgetary terms, they may prove to be more easily disciplined through civil liability and employment incentives, which would lower their true economic cost, making them a viable alternative to regular police at least in some circumstances.

This chapter proceeds by quickly discussing the quasi-experimental literature on police and deterrence as well as some of the attempts to measure the net welfare effects of police spending. We then summarize and extend our previous work on university police as an example of an effective private policing alternative. We contrast this with some new estimates on the deterrence effects of university security guards which indicate no comparable deterrence effects, noting how this distinction in the effectiveness of private police versus private security guards has some support in the existing literature.

2   Police and Deterrence

Examining the relationship between police and crime is difficult given the severe omitted variable bias problems that likely exist, such as reverse causality (places expecting higher crime levels will generally hire more police). While there are examples of field experiments in the literature of deploying more police to high crime areas,[9] these experiments were often under-powered or limited in duration leaving them unable to detect plausible deterrence effects.

Steve Levitt's (1997) paper using election-induced police hiring as a natural experiment to examine the effect of police on crime represents one of the first quasi-experimental designs tackling this issue in the economics literature.[10] Levitt's design, which found large negative elasticities between police and both property and violent crime, was clever and had a large impact on the economics of crime field. Unfortunately, the estimates were wrong, as pointed out by Justin McCrary (2002), due to coding issues. Although Levitt (2002) suggested that his results endured if the coding issues were fixed (and other changes to the research design were implemented), there are many reasons to be skeptical of Levitt's findings.[11]

Subsequent natural experiment papers fared better in their credibility. In a series of papers using police increases after terrorist attacks as natural experiments, Di Tella and Schargrodsky (2004), Klick and Tabarrok (2005), and Draca et al. (2011) all find remarkably similar crime elasticities with respect to police on the order of −0.3 in Buenos Aires, Washington DC, and London respectively.

Finding a similar estimate for the elasticity between property crime and police (though only statistically significant at the 10% level) at a magnitude just under −0.3 and a much larger (and clearly statistically significant) elasticity with respect

---

[9] See, for example, https://www.nationalacademies.org/our-work/proactive-policing-effects-on-crime-communities-and-civil-liberties-in-the-united-states.

[10] Some antecedents in the criminology literature include papers that use natural experiments or instrumental variables designs: see Chaiken et al. (1974); Wilson and Boland (1978). McCormick and Tollison (1984) represents a clever early quasi-experimental study of this issue albeit in a context that did not deal with actual police or real-world crime; instead, it examined the addition of extra referees in college basketball games, finding a significant deterrence effect with respect to personal fouls due to cleaner play.

[11] Our favorite reason to be skeptical is "The Wire" hypothesis otherwise known as "Juking the Stats." In the HBO series The Wire, police administrators were pushed by local politicians to improve Baltimore's crime numbers in advance of elections to give the appearance that the incumbent politicians were being effective. As described in Season 3 Episode 1 (Time After Time): Police Commissioner Burrell relays Mayor Royce's directive by saying, "Gentlemen, the word from on high is that felony rates, district by district, will decline by 5% before the end of the year," followed by his Deputy Commissioner Rawls emphasizing, "We are dealing in certainties; you will reduce the UCR felonies by 5% or more or, I've always wanted to say this, 'let no man come back alive.'" The district majors in the show respond by falsifying the crime data by purposely reclassifying crimes into lesser categories or hiding the crimes altogether in various ways. If this fictional behavior mimics reality, as suggested by series creator David Simon (see, for example, https://www.pbs.org/moyers/journal/04172009/transcript1.html), it would imply that Levitt's natural experiment is potentially conflating two effects of election-induced police hiring: (1) any actual crime deterrence and (2) downward crime measurement error bias.

to violent crime, Evans and Owens (2007) use funding from the federal COPS grant program to serve as the identifying shock in their research design to test if more police reduce crime. Mello (2019) also finds that police hiring through the federal COPS grant program under the 2009 Recovery Act led to significant reductions in crime. Although federal hiring grants are arguably less clearly exogenous than the papers that rely on terrorism as mechanism for identifying changes in police deployment, the hiring grant design has the benefit of estimating the effect of police over a longer time span (years) as opposed to the short interventions examined in the terrorism papers (ranging from just a few days to a few weeks). Examining the longer time frame is likely more relevant for the policy choice of how many police to hire, as the terrorism papers might be capturing the maximal effect of police whereas the average effect is more meaningful in the policy decision. On the other hand, the longer time frame likely means that Evans and Owens (2007) and Mello (2019) are estimating the joint effect of deterrence and incapacitation which could necessitate an untangling when calculating the benefits of police, whereas the terrorism papers likely are capturing just deterrence given the short time periods involved.

Other modern studies have reached similar conclusions when studying quasi-random (MacDonald et al., 2016a) and randomized field experiments regarding policing tactics, such as hot spot policing (Braga & Weisburd, 2022 for a review of the experimental and quasi-experimental hot spot studies). Other studies have examined the effect of policing particular sub-populations, finding largely consistent results.[12]

Chalfin and McCrary (2017) provide an extensive overview of this literature; the punchline is that most credible modern studies find persuasive evidence that police causally reduce crime, and the effect is substantively large. While the negative relationship between police and crime is not observable in naïve correlational analyses, quasi-experimental methods that isolate causal effects are about as close to unanimous in their conclusions as one can expect in an academic literature. Chalfin and McCrary (2018) add another layer of confidence in this literature by directly addressing measurement error in estimating the effect of police on crime by using multiple police measures as instruments for each other, yielding comparable elasticity estimates as those found in the quasi-experimental literature, with much more precise estimates than available in most of the literature.

3 Value of Police

With a reasonably confident estimate of the causal effect of police on crime, it is possible to provide some valuation of the contribution of police. Chalfin and McCrary (2018) provide a rigorous analysis based on their police deterrence

---

[12] For example, see Berk and MacDonald (2010) for an example of police targeting homeless encampments.

estimates and a broad range of estimates for valuing the estimated crime reductions. Using a fully loaded average annual cost of a police officer of $130,000 per year and the mean estimate from the value of a statistical life literature of $7 million per murder deterred as well as standard values for other crimes averted, Chalfin and McCrary find that, in the typical U.S. city in their sample, spending an additional $1 on police yields $1.63 in crime costs avoided if all their estimated crime declines come from deterrence. If they account for the possibility that additional police will lead to the incarceration of more individuals, their estimated return on a dollar of police spending declines to $1.31, an amount that still generates a large net social value increase. Based on these calculations, Chalfin and McCrary conclude that U.S. cities are under policed. This is consistent with an earlier welfare analysis done by Klick and Tabarrok (2010) using a range of elasticity estimates from the literature and a range of crime cost estimates suggesting that an increase in spending on police in the range of 5–155% could be justified based on the existing literature.

While the preceding welfare calculations follow standard benefit-cost methods, they are limited in at least two respects. First, optimality requires an analysis of alternative investments even if we restrict ourselves to a very narrow range of options. Specifically, for our purposes here, it is necessary to examine whether there exist police substitutes that might provide an even bigger return for the investment. Second, the foregoing benefit-cost analyses focus only on budgetary costs of police, when the social cost of police includes more than what merely shows up in a city's books. For example, settlements for lawsuits filed against the police are not typically accounted for in the total costs of policing. These broader social costs, however, are very difficult to estimate and monetize and so we will regrettably largely ignore them even though a thorough welfare analysis needs to reckon with these costs. However, we will categorically note that some portion of these off the books costs of police arise due to misbehavior of the police and these costs are compounded when they go unaddressed due to legal and employment protections police receive.

4 Private Police as an Alternative

MacDonald et al. (2016b) examine the phenomenon of private police. These are police paid by private entities but who otherwise are quite similar to public police and are state certified law enforcement officers. They wear uniforms, carry guns, and make arrests. Given their similarity, it is reasonable to ask whether it is appropriate to treat the private police as a separate security category. We think there are at least a few reasons why private police could be functionally different from public police. Relevant to a concern raised above, because private police do not benefit the employment protections that come with being a civil servant (and a strong police union), the unquantified costs mentioned above might be assumed to be lower.[13] Beyond that, private police operate under different management structures which could make them less (or, perhaps, more) effective than public police.

Specifically, the police studied by MacDonald, Klick, and Grunwald are campus police at the University of Pennsylvania (Penn). Penn police patrol and have arrest powers within a specifically designated boundary around the campus. Past that boundary, the Philadelphia city police have jurisdiction. Although the boundary originally tracked the university's campus fairly well, in the modern day, much of the university activity spills across the historic boundary, though the Penn police must still abide by the boundary. An uninformed visitor would be hard pressed to be able to tell where the boundary even is. Given the relative wealth of Penn, it is not surprising that Penn employs about three times as many police per geographic unit than does Philadelphia. Putting this effectively arbitrary boundary together with the lopsided police coverage generates a plausible regression discontinuity design through which MacDonald, Klick, and Grunwald attempt to isolate the causal effect of private police on crime.

Figure 1 below duplicates the total crime discontinuity graph from MacDonald et al. (2016b) where 0 on the x axis represents the Penn boundary and distance from the boundary is measured in feet along the x axis with negative distances falling within the campus boundary and positive distances extending outside the boundary. Crime is aggregated by physical city block in the Penn patrol zone or university city neighborhood surrounding the campus. The crime data cover the period 2005–2010.

There is a statistically significant increase in total crime when crossing the boundary going outside of the Penn police patrol zone. However, in new graphs Figs. 2 and 3 presented below (not from the original paper), it is reasonably clear that the jump in crime is driven by property crime as opposed to violent crime.

While the discontinuity is evident for the property crime, the violent crime discontinuity is well within the confidence intervals on either side.

Figure 4 provides a more ad hoc grouping of crimes that we dub "street crimes" and includes assaults, burglaries, purse snatching, robberies and theft from vehicles to try to capture the opportunistic nature of these crimes and their potential greater sensitivity to police presence which is largely borne out in the graph.

The more formal regression discontinuity estimates suggest that there is an elasticity of total crime with respect to police on the order of −0.3 with the elasticity ranging from −0.2 for property crime and −0.7 for violent crime with both estimates being statistically significant, although there is variation in statistical significance for specific individual crime categories. The differences in counts of each

---

[13] At least in some instances, these private police do benefit from legal protections such as qualified immunity. See, for example, Fleck v. Trustees of Univ. of Pennsylvania, 995 F. Supp. 2d 390 (E.D. Pa. 2014) which treated private police paid by the University of Pennsylvania as state actors based on the fact that Pennsylvania state law "endows the Penn Police Department with the plenary authority of a municipal police department in the patrol-zone territory, once the 'exclusive prerogative' of the City of Philadelphia," though in the same case, Penn's security guards were not found to be state actors.

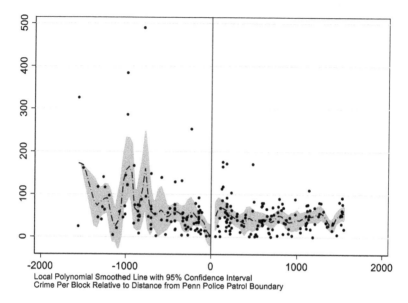

Fig. 1 Total crime as a function of distance to Penn boundary (in ft.)

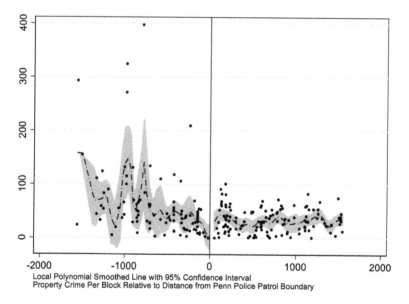

Fig. 2 Property crime as a function of distance to Penn boundary (in ft.)

category means that one cannot directly compare the point estimates from these elasticities. However, the bottom line is that the differences when estimated by a formal regression are all statistically and substantively significant.

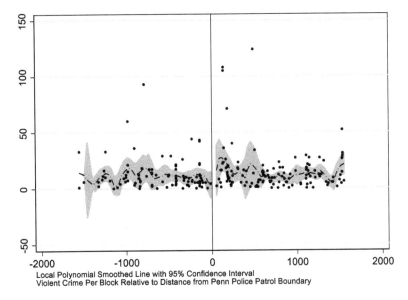

Fig. 3 Violent crime as a function of distance to Penn boundary (in ft.)

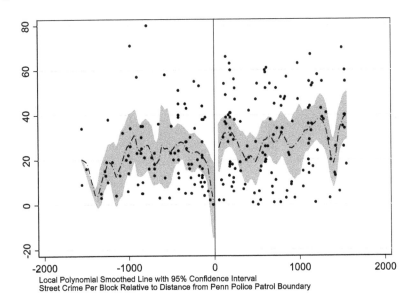

Fig. 4 Street crime as a function of distance to Penn boundary (in ft.)

To avoid the possibility that there are other unobservable changes at the campus boundary, we examined both the issuance of parking tickets (Fig. 5), which is handled by a non-police entity both on Penn's campus and outside of it, and occurrence of traffic accidents (Fig. 6). We examined these falsifications in case there is a hard

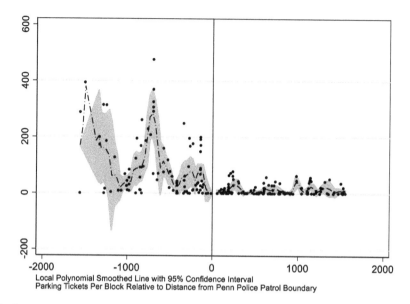

Fig. 5 Parking tickets as a function of distance to the Penn boundary (in ft.)

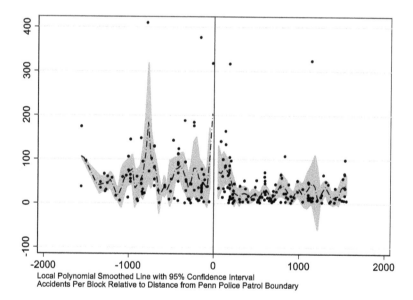

Fig. 6 Traffic accidents as a function of distance to the Penn boundary

to quantify difference in risk-taking propensity or the fastidiousness of rule-following on either side of the boundary as these attributes could also influence crime. In neither case did we observe a statistically significant discontinuity (Figs. 5 and 6).

The falsifications give us no reason to believe our crime estimates are not causal. Given that they are in the range of previous estimates from the literature and that Penn's fully loaded police salary is comparable to the average salary used by Chalfin and McCrary (2018), the net welfare generated by these private police is comparable, perhaps with the benefit that wrongdoing by Penn's private police is more easily remedied and disciplined than it is with public police. The basic design and results of our Penn study were replicated in Heaton et al. (2016) for the University of Chicago's campus police.

5   Private Security Guards as an Alternative

We duplicated our Penn study using data from Johns Hopkins University (main Homewood campus[14]) for the period 2012–2018. Johns Hopkins is interesting since it does not have private police officers but instead has many private security guards that are not state certified law enforcement officers, are unarmed, and have no arrest powers, largely because, at the time, the state of Maryland barred private entities from providing their own police. Like Penn, however, it is an academically rigorous school located in a relatively high crime city.

Studying security guards is useful for several reasons. In the context of this chapter, security guards provide a much cheaper option, with fully loaded salaries well less than half that of their police counterparts, as well as the soft benefits of potentially being able to address professional wrongdoing more easily and quickly. Again, we aggregate crime to the physical city block level over the sample period and we used the distance to the campus boundary as the forcing variable in our regression discontinuity design.

As seen in Fig. 7, we find no discontinuity in total crime at the campus boundary.

Further examination of finer crime categories continued to yield no discontinuity at the campus boundary.

This finding suggests that cheaper private security options that are not publicly certified law enforcement officers do not yield the same (or any) benefits as do private or public police.[15] While having limited power, unarmed security might seem attractive in a debate focused on police misconduct, especially in instances where violence escalates, there is no deterrence and so it is unlikely that private security

---

[14] https://publicsafety.jhu.edu/assets/uploads/sites/9/2022/08/Homewood-Campus-Boundary.pdf

[15] These results bolster the causal interpretation of the Penn police study. If one thought there was something unobservable about behavior on a university campus that was correlated with crime but was not driven by police, we should have expected to find a discontinuity on the Johns Hopkins campus even though they had no police on duty.

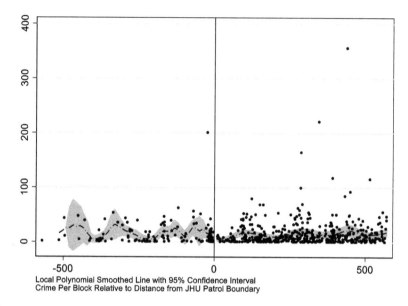

Local Polynomial Smoothed Line with 95% Confidence Interval
Crime Per Block Relative to Distance from JHU Patrol Boundary

Fig. 7 Total crime as a function of distance to the JHU boundary

guards can be justified on a crime basis. These results correspond with those of
Fabbri and Klick (2021) who likewise find that unarmed, limited authority security
guards in a residential neighborhood in Oakland, CA had no enduring effect
on crime.

6 Conclusions

The debate regarding the effect of police on crime has been clouded by a misreading
or unwillingness to acknowledge the research evidence on the deterrent effects of
the police on crime. Bindler and Hjalmarsson (2021) use digitized records of historic crime data and police deployment and find that the creation of the London
Metropolitan Police in 1829 led to a significant decline in crime relative to adjacent
municipalities, suggesting that the deterrent effect of the police on crime is a historical and contemporary reality. Less is known about the deterrent potential of private
police or private security, options that take on increasing importance in an era where
calls for police reform are occurring and the US is experiencing a significant rise in
gun violence in major cities (MacDonald et al., 2022) that is spreading across neighborhoods at a faster rate than cross sectional differences in places (Brantingham
et al., 2021). In this chapter we show that there is a growing body of evidence that
private police are also effective at reducing crime around universities, whereas private security guards appear to have minimal effect. Importantly, the costs of police
are a relative bargain compared to the costs of crime victimization they avert in

society. Private police may even be more cost effective if they are able to innovate and are held more accountable to the public they serve, though this point is speculation and not one that we can settle with empirical evidence at this point. Future work should investigate the optimal set of institutional arrangements that make for cost effect private police that remain accountable to the public.

References

Berk, R., & MacDonald, J. (2010). Policing the homeless: An evaluation of efforts to reduce homeless-related crime. *Criminology & Public Policy, 9*(4), 813–840.

Bindler, A., & Hjalmarsson, R. (2021). The impact of the first professional police forces on crime. *Journal of the European Economic Association, 19*(6), 3063–3103.

Braga, A. A., & Weisburd, D. L. (2022). Does hot spots policing have meaningful impacts on crime? Findings from an alternative approach to estimating effect sizes from place-based program evaluations. *Journal of Quantitative Criminology, 38*, 1–22.

Brantingham, P. J., Carter, J., MacDonald, J., Melde, C., & Mohler, G. (2021). Is the recent surge in violence in American cities due to contagion? *Journal of Criminal Justice, 76*, 101848.

Chaiken, J. M., Lawless, M. W., & Stevenson, K. A. (1974). *The impact of police activity on crime: Robberies on the New York City subway system.* New York City Rand Institute.

Chalfin, A., & McCrary, J. (2017). Criminal deterrence: A review of the literature. *Journal of Economic Literature, 55*(1), 5–48.

Chalfin, A., & McCrary, J. (2018). Are U.S. cities underpoliced? Theory and evidence. *The Review of Economics and Statistics, 100*(1), 167–186.

Di Tella, R., & Schargrodsky, E. (2004). Do police reduce crime? Estimates using the allocation of police forces after a terrorist attack. *The American Economic Review, 94*(1), 115–133.

Draca, M., Machin, S., & Witt, R. (2011). Panic on the streets of London: Police, crime, and the July 2005 terror attacks. *The American Economic Review, 101*(5), 2157–2181.

Evans, W., & Owens, E. (2007). COPS and crime. *Journal of Public Economics, 91*(1–2), 181–201.

Fabbri, M., & Klick, J. (2021). The ineffectiveness of "observe and report" patrols on crime. *International Review of Law and Economics, 65*, 105972.

Heaton, P., Hunt, P., MacDonald, J., & Saunders, J. (2016). The short- and long-run effects of private law enforcement: Evidence from university police. *Journal of Law & Economics, 59*(4), 889–912.

Klick, J., & Tabarrok, A. (2005). Using terror alert levels to estimate the effect of police on crime. *Journal of Law & Economics, 48*(1), 267–279.

Klick, J., & Tabarrok, A. (2010). Police, prisons, and punishment: The empirical evidence on crime deterrence. In B. Benson & P. Zimmerman (Eds.), *Handbook on the economics of crime.* Edward Elgar.

Levitt, S. D. (1997). Using electoral cycles in police hiring to estimate the effect of police on crime. *The American Economic Review, 87*(3), 270–290.

Levitt, S. D. (2002). Using electoral cycles in police hiring to estimate the effects of police on crime: Reply. *The American Economic Review, 92*(4), 1244–1250.

MacDonald, J., Fagan, J., & Geller, A. (2016a). The effects of local police surges on crime and arrests in New York City. *PLoS One, 11*(6), e0157223.

MacDonald, J. M., Klick, J., & Grunwald, B. (2016b). The effect of private police on crime: Evidence from a geographic regression discontinuity design. *Journal of the Royal Statistical Society. Series A (Statistics in Society), 179*(3), 831–846.

MacDonald, J., Mohler, G., & Brantingham, P. J. (2022). Association between race, shooting hot spots, and the surge in gun violence during the COVID-19 pandemic in Philadelphia, New York and Los Angeles. *Preventive Medicine, 165*, 107241.

McCormick, R. E., & Tollison, R. D. (1984). Crime on the court. *Journal of Political Economy, 92*(2), 223–235.

McCrary, J. (2002). Using electoral cycles in police hiring to estimate the effect of police on crime: Comment. *The American Economic Review, 92*(4), 1236–1243.

Mello, S. (2019). More COPS, less crime. *Journal of Public Economics, 172*, 174–200.

Wilson, J. Q., & Boland, B. (1978). The effect of the police on crime. *Law and Society Review, 12*, 367–390.

How to Fight Crime by Improving Police Services: Evidence from the French Quarter Task Force

Wei Long

Abstract This chapter summarizes the findings of a study on the French Quarter Task Force (FQTF), an anti-crime program initiated by a local businessman in 2015 in response to a shortage of police officers and rise in street crimes in the French Quarter, the most popular tourist historical site in New Orleans, Louisiana. The FQTF hires and equips off-duty New Orleans Police Department officers to patrol the French Quarter. The improved police visibility remarkably decreased street crimes such as robbery, aggravated assault, and theft in the French Quarter. Exploiting the change in the FQTF's management, the study finds that the privately managed FQTF, which imposed more monitoring and incentivizing strategies on police officers, reduced more street crimes than the publicly managed FQTF. A back-of-the-envelope assessment further shows that the average efficiency gain by the FQTF far exceeds the estimated operating costs of running this program.

The author thanks Editors Brian Meehan, Simon Hakim, and Erwin Blackstone for allowing to partially reprint the content from "*Improving police services: Evidence from the French Quarter Task Force*", *Journal of Public Economics*, Volume 164, Cheng Cheng and Wei Long, pages 1–18, with permission from Elsevier. The paper also benefits from comments from participants of the virtual conference on Public & Private Security organized by The Institute of Humane Studies at George Mason University.

W. Long (✉)
Department of Economics, Tulane University, New Orleans, LA, USA
e-mail: wlong2@tulane.edu

1   Introduction

A common concern over public provision of local public goods is that it is usually inefficient because the public sector lacks sufficient financial incentive to achieve efficiency.[1] This has been supported by mounting empirical evidence that the public sector is less efficient than the private sector in providing similar goods and services.[2] Police service is one of the most important local public goods and is vital to public safety. Does the public sector provide police service inefficiently? This question has important policy implications. However, there has been little empirical evidence due to the absence of a good benchmark in measuring the potential inefficiency. In a study entitled *"Improving police services: Evidence from the French Quarter Task Force"* which is published in the *Journal of Public Economics,* Cheng and Long (2018) address this issue by exploiting a rare natural experiment that saw the provision of the *same* police service by both the public and private sectors: the anti-crime program in the city of New Orleans called "French Quarter Task Force" (FQTF).

In response to a shortage of police officers and a rise in violent crimes in the French Quarter, New Orleans' historic landmark, FQTF was initiated in March of 2015 by Sidney Torres, a millionaire who lives in that neighborhood. The program uses two simple but innovative means to increase police presence in order to deter violent crimes. The first is to increase police visibility by integrating a proactive patrolling carried out by 3 off-duty police officers at all hours. Second, it launches a mobile app that enables users to instantly report crimes in the French Quarter to the patrolling officers. During the pilot period (March 23, 2015 – June 21, 2015), Torres primarily funded and closely managed the program. Starting from June 22, 2015, FQTF was handed over to and managed by the public sector, including the New Orleans Police Department (NOPD) and the French Quarter Management District (FQMD). This handover of management provides an excellent opportunity to measure the efficiency of providing police service through managing FQTF by the public sector while using the performance of the privately-run FQTF as the benchmark.

Specifically, Cheng and Long (2018) measure the relative effectiveness of managing FQTF between the public and private sectors in reducing violent crimes. In order to distinguish the effect of FQTF on violent crimes from the effect of other confounders, they adopt a difference-in-differences (DD) strategy. This allows them to credibly estimate the treatment effect of FQTF by comparing the violent crime trends between the French Quarter and other New Orleans neighborhoods. The estimates show that while FQTF deterred violent crimes under either public or private management, it was significantly less effective when run by the public sector:

---

[1] The objective of a bureaucrat in the public sector is not cost-effectiveness but usually includes, for example, "salary, perquisites of the office, public reputation, power, patronage, output of the bureau, ease of making changes, and ease in managing the bureau" (Niskanen, 1971).

[2] Mueller (2003) summarizes 71 studies that compare the provision of similar goods and services (e.g., airlines, banks, cleaning services, and electric utilities) by private and public firms. 56 of them find private firms are more efficient in supplying the same good or service than their public counterparts, while only 5 find the opposite results. The remaining 10 find no significant difference in provision efficiency.

Relative to the publicly-run FQTF, the privately-run FQTF led to about 50% reduction in violent crime per month in the French Quarter. Importantly, the empirical evidence points to a causal interpretation of this estimated effect. First, consistent with the DD identifying assumption that requires parallel violent crime trends, little evidence of diverging trends was found before the launch of FQTF. Second, controlling for a wide set of socioeconomic factors does not affect the treatment effect of FQTF. Third, results from a falsification test find expected smaller and insignificant difference in property crime reductions between the public and private sectors. Finally, Cheng and Long (2018) perform statistical inference using the permutation strategy to correct the underestimated standard errors due to that French Quarter is the only treatment group (Conley & Taber, 2011). According to a back-of-the-envelope calculation, this operating inefficiency of the public sector in violent crime reductions translates into an efficiency loss of over $6 million annually. In probing the potential mechanism, Cheng and Long (2018) find the underperformance of the publicly-run FQTF is consistent with evidence of decreased police presence during the public management period, including a considerable drop in patrolling miles and inadequate oversight of police officers. Moreover, the empirical result suggests that the public sector ran FQTF more inefficiently during nighttime and on weekends.

The study on the effectiveness of the FQTF makes several important contributions to the literature. First, it provides the first direct measure of the efficiency of publicly provided police service. This is made possible by exploiting the rare opportunity that the management of FQTF was handed over from the private sector to the public sector. Second, this study joins a broad literature on private provision of public goods (Andreoni, 1988, 1989; Bergstrom et al., 1986) and an emerging literature on private provision of police service specifically (Brooks, 2008; MacDonald et al., 2015). Third, this study contributes to the voluminous literature in economics of crime on the deterrence effect of police on crime (Levitt, 1997, 2002; McCrary, 2002), which recently has obtained more credible evidence of the causal relationship (DeAngelo & Hansen, 2014; Di Tella & Schargrodsky, 2004; Draca et al., 2011; Klick & Tabarrok, 2005).

2   French Quarter Task Force: Background

The French Quarter, a 0.66 square mile neighborhood containing 78 blocks, is the most popular tourist attraction in New Orleans. In 2014 alone, it attracted more than nine million tourists.[3] However, as a "hot spot" for tourists, French Quarter is also a "hot spot" for crime. Around early 2015, several high-profile violent crimes in French Quarter led residents to demand the government to provide more police to protect tourists and locals (Troeh, 2015). However, like many other police departments in the U.S., the NOPD has experienced a shortage of police force due to budget pressure. For example, recruitment of the NOPD has been frozen since 2010

---

[3] http://www.neworleansonline.com/pr/releases/releases/2014\%20Visitation\%20Release_1.pdf

(Amsden, 2015). In light of the surge in violent crimes and police shortage in French Quarter, Sidney Torres, a French Quarter resident and millionaire who made a fortune from the garbage collection business after Hurricane Katrina, decided to launch an anti-crime program called "French Quarter Task Force" (FQTF), which he bankrolled with $380,000 of his own money for the first 91 days.

FQTF is designed to deter crime by increasing police presence through two main channels. First, it increases police visibility by assembling a 24-hour-per-day and 7-day-per-week patrolling group formed by 3 armed off-duty NOPD officers at all hours, who were paid $50 per hour. Second, it launches a mobile app for users to conveniently summon police patrol for crime occurrences, which facilitates crime reporting and reduces police response time. Each officer drives an all-terrain Polaris vehicle that is equipped with an iPad and GPS device, enabling them to promptly respond to crimes reported via the app and 911 calls.

From March 23, 2015 to June 21, 2015, which is referred to as the "private management" period, Torres closely managed FQTF and adopted two main strategies to ensure the operational efficiency. The first strategy is to use the GPS system to track whether the Task Force officers were patrolling their assigned areas and responding to suspicious activities in real time. This is essentially the same strategy he used in his garbage collection business where he tracked locations of his GPS-equipped garbage trucks for supervision and evaluation purposes (Ruiz, 2008). This transparent public oversight that holds patrolling officers accountable is believed to make FQTF "different" (Binder, 2016). Second, Torres managed FQTF the way he ran his private businesses, which was "constantly vigilant about the details" (Binder, 2016). In a New York Times article (Amsden, 2015), Torres explained that he was inspired by Michael Bloomberg, New York City's billionaire former mayor who "popularized the notion that governmental institutions are most efficient when run like businesses". As a result, Torres involved himself in almost everything related to FQTF, such as "[from] hiring the officers to coordinating which routes they patrolled", showing up regularly at the French Quarter police station, "arriving during the shift changes", and "hanging out in the anteroom that was dedicated to his dispatch".

After the pilot period was over, the New Orleans Convention and Visitors Bureau and Mayor Landrieu's Administration both agreed to fund the program for the next 5 years, financed by an increase of 0.2495% sales tax for businesses in the French Quarter. On June 22, the NOPD and the FQMD formally took over the program, entering what we call the "public management" era. Figure 1 depicts the timeline of FQTF. Importantly, since the NOPD *"didn't feel that Sidney needed to continue to monitor a service he wasn't involved in funding or managing"*, it changed the GPS system and cut off Sidney Torres from his connection to the GPS tracker, which prevents external oversight of the Task Force patrolling (Simerman, 2016).

3   Empirical Identification

To evaluate the effectiveness of the FQTF and compare the relative effectiveness of managing FQTF, Cheng and Long (2018) adopt a straightforward difference-in-differences (DD). Conceptually, this strategy compares the change in the number of

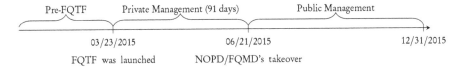

Fig. 1 Timeline of the French Quarter Task Force

violent crimes in French Quarter (treatment group) before and after the adoption of the FQTF, relative to the similar change in 69 other New Orleans neighborhood statistical areas ("neighborhoods" henceforth) (control group). Formally, their theoretical model can be formulated as:

$$Outcome_{imy} = \beta_0 + \beta_1 FQTS_{imy} + \left(\mathbf{X}_i^{2010} \times Year_y\right)\gamma + c_i + T_{my} + u_{imy}, \qquad (1)$$

where $Outcome_{imy}$ is the number of crimes in neighborhood i in month m of year y, $FQTS_{imy}$ is an indicator variable that is equal to 1 for the French Quarter after FQTF was launched and 0 otherwise, $\mathbf{X}_i^{2010}$ is a vector of neighborhood socioeconomic factors measured in 2010 that is interacted with the year trend $Year_y$, c_i is the neighborhood fixed effect, T_{my} is the month-by-year fixed effect, and u_{iym} is the random error term. Therefore, β_1 measures the average treatment effect of FQTF and is expected to be negative if FQTF successfully reduces violent crimes in the French Quarter. Since the spans of the privately-run FQTF (March 23, 2015 – June 21, 2015) and the publicly-run FQTF (June 22, 2015 – December 31, 2015) do not coincide with calendar months exactly, March, April, June, and July are further redefined in order to mitigate measurement error: "March" (March 1 – March 22), "April" (March 23 – April 30), "June" (June 1 – June 21), and "July" (June 22 – July 31).[4] In addition, one empirical concern of using disaggregated crime data at the neighborhood-year-month level is that the estimated effect could be susceptible to crime seasonality. To address this concern, Eq. (1) can be turned to estimate the seasonally differenced model similar to Draca, Machin and Witt (2011):

$$\Delta Robbery_{imy} = \beta_1 \Delta FQTS_{imy} + \Delta\left(X_i^{2010} \times Year_y\right)\gamma + \Delta T_{my} + \Delta u_{imy}, \qquad (2)$$

which is obtained by subtracting $Robbery_{im(y-1)} = \beta_0 + \beta_1 FQTS_{im(y-1)} + \left(X_i^{2010} \times Year_{y-1}\right)\gamma + c_i + T_{m(y-1)} + u_{im(y-1)}$

from Eq. (1).

The focus of Cheng and Long (2018) is to measure the relative effectiveness of running the FQTF by the public sector compared to the private sector. This leads to estimate Eq. (3) by decomposing $\Delta FQTF_{iym}$ in Eq. (2):

---

[4] Under this definition, $FQTS_{imy} = 1$ for French Quarter from "April" to December in 2015.

$$\Delta Outcome_{imy} = \alpha_1 \Delta FQTF_{imy} \times private_{my} + \alpha_2 \Delta FQTF_{imy}$$
$$\times public_{my} + \Delta \left(X_i^{2010} \times Year_y \right) \gamma + \Delta T_{my} + \Delta u_{imy}, \quad (3)$$

where, $private_{ym}$ is an indicator variable that equals 1 for the private management period (from "April" to "June" in 2015) and 0 otherwise; $public_{ym}$ is an indicator variable that equals 1 for the public management period (from "July" to December in 2015) and 0 otherwise. The parameters of interest are α_1 and α_2, which measure the treatment effect of running FQTF by the private and public sectors, respectively. In order to directly estimate the difference in operating efficiency, captured by $\tau_1 = \alpha_1 - \alpha_2$, Eq. (4) can be additional estimated:

$$\Delta Outcome_{imy} = \tau_1 \Delta FQTF_{imy} \times private_{my} + \tau_2 \Delta FQTF_{imy}$$
$$+ \Delta \left(X_i^{2010} \times Year_y \right) \gamma + \Delta T_{my} + \Delta u_{imy}. \quad (4)$$

Therefore, if the public sector is less efficient in managing the FQTF than the private sector in that it reduces fewer violent crimes, then one would expect $\alpha_1 < 0$, $\alpha_2 < 0$, and $\alpha_1 < \alpha_2$ ($\tau_1 < 0$).

There are two major empirical issues that this analysis needs to address in order to interpret the estimated effect as causal. The first is the validity of the DD identifying assumption, which requires that violent crimes in the French Quarter and other neighborhoods should have trended similarly in the absence of the FQTF. Under this assumption, any divergence in the violent crime trend would be interpreted as the causal effect of the FQTF. A natural concern about this assumption is that there might already exist diverging violent crime trends before the FQTF was launched, which biases the DD estimates. This concern can be tested by directly examining if there is evidence of pre-existing divergence with an event study. The second issue is statistical inference arising from the French Quarter being the only treatment group. As demonstrated by Conley and Taber (2011), a small number of treatment groups in a DD framework could greatly overstate the statistical significance even if one uses clustered robust standard errors to account for arbitrary within-group error serial correlation (Bertrand et al., 2004).[5] To address this issue, Cheng and Long (2018) employ the permutation strategy that establishes the empirical distribution for the purpose of inference through random assignment of placebo treatment to control groups, which has been widely applied in economics to obtain correct inference (Abadie et al., 2010; Bertrand et al., 2004; Chetty et al., 2009).[6] In their setting

---

[5] In their Monte Carlo simulations, Conley and Taber (2011) show that using clustered robust standard errors leads to high rejection rates of the null hypothesis at the 5% level when there are few treatment groups. In the case of 100 groups, 6 periods, and only one treatment group, cluster robust inference leads to an extremely high rejection rate of 0.84, which is considerably higher than then benchmark rejection rate of 5%.

[6] The synthetic control method (Abadie et al., 2010) provides an alternative way to estimate the treatment effect when there is only one treatment group. This method constructs a synthetic control group by choosing the best linear combination of untreated groups. Importantly, panel data on

where French Quarter is the only treatment group, this strategy amounts to simply assigning a placebo treatment that mimics the FQTF to each of the other 69 untreated neighborhoods.[7] In each assignment, the placebo treatment effect with one control neighborhood receiving the placebo treatment and other control neighborhoods remaining as the control group is estimated. Thus, the 69 placebo estimates form the empirical distribution and yield the 2-sided empirical p-value for the corresponding DD estimate, allowing researchers to determine whether the estimate is statistically significant.

4 Data

The empirical analysis relies on the measure of monthly violent crimes in the French Quarter and other New Orleans neighborhoods. To construct this measure, Cheng and Long (2018) combine information from two NOPD data resources: the Uniform Crime Reporting (UCR) dataset and the daily 911 call for service dataset. The UCR dataset provides us with the universe of crimes in New Orleans that satisfy UCR reporting criteria set by the Federal Bureau of Investigation (FBI).[8] The 911 dataset contains detailed incident-level information for crimes reported through 911, including time and State Plane Coordinates (SPCs) that identifies the exact crime location. We match both datasets by crime case number and aggregate three violent crimes – robbery, aggravated assault, and homicide – at the neighborhood-year-month level.[9] Figure 2 displays the 72 neighborhoods of the city of New Orleans with the French Quarter colored in red. During the examination period 2013–2015, 8537 out of 8592 (99.36%) UCR violent crimes are matched. Since Cheng and Long (2018) focus on estimating the difference in violent crime reductions between the privately-run FQTF and the publicly-run FQTF, the unmatched violent crime cases could potentially bias their estimate if these cases occurred in French Quarter during the treatment period (March 23, 2015 – December 31, 2015). Cheng and Long (2018) find there are *at most* two such cases according to the UCR dataset: One robbery (December, 2015) and one aggravated assault (December, 2015).[10]

---

covariates (X) for both treatment and control groups in a relatively long pre-treatment period are required to determine the optimal combination. Unfortunately, the most recent neighborhood-level covariate data are only available for the year of 2010, making it infeasible to apply the synthetic control method.

[7] Similar to the real FQTF treatment, a placebo treatment also includes a privately-run period (from "April" to June in 2015) and a publicly-run period (from July to December in 2015).

[8] The FBI uses UCR crime data to measure the level and scope of crime occurring throughout the U.S.

[9] SPCs information on rape in the 911 dataset is incomplete and does not allow users to identify cases at the neighborhood level. Therefore, rape is dropped from the analysis of violent crimes.

[10] The UCR dataset does not have accurate time and location information for each crime case and can only identify a case at the police-district and calendar-month level. However, Police District 8

Fig. 2 The 72 Neighborhoods of New Orleans, Louisiana

Therefore, in the worst-case scenario, the operational difference in managing the FQTF would be underestimated if these two violent crimes, which happened during the public management period, did occur in French Quarter.

Moreover, Cheng and Long (2018) collected data on neighborhood-level demographic controls from the 2010 Census, including proportion of females, percentage of population aged 12–17, percentage of population aged 18–34, proportion of whites, poverty rate, average household income, percentage of population with a high school diploma, percentage of population with a bachelor's degree, wage, percentage of self-employed population, and percentage of population with social security income. While data on these variables are not available during 2013–2015, the authors interact them with the year trend in order to capture their possible time-varying effects in our examination period. In their main analysis, Cheng and Long (2018) only include 69 out of 72 neighborhoods due to missing data for neighborhoods Florida Development and Iberville.

Table 1 presents summary statistics for the full sample, French Quarter, and the other 69 neighborhoods, respectively. As can be seen therein, French Quarter had higher violent and property crime rates than other neighborhoods of New Orleans over the sample period.

only contains two neighborhoods including French Quarter and Central Business District, which allows the authors to identify a much smaller subset of crimes that could occur in French Quarter.

Table 1 Summary statistics

Variable	Full Sample			French Quarter			Other Neighborhoods		
	Mean	S.D.	Observations	Mean	S.D.	Observations	Mean	S.D.	Observations
Crime			2520			36			2484
Violent Crime	3.38	4.56	2520	17.89	6.60	36	3.17	4.17	2484
Robbery	1.62	2.55	2520	10.94	5.42	36	1.48	2.21	2484
Aggravated Assault	1.59	2.33	2520	6.75	2.78	36	1.52	2.24	2484
Homicide	0.17	0.48	2520	0.19	0.40	36	0.17	0.48	2484
Violent Crime (Daytime)	1.41	2.10	2520	4.78	2.89	36	1.36	2.05	2484
Violent Crime (Nighttime)	1.97	2.91	2520	13.11	5.39	36	1.81	2.52	2484
Violent Crime (Weekday)	2.29	3.15	2520	10.83	4.23	36	2.16	2.95	2484
Violent Crime (Weekend)	1.09	1.81	2520	7.06	3.66	36	1.01	1.61	2484
Property Crime	18.29	21.91	2520	102.83	18.52	36	17.06	19.42	2484
Larceny & Theft	11.57	17.12	2520	91.83	17.95	36	10.41	14.08	2484
Burglary	3.78	5.09	2520	3.72	2.78	36	3.79	5.11	2484
Auto Theft	2.93	3.64	2520	7.28	4.08	36	2.87	3.59	2484
Controls									
% Female	51.63	3.74	70	39.30	–	1	51.81	–	69
% Age 12–17	6.71	2.72	70	0.80	–	1	6.79	–	69
% Age 18–34	28.48	7.36	70	23.40	–	1	28.55	–	69
% White	33.14	31.06	70	87.60	–	1	32.35	–	69
Poverty Rate	28.39	14.95	70	11.70	–	1	28.63	–	69
Average Household Income	62785.65	36269.92	70	123253.77	–	1	61909.3	–	69
% High School Diploma	24.28	10.13	70	10.90	–	1	24.47	–	69
% Bachelor's Degree	18.61	11.41	70	29.50	–	1	18.45	–	69
% Wage/Salary Income	70.25	8.83	70	69.01	–	1	70.27	–	69
% Self Employed	9.40	4.70	70	20.66	–	1	9.24	–	69
% Social Security Income	26.21	7.78	70	29.04	–	1	26.16	–	69

5 Results

5.1 Event Study

In order to motivate the regression analyses that follow, an event study is conducted to examine the evolvement of the violent crime difference between the French Quarter and other neighborhoods in New Orleans. This provides an opportunity to assess the validity of the common trend assumption of the DD strategy. Specifically, Cheng and Long (2018) add leading indicators Pre_{iym}^q s in Eq. (3) and estimate the following equation:

$$\Delta Outcome_{iym} = \sum_{q=1}^{6} \theta_q^{Pre} \Pr e_{imy}^q + \theta_1 \Delta FQTS_{imy} \times private_{my}$$
$$+\theta_2 \Delta FQTS_{imy} \times public_{my} + \Delta\left(X_i^{2010} \times Year_y\right)\gamma + \Delta T_{my} + \Delta u_{imy}, \tag{5}$$

where Pre_{iym}^q $(q = 1, 2, \ldots, 6)$ equals 1 for the French Quarter in the qth quarter prior to the adoption of the FQTF. Therefore, θ_q^{Pre} s measures the pre-treatment quarterly violent crime differences between French Quarter and other neighborhoods *relative* to similar difference in the omitted period (2013Q1 – 2013Q3), after adjusting for seasonality and neighborhood-level controls. Along similar lines, θ_1 and θ_2 measure the relative violent crime differences in the private and public management periods, respectively. Figure 3 plots the event study estimates and their 95% empirical confidence intervals obtained from the permutation strategy. The graphical evidence supports the DD research design as the pattern of the plotted estimates does not suggest diverging trends before adopting FQTF. Moreover, it becomes clear that violent crimes in French Quarter experienced a structural relative decline when FQTF was launched and managed by the private sector. In comparison, the relative decrease in violent crimes was much smaller once the FQTF was taken over by the public sector, suggesting the relative inefficiency of operating the program by the public sector.

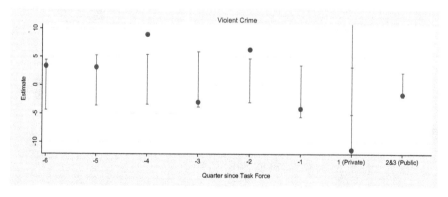

Fig. 3 Estimated Differences in Violent Crimes between French Quarter and Other New Orleans Neighborhoods before and after the Launch of FQTF

5.2   Main Estimates

This section presents the main regression results for the treatment effect of the FQTF on violent crimes based on seasonally differenced models. The OLS estimates are documented in Table 2, in which the empirical p-values calculated using the permutation strategy are reported in parentheses. Column 1 estimates the average treatment effect based on Eq. (2); it is the most parsimonious specification that only includes neighborhood and month-by-year fixed effects. Combined with the graphical evidence from the event study, the negative and significant estimate suggests a causal interpretation that FQTF on average led to about 29% reduction in violent crime in the French Quarter every month, showing the effectiveness of increased police presence through proactive patrolling and easier crime reporting via the mobile app. This deterrence effect is consistent with findings in recent economics studies that provide causal estimates of the police-crime relationship such as Di Tella and Schargrodsky (2004) and Draca, Machin and Witt (2011).

Next, Cheng and Long (2018) examine whether the public sector managed FQTF inefficiently and deterred fewer violent crimes than the private sector. They first examine if the FQTF was able to deter violent crimes when operated by either the private or public sector based on Eq. (3), which is confirmed by the two negative and significant estimates in Column 2. These estimates stay largely unchanged when a variety of socioeconomic factors is controlled in Column 3, including proportion of females, percentage of population aged 12–17, percentage of population aged

Table 2 Effect of FQTF on violent crimes

	OLS				WLS			
	1	2	3	4	5	6	7	8
FQTF	−5.18				−5.27			
	(0.00)				(0.00)			
FQTF × Private		−11.67	−11.69			−11.68	−11.35	
		(0.00)	(0.00)			(0.00)	(0.04)	
FQTF × Public		−1.93	−1.95			−2.06	−1.72	
		(0.07)	(0.09)			(0.04)	(0.13)	
FQTF × Private − FQTF × Public				−9.74				−9.62
				(0.00)				(0.00)
Observations	2520	2520	2520	2520	2520	2520	2520	2520
Neighborhoods and Month-by-Year FEs	Yes	Yes	Yes	Yes	Yes	Yes	Yes	Yes
Controls			Yes	Yes			Yes	Yes

Notes: Each column represents a separate regression. The unit of observation is neighborhood-year-month. Empirical p-values are reported in parentheses. Controls include proportion of females, percentage of population aged 12–17, percentage of population aged 18–34, proportion of whites, poverty rate, average household income, percentage of population with a high school diploma, percentage of population with a bachelor's degree, percentage of population with wage/salary income, percentage of self-employed population, and percentage of population with social security income. WLS uses neighborhood population as the weight

18–34, proportion of whites, poverty rate, average household income, percentage of population with a high school diploma, percentage of population with a bachelor's degree, percentage of population with wage or salary income, percentage of self-employed population, and percentage of population with social security income. Importantly, the two estimates suggest considerable disparity in deterrence effects: FQTF under private management reduced 11.69 violent crimes each month, while it only deterred roughly 1.95 violent crimes when run by the public sector. Relative to the average monthly violent crimes in French Quarter before the FQTF (18.44), these estimates translate into a sizable 63% violent crime reduction by the private force and a relatively modest 10% violent crime reduction when FQTF was under public oversight. Column 4 presents the preferred estimate based on Eq. (4), which directly shows that the difference in violent crime reductions (9.74) is statistically significant at the 1% level. Finally, Columns 5 through 8 report parallel weighted least squares (WLS) estimates with neighborhood population as the weight, which are almost identical to OLS estimates in the first four columns. Taken together, the estimates suggest strong evidence of the relative operating inefficiency of the public sector.

Since the effectiveness of the FQTF in reducing violent crimes comes from increased police presence, the estimated operational difference should reflect the discrepancy in police presence between the private and public management of the FQTF. This is evidenced by a sizable 20% drop in Polaris vehicle patrol miles after the FQTF was taken over by the public sector: falling from 5116 miles per month to 3835 miles per month.[11] Along similar lines, the relative operational inefficiency of the publicly-run FQTF was also observed by Sidney Torres. In his open letter issued in December 2015, Torres said he found Polaris vehicles were sitting unused and he even provided photographic evidence of on-duty Task Force officers idling instead of patrolling.[12] These findings, along with the regression estimates, are in line with the fact that the two main strategies that allowed Torres to manage the FQTF efficiently were no longer feasible during the public management period. First, the new GPS system prevented external oversight of patrolling officers, lowering the cost of underperformance for patrolling officers. Second, and most importantly, the FQTF was not managed like a private business and therefore lost efficiency in reducing violent crimes. In order to further understand when the publicly-run FQTF became more inefficient, Cheng and Long (2018) explore whether the difference in violent crime reductions is heterogeneous across time. Using the deterrence effect of the privately-run FQTF as the benchmark, the smaller negative estimates in Columns 2 and 4 in Table 3 imply that the public sector ran FQTF more inefficiently during nighttime (compared to daytime) and on weekends (compared to weekdays). The differences in magnitude between daytime and nighttime, and weekday and weekend indicate the different crime levels across time, which should not be unexpected

---

[11] Monthly patrol miles are calculated using data obtained from the FQMD's report "French Quarter Task Force Overview and Evolution".

[12] http://thehayride.com/2016/01/heres-the-unbelievable-story-of-how-the-nopd-is-destroying-sidney-torres-french-quarter-task-force-with-incompetence/

Table 3 Difference in violent crime reduction between the public and private sectors (by time)

	Daytime	Nighttime	Weekday	Weekend
	1	2	3	4
FQTF × Private − FQTF × Public	−3.26	−6.48	−2.63	−7.11
	(0.01)	(0.01)	(0.10)	(0.00)
Observations	2520	2520	2520	2520
Neighborhoods and Month-by-Year FEs	Yes	Yes	Yes	Yes
Controls	Yes	Yes	Yes	Yes

Notes: Each column represents a separate regression. The unit of observation is neighborhood-year-month. Empirical *p*-values are reported in parentheses. Controls include proportion of females, percentage of population aged 12–17, percentage of population aged 18–34, proportion of whites, poverty rate, average household income, percentage of population with a high school diploma, percentage of population with a bachelor's degree, percentage of population with wage/salary income, percentage of self-employed population, and percentage of population with social security income

considering that the French Quarter is famous for night life and attracts more residents and tourists during weekend, and thus witnesses more crimes during nighttime and weekend. In addition, this pattern is in line with the fact that the two nighttime FQTF shifts (7 pm–11 pm and 11 pm–3 am shifts) were fully filled with three officers, which generated the strongest FQTF police presence.

Finally, a back-of-the-envelope calculation is conducted in order to quantify the efficiency loss of the publicly-run FQTF. To do so, Cheng and Long (2018) first separately estimate the difference in crime reductions for all three violent crimes: robbery, aggravated assault, and homicide. Results are summarized in Table 4, where one can find the difference in monthly violent crime reductions (9.74) is driven by robbery. Specifically, the privately-run FQTF significantly reduced 7.37 more robberies and 1.85 more aggravated assaults than the publicly-run FQTF, while the effect on homicides is close to zero and statistically insignificant. Cheng and Long (2018) additionally provide a conservative estimate on the social loss of the unprevented robberies and aggravated assaults. Based on the cost-of-crime estimates from McCollister, French and Fang (2010), $42,310 per robbery and $107,020 per aggravated assault, both in 2008 dollars, these estimates translate into an efficiency loss of $560,793 (in 2015 dollars) each month, or approximately $6.7 million (in 2015 dollars) per year.[13]

---

[13] The estimate of efficiency gain is larger (nearly $9 million per year in 2015 dollars) if the cost-of-crime estimates are based on the estimates reported by Heaton (2010): $67,277 per robbery and $87,238 per aggravated assault, both in 2007 dollars. Heaton's estimates are obtained by calculating the average cost estimates from three other studies.

Table 4 Difference in violent crime reduction between the public and private sectors (by type)

	Robbery	Aggravated Assault	Homicide
	1	2	3
FQTF × Private − FQTF × Public	−7.37	−1.85	−0.53
	(0.00)	(0.10)	(0.13)
Observations	2520	2520	2520
Neighborhoods and Month-by-Year FEs	Yes	Yes	Yes
Controls	Yes	Yes	Yes

Notes: Each column represents a separate regression. The unit of observation is neighborhood-year-month. Empirical *p*-values are reported in parentheses. Controls include proportion of females, percentage of population aged 12–17, percentage of population aged 18–34, proportion of whites, poverty rate, average household income, percentage of population with a high school diploma, percentage of population with a bachelor's degree, percentage of population with wage/salary income, percentage of self-employed population, and percentage of population with social security income

5.3   Additional Checks

Furthermore, Cheng and Long (2018) provide additional evidence for the estimated causal effect on violent crimes by undertaking a set of falsification type tests. They do so by examining the effect on property crimes. Since FQTF mainly targets violent crimes, the operational difference in reducing property crimes is expected to be much smaller, if any. This is confirmed by Column 1 estimate (−3.78) in Table 5, which is much closer to zero compared to its counterpart estimate for violent crimes (−9.74). More importantly, this estimate is statistically indistinguishable from zero. Estimates for larceny and theft, burglary, and auto theft in the last three columns also suggest a similar story, indicating that the FQTF effect is similar during both periods, except for auto theft which is marginally significant at the 10% level. One explanation for this result is that larceny theft is more common in the French Quarter but less likely to be perceived by victims, and burglary primarily occurs at night and in private dwellings, making both crime types less susceptible to a public deterrence technology, which is in line with the findings in Draca et al. (2011). Overall, these estimates provide further confirmation that the estimated relative inefficiency in managing the FQTF by the public sector is causal.

Next, Cheng and Long (2018) check the sensitivity of the estimated effect in Table 6, where they report the preferred estimate (from Column 3 in Table 2) in Column 1 as the baseline estimate. Column 2 adds back two neighborhoods that are excluded in our main analysis due to missing data on covariates. This yields an uncontrolled estimate that is almost the same as the baseline estimate. Column 3 investigates the potential confounding effect of spatial crime displacement. If the FQTF drove criminals out of the French Quarter to adjacent neighborhoods, then one would expect to see a larger displacement effect during the private management period compared to the public management period in response to the more efficient

Table 5 Difference in property crime reductions between the public and private sectors

	Property	Larceny & Theft	Burglary	Auto Theft
	1	2	3	4
FQTF × Private − FQTF × Public	−3.78	1.2	−1.79	−3.18
	(0.46)	(0.68)	(0.42)	(0.10)
Observations	2520	2520	2520	2520
Neighborhoods and Month-by-Year FEs	Yes	Yes	Yes	Yes
Controls	Yes	Yes	Yes	Yes

Notes: Each column represents a separate regression. The unit of observation is neighborhood-year-month. Empirical *p*-values are reported in parentheses. Controls include proportion of females, percentage of population aged 12–17, percentage of population aged 18–34, proportion of whites, poverty rate, average household income, percentage of population with a high school diploma, percentage of population with a bachelor's degree, percentage of population with wage/salary income, percentage of self-employed population, and percentage of population with social security income

privately-run FQTF. As a result, the estimated difference in violent crime reductions could be overstated. They examine this possibility by excluding five districts adjacent to the French Quarter, a strategy similar to Di Tella and Schargrodsky (2004) and Draca, Machin and Witt (2011). If the displacement did occur, then excluding the five districts should significantly decrease the magnitude of the DD estimate. However, we find the estimate in Column 3 is very similar to the baseline estimate, suggesting no evidence of spatial crime displacement. Column 4 additionally allows neighborhoods to follow differential linear time trends in violent crimes, which does not affect the estimate. Column 5 uses violent crime rate (violent crimes per 1000 population) as the alternative outcome measure. It shows the corresponding estimate is still negative and significant at the 1% level, providing further evidence of the inefficiency of the public sector in managing the FQTF. Finally, Column 6 re-estimates the main effect without accounting for crime seasonality by using the non-differenced version of Eq. (4); the significant estimate stays robust though suggesting a slightly smaller effect. Taken together, all these results show that the estimated inefficiency of the publicly-run FQTF is very robust.

In addition, Cheng and Long (2018) interpret the FQTF's better crime prevention during the private management period as due to the use of more effective monitoring and performance incentives, which appears to be the main difference between the privately and publicly managed FQTF. Still, there are several major alternative interpretations. First, one might worry that the "novelty effect" drove the difference in crime reductions: the novelty of the FQTF would have gradually worn off, even if there were no program takeover. This does not seem to be the case, as we find that the privately managed FQTF reduced more and more crimes over time. Second, we ask whether the observed superior performance of the privately managed FQTF could be attributed partly to faster response time, along with increased police presence. To do that, we compute the FQTF response time to robbery and aggravated

Table 6 Robustness checks

	Baseline	Adding Two Dropped Neighborhoods Due to Missing Data on Controls	Using Conley-Taber Empirical p-Value	Adding District-Specific Linear Time Trends	Outcome: Violent Crime Rate	Non-Differenced Model
	1	2	3	4	5	6
Panel A. Robbery						
FQTF × Private − FQTF × Public	−7.37 (0.00)	−7.38 (0.00)	−7.37 (0.00)	−7.37 (0.00)	−1.95 (0.00)	−5.81 (0.00)
Panel B. Aggravated Assault						
FQTF × Private − FQTF × Public	−1.85 (0.10)	−1.86 (0.17)	−1.85 (0.09)	−1.85 (0.10)	−0.46 (0.16)	−1.56 (0.06)
Panel C. Theft						
FQTF × Private − FQTF × Public	−1.98 (0.64)	−1.95 (0.63)	−1.98 (0.65)	−1.98 (0.64)	−0.64 (0.55)	−8.78 (0.06)
Observations	2520	2592	2520	2520	2520	2520
Neighborhood and Year × Quarter Fixed Effects	Yes	Yes	Yes	Yes	Yes	Yes
Controls	Yes	−	Yes	Yes	Yes	Yes

Notes: Each column represents a separate regression. The unit of observation is neighborhood-year-month. Empirical *p*-values are reported in parentheses. Controls include proportion of females, percentage of population aged 12–17, percentage of population aged 18–34, proportion of whites, poverty rate, average household income, percentage of population with a high school diploma, percentage of population with a bachelor's degree, percentage of population with wage/salary income, percentage of self-employed population, and percentage of population with social security income

assault reports; we find that it was similar in the private and public management periods (2.13 min and 2.09 min, respectively). Finally, it is possible that our result is driven by a rational response from the FQTF officers. Specifically, the Task Force officers might begin by performing effectively in response to the privately managed FQTF's monitoring and incentives, only to ensure that the public sector later would take over the management and be more likely to tolerate the officers' inefficient patrol performance. However, this potential behavioral change, provided that it existed, would demonstrate the relative effectiveness of more monitoring and incentives in preventing shirking behaviors. In summary, these findings suggest that alternative interpretations are unlikely to explain the distinctive deterrence effects during the public and private management periods.

6 Conclusion

As one of the most important local public goods, police services are crucial for ensuring public safety and social stability. However, there is little empirical evidence on its effectiveness when it is provided and managed by the private sector. The study by Cheng and Long (2018) bridges the gap by comparing the efficiency of managing the anti-crime program FQTF in New Orleans in reducing violent crimes between the public and private sectors. Their estimates suggest that the FQTF – which increased police visibility in the French Quarter – reduced violent crimes in the French Quarter. In particular, FQTF successfully deterred more robberies and aggravated assaults. The deterrence effect of FQTF is more substantial when it is run by the private sector, although the distinctive effects become indistinguishable on property crimes such as burglary and larceny/theft. The crime reductions could translate into an annual efficiency gain of $6.7 million, far exceeding the cost of running the FQTF.

The handover of management on FQTF provides a valuable opportunity for researchers to compare the performance of private and public sectors in providing police services. Cheng and Long (2018) argue that the more pronounced deterrence effect during the private period comes from using more effective monitoring and incentive strategies, which appear to be the only major difference between the privately and publicly managed FQTF. They find consistent evidence of shirking behavior during the public management period, when there was less monitoring and weaker performance incentives. They further rule out major alternative explanations, including officers' rational response and the novelty effect. In summary, the study on FQTF suggests that monitoring and incentive strategies, when used appropriately, have the potential to further improve police services.

References

Abadie, A., Diamond, A., & Hainmueller, J. (2010). Synthetic control methods for comparative case studies: Estimating the effect of California's Tobacco Control Program. *Journal of the American Statistical Association, 105*(490), 493–505.

Amsden, D. (2015). *Who runs the streets of New Orleans?* Accessed 14 Mar 2016. http://www.nytimes.com/2015/08/02/magazine/who-runs-the-streets-of-new-orleans.html?_r=1

Andreoni, J. (1988). Privately provided public goods in a large economy: The limits of altruism. *Journal of Public Economics, 35*(1), 57–73.

Andreoni, J. (1989). Giving with impure altruism: Applications to charity and Ricardian equivalence. *The Journal of Political Economy, 97*(6), 1447–1458.

Bergstrom, T., Blume, L., & Varian, H. (1986). On the private provision of public goods. *Journal of Public Economics, 29*(1), 25–49.

Bertrand, M., Duflo, E., & Mullainathan, S. (2004). How much should we trust differences-in-differences estimates? *Quarterly Journal of Economics, 119*(1), 249–275.

Binder, J. (2016). *Here's the unbelievable story of how the Nopd is destroying Sidney Torres' French Quarter Task Force with 'Incompetence'.* Accessed 14 Mar 2016. http://thehayride.

com/2016/01/heres-the-unbelievable-story-of-how-the-nopd-is-destroying-sidney-torres-french-quarter-task-force-with-incompetence/

Brooks, L. (2008). Volunteering to be taxed: Business improvement districts and the extra-governmental provision of public safety. *Journal of Public Economics, 92*(1), 388–406.

Cheng, C., & Long, W. (2018). Improving police services: Evidence from the French Quarter Task Force. *Journal of Public Economics, 164*(8), 1–18.

Chetty, R., Looney, A., & Kroft, K. (2009). Salience and taxation: Theory and evidence. *American Economic Review, 99*(4), 1145–1177.

Conley, T. G., & Taber, C. R. (2011). Inference with "difference in differences" with a small number of policy changes. *Review of Economics and Statistics, 93*(1), 113–125.

DeAngelo, G., & Hansen, B. (2014). Life and death in the fast lane: Police enforcement and traffic fatalities. *American Economic Journal: Economic Policy, 6*(2), 231–257.

Di Tella, R., & Schargrodsky, E. (2004). Do police reduce crime? Estimates using the allocation of police forces after a terrorist attack. *The American Economic Review, 94*(1), 115–133.

Draca, M., Machin, S., & Witt, R. (2011). Panic on the streets of London: Police, crime, and the July 2005 terror attacks. *The American Economic Review, 101*(5), 2157–2181.

Heaton, P. (2010). *Hidden in plain sight: What cost-of-crime research can tell us about investing in police*. RAND Corporation.

Klick, J., & Tabarrok, A. (2005). Using terror alert levels to estimate the effect of police on crime. *Journal of Law and Economics, 48*(1), 267–279.

Levitt, S. D. (1997). Using electoral cycles in police hiring to estimate the effect of police on crime. *The American Economic Review, 87*(3), 270–290.

Levitt, S. D. (2002). Using electoral cycles in police hiring to estimate the effects of police on crime: Reply. *The American Economic Review, 92*(4), 1244–1250.

MacDonald, J. M., Klick, J., & Grunwald, B. (2015). The effect of private police on crime: Evidence from a geographic regression discontinuity design. *Journal of the Royal Statistical Society: Series A (Statistics in Society), 179*(3), 831–846.

McCollister, K. E., French, M. T., & Fang, H. (2010). The cost of crime to society: New crime-specific estimates for policy and program evaluation. *Drug and Alcohol Dependence, 108*(1), 98–109.

McCrary, J. (2002). Using electoral cycles in police hiring to estimate the effect of police on crime: Comment. *American Economic Review, 92*(4), 1236–1243.

Mueller, D. C. (2003). *Public choice III*. Cambridge University Press.

Niskanen, W. A. (1971). *Bureaucracy and representative government*. Aldine-Atherton.

Ruiz, R. (2008). *The Trash King of New Orleans*. Accessed 14 Mar 2016. http://www.forbes.com/2008/09/03/new-orleans-gustav-biz-logistics-cx_rr_0904nola-cleanup.html

Simerman, J. (2016). *Sidney Torres says the mobile french quarter police detail he created 'is not working'*. Accessed 14 Mar 2016. http://theadvocate.com/news/neworleans/neworleansnews/14549060-186/sidney-torres-says-the-mobile-french-quarter-police-detail-he-created-is-not-working

Troeh, E. (2015). *French quarter sees violent crime surge; residents demand changes*. Accessed 14 Mar 2016. http://www.npr.org/2015/01/20/378567168/french-quarter-sees-violent-crime-surge-residents-demand-changes

Public Security Enhances the Effectiveness of Private Security in Reducing Maritime Piracy Harm

Benjamin Blemings, Gregory DeAngelo, Taylor Smith, and Alexander Specht

Abstract Private security outnumbers public security, yet little is known about how private security complements public security to mitigate the severity of damage caused by criminal actors. A noteworthy context in which private and public security interact is on the high seas where vessels face danger from maritime pirates. This paper quantifies the relationship between public security in aiding private security to enhance the safety of passing vessels, as measured by the likelihood of boarding and hijacking respectively. We hypothesize that on-board private security reduces boarding and hijackings, while public security can deter hijacking of anchored vessels. Our empirical estimates find that public security amplifies the effect of private security, increasing its effectiveness by an additional 29 percentage points (pp) in aggregate. However, there is meaningful heterogeneity in the quality and size of the moderating effects of public security. Low-intensity public security, measured by a country's military expenditures or patrol boats, only amplifies private security's effectiveness against boarding by 21–23 pp, while high-intensity public security amplifies private security's effectiveness by 56–77 pp. Thus, the likelihood that a vessel with private security and high-intensity public security is boarded is nearly zero. There are no significant differences in hijacking, which is a relatively rare event. A likely interpretation is that private and high-intensity public security have complementary skills, such as public security offering air support and private security offering a more permanent and responsive presence.

B. Blemings
Dyson School of Applied Economics and Management, Cornell University, Ithaca, NY, USA
e-mail: btb77@cornell.edu

G. DeAngelo (✉) · A. Specht
Department of Economic Sciences, Claremont Graduate University, Claremont, CA, USA
e-mail: alexander.specht@cgu.edu

T. Smith
DWS Group, Chicago, IL, USA

© The Author(s), under exclusive license to Springer Nature Switzerland AG 2023
E. A. Blackstone et al. (eds.), *Handbook on Public and Private Security*,
Competitive Government: Public Private Partnerships,
https://doi.org/10.1007/978-3-031-42406-9_14

297

1   Introduction

Safety is often provided publicly because there is an assumed market failure that requires a unifying agency (government) to coordinate resources to protect the interests of the public, be it personal or public safety. This is often achieved through the designation of a law enforcement authority to ensure that citizens obey the law.

In some instances private agents (community members, firms, etc.) believe that the publicly provided level of safety falls short of their desired level of safety (Bergstrom & Goodman, 1973). These situations often arise in scenarios where a private agent believes that they can localize the benefits of security by providing private security. Examples include hiring private security detail for a person, retail store, neighborhood, and so on (Nicholson-Crotty et al., 2004; Renauer et al., 2003; Tolman & Weisz, 1995; Weitzer et al., 2008; Zhao et al., 2002).

Actual or perceived market failures are more common in some environments. International territories tend to be one such environment. Consider international waterways that cargo ships traverse when shipping goods globally. Specific waterways (e.g., China Sea, Malacca Straits, Gulf of Aden) are often populated with pirates that aim to hijack vessels and loot the goods onboard. While navies are often deployed to deter piracy activities in these regions, the vastness of the ocean reduces the effectiveness of navies in preemptively deterring pirate attacks, instead resorting to engaging in post-attack response initiatives.

While navies can be effective in diffusing attacks after they have occurred, shipping companies still have a desire to deter pirate attacks and, at the very least, prevent pirates from being able to board a vessel. As noted by an industry expert, "a ship's master was advised to stick to routes patrolled by naval forces, use razor wire and water cannon to prevent pirates from boarding and — crucially — keep the vessel moving." But, as was noted in 2011, "dozens of warships from the world's navies have failed to stem the attacks leading to a growing number of shipowners to turn to private security companies" Company (2011). The desire to avoid pirates from boarding a vessel and inability of a navy to preemptively prevent piracy attacks gives way to shipping companies implementing private security to ensure the safety of both the crew and goods onboard.

Indeed, private security is likely to provide specific deterrence by discouraging pirates from attacking a specific vessel. As noted in DeAngelo and Smith (2020), there is also a possibility that private security can generate positive externalities by discouraging the overall level of piracy on the waterways. If such externalities exist and are salient to pirates, private security could produce a partial solution to discouraging illegal and violent behaviors on the high seas.

To the extent that private security creates spillover benefits in the form of reduced piracy, restrictions that do not allow private security could be creating a haven for illegal, dangerous behavior to persist. In this way, the market failure in the provision of safety on the high seas could be guaranteed by regulations which ensure that a private solution in the provision of public safety cannot be achieved.

The research question that we address is whether the presence of private security is relied on as a substitute for public security (navies) or if it has a complementary effect on reducing the severity of damage, measured by boarding and hijacking, of attempted pirate attacks. This leads to a simple interaction between private security and naval security, both of which we measure in several ways. Heterogeneity in the effect of public security is then examined by using a country's military expenditures to separate those with stronger or weaker public security.

The remainder of the chapter proceeds as follows. Section 2 begins with a discussion of ineffectively governed territories and violence, emphasizing the context of maritime piracy. Next, Sect. 3 details several sources of piracy and security data. Then, Sect. 4 explains the method for disentangling the complementarity of public and private security. Section 5 presents the results, beginning with the full data and then subsampling by terciles of military expenditure to understand the heterogeneous effects of public security funding. The paper concludes, in Sect. 6, with a brief discussion and avenues for future research.

2 Background

Certain conditions have been found to create an environment that allows illicit actors such as terrorist groups and other criminal organizations to plan and operate relatively freely. Poverty is often cited as a principal cause leading to terrorism and other crime. However, research on poverty and terrorism is largely mixed regarding the causal connection between the two (Abadie, 2006; Angrist, 1995; Khashan, 2003; Krueger & Laitin, 2008; Piazza, 2006). Different explanations offered for terrorism and other types of violent crime are not always mutually exclusive. For example, poverty may be linked to institutional factors, such as weak state governance where power vacuums are filled by non-state actors (Graff, 2010). Poor countries also do not provide the principal governing entity with the tax revenues necessary to combat terrorism and other crime or to provide the populace with the public goods necessary to keep people from supporting other organizations that fill these governance gaps.

Piazza (2008) argues that ineffective governance may in fact be the link between poverty, terrorism, and other types of violence. For example, empirical evidence supports the claim that ineffectively governed geographical areas, which are characterized by high levels of poverty, are a significant predictor of terrorism. Countries labeled by the Fund for Peace's Failed State Index as at highest risk of state failure (Somalia, Zimbabwe, Sudan, Chad, Democratic Republic of Congo) are three times more likely to experience a terrorist attack than the categories of strongest states (Norway, Finland, Sweden) Piazza (2008). The likelihood of terrorism also increases along with political instability, civil war, and guerilla warfare – characteristics of ineffectively governed states (Campos & Gassebner, 2009).

2.1   Safe Havens as a Result of Ineffective Governance Serve as Incubators for Illicit Non-state Actors

According to Lamb (2008), safe havens are geographic locations that allow illicit actors to operate with impunity, evade detection or capture. These can often be found in ungoverned, under-governed, misgoverned, or contested physical areas that allow these actors to organize, plan, fund, communicate, recruit, train, and operate in a relatively secure environment. Lamb (2008) explains that safe havens arise because of various gaps in governance where a central government does not effectively provide the necessary security, legal, economic, and political functions that legitimate governments are expected to provide the population living within its borders.

Somalia is usually considered a stereotypical safe haven characterized by a large ungoverned area, with no real central government control and widespread localized contests for power over small geographical areas (Lamb, 2008). While Somalia is a clear example of an ungoverned area, safe havens often exist in under-governed areas where a central government exerts only partial control, such as some smaller islands in Southeast Asia. Safe havens also arise in misgoverned areas controlled by a central government made up of negligent, corrupt, or intimidated officials who do not prevent illicit actors from operating (Lamb, 2008).

Areas where a weak or failed state does not govern effectively create an environment that allows illicit actors to pursue activities such as terrorist training and recruiting, arms trading, drug and human trafficking, and maritime piracy. Ineffectively governed areas with porous borders serve as safe havens for violent organizations and allow materials and individuals to easily move in and out of the territory (Graff, 2010).[1] Furthermore, lack of state control over a geographical area can allow violent actors to establish training camps and headquarters from where they can plan violent attacks. Graff (2010) further explains that these areas are often associated with violent conflict which leads to power gaps in the provision of public goods such as law and order as well as an environment where groups have access to weaponry and potential battle-hardened recruits.

Under-governed areas where a central government performs only some governance functions effectively create an environment where illicit actors can exploit governance gaps, providing basic services such as law and order. Ineffectively governed areas in which organized criminal and terrorist groups operate, often end up becoming state- like territories controlled and governed by illicit actors (Sullivan & Bunker, 2002). Most safe havens are currently located in under-governed areas (Graff, 2010).

---

[1] One example is the Durand Line, the notoriously porous border between Pakistan and Afghanistan.

2.2 Maritime Havens and Piracy

Traditionally, ineffectively governed areas and safe havens have been thought of as definite remote physical locations. However, maritime havens also provide the environment necessary for illicit actors to thrive. Maritime havens allow illicit actors to move between land areas (e.g., islands), taking advantage of wide ocean spaces that are often poorly monitored and not governed by individual states (Graff, 2010). In areas where a central government cannot effectively maintain a security presence, maritime havens may arise and attract illicit actors.

Along with civil war, terrorism, and widespread organized crime, maritime piracy is often a feature of ineffectively governed states with maritime borders (Daxecker & Prins, 2021). Political and economic weakness often leads to government corruption and criminality, which serve to encourage maritime piracy (Prins, 2014). Daxecker and Prins (2017a) note that weak states allow pirates to plan and execute attacks relatively easily and reduces the risk of capture, especially if pirates operate at considerable distance from effective state authority. As a result, states that enjoy intermediate levels of state capacity, but which are characterized by limited reach, such as Indonesia and Venezuela, often experience a significant amount of maritime piracy.

Daxecker and Prins (2021) find that pirates generally do not operate in the least governed territorial areas of weak states, instead opting for areas where corrupt officials and police can be bribed and where roads, ports, and markets are available. Pirates can effectively operate relatively close to state capitals in weak states where central governments lack effective control over these capital areas. However, as a central government's control over capital areas increases, pirates will locate further from state power centers (Daxecker & Prins, 2015).

2.2.1 The Additional Impact of Maritime Piracy on Other Categories of Violent Conflict

In general, countries that suffer from high incidence of maritime piracy and high levels of other types of violent conflict, are categorized as ineffectively governed states. As noted by Daxecker and Prins (2017b), natural resources are often used to finance rebellion and terrorist activity in ineffectively governed areas of the world and allow illicit actors to purchase weapons, buy community support, and hire fighters with the revenues that the sale of natural resources brings. Furthermore, Daxecker and Prins (2017b) find that maritime piracy is an additional funding strategy that supports armed conflict. Maritime piracy has been connected to arms trafficking, the narcotics trade, and slavery, with revenues often being used to finance terrorist groups and armed rebellion. In this way, maritime piracy may serve to increase the intensity of other types of armed conflict in different parts of the world.

3 Data

Our research focus is how the interaction of public and private security leads to safety from maritime pirates. This requires having measures of both types of security and safety-related outcomes, such as ship boarding or hijacking. The primary obstacle to having appropriate data is the classic concern that only attacks that are recorded or caught by law enforcement are included. Our analysis side-steps this concern by conditioning the analysis on an attack occurring. In this way, our results can provide novel insights on how security affects the severity of the damage from criminal activity. This stands in contrast to the typical focus on deterrence, the extensive margin of a crime occurring or not.

3.1 Piracy

Data on piracy attacks are sourced from two locations. First, the sample of pirate attacks is drawn from Open Humanities Data, which combines data from the International Maritime Organization (IMO) and the Maritime Piracy Event Location Dataset (MPELD). This database includes the exact location of the attack and whether the vessel was boarded or hijacked. The first recorded pirate attack in the data is in 1993 and the last one is in 2020. In order to incorporate the legality of private security, we need to merge to another data source which only runs from 1993 to 2014.

3.2 Private Security

The legality of private security depends on which country the vessel is registered in. The data on which countries allow private security on marine vessels is gathered from the American Club.[2] This information is then added to the attacks and a dummy variable, private security allowed, is created which equals 1 if a vessel is registered in a country which allows private security on boats.

On-Board Private Security One possible issue with the measurement of private security's onboard legal status is that rules of the host country do not necessarily lead to on board private security presence. If private security is allowed, it does not necessarily mean the boat employs private security. While this measure of private security is interesting since policymakers control the legality of private security, the estimate may be biased if the legal option to employ private security only weakly translates into the presence of private security onboard. To understand effects of

---

[2] See https://www.american-club.com/files/files/Piracy_FAQ_Appendix_5.pdf for information about the legality of private security and https://www.american-club.com/page/about-the-club for information about the American Club.

Table 1 Descriptions of representative attacks

Event Label	Description
Showing	Seven pirates in a white-blue coloured skiff armed with an rpg approached the tanker underway master raised alarm, sounded ships whistle, activated fire hoses and fired two parachute rockets the armed security team onboard noticed a ladder on the skiff and showed their weapons resulting in the skiff aborting the approach and moved away.
Typical	Pirates in a boat chased and fired at the ship underway master raised alarm and crew locked themselves in the citadel security team on board the ship fired warning shots the pirates escaped
Warship Arrives	Pirates in two high speed boats chased and fired on the ship underway master increased speed, raised alarm and crew musterered in safe room, except bridge crew and security team a warship in the vicinity was informed when the warship arrived at the location, pirates moved away
Helicopter Arrives	A skiff was noticed approaching the tanker underway the d/o raised alarm, informed the master and security team the master increased speed, altered course and contacted warship for assistance about five to six pirates armed with guns and rpg in the skiff closed in to four to five cables and fired on the tanker the onboard armed security team returned fire, resulting in the pirates aborting the attack and moving away a warship dispatched a helicopter to the location to assist no injuries to the crew.
Notifies Navy	Pirates armed with rocket propelled grenades and guns in 20 skiffs approached the ship underway near the port bow at a distance of 3 nm around five to seven pirates were in each skiff armed security team on board the ship fired warning shots master informed a warship in the vicinity and all ships in the area via vhf ch. 16 eventually pirates abandoned attempted boarding

Note: The Description column comes from the textual data for each incident. The column combines the incident descriptions and the crew action taken variables. The text is lower-case, because this makes the regular expression extraction most accurate. In the first row, second column, "rpg" stands for rocket-propelled grenade. In the last row, second column, "vhf ch. 16" means specific communication technology

private security on board, the textual description of the attack is used to find the attacks in which private security is actually present on an attacked vessel. There appears to be little heterogeneity in the intensity or amount of security on these vessels. For descriptions of some representative attacks, see rows 1 and 2 of Table 1.

3.3 Public Security

We identify public security, in this instance, as naval vessels procured by countries.[3] The time and location of these vessels are not easily obtainable and are likely unavailable in sufficient detail to allow them to be included as variables in a

---

[3] These countries acquire vessels for both inter and intra state conflicts. An example of naval vessels procured for inter-state conflict are aircraft carriers which are bought by the U.S. Navy and an example of naval vessels that specialize in intra-state conflict would be patrol boats that are bought by the U.S. Coast Guard for drug interdiction tasks.

regression. A different measure of the presence of public security is the distance from a country's coastline. We assume that there are fewer patrol boats farther away from the coast since a country's economic interests decline with distance from the coast.

There are two cutoffs in distance to shore that are defined by the UN Convention on the Law of the Sea (UNCLOS). First, within 12 nautical miles of the coastline is considered a country's territorial waters. Within the territorial waters countries are free to set laws, use resources (fish, minerals, etc), and regulate use so they have an incentive to provide security in this area. Second, within 200 nautical miles of the coastline is considered a country's exclusive economic zone (EEZ).[4] Using the distance to shore in nautical miles of an attack, two dummy variables are created for whether an attack occurred within the territorial waters and whether the attack occurred within a country's EEZ.

Public Security Intensity Next, we recognize that not all nations possess equally capable public security forces. If unaddressed, this could lead to heterogeneity bias. To assuage these concerns, we also collect data on military expenditures from the Stockholm International Peace Research Institute (SIPRI), patrol boat inventory in 2022 from Global Firepower (GF), and country coastline length from the CIA World Factbook. The SIPRI data are country-year level military spending in 2020 US dollars. Patrol vessels, consisting of vessels that are likely to be used in anti-piracy operations such as patrol boats/vessels, fast-attack craft, gunboats, and missile/torpedo boats, are called upon to defend offshore areas of importance and are the smallest naval vessel recorded by GF. As shown in Sect. A.1, there is strong, positive, and statistically significant relationship between average military expenditure from 1994 to 2014 and patrol vessels in 2022.[5] We use military expenditure and patrol boats per coastline as plausible, arguably imperfect, measures that capture important, relevant aspects of the intensity of public security near country shorelines. Using either measure returns qualitatively similar conclusions.

3.4 Summary Statistics

Our dataset consists of a cross-section of 1651 pirate attacks.[6] Summary statistics for these attacks are presented in Table 2. On average, attacked vessels are boarded 65% of the time and vessels are hijacked 6% of the time.

---

[4] Inside a countries' EEZ, the country has sole rights to natural resources.

[5] The GF data on patrol boat inventory is not available over time. We recognize that military expenditure and patrol vessels are measured at different times, but do not believe this an issue. In fact, this is likely more of an accurate model of reality since patrol vessels are durable capital and previous expenditure is likely to be predictive of future military assets.

[6] This is the sample of vessels where the vessel registration/flag is known, which is crucial for knowing whether private maritime security is allowed. As shown in Fig. 1, the number of attacks in the universe follows the same trends as the sample that merges to country flags.

Table 2 Summary statistics

	Mean	Median	SD	Min	Max	Count
Boarded	0.65	1.00	0.48	0	1.00	1651
Hijacked	0.06	0.00	0.24	0	1.00	1651
Distance to Shore (nm)	37.60	6.34	83.91	0	543.47	1651
Within Territorial Waters (12 nm)	0.62	1.00	0.48	0	1.00	1651
Within EEZ Waters (200 nm)	0.94	1.00	0.23	0	1.00	1651
Flag Allows PMSC	0.70	1.00	0.46	0	1.00	1651
Private Security On Board	0.04	0.00	0.21	0	1.00	1651
Territorial * PMSC	0.43	0.00	0.50	0	1.00	1651
EEZ * PMSC	0.67	1.00	0.47	0	1.00	1651
Priv. Security * Terr. Waters	0.01	0.00	0.10	0	1.00	1651
Priv. Security * EEZ Waters	0.03	0.00	0.18	0	1.00	1651
Vessel Moving	0.44	0.00	0.50	0	1.00	1595
Arabian Sea	0.03	0.00	0.18	0	1.00	1267
China Sea	0.36	0.00	0.48	0	1.00	1267
East Africa	0.23	0.00	0.42	0	1.00	1267
Indian Ocean	0.13	0.00	0.34	0	1.00	1267
Malacca Straits	0.08	0.00	0.27	0	1.00	1267
West Africa	0.16	0.00	0.37	0	1.00	1267

Note: Table shows summary statistics for variables used in the analyses. Data comes from Open Humanities Data, the Maritime Piracy Event Location Dataset, and the International Maritime Organization. See Sect. 3 for additional details. See Table 6 to see disaggregation by whether the vessel is moving

The vessels are an average of 37.6 nautical miles away from the shore, but the median attack occurs 6.34 nautical miles from shore. We also describe the waterways where attacks occur in a couple of ways. First, we note that attacks occur within territorial waters 62% of the time and within at least 1 EEZ 94% of the time. Second, we examine the geographic location of the attack, noting that the majority of the attacks in our data set occur in the China Sea (36%), East Africa (23%), the Indian Ocean (13%) and West Africa (16%).

We also examine the presence of private security onboard a vessel. We measure private security in two ways. First, we identify whether the country where the ship is registered (Flag) permits private security (PMSC). Second, we create a regular expression extraction from the description of the attack that identifies whether private security is described as being onboard the vessel. These two measures of private security indicate that 70% of attacked vessels permit private security, but only 4% of these attacks describe having private security onboard. As shown in Table 6, nearly all attacks where private security was on board occurred on a moving vessel.

Finally, we examine the overlap of our two measures of private security with territorial waterways and EEZ's. Approximately 43% of attacked vessels occur within territorial waterways against a vessel where private security is permitted, and 67% occur against vessels in an EEZ when private security is permitted. Alternatively, private security is onboard the attacked vessel in territorial waterways and EEZ's 1% and 3%, respectively.

4 Method

Our goal is to estimate whether the effectiveness of private security depends on the presence of public security. Within our data, there are attacks on vessels that allow private security, attacks on vessels that are within territorial waters where public security is most intense, and there are attacks on vessels with both public and private security. So, to identify the effect of private and public security, we employ the following baseline model:

$$y_a = \beta_1 \, Pr \, ivate \, Legal_c + \delta \, Territorial_a + \tau \, P^*T_{ca} + \rho_y + \eta_m + \mu_s + u_a, \qquad (1)$$

where a stands for attack and c stands for flag country that the boat is registered. The outcomes, y_a, include whether an attempted attack lead to a boarding or a hijacking. In some specifications we substitute $Private \, Legal_c$ with $Private \, On \, Board_a$.

We also include fixed effects that control for unobserved variation in piracy and security over time. Both piracy and security have tended to trend upwards over the length of the sample, which is accounted for by a vector of year fixed effects, ρ_y. Furthermore, weather patterns, which differ by month and affect the likelihood of boarding and attack, are accounted for using a vector of month fixed effects, η_m. In some specifications, the year and month fixed effects are interacted, but this tends to have no effect on our point estimates. Finally, piracy may have regional differences, so body of water fixed effects, μ_s, accounts for these differences.

The three coefficients, β, δ, and τ, are of interest. The effect of private security is represented by β, the effect of public security is represented by δ, and how they interact is represented by τ. The comparison group consists of vessels that are attacked beyond territorial waters which do not have private security.[7]

Before discussing our results, a few items are worth noting. First, there might be a concern that pirates are able to, ex ante, identify whether a vessel contains private security. For example, maritime vessels must register with a country and display that country's flag on their vessel. Some countries permit private security onboard a vessel (e.g. USA, Norway, Hong Kong, India), while others do not (e.g., France, Greece, Germany, Japan, UK).[8] Thus, the country that a vessel owner registers their boat with and the corresponding flag could bias our results. However, in 25% of vessels that are registered in countries that do not permit private security, we observe

---

[7] When examining the statistical significance of these coefficients we employ standard errors that are robust to heteroskedasticity and some forms of mis-specification.

[8] There are also neutral countries where private security is not recommended nor prohibited (e.g. Panama, Liberia, Marshall Islands, and Denmark).

private security onboard the attacked vessels. Therefore, the flag flown on a vessel is likely not predictive of whether the vessel is utilizing private security.

Second, one of the intents of the empirical modeling in this analysis is to identify the effect of private security being legal onboard a vessel separately from private security actually being onboard an attacked vessel. These results are specifically discussed in Tables 3 and 4.

Third, the motivation of this paper is not to examine whether private security deters contemporaneous or future pirate attacks. Indeed, this analysis has already been conducted in DeAngelo and Smith (2020). Instead, the aim of this analysis is to examine how private security being legal, private security being present, and the amount of public security (as measured by naval presence) impacts safety on the waterways.

5 Results

We first estimate the effect of the legality of private security and its interaction with public security. As shown in Table 3, the legality of private security has the expected negative sign on the likelihood of boarding across all sets of fixed effects. Furthermore, the effect of private security also becomes statistically significant in column 6, when anchored boats are excluded.[9] Private security reduces the likelihood of unanchored boats being boarded by 12 percentage points (pp).

The estimate on private security stands in contrast to the effect of public security, which has a positive effect on the likelihood of a vessel being boarded. This is most likely due to the limited range of pirate attacks, as many occur near the shore due to limited pirate naval technology. This effect is statistically significant and relatively large across all sets of fixed effects and samples, being associated with an 18 pp increase in the likelihood of an unanchored vessel being boarded.

Our interest is in the interaction term, which estimates the effect of being in territorial waters where public security is likely to operate and having the legal option of onboard private security. The estimated interaction is not statistically distinguishable from zero at conventional levels and is typically close to zero, with estimates ranging from 3 to 6 pp. This could be due to the legality of private security only weakly translating into actual on-board private security.

As shown in Panel B of Table 3, the legality of private security has no effect on the likelihood of a vessel being hijacked. However, where public security was ineffective at reducing the likelihood of boarding, it is effective for reducing the likelihood of boats being hijacked. Across all sets of fixed effects, public security reduces the likelihood of hijacking by 6–8 pp which is statistically significant. This effect, however, is only for boats that are anchored, since dropping anchored boats

---

[9] We exclude anchored boats since some boats that are in port are boarded and robbed, which are included in the IMO database. Therefore we omit these instances from our data to focus on the main mechanism of interest, which is vessels that are traversing waterways and not anchored boats.

Table 3 The effects of legal private security, public security, and both on boarding and hijacking

	(1)	(2)	(3)	(4)	(5)	(6)	(7)
Panel A: Boarded							
Flag Allows PMSC	−0.06	−0.06	−0.06	−0.07	−0.07	−0.12**	−0.12
	(0.04)	(0.04)	(0.04)	(0.04)	(0.05)	(0.05)	(0.11)
Within Territorial Waters (12 nm)	0.39***	0.36***	0.36***	0.35***	0.22***	0.18**	0.17*
	(0.04)	(0.04)	(0.04)	(0.05)	(0.05)	(0.08)	(0.09)
Territorial * PMSC	0.04	0.03	0.03	0.06	0.06	0.03	0.03
	(0.05)	(0.05)	(0.05)	(0.05)	(0.06)	(0.10)	(0.10)
Within EEZ Waters (200 nm)							0.04
							(0.10)
EEZ * PMSC							−0.00
							(0.13)
Observations	1651	1651	1651	1651	1267	707	707
Year FEs	–	X	X	–	–	–	–
Month FEs	–	–	X	–	–	–	–
YearXMonth FEs	–	–	–	X	X	X	X
Body of Water FEs	–	–	–	–	X	–	–
Boats Not Anchored	–	–	–	–	–	X	X
Panel B: Hijacked							
Flag Allows PMSC	0.00	0.01	0.01	−0.00	0.01	−0.01	−0.02
	(0.03)	(0.03)	(0.03)	(0.03)	(0.03)	(0.04)	(0.08)
Within Territorial Waters (12 nm)	−0.07***	−0.06**	−0.07***	−0.08***	−0.06*	−0.02	−0.01
	(0.03)	(0.03)	(0.03)	(0.03)	(0.03)	(0.06)	(0.06)
Territorial * PMSC	−0.01	−0.01	−0.01	0.01	0.01	0.03	0.02
	(0.03)	(0.03)	(0.03)	(0.03)	(0.04)	(0.06)	(0.07)
Within EEZ Waters (200 nm)							−0.04
							(0.07)
EEZ * PMSC							0.02
							(0.09)
Observations	1651	1651	1651	1651	1267	707	707
Year FEs	–	X	X	–	–	–	–
Month FEs	–	–	X	–	–	–	–
YearXMonth FEs	–	–	–	X	X	X	X
Body of Water FEs	–	–	–	–	X	–	–
Boats Not Anchored	–	–	–	–	–	X	X

Note: * $p < 0.1$, ** $p < 0.05$, *** $p < 0.01$. Standard errors are in parentheses and are robust to heteroskedasticity. All columns are estimated by the linear probability model described in Eq. 1. In Panel A, the dependent variable is a binary variable that equals 1 if the ship is boarded by pirates. In Panel B, the dependent variable is a binary variable that equals 1 if the ship is hijacked by pirates. Flag Allows PMSC is a binary variable that equals 1 if the country that a boat is registered in allows private maritime security. Within Territorial Waters is a binary variable that equals 1 if the location of the attack is within the territorial waters of a country. Within EEZ Waters is a binary variable that equals 1 if the location of the attack is within the exclusive economic zone of a country. Territorial waters is anywhere within 12 nautical miles of the coastline of a country and the

(continued)

Table 3 (continued)

EEZ extends 200 nautical miles from the coast, as defined by the U.N. Convention on the Law of the Sea (UNCLOS). These distance cutoffs are measures of public security, since countries have incentives to keep their territorial waters safe for economic activity such as fishing and resource extraction. Body of water fixed effects include the following bodies of water: Arabian Sea, China Sea, East Africa, Indian Ocean, Malacca Straits, and West Africa. This information is missing for some vessels. Boats not anchored refers to whether a boat is anchored or not at the time of an attack, only unanchored boats are used in columns 6 and 7. See Sect. 3 for additional data details and Sect. 4 for additional estimation details

Table 4 The effects of on-board private security, public security, and both on boarding and hijacking

	(1)	(2)	(3)	(4)	(5)	(6)	(7)
Panel A: Boarded							
Private Security On Board	−0.39***	−0.40***	−0.39***	−0.35***	−0.20***	−0.24***	−0.20*
	(0.03)	(0.04)	(0.04)	(0.05)	(0.05)	(0.06)	(0.12)
Within Territorial Waters (12 nm)	0.40***	0.37***	0.37***	0.37***	0.28***	0.23***	0.23***
	(0.02)	(0.02)	(0.02)	(0.03)	(0.03)	(0.05)	(0.05)
Priv. Security * Terr. Waters	−0.43***	−0.41***	−0.41***	−0.41***	−0.35***	−0.31***	−0.29***
	(0.03)	(0.04)	(0.04)	(0.07)	(0.08)	(0.09)	(0.09)
Within EEZ Waters (200 nm)							0.01
							(0.07)
Priv. Security * EEZ Waters							−0.06
							(0.12)
Observations	1651	1651	1651	1651	1267	707	707
Year FEs	–	X	X	–	–	–	–
Month FEs	–	–	X	–	–	–	–
YearXMonth FEs	–	–	–	X	X	X	X
Body of Water FEs	–	–	–	–	X	–	–
Boats Not Anchored	–	–	–	–	–	X	X
Panel B: Hijacked							
Private Security On Board	−0.12***	−0.12***	−0.13***	−0.11***	−0.16***	−0.06**	−0.10**
	(0.01)	(0.02)	(0.02)	(0.02)	(0.03)	(0.03)	(0.05)
Within Territorial Waters (12 nm)	−0.08***	−0.08***	−0.08***	−0.08***	−0.05**	0.00	0.01
	(0.01)	(0.02)	(0.02)	(0.02)	(0.02)	(0.04)	(0.04)
Priv. Security * Terr. Waters	0.08***	0.08***	0.08***	0.05	0.01	−0.01	−0.02
	(0.01)	(0.02)	(0.02)	(0.03)	(0.04)	(0.05)	(0.05)
Within EEZ Waters (200 nm)							−0.04
							(0.05)
Priv. Security * EEZ Waters							0.05
							(0.05)
Observations	1651	1651	1651	1651	1267	707	707

(continued)

Table 4 (continued)

	(1)	(2)	(3)	(4)	(5)	(6)	(7)
Year FEs	–	X	X	–	–	–	–
Month FEs	–	–	X	–	–	–	–
YearXMonth FEs	–	–	–	X	X	X	X
Body of Water FEs	–	–	–	–	X	–	–
Boats Not Anchored	–	–	–	–	–	X	X

Note: * p < 0.1, ** p < 0.05, *** p < 0.01. Standard errors are in parentheses and are robust to heteroskedasticity. All columns are estimated by the linear probability model described in Eq. 1. In Panel A, the dependent variable is a binary variable that equals 1 if the ship is boarded by pirates. In Panel B, the dependent variable is a binary variable that equals 1 if the ship is hijacked by pirates. Private security is a binary variable that equals 1 if the boat has private maritime security. Within Territorial Waters is a binary variable that equals 1 if the location of the attack is within the territorial waters of a country. Within EEZ Waters is a binary variable that equals 1 if the location of the attack is within the exclusive economic zone of a country. Territorial waters is anywhere within 12 nautical miles of the coastline of a country and the EEZ extends 200 nautical miles from the coast, as defined by the U.N. Convention on the Law of the Sea (UNCLOS). These distance cutoffs are measures of public security, since countries have incentives to keep their territorial waters safe for economic activity such as fishing and resource extraction. Body of water fixed effects include the following bodies of water: Arabian Sea, China Sea, East Africa, Indian Ocean, Malacca Straits, and West Africa. This information is missing for some vessels. Boats not anchored refers to whether a boat is anchored or not at the time of an attack, only unanchored boats are used in columns 6 and 7. See Sect. 3 for additional data details and Sect. 4 for additional estimation details

(columns 6 and 7) reduce the effects of public security to nearly zero and they are statistically insignificant. The interaction term is also economically and statistically insignificant across all fixed effects and samples.

5.1   On-Board Private Security

One main concern with the estimates presented in Table 3 is that the legality of private security only weakly translates into the actual presence of onboard private security. To address this concern, Eq. 1 is estimated with private security onboard as the measure of private security.[10] As shown in Table 4, the coefficient on private security is larger compared to merely measuring the legality of private security for boarding, ranging from 6–12 pp in Table 3 to 20–40 pp in Table 4. Furthermore, this effect is statistically significant across all sets of fixed effects. Thus, measuring private security by the actual presence of onboard security addresses concerns with the legality variable.

---

[10] This means that the estimate is no longer just the policy, but the effect of the presence of private security.

The interaction between private and public security is also negative and statistically significant across all sets of fixed effects. This suggests that public security complements the effect of private security, amplifying its effectiveness. Focusing on column 5, when public security is also present, the effect of private security is 35 pp stronger, causing even larger reductions in the likelihood of boarding. This also applies purely to boats that are not anchored, where public security increases the effectiveness of private security by 29 pp.

As shown by Panel B of Table 4, private security onboard also reduces the likelihood of a vessel being hijacked. This effect is statistically significant across all sets of fixed effects and ranges from 6 pp to 16 pp. The interaction term loses statistical significance in more saturated models. It does have the expected sign for boats that are not anchored, although that too is not statistically significant.

5.2 Heterogeneous Moderation Effects of Public Security

A possible issue so far is that not all public security is equally effective at foiling the efforts of pirates. This could result in biased estimates of the effectiveness of public security and its moderating effects. To address this threat of bias, we produce results using country-level military spending from SIPRI as a proxy for the intensity of public security.

As shown in Panel A of Table 5, the independent effect of public security on boarding does not depend on military spending. In column 1 we find that attacks occurring near countries in the lowest 2 terciles of military spending are included.[11] The effect of being in territorial waters is to increase the likelihood of being boarded by 24 pp. In column 2 we only include attacks that occurred near countries in the top tercile of spending, and find that public security increases boarding by 21 pp.

While higher public security spending does not reduce the likelihood of boarding alone, it does matter for how public security amplifies the effectiveness of private security. In column 1, lower-intensity public security makes private security 21 pp more effective. In column 2, high-intensity public security makes private security 60 pp more effective, which is 3 times as large an effect as lower-intensity public security. Thus, the interaction effect of private and public security is much larger (more negative) in regions where greater public security spending exists.

The moderating effects of public security on hijacking are less clear. There is some suggestive evidence that high-intensity public security is more effective at reducing hijacking by 7 pp. The low-intensity public security has the same magnitude, but it is not statistically significant at conventional levels. This could be due to small differences in sample size. Neither interaction term is statistically significant,

---

[11] It is important to note that this is not the universe of countries. It is the top tercile of countries where an attack occurred off that country's coast. For example, no landlocked countries are counted.

Table 5 The effects of onboard private security and public security by military spending and patrol boats terciles

	Military	Spending	Patrol Boats / Coast	
	(1)	(2)	(3)	(4)
Panel A: Boarded				
Private Security On Board	−0.17***	−0.31***	−0.25***	0.05
	(0.05)	(0.10)	(0.04)	(0.28)
Within Territorial Waters (12 nm)	0.28***	0.24***	0.23***	0.34***
	(0.05)	(0.04)	(0.03)	(0.08)
Priv. Security * Terr. Waters	−0.23***	−0.56***	−0.23***	−0.77**
	(0.07)	(0.12)	(0.05)	(0.30)
Observations	503	764	1055	212
Top Tercile of Military Expenditure	–	X	–	X
Top Tercile of Patrol Boats Per Coastline				
Panel B: Hijacked				
Private Security On Board	−0.18***	−0.17***	−0.17***	−0.13
	(0.03)	(0.05)	(0.03)	(0.08)
Within Territorial Waters (12 nm)	−0.05	−0.05**	−0.05**	−0.05
	(0.04)	(0.02)	(0.02)	(0.04)
Priv. Security * Terr. Waters	0.07	0.12	0.04*	−0.00
	(0.05)	(0.07)	(0.02)	(0.09)
Observations	503	764	1055	212
Top Tercile of Military Expenditure	–	X	–	X
Top Tercile of Patrol Boats Per Coastline				

Note: * $p < 0.1$, ** $p < 0.05$, *** $p < 0.01$. Standard errors are in parentheses and are robust to heteroskedasticity. All columns are estimated by the linear probability model described in Eq. 1. All columns include year, month, and body of water fixed effects. In Panel A, the dependent variable is a binary variable that equals 1 if the ship is boarded by pirates. In Panel B, the dependent variable is a binary variable that equals 1 if the ship is hijacked by pirates. Flag Allows PMSC is a binary variable that equals 1 if the country that a boat is registered in allows private maritime security. Within Territorial Waters is a binary variable that equals 1 if the location of the attack is within the territorial waters of a country. Within EEZ Waters is a binary variable that equals 1 if the location of the attack is within the exclusive economic zone of a country. Territorial waters is anywhere within 12 nautical miles of the coastline of a country and the EEZ extends 200 nautical miles from the coast, as defined by the U.N. Convention on the Law of the Sea (UNCLOS). These distance cutoffs are measures of public security, since countries have incentives to keep their territorial waters safe for economic activity such as fishing and resource extraction. Body of water fixed effects include the following bodies of water: Arabian Sea, China Sea, East Africa, Indian Ocean, Malacca Straits, and West Africa. This information is missing for some vessels. Boats not anchored refers to whether a boat is anchored or not at the time of an attack, only unanchored boats are used in columns 6 and 7. See Sect. 3 for additional data details and Sect. 4 for additional estimation details

suggesting public security does not amplify the effects of private security for reducing hijacking. Again, this could be due to few attacks ending in hijacking since only 6% of all attacks end with a hijacking.

We are sensitive to the concerns that military expenditure does not capture all aspects of near-shore public security. To address this, we present results in columns 3 and 4 that split the sample into the top and non-top terciles of patrol boats per coastline. As can be seen, the results are qualitatively similar when using this alternative measure of the intensity of public security.

A possible interpretation of these results are that higher spending on/intensity of public security and private security have different capabilities that are complementary. The first 2 rows of Table 1 show that private security is advantagous for responding to piracy, because it is always present and therefore able to respond to attacks. Nevertheless, as shown by the last 3 rows of Table 1, sometimes pirates do not immediately give up upon spotting private security. In these cases, higher-spending public security is able to provide air support and other higher-end capabilities that cause pirates to give up. While we are unable to rule out other interpretations, we can provide case-level knowledge that supports this one.

6 Discussion

Maintaining the safety of territorial and international waterways is critical for personal safety as well as economic well-being, as the global economy depends critically on shipping logistics. To ensure the safety of the waterways numerous countries and agencies have worked together to deploy naval forces in an effort to deter piracy. The difficulty of relying on navies, alone, to deter piracy-related activities is that navies are reactive to pirate attacks, which could produce a general deterrence effect. However, naval ships are unlikely to produce specific deterrence since waterways are vast and navies can only monitor a small fraction of the waterways.

In response to growing safety concerns, commercial and private vessels began utilizing private security when traversing treacherous waterways that have experienced pirate attacks. While private security is almost certainly deployed for personal safety, DeAngelo and Smith (2020) establish that private security also produces public safety by reducing overall pirate attacks. We build on this work to examine whether private security, in conjunction with expenditures on public safety (navies), further enhances the safety of the waterways.

To explore the separate and combined effect of public and private security on waterway safety we explore two measures of private security. The first is an intentto-treat measure of private security, which identifies whether an attacked vessel is legally permitted to have private security onboard. Our second measure examines the text associated with the attack to determine if private security is mentioned.

While private security being legal onboard a vessel is not associated with reductions in the likelihood that a vessel is boarded or hijacked, actually having private security onboard significantly reduces the likelihood that a vessel is either boarded or hijacked.

We also examine whether the effectiveness of private security is impacted by the level of military expenditures. We find that private security in conjunction with increased military expenditures significantly reduces the likelihood that a ship is boarded, but not hijacked. This result is likely because vessels are hijacked so infrequently. These results shed new insights into the effectiveness of private security and the role that public and private security play in reducing pirate-related activities.

Appendix: Additional Tables and Figures (Fig. 1, Table 6)

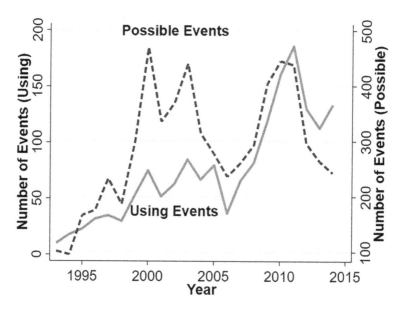

Fig. 1 Trends in possible attacks and using attacks. **Note**: Figure shows the number of pirate attacks by year. The attacks that are used in estimation are shown in the orange, solid line and are on the left y-axis. The total possible number of attacks are shown by the blue, dashed line and are on the right y-axis. They differ in number due to issues merging in the flag country of boats, but follow similar overall trends

Table 6 Summary statistics by vessel moving

	Mean	Median	SD	Min	Max	Count
Panel A: Moving						
Boarded	0.36	0.00	0.48	0	1.00	707
Hijacked	0.10	0.00	0.30	0	1.00	707
Distance to Shore (nm)	78.44	31.65	115.00	0	543.47	707
Within Territorial Waters (12 nm)	0.27	0.00	0.45	0	1.00	707
Within EEZ Waters (200 nm)	0.87	1.00	0.34	0	1.00	707
Flag Allows PMSC	0.71	1.00	0.46	0	1.00	707
Private Security On Board	0.10	0.00	0.30	0	1.00	707
Territorial * PMSC	0.18	0.00	0.39	0	1.00	707
EEZ * PMSC	0.62	1.00	0.49	0	1.00	707
Priv. Security * Terr. Waters	0.02	0.00	0.14	0	1.00	707
Priv. Security * EEZ Waters	0.08	0.00	0.27	0	1.00	707
Arabian Sea	0.07	0.00	0.25	0	1.00	601
China Sea	0.21	0.00	0.41	0	1.00	601
East Africa	0.46	0.00	0.50	0	1.00	601
Indian Ocean	0.08	0.00	0.27	0	1.00	601
Malacca Straits	0.09	0.00	0.28	0	1.00	601
West Africa	0.09	0.00	0.29	0	1.00	601
Panel B: Still						
Boarded	0.87	1.00	0.33	0	1.00	888
Hijacked	0.02	0.00	0.15	0	1.00	888
Distance to Shore (nm)	6.41	2.73	13.83	0	183.37	888
Within Territorial Waters (12 nm)	0.90	1.00	0.30	0	1.00	888
Within EEZ Waters (200 nm)	1.00	1.00	0.00	1	1.00	888
Flag Allows PMSC	0.70	1.00	0.46	0	1.00	888
Private Security On Board	0.00	0.00	0.05	0	1.00	888
Territorial * PMSC	0.62	1.00	0.48	0	1.00	888
EEZ * PMSC	0.70	1.00	0.46	0	1.00	888
Priv. Security * Terr. Waters	0.00	0.00	0.05	0	1.00	888
Priv. Security * EEZ Waters	0.00	0.00	0.05	0	1.00	888
Arabian Sea	0.00	0.00	0.07	0	1.00	649
China Sea	0.50	0.00	0.50	0	1.00	649
East Africa	0.02	0.00	0.15	0	1.00	649
Indian Ocean	0.18	0.00	0.39	0	1.00	649
Malacca Straits	0.07	0.00	0.26	0	1.00	649
West Africa	0.22	0.00	0.41	0	1.00	649

Note: Table shows summary statistics for variables used in the analyses. Data comes from Open Humanities Data, the Maritime Piracy Event Location Dataset, and the International Maritime Organization. See Sect. 3 for additional details

The Empirical Relationship Between Patrol Vessels (Public Maritime Security) and Military Expenditure (Figs. 2 and 3)

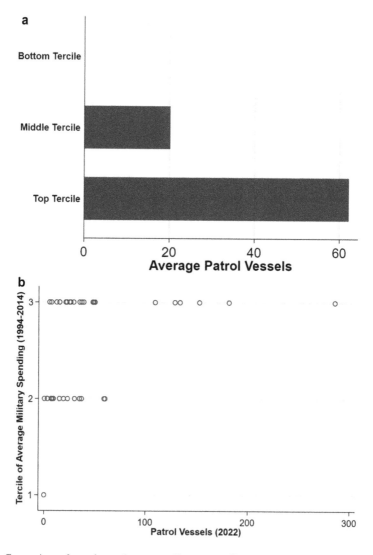

Fig. 2 Comparison of patrol vessels across military expenditure terciles. **Note**: (**a**) shows average patrol vessels (2022) by terciles of average yearly military spending (1994–2014). (**b**) shows the number of patrol vessels of each country, by terciles of average yearly military spending

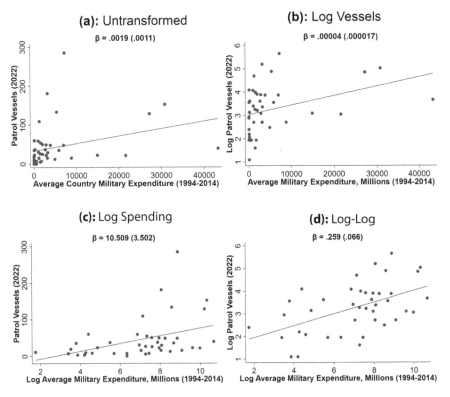

Fig. 3 Scatterplots of military spending and naval patrol vessels inventory by country. **Note**: Scatterplots show the correlation between average military spending (1994–2014), on the x-axis, and patrol vessels (2022) on the y-axis. (**a**) shows untransformed variables. (**b**) shows log vessels on spending. (**c**) shows vessels on log spending. (**d**) shows log boats on log spending. All figures include a linear line of best fit

References

Abadie, A. (2006). Poverty, political freedom, and the roots of terrorism. *American Economic Review, 96*(2), 50–56.

Angrist, J. D. (1995). The economic returns to schooling in the West Bank and Gaza Strip. *The American Economic Review, 85*, 1065–1087.

Bergstrom, T., & Goodman, R. P. (1973). Private demands for public goods. *The American Economic Review, 63*(3), 280–296.

Campos, N. F., & Gassebner, M. (2009). International terrorism, political instability and the escalation effect. IZA Discussion Paper.

Company, N. B. (2011). *As pirate attacks grow, shipowners take arms*. https:// www.nbcnews.com/ id/wbna42883467. Accessed: Apr 2022.

Daxecker, U., & Prins, B. C. (2015). Searching for sanctuary: Government power and the location of maritime piracy. *International Interactions, 41*(4), 699–717.

Daxecker, U., & Prins, B. C. (2017a). Enforcing order: Territorial reach and maritime piracy. *Conflict Management and Peace Science, 34*(4), 359–379.

Daxecker, U., & Prins, B. C. (2017b). Financing rebellion: Using piracy to explain and predict conflict intensity in Africa and Southeast Asia. *Journal of Peace Research, 54*(2), 215–230.

Daxecker, U., & Prins, B. (2021). *Pirate lands: Governance and maritime piracy.* Oxford University Press.

DeAngelo, G., & Smith, T. (2020). Private security, maritime piracy and the provision of international public safety. *Journal of Risk & Uncertainty, 60*, 77–97.

Graff, C. (2010). Poverty, development, and violent extremism in weak states. In *Confronting poverty: Weak states and US national security* (pp. 42–89). Brookings Institution Press.

Khashan, H. (2003). Collective Palestinian frustration and suicide bombings. *Third World Quarterly, 24*(6), 1049–1067.

Krueger, A. B., & Laitin, D. D. (2008). Kto kogo?: A cross-country study of the origins and targets of terrorism. *Terrorism, Economic Development, and Political Openness, 5*, 148–173.

Lamb, R. D. (2008). *Ungoverned areas and threats from safe havens* (Tech. Rep.). Office of the Deputy Assistant Secretary of Defense for Policy Planning.

Nicholson-Crotty, S., O'Toole, J., & Laurence J. (2004, January). Public management and organizational performance: The case of law enforcement agencies. *Journal of Public Administration Research and Theory, 14*(1), 1–18. https://doi.org/10.1093/jopart/muh001.

Piazza, J. A. (2006). Rooted in poverty?: Terrorism, poor economic development, and social cleavages. *Terrorism and Political Violence, 18*(1), 159–177.

Piazza, J. A. (2008). Incubators of terror: Do failed and failing states promote transnational terrorism? *International Studies Quarterly, 52*(3), 469–488.

Prins, B. (2014). *What drives maritime piracy in sub-saharan Africa?* http://piracy-studies.org/what-drives-maritime-piracy-in-sub-saharan-africa/

Renauer, B. C., Duffee, D. E., & Scott, J. D. (2003). Measuring police-community co-production: Trade-offs in two observational approaches. *Policing: An International Journal of Police Strategies & Management, 26*(1), 9–28.

Sullivan, J. P., & Bunker, R. J. (2002). Drug cartels, street gangs, and warlords. *Small Wars and Insurgencies, 13*(2), 40–53.

Tolman, R. M., & Weisz, A. (1995). Coordinated community intervention for domestic violence: The effects of arrest and prosecution on recidivism of woman abuse perpetrators. *Crime & Delinquency, 41*(4), 481–495.

Weitzer, R., Tuch, S. A., & Skogan, W. G. (2008). Police–Community relations in a majority-black city. *Journal of Research in Crime and Delinquency, 45*(4), 398–428.

Zhao, J., Scheider, M. C., & Thurman, Q. (2002). Funding community policing to reduce crime: Have cops grants made a difference? *Criminology & Public Policy, 2*(1), 7–32.

Part IV
Police and Private Security Perspectives

What We've Learned: Lessons from the World's Leading Security Companies on Partnerships and Privatization

Garett Seivold

Abstract Faced with growing protection needs, competing priorities, and limited resources, many governments and municipalities around the world leverage private security resources to enhance public safety. One option is to outsource tasks traditionally performed by the public police through privatization of select functions. Another is to engage in partnerships that include police and private security service providers among the participants. Both types of arrangement often result in greater safety at lower cost—but not always. This chapter details cumulative lessons learned and shared experiences from member companies of the International Security Ligue, including what the world's leading private security firms have identified as critical features of success in the privatization of public security and in public-private security partnerships.

There is a long history of governments partnering with the private security industry, and the evolving threat environment suggests that such collaborations could be even more critical in the years ahead. Information sharing, cross-training, lending of expertise, and technological support are all expected to be needed to meet future security challenges. Security firms are meeting this challenge by increasing proficiencies, investing in technology, and widening areas of expertise, and government and business customers are leveraging them to improve efficiency, enhance services, and for tangible and substantial financial gain. Through its investments and enhanced professionalism, the private security industry has positioned itself as an alternative to stretched police forces and capable of providing functions that have traditionally been the domain of law enforcement and to be more valuable security partners. Indeed, while traditional interest in leveraging private security tended to be for rudimentary functions, such as alarm response, there is now a desire to utilize the specialized skills, knowledge, and technology that have been central features of the private security industry's evolution.

G. Seivold (✉)
International Security Ligue, Zollikofen, Switzerland
e-mail: Garett.seivold@security-ligue.org

© The Author(s), under exclusive license to Springer Nature Switzerland AG 2023   321
E. A. Blackstone et al. (eds.), *Handbook on Public and Private Security*,
Competitive Government: Public Private Partnerships,
https://doi.org/10.1007/978-3-031-42406-9_15

Success of public-private partnerships or outsourcing security arrangements is not guaranteed, however. The experience of the leading security firms of the world indicate the importance of several key factors: Leadership from individuals with security expertise, rather than allowing administrators direct deployment of security resources; a regulatory regime that is sufficient to prevent bad actors from participating in the industry and purposefully aims to enhance public trust in the professionalism of security officers; planning to ensure flexibility in security arrangements to assure public safety during natural or human-caused crises; greater public investment in the study and understanding of private security to drive a fuller understanding of the jobs they do and improve design of partnerships; clarity on the role and responsibilities of public police to allow municipalities to identify how they can most effectively leverage private sector partnerships; application of sustainability principles to security arrangements; focusing on quality, experience, and expertise, rather than using cost to drive selection of private security partners; detailed due diligence investigations of prospective private sector security partners; evaluation of security firm training programs and safety records; comprehensive service level agreements to clarify expectations, measure performance, and drive continuous improvement; and oversight of security arrangements to get early indicators of problems.

1 Introduction

Founded in 1934, the International Security Ligue is a global network dedicated to advancing professionalism within the private security services industry. Every day, more than one million employees from its 28-member companies engage in protection activities around the world.

Many of these are of the type that may generally come to mind: patrolling a university campus, controlling access to an office building, and monitoring deliveries at a warehouse. They are frequently in public spaces as well, maintaining societal order in shopping malls, entertainment venues, and sports stadiums; ensuring security at airports, train stations, and other transportation centers; and providing services in leisure centers, at beachfronts, and in mountain resorts.

The Ligue has been and continues to be a driving force for enhanced professionalism in private security. It recognizes that increased responsibility demands enhanced investment, in both training of personnel and investment in technology. As the world leans more heavily on the expertise of private security professionals, the industry must live up to the enhanced trust that society places in it.

Responsible regulation of the industry is an important part of ensuring that private security firms can meet the growing needs of society for its services. It also requires public institutions and municipalities to approach private security services with the goal of leveraging expertise to enhance public safety, rather than simply as a strategy to save money or shift responsibility.

Additionally, it is important for society to acknowledge and appreciate the substantial resources that are required of private security firms for them to deliver effective security in more complicated and technologically advanced environments. Security firms are meeting this challenge by increasing proficiencies, investing in technology, and widening areas of expertise—and these expenditures must be willingly shouldered by all who rely on them.

Globally, most joint arrangements occur on a local level and in the absence of defined frameworks, which increases the need to consult best practices extracted from successful partnerships, as well as to heed the lessons from arrangements that failed to meet their objectives. The lessons shared in this chapter, from the world's leading security firms, aim to improve public-private security arrangements so that societies may maximally benefit from the utilization of private security.

2   Evolving Relationships

The clear division of responsibility that societies have traditionally operated under—companies hire security firms to protect their properties and assets while police protect public areas—has dissolved over time. Advancing in its place has been a shared security model, one that relies more heavily on the presence of private security forces in public spaces and leverages private security resources for public good.

Although police in some countries have resisted the idea in principle, it has also become clear that some concerns have been misguided. The move to incorporate private security forces for public benefit is not about taking jobs away from the police, but rather freeing sworn officers to perform tasks that match their specific training. Over time, law enforcement administrators have come to see privatization and partnerships with private security as an operational solution to release sworn personnel from functions that others can do.

Most early Law Enforcement-Private Security (LE-PS) partnerships were established by law enforcement—or by law enforcement and private security together—and then led by law enforcement, which would typically provide information targeted to the partnership's members. It was typically uncommon for partnerships to be led by private security, but that has gradually changed. Today, many LE-PS partnerships are the idea of private entities which, with the support of their private security partners, form partnership organizations and then ask law enforcement to join. Such partnerships are typically funded and administered solely by private entities, and law enforcement serves as one member among many.

There are no good global data on what type of partnerships are most common, but the experience of Ligue-member companies suggest that public-private partnerships take myriad forms. Any security challenge is potentially better addressed through the coordination of multiple stakeholders and the range of activities in LE-PS partnerships has broadened over the years. Some LE-PS partnerships originate as a means to improve relationships, build awareness, or jointly address a specific problem, and then evolve and expand over time, increasing their value to participants and the public. A small relationship-building exercise, for example, can evolve over time to involve many activities, including dissemination of crime information, the provision of specialized training for private security officers on such topics as protecting crime scenes, and joint emergency response planning.

Globally, there are many types of LE-PS partnerships, in which information sharing is a predominant feature. Terrorism threats, crime trends, and information on financial crimes are among the types of information now flowing more freely between LE and PS through partnerships. Technical expertise is another item that is frequently shared, such as education by private security firms to law enforcement on unique safety and security procedures associated with different private sector critical infrastructure. Private security operations also extend resources to public law enforcement, including the donation or loaning of equipment to support crime prevention, enhance law enforcement field operations, bolster investigative capabilities, or support other mutual goals.

Below are a few examples of resources that private security firms commonly extend to police to support public safety through today's partnerships:

- Offering the services of their forensic laboratories (used to enhance video) to law enforcement agencies, especially those that lack advanced forensic labs of their own.
- Lending generators and other equipment to assist in emergencies.
- Donating video equipment, cell phones, and computers.
- Donating logistical support (food, meeting space, and so on) for partnership meetings and training events.

One common source of partnership involves providing access to images from private-sector surveillance systems for use in police investigations. It is common for major cities to conjoin public and private security cameras to form a widespread camera network and create security operations centers staffed by both police and private security personnel. Two-way video sharing with public law enforcement allows law enforcement to access a private facility's security video in an emergency or for investigation, and private security forces can receive relevant feeds from public CCTV.

Such efforts have grown more popular over the years because of the effectiveness of such systems in deterring crime and identifying suspects. It has helped to spur city ordinances that require certain types of businesses to have surveillance video, which may then feed into citywide systems to make them an even more effective crime fighting tool.

There are countless examples from around the world where cities have initiated joint projects to cut crime, relying heavily on private security officers and on security technology owned and operated by private companies to do so. Because such projects coordinate the efforts of private security and police, the extent to which it is successful directly impacts the threat environment.

Partnerships have also been popular with private sector businesses for this very reason, as this model can give them greater influence on the provision of security services in the public domain and foster cohesive business districts that improve the business climate. Private security's expansion into public spaces often grows out of the public-private partnerships that exist in business improvement districts (BID) and afford businesses greater opportunity to shape community safety. Private companies want to create better business conditions, and private-public security partnerships provide them an opportunity to do so.

Just as LE-PS partnerships have become more common and grown more diverse, public policing worldwide has been undergoing a restructuring over the past several decades. While the exact shape and consequence of changes vary, it has impacted the very structure and delivery of public safety.

The distinguishing features of this evolution are a separation between those who authorize policing from those who do it and the transference of both functions away from government. "Privatization" may not be quite the right word for the transformation because the distinction between public and private domains is often muddy, but a transfer of responsibility is indeed at the heart of the change.

Policing—the activity of making societies safe—is often not carried out by governments. Indeed, it is a legitimate question as to whether governments are even the primary providers of public safety. And this transfer of responsibility is seen worldwide despite differences in wealth and economic systems.

From Sweden to Singapore, the private security industry has taken on a leading role in enhancing public safety. Countries around the world rely heavily on private security to perform duties formerly the domain of the police. Private security officers can increasingly be seen patrolling city centers, local squares, neighborhoods, and large parts of inner-city areas. They are keeping peace inside municipally owned and operated homeless shelters, ensuring security at refugee centers, and managing operations at prisons. They assist with managing refugees and other displaced persons and assist communities in responding to crisis events. In many countries, private security officers now outnumber police officers. Singapore's 270-plus guard companies employ nearly 29,000 personnel, three times that of police officers (Lim & Nalla, 2014).

In many cases, the distinction between police and private security has blurred. For example, in some regions, private security companies are granted police powers by the state. After completing the same basic training as public officers, they have full police powers on the property they are hired to protect.

Around the world, numerous and diverse forces are contributing to this shift of public safety into the hands of private security. One common driver is a lack of availability of public resources to fund community policing, which has allowed law enforcement to have a presence in communities so they can work effectively with the citizenry to meet their specific crime and social disorder challenges. Funds for community policing have been depleted, with more of available monies put toward national security and first responder technology, as opposed to local law enforcement personnel. Communities have often been left wanting as a result, looking for novel solutions to their safety challenges.

Shrinking government and municipal resources for community policing also increasingly leave private businesses to fend for themselves. It can be observed in less aggressive law enforcement response to alarms or to low priority calls for service like a non-violent store thief.

For example, the average response time of police officers to the most serious 999 calls in Greater Manchester, England, has nearly doubled in recent years, according to data compiled by the BBC (BBC News, 2019). Additionally, the time to respond to "grade two" calls has skyrocketed, from around 48 minutes in 2011 to an average of 7.5 hours in 2017–2018.

Similar trends are reflected in data from major metropolitan areas in the US. An investigative report by the *Milwaukee Journal Sentinel* found police response had slowed in 13 of 15 major call categories. When a man armed with a sawed-off shotgun robbed the Split Endz beauty salon, it took 34 minutes for police to arrive on the scene, for example.

Public security investment is eroding in many countries and is expected to decline even further. Ligue members report witnessing declining numbers of fraud detection and investigation units in countries of operations, a trend that began as far back as 2007 when the *Washington Post* observed that federal officials had begun to ask banks to conduct their own probes, including those of identity-theft rings (Goldstein, 2007).

It is not just resources that are lacking. In the UK, for example, a review found law enforcement response to fraud is disjointed and ineffective, an ineffectual use of intelligence products, a lack of clarity around roles and responsibilities, and that some forces seek reasons not to investigate allegations of fraud (Her Majesty's Inspectorate of Constabulary and Fire & Rescue Services, 2019).

Often, the message sent today to private businesses is that if they want to chase down sophisticated crime rings, it is up to them to do the legwork. The consequence of this shift puts the security of organizations—and the safety of the citizens who work in them—in their own hands. It increasingly depends on how much they are willing spend. In this way, some see public police increasingly becoming like many public health systems, in which governments may provide a certain basic level of care but those wanting more need to pay for it themselves.

At the heart of this transformation—what has made it possible—has been a new model of societal security based on the goal of public safety, as opposed to the incentives of crime or urban deterioration. This has allowed the use of alternative, privatized arrangements for public spaces to flourish, along with greater use of technology in the public domain.

The private security industry has helped to accelerate the transformation. While law enforcement, generally, has moved away from a more-cops-on-the-beat model, private security companies have grown more professional and capable to fill the void. They have widened their areas of competence and invested in tools that allow them to provide value in more settings. The industry has positioned itself as an alternative to stretched police forces and enhanced training and skills to be capable of providing functions that have traditionally been the domain of law enforcement.

Indeed, while initial interest in leveraging private security tended to be for rudimentary functions, such as alarm response, there is now a desire to utilize the specialized skills and knowledge that have been central features of the private security industry's evolution.

Technology has helped to catalyze the interest of public entities in private security, as private security companies can now provide value across operations, from business expertise to security system integration, in addition to the traditional human security offering that is increasingly professional and efficient.

Major contract security companies typically possess more state-of-the-art technology for handling today's security challenges than public police agencies, as described in an industry market report by Robert H. Perry & Associates (2020): "Public police forces are, in most cases, operating on limited budgets with outdated equipment," it explains. By comparison, it finds that the world's leading security companies "have been investing heavily in technology that enhances the security service delivery and are greatly expanding these services being offered to the customer."

Technical applications such as analytics and artificial intelligence hold enormous potential to enhance security and crime fighting but are often too significant an investment for private companies or government agencies to make.

The world's leading firms, represented by the International Security Ligue, have been investing heavily in technology to meet the growing need for municipal clients to build resiliency against major crises, and these same technologies are providing value beyond just protection. Government and business customers are leveraging them to improve efficiency, enhance services, and for tangible and substantial financial gain.

A security system integrated with an analytics engine, for example, can provide details about how a facility is being utilized, such as trends in building traffic flow and when different areas are—and are not—being utilized. This knowledge has obvious security value, and security firms can organize protection with these data in mind, but the information can also provide clients the ability to make smarter building management decisions, such as devising optimal cleaning schedules or to improve heating and cooling and lighting system operation. It also permits better personnel management, by indicating the optimal allocation of people or by monitoring their compliance with standards, policies, and procedures. It can even suggest to an organization if it is underutilizing its real estate to the extent that it should consolidate operations and sell a building. Information that—by itself—would provide direct financial benefit that is potentially worth millions.

Here is just one case study: Facing a growing counterfeit drug market, a global pharmaceutical firm knew it needed to increase its intelligence gathering. For less than $500, it's possible to purchase a pill press and a counterfeit pill mold and turn cheap, readily available, unregulated ingredients into a money-making counterfeit operation. From 2014 to 2018, total incidents of counterfeiting increased by 102%, according to a 2020 report from the European Union Intellectual Property Office, Trade in Counterfeit Pharmaceutical Products. Both illicit grey-traded goods and product counterfeiting risked diluting the company brand, raised liability issues, and was potentially ruinous to profits by eroding consumer confidence.

To address the challenge to its business, the company enlisted its security firm's monitoring tool which runs non-stop and harnesses sophisticated algorithms, artificial intelligence, and massive computing power to search both the surface Internet and its dark corners for early indicators of illicit sales, such as a suspicious product formulation or a too-low price point. Analysts investigate potential hits and quietly and discreetly shut down operations; searching out risks before they become problems, rather than waiting for a disgruntled customer to call a hotline to complain about buying a bogus batch of product.

Coupled with improving security technology is growing public acceptance. Fear of crime, attention to terrorism, and personal familiarity with technology have helped to tilt opinion worldwide in favor of security technology, including the extensive use of public surveillance systems in metropolitan areas.

Even opposition to controversial technologies like facial recognition has waned, as people routinely use their face to unlock and securely sign-in to their phones or computers or use face authentication to access mobile applications. A 2018 survey by the Center for Data Innovation, for example, found that only 24% of Americans support strict limits on facial recognition if were to prevent stores from using the technology to stop shoplifting, while 49% said they would oppose limitations if that was the result (Castro & McLaughlin, 2019). And, concerned about fraud in online transactions, 93% of consumers in Brazil say they'd like more sophisticated security in the form of facial recognition, according to Experian's Global Identity and Fraud Report (February 2020).

Broad acceptance of surveillance video and other technology, such as automated license plate readers, as well as the general perception that such tools are valuable in fighting crime and enhancing public safety, is encouraging cities to partner with firms that have advanced technology in their arsenal.

Because public reliance on the private security industry has grown, it is critical to society for LE-PS partnerships to be successful and for municipalities to effectively procure and manage private security contracts.

3   Case Study: Beverly Hills, California (USA)

Currently, the city of Beverly Hills, Calif. (US), provides an example of just how high the stakes are for operating effective public-private partnerships.

With the famous Rodeo Drive as its centerpiece, Beverly Hills, Calif., is a global tourist attraction and shopping destination. Since the pandemic, however, it has become a common occurrence for thieves to follow shoppers from its famous stores and rob them as they walk down neighboring streets. Incidents receive significant attention on mainstream and social media, such as when a man dining outdoors at an Italian restaurant had a gun placed to his head and a $500,000 watch stolen off his wrist.

Smash-and-grab theft has also become problematic in the city. In one 2-month span, high-end retailers—in a town of 30,000 people—were hit six times in such attacks, often caught on security video and replayed on television and online. It became routine to see cars slow to a stop alongside luxury shops in the early morning hours, for crews armed with sledgehammers to hop out, and for the thieves to smash their way through display windows. Disappearing just a few minutes after the assault began, thieves would make off with thousands of dollars' worth of designer clothes or stolen gems worth millions.

This rise in crime was so significant it sparked the Los Angeles Police Department to initiate a task force at the end of 2021 to examine the sudden surge in "follow-home," or "follow-off," robberies in wealthy neighborhoods. "There's no chance or opportunity for these victims even to comply. They're just running up to people and attacking them," said Capt. Jonathan Tippet, who spearheads the task force. "In my 34 years on the job, I've never seen anything like this" (Blasey & Limón, 2022).

The surge in crime put residents in the tony town on edge and caused city officials to fear that the city's reputation as a shopping destination was being tarnished. In response, the city announced the hiring of 12-armed private security guards for the foreseeable future to protect and patrol the city's shopping district and contemplated having private security personnel monitor security feeds from cameras, drones, and license plate readers and utilize artificial intelligence to flag suspicious activity. The city's Police Chief suggested that the addition of private security was an investment in the city's financial future by letting "the world know that Beverly Hills is a very safe community."

Many city residents expressed gratitude for the city's efforts to make security a priority, but there was also some apprehension expressed at council meetings that hinted at the stakes involved. Specifically, the plan to add more video surveillance and rely on automated technologies and private security contractors unnerved some residents who worry about privacy and data being put in the hands of private companies.

Whether Beverly Hills is successful in reducing crime, maintaining its status as a global tourist attraction, and meeting the expectations of residents, will significantly depend on its choice of private security partners, their level of expertise, and their compliance with safeguards being put in place. More broadly, the Beverly Hills case study reflects just how important private security has become—not just for the safety of residents and the viability of commercial districts, but for the lasting reputation of municipalities, impacting everything from real estate prices to whether a city is one in which people want to live and work.

4 Capturing Benefits

Police-Private Security partnerships and reliance on private security to enhance public safety is critical for community safety and to address issues of crime and social disorder. It is also vital for providing citizens with the feeling of safety and security that they need and demand and which has traditionally been derived from public safety and law enforcement.

Although the idea of private security policing public spaces has at times been met with resistance, the advantages to citizens and private entities has typically been sufficient to overcome it. Once citizens and businesses enjoy the benefits of greater security without additional costs to them, complaints typically dissipate.

For example, experience has shown that companies will often enjoy multiple advantages from arrangements that allow for private security to protect public spaces:

- It expands a company's security perimeter beyond its property line or building and farther away from the assets they're trying to protect.
- It can give a company greater influence over how and how much surrounding areas are protected.
- It improves the general safety of areas around company facilities.
- It can result in quicker response to calls for service from police when needed. (Police have discretion over patrols and may scale back alarm response in many areas; areas that also contract with private security to perform these functions often enjoy greater deterrence from patrols and faster police response, as law enforcement has greater trust in the veracity of alarms.)
- It may not require additional spending. This model typically allows groups of businesses to divert a portion of property taxes toward collective security initiatives.
- It creates economies of scale. A business service area that pools resources to contract for patrols and security service can do so more cost-effectively than as a single entity.
- It may prevent a security "arms race." When a business has less imposing visible security than other nearby businesses, it can become a target of criminals, which may cause it to over-fortify their site in a way that is inconsistent with area crime. Other area businesses may then feel pressure to match those security measures, touching off an "arms race" of security investment that is costly to all area businesses and ultimately harms a commercial area more than it does to protect it. When engaged in security partnerships, a business area is more able to correctly align protection with risk.

As police presence fades and technology and private security does more of the heavy lifting, public attitudes can shift. Whether they change for the better or result in a less productive and more fearful society depends on the effectiveness of partnerships and whether the transition of duties to private security is constructive. Experience has shown the substantial contribution that private sector security makes to policing internationally, but public agencies need to take specific steps to maximize its benefit to societies, businesses, and citizens. The following will briefly describe the keys to successful public private partnerships in security based on our experience.

5 Leadership

When a community is confronted with a security challenge or a business group cites crime or security concerns as a problem, a coalition will frequently develop, followed by the concerned group approaching public leaders to say, "here are our problems, these are our concerns," and to ask for help. Such situations are ideal for police-private security partnerships.

For an effective partnership, private sector security representatives—both contract and proprietary personnel, if applicable—will need to act as the liaison between the community and law enforcement. Private sector security leaders need to be the driving force in coordinated policing arrangements because, as subject matter experts, they have the respect of both community and business groups and law enforcement.

Absent private security leadership, it is typically community organizers or business administrators—who lack the respect of law enforcement and possess little knowledge of security—who will ultimately make decisions on how to complement police or fill the void created by their absence. Rarely do such arrangements result in meeting stakeholders' needs or solving their problems.

With private security leadership, however, community and business groups are often able to successfully address their joint security problems, as well as establishing a foundation that they can use to address future challenges. With the leadership of private security personnel, communities and business groups can leverage partnerships to engage more directly with public police, expand their security perimeter, and increase influence over the safety of their operations.

6 Regulation

It is in every municipality's best interest to investigate potential collaboration between public law enforcement and private security to assess if it might improve public security, aid in combating and investigating crimes, help manage fluctuations in the need for police services, and strengthen preparation for critical incidents. Given the significant expertise of leading private security firms and the advanced technology they can bring to a partnership, there is a potential for significant enhancement to public safety.

The use of private security services for policing does carry risk, however. Specifically, because it is not always the case that regulatory standards for private security firms are sufficient to ensure a quality provision of services. A lack of uniform laws or standards governing the global security guard industry has resulted in significant disparity in the level of service that companies provide, and the regulation that does exist often sets the bar too low to ensure either satisfactory performance or qualified personnel.

This presents an important challenge for government officials charged with developing policy related to public safety and emergency preparedness. Namely, to optimize the role of private security by ensuring that standards for training and protocols for oversight are in place and are rigorous enough to facilitate effective development and maintenance of public law enforcement-private security (LE-PS) partnerships and collaboration.

Ligue members around the world have seen how the development of country-wide or regional standards and uniform accreditation certification processes can help maximize LE-PS partnerships, by helping to ensure that private security companies are not vulnerable to organized crime or unethical and/or illegal behavior.

In fact, unscrupulous security companies are identified by Ligue members as the gravest threat to the private security industry. Thirty-five percent of respondents to the Ligue's Survey on Industry Challenges, taken during the Ligue's 2019 General Assembly, said that bad actors within the security industry are an "extreme" risk to the industry's financial prospects. Another 28.6% believe such companies pose a "significant" risk. Out of 11 identified risks facing the private security industry, this is the most worrisome, according to poll respondents.

Compounding the risk from bad actors is the fact that the global private security industry is still largely fragmented, which puts the overall reputation of the industry in the hands of many players. And any harm to the private security sector generally lessens the effectiveness of LE-PS partnerships and the ability to successfully transfer public security services to the private sector. The public must have trust in the private security industry for such arrangements to work.

Given that private security guards are a visible presence in society and regularly interact with the public, it is important for governments to understand citizens' level of trust with private security agents and to develop regulatory frameworks designed to improve it; for example, by supporting "differentiating standards" that allow security firms to achieve a high-end designation after a rigorous review of their operations and management systems. Such designations help promote professionalism and accountability, which are good predictors of how citizens feel toward private security officers.

7 Planning

In a major disaster—a citywide flood, for example—some businesses may be able to lock up and leave and return only after the water has receded and operations can resume. But others may be counted on to remain open and/or require high-level protection in the interim, such as food stores, pharmacies, and critical infrastructure. For these establishments, there is likely to be a lack of available public law enforcement to provide protection as they tend to other aspects of disaster response.

Community crisis planning must ensure flexibility in security arrangements to assure public safety during natural or human-caused crises and the same is true for government departments responsible for matters of public safety, emergency management, national security, and emergency preparedness.

Expectations for security and peace in society have grown substantially as many categories of violence have declined in recent decades, but these are likely to be tested by an increasingly complex security and safety environment. There is ample evidence that the current increase in worldwide health, safety, and security risks is not a spike in cyclical pattern, but rather a harbinger of shifts in the global threat environment.

The timeline for feeling the security effects may be shorter than many think. By 2025, two-thirds of the world's population may face water shortages, according to a consensus of scientists' estimates. Water scarcity isn't a sure-fire recipe for conflict everywhere it occurs, but resource scarcity always has the potential to be a contributing factor to conflict and instability.

"Based on our research, we have determined that even at scenarios of low warming, each region of the world will face severe risks to national and global security in the next three decades," according to *A Security Threat Assessment of Climate Change*, published by the Center for Climate and Security (CCS, 2020). "Higher levels of warming will pose catastrophic, and likely irreversible, global security risks over the course of the 21st century" (CCS, 2020, p. 6).

As noted in the United Nations Framework Convention on Climate Change and in other global studies, "perfect storm" scenarios grow more likely as globalization collides with the consequences from a warming world. Projected climate change poses the most serious security threats in the world's least developed and already volatile regions. Extremism and conflict are likely to erupt in these regions as food production declines, disease increases, clean water grows scarce, and large populations move in search of resources.

As an essential source of protection for societies and economies, the world will need to lean heavily on the leading private security companies to mitigate the most immediate and troubling ramifications of more frequent crises. Businesses and community leaders must acknowledge that local law enforcement and public response agencies are likely to be overwhelmed in crisis events and probably not able to help. Fundamentally, leveraging private security to assist in protection and crisis recovery efforts needs to be written into the disaster plans of communities, governments, and private businesses.

Practical arrangements should be made well in advance of disaster events. There is immense value in pre-planning and making it part of continuity efforts, as experience has shown that during the storm or in its aftermath is not the time to be reaching out to the private security sector for assistance. Companies and public agencies need to be sure to already have in place well-thought-out arrangements with contract security firms that address practical matters, such as check-in procedures for security contract workers at a crisis staging area and verification of credentials. It is important to spell out the basic security functions that emergency security workers will be asked to perform, and it helps to provide security firms with a Statement of Expectations that address basic expectations for punctuality, ethics, appearance, and similar issues. Failure to work out such details with a security partner in advance of a crisis event will slowdown disaster response and limit the value of such arrangements.

While daily operations may not require it, businesses must be prepared to manage a sudden need to ramp-up security in a crisis event, such as when a criminal gang strikes a business just a few hours before opening. In these cases, the ability to immediately deploy a uniformed private security officer to the scene helps to quickly secure the location, provides professional security coverage, and may help to ease employees' peace of mind as businesses push to reopen. Such a deployment can demonstrate a company's commitment to employee safety, provide peace of mind, and give store associates the sense that "whatever happened last night, I'll be safe today."

8   Insight

Protection officers' roles and responsibilities have been adapting to a changing and heightened threat environment and suppliers of protection officers have been employing advanced training to ready personnel for whatever public security assignments arise and to be more valuable partners in joint security arrangements. Yet, these changes and differentiations often go unrecognized.

To maximize the value of security partnerships and private sector performance of public safety services, governments must improve their understanding of private security roles and duties and enhance their collection of data related to it. The lack of good data is reflected in the outdated taxonomy that governments frequently use to describe the industry.

No two security jobs are alike. Yet, government agencies around the world often lump together individuals who perform myriad different security functions under a single "security guard" classification. The lack of distinction among security jobs ignores the vastly different skills and mindsets that different security jobs demand, and it hurts both research into the profession and security partnerships. Even security guard positions within the same business vary wildly, depending on whether it's a day or night position, whether the job entails interaction with high tech tools, or whether public contact is a feature of the position. For example, private security officers who patrol public shopping districts and those who operate surveillance equipment may serve the same mission in the same environment, but the positions are hardly analogous.

Society could benefit more from private sector security if more detailed job descriptions of security positions were conducted whenever appropriate. By striving to accurately differentiate between security positions, governments are better positioned to ensure proper selection of individuals, appropriate training, and set appropriate performance expectations.

By increasing attention on the diverse and unique duties of private security professionals, governments and society may gradually come to a fuller understanding of the jobs they do, allowing for better design of LE-PS partnerships.

9   Reputation

The reputation of the private security industry is not uniform across the globe. A study in the Netherlands, for example, found that Dutch citizens have mixed opinions about private security guards, with contact being a key predictor of satisfaction (Van Steden & Nalla, 2010), while a study of Russian students found greater dissatisfaction with security guard services (Nalla et al., 2017). A study in India concluded—relative to findings in similar research conducted in other countries—that Indian citizens have a higher degree of trust in the security guard industry and in security guards themselves (Nalla et al., 2013).

Differences in public opinion toward private security underscores the fact that governments give shape to those attitudes, through the standards they set and by whether they aggressively regulate bad actors in the industry by investigating consumer complaints and enforcing licensing requirements. Findings from a study in the city of Porto, Portugal, for example, suggest that professionalism and accountability appear to be good predictors of how citizens feel toward private security officers (Moreira et al., 2015).

It is also a clear indication that governments have an interest in a thriving, respected, and trusted private security services industry. Because of the importance of LE-PS partnerships, any harm to the private security industry harms the ability of governments to effectively protect its citizens.

Where negative public opinion about private security exists, they have less authority and status in the eyes of private citizens. This hurts the legitimization of the private security sector generally and harms the effectiveness of LE-PS partnerships.

If governments want to maximize the value of partnerships, regulators must examine their regulatory framework to ensure that it helps to enhance the image of the industry by not allowing a small percentage of substandard firms to harm the reputation of the entire industry.

Citizens' perception of private security guards is highly relevant for governments since they are the regulators of the private security sector as well as its customers and partners. Because of the role private security plays in public safety, governments need to regard the opinions that citizens hold of private security and to help steer those attitudes in a positive direction.

10   Management

Members of the International Security Ligue report that management is a critical factor for successful joint security arrangements, especially an administrative structure that encourages and facilitates open communication among the parties; helps to maintain the integrity of the initiative; and creates processes for evaluating progress toward the initiative's goals.

It is also important for public agencies or municipalities to look inward to work more effectively with outside partners, a key step that is sometimes missing from these arrangements.

Specifically, experience has shown that it is beneficial when agencies define the core functions of public police and the parameters of its role and responsibilities as a precursor to effective partnering with private security. Without this step, it is harder for municipalities to subsequently identify how private security can be most effectively utilized in partnership with public law enforcement. Expansion of private security in the public sphere offers society enumerable benefits, but they are more easily captured when government officials are strategic in their pursuit.

Finally, the experience of Ligue members supports what academic scholars have found to be other key factors to successful police-private security partnerships. They include:

1. Clarity on specific areas of common interest, such as reducing a specific crime or set of crimes.
2. Effective leadership, with personnel with authority from each partner organization driving participation.
3. Mutual respect.
4. Information sharing based on a high level of trust in confidentiality.
5. Formal consultation and meetings and frequent communication.
6. A willingness to experiment and to consider all ideas.

This last point is especially important as joint partnerships evolve to include more advanced technology. The potential for societal benefits from joint security arrangements are limitless and creative thinking is necessary to make use of advanced technological capabilities.

11   Principles

Foundational to the successful expansion of private security is a commitment by public officials to only engage in partnerships with security contractors that are committed to human rights and dedicated to sustainable values and ethics. This is especially important in jurisdictions that lack strong legislative and policy frameworks that provide oversight of private security firms and ensure governance, accountability, and transparency of their operations. When sourcing private security services, cities should look for tangible evidence that a security contractor is committed to ethical principles, such as those outlined in the International Security Ligue's Code of Conduct and Ethics.

A commitment to sustainability has become an expectation of governments in areas including carbon emissions, waste, and water. This same dedication to sustainability principles should be reflected in the choice by governments of private security contractors. While budget pressures may entice public authorities to align with unproven security operators, such arrangements are rarely sustainable. It may address near-term security requirements but ultimately increases a municipality's exposure to risk by creating linkages to an entity over which it cannot exert control.

When governments hire a security contractor that is committed to human rights and dedicated to sustainable values and ethics—rather than just picking the lowest-cost operator—it is an important indicator of its commitment to social responsibility. Saving public sector resources by economizing on security contracts could also be argued to be a commitment to social responsibility. These resources could be used for other things, like public health, for instance.

Additionally, because of a choice based on quality, governments can expect to benefit from a "sustainable" approach to security, one that: reduces risk from excessive use of force and other problematic outcomes; enhances alliances; facilitates opportunities; builds—rather than erodes—trust in government; and positively influences the communities in which the contractor operates.

When deciding whether to partner with a prospective security contractor, public officials should review its record in key areas that reflect its principles, including:

- Human rights. A commitment to support and respect the dignity of all human beings and to endeavor to observe all applicable international humanitarian and human rights laws.
- Laws and regulations governing private security. Compliance with all applicable laws and regulations and, when absent or insufficient, adherence to a set of minimum standards to ensure the provision of quality and professional services.
- Business ethics. These include proper conduct in its treatment of personnel, customers, and business partners and in interactions with competitors. Included in the company's statements should be a commitment to non-discrimination; prohibitions against taking or soliciting bribes; avoidance of conflicts of interest; protection of confidential information from disclosure; transparency; and to allow its personnel, without fear of reprisal, to raise concerns about suspect business practices.
- Working conditions. A security contractor should have signed a statement that acknowledges its obligation to protect employees from unsafe working conditions and to treat them fairly. Such a statement should describe its commitment to: prohibit any kind of unlawful discrimination; provide necessary instructions and training; conduct employee screening and selection in compliance with applicable regulations; adhere to established procedures for responding to grievances; and pay a fair wage at least to the minimum prescribed by law.
- Environment. Any security contractor under consideration should express a commitment to take the environmental impact of its business into account. The Code established by Ligue members, for example, includes a stated goal to: "continuously seek ways to reduce the consumption of resources, emissions, and waste."

It is important to review both the stated commitments a security company has made and its record of performance. Before hiring a security contractor, due diligence should be conducted to ensure that rhetoric on the subjects of human rights and ethics are matched by past performance. For example, procurement managers might want to: research for a record of excess force and abuse claims; examine occupational health and safety data; and request data on the percentage of employees provided awareness training in business ethics and human rights.

12   Quality

Growing professionalism in the contract security industry does not diminish the need for public authorities and municipalities to be deliberate in selecting a security firm. The contract security marketplace is not homogeneous. The level of excellence has risen substantially but it is not universal—and substandard providers do persist.

Because the contract security industry has improved, the stakes are higher for an agency of government when it outsources public safety functions to a private security firm or works with them in a joint security arrangement: (a) because industry improvement has exacerbated the difference in the level of service one can receive; and (b) because selecting a suitable security partner is necessary for societies to fully benefit from the gains that the industry has made.

Additionally, because excellent providers are available, it is no longer possible to lay blame on "private security" in the wake of a failed contract arrangement. Instead, a failed contract will suggest internal mistakes by government employees who neglected to do their due diligence.

Cost is a primary driver for the desire to utilize private security services. There is tangible evidence, however, that when clients select the lowest contract bid, they are less happy with the results. For example, the Institute of Finance and Management (IOFM) studied hundreds of contract security arrangements and asked clients to rate their security firm's officers on dozens of criteria, from verbal communication skills, to adherence to post orders, to reliability. The study then analyzed client ratings against whether security firms with the lowest bid had been awarded the contract (Security Guard Firm Ratings & Benchmarks Report, IOFM, 2010).

The results were dramatic. For example, the average rating for contract officers was lower—in every one of the 22 performance areas examined—in service arrangements in which the low-bid contract was selected, prompting the report to conclude that "if you focus on bid price, you will likely be less happy with the officers sent to protect your facility." In short, price is an inevitable criterion in a bid selection process, but it can't be allowed to hijack it.

Ligue members have seen partnerships thrive when government agencies adopt a comprehensive approach to evaluating security partners, one that incorporates factors such as quality and the track record of a potential partner. Lesson learned suggest that at least half of a contract should be awarded on the basis of quality criteria.

As such, agencies should identify specific steps it will take to prevent the bottom-line contract bid from consuming attention during the selection process. For example, selection teams often find it helpful to separate the portion of the Request-for-Proposal that specifies contract requirements from the cost proposal. This strategy compels an agency to examine only bids from security firms that successfully meet its minimum qualifications.

Municipalities have also run into trouble when using online competitive bidding, a procurement method that increases visibility and compels vendors to compete against one another to drive down the overall cost of security contracts and specific line items. It incentivizes a "race to the bottom," which inevitably leads to a deterioration in quality.

Cost containment is a critical issue, of course, but there are actions municipalities can take in this regard that won't also result in disappointment in the level of security service they receive. For example, municipalities should measure contractor performance on whether the security firm continuously identifies opportunities to deliver better service more cost-effectively, even in small ways. For example, by improving the efficiency of patrol routes or vehicles to save money on gas or providing hand-held devices to officers conducting audits to ease data collection and eliminate data entry and administrative costs.

13   Due Diligence

Because a contract security provider can reflect positively or negatively on a municipality or public agency—and perhaps even alter public perception of government services generally—it is imperative to sufficiently review a security company's background to be comfortable with its reputation, viability, and business ethics before contracting it for services or entering a joint security arrangement. If a company is too new or has too few clients to paint a reliable picture of its reputation, this should be factored into the choice of private security partner.

Ligue members have seen that the following elements should be included as part of a due diligence investigation to identify the most appropriate private security partner.

- History. Identify how many years the firm has been established in the service area.
- Reference checks. Requests for Proposals might request a minimum of three references that government officials can then contact. Additionally, a municipality may choose to identify and consult with other clients that the company does not offer as a reference. It may be possible to ascertain a client list from the security company's website, networking, or other means.
- Financial health. This should be examined even if a company's record of accounts suggests it can provide an agency with the services it promises, as even companies with a record of clients may have suspect underlying financials.
- Workforce stability. If it can be attained, data on officer turnover and average length of employment are useful indicators.
- Customer complaints. A thorough record review should be made to ascertain whether a company has a satisfactory record of dealing with clients or if it suffers from an unusual volume or pattern of complaints.
- Lawsuits and negligence claims. Investigate for a recent history of valid or successful lawsuits filed by clients or employees, as it is particularly important to know if a contractor has a history of negligence. A contractor should provide prospective clients with information regarding its liability insurance claims

history and legal representatives can then review each case or report to assess its significance.

- Publicity. News accounts and even social media can highlight potential issues of concern. While a disgruntled employee can make unfounded allegations and news accounts can misrepresent a security case or situation, investigating what is being said about a particular firm can raise issues that a prospective client may wish to ask about during contract negotiations.

14 Safety

A check of a company's health and safety record is a particularly critical point of investigation that a municipality should make prior to partnering with a contract security firm. A demonstrable commitment to reducing injuries is a good proxy for measuring its values and dedication to its employees.

Municipalities should refuse to select a security company that is unable to demonstrate a strong safety record and a commitment to reducing injuries. Members of the International Security Ligue, for example, have embarked on a cooperative campaign to enhance safety through benchmarking, case studies, and the sharing of expertise (A Commitment to Reducing Injuries in the Global Security Industry, 2020).

At a minimum, review for compliance with local laws and regulations, which can be observed through random sampling, audits, and compensations claims. One should also find out if the prospective partner has internal policies, programs and processes for quality assurance, feedback management, and continuous improvement. Additional information is available by making visits to reference-customer sites to obtain a picture of the service provider's "live operations." In terms of occupational health and safety, a municipality should look carefully at the provider's internal rules for creating a risk assessment, and it must be deemed suitable for the work that is to be performed.

Certification to international standards and globally recognized management systems, such as OHSAS or ISO certification, is also a reasonable safety indicator and provides another way to distinguish between prospective security partners on the criteria of safety. Certification provides a measure of assurance that a provider has the structure necessary to address occupational health and safety, accident prevention, and employee protection. Finally, a municipality should ask questions about a security provider's safety program, including in areas of communication, employee involvement, and executive leadership.

15 Training

Public policing functions are increasingly being performed by private security firms, a fact that should cause public officials to ask: Which firm can best meet the responsibilities of the assignment? Are we confident a prospective contractor can deal with its challenges?

To set the stage for success in a privatized security arrangement, it is incumbent upon governments that use contract security personnel to assess whether they are comfortable with the training and management programs of firms with which they do business and whether they seem intended to raise the level of proficiency among staff. Although there is consensus that the training of contract security officers has improved, the failure of some security arrangements indicate that problems can still arise.

Municipalities should look for indications that firms invest in their officers, such as the existence of formal programs to provide recognition; ensure regular training and skills upgrading; offer career development; and solicit feedback. More broadly, it is important to gauge if a security firm effectively communicates with and engages its frontline security officers. If they don't, there is potential for a disconnected security force that distrusts leadership, ignores the strategic mission of both the firm and client, and is less loyal and more likely to act in their own self-interest—or even unethically.

It is advised to partner with security firms that exhibit strategies designed to encourage engagement among their security officers in three areas:

- Meaningfulness. Security officers should receive feedback that they are valuable and significant to the organization and that their engagement is being rewarded.
- Support. It is important to examine whether companies promote loyalty by focusing and nurturing positive characteristics as much as correcting problem behavior.
- Resources. To feel engaged, security officers must feel they will be given the necessary tools to do their job well (training, equipment, guidance, etc.) and have an ability to seek recourse through internal whistleblowing channels.

Based on the complexities and needs of the assignment, municipalities and public authorities should identify the basic training requirements for contract security officers. Contractors should also be asked to make training records, programs, and any certifications available for review. Specific training requirements will vary substantially by assignment and environment, but often include diverse subject areas, such as: patrolling techniques and responsibilities; recording of information, taking statements, and writing incident reports; use of interpersonal skills, verbal skills, de-escalation, and nonverbal actions; customer service; self-defense; and authority and jurisdiction.

Expectations are growing for security officers, which increases the need to assess the training that officers receive. Long ago, when all that officers were expected to do was provide deterrence with their presence, an elevated level of professional security training was perhaps not necessary. But that is not what public agencies need from contract officers in today's security environment.

Driven by a more complex risk environment and better and more affordable technology, security officers today are less necessary for mere deterrence and more important for their ability to manage incidents and proactively act in service of the protection mission. Officer training programs must evolve to reflect the new job weighting. More than ever, training programs must seek an answer beyond, "Do officers know the right thing to do?" It must include: "How well will they do it?"

Public procurement teams charged with selecting a security firm need to be sure that the content of a security firm's training program focuses on tackling specific organizational needs and improving competencies for handling situations they face. In addition to measured competency testing, a municipality might examine the extent to which a prospective security firm utilizes scenario-based training that is relevant to its specific security needs. More than lecture or video, active training through exercises and simulations helps ready staff to meet the demands of their assignment and drives higher standards of service.

Scenario-based exercises: (a) make it possible to see how officers are likely to act in different situations and identify problems before an actual event; (b) make officers more likely to carry lessons learned into real events. It is especially appropriate when there is a physical response component, making it suitable for many areas of training, including: emergency medical response, physical penetration exercises, fire evacuation, unauthorized person reports, report writing, bomb search techniques, customer service, conflict resolution, disaster response, and patrol techniques.

16 Clarity

Whether contract security is used to support or assist public safety agencies or is contracted to be the primary provider of a specific security service, clarity of expectation is a vital component of a successful arrangement. At the outset, a Service Level Agreement (SLA) should be developed to detail—in plain language—the expectations of the services to be provided by the contractor company.

A comprehensive SLA should spell out the service elements public agencies expect for every area in which contract guards perform any type of service. It should include service elements in the areas of training, pre-employment screening, and communications. It may also include service level expectations in areas such as deliveries, searches, vehicle control, or any other function contract officers are expected to perform. For example, "Access Control" is a typical service provided by private security, and a description of the service level may be "to restrict access to premises to only those displaying a current staff, contractors, or visitor badge."

SLAs serve to define the scope of the security provision, identify performance objectives for the delivery of the security provision, and document the entity and individuals who are responsible for meeting specific SLA conditions.

They are especially important as a document to manage change, which is frequently needed because security conditions are highly variable. An SLA can be used to capture changes in service expectations that may differ from those in the original contract—something that can become critical if an incident review is necessary to learn whether responsibilities for service were being met.

The SLA also plays a significant role in developing meaningful Key Performance Indicators (KPIs). For each element of service defined in the SLA, public agencies, in conjunction with their private security partner, should identify a list of KPIs. These indicators, which may be referred to as performance metrics or performance measures, allow both the public agency and the private security firm to track if performance expectations in the different service areas are being met.

Identifying appropriate KPIs is important to ensure that a government agency's expectations for security service are clearly defined and so its security partner understands the standards by which its performance will be appraised. Using service-specific KPIs—rather than generic measures of performance—enhances the value of a security provision and has been seen to improve success in public-private partnerships and in the privatization of public safety functions.

Which KPIs are appropriate will vary depending on the service arrangement, so municipalities should demand an opportunity to sit down with a security partner to establish performance indicators that are relevant, important, and measurable. Areas in which performance measures are commonly developed include officer turnover, training, incident responsiveness, and productivity. For example, with regards to "staffing," KPIs might include the percentage of officers that are on-time for assignments, the rate of officer replacement, and days missed by security officers.

The experience of the world's leading security firms show that clarity of responsibilities and expectations are a precursor to effective leveraging of private security for public safety and for driving an effective relationship between government agencies and their private security partners. Detailed SLAs are important for establishing clarity, and topics to address might include: responsibilities of the supplier; responsibilities of the municipal client; performance reviews (systems, frequency of reviews); problem management; security management; setting priority or severity levels; service level incentives and penalties; and Key Performance Indicators or performance metrics.

17 Oversight

When a public agency puts an aspect of security in the hands of a private sector contractor, it's tempting to turn attention elsewhere—but a lack of oversight can have dire consequences. Critical problems can be avoided, however, through use of an explicit oversight protocol and a detailed contract, service agreement, and performance indicators.

As a starting point, it is important to have confidence in the quality of a security firm's management program, and in its resiliency. For example, ISO 22301 is the international standard for Business Continuity Management, and a firm's certification suggests its ability to prevent, prepare for, respond to, and recover from disruptive incidents.

Contract monitoring is also important and lax oversight is a mistake any government agency can make. Goldstein (2009) for example, discovered that 62%, or 411 of 663 private security officers deployed to a federal facility in the U.S., had at least one expired certification, in areas such as firearms qualification, background investigation, domestic violence declaration, or CPR/First Aid training certification.

Frequent inspections and audits are an important part of ensuring a successful partnership. Without a strict audit regimen, a government has limited assurance that private security contractors are complying with post orders.

Oversight programs need to be thoughtfully developed and delivered in a uniform manner across jurisdictions. For example, for convenience and to reduce overtime expenditures, it may be tempting to exclusively conduct post inspections during normal business hours, but it is common to discover instances of noncompliance more often when post inspections are performed after-hours.

To get early warning of potential problems, and get a complete picture of performance, government agencies should ensure that all individual facilities complete required security contract performance evaluations. Standardized recordkeeping—to ensure that all contract files have required documentation—is also a clever idea. Setting inspection targets—and ensuring that each government facility or agency follows them—is also vital.

It's also helpful for a municipality to explicitly identify what an "inspection" should entail. Without identifying how to conduct a review, local managers may make cursory post inspections and the quality of inspections are likely to vary from region to region. Some government staff may conduct little more than a uniform check, while others may conduct a more robust inspection of officer certifications, knowledge of post orders, uniform and equipment checks, and inspection of the post station and timecards.

Lastly, municipalities can encourage better oversight of security contracts by making communication between site management and contract security firms a focus of the service level agreement between the two parties. These may include a timetable for conducting performance monitoring meetings between representatives of the public agency and the security firm; clear standards for handling complaints, including a timeframe for reporting them; an agreement on the frequency of supervisory visits to contract security officers and what will occur during the visits; and documentation requirements, such as a timetable for service reports.

18   Concluding Remarks

As crises become more routine, as crime and incivility threaten daily life, and as extremism and conflict erupt in a world competing over dwindling natural resources, private security services will be needed to play a leading role in ensuring peaceful societies. From helping to manage the millions of climate refugees that a country may encounter to ensuring businesses can operate successfully in destabilized regions, private security services are—and increasingly will be—critical to public safety.

Success in this regard requires (a) the security industry to continue its drive toward excellence, and (b) governments and public agencies to recognize that signing a contract or forging a partnership is only the starting point for building a successful relationship, not the fine print on a completed process.

Historically, much of the blame for the failings of the private security services industry has fallen on providers, their low wages, and lack of sophistication. In the last two decades, however, the world's leading security companies have steadily raised the bar for the industry. These firms have expanded their list of services, enhanced their internal expertise, and made significant investments in advanced security technology. Top performing security firms have also made vast improvements to training programs and management processes and raised hiring qualifications, which has lifted the level of professionalism and allowed them to be more responsive to client needs.

Consequently, when private-public security partnerships or outsourcing arrangements fail in the current environment, it is often because government end-users contribute to it.

Perhaps primarily, failed partnerships result because public agencies resist efforts to align compensation with the more highly skilled and trained officers that now perform security work. They may instead insist on partnering with security providers that pay substandard and unsustainable wages. Failing to pay for private security at a reasonable rate puts public safety at risk in the near term and risks lasting harm to societies. If the private security industry fails to attract talent—just as governments rely more heavily on them—the result will be catastrophic.

Partnerships can also fail because of unreasonable expectations; unclear contract specifications; a failure to articulate strategic goals, objectives, and standards; or lax contract oversight.

This chapter has detailed multiple strategies to avoid such problems, critical actions that the leading security companies of the world—represented by the International Security Ligue—have seen as helpful in forging successful partnerships between public agencies and private security partners.

The experience of Ligue member companies shows that by taking specific actions during procurement and contract development and management phases, that public agencies can substantially raise the odds of a good outcome in privatizing aspects of public safety or in public-private partnerships. Clear lines of responsibility are critical, and so is trust, giving a supplier necessary support, and creating measurable standards of quality. Paying a fair contract price to match the security industry's investment in technology and its people is necessary, and so is consistent engagement with security partners to catalyze improvement.

Local governments and municipalities must act diligently to ensure security firms meet the terms of contracts and intercede promptly when noncompliance is identified. However, public agencies must also do their part to facilitate a strong working partnership and nurture relationships to ensure greater public safety. In short, the utilization of private security services for public safety should be perceived as an opportunity to contract for expertise, not eliminate responsibility.

Private security is already playing a significant role in the safety and security web in countries around the world, and there are numerous examples from countless jurisdictions of the public police working in effective partnerships with private security. Moreover, joint private-public initiatives are likely to have a greater impact on the security of societies in the future. Consequently, how they develop—and how effectively they operate—should be a significant concern to all stakeholders: governments, private companies, and the public.

References

BBC News. (2019, March 15). Police 999 response times almost double in seven years. *BBC News*.

Blasey, L., & Limón, E. (2022, April 22). 17 L.A. gangs have sent out crews to follow and rob city's wealthiest, LAPD says. *Los Angeles Times*.

Castro, D., & McLaughlin, M. (2019, January 7). *Survey: Few Americans want government to limit use of facial recognition technology, particularly for public safety or airport screening*. Center for Data Innovation.

Center for Climate and Security. (2020). *A security threat assessment of global climate change: How likely warming scenarios indicate a catastrophic security future*.

Goldstein, A. (2007, January 2). The private arm of the law some question the granting of police power to security firms. *Washington Post*.

Goldstein, M. (2009, July). *Preliminary results show Federal Protective Service's ability to protect federal facilities is hampered by weaknesses in its contract security guard program* (GAO-09-859T). Government Accountability Office.

Her Majesty's Inspectorate of Constabulary and Fire & Rescue Services. (2019, April). *Fraud: Time to choose – An inspection of the police response to fraud*. HMICFRS. ISBN: 978-1-78655-784-1.

Lim, S. S. L., & Nalla, M. K. (2014). Attitudes of private security officers in Singapore toward their work environment. *Journal of Applied Security Research, 9*(1), 41–56. https://doi.org/10.108 0/19361610.2014.851579

Moreira, S., Cardoso, C., & Nalla, M. K. (2015). Citizen confidence in private security guards in Portugal. *European Journal of Criminology, 12*(2), 208–225.

Nalla, M. K., Ommi, K., & Sreemannarayana Murthy, V. (2013). Nature of work, safety, and trust in private security in India: A study of citizen perceptions of security guards. In *Crime and justice in India* (pp. 226–264). Sage.

Nalla, M. K., Gurinskaya, A., & Rafailova, D. (2017). Youth perceptions of private security guard industry in Russia. *Journal of Applied Security Research, 12*(4), 543–556. https://doi.org/1 0.1080/19361610.2017.1354277

Robert H. Perry & Associates. (2020). *U.S. Contract Security Market White Paper*.

Van Steden, R., & Nalla, M. K. (2010). Citizen satisfaction with private security guards in the Netherlands: Perceptions of an ambiguous occupation. *European Journal of Criminology, 7*(3), 214–234. https://doi.org/10.1177/1477370809359264

Improving Public Safety Through Law Enforcement and Private Security Partnerships

Steve Jones

Abstract People are safer when law enforcement and private security work together. This chapter explores how public-private partnerships can provide a complete solution that addresses many of the challenges facing law enforcement today. Featuring multiple real-world case studies and seasoned perspectives from top leaders in security and law enforcement, it illuminates the success factors in existing partnerships and proposes innovative new areas for collaboration. It demonstrates how public-private security partnerships can provide significant value in budgets, recruiting, responding to mental health and drug crises, airport or campus security, prisoner transport, transit security and many other service areas. Additionally, it offers guidance for improving the functioning and effectiveness of PPPs, as well as considerations for budget, jurisdictional issues and legal liability – all with actionable pathways that any public and private force can follow to achieve unprecedented levels of service and efficiency in today's rigorous social and budgetary environment. The result: a win-win for all law enforcement organizations and the communities they serve.

A city-owned executive airport near Chicago had a problem: It needed to source more police staff in a very tight market of qualified personnel. The airport brought in a private security advisor, which was able to reach out to nearby jurisdictions to bring in personnel whom they cannot directly access. The private firm scheduled the additional officers, providing the much-needed additional active-duty police with full law-enforcement powers to perform critical functions at that facility.

Further south, in the immediate aftermath of 2022s Hurricane Ian the citizens of southwest Florida needed immediate, often life-saving assistance. Local police and other first responders were overwhelmed amidst a vast area of flooding and general destruction that covered 3500 square miles and caused an estimated $67 billion in

S. Jones (✉)
Allied Universal, Conshohocken, PA, USA
e-mail: Brent.OBryen@aus.com

insured losses.[1] *Local public authorities deployed scores of highly skilled private security personnel to work closely with law enforcement and other private companies to not only protect government facilities and business properties, but go out on search and rescue operations using trucks, boats, rafts, chainsaws and every other tool at their disposal to save lives. Their efforts freed law enforcement to focus on its core functions – securing transportation, preventing opportunistic looting and other crimes, and generally maintaining order while the area began to recover.*

These examples make clear that people are safer when law enforcement and private security work together. That is especially true today, where against a backdrop of increasing social unrest, rising crime, and natural disasters, police department staffing has been trending in the wrong direction. In early 2022 Capitol Police Chief Thomas Manger told *Politico* that the department was "probably 400 officers down from where we should be."[2] A June 2021 national survey by the Police Executive Forum (PERF) found that departments around the country had experienced a 44% increase in retirements while resignations had risen 18%.[3] According to PERF, Minneapolis Chief of Police Medaria Arradondo even told a city council panel that reduced staffing is making his department "one-dimensional," with officers mostly responding to 911 calls and not having time to do proactive policing.

At the same time, we're asking our law enforcement officers to fulfill a substantial number of roles outside of their core mission – from event guards and ticket-writers to guidance counselors and mental health counselors. While officials struggle to address these problems, they have been forced to look for alternative models for security – to find a *public safety multiplier* that will alleviate the unprecedented pressure on law enforcement personnel and administrative costs while enhancing public safety.

It's clear that a public-private partnership (PPP) between sworn law enforcement and private security companies can be a powerful strategy for enhancing public safety. Today private security forces are better trained, more sophisticated and more capable than ever before, expanding law enforcement and public safety capabilities in hundreds of communities and private industries throughout the United States and the world.

---

[1] "RMS Estimates US$67 Billion in Insured Losses from Hurricane Ian," Risk Management Solutions, Inc., October 7, 2022. https://www.rms.com/newsroom/press-releases/press-detail/2022-10-07/rms-estimates-us67-billion-in-insured-losses-from-hurricane-ian#.

[2] Daniel Lippman and Nicholas Wu, "Capitol Police union douses private security proposal," *Politico*, January 3, 2022. https://www.politico.com/news/2022/01/03/capitol-police-union-private-security-proposal-526395.

[3] Police Executive Research Forum, "PERF Special Report," June 11, 2021.

1 In This Chapter

This chapter explores how PPPs can provide a complete solution that addresses many of the challenges facing law enforcement today. Featuring multiple real-world case studies and seasoned perspectives from top leaders in security and law enforcement, it illuminates the success factors in existing partnerships and proposes innovative new areas for collaboration. It demonstrates how public-private security partnerships can provide significant value in budgets, recruiting, responding to mental health and drug crises, airport or campus security, prisoner transport, transit security and many other service areas. Additionally, it offers guidance for improving the functioning and effectiveness of PPPs, as well as considerations for budget, jurisdictional issues, and legal liability – all with actionable pathways that any public and private force can follow to achieve unprecedented levels of service and efficiency in today's rigorous social and budgetary environment. The result: a win-win for all law enforcement organizations and the communities they serve.

2 Partnership as a Public Safety Multiplier

When done right, law enforcement and private security working together can be a *public safety multiplier*, enhancing the capability to have additional eyes and ears observing and reporting throughout a defined area or jurisdiction. Adding a private component to law enforcement will help any public safety entity spot activities that are out of the ordinary in a way that a conventional force may not be able to detect. It also provides the ability to have ambassadors on the street, on the train or in any number of additional environments and situations. In many locals and venues around the country, private security can even function as sworn, armed law enforcement officers, supported by their years of rigorous training and real-world experience in the field.

Today's contract security industry has invested in training, management, recruiting and screening best practices that have that have transformed its professionals into a highly trained, multiple-capability force ready to compliment the efforts of traditional law enforcement. That, in turn, is enabling mutually respectful productive partnerships that are extending the reach and effectiveness of public safety efforts.

> A partnership with private security can put those highly trained and vetted private-force individuals in an omnipresence situation that the police department can really rely on.

From the police side it makes sense to partner with private security. A critical part of policing is having a force that can respond quickly, grow quickly as needed, or scale down just as fast. For example, Allied Universal the ability to surge personnel when needed very, very quickly. That's a plus, and a partnership with private security can put those highly trained and vetted private-force individuals in an omnipresence situation that the police department can really rely on. With close coordination with traditional forces, they can be the eyes and ears for nearly every location and situation, able to handle things that currently take up a lot of obligated time from sworn officers.

2.1 Misconceptions and Benefits

PPP is a powerful model that can be utilized on all verticals and levels of government. Still, its widespread acceptance has required breaking down some long-held misconceptions about private security:

- **"Private security officers are just 'guards.'"** The largest misconception is that private security is simply guards rumbling around with keys. This description is a far cry from today's not private security forces, which are nimble, high-tech, and much better educated than those of the past. This preconception radically changes when you bring officials to your private security facilities and show them what you do.
- **"They don't have the same level of sophistication and professional training."** Sometimes public safety officials and police commanders are under the impression that private security is there to be the secondary police force and that's not up to the challenges. In fact, many of our officers have served honorably in the military, police, fire, and rescue – quality, highly trained professionals who for any number of reasons chose to transfer into private security. A lot of them have years of experience in running very secure, critical infrastructure.
- **"We're here to take your job."** Yet another misconception is police personnel assuming that private security in these situations may be infringing on their turf – trying to take their jobs. The world we live in today demands that both entities be partners, not competitors. In an environment of greater social polarization, heightened social unrest and more destructive and frequent natural disasters, private security can offload non-critical tasks from sworn law enforcement, freeing them to focus on their core mission.
- **"They won't be a fit for us."** There is a widespread myth that private security is a rigid model – a "one size for all" proposition – but nothing could be further from the truth. Leading security providers like Allied Universal will collaborate with public entities to determine the unique, optimal solution for their needs, drawing on their extensive knowledge of nuances for any particular vertical, cutting-edge latest technology and a range of capabilities in all areas of law-enforcement and counterterrorism.

In the partnership model private forces can be beneficial within the parameters of the law and to do things that will greatly benefit regular forces by releasing their obligated time. Those benefits are augmented further by the deterrence effect created by simply having more visible officers on site. For example, an analysis conducted at railroad stations in southwest England found that 41% more patrol visits and 29% more minutes spent by security agents led to a significant 16% reduction in victim-generated crimes at the entirety of the stations' complexes, with a 49% increase in police-generated detections at the target locations.[4]

Following are several examples of the public safety multiplier in different public and private verticals.

2.2 Government Buildings and Sites

Government buildings are often vulnerable to unlawful entry, terrorism, and large protests. Assessment and protection of these sites is often performed by private security forces, which under the terms of their contracts may have the full arrest and detaining powers of sworn law endorsement. This is particularly true in federal districts and facilities, but also in states such as North Carolina, South Carolina, Texas, and others where law permits. This presents a prime opportunity for private security to take a leading role in partnership security. They're trained in all facets of policing, including anti-terrorism, and incorporate seasoned off-duty officers (ODO) and other specialists in their forces. They are also up to speed with the latest practices and technologies used in the private sector, or with the lessons that can be learned from other jurisdictions. All of these attributes provide a significant advantage.

> When an event occurs, we have to have those existing relationships with law enforcement agencies from top to bottom in order to be an effective partner for our client.

"In the event of an emergency, private security forces are often the first people on the site," notes Charles Bohnenberger, Allied Universal's Senior Vice President of Government Services. "When an event occurs, we must have those existing relationships with law enforcement agencies from top to bottom in order to be an effective partner for our client. And when the police arrive, we draw a big bright red line and distinction that we are not law enforcement officers."

Nicholas Paros served under Maryland Governor Robert Ehrlich on the Law Enforcement Coordinating Council in 2004. At that time the Department of Natural resources had two police departments, the Natural Resources Police and Park Rangers. The governor couldn't understand why they had two full-service police departments under the Department of Natural Resources. He asked Paros to lead the Maryland Park Rangers/Maryland Natural Resources Police merger, which removed law enforcement officers from the Park Ranger service, embedding them in the Maryland Natural Resources Police, and used a civilian force for the Park Ranger Service. Says Paros, who now is Allied Universal's Regional Vice President, "This saved the state $38 million over time and ended the waste of resources entailed by having sworn law enforcement officers in the parks manage non-critical everyday tasks such as ensuring safety and compliance with park rules."

---

[4] https://journals.plos.org/plosone/article?id=10.1371/journal.pone.0187392

The Role of Off-Duty Officers (ODOs)

Not everyone is aware of the key role off-duty police officers (ODOs) play in private security. In fact, ODOs make up a significant part of the force. Working alongside highly trained traditional security personnel, they help safeguard employees and visitors in nearly every government and industry sector. Today security companies are receiving unprecedented requests for ODO services.

A mantra among police is "you're never off duty." That's because ODOs are always armed and have powers of arrest, as well as an obligation to enforce the law. If an ODO observes a crime against a person in progress, they are obligated to act. Their advantage over a traditional security officer in a high-crime area is their law enforcement powers with authorization to act. That resource can pick up the phone and call and ask somebody to respond. When an off-duty officer calls the precinct to report a robbery in progress and ask for backup, they generally are going to get their request fulfilled immediately because it's blue on blue.

In numerous cities Allied Universal provides security officers and manages the off-duty police program. Our team, for example, works closely with the Fort Worth Police Department to provide off-duty, police officers for a set number of shifts during any given loop. "When it comes to law enforcement, these people provide some of the largest benefits we've ever seen as public safety multipliers, because they're literally sworn police on the street, but administered in a highly efficient way by private security providers," says Marcus Perdue, Allied Universal's Senior Vice President of Risk Consulting. "When one of our big business lines is employing off-duty police for private businesses we work directly with the police department." Allied Universal also has the capability to reach out to officers in different forces and jurisdictional levels to get the very best personnel for the job at hand, taking a load of administrative duties off the desks of public employees so that they can focus better on their key mission.

Private security companies like Allied Universal have existing infrastructure and know law enforcement agency policies. They can manage sworn police officers on site, alleviating the police department of that task. However, not all jurisdictions allow ODOs to work private security details – a potential issue on which your security provider will be able to advise.

2.3   Healthcare

Healthcare is an optimal setting for public-private security partnerships, but also presents a highly complex regulatory environment. By their very nature healthcare facilities are centers for high stress and emotional reactions – places where workplace violence is most likely to occur. They also are critical points of activity whenever there is a disastrous event, whether a nightclub shooting, a public gathering gone awry, a riot, fire or weather event. Their public safety concerns reached an even higher level with the onset of the coronavirus pandemic when their security had to implement new protocols and processes almost overnight. Suddenly, they had to enforce masking policies, expanded restricted areas while limiting visitations from family members. Meanwhile, social unrest centered around vaccines, social distancing and masking flourished. As the pandemic progressed health facilities often had to construct, staff, and secure large outdoor vaccination sites. During this period a survey by National Nurses United found 31% of hospital RNs reported an increase in workplace violence.[5] Clearly, this perfect storm of controversary, instability and increasingly complex safety management called for the public safety multiplier made possible through partnership with private security.

Direct Costs of Workplace Violence – COVID-19

Hospital Violent Crime Increased 47% Last Year

IAHSS's 2022 Crime Survey found that the rate of murders, rapes, robberies, and aggravated assaults at U.S. hospitals dramatically increased in 2021 (a record 2.5 incidents per 100 beds)

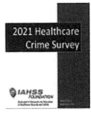

2021 Healthcare Crime Survey

Houston Methodist Hospital faced this environment with a hybrid approach to security staffing, encompassing private forces and off-duty officers from the local law enforcement agencies on its security team. The hospital actually has a substation where police officers work full time in an off-duty capacity. A police coordinator manages this ODO program for Houston Methodist. Because officers are working on an off-duty capacity in the hospital systems that are not owned their privatized, they are mostly working four to 6-hour shifts in constant rotation.

"Hybrid programs provide unbelievable flexibility and allow each member of the team to focus on – and excel in – their particular part of the bigger picture," says

---

[5] "National Nurse Survey Reveals That Health Care Employers Need to Do More to Comply With OSHA Emergency Temporary Standard". National Nurses United, September 27, 2021. https://www.nationalnursesunited.org/press/national-nurse-survey-reveals-health-care-employers-need-to-do-more-to-protect-workers.

John H. Dailey, Chief of Police, Duke University and Duke University Hospital. "For example, our sworn law enforcement personnel have specific training and capabilities that allow them to handle complex investigative and policing functions, while our Allied Universal contract security personnel provide a layered approach to proactive community engagement while maintaining the flexibility to staff up for planned and unplanned events."

The healthcare environment is highly regulated in the U.S. under the Center for Medicare and Medicaid Services, and about 98% of the hospitals in the country receive federal funding. Because of that, healthcare facilities and personnel are subject to *conditions of participation* – regulations designed protect patient health and safety and ensure quality of care. For example, patients have a right to refuse care, and need to be treated from both a therapeutic standpoint and from a regulatory standpoint. These types of considerations significantly impact the parameters for on-site security.

"When patients become violent we've got to be able to discern the difference between clinical aggression and criminal aggression," says Lisa Terry, VP, Vertical Markets – Healthcare, Allied Universal, and author of *Active Shooter Response Handbook for Healthcare Workers*. "For example, on the street there are certain actions a police officer takes when someone becomes aggressive or becomes a threat to them, but in the healthcare environment, those same actions may not be appropriate. That said, it may be appropriate for officers who are well-trained in conflict management and non-escalation/de-escalation to be a part of that intervention team."

Terry explains that clinical aggression may be the result of a patient's unique situation, such as a brain injury, the influence of an impairing substance, or any number of other medical reasons. These situations most often require a therapeutic approach. "When officers are working in the healthcare environment, they must be extremely well-trained and understand how to respond to each situation," she adds. "The healthcare security and police officers should work closely with the clinical professionals to ensure a proper response to the violent behavior."

The Health Insurance Portability and Accountability Act of 1996 (HIPAA) creates additional conditions that govern a law enforcement response. For example, when investigating an active shooter situation, where the alleged perpetrator is in the emergency department being treated, we are highly constrained in our information gathering if the patient, doesn't want to give permission to talk.

2.4   Schools: From K12 to Higher Ed

Schools are a significant vertical for the public-private security partnership. The U.S. Department of Justice has reported that 92% of all public colleges and universities have their own sworn and armed campus officers.[6] Others primarily use their

---

[6] "Campus Law Enforcement, 2011–12". *Bureau of Justice Statistics*. Retrieved October 21, 2021.

local police department with private security taking a valuable supplemental role – for example, unlocking rooms for students who have lost their keys, checking IDs at residence halls, walking people home at night – services that are not cost-effective for conventional police to handle.

"The main challenge in education is staffing, so schools on all levels look to us to augment their capabilities," says Masha Karimi, Manager of Education for Allied Universal. "Each institution of higher education is unique in how they approach public safety, and whether they have security, their own police department, or a combination of the two."

Effective campus safety also means protection from mass violence, as well as working holistically to prevent and reduce emotional, environmental, organizational, medical, and social hazards campuses face daily. Having a trained, experienced, and dedicated armed or unarmed safety and security professional to serve as a liaison between students, staff and external law enforcement can significantly improve campus protection.

At Texas A&M Law School Allied Universal has served as the sole campus security provider. This model is especially effective for smaller campuses where budgets may be constrained. It's very costly to have a full working police department, so a partnership in that case can provide a tremendous cost savings – all under the leadership of their vice president of security.

> K-12 has its own contours because you're dealing with minors with a significantly different set of issues. This requires highly specialized skills for private security officers.

Texas Southmost College (TSC) in Brownsville provides another example of collaboration with law enforcement to ensure a safe and secure environment for its campus community. There Allied Universal has worked with their administration to identify staffing levels and patrol schedules to maximize security in an efficient manner, including an evolving patrol plan to ensure maximum coverage for its campus. The partnership also has incorporated a leading employee-sourced risk technology platform with Allied Universal's HELIAUS® reporting system to help prevent serious safety and security incidents on campuses.

PPP works for K-12 as well. That sector has its own contours because you're dealing with minors with a significantly different set of issues, requiring highly specialized skills. For this sector, what sets leading security agencies like Allied Universal apart is the amount of training given to officers before they even step foot on the property of any school. These individuals not only receive onboarding officer training, but also must go through specialized K through 12 training.

In most cases dedicated campus safety professionals become trusted advisors for students, parents, and the administration. This allows them a much more complete view of campus activities and dynamics. As a result, they are often the first to recognize and help address a threat before it evolves into a bigger crisis.

2.5 Business Improvement Districts

Business Improvement districts are a ubiquitous part of most municipalities. These areas are particularly well-suited to the PPP model. There are nearly 50 such districts just in New York City, and they can be found in more than 1200 municipalities throughout the country, according to Cornell University.[7] These districts are essentially communities within communities. A private security presence in these areas provides public ambassadors – people who greet and provide guidance to tourists. But the most important thing that they are doing is enhancing public safety. They do that by looking for anomalies, whether graffiti and gangs in higher gang-activity locations or working with social services to manage and help mitigate homelessness. They're also looking for drug usage, effectively responding to opioid overdoses when required.

They're looking for additional unsavory element that can impact the safety and attractiveness of the area, but with a softer approach than traditional law enforcement. For those in need of assistance, someone in a golf shirt looks more approachable than a traditional security or police officer, and that clearly offers advantages.

In places like Brooklyn multiple special business districts are cooperating to enhance the resources that are not as a readily available from municipalities than maybe they used to be. So they're addressing graffiti or cleaning up the sidewalks. They're making certain that trash picked up, looking for broken light bulbs or non-functional streetlamps. By doing all this they are making these business Improvement districts better – creating environments where there is enhanced public safety and a better experience for all.

2.6 Public Transit

Public transit is another area where a PPP can provide a public safety multiplier. Major metropolitan transit systems often find themselves not being able to hire enough police officers under their budget, and yet they need the security presence. Facing rising crime, New York City's Metropolitan Transit Authority (MTA) in 2021 announced a plan to spend $2.2 million each month on private security officers to address a 40% rise in crime across the 472 stations and 665 miles of track that comprise its subway system.[8]

In these cases, Allied Universal works with transit systems to design a specific criterion as part of the initial request for proposal (RFP) process. They tell us about their needs and criteria, and then train accordingly to match those and provide the

[7] Mildred Warner, et al., "Business Improvement Districts: Issues in Alternative Local Public Service Provision" Cornell University, Ithaca, NY, June 2002.

[8] Paul Berger, "New York City Subway Hires Security to Improve Safety," *The Wall Street Journal*, May 24, 2021.

appropriate bill rate. We're a major participant in the International Association of the Chiefs of Police transit meetings. We're involved in sponsorship and participation as an equal in the American Public Transit Association pier advisory group for security. That has allowed us to stay intimately involved with the customer base and adapt training to the current needs of mass transit across the U.S. That includes dealing with homeless and emotionally disturbed individuals, including first responder training for administering NARCAN® for opioid overdoses.

Southern California' Metrolink has seven lines and 62 stations operating on 534 miles of rail network, with close to 754,000 weekday riders as of the second quarter of 2022.[9] Metrolink contracted for such services with Allied Universal because L.A. County Sheriff resources were so expensive. Allied Universal personnel were placed on some of the higher-crime lines to provide a constant presence, providing a public safety multiplier without the dollar multiplier.

Allied Universal also provides security and sworn law enforcement officers for San Jose, California's transit system, including those who are armed. There our account managers sit right next to a captain from the sheriff's office, working in tight coordination.

2.7 Aviation

Operating under Federal regulations, airports have both traditional security and law enforcement as part of their plan. With a few exceptions, about 90% is the law enforcement component, which is either provided by an airport police department, or a contract with their municipal police department. For example, the Dallas Fort Worth Police Department has a presence at the airport, but the security component is 90% provided by contract security.

As mentioned at the top of the chapter, the smaller, executive airport in Rockford, Illinois looked to Allied Universal to source the police function of their security program at that airport since the local PD didn't have enough personnel to meet their needs. So, they engaged with us to coordinate with other jurisdictions to bring in personnel whom they cannot directly access. We pay and schedule these personnel because it's really the only way the airport can get enough active-duty police with full authority in that jurisdiction.

---

[9] Metrolink, "Quarterly Fact Sheet 2022."

2.8   Port Protection

PPPs are an effective fit for port authorities throughout North America, where polic-ing requires deep knowledge of compliance requirements, physical security, and other industry challenges. We partner with port operators, cruise ship operators, and cargo shipping companies across the country to provide U.S. Coast Guard Maritime Security (MARSEC)-compliant security programs. Our dedicated team of maritime security and subject matter experts provide nationwide support and best practices for safety and security in a maritime environment.

At Maryland ports 165 unarmed private security personnel from Allied Universal control critical access points, fulfilling requirements mandated by the Maritime Transportation, Security Act of 2002, which trickles down to 33 federal codes regu-lated by the US Coast Guard. There they work with port police, the Maryland Transportation Authority Police Court attachment.

> To augment the police functions or to offload some administrative tasks we utilize Allied Universal, primarily at our access control points – a wall of security, which is very important.

"We have the police doing police work – patrolling, making arrests inspecting, pro-viding forensics, a SWAT team, and other criminal investigations as necessary," explains David Espie, Director of Security for the Maryland Port Administration. "To augment the police functions or to offload some administrative tasks we utilize Allied Universal, primarily at our access control points – a wall of security, which is very important. These critical forces are providing access control at all our six state terminals."

Undeclared passengers hidden in entering vehicles is one area where private security forces are key. In these cases, a person without proper credentials is hidden within the vehicle. At certain locations inbound secondary inspections will detect the undeclared passenger, who will be detained. The security breach will result in a report and further investigation that includes photos, the company name on the truck, and other elements. That will be followed up with a phone call to the police and further investigation.

2.9   Disaster Recovery

In 2022 Hurricane Ian caused over $60 billion dollars of damage in southwest Florida.[10] Private security working with local authorities augmented recovery efforts.

Allied Universal brought 64 off-duty police officers from out-of-state to the disaster area, augmenting the 50 personnel the company already had down there

---

[10] Ian Livingston, "What Made Hurricane Ian So Intense: By the Numbers," *The Washington Post*, October 4, 2022.

who were providing contracted security for private entities – mostly for large national retailers with whom we've had long-standing agreements.

"We sourced people from other jurisdictions," says Bohnenberger. "They worked for us for a long time and they have RVs and boats and chainsaws and generators and everything they need. They've done this for a while and they're kind of tip of the spear." These private teams go to a safe place that is close to the storm, and as soon as it passes they are first on scene.

"They're kind of viewed as almost a relief agency at that point," Bohnenberger adds. "You'll have 100 people in line waiting to pick up plywood and other supplies, and they manage all that and guard the fuel trucks. They do it all day, as well as search and rescue." They also will monitor the lists of employees who haven't checked in with the company, and after 48 hours have passed will travel to the person's home address, via a small boat of necessary. In the aftermath of Ian, these Allied team members rescued multiple people from their homes in places local law, enforcement hadn't gotten to yet. In all of these search-and-rescue scenarios these officers can communicate and coordinate regularly with county deputies.

2.10   Additional Innovative Collaborations

The scenarios in which a public-private partnership can bring benefits to public safety go far beyond the examples listed above. Other innovative examples include:

- **Sporting Events and Concerts:** For sporting events and concerts Norfolk, Virginia employs Allied Universal's Event Services Group as traditional screeners, *and* they outsource the PD function to us as well. We do that across the country. For example, at the Alamodome in San Antonio, the police function is outsourced to us. We manage and pay the police officers on behalf of the city, relieving it of significant administrative and personnel overhead while maintaining the same level of service.
- **Mental Health and Drug Response:** Mental health transport is a growing trend in public safety PPPs across the country. Currently police have to sometimes sit for 24 hours straight with a mental health patient prior to them being evaluated, then either committed or released. With staff shortages and tight budgets, they are stretched very thin performing that function. In numerous states that is being turned over to private security. We happen to be developing entire programs around this for non-violent patients, especially with regard to facility-to-facility transport. This model is under evaluation for greater use in the private sector, with our partnership experiences providing with a lot more clarity to help manage that problem.
- **Booking Services:** Where allowed under law, highly trained private security professionals, often off-duty officers, or police department veterans, can be employed to provide booking services at precincts, freeing law enforcement staff to focus on their core duties.

- **Managing Disabled vehicles:** Depending upon the jurisdiction, private security can respond to disabled vehicle and accident calls, providing the public safety multiplier to highways.

These represent just a few of the possible PPP collaborations. They all depend on establishing credibility as a partner, building consensus on the goals of the assignment, the endgame. Then, it really comes down to delivering on quality and demonstrating what the partnership looks like in action. At the end of the day, all factors must be aligned with the outcomes of what we're trying to achieve with the client and a law enforcement agency.

3 Real-World Considerations and Challenges

Embarking on enhanced public-private partnerships requires careful consideration of multiple, complex real-world issues. No two locales or situations are exactly alike, and their solutions will be shaped by jurisdictional issues, budget considerations, and the political environment.

Understanding "Partnership"

Plenty of well-meaning people may not fully understand the term "partnership." Private security work, whether it be for a private sector client or the government, is usually under the auspices of a contract. Allied Universal works with over 1000 government agencies across the United States, Canada, and approximately another 500 in Europe. Many of our government and private sector clients work in a spirit of partnership to find solutions to a problem. But perhaps just as many at least on the government side look at the relationship in a more conventional way.

You hear this quite a bit: "It's strictly an employer-contractor dynamic." Considering any kind of public-private partnership in that light would be a mistake, depriving you of maximizing all the potential benefits that would stem from the relationship. Of course we all comply with the terms of the contract, but real life can change rapidly, requiring effective, immediate responses – just look at Covid and how the world turned on a dime. This requires approaching the collaboration as dynamic partners focused on identifying solutions through ongoing, creative communication, rather than pointing to a particular numbered paragraph in your agreement.

3.1   Jurisdictional Considerations

The contours of public-private law enforcement partnerships in the United States and around the world are largely shaped, or constrained, by the laws in specific jurisdictions. Overall, about 17 states in the U.S. have laws that provide some degree of traditional law enforcement powers to private security.

In North Carolina, chapter 74E of the Company Police Act permits private-company police departments. There, we have a bona-fide police department of 170 sworn law enforcement officers assigned to a variety of client security programs across the state, from serving as the police department at a community college to transit police. In other markets it may be a modified law enforcement authority. These forces – whose training meets or exceeds the certification requirements as any state law, county or municipal law enforcement officer – have all of the same powers as "regular police," able to make arrests and write citations for violations of the law in the jurisdictions they have been contracted to protect.

> Overall, about 17 states in the U.S. have laws that provide some degree of traditional law enforcement powers to private security.

In South Carolina private security officers are considered law enforcement and have the same authority as sheriff's deputies – able to run traffic radar, make arrests and use blue lights. In Tennessee, after our officers are trained and have passed background checks, they are deputized by the state's public safety director to provide the security of all state buildings. On property, they are sworn law enforcement officers with limited duties, so it's truly more accurate to call them special police.

In Washington, D.C. special police officers have full law enforcement authority on the properties they are assigned to protect. In fact, no armed security guard in Washington. D.C. must be a special police officer, which requires a different level of training. These special forces include the Metro Special Police, the University of the District of Columbia Police, DC Library Police, and other special forces. They all have the authority to make arrests for felonies and misdemeanors, and to utilize blue and white lights on their vehicles.

Privately supplied officers on the Denver transit system must be graduates of a bona fide law enforcement academy. They're armed guards working under the direction of a police department of about 10.

"Any law enforcement officer in the State of Texas is considered a licensed, certified peace officer," notes Tracy Fuller, President, Government Services, Allied Universal. "They have authority throughout the entire state for powers of detaining and arresting. Conversely, in Florida you actually cannot cross the Dade County line into Broward County as a law enforcement officer and detain somebody. You are considered out of jurisdiction and would be able to act only in the capacity of a private citizen."

While jurisdictional nuances can impede law enforcement across local borders and in terms of sourcing personnel, these challenges often can be mitigated by the private component. One example is the public safety multiplier capacity for such public entities as public transit systems that cross multiple jurisdictions. In New York City, for example, The MTA police is a privatize police force that gets state funding. It is part of the New York City Transit Authority Police also extends to the Long Island Railroad.

> Training is a huge component because you're looking for mental illness, drug use, and bad actors, engaging your law enforcement colleagues to serve I the capacity for which they have been trained.

Transit Police typically have authority across the entire system, giving them the ability to not only serve as eyes and ears, but to write citations. "As in other verticals, training is a huge component because you're looking for mental illness, drug use, and bad actors, and engaging your law enforcement colleagues to serve in the capacity for which they have been trained," says Fuller.

A private component to law enforcement also enables personnel sourcing opportunities that may be out of reach for public police forces. "In this model we could reach out to nearby jurisdictions, such as the County Sheriff's office," Perdue explains. "If we're providing service to the Rockford, Illinois airport, for example, we would obtain permission from the Rockford PD to allow those outsources Sherriff's Department personnel to operate within that area. Generally, our approach would be to use a combination of state, county, and local PD, providing off-duty officers in the jurisdiction we're serving while managing all of the administration.

3.2   Liability Issues

As security contractors and providers, we need to be mindful of whether or not a partner is taking on liability in a particular setting. Despite the effort in some communities to undermine qualified immunity – a legal defense that protects sworn police officers from lawsuits due to their actions – the reality is that most jurisdictions are statutorily required to defend and indemnify individuals acting within the scope of their duties unless they clearly showed malice in their actions. In fact, a 2020 national study found that 99.98% of all damage awards in police misconduct litigation (including verdicts and settlements) were in fact paid by the employing public entity.[11]

There is a similar situation with private security forces participating in PPPs in that public agencies will sometimes provide some form of immunity to those contracted to work for them. The key question to ask is does that entity's sovereign immunity extend to the contracted security provider? That is something that can be mitigated in any number of ways, including contractual language, safety programs,

---

[11] Bruce Praet, "Should Cops Buy Liability Insurance?," *Police 1*, September 28, 2020. https://www.police1.com/police-products/financial-services/articles/should-cops-buy-liability-insurance-qVvzG9feh48ErVup/.

and claims management, but the devil is in the details that must be defined, negotiated if necessary, and put in writing before any engagement is contracted.

Social media adds a new wrinkle to liability and public perception exposure in general. That's directly related to the public aspect of what we do when partnering with law enforcement – especially at government facilities and stadiums. When you're standing outside at a sporting event or large concert and something bad is happening, there likely will be a lot of people watching and recording on their phones. It therefore is imperative that private security personnel are properly trained to the highest standards so that they react properly to any conceivable situation.

3.3   Training, Firearms, and Unions

Most states have strict requirements for law enforcement personnel regarding minimum physical, medical, educational, and criminal history standards for anyone performing public safety duties. These don't apply to the private sector, so assure that personnel involved in a PPP for law enforcement fully meet or exceed all requisite legal standards.

All states have rather extensive standards for completion of 16–24 weeks of basic police training at certified academies. While some private security companies have developed equivalent training programs or employ ODOs among their employees, contractors will want to make sure those courses meet state- mandated requirements for content and length.

Firearms are another point of concern when private employees are in the equation. While regulations vary from state to state, they are prohibited and illegal in many public and private locations. Our Special Police can carry firearms anywhere a traditional police officer can, exempted from the legal status due to being a fully sworn law enforcement officer.

Law enforcement unions have sometimes been a challenge for agencies and communities seeking to expand efforts to work with public/private police partnerships, especially in the northeastern U.S. Elsewhere there may be professional associations for sheriffs and other sworn law enforcement that lobby extensively against the inclusion and expansion of private police forces. "Police unions and employee organizations have traditionally resisted any attempts to supplement police departments with private non-union employees," notes Jay S. Berman, Ph.D., Professor Emeritus, Department of Criminal Justice at New Jersey City University and author of *Police Administration and Progressive Reform.* "These are seen as threats to employment opportunity and job security, so prohibitions or limitations are often included in collective bargaining agreements."

"In places where employees are heavily unionized, we take the collective bargaining agreement and will negotiate with union at the same time that we're negotiating with a client on the scope of the contracted work as allowed by state and local law," says Robert Quackenbush, Vice President of Operations, Allied Universal Security Services, and Chief of Police, Allied Universal Special Police.

3.4   Public Policy and Community Issues

Public policy and community issues may arise as well. These are private settings where members of the community may feel uncomfortable with a law enforcement presence. Conversely, there can be community objection to private for-profit companies taking on public roles and making money through tax dollars. These are the sort of public policy and community reactions that I think must be assessed whenever we get a private enterprise working with public agencies.

Remember that if a legal issue arises, whether it's a claim or incident or contract question because it's a public arena, it can very quickly become a political or reputational issue. The contract is a way to mitigate that somewhat.

"I encourage security partners to focus on reputational and political risk," advises David Buckman, Allied Universal's General Counsel. "First and foremost, that often is the most immediate and most meaningful risk in addition to any legal liabilities. That makes it critical to understand what community members are concerned about – and those kinds of issues can become difficult. Any time you are dealing with a distressed population, for example the homeless, you must remember that you're dealing with people who are availing themselves of government safety net services because they've experienced difficulties in their lives. Even people receiving medical care in distressed communities may be challenging, so you have to be prepared to handle difficult situations, and handling them appropriately. Make sure you are doing the right thing in the context of those populations."

3.5   Contracting Considerations

At a certain level, contracting in a PPP is not unlike engaging with any service provider, whether you're hiring from the public or public side – often you get what you pay for. But in this case the stakes can be high, directly impacting public safety and the wellbeing of the community.

Contract liability language generally is pretty standard, and the contracting process often revolves around working through the limits on liability. However, you also should pay careful attention to the specifics of all requirements, including the essential task of rigorously focusing at the outset on a clear, concise scope of work. Any violation or in deviation from that tends to invite a lot of scrutiny. "We see a lot of government-favored contract language that exposes the private organization to probably more significant risk than we would take on in the private sector," says Perdue. "And so, in the private sector, we could often negotiate terms conditions in a way that limits liability to our negligence, for example, rather than just broad liability for anything that happens."

So ask yourself: Does the public entity have a clear enough understanding of precisely what is expected of the private provider? If you don't have that level of that detail initially in the agreement, itis likely to open an issue down the road if there is an incident.

Any government entity also should carefully vet and screen the provider candidate to ensure that the company aligns with community values in terms of diversity, their approach to safety, how they go about their operations, their overall approach and training on the use of force, and how they think about cultural sensitivity in the communities they serve. Make sure you are aligning with the right vendors in terms of those factors.

Another factor to consider is that changes to major procurement documents and contracts must be approved by the city council. In some of those cases attorneys may be very reluctant to make any changes to what is already is in a contract – factors that will be critical to the work we will be doing and its outcomes. If we were to have a serious incident, the parties may be exposed.

The bottom line: When you sit down with somebody for initial discussions or as you're working through your agreement, make sure there's full communication and the respective responsibilities of the entities involved are in writing.

3.6   Budget Considerations

Be wary of being too focused on short-term costs versus longer-term risk and negative outcomes. Even if the short-term investment seems high, keep in mind that the public safety multiplier that comes into play. If you don't take all the necessary precautions for optimal security levels now and you have a problem down the road, it could end up being a much greater magnitude if there's some kind of issue that happens because you aren't adequately staffed and covered.

This obviously can be challenging because public agencies go through competitive bid processes and tend to use the standard of *lowest responsible bidder*, meaning lowest price among bidders that meet certain qualifications. That frequently can be a healthy balance, but lower fees tend to predominate, and the criteria are not always sufficiently rigorous for the task.

Certainly, cost matters, taxpayer dollars must be managed carefully, but all parties need to spend more time and thought with good industry experts on what *is* a responsible bidder, while making sure the bar is high enough to fulfill their needs. That's because at the end of the day, when it's the city council, selection committee or some board is about to decide, you can't at that stage start trying to raise the bar on the qualifications. If anyone has checked the boxes that were selling it early on, that's going to drive the outcome.

We had a port client in California port that had a security issue. Not a big one, but it was big enough from a regulatory perspective that we brought it to their attention. We said, "Look, you should address this with 'xyz' technology, because as currently covered if somebody wants to stick it to you, they can." They didn't take our advice because they looked at this proactive security measure as simply a $10,000 expenditure. That was not a prudent decision because their state of non-compliance was

subject to a $30,000 fine. Sure enough, there was a breach, and the breach was origi-
nally focused on us, because our guard "let someone through." But the reality was
that it was a bicycle rider who went through the exit lane where we had told them
they needed those controls. In this situation our people were not tasked to check
credentials at that location – in fact, we weren't even contracted to staff that part of
their security. And what happened was that a $10,000 solution suddenly became an
exponentially a more expensive problem because the Coast Guard was about to shut
the port.

The bottom line: Always consider your investment in terms of the broader risk
and benefits. In New York City there are a lot of conversations about the subway
system and what the mayor and transit police are doing to keep the public safe. The
concerns keep people off the subway, which in turn has broader economic impact.
When you enhance that with a private partnership, you gain the full public safety
multiplier. It has economic benefits to the end user and all those different things that
carry over.

3.7   The Need for Collaboration

"I think the largest challenges always exist from the disconnect between law
enforcement and security," says Fuller. "Law enforcement does not think of themselves as being a security function and they don't simply think of security as being
contributors. So, part of it is bridging, that gap is building those alliances that allow
them to thrive together versus Live separately and any good public-private partnership? It's given taken to the sharing of information It comes down to the three Cs:
collaboration, communication, and coordination."

4   Utilizing Liaison Organizations

Several national organizations offer councils and committees dedicated to fostering
dialogue between public and private entities. Joining and working closely with these
organizations can help in defining solutions and sourcing the right resources for putting together a successful partnership.

4.1   ASIS International's Law Enforcement Liaison Council (LELC)

This organization helps create strategic alliances among organizations of all sizes exploring public- and private-sector security issues related to law enforcement. It supports external public-private partnership initiatives and transition training – exactly the kinds of things discussed in this chapter. LELC fosters alliances between law enforcement, business, and security stakeholders to advance critical infrastructure protection, business recovery, and assess protection efforts by identifying best practices and facilitating opportunities for networking. ASIS offers multiple levels of certification to security personnel, all of which require field experience and a written exam on crime prevention, evidence handling, the use of force, and emergency response.

From our perspective ASIS has been a great partner, full of what I would call very thoughtful public servants. This committee has always been welcoming to us as an industry, but every year over time they have become even more deeply involved in finding partnership solutions to the security issues we all face. It also fields breakout groups, such as one for the transit police, university police, large cities and small cities. We participate in all of those, and there is a great interaction between us. Website: community.asisonline.org

4.2   International Association of Chiefs of Police (IACP) Private Sector Liaison Committee

Everyone in our sector is familiar with IACP, and this committee, composed of representative members from all facets of the private security sector and the law enforcement community, can serve as a valuable resource for all stakeholders The committee promotes dialog, research, education, and training with a focus on today's most pressing issues. (http://www.theiacp.org.)

4.3   International Downtown Association (IDA)

The International Downtown Association (IDA) focuses on bringing enhanced safety and livability to communities of all sizes throughout the United States and the world. Through its research, white papers, and briefs, it provides data-driven insights to its membership. Member resources include case studies and best practices in the organization's Knowledge Center. IDA regularly issues public safety initiatives briefs and also offers its Vitality Index, utilizing data from 44 downtowns across the U.S. to benchmark livability factors such as economy, inclusion, and vibrancy. Website: www.downtown.org

4.4   The National League of Cities (NLC)

This well-known national organization brings together more than 2700 municipalities across the country with the mission of working together to influence federal policy, strengthen local leadership and drive innovative solutions. NLC does this through Federal advocacy committees, blogs, podcasts, newsletters, workshops, and scores of other resources. The organization's The Public Safety & Crime Prevention (PSCP) Committee develops policy positions on a range of security issues, including homeland security, domestic terrorism, crime prevention, corrections, court systems and other areas central to public-private security partnerships. Website: www.nlc.org

5   Making it Happen

In 2009 the Law Enforcement-Private Security Consortium identified five key components for law enforcement PPPs.[12] The following is my take on each of them, based on today's realities and needs.

1. **Compelling Mission:** When embarking on a new public-private partnership, the first thing is to do an assessment of your mission, based on your risks and needs. What problems are you experiencing? Is it an issue of homelessness? Vandalism? Violent crime? In what areas or in how much of your region are these issues occurring?
2. **External Support or Models for Formation:** Once you have completed your assessment, study how other communities have developed highly effective PPPS. What models are likely to have the beat application to your situation. Consider your stakeholders – whether business Leaders or elected officials – their specific needs and their willingness to take part in the initiative. If your situation is like most, the solution will not be to increase your sworn police presence, just because forces are stretched so thin these days.
3. **Founders, Leaders, and Facilitators as Active Enablers:** You also should appoint a champion and/or group dedicated to development of the partnership. Gather and empower all stakeholders with regular meetings and other communications. You're going need to get consensus, so come to the table with an open mind, strategically prioritizing those that will be the best fit for a partnership. Consider what tools you can deploy to solve those problems? There's an old joke that if you have is a hammer, then every problem is a nail. But in this case you don't just have a hammer – you have an entire toolbox from the private sector

---

[12]The Law Enforcement-Private Security Consortium, "Operation Partnership: Trends and Practices in Law Enforcement and Private Security Collaborations," August 2009.

and the public sector that can be used with us those challenges. Commit to using the whole toolbox.

4. **Means of Communication:** Reach Out. Communicate. Sit down with industry experts and major providers and have a candid conversation. Ask your questions, raise your concerns, do your homework, get input. Get to know the providers get to know what they do. You know visit places where they operate. Don't simply write an RFP in the laboratory and mail it out to a bunch of addresses you got off a list. Dig deep to fully understand the organizations with which you're looking to partner. Have a dialogue with them, learn from them and make sure they're learning from you

5. **Sustaining Structure and Resources:** As discussions progress, continue working closely with all stakeholders to help ensure buy-in of the overall governance framework, standards, and best practices, and how the entire program will be administered. Make sure you are extremely detailed in defining the scope of the mission, the division of responsibilities and collaborations, and contingencies for when things don't go exactly as planned.

The NYPD Shield Program

The New York Police Department's Shield program is a large, successful private-public partnership focused on counterterrorism, based on the knowledge that planning for an attack does not necessarily occur in the target city. NYPD Shield is the flagship organization of the Global Shield Network (GSN) with more than 20,000 members in 50 U.S. states, 54 countries. Its ranks include 100,000 individuals – primarily security directors, law enforcement, and government agency personnel. Membership comes from the corporate, private security, and management sectors, approximately 7000 organizations in all.

Communication and training by the NYPD are key components of the program, provided to members and non-members alike. NYPD Shield shares open-source intelligence, information, and resources on emerging and evolving threats and counterterrorism conditions within New York City (active shooter incidents and detecting hostile surveillance) via its website, seminars, conferences, and other communications platforms. It also provides table-top exercises and live drills.

One of the best PPP implementations out there, NYPD Shield allows law enforcement and the private sector – including the nation's 1.5–2 million security professionals – to leverage their resources for the safety of all – truly a public safety multiplier. Website: www.nypdshield.org

5.1   Clear Communication at the Outset

Government procurement officials can have wildly different approaches on how to go about selecting a security partner. I have seen a broad disparity of requests for proposals (RFPs) – from those that are well thought out and ask the right questions, to those that fail to disclose the necessary information required to submit a comprehensive bid. For example, government agencies should be clear as to how many armed and unarmed security professionals will be needed and for what shifts. They also should be as specific as possible about whether they require sustainable security solutions, as well as necessary certifications and qualifications for personnel, any special training requirements, required clearances and other recruiting specifications so that there are no misunderstandings or assumptions of what can or can't be done by any of the parties.

Ideally the government agency should also consider inviting the vendor to visit the site or venue where the service will take place. That allows all parties to ask questions and discuss nuances of the solutions – opening the door for more strategic choices and a clearer view of who will be the best match as a partner. Agencies also can issue draft RFPs to seek industry input before issuing a final solicitation. Potential private security partners as well as security industry associations can provide additional guidance as to what information should be covered.

> When exploring any partnership, and especially where there is great political sensitivity, ask those tough questions at the outset.

"When exploring any partnership, and especially where there is great political sensitivity, ask those tough questions at the outset," advises David Buckman, Allied Universal's General Counsel. "The security provider should consider the following when having conversations with a government entity: What they're really looking for? Are they laser-focused on the scope of work? If they are, what does the contract say? If we're not talking about the scope, and instead we're talking about the language in the contract, that's potentially an issue you need to mitigate. Having an understanding at the outset of what the end result is for both parties is really important."

Ultimately, all parties around the table should be open to new ways of looking at security. In the current climate, forward-thinking chiefs and elected officials should begin by holding public forums and meetings where they would invite all stakeholders, public and private, to express their thoughts on how they think a partnership will work. You can begin privately. It starts with a conversation, and then you need to expand it from there.

6   Summary: The Public Safety Multiplier

Effectively facing today's unprecedented economic and social realities through a public-private partnership requires a mutual understanding of roles and benefits it entails. That entails respect among all parties, and fully understanding your and other stakeholders' roles in working together. It must be an equal partnership. You can't have a private organization or government organizations law enforcement and security working at cross-purposes. There has to be an attitude of "We're in this together to make it successful; we're equal partners in the effort." So how does it work? What is my role? What's your role?

In the private sector, you must be politically astute. You must really understand the agency to deal with, along with its communities and constituencies – their pain points and sensitivities. You must walk in their shoes and sit in their seats.

All parties in the PPP should stay focused on the key factors that make these partnerships successful:

- **Leadership Support:** When public and private forces work in unison, they create solutions stronger than either can do alone. A robust commitment from police leadership is the cornerstone of crime prevention. The same type of dedication and a strong display of support is necessary for a public-private partnership to flourish.
- **Collaboration, Not Competition:** Private security can support police agencies by relieving them of routine calls and responsibilities. In most locales security officers are not police officers – their role is not to replace but to supplement police officers who can then focus solely on their law enforcement duties. They are a public safety multiplier.
- **Quality and Professionalism:** The security services industry has rapidly evolved. These highly trained professionals often share many of the same skills as police. In some contracted services, the required qualifications for security officers are the same as they are for police officers. They must have graduated from a recognized police academy, pass the same background checks, and even have a few years of police experience. In addition, many private security personnel have prior military or law enforcement experience.
- **Security Officer Capabilities:** Whether there's a need for crowd control, campus, or business district patrols, lock out assistance or customer service, security officers can work in tandem with police officers in many ways, creating more opportunity for police to focus their attention where it is needed most.

Through every level of partnership – from information sharing and casual interaction to formal contractual collaboration – police and security working together will always benefit our communities. This can be a real win for governments and communities, while helping to make government be more responsive, effective, and fiscally efficient.

"In this day and age, with domestic terrorism, mass shootings and other threats, there's definitely a need for a better working relationship between the public and private sector, but it has to occur on the local level," advises Bruce McBride, former Police Commissioner for the State University of New York (SUNY), which encompasses 64 campuses statewide. "You can talk as much as you want a thousand feet up, but unless the trust occurs in precincts and with the local police chief – a real partnership just won't exist."

As a public safety multiplier, we can do the right things for the right people, but there's got to be buy-in from not only those local police level, but from political leaders and the public. When you attain those three things and execute with the best model, training, and expertise for the mission at hand you're going to give yourself the very best opportunity to succeed every time.

The Importance of Public-Private Partnerships

Steve Somers, David R. Hines, Terry L. Sullivan, and Colleen Arnold

Abstract This chapter highlights cooperative arrangements between GardaWorld private security services and federal, provincial, state, and local law enforcement agencies in the U.S. and in Canada. These arrangements come in the form of information sharing, training, and security service specialization and collaboration. These cooperative arrangements between public and private security create what is called a "Force Multiplier" that can be an important amplifier for crime deterrence. The chapter also provides perspectives on public private partnerships in security from two police officers from U.S. Sheriff's departments that have partnered with GardaWorld.

GardaWorld is a global champion in security services, integrated risk management and cash solutions, operating in 45 countries, serving more than 30,000 clients, and representing CA$5 billion in sales.

Founded in 1995 by Canadian entrepreneur Stephan Crétier, GardaWorld became a Canadian success story when Mr. Crétier founded the Groupe de Sécurité Trans-Québec with a $25,000 down payment. In 1999, he acquired the security company Garda, a security leader in eastern Canada.

Agile and responsive, we have grown from a small operation based in Montreal, Quebec, Canada, to a robust service business employing over 132,000 people. Our expansion combines a disciplined approach that includes strong organic growth and strategic acquisitions.

Our performance track record and commitment to customers is why we have continued to grow through the years. These strengths, combined with a focus on

S. Somers
GardaWorld, Operation-Security Services U.S., New York, NY, USA

D. R. Hines · T. L. Sullivan (✉)
Hanover County Sheriff's Office, Hanover, VA, USA
e-mail: tlsullivan@hanovercounty.gov

C. Arnold
GardaWorld, Customer Services Excellency, Quebec, Canada

best-in-class operating performance and sustainable business practices, will continue to drive our growth.

For several years now, GardaWorld has been a key partner with police services. A number of police officers have even left their police organizations to help grow the security industry and establish trusting relationships with their former colleagues.

GardaWorld has a wide range of expertise to support partners in the public safety domain. We provide a variety of services including security guards, mobile security, risk management, risk alerts, crowd management, video monitoring and virtual surveillance, investigation services, emergency medical support, turn-key mobile base camps, response logistics, specialized transportation, custody services, road flagging, executive protection, and talent management.

In order to give a comprehensive overview of public-private partnerships, we felt it was important to offer a perspective from both the public and private sector. For this reason, we requested assistance on this chapter from Sheriff David R. Hines and Captain Terry Sullivan of the Hanover County Sheriff's Department, with whom GardaWorld is a partner.

Colonel Hines, an elected sheriff in Hanover County, Virginia, is a true thoughtful leader in this area and has spent a great deal of his 39-year career dedicated to establishing and expanding these important relationships. Capt. Terry Sullivan is the founding president of the Global Shield Network (more to come later) and leads the Sheriff's Office information and intelligence services. Their combined almost 70 years' experience building these types of partnerships qualifies them as subject matter experts. I am honored by their continued partnership in providing public safety and developing open lines of communication between the sectors.

As you will note later in this chapter, the Hanover County Sheriff's Office is a critical part of the Global Shield Network. This agency has taken a well thought out program, originally developed by the NYPD Shield Program, and expanded its content, delivery, reach, and process. This program considers not only the private sector but also the community at large: local houses of worship, community associations, schools, higher education, and much more.

This program has been so well received that it won the ASIS Foundation Public Private Partnership in Excellence Award in honor of LEO Matthew Simeone in 2021.

1 Perspective

In the United States, 85% of the nation's infrastructure is protected by private security officers, either contractual or proprietary. This is an important fact to remember as we proceed with this chapter. The importance of establishing public-private partnerships should be a critical component of any security program.

For a U.S. security practitioner, the perfect security program would completely lock down the assets we are protecting—a police state of cameras, electronic countermeasures, barbed wire, armed guards, and limited access by only a select group.

The problem is that really can't be accomplished in today's environment. It's unsustainable and unrealistic. We need to develop programs that are flexible yet effective, and that consider the needs of the community they are established to protect.

We need to establish partnerships within the community, both on the public and private side.

2 Why the Need

Almost 80% of the terroristic threats uncovered since 9/11 have been because of information received from the private sector—not through intelligence agencies.

A comprehensive security program encompasses a variety of protection options that are designed to offer a secure yet flexible approach to protect assets. Today's security design is one that incorporates architectural and environmental design, and presents as layers of security rather than one solid line. Developing this holistic approach allows for the utmost protection, by considering all the different threats to security.

To properly accomplish this, we must consider the need, the asset, and the expected results. What is the physical security need? Is it manned guarding, remote monitoring, and electronic countermeasures? Is it intelligence as well as a plan for integrated risk management?

Additionally, we need to develop a network that allows us to collaborate with law enforcement on the local, state, and federal level. These relationships are critical to the success of any security program, but also benefit the local community through information sharing, training, and open lines of communication.

These relationships must be developed. They are critical to the core mission. These relationships are called public-private partnerships and for the last 20 years, GardaWorld has been actively involved in establishing, leading, and expanding these all over the country.

3 Historical Perspective

The historical background of public-private partnerships dates back centuries, but as financial demands have increased in recent years, these partnerships have rapidly expanded.

In the 1980s, partnerships between public law enforcement and the private sector began to open. Some were based on the private sector offering guidance, resources, and recognition to the government agencies. These partnerships, whether using Foundations or other fund-raising opportunities, have allowed private funds to help purchase equipment, develop community programs, and fund training initiatives that fall outside public budget. These important partnerships grew out of necessity but fell directly into the Community Policing Model. Partnerships are an equal, open relationship built on trust, which allows for the dissemination of information.

In 1989, the first legislation designed to support public-private partnerships was passed in California. In 1995, the Commonwealth of Virginia passed similar legislation and in 2011, 18 other states followed suit. By late 2012, 32 U.S. states and Puerto Rico had enacted legislation to enable the use of public-private partnerships (Geddes & Wagner, 2013).

These partnerships were established to open collaboration between government agencies and the private sector. This allowed the private sector to finance, build, and operate large projects on the government's behalf, resulting in cost savings and quicker development of desired projects.

Prior to 9/11, the International Association of Chiefs of Police (IACP), the National Sheriffs' Association, and ASIS International (formerly the American Society of Industrial Security) joined forces with funding from the Department of Justice to launch "Operation Cooperation". It was a national effort to increase collaboration between law enforcement and the private sector.

Since the attacks of September 11, 2001, the partnership between private security and law enforcement has become a critical component to fighting terrorism. An offspring of these partnerships is the open lines of communication they have established. This open communication and trust have helped to reduce crimes in those areas that support these public-private partnerships.

Excerpt from Public-Private Partnerships: Community Partnerships Evolving into Uncharted Territory—"Public-private partnerships with law enforcement have been going on since the birth of our country. When the Sheriff or Marshal of a territory needed additional manpower he would reach out to local businessmen or townspeople to create a posse. Even today, public-private partnerships still exist and there appears to be no end in sight. Chief Joseph C. Carter, Massachusetts Bay Transportation Authority and President of the International Association of Chiefs of Police (IACP) discuss increased responsibilities and a need to work closely with private companies in the aftermath of the September 11, 2001 tragedies. Chief Carter says, "… a growing number of private companies have been awakened to a sense of corporate citizenship—meaning a sense of responsibility to share their resources and expertise for the greater good of the United States." (Brown, 2011)

The focus today is very different from years ago; law enforcement is now a highly educated profession, well versed in the areas they previously needed guidance through.

The need for public-private partnerships is also more important today than in any other time in history. Rising crime, defunding of police, sophisticated criminal enterprises, more radical hate groups, growing violent crime in our communities, and the continuing terroristic threat, whether internal or external, of our borders. The need to develop strong partnerships throughout our communities and with local, state, and federal agencies is critical to our ability to reduce the threat and fight crime.

> Government at the federal, state, and local level must actively collaborate and partner with the private sector, which controls 85 percent of America's infrastructure ... the nation's infrastructure protection effort must harness the capabilities of the private sector to achieve a prudent level of security without hindering productivity, trade, or economic growth. (The President's National Strategy for Homeland Security)

> Police are not experts when it comes to site security. Partnerships between the police and private security are necessary to assist in these types of homeland security efforts. (Post-9/11 Policing Roundtable participant. Morabito & Greenberg, 2005).

Developing these relationships can be difficult, but you need to be persistent. Remember, opening these lines of communication and building a relationship based on trust and mutual respect won't happen overnight. But once established, they will offer mutual support. Trust must be built on both sides of the equation.

Over the past 20 years, we have focused a great deal of attention on building these relationships around the world. In this chapter, however, we focus on what we have done to develop relationships specifically in the United States and Canada. The United States is a different equation as law enforcement is more localized and those relationships need to be developed at the local level wherever you operate.

A historical challenge for sustaining long-lasting public-private engagement has been ensuring that both parties and the community at large see the value of the partnership. In order to keep these relationships strong, public-private partnerships need to stay relevant to the trends of the day and have an understanding of shared risk. Through communication and an environment that encourages collaboration, partnerships do not become stale but instead remain vibrant and active through valued intelligence, resource identification, and networking opportunities.

These partnerships are unique and offer access to information that is most often accurate and the source dependable. The partnership between our organization and the public sector allows for intelligence sharing, a better response to perceived threats, and a working knowledge of how law enforcement responds to active threats. This, coupled with limitless training opportunities such as desktop initiatives, hands-on scenarios, and classroom and virtual training allow our team the most robust training curriculum possible.

GardaWorld is involved with numerous public-private partnership organizations that work diligently to further develop and expand these critical partnerships. In turn, this allows us the ability to provide a best-in-class service to our clients.

4   Force Multiplier

In the United States, we have over 800,000 sworn members of law enforcement and more than 1,100,000 security professionals. There are 18,000 federal, state, and local agencies supporting those 800,000 law enforcement officers, and just under 12,000 private security companies supporting the 1,100,000 security officers. This does not include proprietary programs which would significantly increase these numbers.

The partnership between public and private partners establishes a Force Multiplier. Just think if we could tap into all the resources available in both the public and private sectors to not only deter crime but fight it.

5 Benefits

- Better communication
- Leveraging of resources
- Information sharing
- Enhanced training opportunities
- Collaboration
- Better emergency response
- Cost savings

In the United States, most local, state, and federal policing agencies offer some sort of partnership.

For example, federal agencies such as the FBI offer InfraGard and the Domestic Security Alliance Council (DSAC). These programs can be coordinated through the Office of Private Sector (OPS) and each field office hosts their FBI Citizens Academy, which feeds membership to the National Citizens Academy Alumni Association. Every field office has a Private Sector Coordinator (PSC) and an Academia Coordinator (AC).

https://www.fbi.gov/file-repository/ops-fact-sheet-121222.pdf

The US Secret Service offers the Electronic Crimes Task Force, employing public-private partnerships to combat cybercrime. The Financial Crimes Task Force (FCTF) combines the resources of the private sector and other law enforcement agencies in an organized effort to combat threats to U.S. financial payment systems. Today the Secret Service has 46 FCTFs located across the country.

https://www.secretservice.gov/contact/ectf-fctf

The Department of Homeland Security (DHS) offers numerous outreach programs across the country. Please contact your local agency for more information.

https://cops.usdoj.gov/RIC/Publications/cops-p169-pub.pdf

One of the largest formal partnerships is the New York Police Department's (NYPD's) Shield program, a private-public partnership liaison program with close to 20,000 members in 50 U.S. states, 54 countries, and more than 7000 organizations.

The program's focus is counterterrorism through information-sharing via the Shield website, seminars, conferences, and digital communications, as well as table-top exercises and live drills.

https://nypdshield.org/public

In Baltimore County, MD, the police department has the Baltimore County Police Foundation, formed in 1979 as a private, business-sponsored non-profit organization dedicated to improving the quality of police services to its citizens and developing the relationship between law enforcement and the business community.

https://TheBCPF.com

The Washington DC Police Foundation was established to expand public safety awareness and advance public safety initiatives through public and private partnerships.

https://dcpolicefoundation.org

In Philadelphia, PA, the Citizens Crime Commission of the Delaware Valley was created in 1955 to improve the quality of life for citizens in the Delaware Valley, with ongoing outreach, community programs, and the latest safety and security initiatives.

http://crimecommission.org

ASIS International and the International Association of Chiefs of Police (IACP) work diligently to establish a working relationship between the public and private sector. ASIS, for example, established a steering committee responsible for developing partnerships. The Law Enforcement Liaison Committee is a mix of law enforcement and private sector security practitioners.

http://ASISonline.org and https://IACP.org

6 Canadian Perspective

Canada has three levels of police services: municipal, provincial, and federal. The Royal Canadian Mounted Police (RCMP), Canada's national police force, is unique in the world as a combined international, federal, provincial, and municipal policing body.

As in the United States, public-private partnerships in Canada have become more and more interesting as budgets tighten, the work force numbers decrease, and crime increases. Police forces are stretched past their limits and spend countless manpower hours on non-core functions.

GardaWorld is well-positioned to support policing agencies to ensure citizens receive, and public organizations can deliver, the quality services required. In 2020, the cost of a security guard represented approximately 60% of the average police officer salary. Municipalities and provinces could realize savings of up to 40% that could be reallocated to critical public safety initiatives.

Governments across Canada are recognizing the opportunities and several provinces are reviewing policing acts.

For example, in March 2019, the Ontario government passed the Community Safety and Policing Act, 2019 (CSPA), as part of the Comprehensive Ontario Police Services Act, 2019. The CSPA will replace the current Police Services Act (PSA). The CSPA is an opportunity to modernize policing and enhance community safety in Ontario.

Further, in 2019, with the passage of Bill 68, the CSPA was amended to include a refined definition of "adequate and effective policing". The CSPA states that court security and the enforcement of municipal bylaws are not functions which are included in the definition of adequate and effective policing. This allows for the possibility of a different delivery of some of these services, rather than requiring the use of members of the police service. Court security remains a responsibility of the police service board.

In Canada, GardaWorld supports various policing agencies with courthouse security, parking enforcement, issuance of trespassing notices, municipal mobile patrols, static security presence at municipal high-risk respite centers, security presence at vaccine centers, and comprehensive security coverage at federal immigration centers including detainee transport, to name but a few.

Specifically, in Ontario, there are numerous police services using varying versions of police partnerships or re-allocating sworn front-line police personnel away from less urgent calls — resulting in cost-saving and improved efficiency.

The police services currently using this practice include Peel Region, Coburg, Waterloo and Durham, Toronto, and York.

The Cobourg Police Association used a community wellness plan to enhance their services by using special constables. The aim was to support the physical and mental health of those on the front lines and reduce the potential for burnout, while allowing the special constables to apply their expertise and training on critical activities.

Peel Police sought approval from the Solicitor General's office for the expanded use of special constables and received their appointments back within 48 h—this shows the value of partnerships being developed.

In Quebec, an advisory committee on policing released a report in May 2021. The question is no longer whether there will be a greater role for external partners to support our police services, but when and how should this be done?

There are five recommendations from this report:

1. Introduce into the Police Act the principle that certain duties related to police activity may be performed by civilians or employees of private security agencies.
2. Identify, in collaboration with key stakeholders (police, private security agencies, unions, etc.), duties to be performed by a police officer and those that may be assigned to civilians or security agency employees in relation to police activity.

3. Enshrine in regulation tasks that can be performed by civilians or private security agency employees.
4. Subject private security officers linked to a police service, the police ethics regime, and the Office of Independent Investigations.
5. Amend the Private Security Act to include the creation of a national joint Bureau de la sécurité privée and Minister of Public Security (BSP-MSP) accountability commission requiring private agencies to submit an annual activity report that includes aggregate complaint data (Gouvernement du Québec, 2022).

GardaWorld is positioning itself as a privileged partner to improve public safety services in Quebec. Projects are being discussed in connection with the recommendations of the report of the advisory committee and, more specifically, with the Quebec Ministry of Public Safety.

Our approach with the provincial government is to discuss the role of private security in this partnership and our contribution. The shortage of police officers, combined with the increase in crimes against the person and the evolution of the various tasks required of police officers (whether administrative, prevention, or repression of crime), calls for a new approach.

Redistributing tasks to private security can optimize the work of police officers. Outsourcing tasks would allow police to focus on their core functions that require specific training. In addition, budget savings could be reinvested to acquire technological tools to support their primary mission.

Examples of tasks that could be assigned to private services, which have been trained and are supervised by the competent authorities, include:

- Fingerprinting
- Transport of inmates
- Interview transcript
- Criminal background checks
- Road flagging/Traffic control
- Electronic offence tickets
- Photographic radars
- Administrative management
- Escort service and secure transportation
- Securing crime scenes
- Searching for cameras and extracting crime scene images

Tasks operationalized by security professionals, formerly dedicated to policing, are performed by appropriately trained personnel. Specific training is provided by the Gardaworld Campus and these trainers are recognized by the Office of Private Security. (Provincial Safety Industry Self-Regulatory Organization).

Both in Quebec and in other Canadian provinces, GardaWorld contributes to public safety and increases citizens' sense of security. Our operations in several municipalities prove that private security plays a key role.

Here are some examples of the work done at the municipal level in collaboration with municipalities and municipal police services:

- Alarm
- Preventive patrol in parks, schools, and residential areas
- Access control in public places
- Ensuring compliance with bylaws
- Issuing circulation tickets
- Vandalism prevention
- Traffic management at special events

And at the federal level with the Canada Border Services Agency, GardaWorld provides:

- Transportation of inmates
- Management and operations of the Canada Immigration Detention Centre

The trust Garda has established with Canadian police organizations and the Ministry of Public Safety is not simply about securing specific contracts, but to fuel the Minister's reflection on the various tasks that could be performed by private security.

This responsible approach will lay the foundation for lasting collaboration with the various police forces.

Transparent communication at all levels and by all stakeholders is critical in ensuring a cooperative transition to a tiered model of policing.

7 Outsourcing Opportunity

The opportunity for developing even more partnerships resides in law enforcement's ability to outsource certain functions that could be supplied by the private sector, to reduce budgetary requirements.

In Canada, the local Police Services Acts regulate which services must be provided by police and which services can be contracted out. Some agencies are already outsourcing positions to private companies and many use non-sworn civilian resources. The advantage of outsourcing these positions is reduction in costs associated with recruitment, screening, training, benefits, management, and retirement.

There are several stages to the process that will allow you to make informed decisions as to what services can be outsourced. This can be accomplished by partnering with an experienced service provider that can assist you with the evaluation process.

Your private sector partner will work with you to develop the necessary steps to evaluate the proposed positions, review any legal restrictions, and develop a strategic plan outlining the entire process.

1. Planning
2. Analysis
3. Design

Once you have analyzed the data the next steps would be:

1. Decision

2. Transition
3. Operation

Below is a limited list of positions that might be considered:

• Crime scene investigators	Death investigators
• Dispatch operators	Background investigators
• Detention officers	Prisoner transport
• Crossing guards	Parking enforcement
• Community service officers	Budgeting analysts
• Clerical support	Crime lab technicians
• Technology technicians	Code enforcement
• Case managers	Liquor regulatory officers
• Police records custodian	Quarter master
• School resource officers	PPP coordinators
• Recruiting	Human resource management

The list is endless and the ability of the private sector to fill these roles successfully is clear. This would allow sworn personnel the opportunity to fight crime and support the public's need.

Outsourcing can also lead to innovation and performance improvement, as outside expert perspectives are introduced. At GardaWorld, we have a proposed performance incentive plan on several contracts to encourage this:

- CCP-Contract Compliance Program: A certain percentage of overall revenue is awarded to the contractor if they meet pre-determined contract requirements (e.g., staffing levels, certifications/licenses, reporting cadence, etc.).
- Excellence Program: A certain percentage of overall revenue is awarded to the contractor for meeting pre-determined key performance indicators (KPIs) or proposing innovative processes or solutions that save the client money or make the operator more efficient.

In order to make this type of incentive program financially viable for the client, the base rates must not include a profit margin. Instead, profit is earned through the Contract Compliance and Excellence programs.

We've found in Canada that smaller jurisdictions have been more progressive on contracting out services due to budget constraints. For example, in Toronto, Canada's largest city, the budget has exceeded $1 billion for 2023, while a labour shortage and reduced access to resources has made staffing difficult. All parties are interested in finding solutions. For more information, visit Toronto Police Services Board – I Adequacy Standards Compliance Framework.

Public-Private Partnerships: Making Them Last
Colonel David R. Hines & Captain Terry Sullivan
Hanover County Sheriff's Office

8 Law Enforcement Perspective

Trust is the most advantageous asset in any partnership. It is the glue that keeps partnerships strong and long-lasting. It is a prediction of reliance on each other.

Partnerships depend on trust between groups or individuals to get their tasks accomplished. Without reliance on the other partner, most relationships fail because the partner does not feel useful or needed.

In Hanover County, our sworn law enforcement officer complement is a fraction of the county's entire population. This is typical for any law enforcement agency. When considering reliance on each other, understanding this concept reveals how important it is for law enforcement to work closely with their communities and the private sector.

What this means is, to be successful, public-private partnerships are not an option; they are a requirement. We must guard against a culture that would promote separation from the community. We must empower our officers by providing opportunities for them to work directly with the private sector and encouraging them to build those lasting partnerships that are at the foundation of any law enforcement agency's success.

We have discovered through the process of building partnerships over several decades that one of the most challenging times to retain partnerships occurs in the absence of a high-profile community need. Time is a valuable commodity today and many partners have little to spare. Time spent together must be of value, and opportunities to build the partnership should transcend a response to a community emergency alone. We must find ways to stay relevant for each other not just on occasion, but with frequency. If we do not, then when a crisis occurs, valuable time will be lost if public-private partnerships are in their infancy.

Unfortunately, some organizations build partnerships only in the shadow of a high-profile need. It is important to understand that, by establishing a philosophy of continually building partnerships in both crises and daily operations, a solid foundation can be created, making it possible to avoid the challenges of creating new relationships that are not as strong as those with a long history of trust.

The way the Hanover County Sheriff's Office has achieved success in this area is through effective continual communication and by remaining relevant.

9 Effective Communication

Arguably the most important element in a relationship is communication. Effective communication works to build foundations and seeks to include all involved. It creates transparency and accountability. We know what the other partner is doing, thinking, and routinely working on. This creates a tangible awareness of each other's commitment to the partnership.

We communicate in various ways. Verbal communication is the most common, but one that is often forgotten is communication through not only our actions but our inaction as well. Being intentional in four critical areas strengthens our opportunity for long-lasting partnerships:

1. Meetings
2. Phone Calls
3. Emails
4. Presence

1. Meetings

One of the worst things you can do to damage a private sector partnership is to miss a meeting without good cause. This can very rapidly send a signal of apathy or lack of interest to your partner. Taking the time speaks volumes and lets the partner know you have a sincere interest in a lasting partnership.

2. Phone Calls

For some of us in the law enforcement community, our positions can serve as a communications gathering point. That means we can receive a massive number of calls and voicemails throughout the day. While it is a challenge to get them returned in a fast-paced environment, a partner will feel valued when you are readily responsive to their outreach.

We strongly believe in this concept and, in most cases, will do everything possible to not miss a call the first time. If we do miss the call, then it is recognized as a priority to return the call as soon as possible. This works well for us, and it allows another opportunity to show our private sector partners how important they are to us.

Every time you fail to return a call, you have missed an opportunity to connect. We cannot afford to send a signal of complacency, lack of transparency, or disorganization into the community. We must return the call quickly and be professional, courteous, and ready to serve in our response.

3. Emails

An ignored email can have the same results as an unanswered phone call. In this world of electronic communications, an untimely response to or a complete disregard of an email can leave the person on the other end feeling neglected. The email to you has launched a conversation. That initial expectation is that you will enter into the conversation. Not answering the email is the same as walking away in the middle of a conversation. The traditional etiquette defined is that once in receipt of an email, we should respond as soon as we can.

4. Presence

In this age of virtual communication and increased access to information, we need to have both content expertise as well as "physical presence" to instill confidence in the communities we serve. This means being an effective communicator who is knowledgeable on the information available and expanding your communications "toolbox" by meeting in person instead of only via emails and phone calls. It is about bringing a reliable perspective to the conversation face to face, so your value and commitment to the partnership can be seen firsthand. This brings increased confidence in the information being shared and furthers knowledge of its intent and purpose.

Here is where public-private partnerships really find their value. Each of us has particular areas of expertise. Our private sector partners are often on the cutting edge of innovation. Government has traditionally been trailing in this area; however, government has access to resources coupled with duty, responsibility, and jurisdiction. When you combine duty, responsibility, and jurisdiction (government) with innovation (private sector), there are very few challenges that cannot be overcome.

So how do the public and private sectors begin to work together in these areas leading to success?

- We begin by having a genuine interest in each other.
- We become flexible in our ability to discuss many different things.
- We acknowledge that we might not have all the answers.
- We work to make connections and discern trends.
- We are humble in asking questions and seeking understanding.
- We pursue long-lasting partnerships.
- We clearly communicate our goals.

Clearly communicated goals can inspire a partnership. One of my favorite inspirational stories is about a man who was called to rebuild an ancient city. The city was destroyed and for almost two decades was in ruin. The people tried to rebuild shortly after the destruction initially occurred but eventually stopped. Many have speculated as to why the building stopped, and one of the predominant theories is that it was due to lack of leadership and clear articulable goals.

Many years later, a leader arrived in the city and, in secret, surveyed the damage, taking notes as to what needed to be done. It appears he did this in an effort to bypass those within the city who might have tried to cloud the mission or confuse the goals. Once he completed his survey, he called the people together and shared with them, in detail, the destruction he observed and the many problems the people were experiencing.

It was interesting that this leader went into detail on each of the problems. Didn't the people live there, and wouldn't they know what the problems were? Why would he need to reiterate something everyone was aware of already? Ingeniously, what he was doing was outlining every issue at hand and clarifying the goals to be achieved. Through his delivery, presence, and reputation, he was inspiring the people to join together and be part of the solution. The response of the people in hearing him clearly state the goals and objectives was, "Let us rise up and let us build."

In this particular text, the Greek translation literally meant, "They rose up to rise up," indicating that they were not only ready to begin the task at hand, but were ready to establish a long-lasting partnership with each other. They no longer were content with sitting idly by as things continued to worsen. In declaring these common goals with confidence and authority, the community who had sat idly by for almost two decades was inspired to stand up and, through partnership, make a difference.

When public and private sector partners establish common goals, then the steps to move forward become clearer. It sets the groundwork on how to work together. When the goals are inspirational, they create a synergy that can inspire an unyielding movement towards success! This in turn creates relevance in the partnership, which brings value and strength.

10 Remaining Relevant

Sometimes well-intentioned public-private sector teams begin an initiative, but do not quite achieve collaboration. In some cases, the problem is the lack of a real understanding of what collaboration is, let alone how to achieve it. The confusion is easy to understand. While collaboration entails communication, coordination, and cooperation, achieving any one of these outcomes alone will not produce a partnership.

When it comes to achieving objectives, collaboration is the most comprehensive way to do just that. A good communication plan, cooperation between individuals, and coordinated efforts of partner agencies all make working relationships more effective. But this collaboration requires a concentrated effort to achieve and sustain it.

These partnerships, not unlike other working relationships, inevitably experience very productive as well as unproductive times. Working in cooperation, however, can generate results that, in many cases, we could not even hope to achieve on our own. The strength of a partnership comes from hard work and by continually applying these principles of working in cooperation. To make this a reality, we must all continually enhance teamwork strategies, expand expertise, improve communication, involve new partners, sustain trust, seek additional resources, and diagnose how well the collaboration is working.

It is here that the Hanover Sheriff's Office strategy, "Strong Partnerships Create Safe Communities," was born. We work closely with many community and private sector partners. Neighborhood Watch, Worship Watch, and Business Watch encompass many of our formal partnerships; however, we also connect further with critical infrastructure, private security professionals, medical, hospitality and so many more.

Through partnerships with groups such as ASIS, we are connected into an international private security professional network. We work with multiple bankers' associations, the Hanover Chamber of Commerce, Airpark Association, Retail Merchants Association, and this list could go on and on. Every day we intentionally look for opportunities to build new partnerships, and when we say we partner with the private sector, it's not just on paper to check a box. We are training with them, collaborating on best practices to prevent crime, and collectively working together to bring a shared success.

As a result, through our intensive efforts to partner with the community and private sector, we are able to support a communications network that can connect with approximately 70% of our population in addition to a state, national, and international expanded network.

To develop this innovation further, HCSO SHIELD was born. HCSO SHIELD is part of the Global SHIELD Network (GSN). The GSN was developed by multiple law enforcement agencies working together in partnership with the New York City Police Department (NYPD) to build on their original SHIELD model. Shortly after the 9/11 attacks, the NYPD developed SHIELD as a formal method to partner with the private security sector. This partnership method was designed to open communication by providing resources of interest to the private sector. In 2015, the Hanover Sheriff's Office, alongside multiple agencies, worked with the NYPD to expand this concept to additional private sector partners such as the business, faith, and critical infrastructure communities.

SHIELD became a national initiative in 2017 and then very quickly became global in 2018 after the Hanover Sheriff's Office hosted the first international conference. In addition, the Hanover SHIELD initiative is not simply a program; it is a formal culture of connecting with the private sector. It serves as an umbrella concept connecting all Sheriff's Office community and private sector programs to a central communication point while creating a sharing mechanism through partnerships on trusted information, crime trends, and matters of homeland security. It incorporates all of our Neighborhood Watch, Business Watch, and Worship Watch members as well as offers an opportunity for any citizen to partner with the Sheriff's Office. It establishes a platform connected to a global network to keep our community partners informed as to what is occurring in our community and abroad. The initiative is designed with an understanding that crime and terrorism events throughout the region, state, nation, and even the world, can have an impact on our Hanover community. This creates relevancy and, as a result, inspires long-lasting public-private sector partnerships. More information on SHIELD can be found at www.hanover-sheriff.com/362/HCSO-SHIELD-Program and www.globalshieldnetwork.com.

This strategy ensures opportunities are available for the private sector to partner and communicate with the public sector. These additional resources and opportunities to share create value in the daily communication. Partnerships between the public and private sectors are no longer reliant on crisis planning alone. Intentionally looking for elements of interest to share with each other, elements that support the success of both the public and private sector, remains the key to lasting partnerships.

It is clear: no single agency has the ability to respond to every threat alone. Today more than ever, the public must trust law enforcement agencies and know where to find reliable information. They need to feel they can count on us like a friend or someone they hold in high regard. Every private sector partner needs to feel that they are respected and that they are part of the team. As a result, we are more apt to share information, work together, and build partnerships with each other. Success is not found in a silo, but by a community working together.

Ultimately, the widespread pursuit of public-private partnerships is one of the most significant advancing trends in community organizing and development since the advent of community policing. Whether it is collaboration among the private security profession or efforts to bring together neighborhood residents, there is much to be gained in recognizing the importance of partnerships when leveraging resources and achieving meaningful and positive community change.

References

Brown, C. H. (2011, September). *Public-private partnerships: Community partnerships evolving into uncharted territory.* https://www.fdle.state.fl.us/FCJEI/Programs/SLP/Documents/Full-Text/Brown,-charles-paper.aspx. Last visited January 25, 2023.

Geddes, R. R. G., & Wagner, B. L. (2013). Why do U.S. states adopt public–private partnership enabling legislation? *Journal of Urban Economics, 78*, 30–41.

Gouvernement du Québec. (2022, November 25). *Réalitié policière au Québec.* https://www.quebec.ca/gouvernement/ministere/securite-publique/publications/realite-policiere-quebec. Last visited January 25, 2023.

Morabito, A., & Greenberg, S. (2005, September). *Engaging the private sector to promote homeland security: Law enforcement-private security partnerships.* https://www.ojp.gov/pdffiles1/bja/210678.pdf. Last visited January 25, 2023.

New Realities and New Solutions in Public and Private Policing

Erwin A. Blackstone, Simon Hakim, and Brian Meehan

Abstract This chapter provides an overview of the contributions to this volume and draws suggestions for improving security and police performance with respect to their primary mission of deterring and responding to criminal events. In the context of recent increases in U.S. crime and public concern about police behavior, the role and responsibility of public and private police are important matters. Moreover, private security is becoming an important component of overall security, as police resources are stretched to fulfill a variety of obligations, some of which are not perfectly aligned with serious crime prevention. Throughout this chapter we explore the following options for security provision between public police and private security:

1. Services provided exclusively by police and financed by public funds.
2. Contracting out of security services. Private security companies and police can bid to provide security services based on measurable outputs (arrests, crime rates, response times for example). Winning contracts would stipulate the preferred bundle of these outputs and cost. These would be paid for by public sector funds.
3. Police shedding of security services. Police allow private security, volunteer groups, and individual consumers of security services to contract with each other; this does not require public funds. Police could also bid to provide some of these services, but financing comes privately not from the public sector.
4. Public Private Partnerships (P3). Police work together to provide security services, contracts and agreements outline the rules and roles of each side. For

E. A. Blackstone · S. Hakim
Department of Economics and Center for Competitive Government, Temple University, Philadelphia, PA, USA
e-mail: erwin.blackstone@temple.edu; Hakim@temple.edu

B. Meehan (✉)
Department of Accounting, Economics, and Finance, Campbell School of Business, Berry College, Mount Berry, GA, USA
e-mail: bmeehan@berry.edu

© The Author(s), under exclusive license to Springer Nature Switzerland AG 2023
E. A. Blackstone et al. (eds.), *Handbook on Public and Private Security*,
Competitive Government: Public Private Partnerships,
https://doi.org/10.1007/978-3-031-42406-9_18

example, police could call on private security to assist when demand for services is extremely high (a natural disaster for instance) and agree upon payments and goals via contractual agreements.

1 Introduction

In Part I of the volume, the chapters focus on solutions to crime when public and private entities cooperate. In chapter "Allocating Police and Security: Comparing Public and Private Processes and Consequences", Bruce Benson reviews the economic literature on existing public and private goods and their relationship to police functions. Markets often have difficulty providing public goods[1] because benefits from their provision are non-rival (jointly consumed), and exclusion is prohibitively expensive. So, individuals can't be excluded from enjoying the benefits even if the individual is unwilling to pay. The police provide many services that are private in nature, which divert police resources away from other activities, while some individuals receive private benefits paid by public funds. Thus, these services could be shed by police and be competitively provided, allowing police to participate, if they wish, under "level playing field" conditions.

The increased share of private provision in security services may reflect dissatisfaction with public police or insufficient provision compared to what consumers want. In any event, Benson concentrates on contracting out to private companies many activities traditionally provided by government. This trend has often resulted from rising concerns of voters about monopolistic police spending and service provision. Examples of contracting out of public police services to private security include guarding courthouses, transporting prisoners, parking control, patrolling, and even 911 dispatching services (Koeske, 2020). Benson concludes that market-based provision of security services is possible and desirable, and that regulation should not be used to stifle desirable competition between both sectors. In essence, a "level playing field" should exist for public police and private security when police desire to maintain such services. Thus, if public police can offer services cheaper or better than private police, they should perform the functions and of course should be funded accordingly. The underlining element in Benson's argument is that public police should be exposed to competition for services. We would expand Benson's argument to suggest that much police activity involves private goods, which could be shed by the police. For example, if burglar alarms required verification from private security or citizens, then police could respond only after a private entity verifies that the burglar alarm activation is not false. Initial response is then shed by police (see current Verified Response arrangements in chapter "An Overview of Private Security and Policing in the United States"). The budgetary resource savings

---

[1] Markets sometimes get around free rider problems associated with public goods. For example, broadcast TV and Radio, which are both non-excludable and non-rival, use advertising to fund their activities.

for this move means that police could add nationally the equivalent of 35,000 officers (Blackstone et al., 2020); police could then concentrate on their core functions of deterring violent and property crime and arresting criminals. Response time to all police calls could decline, further benefiting the entire community while individual non-public goods are excluded from police services. To conclude, private services should be shed, and public good services could be considered for being contracted out while police, if desired, could compete with private security to provide both types of services. Contracting out services is best accomplished when the outputs are specified, and if the police wish to compete, an independent budget for the service should exist to avoid cross subsidization with the public arm of police.

Tim Prenzler and Rick Sarre in chapter "Public Space Crime Prevention Partnerships: Reviewing the Evidence" address private security contracted out by private entities. They suggest avenues of cooperation that are often initiated by third parties that lead to reduced crime. Police are reluctant to initiate cooperative arrangements, perhaps believing private security is insufficiently trained or because they fear competition. Based on a UN report, the authors suggest government involvement in licensing of private security companies, regulating and managing ethical risks like police officers working overtime for private security companies, or police officers holding financial interests in such companies. Prenzler and Sarre suggest cooperative mechanisms for crime control by police and private security companies, subject to government regulation and control. Their approach calls for a more centralized regulatory approach relative to the plan outlined by Benson in the previous chapter. They argue that regulation should not be used to prevent desirable competition. For example, it might be appropriate for regulatory authorities to require background checks to prevent those with criminal records from guarding financial institutions or child molesters from working near children. Those who want to be armed might be required to have gun safety training. Such regulation may encourage police to be more receptive to partnerships with private security but can also crowd out reputational effects from certification or high-quality name brands.[2] In any case, regulation should not create onerous obstacles for security companies' entry and competitive activities, as some of these regulatory obstacles have been associated with reduced entry and subsequent property crime increases (Meehan & Benson, 2017).

In the following chapter (chapter "Australian Public and Private Crime Prevention Partnerships in Cyberspace"), Rick Sarre and Tim Prenzler discuss the exponentially growing problem of cybercrime where public private partnerships are essential in tackling it. Public agencies need private companies to manage and secure

---

[2] Certification can serve as a substitute for government occupational regulations (occupational licensing), as it can provide a signal of quality. Name brands also can serve as a signal of quality. When regulation is used to require occupations to meet licensing standards, firms and consumers are less likely to rely on name brands or certification when making buying and hiring decisions. Economic research examining occupational licensing has overwhelmingly found that licensing acts as a barrier to entry, reduces competition, and increases prices, without having a large impact on quality (see Kleiner, 2015).

their databases. For example, cooperation should exist in collecting, using, and the storage of metadata. However, the danger of hacking data requires the government to exercise control and make sure that the private partners comply in maintaining surveillance tools. Government must enhance the capacity of potential victims to adopt self-policing that will allow governments to reduce their involvement. For example, the government could encourage the use of multi-factor authentication and frequently changing passwords. The international nature of cybercrime requires close regulation of the private entities that confront such crimes to ensure that legal and ethical boundaries are not crossed. Public entities may cross legal and ethical boundaries themselves if the incentives of public figures push them in that direction. Indeed, the problem is that under the current situation, victims of cybercrimes, unlike victims of "traditional" crimes, have limited access to public agencies' support and involvement. Local police have limited capacity and interest to deal with such problems where most victims and perpetrators are outside their jurisdiction. However, investigating and punishing offenders of most cybercrimes embody public attributes while public agencies are frequently limited in addressing the crime since perpetrators are often in other countries. The authors suggest that regulation of private providers is indeed necessary to ensure the non-crossing of legal boundaries. The significant issue of funding activities related to such crimes remains open. We would add that international cooperation, at least those cooperating nations or by UN agencies, is probably a necessary element in attacking cybercrime. Offenders are often located outside the jurisdiction of the FBI or other national police forces. While private cyber security is often unable to apprehend and punish offenders, the private security sector is very active in preventing cybercrimes through software and technology solutions. As indicated in chapter "An Overview of Private Security and Policing in the United States", private cyber security employment and wages have grown as demand for these services has increased. Online commerce has also relied on reputation mechanisms and authentication to reduce the risks of cybercrime. The future of cybercrime prevention may be with these private solutions. Cooperative international governance solutions may also help with inter-jurisdictional apprehension and punishment.

In chapter "Private Security Confounds Estimates of Public Police and Crime", Benjamin Blemings et al., conducted empirical analysis based on county data for the entire U.S. to determine whether private security is a substitute for or complementary to public police. Their results suggest that private security is complementary to police, and private security is significantly more negatively correlated with property crime than with violent crime. This result is consistent with previous evidence (Meehan & Benson, 2017). Violent crimes are usually difficult to prevent since they often occur among acquaintances and in unpredicted locations and thus are difficult to prevent and deter. Also, from the demand side, private security is mostly charged with prevention and deterrence of property crimes. It is possible, however, that when private police operate in an area, public police resources could be shifted to deal with other crimes, including violent crimes or crimes in other high crime areas of the jurisdiction. This could explain why lower levels of police density result in stronger negative correlation between an increase in private security and crime. In counties where the density of public police is high, private security deterrence is almost zero. The authors suggest that discussions on changes in funding public police in any jurisdiction should consider the extent of the complementary private security operating there. An implication of this empirical study suggests that the increase of private security does and could lead to lower public police spending, or reallocation of police resources toward violent crime prevention.

Frank Vram Zerunyan, in chapter "Public-Private Security Partnerships. Can They Meet the Growing Challenges of Law Enforcement?", notes that towards the end of the Civil War, the private security firm Pinkerton had extensive policing powers, including protecting President Lincoln and guarding banks. However, over time with the advancement of public police, the powers of private police have diminished. Much of this diminished power has come through regulatory restrictions. Today, the powers of private police, unless specifically authorized by state laws or municipal authorization, are limited to citizen's arrest, which is the same arrest power that all citizens enjoy. The growing demand for security by institutions like universities, hospitals, central business districts, and gated communities has led to a recent expansion of legal powers including that of private sworn officers. In particular, the rise of cybercrimes like identity theft, credit card fraud, and illegal computer hacking, resulting from a lack of interest in and professional knowledge of public police, has led to increased demand for private services. Zerunyan suggested that relevant laws and regulations need to be changed to enable better cooperation between public police and private security companies that specialize in preventing and investigating such crimes. This could be exercised following various models of such cooperation that already exist in the form of teen courts and mental health response.

Pieter Leloup's chapter "The COVID-19 Pandemic and Its Impact on Public-Private Partnership in Policing: Experiences from Within the Belgian and Dutch Security Industry" is the first in part II of this Handbook that explores national public-private partnership (P3) experiences. He analyzed the impacts of the COVID-19 pandemic on police and private security cooperation in Belgium and the Netherlands. The governments of both of these countries (as well as many other European nations) recognized private security as an essential service during the pandemic. Because of this, the private security industry was able to expand operations by enforcing health and safety measures alongside the police. This chapter deals mostly with the private security involvement in the protection of vaccination centers in these two countries. The interviews which were conducted with European officials and two national private sector representatives showed that their actual involvement in managing the activities has not led to greater recognition of private security or to the establishment of structural partnerships between police and private security. Leloup suggested that such partnerships should still occur, be evaluated, and enable the two sectors to learn about each other's abilities and activities. He noted that legal constraints now inhibit some public information from being provided to private entities. It is noteworthy that private security may handle such activities as maintaining order at vaccination sites better than police who may evoke more hostility and create a more threatening environment. Should a disturbance occur, police can respond at high priority when dispatched by private security.

Logan Puck, in chapter "Incorporating Non-state Security Actors into Public Security: Mexico's Failed Experiment" analyzes the incorporation of the private security watchmen into the then allegedly corrupt and abusive State police force of Mexico City. The State objectives in this incorporation were to improve the delivery of public security services and to neutralize entry efforts of private security companies that threatened the public police monopoly. Both objectives were not achieved, as incorporation of private security night watchmen into public police via Policía Auxiliar (Auxiliary Police) decreased performance and increased corruption within this organization. Puck suggested that improvement of the public police should be done from within the force and not by incorporating external forces. Prior to being absorbed by the public police, the watchmen had a better relationship with the public and were more effective. These results have a similar flavor to chapter "How to Fight Crime by Improving Police Services: Evidence from the French Quarter Task Force" evidence on the public takeover of private security forces in New Orleans, as post incorporation effectiveness of this organization fell. Moreover, we argue that keeping the private watchmen separate could increase competition and provide a greater check on the public police, possibly improving their performance. This chapter also illuminates some of the missteps that can potentially come from P3s and contracting out, supporting Benson's arguments from chapter "Allocating Police and Security: Comparing Public and Private Processes and Consequences".

In chapter "The Substitutability and Complementarity of Private Security with Public Police: The Case of Violence Against Women and Girls in the Rail Network of the United Kingdom", Barak Ariel analyzes the substitutability and complementarity of public and private police in the case of violence against woman and girls (VAWG) on the rail network of the UK. Ariel's review of past studies revealed that when these two sectors did cooperate, public expenditures were reduced. Also, he showed that when such cooperation exists, many private agents, like security guards and place managers, were as or even more effective than police in crime management and security services. Ariel argues, based on this previous work, that using "Hot Spot" policing strategies combined with the use of private security can reduce VAWG. He presents evidence which indicates that "Hot Spot" private policing strategies reduced crime in train stations in the UK relative to areas that did not employ private security in these crime hot spots. We would note that since most UK police, like private security, are unarmed, they are more comparable than in the US.

In chapter "Working with Private Policing to Enhance Public Policing: The Case of the United Kingdom", Mark Button showed that private security in Great Britain provides the whole gamut of unarmed services from uniformed security in private places like shopping centers and office buildings, to the more controversial custody of prisoners, and to the often-complex investigating services of fraud, corruption, and cybercrimes. The chapter suggests a typology of three categories for private security involvement: state facilitation created standards and schemes for the two sectors to work together, state delegation where the private security companies are delivering state services, like contracting out prison transport and custody suites, and finally state reinforcement where the state encourages, through contracting out, entry of private security companies to provide services that police are less trained for, like investigations of fraud and cybercrime. Button argues that the public sector plays an important role in facilitation, delegation, and reinforcement, and that by appropriately emphasizing these roles the public sector can bolster the "essential" contribution of private security to public safety.

The chapters of Part III describe and evaluate local public and private relationships, and present case studies examining these relationships. Edward Peter Stringham and Louis B. Salz analyze in chapter "Private Law Enforcement in New York City" private alternatives to government policing and cooperative arrangements between private security companies and police that enhance safety. Examples include gated communities, housing development, a food distribution hub, volunteer community guards, a governmentally owned corporation, and a rapid transit company special police, all in New York City. Chapter 11-A, Part 1 of the Consolidated Laws of New York authorizes and distinguishes 85 different types of police officers. The State allows for varying ability to be armed, use force, and make arrests. Stringham and Salz suggest that communities should be allowed to maintain different types of forces for their specific needs. Indeed, there is no reason to impose a unified law on all private security forces. Employers of such forces or residents of neighborhoods should be allowed to protect themselves to the extent they desire. The package of security services demanded from different communities will be contingent on price, risk, perceived customer service, and the quality of crime deterrence provided. From a risk perspective, insurers of private security charge different premiums depending on the risk they incur. Clearly, insurers will evaluate the attributes, training, and accumulated experience of the guards and the company that employs them in the premium they charge. These insurance companies incentivize relatively good performance, more training, and less risky actions, as this will reduce premiums and allow companies to charge less for their services, which increases the quantity of services demanded from these private police. Insurance contracts also act as a signal to potential clients that damage will be covered, and risks mitigated, which increases demand for security services. Thus, insurers help establish responsible private security. But government at both the local or state level often intervenes by requiring attributes like basic training or non-criminal background of the employees. The motives for this government intervention could be for public safety, or to restrain entry to reduce competition, as licensing boards that institute these training requirements are often made up of currently licensed private security guards that would prefer to have less competition for their services (Meehan & Benson, 2015).

In chapter "Private Security and Deterrence", Jonathan Klick and John MacDonald analyze armed private police at The University of Pennsylvania compared to unarmed private security guards at Johns Hopkins University in Baltimore. Penn employs armed private police that are also sworn officers to provide security around campus, while Johns Hopkins employs unarmed non-sworn security guards for the same purpose. They find that the Penn armed private police deter crime without displacement, and they accomplish this at a similar magnitude to armed public police in the U.S. They conclude that both armed private university police and the public police were a bargain in comparison to the expected costs of their crimes they prevent. With respect to costs and benefits, private security or private police are more cost effective than public police due to their lower employment costs. Private security guards who are paid by their employers often do not enjoy the employment protection of their public police counterparts. Klick and MacDonald also find that the unarmed security guards at Johns Hopkins have a more limited effect in reducing crime. We would add that the University of Pennsylvania police apparently reduced crime in their patrol zone to a greater extent than public police elsewhere in Philadelphia, partially because there are more officers per capita in the University of Pennsylvania patrol zone than in Philadelphia proper. Overall, the evidence supports the idea that sworn, armed police (public or private) reduce crime, while unarmed privative security without arrest powers do not deter crime at the same level.

In chapter "How to Fight Crime by Improving Police Services: Evidence from the French Quarter Task Force", Wei Long presents his empirical findings from a unique experience in the French Quarter of New Orleans, where a local entrepreneur privately funded and closely managed three off-duty highly visible New Orleans officers proactively patrolling the Quarter all hours of the day. He also launched a mobile app that enabled residents to report crime directly to the patrol force rather than through the 911 system. Long compared the effectiveness of public versus private managed forces in deterring violent crimes. The public management of the program was conducted by the New Orleans Police Department and the French Quarter Management District. The empirical results showed that more robberies and aggravated assaults were deterred when the force was private, being actively managed by a local entrepreneur who lived and owned other business within the French Quarter. The effect on property crimes is indistinguishable between public management and private management. The welfare gain from this private management in terms of reduced violent crime was estimated at $6.7 million a year, far exceeding the costs of running the program. The program's success reflected in the savings is attributed to the close private management in comparison to public police management. The success of the program was reduced when the public sector took over the management and funding of the program. The public police oversight did not create the same incentives for quick response as the private management did, while all the technology and equipment remained, the effectiveness and thus the crime deterring impact diminished. During the private management period the founder of the Task Force closely monitored response times by each of the police officers employed and was closely involved in officer security assignments, employment hours, and hiring of officers based on their performance. He was able to run the Task Force like it was his own business. Under public management this oversight and incentive compatibility was lacking, reducing the overall effectiveness of the program.

In chapter "Public Security Enhances the Effectiveness of Private Security in Reducing Maritime Piracy Harm", Benjamin Blemings et al. address the complementarity of private and public security in preventing boarding and hijacking passing vessels. They find that strong public security increases the effectiveness of private security by 29%. Low intensity public security amplifies private security against boarding by 21–23% while high intensity public security amplifies the impact by 56–77%. The likelihood that vessels with private security and high intensity public security are boarded by pirates is near zero, reflecting highly complementarity efforts. In the case of hijacking the vessel, which involves boarding and then taking control of the vessel, the presence of private security reduces the probability that a vessel is hijacked, but the presence of public security (in terms of military spending) does not appear to reduce the probability of hijacking. This could be because of how rare it is for a vessel to be hijacked. Taken together the evidence suggests that private security reduces and deters maritime piracy, and that public security can act as a complementary deterrent. Thus, the presence of both has the most promise for reducing piracy.

Part IV includes chapters by a private security association and some major international security companies. In chapter "What We've Learned: Lessons from the World's Leading Security Companies on Partnerships and Privatization", Seivold Garett from the International Security Ligue, which includes 28 companies, suggests criteria contributing to success and failure for such partnerships including public contracting out arrangements. He distinguishes between outsourcing traditionally performed police services to private security and partnerships of the two sectors. Private companies' less successful operations in the twentieth century are attributed to their low wages and the consequent lack of sophistication of their personnel. From the start of the twenty-first century, firms expanded their services, enhanced their professional expertise, invested in relevant technology, improved their training programs, and enhanced their management style. Public agencies lack the ability to compensate highly sophisticated professionals that are needed in today's technological world and thus they could partner with the appropriate private security companies. Many current partnerships fail because of unreasonable expectations, unclear contract specification, failure to articulate strategic goals, objectives, and standards or weak contract oversight. Garett suggests that improving such partnerships requires clear lines of responsibilities, measurable standards of quality, and incentives to catalyze improvements with the security partners outlined within contractual arrangements.

In chapter "Improving Public Safety Through Law Enforcement and Private Security Partnerships" Steve Jones, the CEO of Allied Universal, addresses the common problem of peak time demand for security during natural disasters, periods of social unrest, and rising crime conditions, when significant shortages of police exist. Accordingly, private security personnel are necessary to supplement security needs. Such needs commonly exist when police are busy responding to 911 calls, precluding them from proactive policing. The chapter also addresses the complementarity between police and private security in securing healthcare facilities, government buildings and other sites, schools, business improvement districts, public transit, sporting events and concerts, handling mental health and drug incidents, and responding to disabled vehicles and accidents, among many other services. This suggestion is realized by recent findings from Rayasam (2023), who find that hospitals are increasingly establishing their private sworn officer forces to confront the surge of violence within their facilities. Successful partnerships require the following conditions: a robust commitment from police leadership to the P3, collaboration and not competition, and quality personnel along with appropriate training and background checks for private security personnel like those for police.

Chapter "The Importance of Public-Private Partnerships" by Steve Sommers, a Vice President of Garda, and David R. Hines, Hanover County, Virginia Sheriff et al. highlight public private security partnerships where police contract out specific services that do not need to be performed by the significantly more expensive sworn public police officers. To address the feasibility of these partnerships, two public police officers that frequently interact and partner with Garda co-authored this chapter. The Garda authors suggest that state and local jurisdictions could outsource tasks to private security companies to address such activities as fingerprinting suspects, transport of inmates, criminal background checks, road flagging/traffic control, electronic offence tickets, securing crime scenes, and searching for cameras and extracting crime scene images, among other activities. Specific activities that could be contracted out to private security include preventive patrol in parks, schools, and residential areas, access control in public places, ensuring compliance with bylaws, vandalism prevention, traffic management at special events. Federal services that could be contracted out include transportation of inmates, and management and operations of immigration detention centers. Garda's suggestions relate to the Canadian experience but are relevant to other nations. Indeed, it is likely that shifting services that do not require sworn officers from monopolistic police to the more competitive security companies will encourage innovation, improved efficiency, and lower costs.

2   Security Services and Policy Options

We attempt to integrate the findings from these chapters along with other research into a table that details common police activities and suggests criteria for more efficient provision. As was outlined at the beginning of this chapter, potential supply arrangements for security services include pure public goods produced exclusively by public police, public goods that are contracted out to private security services, public-private partnerships (P3), and services shed by police to private security or partnership with volunteer groups. In all cases of contracting out, we suggest that "managed competition" is allowed where police can compete with private providers for service delivery under several conditions. These include the requirement that the deliverables or the outputs are measurable for appropriate competitive pricing, that the operation by police is by a budgetary unit separated from the budget of the public services, so that no cross subsidization exists from the public to this specific "private" arm of police, and where all operations and control are subject to "level playfield conditions."

The detailed evaluation and suggested forms of provision are largely based on the evidence provided in the chapters of this Handbook. Some additional evidence is provided where appropriate.

Table 1 Delivery of Security Services and policy options

Type of service	Impact on public safety	Potential measurement of output	Does private security provide services?	Is public police involvement required?	Policy prescription
Conducting patrol	Deterrence via increasing probability of apprehension	Pre and post patrol crime rates, although these might be difficult to tie directly back to patrol	The public sector has contracted out for patrol in many areas (Benson chapter "Allocating Police and Security: Comparing Public and Private Processes and Consequences", Garda chapter "The Importance of Public-Private Partnerships"). Pure market based private patrol exists in many communities. New Orleans Task Force (Long chapter "Private Law Enforcement in New York City") provides evidence that private management deterred more violent crime than public management for emergency response and patrol in New Orleans	If needed, police can respond in high priority cases	Benson (chapter "Allocating Police and Security: Comparing Public and Private Processes and Consequences") suggests increased private provision via reducing occupational licensing barriers to entry and expanding arrest powers for private security in the U.S. He also suggests reducing liability protections for police (eliminate qualified immunity) and allowing private and public security to compete to provide services. The public sector could be less resistant to contracting and partnering with private providers as outlined by Garda (chapter "The Importance of Public-Private Partnerships"). Encourage more private management and incentive structures al la New Orleans Task Force (Long, chapter "Private Law Enforcement in New York City") and Mexico City's Watchmen (Puck, chapter "Incorporating Non-state Security Actors into Public Security: Mexico's Failed Experiment"). Since private security agents working in these areas are much cheaper than public police on average, resource savings could be substantial

(continued)

Table 1 (continued)

Type of service	Impact on public safety	Potential measurement of output	Does private security provide services?	Is public police involvement required?	Policy prescription
Crime investigations	Deterrence via increasing probability of apprehension	Clearance rates. If investigation is of higher quality crimes should be cleared at a higher rate	Private detective and investigative services exist, but contracting out by public authorities for these services is limited. Button (chapter "Working with Private Policing to Enhance Public Policing: The Case of the United Kingdom") shows that private investigators are used to detect and deter cyber crime, corruption, and fraud in the UK	Increased contracting out could allow both private and public investigators to increase specialization. Perhaps cyber crimes and high-tech white color crimes could use private investigators (Garett, chapter "What We've Learned: Lessons from the World's Leading Security Companies on Partnerships and Privatization"; Button, chapter "Working with Private Policing to Enhance Public Policing: The Case of the United Kingdom"), while public sector could focus on violent crime investigation	It is possible to contract out complicated cases to specialized private companies and other cases where market prices and quality of service warrant it (Garett, chapter "What We've Learned: Lessons from the World's Leading Security Companies on Partnerships and Privatization"; Button, chapter "Working with Private Policing to Enhance Public Policing: The Case of the United Kingdom")
Response to burglar alarms activations. (10% of police calls for service)	For valid alarms: Deterrence via increasing probability of apprehension. Limiting damage and theft via quick alarm response	Response times	Verified Response (VR) exists in many countries. This sheds the initial response to an alarm to private security, if verified sworn public officers respond	VR: Initial and false alarms: No Police involvement For verified alarms public police respond, and in this way, they can act as complements (Blackstone et al., 2020, Blemings et al., chapter "Private Security Confounds Estimates of Public Police and Crime").	Shedding or managed competition of initial response. Expand cities with VR policies to free up police resources, reduce response times, and reduce burglary (See Blackstone et al., 2020 and chapter "An Overview of Private Security and Policing in the United States"). If arrest powers for private security are expanded, as suggested by Benson (chapter "Allocating Police and Security: Comparing Public and Private Processes and Consequences"), full alarm response could be conducted by private contracting

Emergency response calls. (80% of police responses)	Deterrence via increased probability of apprehension if call is crime related. But, in the U.S., less than 3% of 240 million annual calls involve violent crime; Only 37.4% in a sample of 9 cities involve criminal situations requiring police (Vera, 2022)	Response time. Improvements in response could be tracked using mortality rates in the case of emergency medical responses	Private emergency response services exist. For example, Shomrim Volunteer Security (Stringham and Salz, chapter "Private Law Enforcement in New York City"). Non-police emergency response including mental health response is becoming more common (Zerunyan, chapter "Public-Private Security Partnerships. Can They Meet the Growing Challenges of Law Enforcement?"). New Orleans Task Force (Long, chapter "Private Law Enforcement in New York City") provides evidence that private management deterred more violent crime than public management of emergency response and patrol in New Orleans	When crime and life-threatening or crime related police respond. Non-emergency services could be shed to private security. Private security and public police can act as complements (Blemings et al., chapter "Private Security Confounds Estimates of Public Police and Crime") in a similar way to verified burglar alarm response (Blackstone et al., 2020)	Public Police dispatcher filtering could be used to appropriate public or private service. If call is related to crime or life-threatening condition public police respond. If medical or mental health emergency a P3 with mental health professional could be used. (Zerunyan, chapter "Public-Private Security Partnerships. Can They Meet the Growing Challenges of Law Enforcement?"). For non-emergency-private security contracted response. In the case of mental health or non-emergency calls, improved mental health outcomes with less reliance on incapacitation, for non-emergencies public sector resource savings as contracted security are cheaper than sworn police. Psychologist's and mental health professions employed by police or contracted out can also help with emergency response to domestic disputes (Reaves, 2017)
Protecting individuals; bodyguards or police escorts	Very little, the benefits and the costs are internalized by market participants	Based on market reputation. A lack of measurable outcomes is a good thing for business	Yes, bodyguards are primarily private security services (see for example Tactical Response Security Consulting 2023) for private citizens. Contracting out could exist for public authorities	Only in emergency situations. Not for routine operations	Expand contracting out. Managed competition is possible (Garda, chapter "The Importance of Public-Private Partnerships") For any non-governmental protection private security can be contracted via the market
Processing suspects: Interviews, providing transcripts, fingerprints, put into custody	Accuracy and safety. Aligning arrests with actual crimes provides deterrence via increasing probability of detection	Preparation for possible arrest	See Garda (chapter "The Importance of Public-Private Partnerships") and Benson (chapter "Allocating Police and Security: Comparing Public and Private Processes and Consequences") for details	If processing is contracted out with private security firms, they will have to work closely with local police departments for information sharing and eventual incapacitation (jail)	Expanded contracting out for these services as suggested by Garda (chapter "The Importance of Public-Private Partnerships") and Benson (chapter "Allocating Police and Security: Comparing Public and Private Processes and Consequences"). Probably more significant resource savings for large police departments

(continued)

Table 1 (continued)

Type of service	Impact on public safety	Potential measurement of output	Does private security provide services?	Is public police involvement required?	Policy prescription
Parking enforcement	Managing street parking. Deterring illegal parking via punishment (fines) and increasing probability of apprehension	Parking fee revenues, capacity utilization, and vehicle turnover	See Garda (chapter "The Importance of Public-Private Partnerships") for details	No	Expand contracting out (Garda, chapter "The Importance of Public-Private Partnerships")
Traffic Enforcement	Manage traffic when a problem occurs	Safety and improved traffic conditions	See XPressGuards (2023) for an example of these services	Yes	Expand contracting out (Garda, chapter "The Importance of Public-Private Partnerships")
Conducting search & rescue operations	Emergency activity usually with limited professional skills required	Successful search or rescue	Jones (chapter "Improving Public Safety Through Law Enforcement and Private Security Partnerships") provides description of private search and rescue operations	Police respond only if crime is determined	Increased shedding of these services. (Jones, chapter "Improving Public Safety Through Law Enforcement and Private Security Partnerships".) Allow volunteers to join
Managing emergency conditions	Serving in disasters	Saving lives & property	Contract out. In disaster prone areas adopting volunteer groups	PPP relationships will be necessary. Police and Private security will have to work together during these situations	Contracting out or PPP including volunteers (Blackstone et al., 2017; Wallace, 2009). Jones (chapter "Improving Public Safety Through Law Enforcement and Private Security Partnerships") suggests contracting with private security companies during emergency situations to supplement police, as there will be excess demand for these services

Security for Public Transport Hubs	Deter victimization of vulnerable groups in vulnerable situations	Public transport area crime rates and complaints lodged	Ariel provides evidence that private security deters violence against women and girls for UK rail network hubs (chapter "The Substitutability and Complementarity of Private Security with Public Police: The Case of Violence Against Women and Girls in the Rail Network of the United Kingdom"). Rapid Transit Authority Special Police (Stringham et al., chapter "Private Law Enforcement in New York City"). Jones (chapter "Improving Public Safety Through Law Enforcement and Private Security Partnerships") also recommends more private security involvement with public transit	Only in emergency situations	Increased shedding of these services by police to enhance private competition. Public transit hubs can contract with individual security services and not rely on public police. "Hot Spot" policing strategies should be used by security companies (Ariel, chapter "The Substitutability and Complementarity of Private Security with Public Police: The Case of Violence Against Women and Girls in the Rail Network of the United Kingdom")
College/university/ higher ed. security	Deterrence via increasing probability of apprehension	Crime and clearance rates in and around the college	Klick and MacDonald (chapter "Private Security and Deterrence") provide empirical results for armed private University of Pennsylvania Police and unarmed security guards at Johns Hopkins University	Only in emergency situations. Not for routine operations	Klick and MacDonald (chapter "Private Security and Deterrence") show that armed and sworn (with arrest powers) private university police deter crime in and around The University of Pennsylvania, while unarmed security guards at Johns Hopkins did not deter crime at the same level. Expanding private security arrest powers (Benson, chapter "Allocating Police and Security: Comparing Public and Private Processes and Consequences") and allowing them to be armed may increase deterrence at institutions of higher ed. Institutions of higher ed. could hire armed sworn officers instead of unarmed guards for security purposes

(continued)

Table 1 (continued)

Type of service	Impact on public safety	Potential measurement of output	Does private security provide services?	Is public police involvement required?	Policy prescription
Transportation of inmates	Deterrence via increasing and securing punishment and strengthening the incapacitation effect	Number of successful trips. Complaint/failure rates	A task usually conducted by sheriff but yes it can be provided privately via contracting out (Garda, chapter "The Importance of Public-Private Partnerships")	Only for receiving the prisoners	Contracting out is common (Garda, chapter "The Importance of Public-Private Partnerships"), could be bundled with guarding police stations and more
Investigating cyber crimes	Involves significant capital equipment, specialized employees, and evolving technology	Number of cases resolved, or clearance rates	Blackstone et al. (chapter "An Overview of Private Security and Policing in the United States") provide data on the rise of private cybercrime investigation and security over the past few decades	Major federal and state security organizations engage in these investigations but could be aided by high tech private firms	Increased contracting out or Public Private Partnerships with federal agencies like the US FBI. (Blackstone et al., chapter "An Overview of Private Security and Policing in the United States", Garett chapter "What We've Learned: Lessons from the World's Leading Security Companies on Partnerships and Privatization")
Maritime piracy security	Deter pirating activity, reduce probability of boarding, hijacking, and theft	Rates of boarding, hijacking, and theft rates	Yes, see Blemings et al. (chapter "Private Security Confounds Estimates of Public Police and Crime")	Public security amplifies the deterrence impact of onboard private security. (Blemings et al., chapter "Public Security Enhances the Effectiveness of Private Security in Reducing Maritime Piracy Harm")	Private security can reduce incidence of hijacking and boarding, yet some nations ban the use of private security onboard ships (Blemings et al., chapter "Public Security Enhances the Effectiveness of Private Security in Reducing Maritime Piracy Harm"). The first policy prescription is to legalize private security for maritime use. Second, strong public expenditures work as complements to private security to deter boarding of vessels. Establish partnerships between the two allows them to work together
Bounty hunters	Deter bail jumping and improve the apprehension to penalty/incapacitation	Rate of retrieval of offenders	Helland and Tabarrok (2004) provide evidence that private bounty hunters hired by private bail bondsman retrieve offenders at much higher rates than public police attempting to engage in the same retrieval process	On the receiving end of the retrieval process, public authorities must have a working relationship with private bounty hunters	Increased use of cash bail combined with increased use of private bounty hunting contracts (Helland & Tabarrok, 2004)

| Hospital, clinic, and health care center security | Deter vandalism and theft and provide immediate safety for vulnerable groups | Victimization rate, theft/burglary rates | Guarding of vaccination centers in Belgium and the Netherlands (Leloup, chapter "The COVID-19 Pandemic and Its Impact on Public-Private Partnership in Policing: Experiences from Within the Belgian and Dutch Security Industry") | In case of emergency situations | Shed these services, allow health care institutions to contract with private security agencies or allow hospitals to create private sworn officer police forces with arrest powers (Rayasam, 2023). Reduce informational and structural barriers between private security and police (Leloup, chapter "The COVID-19 Pandemic and Its Impact on Public-Private Partnership in Policing: Experiences from Within the Belgian and Dutch Security Industry") |

Table 1 provides a short summary of the security services presented in the book, police and private security often provide these goods independently, via public private partnerships, or via contracting out. We highlight situations where production or provision can be contracted out, shed completely, or where partnerships could be enhanced. If the desired output is measurable and dictated in a contract, and the transaction costs of shifting the service are lower than the savings from existing police provision, it makes contracting more straightforward. The requirement of measurable output helps with the contracting out process, as the security outcome can be more accurately delivered by the private service. Some private security investments, like cameras associated with a response team can be both a substitute and complement to patrol and may make it easier to monitor and contract out patrol. Further, police may compete at the contracting stage with other providers if they can provide the services more efficiently and if cross subsidization is avoided by, for example, having a separate budgetary unit.

3   Final Thoughts

The main objective of security services is to deter, prevent, and investigate crime. The initiation of the 911 system was intended to reduce response times for medical emergencies and interrupt and deter criminal events. However, several studies have analyzed 911 calls in 15 cities and reveal that 32–75% of responses are for non-criminal events that do not require sworn officer participation (Asher & Horwitz, 2021; Tabachnik, 2020; Vera, 2022a). Tabachnik (2020) calculated the number of minutes officers were involved in various activities during a typical day in three cities. Our conservative estimates using Tabachnik data reveals that non-criminal activities occupied between 27.5% and 35.9% of police officers' time. These non-crime activities that police address are administrative, personal, legal, and medical assistance. Tabachnik adds that other services that include significant non-crime activities include traffic control, which occupies 11–19% of calls. Traffic control includes parking complaints, and abandoned vehicles, neither of which require involvement of sworn officers. Kanu (2022) finds that 75% of Sacramento police officers' traffic activities result in warning or no action at all. Blackstone et al., show that police response to burglar alarms takes 10% of patrol officers' time, and 94–99% of these alarms are from false activations and do not require sworn officers' response. These responses should be paid for by the alarm owners.

We reviewed six surveys to approximate the percent of 911 calls or the time involved that do not require exclusive police response. We then suggest whether police, private security or some combination should respond to lower response time or reduce costs of response. The surveys include Asher & Horwitz, 2021; NICJR, 2021; Tabachnik, 2020; Terrill et al., 2014; Vera Institute of Justice, 2022a, Messinger et al., 2013.

Police response to non-crime events includes a significant number of false 911 calls. Police should respond only to verified actual crimes or attempted intrusions.

Blackstone et al. (2020) showed that when police respond only to valid burglar alarms via a Verified Response (VR) policy, as adopted in Salt Lake City, there was an 87% reduction in police responses to burglar alarms, and 26% reduction in burglaries. Further, when a designated agent of the alarm owner checks the periphery of the property and then subsequently dispatches police when a verified burglary occurs, police response time to high or priority 1 calls declined from 12:04 minutes to 5:32 minutes, and for the lower priority 2 responses, the decline in average response time was from 11:54 to 8:42 minutes. The reduced response time provides benefits to the entire community (Blackstone et al., 2020).

Police now respond to most emergency calls. We will attempt to create a back-of-the-envelope estimate for the police resources saved by allowing private security or other private entities to provide initial response in situations where police are not necessary. The six sources we consulted suggest that non-criminal responses comprise between 43% and 80% of the total police responses (Sumirall, 2022 estimated 80% for Seattle). These include response to burglar alarms, search and rescue, disturbance or nuisance, deceased person, damage or vandalism or mischief, missing or runaway or found person, and welfare checks. The calculation from Messinger et al. (2013) for these categories, which don't require police response, yields 43% of total police calls, which is the most conservative of the estimates examined. If we use data from the Salt Lake City Verified Response (VR) program mentioned above, we observe that, after VR went into place, police still responded to 13% of burglar alarms, which amounts to an 87% reduction in police responses once the initial responses were shed to private security or alarm owners (Blackstone et al., 2020). Thus, using this 87% reduction estimate as a rough guide to how other calls to police would look after the initial responses are shed, combined with the overall number of calls that don't require police (43%) provides a rough estimate to the amount of police time that could be saved. By multiplying 87% (reduction in calls after initial response is shed) × 43% (types of calls that don't initially require police) we obtain an estimate of 37%. This is the amount of police officer resource time that could be saved by shedding initial responses for calls, that do not require police response. The largest categories are disturbances and nuisance and burglar alarms (Messinger et al., 2013; Blackstone et al., 2020). If we multiply this estimated 37% of police officers' time used engaging in these activities, we can approximate the police resource savings that could be freed up by contracting out or shedding these services. Nationally in 2021, there were 684,900 police and sheriff patrol officers (US Department of Labor, 2022). Multiplying the total patrol officers by the 37 of time devoted to these response activities yields the time and resource equivalent of 253,413 officers. In other words, by our rough calculation, enabling initial verifying response by private non-sworn police officers to these events, could save the equivalent of about 253,413 officers that could be shifted to enhancing security in other areas.

Police involvement in traffic occupies 9–13% of patrol officers' calls and time (Asher & Horwitz, 2021; NICJR, 2021; Tabachnik, 2020; Terrill et al., 2014; Vera Institute of Justice, 2022a; Messinger et al., 2013) including motor vehicle collision investigation, abandoned vehicles, moving and parking violations, assisting motorists, and directing traffic. In fact, minor or only property damage motor vehicles accident are private goods and should be shed by police. In Philadelphia Pennsylvania, for example, Police no longer respond to calls for non-injury traffic accidents, allowing self-reporting or insurance companies to handle the cases (Weitzman, 2010). Dealing with abandoned cars could be contracted out under general police supervision. Parking violations are often contracted out (Sheyner, 2015). Moving violations, like impaired or drunk driving, entail significant negative externalities and should remain with sworn officers. Directing traffic can be contracted out to private security companies.

Police response to medical emergencies is common in the U.S. since patrol is often available in most communities for more immediate assistance than paramedics. As of now, police are reasonably well trained and experienced in providing emergency first aid.

We recommend in this chapter that over 43% of police-provided services be considered for contracting or shifting to competitive private and public providers. Some of these services may not be economically viable as stand-alone services; however, the shift of several services could lead to economies of scope attributed to their bundling under one provider. Thus, this significant shift of services from monopolistic police to competitive providers may, in the long run, enhance both technological innovations and the efficient use of resources that improve their delivery to the public at lower costs. The shift of emergency first aid from police to the more private provisions exists in some areas (Stringham and Salz, chapter "Private Law Enforcement in New York City") but could expand in the future with economies of scope. Contracting out could be under managed competition where private entities and local police or any other public agency like an adjacent police or fire departments may compete. However, since it is a private service, a fee should be charged to the patient. In any event, private services should be shed to reduce police response time to actual criminal acts.

A special case of responses by police within 911 calls is behavioral health, as these cases commonly involve negative externalities. A Vera analysis (2022b) includes public intoxication, public urination, vagrancy in addition to other antisocial behavioral activities. In the nine cities analyzed, 19% of all 911 responses were related to behavioral health. Thus, it is recommended that in large jurisdictions initial responses should be done by trained civilian professionals and not by police. Police can then be dispatched at high priority if a need arises. In Denver, Colorado since 2016 police have been accompanied by professional clinicians to 911 mental health calls. In a 2020 pilot study, 350 such calls were responded to by a clinician and a paramedic without accompanying police with no reported problems (Tabachnik, 2020). Such a reform should be seriously considered by all U.S. communities, since the U.S. government subsidizes 85% of mobile civilian crisis responders under the 2022 American Rescue Plan (Vera, 2022b).

The more services that are subject to contracting out and shedding, the more likely they could be bundled, and thereby possibly enjoy economies of scope. These former police services are complementary, and can be provided by the same inputs, and can be switched from one output to another. The objective is to move from monopolistic police provision to competitive firms and possibly enjoy economies of scope, more efficient production, and the innovations that competition yields. Thus, the more services are offered, the more likely economic viability is achieved, and more public and private entities compete. Also, such bundling could be more successful as the size and income of the community increases. However, even if scope economies are absent, the arguments for contracting out or shedding still apply. The competition through contracting out these services could yield both greater productivity and technological and managerial innovations in the methods of delivering them. Finally, if police only respond to real criminal events, resource pressures on police will be reduced, and their response time should also be reduced, enhancing security for the entire community. In an environment of increasing crime, enabling police to focus on crime seems highly desirable.

The suggestions made here for revision of security services, especially for local government for shedding, contracting out and establishment of PPPs of police and other related services are based on evidence provided in this Handbook and other sources. We invite researchers, policy makers, and national/local/and regional authorities to recognize that these suggestions need to be tested. Pilot studies, as in the example above from Denver, could be useful. Local variation in contracting out and shedding police services could allow for natural case studies to examine the effectiveness of these suggestions.

References

Asher, J., & Horwitz, B. (2021). How do police actually spend their time? *New York Times*, updated November 8. Originally published on June 19, 2020. https://www.nytimes.com/2020/06/19/upshot/unrest-police-time-violent-crime.html Accessed 13 Apr 2023.

Blackstone, E., et al. (2017). "A regional, market oriented governance for disaster management: A new planning approach" (with Hakimand Meehan). *Evaluation and Program Planning, 64*, 57–68. https://www.sciencedirect.com/science/article/abs/pii/S0149718917300022

Blackstone, E., et al. (2020). Burglary reduction and improved police performance through private alarm response. *International Review of Law and Economics, 63*(September), 1–13. https://www.sciencedirect.com/science/article/pii/S0144818820301435

Helland, E., & Tabarrok, A. (2004). The fugitive: Evidence on public versus private law enforcement from bail jumping. *The Journal of Law & Economics, 47*(1), 93–122.

Kanu, H. (2022, November 2). Police are not primarily crime fighters, according to the data. *Reuters*. https://www.reuters.com/legal/government/police-are-not-primarily-crime-fighters-according-data-2022-11-02/#:~:text=Police%20spend%20most%20of%20their,%2C%20and%20New%20Haven%2C%20Connecticut. Accessed 13 Apr 2023.

Kleiner, M. M. (2015, January). *Reforming occupational licensing policies, The Hamilton Project.* Brookings Institution Discussion Paper-01.

Koeske, Z. (2020, August). City lays off dispatchers in move toward outsourcing 911 services. *Government Technology*. See https://www.govtech.com/em/safety/city-lays-of-dispatchers-in-move-toward-outsourcing-911-services-.html Accessed 11 Apr 2023.

Meehan, B., & Benson, B. L. (2015). The occupations of regulators influence occupational regulation: Evidence from the US private security industry. *Public Choice, 162*, 97–117.

Meehan, B., & Benson, B. L. (2017). Does private security affect crime?: A test using state regulations as instruments. *Applied Economics, 49*, 48.

Messinger, S., et al. (2013). The distribution of emergency police dispatch call incident types and priority levels within the police priority dispatch system. *Annals of Emergency Dispatch and Response, 1*(2), 12–17.

NICJR. (2021). Seattle calls for service analysis. National Institute for Criminal Justice Reform. See https://herbold.seattle.gov/wp-content/uploads/2021/07/Attachment-3-Seattle-Calls-for-Service-Analysis-Report-with-Appendices-NICJR-June-2021.pdf. Accessed 23 Apr 2023.

Rayasam, R. (2023, May 28). Hospital police pitfalls feared. Philadelphia Inuirer:G4.

Reaves, B. A. (2017, May). *Police response to domestic violence, 2006–2015.* Office of Justice Programs, Bureau of Justice Statistics, US Department of Justice. Accessed 3 Apr 2023.

Sheyner, G. (2015, June 30). City contracts out parking enforcement for a new downtown program. *Palo Alto Weekly.* https://www.paloaltoonline.com/news/2015/06/30/city-contracts-out-parking-enforcement-for-new-downtown-program. Accessed 31 May 2023.

Sumirall, F. (2022, May 19). SPD report discovers 80% of 911 calls were for non-criminal events. *MYNorthwest.* See https://mynorthwest.com/3479482/spd-report-discovers-80-of-911-calls-were-for-non-criminal-events/. Accessed 19 Apr 2023.

Tabachnik, S. (2020, September 6). …How do cops spend their time: As Denver debates police funding, these numbers offer an inside look. *Denver Post.* https://www.denverpost.com/2020/09/06/denver-police-officer-time-job-funding-data/. Accessed 13 Apr 2023.

Tactical Response Security Consulting. (2023). https://tacticalresponsesecurity.com/executive-protection-services-philadelphia-pa/?utm_source=TPA%20On%20Google%20Search&utm_campaign=TPA%C2%AE%20New%20Jers. Accessed 2 June 2023.

Terrill, W., et al. (2014). Police service delivery and responsiveness in a period of economic instability. *Police Practice and Research, 15*(6). https://www.tandfonline.com/doi/abs/10.1080/15614263.2013.829606 Accessed 18 Apr 2023.

US Department of Labor. (2022). Occupational Outlook handbook. Protective Service Occupations. https://www.bls.gov/ooh/protective-service/home.htm. Accessed 23 Apr 2023.

Vera Institute of Justice. (2022a, April). 911 analysis: Call data shows we can rely less on police. *Vera Institute.* https://www.vera.org/downloads/publications/911-analysis-we-can-rely-less-on-police.pdf Accessed 4-13-2023.

Vera Institute of Justice. (2022b). *911 analysis: How civilian crisis responders can divert behavioral health calls from police.* https://www.vera.org/downloads/publications/911-analysis-civilian-crisis-responders.pdf. Accessed 6 May 2023.

Wallace, D. G. (2009). Local government contingency planning for public security and public safety. In S. Hakim & E. A. Blackstone (Eds.), *Safeguarding homeland security: Governors & mayors speak out* (pp. 87–98). Springer.

Weitzman, D. (2010, May 3). *Drivers beware: What it means for you now that the Philadelphia police no longer respond to minor traffic accidents.* https://www.myphillylawyer.com/2010/05/03/drivers-beware-what-it-means-for-you-now-that-the-philadelphia-police-will-no-longer-respond-to-minor-traffic-accidents/. Accessed 31 May 2023.

XPressGuards. (2023). https://xpressguards.com/traffic-enforcement-security-guards/

Printed in the USA
CPSIA information can be obtained
at www.ICGtesting.com
LVHW010852241123
764805LV00005B/63